THE Encyclopedia
OF
Dim-Mak

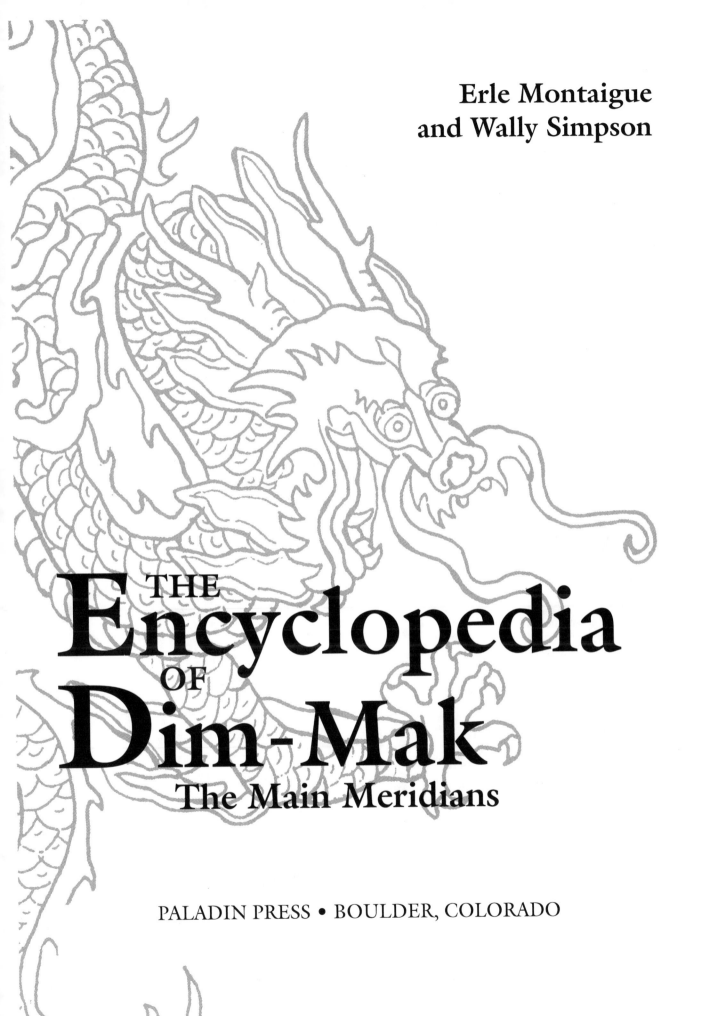

Erle Montaigue
and Wally Simpson

The Encyclopedia of Dim-Mak
The Main Meridians

PALADIN PRESS • BOULDER, COLORADO

Also by Erle Montaigue:

Advanced Dim-Mak:
   The Finer Points of Death-Point Striking
Baguazhang: Fighting Secrets of the Eight Trigram Palms
Dim-Mak: Death Point Striking
Dim-Mak's 12 Most Deadly Katas: Points of No Return
The Encyclopedia of Dim-Mak:
   The Extra Meridians, Points, and More
Power Taiji
Secrets of Dim-Mak: An Instructional Video (video)
Ultimate Dim-Mak: How to Fight a Grappler and Win

The Encyclopedia of Dim-Mak: The Main Meridians
by Erle Montaigue and Wally Simpson

Copyright © 1997 by Erle Montaigue and Wally Simpson

ISBN 0-87364-923-0
Printed in the United States of America

Published by Paladin Press, a division of
Paladin Enterprises, Inc., P.O. Box 1307,
Boulder, Colorado 80306, USA.
(303) 443-7250

Direct inquiries and/or orders to the above address.

PALADIN, PALADIN PRESS, and the "horse head" design
are trademarks belonging to Paladin Enterprises and
registered in United States Patent and Trademark Office.

Visit our Web site at www.paladin-press.com

Contents

Introduction 1

Introduction to Traditional Chinese Medicine 11

The Gallbladder Meridian 27

The Liver Meridian 109

The Bladder Meridian 131

The Kidney Meridian 203

The Stomach Meridian 231

The Spleen Meridian 273

The Heart Meridian 297

The Small Intestine Meridian 309

The Lung Meridian 329

The Colon Meridian 343

The Triple Heater Meridian 365

The Pericardium Meridian 389

Medical Glossary 401

Glossary 409

Bibliography 415

About the Authors 417

Warning

On Misuse of this Information

The techniques discussed in this book can be extremely dangerous and even deadly. It is not the intent of the author or publisher to encourage readers to attempt any of them without proper professional supervision and training. Attempting to do so can result in severe injury or death. Do not attempt any of the techniques described without the supervision of a certified instructor or acupuncturist.

The author and publisher disclaim any liabilityh from any damage or injuries of any type that a reader or user of information contained within this book may encounter from the use of said information. *This book is for information purposes only.*

On Plagiarism

The information on dim-mak provided in this book is protected under international copyright law and may not be used in any other publication without permission from the author. This statement is necessary here to because there are those who will consider plagiarizing the information—changing it slightly, perhaps—and then claiming that it was common knowledge. However, the information on dim-mak in this book is not common knowledge, as this is the first time it has ever been presented in physical form. Prior to this publication, this knowledge was only ever passed on by word of mouth and personal teaching from master to student. So when any of the dim-mak point information turns up in other publications, it shall be clear where it came from, no matter how hard the plagiarizer tries to hide the fact.

Anyone who wishes to include this information in any publication, be it a national magazine, an in-house newsletter, or a book, must contact the author, Erle Montaigue, prior to doing so. In most cases permission will be granted just as long as acknowledgment of the information's origin is included.

Preface

The Montaigue Encyclopedia of Dim-Mak

First and foremost, I want to issue a warning to all who read this book about the dangers of abusing their knowledge of dim-mak techniques.

There was a time when only those who had achieved an advanced level of training were given the most deadly ways of fighting—and then only after they had learned about the basic ways of healing.

In modern times we have seen certain people who have come across a minute part of dim-mak—such as the ability to cause knockout (KO) very easily by striking certain points on the body—go out and teach this openly to anyone who would pay the money. We have seen these same people giving others very high dan rankings after only a relatively short period of time. Worse, we have heard these people saying that striking to cause KO is not dangerous and that anyone can do it!

Sure, anyone *can* do it after only a few minutes of training, but *it is extremely dangerous* (especially when the person executing the strike does not know what he is doing or how to heal the result of such strikes)! We had a case here in Australia where after only one seminar, one chap was going around striking friends and relatives, even strangers, in kidney points to show how good he was at the martial arts. The recipients of these strikes were urinating blood that evening! Here is the classic example of someone who receives a limited amount of information from someone who does not know the full score himself and then goes out and applies it without knowing the dangers.

I began publishing information on dim-mak back in 1986 when I wrote my first article on basic dim-mak for the magazine *Australasian Fighting Arts*. It was my intention to introduce these deadly strikes to the general martial arts public gradually and educate people about the dangers of such strikes.

At that time, the only books on dim-mak were a couple of very basic books in Chinese, which were later translated into English and really taught nothing at all. There were also a couple of responsible teachers of the karate version of dim-mak called *tuite*, like Sensei Oyata, who was only teaching his most advanced students these methods. A few other schools in Japan, like the Shorinji Kempo school of Sensei Bando, were teaching some of the neck strikes only to their most advanced students.

Unfortunately, there were those who took the opposite tack and openly taught a few very dangerous strikes that look very impressive to the novice. Slowly but surely, some information got out and was being taught to anyone. Seeing this, I decided to fast-track the information so that people would know the dangers of these strikes.

Before I began writing about dim-mak, very few people, if any, actually used the Chinese terms for the strikes, such as Stomach 9 (St 9). They would simply call them "nerve strikes" or something similar.

Now, as a result of my writing, everyone knows that the easy knockout strike is to a point on the neck called St 9. My articles also educated people about exactly why the strikes to the neck work so well for achieving knockouts. Some martial artists knew the strikes worked, but few knew why. So, taking my own training and using the knowledge of some of the world's leading minds on cardiology, neurology, and physiology, combining modern science with ancient Chinese knowledge of the energy systems of the body, I set out to educate the martial arts public as to why the strikes worked. My goal was to tell people that even the lightest strike was dangerous!

In late 1995, with four books on dim-mak and around 110 video titles, I realized it was about time to write an encyclopedia on dim-mak—an enormous task, but an important one. Until now, martial artists have had to rely on acupuncture texts for information on the points, which was inadequate for a number of reasons. Primary among them was that acupuncture texts were not written with the martial artist in mind: they did not show the correct directions for striking, the proper techniques to get at the points, the effects of the point strikes, or the antidote points.

This book is purely for martial artists who wish to know more about dim-mak, either for hurting or for healing. It will also be of interest to acupuncturists, because it gives an added dimension to their craft that is not covered in any of the acupuncture texts.

The coauthor of this book, Wally Simpson, has been a student of mine for many years, and he is regarded in Australia as one of the foremost acupuncturists. He has had his own practice for several years and is the principal instructor of traditional Chinese medicine (TCM) for the World Taiji Boxing Association. Because he has a sound knowledge of all aspects of TCM, including the herbal area and *tui na*, or Chinese massage, and since I have only a basic knowledge of acupuncture, I asked him to contribute to this book. In every chapter there are sections for each point called "Chinese name," "Point location," and "Healing,," which Wally wrote. He also wrote the Introduction to Traditional Chinese Medicine that follows my introduction.

This is the first time in history that anyone has attempted to cover all of the major dim-mak points in the body in an encyclopaedic manner. It has been a labor of love—a mammoth task involving sleepless nights, hard work, and a lot of research, but it is worth it in the long run just to get this much-needed information out to the martial arts and general public.

The future of dim-mak is looking good. Many people are now attempting to find out more. In doing so, they enhance their own martial systems. More and more information is coming out as a result of people such as myself researching and trying out old methods to see if they really work, working with others in related areas of expertise such as acupuncture. In this way, dim-mak is being brought back from the brink of extinction so that it now has more followers than ever before in history. This has happened simply because the information is no longer secret (bar a small number of advanced methods, like the Wutan Shan system).

Acknowledgments

My old, faded, and dog-eared copy of *Point Location, and Point Dynamics*, by Carole and Cameron Rogers (to which I wrote the foreword), is still the best reference work on acupuncture point location and one I refer to daily. Should you wish to obtain a copy, please write to me, c/o Paladin Press, P.O. Box 1307, Boulder, CO 80306.

Wally Simpson, a fine student and friend, has contributed much to my knowledge of acupuncture and Chinese medicine in general.

Chris Madden was my first "teacher" of Chinese medicine at an informal, friendship level.

And Chang Yiu-chun passed on to me knowledge that could not be bought.

INTRODUCTION

I have always put forth the view that the "internal Chinese martial arts," such as taijiquan and bagwazhang, are the most deadly arts ever invented, and that these same arts, along with the practice of *qigong*, also represent the very tip of the mountain as far as self-healing and medical healing go.

And yet, looking around at what most people put forth as being representative of these arts, I wonder about this.

At one time, taijiquan, for instance, was regarded as the "supreme ultimate boxing" system of China. Now the internal arts of China look very different. We see men playing little boy's games, dressing up in funny suits that have not been worn for centuries in China, all trying to show how good they are at their art and how much better they are than everyone else. They all go to the same meetings and competitions to show their wares, they all have the same serious expressions on their faces, they all write the same articles for magazines about how these arts should be used, and they all take themselves and their arts very seriously. But not many, if any, have a clue as to the true nature of the internal martial arts.

These once-great arts rise high above the way most people practice and propagate them today. Dim-mak is one of these great internal martial arts—one that almost became extinct, having left behind only a shadow of its former glory in the form of taijiquan or t'ai chi. Once a great fighting art, taijiquan in particular took a beating when it entered the modern Western world and was adopted as part of the "New Age" movement. Only a handful of dedicated instructors persevered with trying to reveal the true nature of this art.

Now, largely because of their efforts, taijiquan is being revealed for the first time in modern history as the great fighting, self-defense, and healing art that it once was. Before this, most people only ever saw a fraction of taijiquan—i.e., the self-healing area—the slow movements we have become familiar with. Few people ever saw the real martial arts applications, and even fewer got to see the "medical" area of the art.

THE THREE AREAS OF EXCELLENCE

Like all great internal martial arts, taijiquan originally comprised three areas of excellence.

The first of these is the *self-healing* area. (Obviously, one has to be healthy in order to practice a self-defense art.) This area consists of practicing the forms and the pushing hands movements. There are slow forms, medium-paced forms, and explosive forms. In addition, there are two-person fighting sets, also for self-healing.

1

At its highest level, the original Yang style of taijiquan founded by Yang Lu-ch'an (which was first called *hao ch'uan* or loose boxing) becomes an explosive set of movements, or *fa-jing* shakes, causing the practitioner to look like a rag doll. (It was later, as Yang's grandson took over the school, that the form was altered, leaving only the slow movements.) In order to become healthy through movement, we must have slow, graceful movements as well as explosive, powerful movements. This gives us a complete set of movements based upon the yin and yang theory.

Part of the reason taijiquan has been bastardized as it has is that there have been so many mistranslations of the "classics" (sayings by old masters that were documented to provide a better understanding of taijiquan) handed down over the years that we just don't get their true meaning. One such mistranslation, affecting the very way that taijiquan is practiced today, can be found in the classic saying, "Move like the great river." Most people have interpreted this to mean that we move slowly and calmly as a gently flowing river. But when the Chinese talk about the "great river," they are referring to the Yellow River, which in parts is barely navigable because it is so wild and explosive. So, yes, we must perform the taijiquan forms like the great river, sometimes slow and calm flowing, sometimes explosive and dangerous.

The second area is the *martial* area—not that which is presented by most taijiquan instructors, where we block and evade, then reattack, and so on, but the extremely deadly use of dim-mak, or death-point striking. This is more than just striking to very dangerous points, it's the *way* that we strike them and the explosive method we use to attack before an attacker even has time to react to our defense. Taijiquan, when done at its original level, deserves the name "Supreme Ultimate Boxing." But when done as some sort of health dance or mystical experience, it cannot be labeled as such. No forms are practiced in the martial area, although the original forms from the self-healing area become important here in giving us timing and coordination. In the self-defense area we practice "training methods," which give us the ability to react at a reflex level, attacking the attacker rather than defending against him.

The third area of excellence achieved through training in the internal martial arts is the *medical* area. I

Figure 1

Figure 2

regard this as the highest level of one's training. When I say "medical," I mean that the practitioner of taijiquan can actually use the postures on someone to affect a healing. This is more than just giving the person a posture that will heal some ailment; it is actually *doing* something to that person. This area takes many years to master, and then some.

However, to use taijiquan for healing others all one really has to know are the self-defense applications at a dim-mak level, for two reasons. The first is that when we train in taiji at its highest martial levels, we develop an internal energy that attaches us directly to the ground via "energy (qi) roots." These roots then direct what is called "ground energy" up through our own body and into the one we are trying to heal. The second reason is that once we know the self-defense applications of dim-mak, all we have to do is use those exact same movements, only on a healing level (not at a martial level, of course, because we would kill our patient instead of healing him).

Take, for instance, the posture known as *p'eng* (fig. 1). In a self-defense application, we defend against an attack using a low block to our right side, damaging our attacker's heart/lung meridian and thus draining energy from his body (fig. 2). Then we further drain qi from the heart/lung meridian by hammering onto the wrist points of Heart 5 (Ht 5) and Lung 8 (Lu 8), using a violent grab with our right palm (fig. 3). Then we strike to his "mind point" on the side of his jaw with our left backfist, thus causing him to lose consciousness as the action of the strike causes his central nervous system to stop sending signals to his brain (fig. 4). Then, to further the damage, the left wrist attacks to Conceptor Vessel 22 (Cv 22) point, thus causing death (fig. 5).

We can use this exact method on a healing level to cure someone of low energy, listlessness, and so on, as well as to help someone who has emotional problems resulting from some childhood trauma, such as sexual or other abuse. This still involves striking the heart and lung meridians (fig. 6), but only very lightly. Then there is the light grab on the wrist, followed by the left palm scraping over the patient's left cheek and out over the head, as in Figure 7. (I am in the process of writing a book on medical taijiquan, which will show all of the applications from taiji used in this way.)

Figure 3

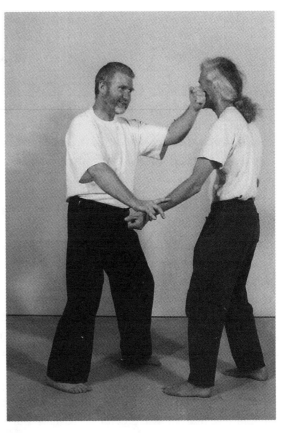

Figure 4

Figure 5

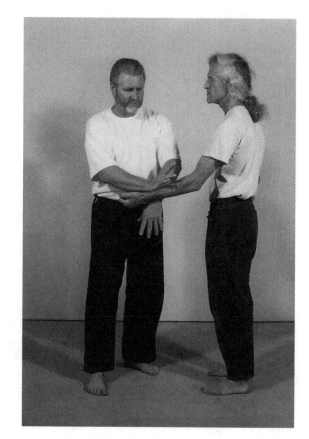

Figure 6

This is why the healing area should never be taken away from the martial area. The medical area is the highest level of one's martial arts training, but sadly, most systems nowadays have taken only the deadly part of dim-mak. They focus on the more spectacular movements and leave the healing side of their art out completely, thus lessening the greatness of this art.

I believe I am the first person in modern history to be taught this area and, more important, to document it for future generations. The Chinese didn't teach it to the various masters who took what they learned in China and invented their own systems. This was primarily because those people didn't stick around long enough to be ready to receive this information or to use it, because the qi was not at a sufficient level. In addition, the Chinese simply didn't want anyone else to have this information.

So why does a Westerner from Australia have it? The answer to that calls for a bit of background.

HISTORY OF DIM-MAK

The history of dim-mak is quite gray, but we do have *some* information on its origins.

Chang San-feng, the original founder of dim-mak, was born sometime between 1270 and 1347. Most scholars agree that 1270 is the most likely date, and based on that, one could assume that he invented dim-mak around 1300. He and two of his friends, who were acupuncturists, decided to experiment on animals and people to determine the effects of strikes to the acupuncture points. Obviously, other masters of great genius have added to our repertoire of dim-mak point strikes over the years, but it was Chang who got us all started.

Many argue that because the name "taijiquan" is not once mentioned in Chang San-feng's history, he cannot have invented it! In fact, taijiquan is only a recent name given to Chang's original point-striking system of dim-mak, which then became h'ao ch'uan, and only late last century became known as taijiquan. There is plenty of mention in Chang's history of dim-mak, and so each year tens of thousands of Chinese martial artists celebrate Chang's birthday as marking the birth of taijiquan.

Understandably, Chang became a little paranoid at having discovered such power. (Back then, it was a

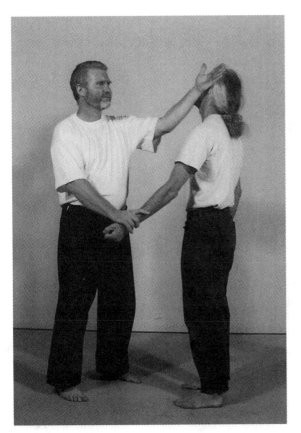

Figure 7

bit like discovering the atomic bomb, in that so much devastation could be caused by even a one-finger strike.) So he invented a way of passing on this information to his most trusted family members without revealing it to others who would try to copy what he had originated. He made up a simple set of movements, like a dance, into which he placed all of his dim-mak strikes, only telling those trusted few exactly what each movement meant. It was this set of movements that was then called h'ao ch'uan, or "loose boxing," and later taijiquan.

Human nature being what it is, students would learn the basic steps from other students and then, thinking that they had received it all, would go out and teach what they had learned. This was the death knell for h'ao ch'uan or taijiquan, for most of them would never reach the highest levels where the dim-mak and dim-mak healing were taught.

Other martial arts systems picked up on the dim-mak strikes that Chang had invented, and because they were more in line with what are known as the "hard styles," actually taught what little they knew of dim-mak openly. So nowadays a number of martial art systems have some semblance of the original dim-mak. Even the Okinawan and Japanese karate schools know a bit of dim-mak. However, it was the original Chang San-feng invention that had the ultimate sophistication and subtlety. The point strikes remain hidden in the modern taijiquan forms or katas, but not many know how to use them, or even wish to know about them. Taijiquan has become a New Age health dance that, when performed 10,000 times, supposedly leads one to enlightenment. (In order achieve this enlightenment, one must also wear a serious "taiji suit" and spout words of wisdom from the masters whenever confronted by people at parties who might be impressed with such profound knowledge.)

The history of dim-mak cannot be separated from the taijiquan lineage, and two names are synonymous with this lineage.

The first is Wang T'sung-yeuh, said to be either a student of Chang San-feng or the student of a student (it is fair to say that there was a direct lineage from Chang). Since Chang did not write anything down since he was paranoid that someone would steal his information and then use it against him, it was Wang who first recorded the exact nature of h'ao ch'uan. His treatise was then filed away and stayed that way, just gathering dust, through successive generations, until its owners did not even know what it was.

The next name is Yang Lu-ch'an. Yang rediscovered the treatise, which had somehow made it to the Chen Village of Shao-lin style martial artists where he was working. Yang did not know what it was all about until a man called Zhiang entered the village. Zhiang happened to be a direct descendant of Chang San-feng, and together he and Yang used the treatise to rediscover h'ao ch'uan. Because the Chen people were kind enough to put both men up and to work, they too enjoyed Zhiang's knowledge, changing their Shao-lin system to be more like h'ao ch'uan. Nowadays, Chen taijiquan is a very popular style, but it retains the hardness of the Shao-lin background and does not have the "soft" and "loose" internal qualities of Yang-style taijiquan. Yang style, in its time, was said to be the very pinnacle of martial arts systems. Most modern styles of taijiquan come from the Yang system invented by Yang Lu-ch'an.

From Old to Modern Taijiquan

Yang Lu-ch'an had six sons, four of whom were murdered in a bloody battle with a rival family. Yang himself preferred to commit suicide rather than be killed by these rivals. Of the two remaining sons, one, Yang Ban-hou, went slightly bonkers after witnessing all of this, and the other, Yang Kin-hou, escaped to a Buddhist monastery to recover.

My lineage comes directly from Yang Kin-hou in two lines.

The first line comes from Kin-hou's first son, Yang Shou-hou, who refused to change his father's and grandfather's system of fighting. He taught only three students, among them Chang Yiu-chun, who became my main teacher.

The second comes from the Yang Cheng-fu side. Cheng-fu, the brother of Shou-hou, changed the original system so that everyone, young and old, could enjoy the great healing benefits of taijiquan. He left out all of the leaping movements and fa-jing, or explosive energy movements. I also learned directly from Yang Sau-chung (the son of Cheng-fu) and from one of his three main disciples, Chu King-hung.

Yang Cheng-fu's system is the most popular system today, and it is said that it represents the maximum that the original could have been changed without having lost its internal essence. (Later "masters" of Yang-style taijiquan further changed the whole system, causing it to become too soft, with little or no martial arts applications, until, nowadays, nothing of its original greatness remains. Because of this association of taijiquan with some sort of health dance, I prefer to call what I teach h'ao ch'uan, which is more in keeping with Yang Lu-ch'an's original idea of a great self-defense/healing system.)

So after much begging, borrowing, and stealing (as well as buying and granting many "favors"), I was taught by some of the very best Chinese teachers, and in 1985 I became the first Westerner to be given the degree of "Master" directly from China. Following that first tour, it took nine years of correspondence before I finally had the chance to go to Wutan Shan and learn these forms of fighting and healing.

Wutan Shan is a mountain range 400 kilometers long in Hupei province. One of these mountain peaks is also called Wutan Shan, and it's here that the original Wutan Shan temple existed. Chang San-feng was said to live at this temple. Nowadays, the "keeper" of the system, Liang Shih-kan, teaches out of his humble abode in a small village at the base of this peak. He has around seven students and teaches on a dirt patch in his backyard.

In May 1995, I was the first Westerner ever invited to Wutan Shan to be taught the original Wutan Shan style of "qi disruption," which involves nine brief katas that are said to be the original forms invented by Chang San-feng. There I learned the remaining five short forms of what I believe is the original Chang San-feng system. (I already knew the first four of these, as taught to me by Chang Yiu-chun.) Normally, only two of these forms are shown to outsiders, even other Chinese. So it was only after nine years of negotiating and sending videotapes, as well as much begging, borrowing, stealing, and buying—and after having to literally defend myself against two of Liang Shih-kan's students on the first morning there—that I was taken to the back of Liang's house to learn these forms. And now that I have had time to study these forms at my own pace, I am seeing where Yang Lu-ch'an's form came from. Each of the nine short, explosive forms has a little of Yang's form in it.

REDISCOVERING THE ORIGINAL ART

It was after this experience, late in 1995, that I decided to undertake the huge task of writing the dim-mak encyclopedia, combining my knowledge of dim-mak with coauthor Wally Simpson's knowledge of acupuncture and Chinese medicine in general. The original inventor of taijiquan (or, rather, its forerunner), Chang San-feng, was an excellent martial artist in the true sense of the word, as well as a great acupuncturist and healer. Chang combined both of his talents to invent the very deadly point-striking art of dim-mak. In publishing this book, I believe that we have rediscovered what Chang San-feng originally invented. You cannot take the healing art away from the martial art; in so doing, you only get half of a great art.

Rather than listing all of the dim-mak points in alphabetical order as the typical encyclopedia would, I have organized this one by meridians.

The chapters in this volume each focus on a major meridian and show the exact location of each of the dim-mak points associated with that meridian; the effect of striking these points in all possible directions; the antidote methods, if any, to revive someone who has been struck in these points; and applications that enable one to get at the points. Where possible (and if necessary), I also talk about "set-up" points as well as other points that will enhance the effect when struck along with the major point. (Note that some of the points—for instance, the gallbladder points at the top of the head—are so close together that striking one will have the same effect as striking another one close to it. So although I cover all of the dim-mak points, some are covered in greater detail.)

There will also be a second volume dealing with things that do not fall neatly into the meridian category, such as multiple strikes. There are, of course, hundreds of multiple point strikes, and we are given the exact points, how to strike them together, and in what order to strike them to do the most damage. Rather than trying to cover these combinations in this volume, which covers the mainstream meridians, I have placed them in a second volume covering the "extraordinary meridians." Apart from the *ren mai* (conceptor vessel) and the *du mai* (governor vessel), the extra meridians are linking meridians that do not have any points of their own, but pass through and link other meridians and take their point names from those points through which they pass.

THE MAIN MERIDIANS

MERIDIAN	ABBREVIATION	COMMON POINT
Gallbladder meridian	Gb	Gb 14
Liver meridian	Liv	Liv 14
Lung meridian	Lu	Lu 1
Colon meridian	Co	Co 10
Kidney meridian	Kd	Kd 1
Bladder meridian	Bl	Bl 57
Stomach meridian	St	St 9
Spleen meridian	Sp	Sp 1
Triple heater meridian	Th	Th 17
Pericardium meridian	Pc	Pc 7
Heart meridian	Ht	Ht 1
Small intestine meridian	Si	Si 16
Conceptor vessel (meridian)	Cv	Cv 14
Governor vessel (meridian)	Gv	Gv 20

Because each meridian is believed more active at particular times of the day, which has great significance in acupuncture, most books on acupuncture begin with the lung meridian (which is most active at dawn, or between 3 and 5 A.M.) and then follow the natural progression through each meridian based upon the body's time clock. However, since this is a book on dim-mak, where time theories are not as significant, I have taken a different tack, beginning with the gallbladder meridian in Chapter 1, because it is the most important in terms of the martial aspects.

In each chapter, I will cover the points in a particular meridian, and each will be presented showing applications in both the martial arts or dim-mak area and the healing area. I will also include all of the following information:

Chinese name: This section gives an inkling of what the point is all about and its location, although sometimes the meaning of the Chinese name is somewhat lost in the translation to English.

Location: This section gives a definite location of the point. Although the points are only the size of a pen end, striking anywhere around the point (for a distance the circumference of a large coin) will activate them. Usually, I give a larger weapon as the attacking weapon so that accuracy is not a problem. However, sometimes, there is just no way around it: some of the points require great accuracy and must be struck with smaller weapons such as a one-knuckle punch. When there is a definite anatomical location, I also give that as a more precise way of locating the points.

Connections: This section gives some idea of the damage that the strikes can do by indicating the point's connections to other meridians. It also gives an indication of the other healing benefits the point might offer.

Direction of strike: This section shows the correct direction for the strikes. Some points only have one direction, e.g., straight in. Other points have several directions of striking, each having different effects.

Damage: This section deals with the type of damage done when the points are struck. From a light to moderate strike to a heavy strike, the effect will vary significantly in most cases. Every dim-mak point has an electrical property. That is, if one is so trained, he or she can affect the qi or energy of that point sufficiently to cause an adverse (as in fighting) or positive (as in healing) effect to the body's qi system. This can either be a qi drainage point, a qi filling point, or a stopping point, as in death.

Physiological points are simply those in the vicinity of an important organ that will have the obvious effect upon that organ when they are struck. For instance, a strike to a point that is directly over the top of an important nerve or sinus in the body will cause adverse physiological things to happen to the body. This section indicates whether the point is also a physiological strike, since all points are electrical strikes. It takes only a few minutes to master the physiological strikes, such as to St 9, which activates the carotid sinus to bring down the heart rate dramatically enough to cause KO. These are the strikes that most people nowadays are well versed in. The electrical strikes, however, take a little more training and are much more sophisticated in application.

Set-up point: Most of the major points have set-up points—those that, when struck a split second before the major point is struck, will enhance the effect of the main strike. There are "utility" set-up points, those that set up most of the major points, and there are specific set-up points, those that are specific to any particular major striking point. The set-up points usually either drain energy or add to the energy, depending upon what you are trying to do. For instance, Gb 14, when struck in a downward way, causes great qi drainage, so the set-up shot to Pc 6 also has to be in an adverse qi flow direction. But if the strike to Gb 14 is in an upward direction, then the set-up strike must also be in a positive qi flow direction to add qi to the point, which sort of causes an explosion, usually in the head, like a balloon that has been pumped up to exploding point.

Antidote: Not all of the points have antidote points—points that one uses to reverse the effect of the initial strike. Some points are just so dangerous that there is no way of revival. This section tells whether there is an antidote point or not and, if so, what it is and how it must be used. Sometimes we use "utility antidotes," such as Gb 20, squeezing inward and upward into the head on both sides of the neck. These points will work in a general sense on many of the points. Sometimes the major point's strike will have its own specific antidote point to use.

Healing: This is a section in each chapter where Wally Simpson gives some of the healing benefits of each of the major points. For each point, he lists current uses and indications as well as traditional functions and indications as specified by ancient Chinese text. Often there is significant overlap. The healing section is geared mostly to the novice. For instance, Wally will provide ways that a nonacupuncturist can effect a healing for headache using finger or palm pressure. However, he will also include some point combinations aimed at the more experienced acupuncturist or student of acupuncture. In order to understand these combinations fully, one will have to be versed in acupuncture. Where multiple points are listed for treatment of a specific condition, the needles are stuck into all of the points at once and left there for a period of time, depending on how serious the condition is.

With the healing aspects of each point, finger pressure is what you should be working toward unless you are taking acupuncture lessons. The greatest therapy that anyone can give to another is to simply touch. Within us all there is the ability to heal with only our hands. Each chapter tells which points to touch to effect a healing for individual disease states. However, in most cases, where the practitioner has been practicing his or her internal martial art, the ability to simply know where the hands should go will grow with training. This growth continues until you are able to tell where a person is sick and know what remedy to give automatically. You will begin to recognize body language that will tell you exactly what is wrong with someone, and your hands will move to the correct position on the body to effect a healing.

NOTE: There is a glossary of medical references and terms at the back of the book, because many readers will not be familiar with the formal or traditional names used for the conditions mentioned under "healing."

Applications: Here I give one or two applications that can be used to get at the points. I try to keep them simple, although sometimes I include some of the more complicated methods for the sake of interest. There are obviously many applications that can be used to get at all of the points shown in this book. I will be giving one or two of the best and easiest methods to get at the points—methods that most people, regardless of experience will be able to understand and use. These come from my own martial arts systems of taijiquan, bagwazhang, dim-mak, and combat grappling. Martial arts practitioners will, of course, be able to substitute applications from their own katas or systems for mine. My ways are just a guide as to how these points should be struck.

The diagrams showing all the points in a particular meridian are located at the end of each chapter. Of course, in each chapter I will mention many points other than those of the particular meridian, but you can look those up in the chapters that cover those specific points.

Introduction to Traditional Chinese Medicine

by Wally Simpson

The first thing I discovered about massage was that if I felt good about doing it, then the person on the receiving end felt good about getting it. This was basic Swedish massage. These days I'm not sure all my clients feel good about getting massage from me, but the majority of them feel good about the results. You don't have to be a professional to give a good massage, as long you feel good about doing it.

I never felt good about doing martial arts; it always seemed a brutal, aggressive sort of thing to do. I was much more into communication with nature through surfing, bush walking, and so on, and though surfing could get a little aggressive at times, it was just the child in us demanding our birthright. (Every wave that we wanted, on our own.) It wasn't in the same league as martial arts, or so I thought. (Isn't youthful innocence amazing?)

Then, after earning a degree in Traditional Chinese Medicine (TCM), I decided that to be the complete doctor of TCM I had to teach people how to heal themselves and stay healthy via life-style (e.g., exercise, diet). Well, the Chinese did t'ai chi, and I was told that t'ai chi is not a martial art, and it didn't look all that aggressive to me. So off I went to learn this new skill. After three years of studying t'ai chi with what I thought was a reputable organization, I was introduced to one of Erle Montaigue's students, who told me that t'ai chi was a martial art and what I was doing looked nice but it wasn't t'ai chi. The concept of t'ai chi as a martial art wasn't easy for me to digest, but after my first lesson in the Yang Cheng-fu form, I knew it was far ahead of what I had been taught as t'ai chi. I guess it took the next 10 to 12 months for me to feel good about doing the small san-sou as well as the form, and it would be two years before I would meet Erle in person (though I had seen him at a couple of camps). Now, after training with Erle personally for three years, I know that it was one of the best things I have ever been fortunate enough to become involved with, and the martial stuff I was so apprehensive about has changed my life for the better in a way that I never could have imagined. It has given me a lot of confidence in myself and in my ability to defend myself and family, as well as to help others toward health and happiness. It has also improved my capacity to heal.

What Erle has given me with t'ai chi was like a seed that sprouted and is now in the process of growing into what will be a source of nourishment for myself, my family, and my many clients and friends for many, many years.

It is a great honor and a privilege to coauthor this book with Erle. The research has taken a large part of my spare time, but the information that I have unearthed (some of it rediscovered) has made it well worthwhile. I hope you gain as much out of these pages as I have. Thanks, Erle, for the opportunity once again for growth.

THE ENERGY MERIDIANS

The belief that the body is traversed by channels of energy and that this energy is the driving force behind the functions and movements of the various organs, muscles, tissue, and cells of all living creatures has been taught by many ancient cultures and has persisted from the earliest times to the present. Nowadays, modern scientists, especially physicists, are discovering through their scientific investigations that these ancient beliefs hold many more truths than was previously believed.

The Chinese called these channels of energy "meridians." In addition to the 12 main meridians covered in this volume, there are also eight extra meridians (including the Cv and Gv channels), *luo* (connecting) channels, tendino muscular channels (relating to the tendons and muscles that relate to the 12 main meridians), and divergent (distinct) channels, all of which will be covered in depth in the second volume of this encyclopedia.

Over many thousands of years the Chinese discovered that these meridians could be influenced, both beneficially and adversely, at certain points along their pathways. Modern science has found that these points, when scanned with apparatuses that measure electrical charge, have a reduced capacity for conductivity. These points are like mini-vortexes of energy spiraling into our body's major energy channels. When struck in a certain way, punctured with needles, pressed, tapped, or rotated, they have a specific effect on both local muscle, tissue, and cells, and other areas enervated, traversed, or influenced by the particular meridian being dealt with by the different methods of intervention.

HEALING AND MASSAGE

Healing and massage work are very much like martial arts; you must move from your center to have real power.

When a martial artist throws a punch and uses only the power from the muscles of his or her arm, the punch lacks any real power, and its penetration will be relatively shallow. Likewise, in massage, if you are just using your arms or hands to perform different techniques, the penetration will only reach the surface muscles, and after you have done three or four one-hour massages you will find that your arms and hands are starting to feel heavy and tired. Whereas, if the movements are coming from your waist or, more specifically, *tantien*, you will find that you can massage all day, and when you go home in the evening you will feel quite invigorated. Your techniques will reach farther into the body to the deeper layers of muscles and tendons, as there is more strength and penetration with movements from the waist.

Your stance is important. I was using a horse stance, but lately I have been using the power stance from advanced push-hands. Whatever your stance, the back should be as straight as possible. Depending on the height of your table and the size of your client, the knees should also be bent. I find that using a slightly lower table is best, so that if clients are quite big and solid, you can get over the top of them without standing on tiptoes, which allows your to bring more weight to bear on the area being worked. With a thin client, the knees can be bent more to keep the back straight. Breathing should be low in the tantien and, if possible, in sync with the person receiving the massage.

You must be able to react to a large variety of variables and respond with the type of movement needed for the present circumstances in both martial art and massage. To have a set approach and be unwilling to modify that approach with different clients/conditions is to severely limit the quality of the results you will achieve. It's like knowing only one or two strikes or blocks from a martial art form: if you are good at them, then you will succeed at times; if you know the whole form and are good at it, you will succeed a lot more. So try lots of different approaches to the same types of conditions in your massage and be flexible in how to treat. Listen to your clients—not just their voices, but what the muscles and points/channels are telling you. Work from both sides of the table, just as you should do martial techniques on both sides to keep your body in balance and be capable of using both hands/legs/feet. If you work only from one side of the table with massage, you will become unbalanced (the lumbar vertebra rotate in the direction you constantly lean) and need treatment yourself.

If you work on the floor, the same principles apply. Work from both sides and bring the movements from your tantien. To do this it is best to kneel beside the client. If you are sitting you can't move well, and you both suffer as a result.

You need to clear your mind of the chatter that normally goes on in there, and focus your attention on what you *intend* to achieve. That is not to say that you massage while spacing out, thinking, "I am going to heal this person" or "I am building yin or yang." Rather, it implies that you have a clear mind and an intention to build yin or yang and heal the individual. It's as in the martial arts—if there is no intent behind a movement, then results are poor. Without intent, there is very little chance of either a strike or a massage technique being successful. In the martial arts, we hear and read a lot about this "no mind" state, where the reptilian brain takes over and there is no conscious control over actions. Well, before that state is reached there must first be intent. A crocodile uses intent as a focus to provide the power and direction for that lunge up the river bank to grab its prey and drag it back to the water—just as you must intend to learn a martial art, or no amount of lessons can turn you into a martial artist. You must intend to help your clients, or no amount of massage will bring them relief from their symptoms.

When you are working with people in a healing capacity it, is possible to pick up negative energy from them, especially if you feel the healing is coming *from* you rather than through you. The *no mind* state mentioned above is the best way to stop that absorption of negative energy. In that state, you become a channel, and that allows energy to flow *through* you, not from you. The no mind state is what allows us to be free of attachment to the outcome. In healing, this means the client can proceed at his or her own pace with healing. It's a bit like saying, "Okay, here is a way out of this mess; I'll open the door, and you walk through when you are ready." Without attachment to the outcome, there is no draining of your energy and, as a result, little likelihood of your picking up negative energy. As martial artists, too, this lack of attachment to the outcome allows us to be ready for whatever happens, and that is a very important contribution to the final outcome.

The point Gv 20 (*baihui*), on top of the head (*sahasrara chakra* in the yogic tradition), is an entry and exit point for qi, as is Kd 1. It is said that the yang qi of heaven condenses and falls to earth to become yin qi, while the yin qi of earth evaporates to rise and become the yang qi of heaven. Mankind stands between heaven and earth and is subject to the qi of both. Yang qi of heaven enters via Gv 20 and exits via Kd 1; yin qi of earth enters via Kd 1 and exits via Gv 20. *Laogong* (Pc 8) is another point where qi can enter and exit the body. Likewise, Gv 4 (*mingmen*) is seen as the point of entry for yang qi at birth.

There are many other points for entry and exit of qi from the body, but those are the only ones I'll mention here. It is a good idea to free up those points so that when you are doing massage or healing work, the qi will flow through you without any effort on your part. The qi of heaven and earth meet in the middle at the *dai mai* (girdle or belt meridian) and can be directed out of Pc 8 to help another being or harm another being, depending on your *intent*. Doing qigong will eventually make you aware of these points, and that is the first step in freeing them up. We have these pathways open anyway, but most of us tend to isolate ourselves from them with the business of the everyday world.

So we have all this healing and martial stuff happening in the no mind state, and it is our intent that gives us direction and impetus. But intent without the ability is like sex without the partner; it mainly happens in your mind. So make sure you do the training to back what you intend to achieve. With massage, this means not only reading and learning how to locate points and what they do, but also doing lots of massage so your hands develop a feel for different conditions.

METHODS OF LOCATING POINTS

There are three methods of measuring where the points are located.

Anatomical Landmarks
The first way is to use physical landmarks such as a depression or a prominence of the bones, a joint or a muscle, the edge of the nail, a skin crease, the hairline, the area between the nipples or to the nipple, the umbilicus, the corner of the mouth or eyes, or a tendon.

Proportional Measurement

A second method is to take the different parts of the body and divide them proportionally. Each division is termed *one cun* (pronounced *tsoone*). For example, the distance from the second finger joint to the first is one cun (diagram 1). The one cun measurement will differ from a large person to a smaller person, as it is taken from anatomical parts of each individual's body.

On the head we have several measurements: from the anterior hairline to the posterior hairline is 12 cun (diagram 2); between the two mastoid processes is 9 cun, as is the distance between both St 8 points.

On the chest we usually base the measurements upon the intercostal spaces, or those between the ribs. From the axillary fold to the 11th rib is 12 cun. From the sternocostal angle to the middle of the navel is 8 cun. From the navel to the upper line of the symphysis pubis is 5 cun. Between the two nipples is 8 cun (diagram 3). Between the scapular medial line and the posterior midline is 3 cun.

On the arm, from the end of the axillary fold to the transverse cubital crease is 9 cun (diagram 4). On the forearm, the distance between the transverse cubital crease (elbow) and the carpal crease (wrist) is 12 cun (diagram 5).

On the thigh (diagram 6), the distance from the pubis to the medial epicondyle of the femur is 18 cun. From the prominence of the greater trochanter on the outside of the thigh to the center of the patella is 19 cun.

For more minute measurements, we use *fen*, which denotes one-tenth of a cun.

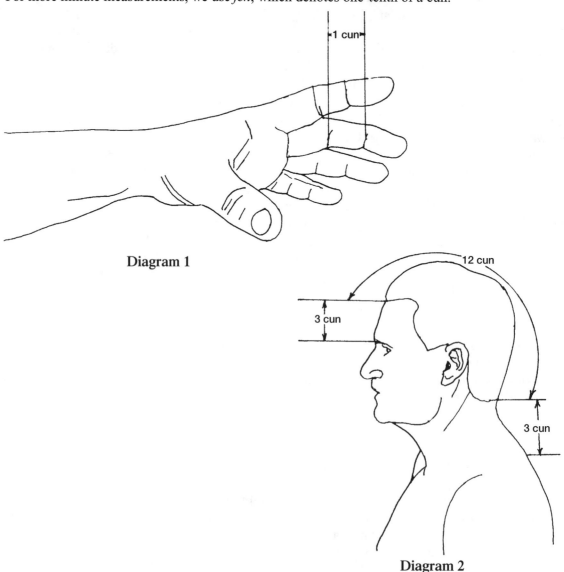

1 cun

Diagram 1

12 cun

3 cun

3 cun

Diagram 2

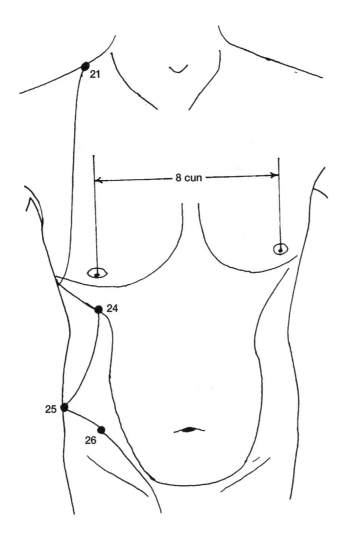

Diagram 3

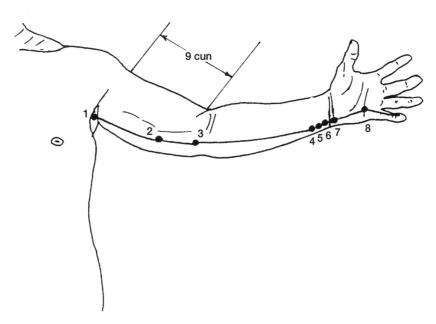

Diagram 4

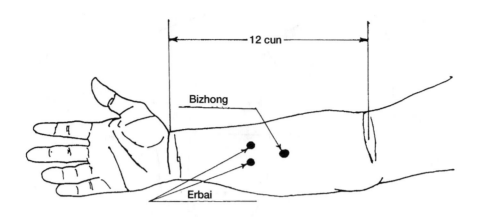

Diagram 5

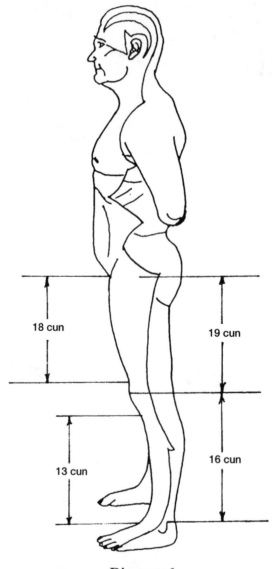

Diagram 6

Measuring with the Fingers

Finally, we use the fingers to locate the points.

When the longest finger is flexed, the distance between the two ends of the creases of the interphalangeal joints is one cun.

The width of the four fingers when they are held together is 3 cun (diagram 7). The width of the thumb is one cun. The width of the index and longest finger taken at the second joint is 1.5 cun.

You might notice a seeming inconsistency between some of the measurements and what you see in the diagrams. For instance, the measurement across the forehead, when looked at on a two-dimensional diagram (diagram 8), looks as if it is not actually 9 cun—in fact, it looks like much less. However, you have to take into consideration that this measurement goes around the forehead from St 8 to St 8. So when you take a piece of string and stretch it from St 8 to St 8, then place that length from nipple to nipple, the distance between which is 8 cun, then you will see that the forehead distance is indeed 9 cun.

Because the Chinese way of measuring depends upon the size of the patient, it is best if you have the experience to know automatically where the points are and only use the measurements as a rough guide. Most acupuncturists prefer to use the anatomical method.

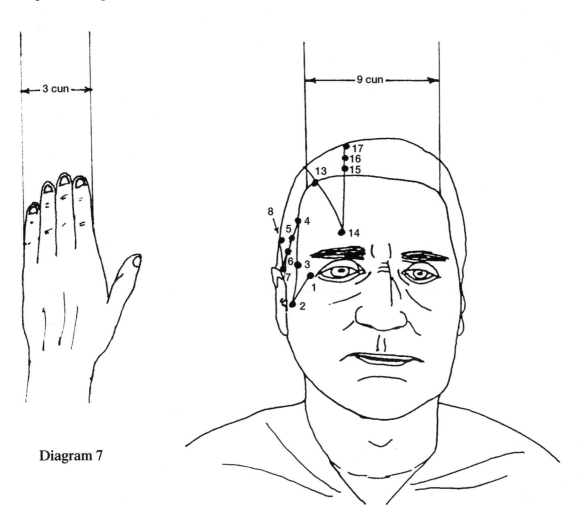

Diagram 7

Diagram 8

STATES OF UNWELLNESS: THE UNDERLYING CAUSES

The Chinese believe that it is some type of disruption to the flow of energy that creates all states of unwellness. Thus, when looking at the cause of a disease, a TCM doctor looks at several broad classifications of conditions. These broad classifications are then further refined by consideration of the syndromes of the organs (*zhang/fu*) or channels and collaterals (*jing/lou*) involved. In the text that follows, we will take a look at those that have the most significance for our purposes in this text.

Xu (Deficient) and Shi (Excess) Conditions

Xu, or deficient, conditions are characterized by weakness, decrease in body function, listless spirit, lethargy, shortness of breath, aversion to speaking, and poor appetite. Pain are dull, vague aches that improve with massage, and you may feel coldness in the problem areas. The face and complexion may be pale, as is the body of the tongue. The tongue may also appear swollen and have scalloped sides. The pulse feels weak.

The "emptiness" (*xu*) may be of qi, *xue* (blood), yin, or yang. Yin xu causes a rapid and weak pulse, and the tongue body may appear red with no coating or a patchy coating. Patients may have a subjective feeling of heat, especially in the afternoon and evenings, or they may have hot flashes and night sweating and appear wasted. Yang xu produces a slow, weak pulse and the tongue body will be moist and may have a thick coating on its surface. Patients may feel cold or cool, even on hot days.

Xu conditions are nourished or tonified with massage that involves clockwise rotations; strong, deep, even pressure; and slow movements in the direction of the channel flow, that is, from the small numbers to the large numbers (referring to the numbers assigned to the acupuncture points along the meridian.)

Xu conditions feel empty on the surface, and as you get deeper you will find an area of consolidation. They often present themselves as flaccid muscles or a depression over the point/area, or even as a wasting of the whole muscle tissue in that region. They are generally pale and feel cooler than surrounding tissue, and the client is likely to report a lack of energy or lethargy either in the area or in general. These areas, while they may be sore and ache, like to be touched and like heat; they are less likely to cause restriction of movement than other types of conditions. Clients will probably experience them as a dull ache or a weakness. Work more slowly over these areas; start gently and move deeper fairly rapidly. While it will probably hurt, clients will report that it is a nice pain; they like to be touched, pushed, and prodded in these areas, so you can stay deeper for longer. As a result, you can generally work there until significant improvement is achieved. Heat, and in particular moxibustion, is wonderful in these types of conditions. Moxibustion is the burning of herbs. The herb mugwort is cured for a long period, made into a stick, and burned on or near acupoints or on needles. Moxa warms cold and builds qi and yang via penetration of heat energy. Moxa is very good to use on yang xu patients.

In xu conditions, where cold and lethargy are a problem, in addition to treating local points/areas with moxa, it is a good idea to use points such as Kd 3, Sp 3, St 36, Bl 23, Bl 20, Th 4, Gv 4, Cv 4, Gv 6, Gv 12, and Gb 25 to help build qi and yang in general. It is yang qi that acts as the first line of defense against pathogenic invasion, cooks the food in the stomach, and extracts the nutrient and sends it up to join with the qi from the air we breathe. Yang qi provides us with warmth and the ability to process fluids, as well as holding things in place and supplying the get up and go for our everyday activity.

Excess, or *shi*, conditions may be the result of a strong external pathogen (e.g., wind, cold, heat, dryness, damp, fire, trauma) attacking a weakened system and penetrating into the body, causing it to become full of perverse energy. These conditions may also occur due to normal body conditions and a very excessive set of circumstances, or as a result of holding onto an emotion for a long time and thus stagnating the free flow of energy (of which emotions are a part).

Shi conditions tend to be of recent onset, acute, and of short duration. Patients may be in good spirits, have a flushed face and a loud voice, and have very severe pain that feels worse with pressure and doesn't particularly like massage. Muscles may appear to be in spasm and rigid and may rebound when pressed. Other signs and symptoms will depend upon what type of fullness is presenting. For instance, heat will cause a redness of both the area involved and the tongue body. The coating on the tongue may be thick and yellow, or black if the condition is very severe. The pulse will be rapid and strong, as is standard in shi conditions. The damaged area or the whole body may feel hot to touch, and there may be a great thirst.

Shi conditions are sedated or dispersed with massage that involves counterclockwise rotations and fast, lighter movements against the flow of the channel (i.e., from the largest numbers to the small numbers.) From my experience, I have found that some individuals with shi conditions of the muscles—where the muscle is hard as a rock and feels bloody awful when pressed—get best results from massage if they concentrate on their breathing and let the doctor work quite deeply. Concentrating on the breathing helps to deal with the pain being inflicted by the massage technique and also helps release the blockage of energy or blood (qi or xue) in the muscle.

Excess conditions feel solid or dense all the way up to the surface. The area may look raised, feel hot, and look red or darkish compared to the surrounding tissues. Normally, these are very painful conditions, causing varying amounts of restriction to movement. They do not like to be touched and may not respond to heat (this varies, depending on the type of shi condition and the duration of the condition; it is possible to get a full cold condition, which will respond well to heat). Work quickly and gently at first over these shi regions, but slowly make your movements deeper. Your client will let you know how deep you can go and for how long you can stay there. It is no good getting too deep too soon, because the client will tense excessively and grit the teeth to stop you from penetrating. This may at times be useful, as when clients become super tense and rigid from your pressure; when you stop pressing, they get a greater degree of relaxation. It can also just tense them up and not produce any relaxation at all. Your client has the final say about the depth you can reach. I find it best to work quickly over these areas and come back to them often. Use points that are on the same meridian pathway but that are located on the extremities to help drain stuck qi and blood out of tense areas (e.g., for extremely tight shoulders, treat local points and then use points like Si 3, Gb 34, Gb 41, Gb 43, Gb 44, Co 4, Bl 60, etc., as distal points).

In shi conditions where there has been a penetration of cold that has resulted in muscle spasm and pain (e.g., wind/cold penetration into the muscles and channels of the neck and shoulders), use points like Gv 14 to warm the cold and free up the channels or Gb 21 to warm the cold and send stagnant qi back down to be dispersed. For cold to have penetrated, there has either been an underlying xu condition or an exposure to extremes of cold over an extended period. So you may need to tonify xu with the above-mentioned points, as well as disperse the cold, warm the yang, and free up the channels.

Some points can sedate shi (excess) as well as tonify xu (deficient) conditions. So you need to be clear on what you are working with.

Internal and External Climatic Conditions

Other factors that influence our lives are the internal and external climatic conditions, and if we are to be successful at treating disease, then we need to be familiar with these conditions and how they interact within the body's landscape. There are six evils (*liu xie*) or pernicious influences: wind, cold, heat or fire, dryness, dampness, and summer heat. An individual with one or more of these conditions will most probably have an aversion to the particular influence involved.

Wind (*feng*) can be of internal or external origin. Wind seldom attacks the body alone; it is usually in the company of another pathogen, such as heat, cold, or dampness. Wind tends to cause symptoms to appear and disappear suddenly. It produces change and a degree of urgency in what is otherwise slow and even. Wind is a yang phenomenon associated with spring, though it can appear in any season (e.g., hay fever is a classic wind-related disease that most often appears in spring but can appear in autumn). Wind tends to affect the upper parts of the body first—skin, face, neck, sweat glands, lungs, and *taiyang* (the most exterior of the six yin and yang divisions, it includes bladder and small intestine and tends to be seen as the first stage of penetration by external pathogenic influences). Wind can cause spasms, tremors of the limbs, twitching, dizziness, tetany, symptoms such as rash or arthritis, or maybe just pain that moves from one place to another (e.g., shingles). With external wind invasion, some people may recall having been exposed to draught, while others won't. External wind invasion is characterized by its sudden onset. It is often accompanied by fever, as the protective (*wei*) qi fights to expel the invading pathogen. This is more simultaneous chills and fever, with the symptom that predominates signaling the type of pathogen that the wind has combined with.

Internal wind is generally of a chronic nature and often involves the liver (e.g., an excess condition of the liver, such as liver fire, can create wind in the same way as a fire creates an updraft, causing symptoms such as migraine or tinnitus, while a deficient condition of, say, liver blood may create empty wind symptoms, such as itchy eyes). Internal wind may include such symptoms as dizziness, tinnitus, numbness of the limbs, tremors, convulsions, or apoplexy.

Cold (*han*) can be of internal or external origin and of an excess or deficient nature. It is a yin pathogen associated with winter in the same way as wind is associated with spring. It can appear in any season (e.g., a cool breeze in summer can generate an attack of wind cold in the body, especially if there is a preexisting condition or a weakness of defensive qi), though it will be aggravated in cold weather. The most reliable sign is that the individual feels cold—the whole or part of the body will feel cold to the touch and/or it may have a pale, frigid look, and the person will have an aversion to cold and actively seek warmth and warm clothes. Cold causes things to contract and so restricts movement and blocks the circulation of qi in the channels, causing sharp, severe cramping pain that will generally respond positively to heat. Cold from external attack will cause symptoms such as aversion to cold and acute severe cramping pain that does not like to be touched but likes heat. There may be chills and fever, with the chills predominating. The pulse will be slow and feel full and floating (it can be felt better at the superficial levels with light touch), the tongue will be pale and moist with a thin white coating (this coating may be thick if there is a lot of damp or phlegm present). There will be body aches, headache, and usually only small amounts of sweating if there is any at all (cold obstructs the pores).

Internal cold is the result of a deficient yang qi. Yang qi is hot and active, so a decline in it causes the body to become cold and slow. Internal cold is generally associated with chronic conditions or the consumption of too much raw or cold food and drink. It is generally related to the kidney or the spleen. Symptoms might include slow, weak pulse; aversion to cold; and a preference for hot drinks and warm clothes. Patients generally like to be touched and respond well to heat. The tongue is pale and moist and has a thin white or patchy coating (or it may have a thick white coating because there is no heat for digestion). Movements will be slow and weak, and there may be copious clear urine and loose stool with food in it (maybe watery stool), discharges will be white or clear and have little or no smell, and the patient may sleep curled up in a fetal position and have a lack of energy, poor digestion, and a slow, deep pulse.

Hot (*re*) or fire (*huo*) can be internal or external in origin and can be of an excess or deficient nature. It is a yang pathogen and, though associated with summer, can occur in any season. Heat is normal in the body; it is the yang aspect that creates activity and warmth for the body. As a pathogenic influence, it causes either the whole body or part of the body to feel hot and to have a red color. The hot pathogen may create irritability and agitation, the patient will dislike heat and prefer cold drinks, and there may be signs of high fever, chills and fever where heat predominates, as well as a red face and a red tongue with a yellow dry or yellow greasy coating, depending on what it combines with (e.g., dryness or damp). The pulse will be rapid; if it is an external pathogen the pulse will also be floating. There will generally be a big thirst, maybe lots of sweating, and perhaps foul-smelling urine/secretions. Urine will be yellow (check that it is not just from vitamin B intake), and the stool may be dry and constipated or loose and smelly (can be explosive). If the pathogen is excess, then it won't like touch, whereas if deficient it will like touch. There may be extravasation of blood (e.g., bloody nose, hematuria).

Heat causes things to dry out, so there can be a lack of or scanty excretions. External excess heat invasion can produce a fast/full/floating pulse, forceful/severe pains, convulsions, very hot dry symptoms, excess thirst, lots of sweat or no sweat, great irritability, and possibly delirium.

Internal heat/fire can be excess or deficient in nature. If excess, it is usually contracted from the liver. The major symptoms of the pathology of liver fire flaring include sudden outbursts of anger, red eyes, irritability, inability to keep still, and violent migraines. Most if not all excess internal heat/fire is the result of emotional suppression or stagnation. Internal excess of liver heat may also result in heavy or irregular periods.

Internal deficient heat or fire is the result of a yin deficiency. There is not enough yin (coolness) to keep the yang (heat, fire) of the body in check, so an apparent excess of yang develops. Deficient heat symptoms include thirst but no desire to drink; red tongue with a thin yellow coating or no coating; afternoon fevers; malar flush; weak, empty, fast pulse; pain that gets better with touch; night sweats; and fear of cold. The flushing of menopause is a deficient heat condition in most cases.

Damp (*shi*) is wet, heavy, and slow. It is a yin pathogen associated with damp, cloudy weather in any season. Living and working in damp surroundings and wearing damp clothes can contribute to a damp condition. A major factor in the generation of damp conditions is the over-consumption of cold food and drink, raw food, or greasy food. Irregular eating habits will weaken the spleen's ability to transform and transport food and fluids effectively. Dampness is heavy, turbid, lingering, and can tend to move things downward, affecting the lower parts of the body first, though when combined with wind, it will affect the upper parts of the body (e.g., headache where the head feels heavy, dull, as though there is a tight band around it). Symptoms could include heavy, sore limbs; excretions and secretions that are often copious, turbid, cloudy, and sticky; eyes that feel as if they have sand in them; urine that is cloudy; stool that could be quite loose or even diarrhea; and maybe heavy vaginal discharge, fluid-filled lesions, or oozing skin eruptions.

External damp may obstruct qi, resulting in fullness in the chest or abdomen and dribbling or incomplete urination and/or defecation. It can also obstruct the qi in the channels causing heaviness, stiffness, and/or soreness and swelling in the joints. If it affects the spleen, it may interfere with the rising of pure qi (extract from food and fluids) and cause loss of appetite, indigestion, nausea, diarrhea, edema, etc. One of the best signs of damp that I come across all the time is when you feel really awful when you first get up after sleep or even just sitting or lying for a while, but start to feel better after moving around a bit. External and internal damp are distinguishable mainly by the speed of onset. External damp is acute and will be accompanied by other external signs; it can easily become internal damp. Internal damp is likely to make the individual more susceptible to external damp. Regardless of where it came from, damp is an insidious pathogen and can last a long time. Mucus or phlegm (*tan*) is a form of internal damp and is generally generated by disharmonies of the spleen and kidney. Dampness can condense when there is heat present or when it has been around for a while. Since phlegm is heavier than damp and much more viscous, so it can easily obstruct the channels, generating lumps, nodules, tumors, etc. In the lungs it causes cough with thick expectoration. In the heart it can obstruct the *shen* (spirit), resulting in muddled thought, stupor, coma-type conditions, madness, or chaotic behavior. Mucus in the channels can cause numbness; paralysis; nodules; soft, mobile tumors; and limbs that ache and feel heavy. The tongue most often has a thick, greasy coating when phlegm is present, though it may just be moist in damp conditions. The pulse is slippery in both.

Summer heat (*shu*) is an external pathogen that is the result of exposure to extreme heat. Symptoms include sudden high fever and heavy sweating; if it enters the stomach it causes nausea and vomiting. Summer heat can easily damage the qi, resulting in exhaustion. It can also damage the fluids, causing dryness. Summer heat often occurs with dampness.

Dryness (*zao*) is associated with autumn. It is a yang phenomenon closely related to heat—heat and dryness are on a continuum, dryness toward dehydration and heat toward redness and hotness. Symptoms of dryness include dry mouth, lips, tongue, and nostrils; cracked skin; and dry, hard stool. External dryness can interfere with the descending and dispersing function of the lungs, causing symptoms such as dry cough, little or no sputum, asthma, chest pain, fever, body aches, and other external symptoms.

It is fairly unusual for these types of pathogens, especially when they are of exterior origin, to attack the body on their own. Most often they combine with wind, such as in the case of *bi* syndrome (the Chinese equivalent of arthritis), where wind/cold/damp or wind/heat/damp, etc. get together to retard the flow of qi and xue, causing pain, swelling, and restriction of movement. It is even possible to have an attack of wind/dryness in one area of the body while experiencing a wind/damp heat attack in another part.

THE 5 ELEMENT POINTS CYCLE OF CREATION OR SHENG CYCLE

The sheng/creation or nourishing cycle is where each element nourishes or creates the next cycle (element)—e.g., fire creates earth. The sequence can be rationalized as follows:

Wood creates fire (the wood is burned to create the fire).
Fire creates earth (fire expends itself, and what is left is ash which become earth).
Earth creates metal (the element metal is found by digging in the earth).
Metal creates water (by melting—solid metals melt to form a liquid). Metal also corresponds to air (in Western astrology), and air condenses to form a liquid.
Water creates wood (by nourishing growth).

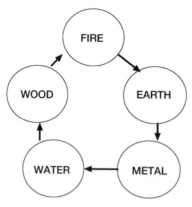

The 5 element points cycle of creation or sheng cycle.

If each element is fed and strengthened, it will feed the next element in the cycle, as a mother feeds a son or daughter; thus it is termed the cycle of creation, and it gives birth to the mother/son theory used in treating disharmonies.

The KO/inhibiting/repressive or controlling cycle is where each element inhibits or controls the element two steps ahead in the sequence. For example, wood controls earth. This is like a grandparent exerting control over a grandchild, and in TCM it is called grandmother/grandson cycle. It works as follows:

Fire controls metal (by melting it).
Metal controls wood (by cutting it).
Wood controls earth (by covering it).
Earth controls water (by damming it).
Water controls fire (by extinguishing it).

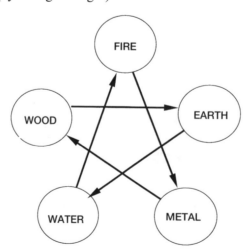

The Ko cycle.

The organ-element relationship is as follows:

ELEMENT	YANG ORGAN	YIN ORGAN
EARTH	STOMACH	SPLEEN
METAL	COLON	LUNGS
WATER	BLADDER	KIDNEYS
WOOD	GALL BLADDER	LIVER
FIRE	SMALL INTESTINE/ TRIPLE HEATER	HEART/ PERICARDIUM

The harmonious balance of the sheng and KO cycles represents the mutual support and control of the five elements. The sheng (creative) cycle ensures that there is continual growth and generation. The KO cycle ensures that there is growth within limits, that growth does not continue unchecked. Thus the two cycles represent the balance of the five elements. Both cycles are natural and positive, unless an imbalance or blockage occurs in the flow, resulting in the generation of a destructive cycle.

The sheng cycle is predominant during the day, and the KO cycle is predominant during the night. Each element has its corresponding color, smell, body organ/channel, etc. that can form the basis of diagnosis. If any concordance tends to predominate or is lacking, a practitioner will be able to diagnose which part of the sequence is disturbed and treat the energies accordingly to open the natural flows.

Another way of using this system is as follows. An inflammatory condition occurring in an organ or tissue can be seen as a fire-type symptom (feels hot, causes irritation, etc.), so using the water point to reduce this fire (inflammation) can have a dramatic and immediate effect on the inflammation. If the inflammation is not completely relieved by the water point, then add a metal point to nourish the water and increase the effect of its action.

As a martial artist, one could do a primary strike on the earth point of the pericardium channel (Pc 7), and then do the next strike on the front *mu* (alarm) point of the heart (Pc 7 and then Cv 14), in order to increase the damaging effect of the strike to the heart mu point. Thus, striking Pc 7 first increases the damage done to the heart when the Cv 14 point is struck. This is using the sheng cycle's mother/son theory, where the son is used to drain qi from the mother. The heart is the yin, or half the yin, of the fire element (pericardium is the other half). The pericardium is also seen as the protector of the heart, so damage here could increase damage to the heart.

Using an example from the KO cycle, one could strike to the metal point of the pericardium channel (Pc 5), then follow with a strike to front mu point of the liver (Liv 14). Here metal is acting to control the wood, and then further striking to a major point affecting the yin organ of the yin element adds insult to injury and results in dramatic results (perhaps liver shutdown). These are just examples of how these cycles might be used martially; there are lots of different combinations that could be used.

There is also a cycle called the reverse KO cycle (or counteracting or rebellious cycle). This is where one element rebels against its natural controller. This is an abnormal cycle and is symbolic of defiance. It may well be that at death the reverse KO cycle comes into play.

The format is as follows:

• Wood counteracts metal (by blunting it).
• Metal counteracts fire (by extinguishing it—cutting off its supply of oxygen).
• Fire counteracts water (by boiling it away if the fire is too vigorous).
• Water counteracts earth (by washing it away if the water is dammed to excess).
• Earth counteracts wood (by providing no foundation for its roots).

THE FIVE SHU POINTS

The five shu points are also called antique points, five element points, command points, and well points. They are all located below the elbows or the knees, since it is here that the energy in the channels is the most superficial, and the energy potential in the channel changes very rapidly in this region.

Thus, these points have a strong effect on the body when used either to heal or to disrupt an individual's energy patterns. These points can be used to disrupt qi flow in a channel in advance of a strike to a major knockout or death strike point, or to create a potentiality for healing by either boosting the qi in the channel or draining excess qi from the channel.

Jing Well Points

Jing well (*tsing, ting, ching*) points are wood on the yin channels and metal on the yang channels. They are located at the beginning or the end of the channel at the extremities of the fingers or toes. They are compared to the welling up of the water course. It is in the region of these points that the changeover of yin and yang qi occurs; the energy is very unstable here, so the use of these points is potentially very powerful.

These points dispel wind and heat. Bloodletting is most often applied to these points to clear heat (prick the point with a sterile needle and extract a few drops of blood). This is indicated for acute attacks of wind/heat or internal wind/heat that has caused loss of consciousness by drying the blood out of the vessels, as well as for heat in the blood that causes toxic skin conditions, bleeding nose, etc. These points also act on the muscle and divergent channels.

Ying Spring Points

Ying spring (*rong, yong, yung,* gushing) points are fire on the yin channels and water on the yang channels. These are located proximally to the jing well points, and it is here that the energy of the channel accelerates, like a spring bursting forth from the soil. They are also called acceleration-of-energy points and can be used to either increase or reduce the qi of the channel. They can be used to cool hot conditions and are usually reduced for this purpose by needling. They can be used with jing well points for draining excess qi from the channel and to treat excess in the muscle meridians. In shi conditions local points are used first, then distal points such as ying spring and/or jing well. Ying spring can also be used as good pep-up points.

Shu Stream Points

Shu stream (*yu,* transporting) points are earth on the yin channels and wood on the yang channels. These points are proximal to the ying spring points, and it is here that a pathogen that has entered a channel gets carried along, like a boat catching a stream. Their function is to eliminate pathogen energy from the channel, especially wind and damp, conditions, such as aching joints, etc. Here a reducing method is used; you can use ying spring and shu stream for this purpose (to treat arthritis that is seen as wind/damp bi syndrome in Chinese terms). On the yin channels the shu stream point is also the *yuan* source point, where the yuan qi (the physiologically active component of jing) resides and can be tapped to replenish and strengthen the vital energy of an organ or channel. Here a reinforcing method is applied.

Jing River Points

Jing river (*ching,* traversing) points are metal on the yin channels and fire on the yang channels. At these points the energy can be deviated out of the channel. They are used to treat cough and asthma (e.g., for cough from lung qi xu, you might use Kd 7 and Lu 9 or Sp 5, Lu 8, Kd 7, and Pc 5).

He Sea Points

He sea (*ho,* uniting) points are water on the yin channels and earth on the yang channels. At these points the qi penetrates deeper into the channel, passing through the internal organs, so these points can be used to stop pathogen energy from going deeper and also to regulate the associated organ. The arm 3 yang channels (Th, Si, and Co) share a more distant relationship with their internal organs than the other channels to their internal organs (*zhang/fu*), so there is an extra point for each on the leg, called a lower he sea point, which is used to treat the related organ (e.g., for the colon, St 37 is used as a lower he sea point).

Healing is the art of building/moving and balancing the body's qi, while martial arts is the art of stagnating, depleting, and scattering the body's qi. If you are going to learn to destroy, then also learn to build.

Bibliography

Beijing College of Traditional Medicine. 1980. *Essentials of Chinese Acupuncture, Beijing First Edition*. Beijing: Foreign Language Press.

Deshen, Wang. 1982. *Manual of International Standardization of Acupuncture Point Names*.

Kaptchuk, T.J. 1983. *Chinese Medicine: The Web That Has No Weaver*. London: Rider & Company.

Legge, David. 1991 to 1995. Seminars. Brisbane, Australia,

Matsumoto, Kiiko. 1995. Seminar. Sydney, Australia.

O'Connor, J., and D. Bensky, eds. 1981. *Acupuncture: A Comprehensive Text*. Seattle: Eastland Press.

Simpson, Wally. 1983 to 1986. Course notes from Acupuncture Colleges Australia/Brisbane.

Chapter 1

The Gallbladder Meridian

The gallbladder meridian is the second longest meridian and has the most usable points in dim-mak. Those points are relatively easy to get at and will all cause a KO when struck in the correct direction and with the correct pressure.

Most of the Gb points work fine on their own, with only the set-up point used to enhance the effect. However, when necessary, I will also include a secondary and tertiary point that can be used in conjunction with the major point to greatly enhance the effect (e.g., Pc 6, Th 12, and Lu 7 used with Gb 5).

The gallbladder stores and concentrates bile, which is used to break down animal fats taken in as food. Bile is made up of bile salts, bile pigment, and cholesterol, and it is produced in diluted form in the liver. Although the liver can secrete bile directly into the system, the diluted form is not really strong enough. So the job of the gallbladder, located on the underside of the liver, is to concentrate the bile into a more usable form.

Western medicine tells us that the gallbladder is not critical for life, but Chinese medicine tells a different story. (And knowing several people who have had their gallbladder removed, I know that it is important for the qi flow in the body and that quality of life usually diminishes after it has been removed.)

THE TCM VIEW

The gallbladder meridian is yang in nature and has a wood element in Chinese element theory. It is the other half of the wood meridian pair, with the liver meridian being the yin half.

The gallbladder is said to be the "controller of judgments." In years gone by, the meridians were likened to a human society, with each meridian having a role to play, like any normal human being within a society. The liver makes the bile, but it is the job of the gallbladder to store and judge when to release it. On another level, the gallbladder has the ability to help the individual with the capacity to confer judgment and make decisions, and so forth. Hence the old saying, "he has a lot of gall," or "he lacks gall."

So, when we attack this meridian, we are indeed attacking a most deadly meridian as it has much to do with the internal physiological workings, as well as the mental and spiritual workings of the body.

GB 1 (GALLBLADDER POINT NO. 1)

Chinese name:

Tongziliao, or bone of the eye.

Location:

.5 cun lateral to the outer edge of the canthus of the eye. (See diagram 10 at the end of this chapter.) The point is in the orbicularis muscle. The nerves in the region include the zygomaticofacial, zygomaticotemporal, and the temporal and frontal branches of the facial nerve.

Connections:

Small intestine and triple heater meridians.

Direction of strike:

This point is usually struck with a one-knuckle punch or with the tips of the fingers, moving from the rear of the head to the front, past the eye. The one-knuckle or the tips of the fingers will slice into the small hollow where the point is located at the corner of the eye.

Damage:

Struck on its own, this point will cause extreme nausea, loss of memory, and possible death. It is very dangerous, even with light strikes. Depending upon the strike used, you can of course do damage to the eyes as well.

Set-up point:

There is no specific point. However, the attacker's arm can be violently rubbed/struck from his elbow down to his wrist on the outside of his forearm. This will affect the qi, enhancing the effects of the major strike. (See the "Applications" section.)

Antidote:

Gently rub Gb 1 backward toward the ear, or press Gv 26, just under the nose (see diagram at the end of the governor vessel chapter), upward and back toward the head. If you are going to use CPR it is best to apply the antidotes first.

Healing:

For headaches, hold both Gb 1 points using your fingertips (fig. 8). For xu (deficient) conditions (see the Introduction to TCM at the beginning of the book), you can rotate your fingertips in a clockwise direction on both sides (i.e., make a circle as if the circle is moving away from you). Or for shi (excess) conditions, make a counterclockwise circle on the point.

You may also palpate the area with light pressure. When you are holding the points, the patient should feel some light pain there. Regarding the amount of pressure to use for this

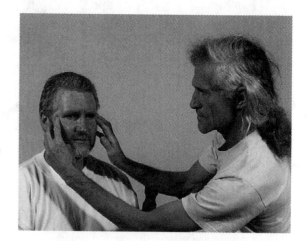

Figure 8

Figure 9

point, it is said that you should use as much as one can stand on the eyeball. I have found, however, that a little harder than this works better.

You can also wipe out from Gb 1 toward Gb 3, which is the temple. (See diagram at the end of this chapter for Gb 3).

This point is used for headache, ophthalmoplegia, failing vision, night blindness, atrophy of the optic nerve, redness of the eye, lacrimation, and keratitis.

Traditional uses include glaucoma, membrane over the eye, excessive tearing, and sore throat. This point is also used to eliminate "wind heat," dispel "fire" and brighten the eyes.

Gb 1 is a point of intersection of the small intestine and triple heater channels with the Gb channel. The liver and triple heater divergent channels also meet here, so it can be used to affect general qi flow throughout the body via the liver divergent channel.

Applications:

1) The opponent attacks with a left straight punch. You should swing both arms out to your right, until your left palm makes contact with his left forearm as your right fingertips slice into his Gb point. Both of your palms are moving in the correct direction, i.e., your left palm is moving down his left forearm from elbow to palm for the set-up, while your right fingers are striking from the back of his head to the front (fig. 9).

2) The opponent attacks with a right straight. You step to your left while parrying and setting up his right forearm (fig. 10). Instantly, your right one-knuckle punch moves in a clockwise direction to strike his Gb 1 point from rear to front (fig. 11).

Figure 10

Figure 11

GB 2 (GALLBLADDER POINT NO. 2)

Chinese name:

Tinghui (confluence of hearing).

Location:

In front of the intertragic notch, directly below tinggong , or Si 19 (see diagram at end of small intestine chapter), at the posterior border of the condyloid process of the mandible. (This is the little "notch" on the edge of the ear, that little triangle that sticks out just above the jaw bone.) Locate the point with the mouth open. (See Diagram 1, end of this chapter).

Connections:

An internal branch to Si 19.

Direction of strike:

This point is usually struck straight in to the head. It is best suited for a one-knuckle punch or using a claw type of hand where the fingertips strike into the point. It is made more effective when Si 19 is also attacked. This can be achieved by the use of the dim-mak claw (fig. 12).

Damage:

Struck on its own, this point will cause extreme nausea and dizziness. Death will occur only if the point is struck really hard.

Set-up point:

Neigwan, or Pc 6 (see diagram at end of pericardium chapter) is struck straight inward just before the Gb 2 strike. (Neigwan is a utility set-up point that can be used to set up many of the major strikes.)

Antidote:

Poke up into St 3, just under the cheekbones, with the index and middle fingertips of one hand, as in Figure 13. (See the diagram at the end of the stomach chapter for the location of St 3).

Healing:

Gb 2 is supplied by an anterior aural branch of the superficial temporal artery and, in the deep position, by the external carotid artery and the posterior facial vein. It is innervated by the great auricular nerve and a branch of the facial nerve.

Gb 2 is used against tinnitus (ringing in the ear), deafness, otitis media (inflammation of the middle ear), deaf mutism, toothache, and facial paralysis.

Traditional indications include mouth and eyes awry, hemiplegia (paralysis of half the body), seizure in which the body is alternately tense and limp, "madly running away" (a Chinese

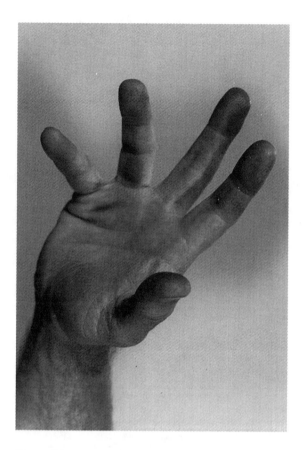

Figure 12

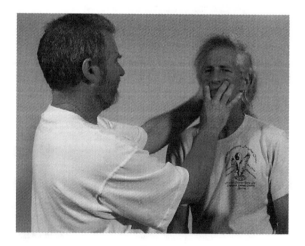

Figure 13

term for something similar to hysteria), dislocation of jaw, swelling of parotid glands, tinnitus, deafness, and toothache.

The massage technique used is to press the points on both sides and hold them, or rotate them as for Gb 1 (clockwise or counterclockwise for either xu or shi conditions).

This point can be used along with tingmia (an extra point located at the lower anterior root of the earlobe), with chinqian, (an extra point .5 cun anterior to Gb 20), or with St 6 and St 4 for apoplectic facial paralysis.

Gb 2 can also be used along with xiaxi (Gb 43) for tinnitus and with foot qiaoyin (Gb 44) for deafness.

Applications:

1) The opponent attacks with a right hook. I will attack his right forearm with my right knife-edge palm to his neigwan point (fig. 14). My right dim-mak claw rebounds in an arc to strike the side of his face with my five fingertips. My middle finger will make contact with Gb 2, while my index finger makes contact with Si 17, my thumb contacts St 9, my ring finger contacts Si 19, and my small finger contacts Gb 1. Obviously, this is the optimal strike but requires great accuracy. Even if you are lucky to get only two of the above points, with one of them being Gb 2, this strike is devastating and will cause death from extreme qi drainage (fig. 15).

2) The opponent attacks with a right straight. My right palm takes his arm, slamming it down the forearm to set up the point (fig. 16). My left palm instantly slams downward on the forearm as well, as my right one-knuckle punch attacks to Gb 2 (fig. 17). You also could have used a palm strike with this method since you do not have to be so accurate using the palm.

Figure 14

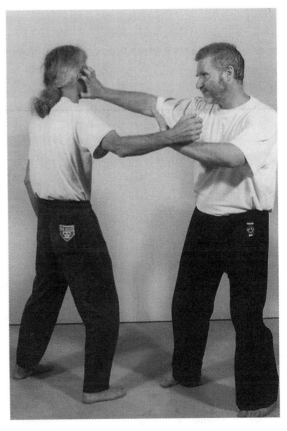

Figure 15

Figure 16

Figure 17

GB 3 (GALLBLADDER POINT NO. 3)

Chinese name:
Shangquan (guests and hosts).

Location:
This is the temple point. It is on the superior border of the zygomatic arch in the depression that can be felt in the bone.

Connections:
Stomach meridian.

Direction of strike:
Straight in to the side of the head using any weapon—in particular, the one-knuckle punch or a palm heel.

Damage:
Being the temple, this is an extremely sensitive area. A hard strike to this point will cause death, and a light or medium strike will cause KOt.

Set-up point:
The set-up point for the temple is a qi-disruptive strike. Briefly, qi disruption occurs when we upset the electrical flow (qi flow) in the body. The qi-disruptive strike must be as close to the skin without touching as possible. (We can do this without touching the attacker when we have attained a high level of training.) To cause qi disruption, the palm or palms are waved violently past certain areas of the body.

There are nine qi-disruptive methods in all. It works like this. We all have electrical channels through which electricity flows. In electrical theory, we can cause an adverse electrical current by waving a magnetic object across a conductor, as in an electrical generator. Our hands have minute magnetism, and when they are waved across certain meridians, they will cause an adverse flow of qi, thus causing the recipient to become weak or even fall down. Experiments have been done in the

United States where by simply reversing what is called "awakening energy," people have been made to either go to sleep or wake up. (The Chinese call this awakening energy, "light qi.") These experiments failed at first because the experimenters were using too high a voltage, but when they used voltages that were equivalent to the normal human body voltage (very low), the effect was attained.

The qi-disruptive set-up strike used in conjunction with Gb 3 is a violent swipe across the attacker's face from his left to right. The direction never changes, nor does the hand with which you perform the strike. We always use the left hand to do this strike. I have tested this particular set-up strike out many times on many different people, and it has not failed once (a certain level of achievement in the internal arts is necessary, though.) You have your partner place his fist onto your chest and punch as hard as he can. The punch is felt to be quite powerful, to the point of knocking the wind out of you. You take his punch again, as soon as you've done the "swipe," and there is no power there at all.

Qi disruption is a complicated area of the martial arts. I have a video series on this in which I demonstrate on all types of people, ranging from gung-fu experts to highly ranked karateka. There are "instant disruptions," where the person will recover from the strike a second or two later; there are short-term strikes, from which he will recover up to four minutes later; and there are long-term strikes, from which he will recover four days later. So we must also know the antidote to these strikes, especially the short- and long-term strikes. We do not want our friends weakened for days after (and this has happened, where people who did not know what they were doing have executed the strike on friends and caused them to become quite ill for days, not knowing the antidotes). For the Gb 3 strike, which is an instant strike, we do not need to do any antidote because the recipient will recover naturally in a second or two. Hence the need, in a real fighting situation, to strike the major point, Gb 3, a split second after the set-up strike.

Antidote:

Although there is an antidote for the set-up strike, there is no antidote point for Gb 3 because it is just too dangerous. You can try CPR and a get the person to a hospital.

Healing:

Innervated by the zygomatic branch of the facial nerve and the zygomaticofacial nerve. Irrigated by the zygomaticoorbital artery and vein.

This point is forbidden for needling. You can hold both points or rotate clockwise or counterclockwise for xu or shi conditions. You might use three fingers, one on Gb 1, the next on Gb 3, and the next on Th 21 (fig. 18).

It is used for ear problems or trigeminal neuralgia (use enough pressure to cause slight pain). You can pinch Gb 3 and St 7 for facial pain. For ear or sinus congestion, you might run a finger with light pressure from Gb 1 through Gb 3, Th 21, Si 19, and Gb 2 down the groove created by the corner of the jaw, and continuing down the sternocleidomastoid muscle, which runs down either side of the neck, to the pit of the throat.

Applications:

1) He attacks using a right hook. You use the set-up qi-disruptive method mentioned above to swipe his face, continuing to slam his right forearm at neigwan or Pc 6. A split second later, your right one-knuckle punch makes contact with Gb 3. This is instant death, so be warned, this point is not for experimentation (fig. 19).

2) Slam his left forearm upward as he attacks with a left straight. Your right palm continues up to strike to Gb 3 (fig. 20).

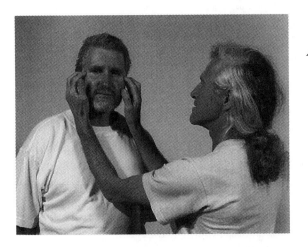

Figure 18

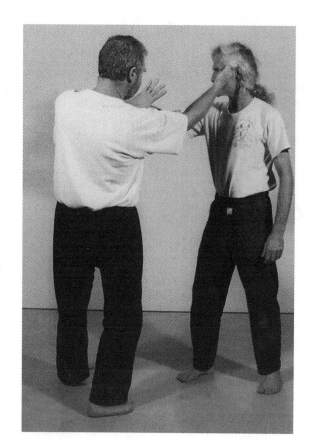

Figure 19

Figure 20

GB 4 (GALLBLADDER POINT NO. 4)

Chinese name:

Hanyan (satisfying jaw).

Location:

Within the hairline of the temporal region, a quarter of the distance from St 8 to Gb 7, or 1 cun below St 8. Movement can be felt at this point when chewing.

Connections:

Stomach and triple heater.

Direction of strike:

Gb 4 is struck straight inward using a palm-heel strike.

Damage:

This point, because of its location, will cause death at most and at the least extreme dizziness that causes the recipient to fall down.

Set-up point:

The set-up point for Gb 4 is neigwan, which is struck straight inward in this case.

Antidote:

Again, we use St 3 as the antidote for this point. Both St 3 points should be pressed upward into the cheekbones. You can also use Gv 20 by pressing downward onto the point to counter the drainage of qi caused by this strike.

Healing:

The region is irrigated by the parietal branches of the superficial temporal artery and vein and is innervated by its location just on the temporal branch of the auriculotemporal nerve.

Indications for use include headache (especially one-sided headache), stiff neck, blurred vision, pain at the outer canthus of the eye, tinnitus, rhinitis (inflammation of the nose), seizures, convulsions, and

Figure 21

Figure 22

Figure 23

conjunctivitis (inflammation of the inner eyelid).

Massage using clockwise or counterclockwise rotations for xu or shi conditions respectively, e.g., headache. Straight push and hold is also very sedating for migraine.

Applications:

1) He attacks with a right hook punch. Slam his neigwan point straight inward, and a split second later strike straight in to Gb 4 using your right palm (fig. 21).

2) In response to his left straight attack, execute a "slip block" (which slips up his attacking arm, thus blocking it from attacking to the major point) with your right palm (fig. 22), which then slides up his arm to attack at the point (fig. 23).

GB 5 (GALLBLADDER POINT NO. 5)

NOTE: Gb 5, Gb 6, and Gb 7 perform much the same as Gb 4; the attacks, directions, and so on are all the same.

Chinese name:
Xuanlu (suspended head).

35

Figure 24

Figure 25

Location:

In the middle of the curve between St 8 and Gb 7. (St 8 is about 1.5 cun above the forward upper corner of the ear, and Gb 7 is about .25 cun above that point on the ear. If you drew a line between the two, the point would be right in the middle.)

Connections:

Stomach and triple heater.

Direction of strike:

Straight inward using either a palm-heel strike or a one-knuckle punch.

Damage:

This point does much the same damage as Gb 4; however, it is a little more effective in causing dizziness and death, depending on how hard it is struck. If Gb 4, 5, 6, and 7 are struck simultaneously, it is a devastating strike.

Set-up point:

Again, strike neigwan straight inward.

Antidote:

Use Gb 20, pressing both sides upward into the head. (This is a utility revival point.)

Healing:

This point is used to heal migraine, pain in the lateral canthus (the side of the eye socket), toothache, edema (fluid retention) of the face, and neurasthenia (a TCM term referring to a range of nervous conditions from neurosis to insomnia to lethargy.). It is forbidden to needle this point more than 3 fen obliquely.

Applications:

This group of points—Gb 4, 5, 6, and 7—is bunched so close together that all of them call for the same methods of attack as Gb 4. However, Gb 5 is also activated by attacking to Th 12 on the back of the triceps.

Figure 26

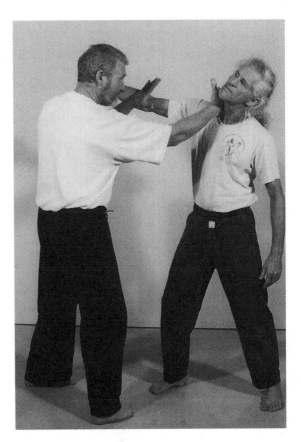

Figure 27

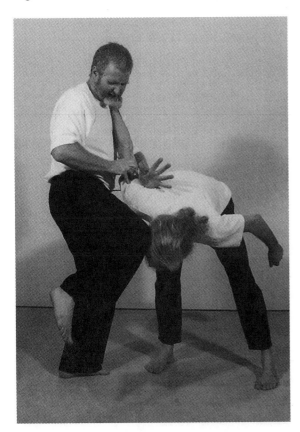

Figure 28

1) He attacks using a right straight. Slam his arm using both of your palms, striking to neigwan with your left palm and to Lu 5 (in the crease of the inside of the elbow) with your right palm (fig. 24). Lu 5 and Pc 6, when struck together, cause a great qi drainage from the "place of power" (lungs). This combination alone will cause a knockout when the strike is fairly hard. The Pc 6 strike sets up the Lu 7 shot. Your right palm immediately reaches around behind his right triceps to strike at Th 12 (just in the horseshoe formed by the triceps), while the left palm pushes away, thus causing great damage to the shoulder joint as well and causing him to move forward and down (fig. 25). Now, your right palm is free to attack to Gb 5 (or to the whole group of Gb points at that area), while your left palm keeps up the pressure on neigwan to keep up the qi drainage (fig. 26).

2) You might use a strike to St 9 to knock him out or make him weak and dizzy (fig. 27). Taking a long arm bar, you could cause him to bend forward, where your right knee is able to attack to Gb 5 or the whole group of points around that region (fig. 28).

37

GB 6 (GALLBLADDER POINT NO. 6)

Chinese name:

Xuanli (suspended balance).

Location:

On the hairline between Gb 5 and Gb 7.

Connections:

Small intestine.

Direction of strike:

Straight in from the side, usually with a palm-heel strike or, to be more accurate, a one-knuckle punch.

Damage:

This point is getting close to a point just above the ear that will cause a "delayed death strike." Delayed death strikes have been talked about in a mystical sense for years. However, the effects of most of these strikes are scientifically proven, as is the case with the strike to Gb 6 and other points in this region of the head. The small middle meningeal artery, which is right in this vicinity, about 3/4 inch above the ear, will burst when struck, causing blood to seep into the brain. It takes around three days to fill the brain sufficiently to cause death. NOTE: If this artery has been broken, it is diagnosed by looking at the pupils to see whether they change in size.

This area of the head also houses a lot of important brain stuff, so a strike here is not only an electrical strike, affecting the qi system of the body, but an excellent physiological strike as well.

Set-up point:

Either use neigwan or Si 8 on the posterior aspect of the elbow joint. Strike neigwan in a downward direction from his elbow down to this wrist, or strike Si 8 straight in. The Si 8 set-up works particularly well because this point has a connection to the small intestine meridian.

Figure 29

Figure 30

Figure 31

Figure 32

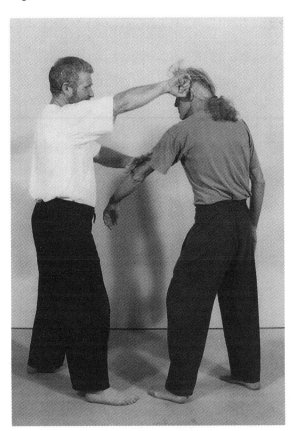

Figure 33

Antidote:

   Either use Gb 20 again, or you can use Bl 10.
   Squeeze in from both sides of Bl 10 on the back of
   the neck.

Healing:

   The healing indications for Gb 6 are the same as
   for Gb 5.

Applications:

1) Because we are getting into the area of a
   delayed death strike, we can use the techniques
   for Gb 5, or we can use what is called a
   percussive strike, which sends a percussive
   wave into the head to increase the damage.

   Take either his right hook or straight
   attack at his neigwan point with your right
   palm (fig. 29). Using the power of your waist,
   violently jerk your waist to your right, thus
   taking your right fist over to your right to
   attack to the point. The fist will flick upward
   upon impact, sending a shock wave up into
   the brain. The last three knuckles are the
   point of impact (fig. 30).

2) Take his left elbow at point Si 8 with your
   right palm, which will damage the energy
   system of the small intestine and break his

arm at the elbow (fig. 31)! Your left palm now slams down onto Si 8, controlling the arm (fig. 32). Using the power of the waist, which turns violently right then left, the right fist performs a "penetration" punch, turning over so that the thumb is underneath, and striking the point with the first two knuckles of your right fist (fig. 33).

GB 7 (GALLBLADDER POINT NO. 7)

Chinese name:

Qubin (crook of the temple).

Location:

On the hairline in front of the ear apex, one finger's width anterior to Th 20.

Connections:

Small intestine.

Direction of strike:

Straight in toward the head.

Damage:

Again, because of the location of this point, a delayed death strike may occur even with a medium-powered blow. A knockout will probably occur because of the action upon the heart through this point's connection to the small intestine. This point is extremely dangerous because of its location at the base of the brain. Other points will also be struck, such as Gb 4, 5, and 6. The damage is even greater when these points are struck at the same time using the palm strike.

Set-up point:

The set-up points for Gb 7 are the same as for Gb 5—neigwan or Si 8.

Antidote:

Either use Gb 20, punching in and upward into the head, or use Gv 20 with pressure down

Figure 34

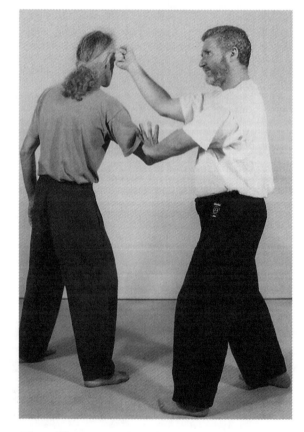

Figure 35

into the head. NOTE: The antidote may not work because of the seriousness of the location of this point.

Healing:

Used to treat migraine, trigeminal neuralgia, and spasm of the temporalis muscle.

Applications:

The applications for this point are exactly the same as for Gb 6, only the effect is slightly different if only Gb 7 is struck with no other points, using for instance a one-knuckle punch.

You could use the posture known as "arn right/left" from the original taijiquan form. He attacks with a right straight, and you parry into the outside of his right elbow, damaging the Si 8 point at the elbow. Notice that the right hand is already moving up on the inside of my left palm, ready to strike (fig. 34). My waist has turned to my left. Now, as my waist turns back to my right, my right one-knuckle punch attacks straight in to Gb 7 (fig. 35).

GB 8 (GALLBLADDER POINT NO. 8)

Chinese name:

Shuaigu (leading to valley).

Location:

Superior to the apex of the auricle, 1.5 cun within the hairline, or 1.5 cun above Th 20, which is on the head where the ear apex would touch if pressed inward.

Connections:

Bladder. There is a connection from the bladder meridian, which crosses Gv 20 and runs down to intersect with the Gb meridian at Gb 8.

Figure 36

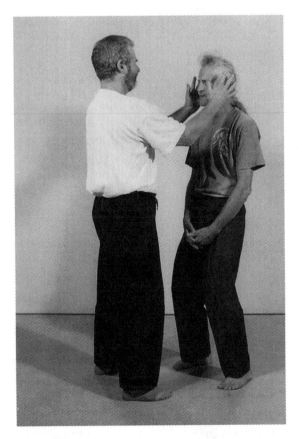

Figure 37

Direction of strike:

There is only one direction for this point: straight in to the head from the side.

Damage:

KO will occur with relatively lighter strikes; medium strikes will cause a loss of the sense of being (the person won't know where he is or even who he is). Death will occur with a very hard blow. This point is also a delayed death strike, being in close proximity to the small artery (middle meningeal artery) mentioned earlier.

Set-up point:

This point works really well with Th 12, struck straight inward, although neigwan will also work very well.

Another point that is not necessarily a set-up point per se, and which works very well with Gb 8, is the "third eye point." Called yintang, it is an extraordinary point situated right over the top of the governor vessel but not actually associated with it. It is located at the medial end of the two eyebrows. This is an "extra point" (one of those that have no actual meridian associated with them). In a healing sense, the yintang point is used to cure headache, insomnia, dizziness, vertigo, and diseases of the nasal cavity.

Antidote:

The antidote to Gb 8 is to squeeze Bl 10, at the back of the neck, inward and upward slightly. If yintang is also struck, you will have to use the qi balancing method as follows. (If, for instance, someone has had a qi-disruptive method performed on him that lasts for a few days and you wish to alleviate this situation, you should also use this method.)

Be calm and relaxed, not thinking about anything at all. (Do not think about the qi coming into your body and then going into the patient's; this will only block the healing.) Place your palms over Gv 20 (the crown) with only the thumb, forefinger, and middle finger touching (fig. 36). Inhale deeply, and then on the exhalation, run both hands in a teardrop shape around the patient's head, as close to the skin as possible without touching it, down the side of the face (fig. 37). Continue over the chin and end up at Cv 14, with the last three fingers touching (fig. 38). Hold this position for a full inhalation and exhalation, then take your palms back up to Gv 20 and begin again. You want to be certain not to rub back over the path that you followed on the way down, so take your palms out fairly far, in big arcs. Do this three times, and it should be enough to fix the strike to the third eye point. It will also help in alleviating the strike to Gb 8, depending upon what physical damage has been done.

Healing:

Gb 8 is irrigated by the parietal branches of the

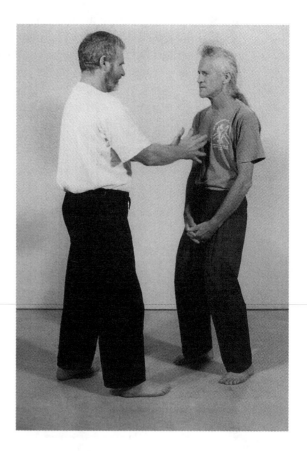

Figure 38

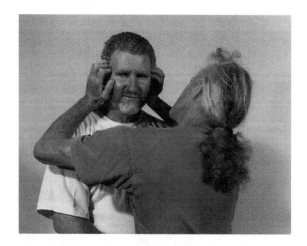

Figure 39

Figure 40

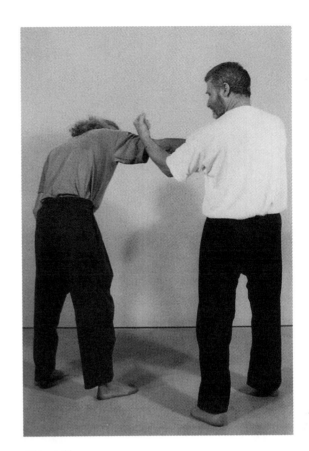

Figure 41

Figure 42

Figure 43

Figure 44

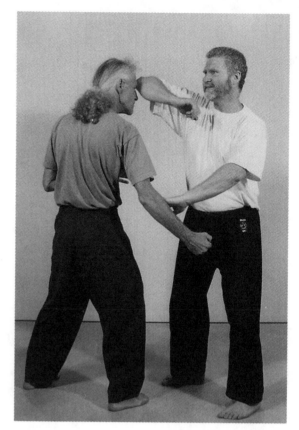

Figure 45

superficial temporal artery and vein and innervated by the anastomotic branch of the auriculotemporal nerve and the great occipital nerve.

It is used to treat migraine headache, vertigo, eye diseases, and facial neuralgia.

You could use it in conjunction with Th 9, Gb 20, Gv 20, Th 3, and *tai yang* for headaches. (Tai yang is an extraordinary or extra point, located out from the outer corner of the eye and at an angle slightly upward, about halfway between the corner of the eye and where that line meets the ear, or at the depression 1 cun behind the middle point between the lateral tip of the eyebrow and the angulus oculi lateralis, or the corner of the eye socket). This point is used alone to cure headache, migraine, common cold, trigeminal neuralgia, toothache, facioplegia (facial paralysis), and eye disease.

Press in a straight line from tai yang out and angled upward to Gb 8 (fig. 39). You can also do clockwise or counterclockwise rotations for xu or shi conditions respectively, or you might just "hold" the point and push lightly.

For the early stages of glaucoma you could combine Gb 8 with an extra point called *qiuhou*, which is at the inferior border of the orbit (eye socket), approximately one quarter of the distance from the lateral edge to the medial edge (just on the eye socket bone under the outside corner of the eye and inward slightly). Continuing the combination, add Gb 20, tai yang, Co 11, and Bl 1. Use clockwise or counterclockwise rotations for xu or shi conditions or vibrate the points (your fingers vibrate over the point).

For conjunctivitis, you could make a line (with your fingers) out and up from tai yang to Gb 8 with press-and-release action. Plus, hold Gb 20 and Co 4. You can also hold Bl 1 or do slow rotations counterclockwise. NOTE: *Be careful not to cross-infect the eyes.*

Applications:

The set-up point for Gb 8 is Th 12. So we make use of this in the martial applications.

1) He attacks with perhaps a right straight. You might use a p'eng-type blocking/striking motion straight upward into neigwan, or that general area (fig. 40). Your right palm instantly rotates over

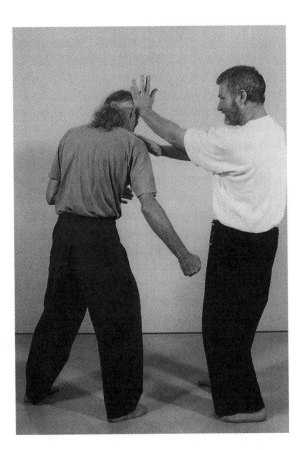

Figure 46

his right wrist to grab neigwan as your left palm strikes across Th 12 (fig. 41). Your left palm now instantly moves backward down his triceps as your right one-knuckle punch or heel palm attacks to Gb 8 (fig. 42).

2) This is a very deadly four-point application, causing instant death. He might attack using a right low hook. You will slam the inside of his right forearm with the back of your right palm, striking to Lu 5 as the set-up point. This will cause KO by itself when struck hard. In this case it is struck hard, as we use what is known in internal martial terms as a "dead hand," where the arm is totally loose and not tense at all, using the rotation of the waist to cause the "dead arm" to be thrown into the elbow crease at Lu 5 (fig. 43). The waist now loads to your right as you cock your right elbow, ready to strike, and your left palm knife edge attacks to St 9 (fig. 44). This will cause KO or death. Next, the waist swings violently to your left, causing your right elbow to strike into yintang, or the third eye point. Your left palm is also loaded, ready to strike (fig. 45). A split second later (if the timing is not right the attacker's head will move backward too far, thus making you

miss with the main shot), your left palm slams into Gb 8 (fig. 46). Just using the elbow to yintang will cause death; the combination is so devastating that it causes instant death. It is known as an irretrievable dim-mak strike (meaning that even CPR or instant medical attention will not reverse its effect).

GB 9 (GALLBLADDER POINT NO. 9)

Chinese name:
Tianchong (heavenly assault).

Location:
.5 cun posterior to Gb 8, 2 cun within the hairline.

Connections:
Bladder.

Direction of strike:
You should strike this point straight in to the head using either a one-knuckle punch or a palm-heel strike.

Damage:
A strike to Gb 9 causes instant KO because of the location of the point; death could occur if it is struck hard enough. This is an energy drainage point.

Set-up point:
Neigwan is again the set-up point, although a "slice" up the outside of the forearm will also work well. Other points that work well with Gb 9 are St 15 and St 16 on the pectoral. When both points are struck just before the Gb 9 shot, the effect of the heart slowing or stopping is greater.

Antidote:
Gb 20 squeezed inward and up.

Figure 47

Figure 48

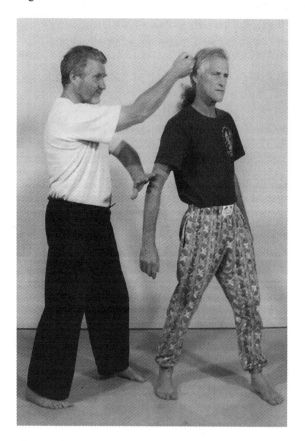

Figure 49

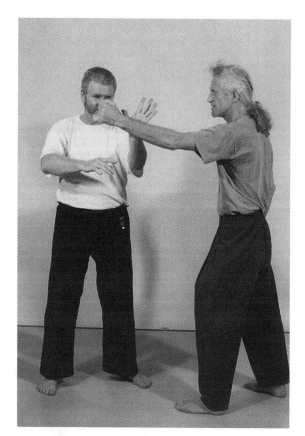

Figure 50

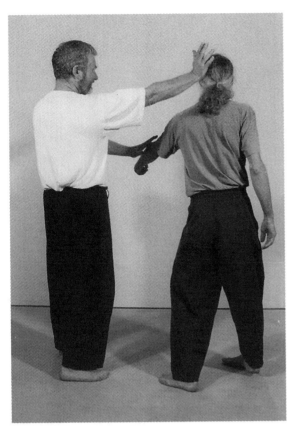

Figure 51

Healing:

Used to treat toothache, painful swelling of the gums, epilepsy, and goiter.

Applications:

1) He attacks with a right hook. Slap his neigwan point with your left knife edge as your right palm slams into St 15 and St 16 simultaneously (fig. 47). Hook your left palm over his right wrist and throw his right arm over to your right, loading your right one-knuckle punch (fig. 48). Turn your waist to your right as your right one-knuckle punch attacks to Gb 9 (fig. 49).

2) He attacks with a left straight. Slam his left neigwan with your left palm (fig. 50). Again, hook it over to your left as your right palm strikes to Gb 9 (fig. 51).

GB 10 (GALLBLADDER POINT NO. 10)

Chinese name:

Fubai (floating white).

Location:

Posterior and superior to the mastoid process, in the middle of the curved line drawn from Gb 9 to Gb 11. An easier way to find it is on a horizontal line drawn at the level of the eyes that runs toward the back of the head. The point is behind the ear on the squamosal suture, which is the joint between the parietal bone and the temporal bone of the skull.

Connections:

Bladder.

Direction of strike:

The direction is straight in, as with most of the head shots.

Damage:

Shocks the brain and affects the motor nervous system. If struck hard enough it will cause death at most and KO at least.

Set-up point:

Gv 26, just over the top lip and under the nose, with neigwan.

Antidote:

Press Gv 26 to deal with the shock that this strike can cause. If the attacker has gone white, the skin is "pasty," and he is perspiring profusely, then he is in shock. Gv 26, pressed with the tip of the thumb, is a good general point for all kinds of shock. Otherwise, the antidote is rest, if he isn't dead!

Healing:

Innervation is by the branch of the great occipital nerve. Irrigation is by the posterior auricular artery and vein.

This point is traditionally used for headache, tinnitus, deafness, and bronchitis. It is also used to treat atrophy of the leg muscles. This is a method of using a branch point to affect the root. (Root points are on the limbs and are close to the beginning and end of the channels, while the branch points are at the other end of the channel on the trunk or head.)

As Gb 10 is an intersection point with the bladder, it can be used to treat diseases involving both meridians. Gb 10 can be used with Co 4, St 44, Gb 14, and Co 3 for toothache.

Figure 52

Figure 53

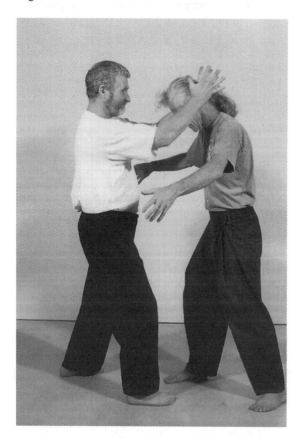

Figure 54

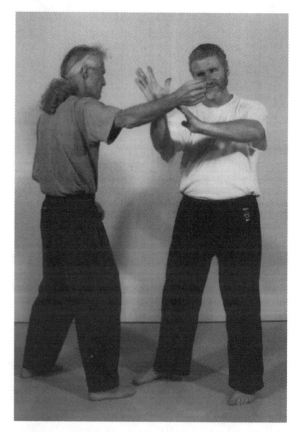

Figure 55

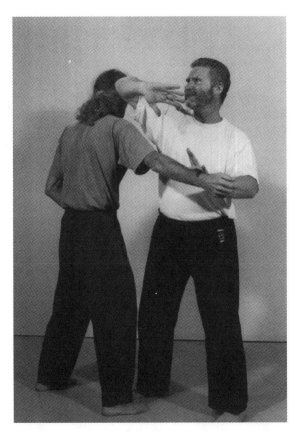

Figure 56

Massage might take the form of a straight press or a press with clockwise or counterclockwise rotation for xu or shi conditions respectively. You might also do fingertip percussion on this point for deafness or tinnitus. For one-sided headache, you could combine Gb 10 with tai yang, Gb 20, or Gb 12 as local points, plus Co 4, Gb 41, or Liv 3 as distal points.

Applications:

1) He might attack with any type of attack that is straight toward you, perhaps with both hands. You should strike with both palms toward his face, thus blocking his attack and, in this case, setting up the point by adding to the qi of the point by rubbing the inside of both of his forearms upward (fig. 52). Your right or left one-knuckle punch will attack to Gv 26 under the nose. This in itself could cause death at most and extreme muscle spasm of the upper body at least (fig. 53). Slam to both sides of his head with both of your open palms at Gb 10 (fig. 54).

2) Block his right attack with your right palm (fig. 55). This loads your right elbow. Twist your waist back to your right violently, thus thrusting your right elbow into the point (fig. 56).

GB 11 (GALLBLADDER POINT NO. 11)

Chinese name:

Qiaoyin (cavity of yin).

Location:

Midpoint on a line connecting Gb 10 and Gb 12. It is found in a small hollow behind the ear.

Connections:

Bladder.

Direction of strike:

Same as for Gb 10, straight inward.

Damage:

The damage is the same as for Gb 10, as it is in the same area of the head.

Set-up point:

To set up this point, you can use neigwan or, again, Gv 26, just under the nose. You can also can rub the outside of his arm violently downward several times before attacking to the point. This has the effect of turning his body to show you the point.

Antidote:

Gb 20, up and in.

Healing:

Used for pain in the neck and head, ear pain, deafness, tinnitus, bronchitis, laryngitis, pain in the chest, and goiter.

Applications:

He attacks with a right straight. We use the "willow tree" method here (a training method from

Figure 57

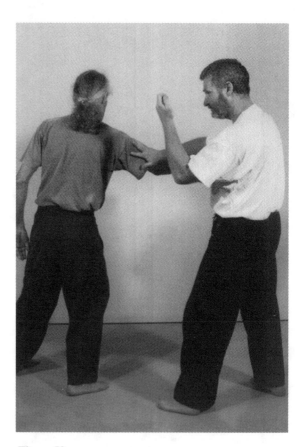

Figure 58

taijiquan). Slap his right forearm with your left palm downward as your right is about to take over this movement (fig. 57). Your right palm now takes over the sliding movement on the arm as your left palm is getting ready to strike (fig. 58). Your left palm makes contact with Gb 11, causing KO or death (fig. 59).

GB 12 (GALLBLADDER POINT NO. 12)

Chinese name:
   Head wangu (finished bone).
Location:
   In the depression posterior and inferior to the mastoid process, 0.7 cun below Gb 11 and level with Gv 16.
Connections:
   Has a connection with bladder meridian and the governing vessel via an internal branch of the bladder meridian that passes through Gv 20 and descends to the region above the ear and connects with the gallbladder meridian at the Gb 7, Gb 8, and Gb 12 points. The tendino-muscular channel of the leg tai yang meridian has a branch that extends from the axilla over the chest upward to

Figure 59

the supraclavicular fossa and terminates at Gb 12. (The pathways of the tendino-muscular channels lie in the superficial regions of the body and constitute the superficial circulation of the qi. They penetrate the skin, muscles, tendons, joints, and body cavities, but not the organs. They follow similar pathways as their main meridian counterparts, and they have branches that at times cross over other channels as well as areas not traversed by their main meridian counterparts.)

Direction of strike:
Inward and slightly upward into the brain.

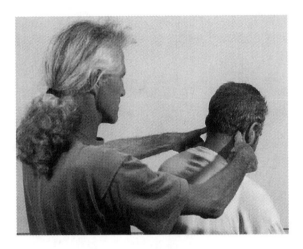

Figure 60

Damage:
A strike to Gb 12 will at least cause KO and at most death. In between these two extremes, you can cause headaches for days after the strike. It takes the qi away (drains it) from the upper body, with even a light blow causing pain and lack of energy for days. When struck upward into the head, this is one of the more dangerous points because of its anatomical location.

Set-up point:
This point has an unusual set-up point, apart from the more normal neigwan. It works particularly well with a qi-disruptive method of violently rubbing the right palm over the skull as close to the hair as possible without touching it.

Antidote:
Gv 20 pressed downward recaptures the yang, i.e., brings the qi back into the upper body.

Figure 61

Figure 62

Figure 63

Figure 64

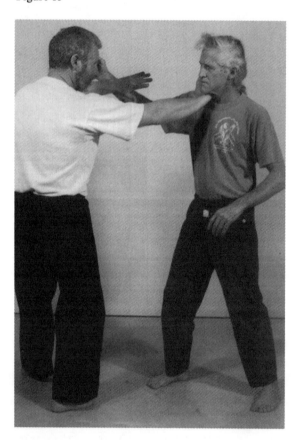

Figure 65

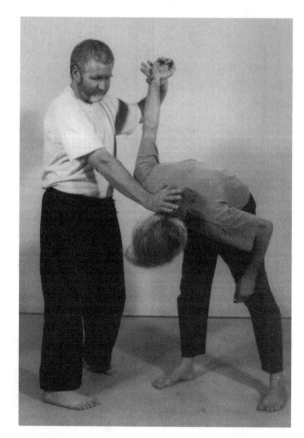

Figure 55

Figure 67

Healing:

Innervated by the lessor occipital nerve. Irrigated by the posterior auricular artery and vein.

Used for headache, insomnia, pain and stiffness of the neck, swelling and pain of the cheek, toothache, facial paralysis, and seizures.

You might use a straight push or clockwise or counterclockwise rotations for xu and shi conditions respectively when treating headache or a stiff, painful neck. You can also do a straight press, then pull the fingers under pressure down the neck along tight muscles to the shoulders. Or you can do a series of presses down into the muscles of the shoulders (fig. 60).

This point is generally included in occipital shiatsu, where you start at the center of the occipital region and do a series of presses out along the base of the skull and down to Gb 12.

Generally, use Liv 3, Gb 41, Gb 34, or Bl 60 as distal points with this point when treating headache or stiffness and pain in the neck.

You can try the following treatment for the mumps: Gb 12, St 6, Co 4, St 5, Th 17, Gb 20, St 36, St 8, St 7, BL 11, and Si 13.

You could also use moxa in this region for whiplash or other muscle spasm problems.

Applications:

1) He might attack with a straight right. You will use a p'eng block to defend (fig. 61). Your right palm grabs his right wrist, and your left palm slams into Th 12, just in the horseshoe created by the triceps (fig. 62). This causes him to drop forward. Step around with your right foot and flick your right palm violently over his skull, not quite touching his hair. (fig. 63). This also loads your right elbow, which now comes back with a turning of the waist to your left to strike Gb 12 with devastating results (fig. 64).

2) Take his right hook punch at neigwan with your left palm and strike him into St 9 with your right (fig. 65). Immediately grab his neck with your right palm, pulling him forward as your left palm lifts up his right arm (fig. 66). Do a swivel on your heels to turn into his head as your left palm slams into Gb 12 (fig. 67).

GB 13 GALLBLADDER POINT NO. 13)

Chinese name:

Benshen (head above the tears).

Location:

.5 cun inside the hairline and .5 cun medial to St 8, directly above the outer canthus of the eye. If you draw a line along Gb 7, 6, 5, and 4, then go another inch up toward the head, this is pretty close to Gb 13.

Connections:

Yang weimai (an extra meridian that runs from the side of the foot right up past the forehead and ends up at the back of the head. Although this meridian is quite long, it only has eight points. It is used traditionally for fever and perspiration of febrile disease, painful swelling of limps and

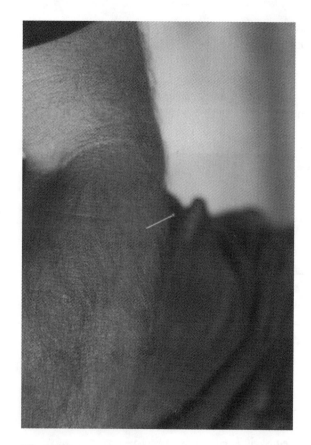

Figure 68

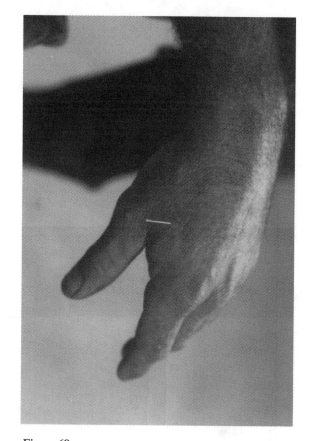

Figure 69

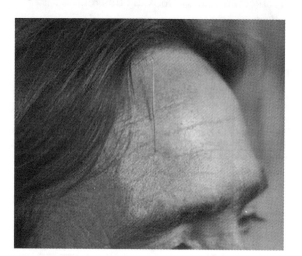

Figure 70

Figure 71

Figure 72

Figure 73

Figure 74

joints, headache and pain in the neck, hot feeling of hands and feet, numbness, pain of muscle and bone in back, hip redness, and swelling of the eyes.)

Direction of strike:

The strike to Gb 13 should be straight in toward the brain.

Damage:

Gb 13 is part of what is called the triangle strike (i.e., the three points form a triangle when joined, so we not only strike to Gb 13 but also hit Gb 14 and 15 at the same time). The combination of the colon strike with the three gallbladder strikes causes what is known as *adverse cyclic qi disruption.* This sends adverse qi (that which causes the body to disintegrate rather than to build) into the head and brain, which will cause not only immediate brain dysfunction but also delayed dysfunction that could last for years if death is not immediate.

Set-up point:

The normal way to strike Gb 13 is including the triangle. The set-up point for this triangle strike is Co 10, on the upper area of the outside of the forearm.

Antidote:

There is only one antidote for this strike. Acupuncture needles must be used because finger pressure does not work in this case. The points to needle (and please ask an acupuncture doctor about the directions, and so on, since an unqualified person could cause damage sticking needles into the wrong places for this state), are Co 10 (straight in), Co 4 (straight in). and Gb 14 (vertically toward the eye), as in Figures 68, 69, and 70.

Healing:

Used for headache, dizziness, stiffness, pain in the neck, pain in the lower chest, epilepsy, and hemiplegia.

Applications:

1) He might attack with a straight right. You slam his Co 10 point with your right backfist as your left palm is loading, ready to strike (fig. 71). Your left palm now slams into his elbow as your right palm attacks to the triangle with great force. The power used must be substantial (fig. 72).

2) He might attack with a two-handed attack. You open up both of your knife edges to attack to both of his neigwan points. (fig. 73). Twisting his right wrist (or left if you are working on the opposite side), your right hammer fist slams

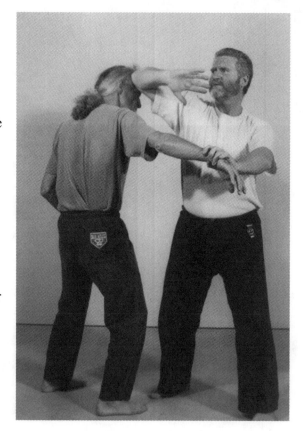

Figure 75

down onto Co 10 (fig. 74). Your left palm now flicks his right arm out to your left, loading your right elbow, which now comes back to your right to attack directly to Gb 13 (fig. 75).

GB 14 (GALLBLADDER POINT NO. 14)

Chinese name:

Yangbai (yang white).

Location:

1 cun above the middle of the eyebrow on a line directly above the pupil of the eye in the depression on the superciliary ridge. It is in the frontalis muscle and is irrigated by the lateral branches of the frontal artery and vein. It is situated directly on the lateral branch of the frontal nerve.

Connections:

This point is the intersection of the stomach and yang linking channels with the gallbladder channel. The yang linking channel is one of the eight extra channels (meridians) and is also called *yang wei mai.*

Direction of strike:

Either upward, downward, or straight in.

Damage:

If this point is struck straight in, it will cause physical damage to the neck. Struck upward, it brings too much yang energy into the head and causes a state similar to sunstroke, with the effects including nausea, blackout, and even death. When struck downward, it causes KO by draining energy from the head. This point is also right over the part of the brain that makes us different from animals, so a strike to it will also affect the way we think, work, move, and so on.

Set-up point:

If you are striking straight in, neigwan is the set-up point. For striking upward, strike the outside of

Figure 76

Figure 77

the forearm downward with the other hand, or strike the inside of the forearm upward from wrist to elbow. If you are striking downward to cause a qi drainage, you strike the outer forearm upward from wrist to elbow or the inside of the forearm downward from elbow to wrist.

Other points that work really well in conjunction with Gb 14 are Gb 13 and 15 (the triangle, as above).

Antidote:

If Gb 14 has been struck upward, apply pressure with both knife edges (strike downward) onto Gb 21, then slice each palm off the edges of the shoulders rapidly. This takes qi out of the head. (This is also a good remedy for sunstroke, which is basically the same condition). If Gb 14 has been struck downward, you must use Gb 20, squeezing inward and up, and also Gv 20, pressing down. If the strike was straight in and the neck is broken, see a doctor!

Healing:

Used for supraorbital neuralgia, facial paralysis, ptosis (drooping of the upper eyelid), eye disease, frontal headache, and facelifts (to maintain facial tone).

Traditional functions are to eliminate wind and to clear the vision.

It is also used for headache, sore eyes, eyelid tic, night blindness, itching eyelids, vomiting, chills, and stiff neck.

To massage, hold both points at once while the patient concentrates on breathing for frontal headache or facial tension, paralysis, and so on. You can rotate clockwise for xu (dull ache) conditions, or counterclockwise for shi (sharp, strong, painful) headache. You can also massage toward the hairline as part of a routine for facelift or wipe out toward the sides of the face for excess worry or facial tension. It is also used as part of a shiatsu facial massage where light pressure is applied first to *yu yao* (the fish's belly point, an extra point found in the middle of the eyebrow, or the fish's belly),then up to Gb 14 and on to Gb 15.

Figure 78

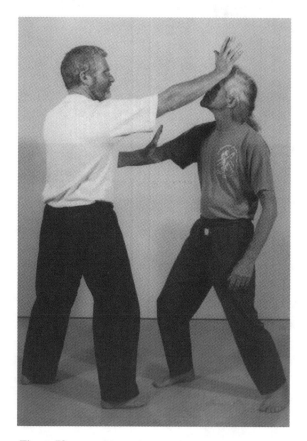

Figure 79

Applications:

Gb 14 can also be used as part of the triangle strike mentioned above. So all of those applications that were used for Gb 13 can also be used for Gb 14. However, Gb 14 has different set-up methods. I will use the right straight attack to show these, although the set-up point used will depend upon the type of attack.

1) He attacks with a straight right. My left palm strikes in an upward direction along the outside of his right forearm from wrist to elbow, just before my right palm attacks in a downward direction over Gb 14 (fig. 76). This strike drains energy from the head, causing KO.

2) He attacks with a straight right, and I attack the inside of his right forearm with my left palm sliding downward this time from elbow to wrist as my right palm strikes downward to Gb 14 (fig. 77). This also causes qi drainage from the head, resulting in KO.

3) He attacks with a right straight. This time I slice his forearm on the outside downward from elbow to wrist. My right palm strikes in an upward direction to Gb 14 (fig. 78). This adds energy to the point, resulting in excessive yang energy in the head, which causes nausea at least and KO or death at most.

4) He attacks with a straight right. I attack to the inside of his forearm in an upward direction from wrist to elbow. My right palm attacks upward to Gb 14. This results in too much yang energy to the head, causing KO, nausea, or death (fig. 79).

GB 15 (GALLBLADDER POINT NO. 15)

Chinese name:

Head lingi (base of God).

Location:

.5 cun inside the hairline and directly above the pupil when looking ahead.

Figure 80

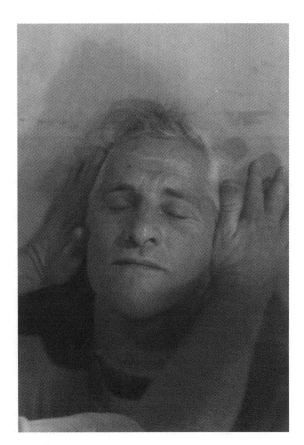

Figure 81

Connections:

Yang wei mai.

Direction of strike:

Since this point is part of the triangle of Gb 13, 14, and 15, it is usually struck along with the other two points in the triangle. However, it can be struck by itself, straight in and slightly downward.

Damage:

Causes the head to feel as if it is swelling up or being pumped up like a balloon. The recipient will not know where he is for a second or two if struck mildly, and he will be knocked out if struck heavily. Of course, any head point will kill if an external weapon is used. I am only covering empty hand methods in this book.

Set-up point:

Neigwan struck straight in to the wrist will enhance the damage done to this point. The "mind point," or *qianzheng*, is a new point and is on no particular meridian. It is found where the little bit of fat is in the hinge of the jaw when the jaw is opened. This point is struck after Gb 15, which further enhances the effect upon Gb 15. Qianzheng alone will cause KO by the action upon the central nervous system. It stops messages getting to the brain, and so the recipient falls down. Used with Gb 15, the fight is over.

Antidote:

Lie the patient down and place both of your palms over his face (fig. 80). Push downward over his face to the ground with mild pressure (fig. 81). You can also use Gb 20 as a utility revival point.

Healing:

Used for vertigo, stuffed nose, nebula, apoplexy, coma, malaria, epilepsy, and acute or chronic conjunctivitis.

Applications:

1)   He attacks with straight right. Your right palm slams straight in to neigwan (Pc 6), as your left

Figure 82

Figure 83

palm attacks to Gb 15 (fig. 82).

2) He attacks with a left hook. Your right palm attacks to neigwan as your left palm slams down onto Gb 15 (fig. 83). Your right elbow now attacks to the mind point (fig. 84).

GB 16 (GALLBLADDER POINT NO. 16)

Chinese name:

Muchuang (window of the eyes).

Location:

1 cun posterior to Gb 15 in a straight line with Gb 14 and 15.

Connections:

Yang wei mai.

Direction of strike:

The direction for this point is straight in on top of the head.

Damage:

This point is particularly nasty because of its proximity to the brain. When struck, the recipient feels immediate local pain because it is also an electrical point. (All dim-mak points are electrical points, in that they cause some damage to the energy system of the body. Some points, however,

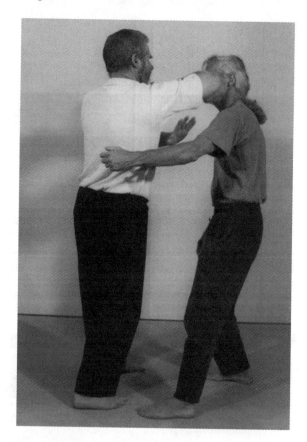

Figure 84

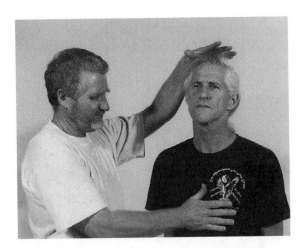

Figure 85

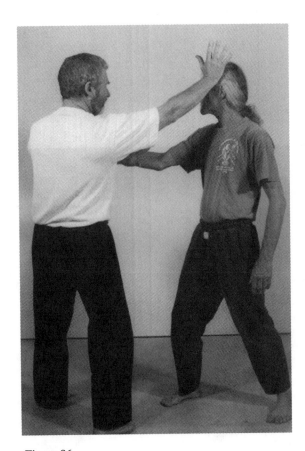

Figure 86

Figure 87

are located over or very near to physiological areas of the body that are particularly sensitive to being struck, like the brain.) The strike is done straight down into the brain, and because of the point's location, very close to the frontal coronal (the sutures formed by the knitting together of the skull plates from birth), this can cause a broken skull! This is also the area just above the hypothalamus, where, among other important things, the reflexes are developed. It is also right over where "premotor" decisions are made (e.g., "I am now going to pick up this cup."). So strikes to this area will affect the reflexes and coordination as well as the ability to simply make decisions.

This part of the cerebrum is also in charge of body movement, so a strike anywhere in this vicinity impairs the same.

Set-up point:

We use the utility set-up point of neigwan. We could also use St 9 to slow the heart just before the strike. This has a devastating effect.

Antidote:

If physical damage has been done, such as a broken skull, then medical attention is needed. If electrical damage has been done (extreme local pain, nausea, scattered mind), we use a balancing method by placing the left hand on Gv 20 and the right palm on Cv 14. As you breathe out, apply pressure to Gv 20 and less pressure to Cv 14. On the inhalation, apply light pressure to Cv 14 and less pressure to Gv 20 (fig. 85).

NOTE: You *should not use the above antidote if physical damage to the skull has occurred!*

Healing:

Used for headache, dizziness, swelling of the head and face, conjunctivitis, toothache, and apoplexy.

Applications:

1) He attacks with a straight or hook right. You simply come straight in and block his right at neigwan with your left palm and strike straight down onto Gb 16 with your right palm. (fig. 86).

2) Strike his left neigwan as that arm attacks, and strike to St 9 with your left knife-edge palm (fig. 87). Your left palm now moves his left arm over to his right while your right palm attacks to Gb 16 (fig. 88).

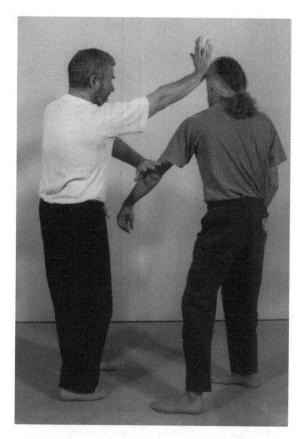

Figure 88

GB 17 (GALLBLADDER POINT NO. 17)

Chinese name:

Zhengyin (principle yin).

Location:

Keep going backward in a line parallel with the skull, 1 cun back from Gb 15.

Connections:

Yang wei mai

Direction of strike:

Straight down into the brain, usually from the side.

Damage:

Much the same as for Gb 16 because of its proximity to the brain parts. A strike to this point has a slightly greater effect upon the reflexes, as Gb 17 is closer to the part of the cerebrum that controls movement, so motor actions are damaged. There will also be local pain through the electrical part of this strike, and, if the strike is very hard, knockout as well as death.

Set-up point:

Again, this point works particularly well with St 9 and neigwan.

Antidote:

The antidote is the same as for Gb 16, using Gv 20 and Cv 14 and breathing. Again, do not use this antidote if physical damage has occurred to the skull. You could also use Gb 20 if KO has occurred.

Healing:

Used for rigidity of the neck, dizziness and vertigo, toothache, and vomiting.

Applications:

1) You could use the "willow tree method" here. He attacks with a straight right. You slam his arm on the outside of his forearm and slide down his arm with your left palm, as in Figure 89. Your right palm comes straight up and over to strike downward into Gb 17 from the side (fig. 90).

2) Your left palm attacks to his right neigwan as your cupped right palm slaps the whole side of his neck, causing a percussive shock wave to go into the whole neck area. This causes KO and is part of the "strike" that evangelists use when "dropping" people at seminars (fig. 91). Your left palm now pulls his right arm over to your right as your right palm strikes down onto Gb 17 (fig. 92).

Figure 89

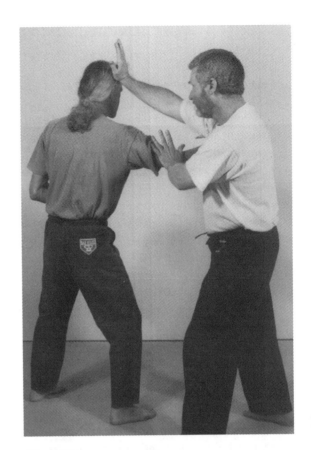

Figure 90

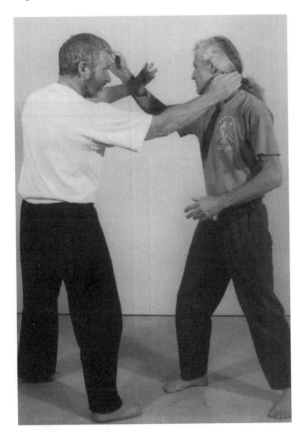

Figure 91

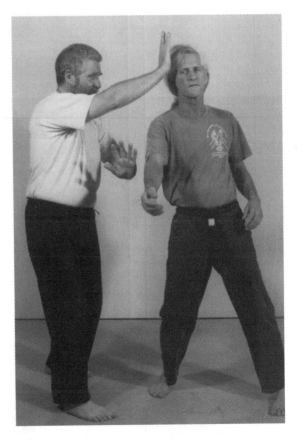

Figure 92

GB 18 (GALLBLADDER POINT NO. 18)

Chinese name:

Chengling (support the spirit).

Location:

1.5 cun posterior to Gb 17 on the line connecting Gb 15 and Gb 20. Approximately 5 cun posterior to the hairline of the forehead, or approximately 1 cun posterior and 1.2 cun lateral to Gv 20.

Connections:

The yang wei mai intersects with the Gb meridian at Gb 18.

Direction of strike:

Strike straight in and down into the head, usually with a palm-heel strike.

Damage:

Even a light blow here can cause a KO. A strike to this point scatters the qi of the upper body, causes nausea, and affects the way the *tantien* distributes the qi. (The tantien is an electrical point about 3 inches below the navel on the midline. This is where the qi comes from and is stored, and so it has great significance in the internal martial arts.) Because of the location over the side of the brain, this point will cause considerable brain dysfunction when struck hard enough.

Set-up point:

You can either use neigwan, or this point works particularly well with a neurological shutdown strike to the side of the face.

Antidote:

Use Gb 20. Squeeze in and upward into the head.

Healing:

Because of its intersection with the yang wei mai meridian, this point can be used to influence the yang wei mai in treating symptoms such as chills and fever, stiffness and pain, muscular fatigue,

Figure 93

Figure 94

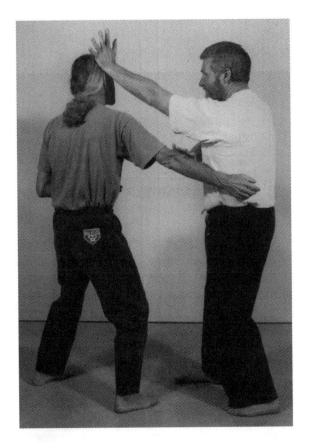

Figure 95

vertigo, and pain and distension (swelling) of the waist.

Gb 18 is innervated by the branch of the great occipital nerve and irrigated by the branches of the occipital artery and vein.

Use this point to treat headache, rhinorrhea (nasal discharge), epistaxis, (nosebleed), occluded nose, common cold, bronchitis, and eye disease.

Generally massage straight in or push or rotate clockwise or counterclockwise to treat xu or shi conditions. The headaches treated by Gb 18 are generally at the top of the head and, as such, are usually liver related, but Gb 18 can be used for headache on the side of the head also. You could use it in combination with Gb 20, Gb 12, Gb 8, Gb 21, Co 4, Liv 3, Gb 41, and Gb 34 for headache.

If treating rhinorrhea, epistaxis, occluded nose, common cold, or bronchitis, you might include points from the Co and Lu meridians. In the case of epistaxis, Sp 10 can also be used.

For eye disease, you could include Gb 1, St 1, Bl 1, Gb 41, Gb 43, and Liv 2.

Applications:

1) He could attack using a right hook, to which you could strike to neigwan with a one-knuckle punch. This will cause him to feel quite nauseated, and he'll have to sit down anyway. So you continue by slamming his right arm over to your right with your left palm and attacking to Gb 18 with a hammer fist (fig. 93).

2) Slam his right straight attack at his forearm outside with your left palm and attack to the neurological shutdown points at the side of the jaw (fig. 94). Your right palm takes over on his right arm as your left palm attacks to Gb 18 (fig. 95).

GB 19 (GALLBLADDER POINT NO. 19)

Chinese name:

Naokong (brain cavity).

Location:

Directly above Gb 20, level with Gv 17 on the lateral side of the external occipital protuberance. Or look at the back of the head just above the neck. The bit that sticks out the most, saying "hit me, hit me" is Gb 19.

Connections:

The yang wei mai intersects with the Gb meridian at this point.

Direction of strike:

Straight in to the back of the head, usually using a palm strike.

Damage:

The damage is immense with a strike to this point. The whole brain is shocked, causing KO even with lighter strikes. Many people have been able to cause a KO on students using this point. However, only irresponsible instructors would use this point to "show of," because although it is such an easy KO, it causes considerable damage long after the strike has been made.

Figure 96

Figure 97

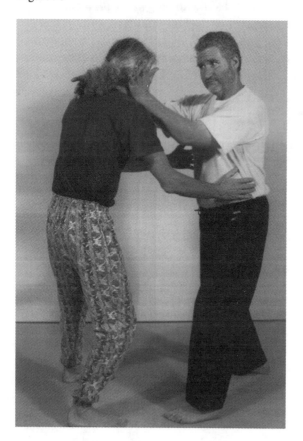

Figure 98

Figure 99

Set-up point:

A strike to Gb 19 needs no other point to set it up, but you could use a slice along the whole arm, from shoulder to wrist. This tends to cause a qi build-up at Gb 19, so that when struck, it sort of "bursts" like a balloon!

Antidote:

There is no antidote for this point, other than rest if the strike was not too hard and hospitalization if it was hard. This point can be struck accidentally when someone simply falls backward onto the head.

Healing:

Innervation is by the branch of the great occipital nerve. Irrigation is by the occipital artery and vein.

Used for headaches, pain and stiffness of the neck, common cold, asthma, seizures, mental illness, palpitations, and tinnitus.

It is used in conjunction with Gv 20 and Bl 10 for dizziness. Another prescription for dizziness that includes Gb 19 is as follows: Gv 24, Gv 23, Gv 22, Gv 21, Gv 19, Gv 20, Gb 19, Si 5, Sp 2, Bl 67, Bl 63, Bl 62, and St 36.

You could use moxa on this point in conjunction with Gb 20, Lu 7, Lu 9, Co 4, and St 41 for lateral or midline headaches.

Massage techniques would be either a straight push or clockwise or counterclockwise rotation for xu or shi conditions. You could use "on-and-off" pressure for headaches or a push where pressure is directed straight in and then dragged laterally.

Applications:

1) You first set up this point by slicing down his left attacking arm with the right palm (fig. 96). Then the left palm also slices down the whole arm. This has turned the attacker so that you are now in back of him so that your right palm can strike straight in to Gb 19 (fig. 97).

2) You might have "closed" with your attacker so that you are both in a grappling type of situation (fig. 98). Start with a quick shot with your left palm to the side of his jaw at the mind point and follow up immediately with the reverse hammer fist to Gb 19 to cause an instant KO. This is a lovely shot that people just don't expect from this grappling-type position (fig. 99).

GB 20 (GALLBLADDER POINT NO. 20)

Chinese name:

Fengchi (pool of wind).

Location:

In the posterior aspect of the neck, below the occipital bone, in the depression between the upper portion of the sternocleidomastoid muscle and the trapezius muscle.

Connections:

Gb 20 has connection with both the yang wei mai and the *yang chiao mai*, both extra meridians. Gb 20 is also one of the points used to access "the sea of bone marrow" (the brain) and is considered a special meeting point because it has direct connections with the Si, Bl, and Gv meridians.

Direction of strike:

Gb 20 must be struck upward into the head using a weapon that is "sharp," such as a reverse knife-edge strike.

Damage:

Again, the damage caused by striking this point in the correct direction is immense. We get not only the electrical disruption but also the physiological damage caused by Gb 20's location at the base of the brain. Even a light to medium strike upward to this point will cause a KO. Very hard strikes will result in brain damage and even death.

Set-up point:

To set up this point, we strike to Gb 1 in the corner of the eye. (See the applications to find out how to do this.)

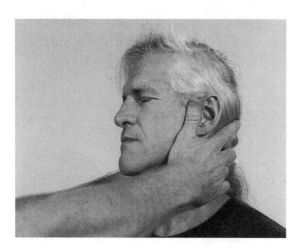

Figure 100

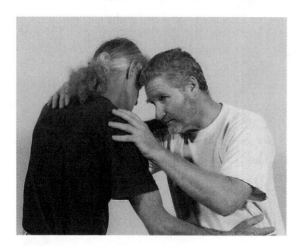

Figure 101

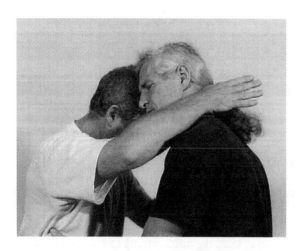

Figure 102

Figure 103

Figure 104

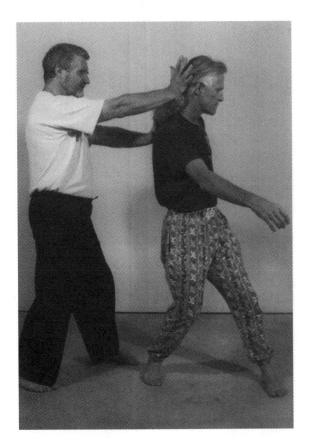

Figure 105

Antidote:

Although Gb 20 is itself a utility revival point, we cannot use it as an antidote when it is struck. We can, however, grab the back of the neck from in front—placing the thumbs just in front of the two ears so that the fingers meet behind the neck—and squeeze (fig. 100). Or you might strike downward onto Gb 21 on the highest part of the shoulders and then wipe off violently to either side off the shoulder. This will take yang qi out of the head. The upward strike adds qi to the head.

Healing:

The point is supplied by branches of the occipital artery and vein and by a branch of the lesser occipital nerve.

Used for the common cold, dizziness, headache, stiff neck, red and painful eyes, rhinitis, tinnitus, deafness, pain of the shoulder and back, and feverish diseases.

Its traditional function is the dispersal of "wind heat" conditions. Gb 20 also benefits the hearing and vision.

Traditional indications include sinusitis; red, sore eyes; deafness; tinnitus; lateral and midline headaches; occipital headaches; insomnia; common cold; tidal fever (a fever that comes and goes with the tide); swelling; or tumor of the neck.

This point can be pressed and held for headaches (rotated counterclockwise if the headache is severe or clockwise if it is dull). You can also put your fingers into Gb 20 on either side and pull them apart. You might even run a line from Gb 20 down to Gb 21 or Si 13 for stiff neck, whiplash, and so on. You can also lift the head with the fingers in Gb 20, holding it at about a 45-degree angle, while the patient concentrates on breathing and relaxing.

Applications:

1) Suppose you are in a grappling situation. You should use the set-up point of Gb 1 by striking it with the right side of your forehead, as in Figure 101. NOTE: never use the centerline of your own head in a head-butt type of attack because this will cause damage to you.) Your right hand is around the back of his neck. As soon as you have struck to Gb 1, your right reverse knife-edge palm strikes upward into Gb 20 with devastating results (fig. 102).

2) Take his right straight with a p'eng block, as in Figure 103. Immediately grab his wrist and elbow and pull him violently around so that you are now in back of him (fig. 104). Strike in an upward way to Gb 20 with your right fist (fig. 105).

GB 21 (GALLBLADDER POINT NO. 21)

Chinese name:

Jianjing (shoulder well).

Location:

Midway between Gv 14 and the acromion of the shoulder, at the highest point of the shoulder.

Connections:

Gb 21 is connected to yang wei mai and the triple heater meridian. There is a branch inside to Gv 14, Bl 10, Si 12, and back to Gb 24.

Figure 106

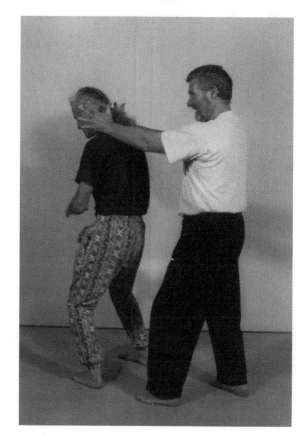

Figure 107

Direction of strike:
This point should always be struck straight down into the shoulder, usually using a knife-edge strike.
Damage:
This point is also a dim-mak healing point in that it is used to heal a strike in an upward direction to Gb 14. It drains qi from the head, and so alleviates the problem caused by the strike. (Sunstroke is also an indication of too much yang qi in the head.) So we also know how to heal this condition with a medium strike down onto Gb 21 followed by a violent swipe out over the shoulders.

However, if too much pressure is used on someone who does not have too much yang energy in the head, then it will drain too much qi from the head, causing lightheadedness at least and a KO at most (although the latter would require a fairly hard strike). Between these two extremes in possible effects of this strike is for the recipient to drop straight down to the ground. Gb 21 is also associated with the accessory nerve, which runs down the back of the neck on the right and left sides. This nerve is also well known for causing knockouts from neurological shutdown strikes to the back of the neck.
Set-up point:
Neigwan is normally used as a set-up point since it is also a traditional qi drainage point and so enhances the effect of drainage. Gb 33 can also be used to great effect when the attacker is kicking, because of its location on the ouside of the leg toward the knee.
Antidote:
Press down on Gv 20 (*bahui*) on top of the head, as this is a universal "lifting" point and tends to bring the qi back into the head and upper body.
Healing:
Innervated by the lateral branch of the supraclavicular nerve and the accessory nerve. Irrigated by the transverse cervical artery and vein.

Used for neck rigidity, pain in the shoulder and back, motor impairment of the hand and arm, mastitis, apoplexy, difficult labor, hemiplegia due to stroke, functional uterine bleeding,

70

Figure 108

scrofula (tuberculosis of the lymph nodes), jaw pain and stiffness, and headache. This point sends qi downward.

Massage can be a light to medium percussion or a straight push. Kneading through this whole area can be painful but gives tremendous relief.

I usually combine this point with Bl 10, Gb 20, Th 15, Si 13, Si 14, Bl 13, Bl 43, Bl 60, Gb 34, and Si 3 for shoulder problems, neck rigidity, and impairment of the hands or arms.

For the common cold, use Gb 21 with Gb 20, Bl 10, Bl 12, Bl 43, Lu 1, Lu 5, Lu 7, Lu 9, Cu 4, St 36, Liv 3, and Cv 17.

For vertigo, combine Gb 21 with Liv 3, Gv 20, Kd 1, Gb 20, Lu 7, and St 36.

Applications:
1) He attacks with perhaps a straight right front kick. Always move in, never away. Slam the side of his knee at Gb 33 with your left palm (fig. 106). You have moved "in a V shape" to his side. This move will also turn him around. You have already loaded your right palm, and as soon as you have struck the leg, your left palm also loads and then strikes straight down onto Gb 21 on both sides using your knife edges (fig. 107).
2) Take his right straight at neigwan using a p'eng type of block (fig. 108). You are already in motion to his rear; get there quickly and strike down onto both Gb 21 points as in the previous method (fig. 107 again).

GB 22 (GALLBLADDER POINT NO. 22)

Chinese name:
Yuanye (gulf's fluids).

Location:
On the midaxillary line, 3 cun below the axilla and in the fifth intercostal space.

Connections:
Lower meeting point of the Lu and Co divergent meridians. (The tendino-muscular meridian of the Gb divides into two branches in the region of Gb 22.) It is also a meeting place with the Si and Ht meridians.

Direction of strike:
Strike straight in to the body from the side, as the point is under the arm.

Damage:
This is a particularly sensitive area, as there are lymph nodes here. It is an extreme qi drainage point, so the recipient cannot carry on after being struck even lightly in this point. If death is not instant, it will occur sometime later, because a strike here causes the heart to falter or stop instantly.

Set-up point:
Ht 1 is the set-up point for this strike.

Antidote:
Use Gb 20 if KO has occurred, or Kd 1 if the person appears to be dead or near death. Strike Kd 1 very hard straight in, or bleed this point. Kd 1 is a classical revival point, as it releases the stored qi from the tantien into the body. You can also press Co 10 and Ht 3 with the thumbs or fingers using mild pressure.

Figure 109

Figure 110

Figure 111

Figure 112

Healing:

This point is irrigated by the thoracoepigastric vein, the lateral thoracic artery and vein, and the fifth intercostal artery and vein. It is innervated by the lateral cutaneous branch of the fifth intercostal nerve and the branch of the long thoracic nerve.

Gb 22 is used for pain in the hypochondriac region, swelling of the axillary region, pleurisy, intercostal neuralgia, pain of the shoulder and arm, and axillary lymphadenitis (inflammation of the lymph nodes).

Massage techniques might include finger pressure on either one or both points for pleurisy or other lung-related problems or neuralgia of the intercostal region. You could also tap through this region to treat those same conditions or for pain of the shoulder and arm. You can trace from the spine along the intercostal muscle through this point for shingles or intercostal neuralgia. You can also do clockwise or counterclockwise rotations for xu or shi conditions.

Applications:

1) He might attack with a right hook low to your left side. You should slam Lu 5 in the inside crease of his elbow with your right back palm (fig. 109). This strike alone is enough to cause serious KO. Your left palm now takes his right wrist and lifts it slightly as your right reverse knife-edge attacks straight upward to Ht 1 (fig. 110). With a quick twist of your waist left and then right, your right knife edge attacks straight in to Gb 22 (fig. 111). Notice that the left foot has trapped his knee to stop further movement to your left.

2) Simply take his right straight attack with your right palm as your left palm comes up underneath to take over the block (fig. 112). Your right palm is now free to strike straight in to Gb 22.

GB 23 (GALLBLADDER POINT NO. 23)

Figure 113

Chinese name:

Zhejin (flanks sinews).

Location:

1 cun anterior to Gb 22, approximately level with the nipple (on a male) in the fourth intercostal space.

Connections:

None.

Direction of strike:

The direction for Gb 23 is straight in.

Damage:

Drains qi from the body. Even a medium-power strike is enough to prevent the attacker from being able to continue. This point is disastrous when struck with Gb 22.

Set-up point:

Set up this point with Ht 1 or neigwan.

Antidote:

Press down onto Gb 20 and squeeze inward onto Bl 10.

Healing:

Used for fullness in the chest, asthma, pleurisy, vomiting, acidic belching, and intercostal neuralgia.

Applications:

1) Because this point is a little farther forward of the nipple than Gb 22, we can use the

Figure 114

Figure 115

following method. He attacks with a straight right. Slam his neigwan point straight in with your right palm and twist your waist back to your right, bringing your right elbow straight in to the point in the correct direction (fig. 113).

2) Slam his right arm at both wrist (neigwan) and elbow crease (Lu 5), as in Figure 114. Grab his arm and violently pull him forward (fig. 115). As he is moving past you, strike to Gb 23 and Gb 22 with your right palm (fig. 116).

GB 24 (GALLBLADDER POINT NO. 24)

Chinese name:

Riyue (sun moon).

Location:

Inferior to the nipple, between the cartilages of the seventh and eighth ribs, one rib below Liv 14.

Connections:

Because the spleen channel passes through it, Gb 24 can affect the flow of qi in the Sp channel. It has a connection with yang wei mai and an internal pathway to Liv 13 and St 30 that meets back at Gb 30.

Figure 116

Figure 117

Figure 118

Direction of strike:
   This point can either be struck straight in (normal) or laterally, either from outside to inside or the reverse.

Damage:
   This is a death point, and just a medium strike will cause a KO.

Set-up point:
   Either use neigwan or St 9.

Antidote:
   Squeeze Gb 20 straight in.

Healing:
   Innervation is by the seventh intercostal nerve. The point is irrigated by the seventh intercostal artery and vein.

   Used for vomiting, regurgitation, jaundice, hiccup, intercostal neuralgia, cholecystitis (inflammation of the gallbladder), acute and chronic hepatitis, and peptic ulcer.

   This is the front *mu* point of the gallbladder. (A mu point is the alarm point of the meridian. Tenderness in mu points denotes that there is something wrong with the organ physically and/or its qi.) So this point's traditional function is to treat all syndromes of the gallbladder, as well as warning of impending symptoms.

   The spleen meridian passes through this point, so it can affect the flow of qi in the spleen channel. This point will speed up contractions of the gallbladder and promote emptying of this organ, as well as strengthening peristalsis in the common bile duct of the Gb and causing an increase in the flow of bile.

   Massage techniques include straight press, clockwise or counterclockwise rotations for xu or shi conditions, and light finger tapping in the region for xu conditions. You could use Gb 24 with Bl 18, Liv 6, Gb 34, Th 6, and Bl 19 for inflammation of the gallbladder or hepatitis. Also use gold moxa on this point for intercostal neuralgia.

For acute cholecystitis, gall stones, or roundworm in the biliary tract, you could use *dannangxue*, an extra point 1.2 cun below Gb 34 (it will be tender) with Pc 6, Gb 34, Gb 24, and St 36, all on the right side. This may give some relief while you go to either an M.D. or a TCM doctor.

For headache caused by arrogant liver rising (a condition that is both excess yang and deficient yin, you could use Gb 24, Liv 14, Liv 2, Co 4, Co 11, Gb 14, Gb 20, Gb 34, and Gv 20.

Applications:

1) He attacks with a straight right. Your left fingers simultaneously block the attack and poke into St 9, causing heart failure or slowing, resulting in KO. A split second later your right palm attacks straight in to Gb 24 (fig. 117).

2) He attacks with a straight right again. You slam his neck at St 9 with your right back palm as your left palm blocks and sets up the major strike by sliding up on the inside of his right forearm (fig. 118). Your right palm now grabs around the back of his neck and pulls him forward onto your right knee, which attacks to Gb 24 (fig. 119). The combination of St 9 and Gb 24 is death.

Figure 119

GB 25 (GALLBLADDER POINT NO. 25)

Chinese name:

Jingmen (door of the capital).

Location:

Located on the lateral sides of the abdomen, on the lower border of the free end of the 12th rib.

Connections:

None.

Direction of strike:

Straight in from the side of the body.

Damage:

Since this is a mu point for the kidneys, any strike here will affect the kidneys. This point in particular will cause great kidney damage wen struck from the side—more so than when the kidneys are struck from the lower back area (traditional kidney strike). From the side, the strike to Gb 25 sets up a shock wave that damages the kidneys. A hard strike will cause death through kidney failure; light to moderate strikes will cause bleeding from the penis and great pain in the kidney area. It is difficult to get an electrical reaction from this point.

Set-up point:

Any of the kidney points will work well as set-up points. They also work well along with a strike to Gb 25. So you could strike Kd 10 at the back of the knee using your foot.

Antidote:

Press Kd 1 inward with great pressure and apply pressure to Kd 10 at the same time if possible.

Healing:

Innervated by the 11th intercostal nerve. Irrigated by the 11th intercostal artery and vein.

Figure 120

Figure 121

Figure 122

Figure 123

Used for borborygmus (intestinal rumbling), diarrhea, abdominal distension, pain in the lower back and hypochondriac region, nephritis (chronic inflammation of the kidney), pain caused by intestinal hernia, and intercostal neuralgia.

Because it is a front mu point of the kidneys, Gb 25 is used traditionally to treat all conditions of the kidneys, including spermatorrhoea (involuntary discharge of semen without ejaculation), impotence, incontinence, and so on.

Massage could include a straight push with clockwise or counterclockwise rotations for xu or shi conditions.

You could also lie the patient on his or her back with your hands under the small of the back and your middle fingers touching the space between the second and third lumbar vertebrae. Then pull your hands apart while pressing with your middle finger, guiding the hands out and around to Gb 25 then on through Gb 26, 27, and 28; abdomen *zigong* (an extra point); St 28; and Kd 13; ending at Cv 4. This is running the *dai mo* (girdle meridian).

A shorter version could start on the side of the body an inch or so back from the free end of the 12th rib and run medially, passing through Gb 25 and on to Gb 26 before pulling the hands away from the abdomen abruptly.

Another alternative is to proceed like the original dai mo run from the spine to Gb 26, then on to Sp 15, St 25, and Kd 16, and ending at Cv 8 (the umbilicus). These types of treatments will help balance yin and yang qi of the body (upper and lower aspects).

You might combine Gb 35 with Cv 12, Liv 13, St 36, and Liv 3 for borborygmus, diarrhea, abdominal distension, and so on, or with Kd 3, Sp 6, Bl 23, and Cv 3 and 4 for kidney xu problems.

Applications:

1) He attacks with an upper attack. Block it and attack to the back of his knee with your instep or ball of the foot (fig. 120). Your right palm now attacks Gb 25 as your left foot steps to the side (fig. 121).

2) He attacks with a straight right. Slam his neigwan point with your right palm as the left palm is taking over the block. (fig. 122). Step closer, as he has been "set up," and strike straight in from the side to Gb 25 with your right elbow. This is a death strike (fig. 123).

GB 26 (GALLBLADDER POINT NO. 26)

Chinese name:

Daimai (girdle vessel).

Location:

Directly below the free end of the 11th rib, where Liv 13 is located, level with the umbilicus. The point lies in the external oblique muscle and the internal oblique and transverse abdominal muscles.

Draw a line across from the navel, and where you touch the ribs, that's the point.

Connections:

Dai mai (an extra meridian that runs around the waistline).

Direction of strike:

Straight in from the side of the body.

Damage:

Causes the whole central torso to be shocked with pain in the gallbladder area; a hard enough strike will cause death, as it will cause the heart to stop.

This point is connected to the girdle meridian, which runs around the waist. This meridian, when struck, causes a disconnection between "upper and lower," so the legs don't know what the arms and torso, etc., are doing.

Set-up point:

Both neigwan points should be struck toward you, i.e., down his inner forearms directed toward the wrists.

Antidote:

Squeeze in at Gb 20.

Figure 124

Figure 125

Figure 126

Healing:

Innervated by the subcostal nerve (the 12th intercostal nerve) and irrigated by the subcostal artery and vein (12th intercostal artery and vein).

Used for irregular menstruation, leukorrhea (abnormal vaginal discharge), hernia, pain in the lower back and hypochondriac regions, endometritis, cystitis, profuse bleeding with leukorrhea, and paraplegia due to trauma.

Traditional indications are include irregular menstruation and red and white vaginal discharge, intestinal colic, diarrhea, and convulsions.

Traditional functions: to regulate the *dai mo* (girdle vessel) and alleviate damp heat.

Massage techniques are similar to those used with Gb 25.

For enlarged thyroid, you might try combining Gb 26 with Bl 10, Gv 12 , Bl 12, Cv 23, St 9, Gv 3, and Gb 26, alternating with Gb 2O, Gv 14, Bl 11, Cv 22, St 10, Gv 4, and Th 3. NOTE: *Be careful when pressing St 9!*

You could use moxa on Gb 26, Cv 4 and Cv 6, and Bl 23 for irregular periods. For leukorrhea, you might combine Gb 26 with Sp 6, Cv 6, Cv 4, Liv 2, Sp 9, St 36, and Gv 20.

Figure 127

Figure 128

Applications:
1) He attacks with both hands. You should slam both of his neigwan points toward you (fig. 124). Both of your knife-edge palms strike back into both of his Gb 26 points (fig. 125).
2) He attacks with a straight right. You should move to the side, slamming his right elbow with your left palm as your right palm percusses onto Gb 26 on one side (fig. 126).
3) Other points that work well with Gb 26 are Liv 14 and Cv 14. He might attack with a straight right; you take his neigwan, slamming it with your right palm. Your left palm takes over the block as your right hammer fist smashes into Gb 26 from the side (fig. 127). Your waist instantly reloads, and your right elbow slams into either Liv 14 or Cv 14 (fig. 128).

GB 27 (GALLBLADDER POINT NO. 27)

Chinese name:
Wushu (five pivots).
Location:
In the lateral sides of the abdomen, in front of the anterior super iliac spine, 3 cun below the level of the umbilicus, approximately level with Cv 4. In the external and internal oblique muscles and the transverse abdominal muscle.
Connections:
Dai mai.
Direction of strike:
Struck straight in from the front.
Damage:
KO or damage to the kidneys. Hospitalization is necessary if the strike is hard.

Figure 129

Figure 130

Set-up point:

Instead of a specific point to set up Gb 27, there is an abstract way of setting it up. We simply surprise or shock the attacker. For instance, he might be getting ready to attack, and we attack high with perhaps a yell, shocking him instantly. Then when the points are struck it will have a far greater effect.

Antidote:

Press inward hard at Kd 1.

Healing:

Innervated by the iliohypogastric nerve and irrigated by the superficial and deep circumflex iliac arteries and veins.

Used for leukorrhea, pain in lower back and hip joint, hernia, endometritis, and orchitis (inflammation of the testis).

Traditional indications include colic, vaginal discharge containing blood, lower back pain, abdominal pain, constipation, and infantile convulsions.

Massage techniques are similar to those used with Gb 25 and Gb 26. This is a great point to press for spasm of the psoas and ileopsoas muscles causing paralysis of the hip and/or pain in the lower back, groin, and extending down the front of the leg and/or inability to flex the leg without pain.

Applications:

He is about to attack. You rush forward, going high with both of your hands (fig. 129). Just before you contact his face, you go low with both palms to both of his Gb 27 points straight inward (fig. 130).

GB 28 (GALLBLADDER POINT NO. 28)

Chinese name:
Weidao (meeting path).

Location:
.5 cun anterior and inferior to the anterior iliac spine.

Connections:
This is another Gb point that intersects with the dai mai.

Direction of strike:
This point can kill when struck from the inside of the body to the outside and into the hip bone.

Damage:
Compared to the other Gb points, Gb 28 more of a physical effect upon the bladder, which can burst when the point is struck in the correct direction as described above.

Set-up point:
Liv 13 can set up Gb 28 nicely when struck straight in.

Antidote:
Kd 1.

Healing:
Enervated by the ilioinguinal nerve and irrigated by the superficial and deep circumflex iliac arteries and veins.

Used for pain in lower back and hip joints, leukorrhea, lower abdominal pain, prolapse of the uterus, endometritis, pain from intestinal hernia, chronic constipation, and adnexitis (inflammation of a gland in this region).

Massage techniques are similar to those used for Gb 25, Gb 26, and Gb 27. For prolapse of the uterus, you might press in the direction of the uterus, directing qi to the uterus, then move the

Figure 131

Figure 132

pressure up and away toward the anterior superior iliac spine and combine with Gv 20, Sp 6, Sp 3, and abdomen zigong, with moxa on Cv 4, Cv 6, and Cv 12

Applications:
You are grabbed from behind. You first attack to Liv 13 with your right elbow (fig. 131). Now your right or left palm slams backward in a lateral direction just above the groin and into the hip bone to Gb 28 (fig. 132).

GB 29 (GALLBLADDER POINT NO. 29)

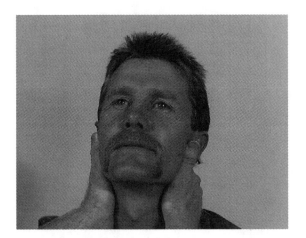

Figure 133

Figure 134

Chinese name:
Juliao (bone of lodging).

Location:
Midway between the anterosuperior iliac spine and the great trochanter. Locate the point with the patient lying on his or her side. Gb 29 is at the anterior margin of the tensor fascia lata and, in its deep position, in the vastus lateralis muscle.

Connections:
This is a point where the Gb meridian intersects with the *yang qiao* channel (one of the eight extra channels).

Direction of strike:
Strike this point straight in to the middle of the leg/pelvis.

Damage:
A strike to this point only will cause paralysis of the upper right side of the body. It will also cause a KO. When combined with a strike to Gb 12, a strike to Gb 29 will cause spasm in the whole upper body.

Set-up point:
Strike straight in to the middle of the biceps, cutting with a knife-edge strike. This will greatly increase the paralyzing effect.

Antidote:
Stand in front of the patient. Place your both thumbs in front of each ear. Touch your fingers together behind the neck and squeeze mildly (fig. 133).

Healing:
Innervated by the lateral femoral cutaneous nerve of the thigh. Irrigated by the branches of the superficial circumflex iliac artery and vein and the ascending branches of the lateral circumflex femoral artery and vein.

Used for pain in the back and lower extremities, paralysis, stomach ache, lower abdominal pain, orchitis, endometritis, cystitis, disease of the hip joint and surrounding soft tissue, imbalance in the length of the left and right legs, sciatic nerve impingement and pain, and

Figure 135

Figure 136

Figure 137

Figure 138

sexual repression with rigidity of lower back and pelvis regions.

Traditional uses include lower back pain and associated lower abdominal pain, paralysis and atrophy of the leg, and diarrhea.

To massage, use a straight press, with clockwise and counterclockwise rotation for xu or shi conditions. You can use fists or knuckles to knead this region, and you might do fingertip percussion on this point. Some people are very sensitive in this region, especially when there are problems with sexual inhibitions, muscle inflammation causing pressure on the sciatic nerve, or a left/right leg length imbalance, so you may not be able to percuss this point very heavily or for too long. It is good to do as much as the person can cope with for as long as is tolerable. You can also get into this point with your elbow, preferably with the patient on his or her side, if it is tolerable.

You could combine this point with Gb 30, Bl 25, Bl 26, Bl 54, Bl 40, and Gb 34 for sciatic pain or lower back pain. For left/right leg imbalance, you might combine it with Gb 30, Gb 34, Gb 31, Gb 32, and Gb 41. For pain associated with blood stagnation causing dysmenorrhea, you could use it with Sp 6, Cv 6, Co 4, Gb 29, Bl 18, Sp 8, Cv 2, Bl 31, Bl 32, Bl 33, and Bl 34. You can use this point with Gb 30, Gb 34, Gb 39, and Bl 25 for arthritis of the hip.

Applications:
1) He attacks with a straight right. You should slam the back of his right forearm at Th 8. This is enough to cause KO in many cases (fig. 134). Your right palm immediately grabs his right wrist and jerks it toward you while your left palm attacks to Th 12 (fig. 135). While your left palm still guards his right arm, your right palm attacks straight in to Gb 29 (fig. 136).
2) The Gb 29 point is the lowest we go using the hands. The rule is, where the hands can reach, use them. Where they cannot reach, use the legs. So anywhere below Gb 29, we usually use the legs to attack to the points. Slam his right inside arm at neigwan point with your left knife edge and the middle of the biceps with your right knife edge. You will access Ht 2 here, as well as taking the arm out through a nerve point strike to the median nerve (fig. 137). Take the back of his upper arm at point Th 12 while still holding his wrist at Lu 8 and Ht 5, and bring your knee into Gb 29 (fig. 138).

GB 30 (GALLBLADDER POINT NO. 30)

Chinese name:
Huantiao (jumping circle).

Location:
At the junction of the middle and lateral thirds of the distance between the great trochanter and the hiatus of the sacrum (Gv 2). To locate this point, lie the patient on his or her side with leg flexed. The point is in the gluteus maximus and inferior margin of the piriformus muscle.

Connections:
This is a point of intersection between the gallbladder meridian and a branch of the bladder meridian.

Direction of strike:
Straight in from the rear into the hollow of the buttock.

Damage:
This will cause a KO and leg damage, along with nausea and perhaps bladder problems—even years after the strike.

Set-up point:
Use neigwan as the set-up point for this strike. Both points are qi drainage points.

Antidote:
Have the patient lie face down and apply pressure all the way up either side of the backbone without touching the backbone. Go from the buttock area to the shoulders and back down.

Healing:
Innervated by the inferior cluneal cutaneous nerve and the inferior gluteal nerve. Deeper, it is right on the sciatic nerve. Irrigation is by the inferior gluteal artery and vein.

Figure 139

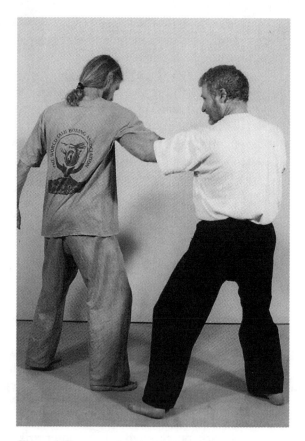

Figure 140

Used for pain in the lower back and hip region, muscular atrophy, motor impairment, pain and weakness of the low extremities, hemiplegia, sciatica, numbness and paralysis of the low extremities, and disease of the hip and surrounding tissue.

Traditional uses include the following: hemiplegia, lower back and groin pain, and "leg qi." (Leg qi is also known as edema of leg or, in Western medicine, beriberi. It is characterized initially by swelling with numbness, pain, and weakness. Spasm, atrophy, fever, palpations, and vomiting will develop if the heart is attacked. Caused by wrong eating habits, damp invasion, etc.)

To massage, use a straight push with clockwise or counterclockwise rotation for xu or shi conditions.

You could combine it with Si 3, Gb 34, Gb 41, Bl 54, Bl 40, and Bl 58 for painful legs.

For leg qi, you might try combining Gb 30 with St 32, Si 3, Sp 6, St 36, and St 40.

Combine with Gb 29, Bl 54, Bl 25, Bl 26, Bl 40, and Th 34 for lower back pain, sciatica, etc.

If the shoulders are stiff and painful, you could use Gb 30 in conjunction with Gb 21, Th 15, Si 13, Si 3, Gb 30, Gb 34, and Bl 60.

Figure 141

86

For rheumatoid arthritis, combine Gb 30 with Co 4, Co 11, Co 15, and St 36. If the wrist is involved, add Pc 7 and Pc 3. If the hip is involved add Gb 31, Bl 54, Gb 29, Bl 25, and Bl 40.

Traditional functions include activating the *jing luo* (all of the 12 main and the collateral channels); removing obstructions; and tonifying the back, waist, and hip joints. Often used for sciatica.

Applications:

He attacks with a right straight. You should block this with a right p'eng (fig. 139). Your left palm now attacks straight up into Ht 1 (fig. 140). Meanwhile, you are moving out to the side past the attacker. You are now in a position to slam him into his right buttock at Gb 30 with your right palm. This is probably one of the only techniques in which the hand is used to strike such a low point, since you are pretty safe in back of him (fig. 141).

GB 31 (GALLBLADDER POINT NO. 31)

Chinese name:

Fengshi (city of wind).

Location:

On the midline of the lateral aspect of the thigh, 7 cun above the transverse popliteal crease. Beneath the tensor faciae latae, in the vastus lateralis muscle.

When standing erect with the hands at the sides, the point is located where the tip of the middle finger touches the leg.

Connections:

None.

Direction of strike:

Strike straight in to the side of the thigh, usually using a ball of the foot type of attack or an instep, round type of low kick.

Damage:

This strike causes a "dead leg," wherein the leg becomes paralyzed. It can cause a KO, as well as affecting the heart by slowing it down or stopping it. In order to affect the heart, though, the strike must be accurate—executed with a small weapon such as the ball of the foot or a big toe.

Set-up point:

Neigwan is struck as the set-up point.

Antidote:

Apply pressure down the front of the thigh, especially to St 32, using the flat of the palm.

Healing:

Innervated by the lateral femoral cutaneous nerve, the muscular branch of the femoral nerve. Irrigated by the muscular branches of the lateral circumflex femoral artery and vein.

Used for hemiplegia, muscular atrophy, motor impairment, pain in the lower extremities, itching anywhere on body, pain of the lower back and leg, and neuritis of the lateral cutaneous nerve of the thigh and a muscle branch of the femoral nerve.

Traditional functions are to dispel wind, relax tendons, invigorate collaterals, and tonify the waist and knees. Much used to dispel wind of herpes zoster (shingles) and wind stroke (another term for stroke or blood clot in the brain is cerebrovascular accident [CVA]).

Traditional uses include soreness and pain in the lower back and leg; numbness and stiffness of leg and foot; hemiplegia; itching on one side of the body; headache; and red, swollen, sore eyes. To massage, use a straight push with clockwise or counterclockwise rotations for xu or shi conditions. You can do a straight push passing through this point, beginning at Gb 29 and moving to Gb 30 and to the head of the femur and straight down the center of the thigh at 1 cun intervals, ending at Gb 33. This will help with lower back and hip problems. Percussion down the Gb meridian of leg as above can also be used.

Combine with Gb 30, Bl 54, Gb 29, Bl 57, Bl 56, Bl 25, Bl 26, Bl 40, and Gb 34 for infantile paralysis of the lower limbs or for sciatic pain. For CVA (stroke) when the legs are involved (hemiplegia), use Gb 31 with Co 15, Co 11, Th 5, Co 4, Gb 30, Gb 31, Gb 34, and Gb 39.

For itch, combine with, Ht 7, Co 4, Co 11, Liv 2, Sp 10, and Gb 20.

Applications:

He might attack with a straight right. You might use a p'eng-type block to his right neigwan, thus setting up the point. Immediately, strike straight in to the thigh at Gb 31, using either the instep for a lesser effect or, if you are accurate enough, using the ball of the foot or a toe to kick (fig. 142).

GB 32 (GALLBLADDER POINT NO. 32)

Chinese name:

Femur zhong (middle ditch).

Location:

In the lateral aspect of the thigh, 5 cun above the transverse popliteal crease, between the muscle vastus lateralis, 2 cun below Gb 31.

Connections:

None.

Direction of strike:

Same as for Gb 31, straight in from the side of the thigh.

Figure 142

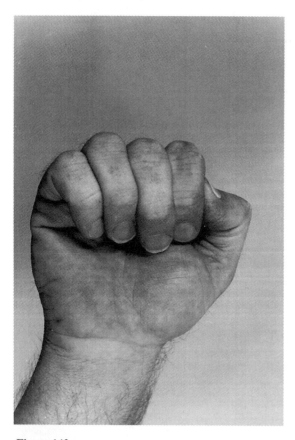

Figure 143

Figure 144

Figure 145

Damage:

Causes KO or takes out the knee on that side. Also affects the heart and causes nausea.

Set-up point:

Use neigwan as a set-up point or, as a secondary strike, Ht 3 in the elbow crease. The latter can cause death by itself since it affects the heart, often stopping it.

Antidote:

Liv 3 is pressed straight in. Liv 3 is a good antidote to all knee and upper thigh ailments.

Healing:

Innervation and irrigation are the same as for Gb 31. Used for muscular atrophy; motor impairment; numbness, pain, and weakness of the lower extremities; leg qi (beriberi); paralysis of the lower limbs; right/left leg imbalance; and sciatic neuralgia (inflammation of the sciatic nerve, also called sciatica).

Massage techniques are the same as for Gb 31.

Applications:

He might attack with a straight right. Your left palm slaps the outside of his right lower forearm as your right thumb (palm is held in the typical taijiquan fist, as in fig. 143) attacks in a line toward you to Ht 3 (fig. 144). Your left foot now attacks to Gb 32 (fig. 145).

GB 33 (GALLBLADDER POINT NO. 33)

Chinese name:

Xiyangguan (yang hinge/gate).

Location:

When the knee is flexed, the point is 3 cun above Gb 34, lateral to the knee joint in the depression between the tendons of the biceps femoris muscles and the femur. In the hollow above the lateral condyle of the femur, at the posterior aspect of the iliotibial band and the anterior aspect of biceps femoris tendon.

Connections:

None.

Direction of strike:

Again, straight in from the side of the knee, just above the patella.

Damage:

KO, plus great tendon damage around the knee (the tendons could be completely torn away from the bone). This is the ideal strike to the leg, because the tendons holding the lower leg on are torn and the recipient cannot carry on with no leg support. This strike will drain qi greatly.

Set-up point:

Th 12 is a good set-up shot for this point, as is neigwan.

Antidote:

Again, use Liv 3.

Healing:

Innervated by the terminal branch of the lateral femoral cutaneous nerve and irrigated by the superior lateral glenicular artery and vein.

Figure 146

Figure 147

Used for pain and swelling of the knee, contracture of the tendons in the popliteal fossa, numbness of the leg, and paralysis of lower limbs.

Traditionally used for inability to flex or extend the knee, progressive pain and swelling of knee, and leg qi (beriberi).

Massage techniques include straight push with clockwise and counterclockwise rotation for xu or shi conditions and percussion with one or two fingers.

You might use Gb 34, Sp 6, Sp 9, Sp 10, St 36, St 34, *xi yan* (the "eyes of the knee," consisting of St 35 and the extra point, xi yan, on the opposite side of the tendon), Liv 3, and Gb 33 for pain and swelling of knee.

Applications:

He attacks with a straight left. You slam his elbow with your right palm as you step to your right side (fig. 146). Your right palm grabs the inside of his left elbow as your left palm takes his wrist. Your left foot has stepped up, and as you push your left palm, your right palm pulls violently as your right heel kicks to the side of his thigh just above the knee at Gb 33 (fig. 147).

GB 34 (GALLBLADDER POINT NO. 34)

Chinese name:

Yanglingguan (fountain of the yang mound).

Location:

In the depression anterior and inferior to the head of the fibula when the leg is flexed. Anterior to the capitulum of the fibula between peroneus longus, and the extensor digitorum longus pedis muscle.

Connections:

None.

Figure 148

Figure 149

Direction of strike:
Kick across the knee at about a 45-degree angle from the front (refer to fig. 147 again for proper angle.)

Damage:
Aggravates the liver greatly so that hospitalization is necessary. Also causes KO and destroys the leg.

Set-up point:
Slap the outside of his forearm from his wrist to elbow (direction of strike is moving away from you). This is an ideal qi drainage set-up.

Antidote:
Hold the back of his head and press inward on both sides of his forehead at Gb 15.

Healing:
This point is found where the common peroneal nerve bifurcates into the superficial and deep peroneal nerves and is innervated by these. It is irrigated by the inferior lateral genicular artery and vein.

Gb 34 is used for hemiplegia, muscular atrophy, motor impairment and/or numbness in the hypochondriac and costal regions, bitter taste in the mouth, vomiting, hepatitis, cholecystitis, roundworm in the bile duct, hypertension, intercostal neuralgia, inflammation of the shoulder, and habitual constipation.

Traditional indications are as follows: distension of mouth, tongue, throat, face, and head; fullness in the chest and ribs; distension of the gallbladder; loss of urine (incontinence); constipation; and leg qi.

This is a he sea point (a uniting point) and an earth point of the Gb meridian and a meeting place of tendons and muscles. Its traditional functions are as follows: soothes liver/gallbladder, relieves damp heat, removes obstructions from the jing luo, activates jing luo, tonifies tendons and ligaments, eliminates phlegm/fire in the stomach, and subdues liver yang.

Massage by using a straight press and hold technique or clockwise or counterclockwise rotation for xu or shi conditions. You might do percussion on this point or press and slide down the pathway of the channel.

You can combine Gb 34 with Liv 14, Liv 4, Liv 2, Liv 3, Liv 13, Liv 8, Gb 24, Cv 12, and St 36 for hepatitis.

Use with St 25, Sp 15, Liv 3, Liv 4, St 37, and Gb 41 for constipation.

Use with Bl 25, Bl 26, Bl 54, Bl 40, Bl 58, Gb 29, Gb 30, Gb 31, Gb 32, and Gb 33 for sciatic pain.

For anterior shoulder pain, combine with Co 15, Co 14, St 38, and Gb 21, and with Th 14, Th 13, Th 15, Gb 21, Si 3, Si 9, and Si 10 for posterior shoulder pain.

For intercostal neuralgia, you could use this point with Liv 14, Gb 24, Liv 3, Gb 41, Ht 1, and *huatuojiaji* points (extra points from T 7 to T 12 associated with the thoracic vertebra).

For inflammation of the gallbladder or gall stones, use with Pc 6, *dannangxue* (a new point found 1 cun below Gb 34), St 36, and Gb 24 on the right side, plus huatuojiaji points from T8 to T9.

Figure 150

Applications:

1) He attacks with a straight right, and you step to your left as your left palm slams his right forearm up his arm (fig. 148). Instantly, your right palm also moves underneath your left palm and slices upward on his forearm as your right heel kicks at an angle into Gb 33 (fig. 149).

2) He attacks with a right hook. You should slam his inner forearm at neigwan and follow with a back kick to Gb 34 (fig. 150).

GB 35 (GALLBLADDER POINT NO. 35)

Chinese name:

Yangjiao (yang's intersection).

Location:

7 cun above the lateral malleolus, on the posterior border of the fibula, within the distance between the tip of the lateral malleolus and Gb 34, level with Gb 36 and Bl 58. In the lateral aspect of the leg, the distance between the tip of the lateral malleolus and the midpoint of the knee is seen as 16 cun.

Connections:

Yang wei mai.

Direction of strike:

Straight in from the side of the calf.

Damage:

This is a particularly nasty strike because its effects occur later in life due to the slow damage caused to the point. All *xie cleft* points react in this way. (A xie cleft point is an accumulation point where qi and blood converge in the channel, and it can be used to treat acute disease states because of this function.) It causes knockout when struck directly with a small weapon. Obvious leg damage is another effect, as is extreme local pain that can cause the nervous system to shut down for a period until the brain works

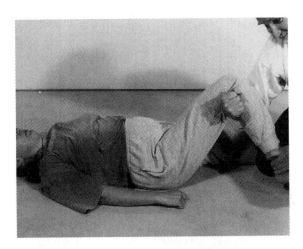

Figure 151

Figure 152

Figure 153

out what is wrong. This point can also be used as a neurological shutdown strike. (Neurological shutdown points are those that, when struck all by themselves, cause the whole nervous system to shut down, dropping the person.)

Set-up point:

A traditional set-up point for this strike is Bl 10 around the back of the neck, closer to the head.

Antidote:

With the patient lying down, pull gently on the leg at the foot. You can also place one arm under his knee and lever downward. (fig. 151).

Healing:

Innervated by the lateral sural cutaneous nerve and irrigated by the branches of the peroneal artery and vein.

Used for fullness in the chest and hypochondriac region, knee pain, muscular atrophy and weakness of the foot, pain in the lateral aspect of the leg, sciatica, and asthma.

Traditionally Gb 35 functions as a xie cleft point of the extra meridian yang wei mai.

Massage techniques might include a straight push, clockwise or counterclockwise rotation for xu or shi conditions, percussion over the point with the fingertips, or a shiatsu progression down from Gb 34 to Gb 39 (you can press with the heel of the hand down the same line). These types of procedures are best performed with the patient on his or her side or lying face down with the leg bent at the knee and the foot placed next to the opposite knee.

You can use this point with Gb 38 , Gb 31, Liv 2, Bl 60, Gb 40, Sp 6, Gb 41, Liv 3, and St 36 for numb feet caused by damp obstructing the flow of qi and blood (peripheral neuritis).

You can also use it with St 41, Gb 40, Kd 3, Bl 60, Kd 8, and Liv 4 for arthritis of the ankle.

Use with Cv 15, Si 3, Kd 1, Bl 15, St 36, Liv 3, Pc 5, Cv 13, Gb 2O, Gv 16, Gv 26, Gv 14, Gb 34, and Liv 5, for epileptic seizures.

For red or white leukorrhea, you can use Gb 35 with Cv 6, Cv 3, Bl 30, Sp 6, Sp 9, Cv 9, and Cv 4.

Applications:

In a grappling situation, you could strike to Bl 10 at the back of the neck (fig. 152). Next use a round-type kick to Gb 35 with either the instep or toe if wearing shoes (fig. 153).

GB 36 (GALLBLADDER POINT NO. 36)

Chinese name:

Waiqiu (outer mold/external region).

Location:

7 cun above the lateral malleolus on the anterior border of the fibula, or midway between Gb 34 and the lateral malleolus, in front of Gb 35 and level to it at the anterior border of the fibula.

Connections:

None.

Direction of strike:

Straight in from the side of the leg.

Damage:

This is also a xie cleft point, so it does much the same damage as Gb 35.

Set-up point:

Bladder 10 will set up Gb 36, as will neigwan.

Antidote:

If no great physical damage has occurred to the lower leg (as this point is closer to the shin), use Gb 20 as a universal revival point in the event of a KO.

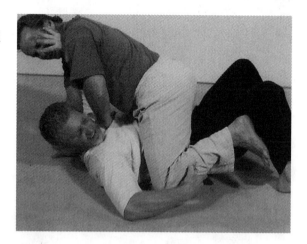

Figure 154

Healing:

Innervated by the superficial peroneal nerve. Irrigated by the branches of the anterior tibial artery and vein.

Used for pain in the neck, chest, and hypochondriac regions; headache; hepatitis; and paralysis of the lower limbs.

Because Gb 36 is a xie cleft point of the gallbladder channel, it is traditionally used for acute injuries of the gallbladder and its channel.

Massage techniques would include straight push, clockwise and counterclockwise rotation for xu or shi conditions, percussion with fingertips over the point and/or in a progression from Gb 34 to Gb 39. You could also press along this same line with the heel of the hand (or rub) down the pathway of the Gb meridian.

For intercostal neuralgia, you might use Gb 36 with Bl 18, Liv 6, Liv 14, Gb 34, Th 6, Bl 19, Gb 24, *jiaji* points (extra points) from the fifth thoracic to the 10th thoracic vertebra, Bl 17, Sp 17, Gb 36, Liv 3, Bl 14, and Liv 13.

For headache, use it with Gb 20, Gb 14, *taiyang* (an extra point just back from Gb 1 around the temple area), Gv 20, Co 4, and St 36.

Figure 155

Applications:

1) Now that we are getting well down the leg, the applications become sparse. However, you can use Gb 36 in a grappling situation where the attacker has pinned you. Gb 36 is a good point to grab and push violently since it sends a shock right up the leg, usually causing the attacker to leap up. I used this point in my wrestling days, and it worked every time. (See fig. 154.)

2) Gb 36 can also be kicked. Should he attack with both hands, you should use both of your hands to defend and kick using the side of your shoe to Gb 36 (fig. 155).

GB 37 (GALLBLADDER POINT NO. 37)

Chinese name:

Guangming (bright light).

Location:

5 cun directly above the tip of the external malleus, at the anterior border of the fibula. Between the extensor digitorum longus pedis and peroneus brevis muscles.

Connections:

Transverse *luo* to Liv 3 and Liv 1. (A luo point or meridian is a connecting point or meridian.)

Direction of strike:

Straight in to the side of the lower shin.

Damage:

When struck very hard with a larger weapon such as the instep kick, this point will cause KO, as well as physical damage to the shin area. When the point is struck directly, it causes great local pain, as well as liver and gallbladder damage. This point is also pertinent to eye damage or healing, depending upon how it is used. Used in a martial way (usually a kick), it will cause severe eye damage slowly over several years. A quick, sharp strike using a small weapon will cause momentary blindness.

Set-up point:

You could use Liv 3 as a stomp, then rebound up with a heel kick to the point. You can also strike Liv 14 from the middle of his trunk to the outside.

Antidote:

Gb 20 for KO, or, for liver problems, treat Liv 3, either using needles or pressure.

Healing:

Innervated by the superficial peroneal nerve. Irrigated by the branches of the anterior tibial artery and vein.

The traditional function of this point is as a luo point of the gallbladder, so it might be used to balance the yin/yang aspects of an element (e.g., Gb with Liv in the element of wood). It also regulates the liver and clears the vision.

Used for pain in the knee, muscular atrophy, motor impairment and pain of the lower extremities, ophthalmoplegia, night blindness, distending pain of breast, atrophy of the optic nerve, cataract, migraine, and pain along the lateral aspect of the calf.

Traditional indications include the following: chills; fever without sweating; soreness of leg and knee; atrophy, blockage, and numbness of the leg; seizures; and pain and itching of the eye.

Massage might include straight push with clockwise or counterclockwise rotation for xu or shi conditions, and percussion with the fingertips. You can also press this point with the heel of hand, press with movement back and forth across the point, or press and slide the thumb up or down the meridian.

You could use Gb 37 with Gb 20, Liv 2, Liv 3, Liv 4, St 1, and an extra point called *qiuhou*, one-third of the distance from Gb 1 to St 1, for early stages of cataracts, blurred vision, and so on. I would use Bl 1 here as well.

Use with Co 4, St 36, St 1, and Bl 1 or with Gb 20, Bl 2, and Bl 1 for optic nerve atrophy and optic neuritis.

Figure 156

Figure 157

Applications:

WARNING: *Although Gb 37 may look like an ineffectual strike aside from leg damage, do not play around with it, because it could cause blindness! This point is an important eye point.*

He might attack with a straight right, so you use a p'eng/hinge method to attack and simultaneously block his attack. Your right p'eng attacks up the outside of his right arm, while your left hinge palm attacks to Liv 13 (fig. 156). Your right heel now stomps onto Liv 3. Then, using the rebound from that stomp, the right heel snaps around to hook kick to Gb 37 (fig. 157).

GB 38 (GALLBLADDER POINT NO. 38)

Chinese name:

Yangfu (yang's help) fire and jing point.

Location:

4 cun above and slightly anterior to the tip of the external malleolus (the outside ankle), on the anterior border of the fibula and the tendons of peroneus longus and brevis.

Connections:

None.

Direction of strike:

Struck down into the leg at an angle. This point doesn't have to be accurate since you kick it with the side of the foot downward into the ankle.

Damage:

KO, when struck in the correct direction, and leg damage—it can break the shin. Also, a good strike here can cause headaches for weeks.

Set-up point:

Gb 15 struck straight in.

Figure 158

Figure 159

Antidote:

Gb 15, massaged upward gently. See a doctor if the leg is broken.

Healing:

Innervation and irrigation are the same as for Gb 37.

Used for one-sided headache; pain at the outer canthus supraclavicular fossa and axillary regions; scrofula; pain in the chest, hypochondriac region (either side of upper chest), or lateral aspects of the leg; malaria; arthritis of the knee; paralysis of lower limbs; migraine; and hemiplegia.

Traditional function is as a *jing* river (traversing) point, so it may be used to deviate pathogenic qi out of the channel. Since it is a fire point of the Gb meridian, it might be used to cool fire in the wood element with Liv 2.

Massage techniques are similar to those used with Gb 37.

Gb 38 could be used with Gb 20, Gb 1, Liv 3, Liv 2, Co 4, Gv 20, and Gb 14 for headache .

You might also use it with Gb 34, Gb 39, and Gb 41 points in the web of toes (a group of extra points called *shangbafeng*); Sp 4; Bl 65; Sp 5; and Liv 4 for arthritis of feet. For paralysis, it can be used with Co 11, Liv 4, Liv 5, Co 4, Th 3, St 36, and Bl 60.

For lower back pain, it can be used with Gb 21, Gb 30, St 33, St 36, Bl 53, Bl 54, Bl 57, Bl 60, Bl 58, Bl 40, Bl 23, Bl 65, Gv 2, and Gv 3.

Applications:

He attacks with a straight right. If you have your left foot forward, you leap into the air, bringing your left foot back as your right foot comes forward (movement from old Yang-style taijiquan, called "sleeves dancing like plumb blossoms"). As you do this, your left palm has slammed down onto his right forearm at Th 8 (fig. 158), causing him to lose energy and probably black out (or close to it). Your right palm now slams down onto Gb 15 just before the right side of your foot scrapes downward over Gb 38 (fig. 159).

GB 39 (GALLBLADDER POINT NO. 39)

Chinese name:

Xuanzhang or juegu (suspended bell).

Location:

3 cun above the tip of the lateral malleus, in the depression between the posterior border of the fibula and the tendons of peroneus longus and brevis. Just above the ankle on the outside of the leg. This is the last Gb point above the ankle.

Connections:

Connects to the three leg yang channels: the gallbladder, stomach, and bladder. Special meeting point of bone marrow.

Direction of strike:

Straight in and down into the ankle.

Damage:

This is an interesting point all by itself. It causes great damage to the brain. At a lesser level, it can make the recipient feel totally disorientated, and at a larger level, it will cause both immediate and delayed mental problems. A strike here will drain energy from the whole leg area immediately, and a few minutes later the whole body will be drained, resulting in KO or death. Do not play around with this point!

Set-up point:

Any Gb point will set up this point, so you could use points on the head, face, back of the neck, torso, and legs. Always strike the set-up point in an "adverse" qi direction (i.e., in a direction that will drain qi and not add it).

Antidote:

Massage the whole back area on both sides of the backbone and down the back of the legs. Then turn the patient over and massage down the front of the legs. See a Chinese doctor for damage to the brain.

Healing:

Innervation and irrigation are the same as for Gb 37.

Used for hemiplegia; neck rigidity; fullness of the chest; distension of the abdomen; pain in the hypochondriac region, knee, and leg; leg qi; migraine; scrofula; sciatica; and ankle pain with damage to surrounding tissue.

Traditional indications include nosebleed, throat blockage, cough, fullness in the chest and abdomen, stiff neck, hemiplegia due to stroke, leg qi, and broken bones.

Traditional functions are to dispel wind and damp, tonify bone marrow, and treat *wei* and *bi* syndromes (Chinese terms for conditions similar to arthritis, although wei syndrome is more like paralysis). It also functions as a meeting point of the marrow and an intersecting point of the three leg yang channels.

Massage techniques include straight press, clockwise or counterclockwise rotation for xu or shi, movement back and forth across the point, clasping of the leg between the thumb and forefinger and squeezing, and using as part of a shiatsu progression down the Gb meridian.

Figure 160

For acute leukemia, use this point with Bl 18, Bl 23, Bl 1, and Liv 3.

Hold Gb 34, Gb 39, and Gb 30 for paralysis of the foot.

For migraine, use it with Gb 20, Gb 15 , Gb 34, Co 4, Gv 20, *taiyang,* Gb 43, and Gb 41.

Use with Gb 11, Th 5, St 36, Th 6, Liv 13, Liv 4, Gb 34, Liv 2, Liv 6, Liv 14, Liv 3, Gb 40, Kd l, Gb 41, Gb 25, and Gb 26 for pain in the sides. related to hepatitis.

Use with Bl 11, Gb 39, Bl 23, and Kd 3, for bone fractures; adding Gv 20, Sp 3, Bl 20, and Gb 34 might treat easy displacement of vertebra, etc.

For hemiplegia with difficulty speaking, you might try Gv 20, Gb 21, Gb 31, St 6, Gb 39, and Co 11. You could also use Co 4, Co 10, Co 11, Gb 21, Gb 30, Sp 10, Gb 34, Sp 9, Liv 4, and Bl 60, with this point for hemiplegia.

Applications:

He attempts a crescent kick. You should simply strike with your left palm to Gb 39 in a downward direction (fig. 160).

GB 40 (GALLBLADDER POINT NO. 40)

Chinese name:

Qiuxu (mound of ruins or grave mold or region of the eminence).

Location:

Anterior and inferior to the lateral malleolus, in the depression on the lateral side of the tendon of extensor digitorum longus. At the origin of extensor digitorum brevis pedis. Side of the foot, forward of the ankle bone.

Connections:

Takes transverse luo from Liv 5.

Direction of strike:

Usually a stomp straight down onto the top of the foot to the side, although you can use finger pressure in a grappling situation.

Damage:

When struck really hard, this point can paralyze the whole body or just the leg being struck. It can also cause heart failure and knockout. WARNING: *Do not play around with this point just to show off; you could do irreparable damage to the energy system of the gallbladder and liver, causing disease in later life.*

Set-up point:

Combine this point with Lu 11 (tip of the thumb), and you make for a really good paralyzing strike. However, it is not easy to get at Lu 11 since it is on the tip of the thumb. So we can also use Lu 8 at the wrist, as in a wrist grab and jerk. This will drain energy from the system so that the major strike will have a far greater effect.

Antidote:

Liv 3 pressed straight in, or Gb 38 pressed straight in. (Of course, if the foot has been broken, see a doctor.)

Healing:

Innervated by the branches of the intermediate dorsal cutaneous nerve and superficial peroneal nerve. Irrigated by a branch of the lateral anterior malleolar artery.

Indications include pain in the neck/chest/hypochondriac region, swelling of the axillary region, vomiting, acid regurgitation, muscular atrophy, motor impairment, weakness and pain in the lower extremities, pain and swelling of the ankle, malaria, cholecystitis, and sciatica.

Traditional indications include rib pain, soreness of the leg from twisted muscles/tendons, or ligaments, tidal fever, distension of the lower abdomen, and colic.

Traditional functions are to promote the functions of the liver/gallbladder channels (Gb 41 is better for internal organs); invigorate the jing luo; ease the joints; treat the aftereffects of wind stroke, infantile paralysis, and wei syndrome; spread liver qi; and benefit the gallbladder. It is a *yuan* source

Figure 161

Figure 162

point (yuan qi is ancestral energy, so a yuan point draws upon ancestral qi), so it can tap the original qi of the organ.

Massage techniques include pressing, rotating clockwise or counterclockwise for xu or shi conditions, and percussion kneading of the point and surrounding tissue.

Applications:

He attacks with a straight right. You should use a p'eng blocking type movement (fig. 161). As your left palm controls his right elbow, your right hand immediately grabs his right thumb, twisting and bending it (fig. 162). Your right heel now stomps down onto Gb 40. The fight is over.

GB 41 (GALLBLADDER POINT NO. 41)

Chinese name:

Zulinqi or foot linqi (near tears on the foot or lying down to weep).

Location:

In the depression distal to the junction of the fourth and fifth metatarsal bones, on the lateral side of the tendon of extensor digiti minimi of the foot. About 2 inches back in a straight line from the little toe.

Connections:

None.

Direction of strike:

Straight down onto the foot.

Damage:

This point is a master point for the extra meridian called *dai mai*, or the girdle meridian that runs around the waist. So a strike to Gb 41 will have an effect on that meridian. One of the dai mai's functions is to control the communication between upper and lower, so a strike to Gb 41 not only

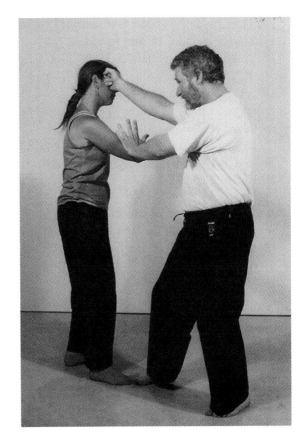

Figure 163   Figure 164

produces great local pain or a KO, it also cuts off communication between the torso and legs, resulting in great uncoordination. For these reasons, you could use this point as a set-up strike to a more deadly blow.

Set-up point:

Ht 1, struck straight up and into the axilla. Also, Sp 17, struck in from the outside of the body.

Antidote:

Liv 3 if there is not too much physical damage to the foot. Sp 21 if there is electrical damage (i.e., the coordination is shot). Press straight in on Sp 21 and/or Liv 3.

Healing:

Innervation is by the branch of the intermediate dorsal cutaneous nerve of the foot. Irrigation is by the ateriovenous network in the dorsum of the foot and the fourth dorsal metatarsal artery and vein.

Used for pain in the outer canthus, blurring of vision, pain in the costal and hypochondriac regions, pain and swelling of the dorsum of foot, distending pain in the breast, malaria, headache, vertigo, conjunctivitis, scrofula, irregular menstruation, breast abscess, and dampness and swelling of foot.

Traditional functions of this point are to promote the free and unrestrained function of liver qi, dispel damp/heat, treat the hypochondrium (hypochondriac region), regulate the dai mai, and spread and drain the liver/gallbladder. It is a wood point and *shu* stream point (transporting point) of the gallbladder meridian, a meeting point of the gallbladder and dai mai, and a master point of the dai mai.

Massage techniques include pressing and rotating clockwise or counterclockwise for xu or shi conditions

Use with Lu 1, Cv 22, Cv 17, Liv 14, Gb 24, kidney points on the chest, Bl 60, Sp 9, Ht 1, Lu 7, Lu 9, and Liv 3 for wheezing. For headache and migraine, use with Gb 2O, Gb 15, Gb 21, Co 4, St 36, Gb 34, Gb 14, yintang, taiyang, and Gv 20.

101

For blurring of the vision, use with Bl 1, *yuyao* (an extra point), Gb 1, St 1, and Liv 14.

For sciatic pain, use with Bl 23, Bl 30, Gb 29, Gb 30, Bl 25, Bl 26, Bl 54, Gb 34, Bl 57, Bl 31, Bl 32, Gb 39, and jiaji points from L 2 to L 5/S 1 (extra points associated with the lumbar vertebra and the sacral vertebra).

For breast pain and distension, use with Liv 14, St 15, Cv 17, Sp 18, Si 1, Pc 6, Th 10, Bl 54, Bl 17, Bl 18, Bl 19, and Gb 21.

Applications:

If you are going to use Gb 41 as a set-up point, you might take his right (or left) straight with your right p'eng-type block and then stomp onto Gb 41 (fig. 163). Follow this with a strike to Gb 3 with the right palm (fig. 164).

GB 42 (GALLBLADDER POINT NO. 42)

Chinese name:

Diwuhui (five terrestrial reunions, earth's fifth meeting).

Location:

On the foot, 0.5 cun anterior to Gb 41, in the space between the 4th and 5th metatarsals.

Connections:

None.

Direction of strike:

Straight down onto the foot.

Damage:

This point is much the same as for Gb 41, except that it can cause disorientation when struck exactly on the point using perhaps the heel.

Set-up point:

This one has an interesting set-up point in Sp 17. There seems to be a connection Gb 42 and Sp 17 because a far greater result is obtained from striking Sp 17 first. Sp 17 must always be struck from the outside of the body to the inside.

Antidote:

For local pain, rub the top of the foot down the foot to the toes gently. For qi damage or KO, press in and upward at Gb 20.

Healing:

Innervation and irrigation same as for Gb 41.

Used for red, painful eyes; swelling of the axillary region; redness and swelling of the dorsum of the foot; distending pain of the breast; tinnitus; and lower back pain.

Massage techniques include pressing and rotating clockwise or counterclockwise for xu or shi conditions.

Use with St 34, Si 1, St 15, Liv 14, and Sp 18 for swelling of the breast.

For red eyes, use with Gv 24, Gv 23, Gv 22, Gv 21, Gv 20, Gb 37, Gb 1, and Liv 2. Adding Gb 20, taiyang, Co 4, Bl 1, and Gb 8 could also help conjunctivitis.

Can be used as a root or distal point with Th 21, the branch point (locally) to treat tinnitus. (Root points can be used to stimulate qi flow through the whole channel rather than just in a local area.)

Figure 165

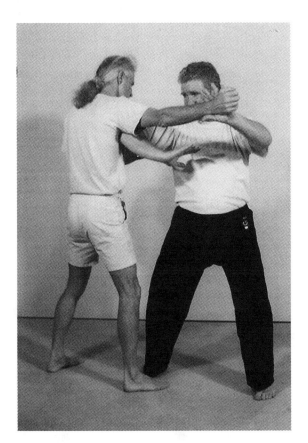

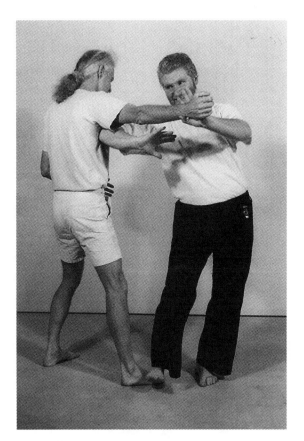

Figure 166   Figure 167

Applications:

Strike his right neigwan with your right palm (fig. 165). Bring your right elbow back into Sp 17 (fig. 166). After this, he will not wish to carry on with the confrontation since he will have to sit down—if he is not knocked out or dead. Now stomp down onto Gb 42 with your heel (fig. 167).

GB 43 (GALLBLADDER POINT NO. 43)

Chinese name:

Xiaxi (harmonious river).

Location:

0.5 cun behind the margin of the web of the fourth and fifth toes. On the crevice between the fourth and fifth toes.

Connections:

None.

Direction of strike:

Stomp down between the fourth and fifth toes.

Damage:

This is a water and *yong* point (stream or spring point), so it can be used to affect many other points. It produces great heating in the head, as if sunstroke has occurred, causing the person to faint. There is local pain as well.

Set-up point:

Because this point causes much the same reaction that an upward strike to Gb 14 has, Gb 14 is also the set-up point, struck upward. Other points that work very well with this point are Liv 13, near the tip of the 11th rib, and Lu 8.

Antidote:

Place pressure on Gb 21, then violently brush outward over the shoulders.

Figure 168

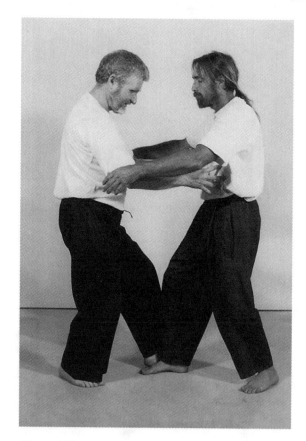

Figure 169

Healing:

Innervation is by the dorsal digital nerve. Irrigation is by the dorsal digital artery and vein.

Used for pain in the outer canthus; blurring of vision; tinnitus; pain in the cheek, submandibular region, and costal and hypochondriac region; febrile disease; migraine; hypertension; and intercostal neuralgia.

Traditional function is as a *ying spring* (gushing) point, so this point is used to increase qi or reduce qi flow in the Gb channel and help drain stagnant qi and blood from a trauma, such as a strike. It is normally used as a distal point for this purpose. Being a water point for the Gb meridian, it can cool heat and reduce or reinforce qi, depending how it is dealt with. It is also a root point for Gb 2 and Si 19 points.

For massage, press and hold the point, or you can do clockwise or counterclockwise rotations for xu or shi conditions.

Use with Gb 26, Liv 4, St 25, St 26, St 27, St 28, St 29, Cv 4, Cv 5, Cv 6, Cv 7, Kd 16, and Kd 27 for pain and or tightness of lower abdomen and menstrual problems.

To help relieve symptoms of the mumps, you might use it with Co 4, St 6, Co 2, Th 17, Th 5, Lu 7, Co 10, St 44, jaiji points from T1 to T4, Gb 20, Co 11, Gb 12, and Cv 14.

For migraine, use it with Gv 23, Gv 21, Si 5, Co 40, Th 1, Gv 20, Gb 20, Bl 60, and taiyang.

For breast abscess, use it with St 16, Gb 41, Kd 23, St 36, St 39, Co 8, Si 1, Lu 10, and Liv 14.

Use with Bl 1, Gb 1, St 1, and Liv 3 for blurred vision, and with Gb 2, Si 19, Th 21, and Th 2, for tinnitus.

Applications:

He might attack with both hands low. You should use both of your knife hands to strike downward onto Lu 8 points on the thumb side of the wrist. (This is a method from bagwazhang called "rooster fighting.") A split second later, you strike to Gb 43 with the ball of your foot or your heel (fig. 168).

104

Now, step forward as he moves back from the strike, and strike with both palms into Liv 13, using the fingers (fig. 169). This series of strikes is very dangerous because you have struck what is known as a "triangle of point," which means death and is irreparable.

GB 44 (GALLBLADDER POINT NO. 44)

Chinese name:
Foot qiaoyin (yin cavity).

Location:
Lateral side of the tip of the fourth toe, 0.1 cun proximal to the corner of the nail.

Connections:
Transverse luo to Liv 5.

Direction of strike:
Stomp on the toe.

Damage:
This is a metal and cheng point (cheng means to complete, or an extremity point; other names are jing point or well point). It has a great effect upon the muscles and tendons, and, therefore, a strike here causes great physical damage to these areas. It is a good strike for setting up a tendon or muscle strike. It causes great local pain, as well as delayed pain in the leg. It also causes extreme nausea through its action upon the liver. Gb 44 can cause KO if struck hard enough.

Set-up point:
Liv 3 is a good set-up point for Gb 44 since it enhances the effect that this strike has upon the liver, although you would have to strike (stomp) on the foot twice in order activate the set-up point. You could also use the utility set up of neigwan.

Antidote:
Rub the insides of both forearms upward from wrist to elbow.

Healing:
Innervation is by the dorsal digital nerve, and irrigation is by the arterial and venous network formed by the dorsal digital artery and vein and the plantar digital artery and vein.

Used for one-sided headache, ophthalmoplegia, deafness, pain in the hypochondriac region, dream-disturbed sleep, febrile disease, hypertension, conjunctivitis, intercostal neuralgia, asthma, and pleurisy.

Traditional functions are as a metal point of the Gb meridian and a jing well point of the Gb meridian, so it is used a lot to reduce stagnation of qi, blood, and heat. This and other jing well points are used to treat superficial problems such as trauma. Jing well points belong to the muscle meridians that flow in the superficial regions of the body; hence their effectiveness in treating the surface and superficial problems (e.g., skin problems, bruises). This point is the root (origin) of the Gb meridian.

To massage, press and hold. Another good method is to use the knuckle of the thumb on the point while clasping the bottom of the toe with the forefinger and squeezing.

Use with Gb 2, Gb 20, Th 17, Si 19, and Th 21 for tinnitus; you might add Kd 3, Bl 23, and Gb 25 to treat deafness.

For painful elbow or inability to extend the forearm, use it with St 42, Co 11, Th 15, Co 10, Co 4, Gb 21, and Gv 14.

For trauma along the pathway of the Gb meridian, you can prick this point and extract a drop of blood, or at least press and hold it till it is quite painful.

Combine with Ht 7 and Gb 21 for dream-disturbed sleep.

Applications:
You could simply stomp onto the Gb 44 point from a grappling situation. Several stomps, in fact, would cause the attacker to become quite nauseated.

We have come to the end of the gallbladder meridian. Remember, any gallbladder point will always cause knockout from the action of the carotid sinus upon the heart. When these points are worked with the set-up points, you will probably never need any other points. It is my advice, however, to choose only two or three of the gallbladder points, as with all of the meridians, and work with them until they become almost reflex strikes. It is not enough just to know the points and what they do; you must be able to fight, first of all.

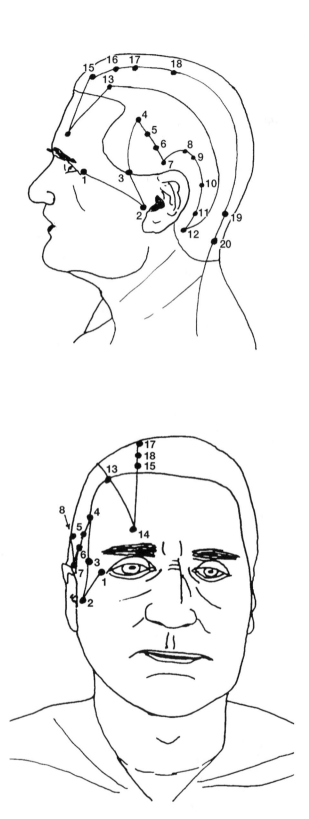

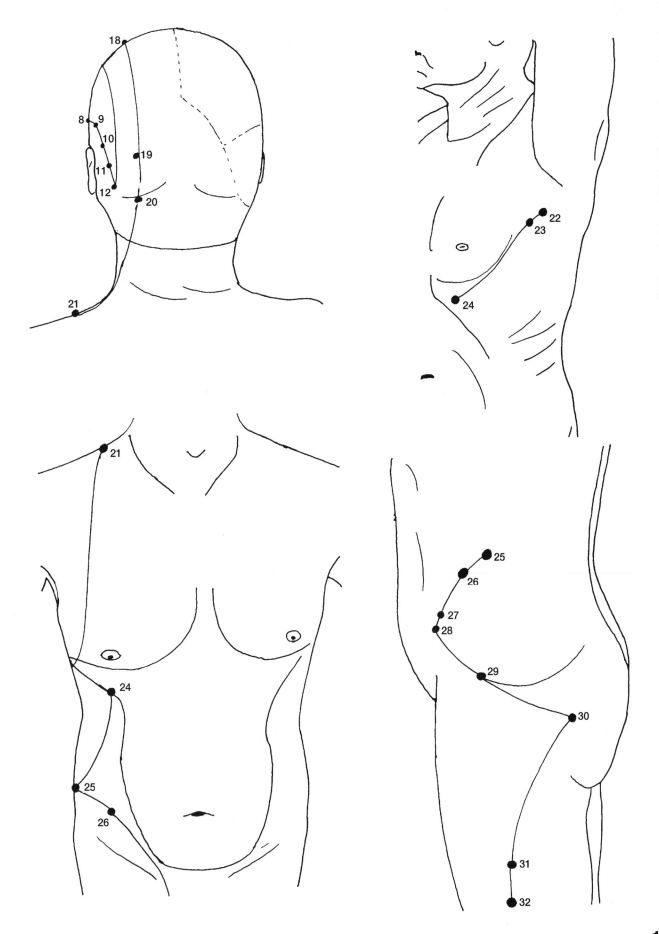

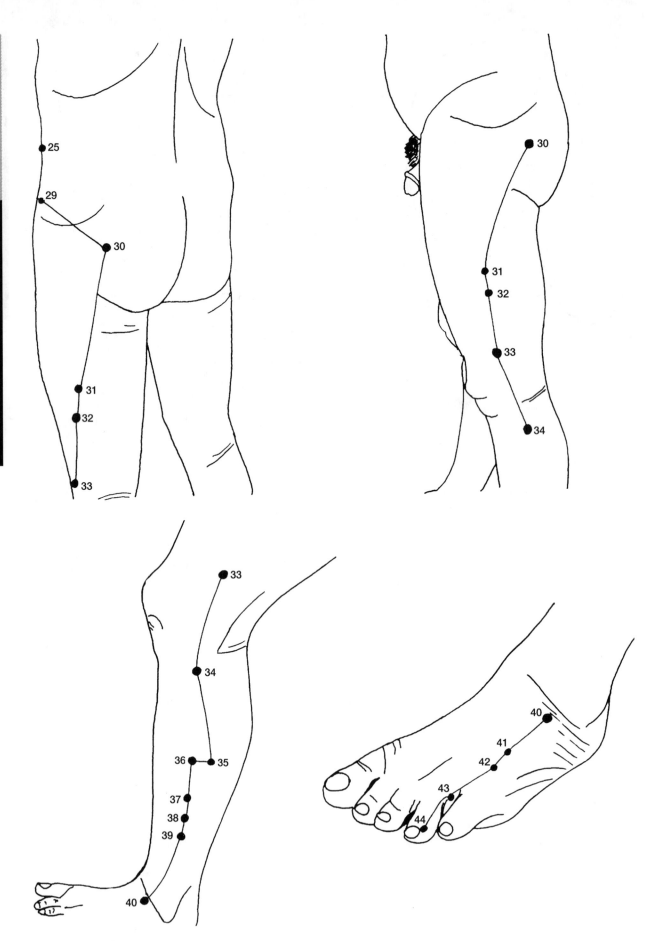

Chapter 2

The Liver Meridian

The liver meridian is the other part of the gallbladder meridian; they are linked as a pair. When we heal someone who has perhaps a liver imbalance, it is not complete if we do not also balance the gallbladder meridian. The liver is yin in nature and has an aspect of wood for its element, as does its other half, the gallbladder. The liver is located more to the right side of the abdomen, above the duodenum. It is the largest of the body's glands and is responsible for several important functions.

The eyes are the doorway to the liver, and, indeed, what we see in the eyes tells us what is happening to the liver. The liver stores the blood and regulates and ensures the free-flowing nature of qi. It is manifest in the nails and dominates the tendons.

The liver is the controller of planning in the body society. When we are active, blood will flow from the liver to make up for this extra activity. When we are at rest, blood flows back to the liver. So the liver has an important function on the physical body.

The liver and gallbladder together are responsible for a number of functions. One of the main ones relates to digestion in the generation of digestive enzymes to be introduced into the small intestine. The liver aids in the digestion of fats by secreting bile into the duodenum. However, the liver also helps control metabolism and works with the immune system to combat rogue cells and organisms that threaten the body (in a process called *phagocytosis*). The liver also destroys red blood cells, forms urea for the excretion of nitrogenous wastes, forms fibrinogen (used in blood coagulation), stores glycogen, helps in the metabolism and storage of vitamins, and produces protective and antitoxic substances, among its many other functions.

THE TCM VIEW

In Chinese medicine, the liver has a great effect upon menstruation. If there is not enough blood in the liver, for instance, menstruation will be scanty. If there is too much blood in the liver, then menstruation will be "hot" or painful.

The blood in the liver also moistens the eyes and tendons. So blood deficiency in the liver could lead to bad vision or tendon contraction. If there is to much blood or there is heat present in the liver blood, then this will lead to a nosebleed or blood in the sputum.

If the blood is either hot (too much) or deficient (too little), this could lead to liver damage, and liver damage could lead to blood abnormality, which will eventually show up in the skin, with certain skin diseases. It is said the skin is a back-up organ for the liver.

The liver has the job of making sure that there is a clear path for the qi to flow along. If this pathway is clear, then life is good and things like emotions all work as they should, arising and dissipating, etc. But if this flow is impeded, then the emotions are the first to go awry, leading to physical symptoms associated with emotional problems (i.e., headache, stuffiness in the chest, and, in women, premenstrual tension).

As you can see, when we strike to liver points, it will have a dire effect upon not only the physical body but also the mental and emotional. Strikes to liver points can cause the person to black out instantly or to break down and cry uncontrollably, either instantly or hours after the strike. Strikes to the liver can even manifest themselves years later.

LIV 1 (LIVER POINT NO. 1)

Chinese name:

Dadun (large hill or great honesty).

Location:

On the lateral aspect of the dorsum of the big toe, 0.1 cun proximal to the corner of the nail.

Connections:

Takes transverse luo from Gb 27.

Direction of strike:

Stomp straight down onto the big toe.

Damage:

Liv 1 is a wood and cheng point. The liver is in charge of sending qi out to all areas. It also controls the defense of the body. A stomp onto the big toe not only produces great local pain, it also damages its ability to send the qi out. So, although a stomp on the toe may sound quite innocuous, it can impair health long after the stomp was done. Immediately, though, it has the power to immobilize the attacker because it is an energy drainage point. So this point would be used mainly as a set-up point.

If stomped all by itself, Liv 1 will cause nausea. Used with Liv 13, it will immediately cause great internal damage as well as qi damage, and it will cause death when Liv 13 is struck hard.

Set-up point:

The old "push on the chest" will set up Liv 1 nicely: a set-up point setting up a set-up point! So even before the fight has started, you should slam him in the chest at Cv 17, downward. This will damage his center of power (diaphragm), thus draining qi from the whole body. When Liv 1 is struck, it further enhances this effect.

Antidote:

Take the patient's forearm and rub it, using medium pressure downward on the outside of the arm and upward on the inside of the forearm. Do this on both arms. The immediate effect of a stomp to Liv 1 is nausea, and this method will treat it (fig. 170).

Healing:

Innervation is by the dorsal digital nerve derived from the deep peroneal nerve. Irrigation is by the dorsal digital artery and vein. Used for prolapse of the uterus, hernia, uterine bleeding, enuresis (incontinence), orchitis, irregular menstruation, and colic.

Traditional function: as a jing point, it is used to drain excess and treat superficial injuries. It is a wood point of the liver channel, and it is the point of origin of the liver channel, but *not* the liver channel's root.

To massage, press and hold the point. You can use the fingertip, thumb tip, or the knuckle of the thumb to press the point, while squeezing upward with the forefinger on the bottom of the big toe.

Use with Liv 14, Gb 24, Gb 25, and Liv 13 to treat pain in the flanks.

For pain and distension of the testicles, use with Cv 4, Cv 3, Cv 2, and Cv 6. You could prick the point and extract a drop of blood for trauma (e.g., from a blow to the genital region).

For urinary dysfunction, use with Cv 2, Cv 3, Cv 4, Cv 5, Ht 1, Cv 6, Bl 23, Bl 27, Bl 17, Bl 20, Pc 5, Sp 10, Kd 7, Kd 2, and Kd 3.

Use with Pc 6, Ht 7, Gv 26, Si 3, Co 4, Liv 3, Liv 11, Sp 6, Co 11, Gb 34, Gb 30, Th 21, Th 17,

Figure 170

Figure 171

Kd 4, Bl 1, Gv 20, and Kd 16 for hysteria.

Use with Cv 6, Cv 4, Kd 10, Liv 3, Kd 2, Sp 6, Sp 2, St 12, Pc 6, and Bl 54 for menstrual irregularities.

Applications:

1) Slam him in the chest at Cv 17. Now stomp on his big toe, particularly the inside of the corner of the toe.

2) He comes at you with both hands low, as if to take you down. Slam both of his forearms at the wrists with both of your knife edges. This will drain qi. Take both hands and thrust them forward into Liv 13 on both sides. Then stomp onto Liv 1 (fig. 171).

LIV 2 (LIVER POINT NO. 2)

Chinese name:

Xingjian (active interval or walk between).

Location:

On the web between the big and second toes, slightly closer to the big toe.

Connections:

None.

Direction of strike:

Again, straight down into the foot.

Damage:

This is a fire and yong point. when used for healing, it eliminates fire and soothes the liver. When used to damage, it causes fire in the liver, thus irritating it greatly. The recipient of a strike to Liv 2 will feel very angry and will be so overwhelmed with these feelings that he will be unable to carry on with the confrontation. The strike also causes local pain and qi drainage.

Set-up point:

Same as for Liv 1.

Antidote:

Lie the patient down and massage around Liv 13 inward and out to the sides (fig. 172).

Healing:

Innervation occurs by this point's location where the medial branch of the deep peroneal nerve divides into the dorsal digital branches.

It is used for menorrhagia (abnormally profuse menstrual flow); enuresis (incontinence); retention of urine; urethralgia (pain in the urethra); hernia; deviation of the mouth; redness, swelling, and pain of the eye; pain in the hypochondriac region; headache; blurring of vision; epilepsy; convulsion; insomnia; vertigo; glaucoma; night sweating; intercostal neuralgia; orchitis; and abnormal uterine bleeding.

Traditional indications include abnormal uterine bleeding; pain in the penis; cloudy urine and urethral discharge; red, swollen eyes; rib pain; insomnia; vomiting; colic; distension in the lower abdomen; and seizures.

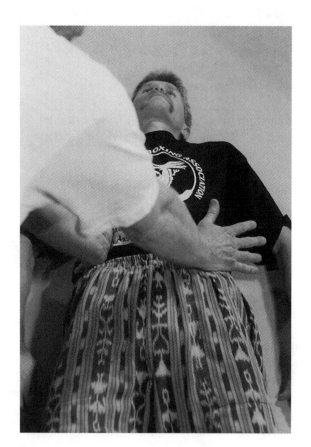

Figure 172

Figure 173

Traditional functions: (1) a fire point of the liver channel, used to drain fire from the liver; (2) a ying spring point, used to soothe the liver, remove stagnation of qi (not as strong as Liv 3, and clear the low heater; stronger than Liv 3 at sedating liver fire).

Massage techniques include pressing and holding the point, rotating clockwise or counterclockwise for xu or shi conditions, and tapping with the fingertips on the point.

Use Ht 5, Sp 6, Cv 4, and Cv 6 with this point for excessive uterine bleeding.

For lower back pain with difficulty moving, use Liv 2 with Gb 31, Gb 30, Gb 29, Bl 25, Bl 26, Bl 54, Bl 40, and Gb 34 for lower back pain with difficulty in moving.

Use with Bl 1, Gb 1, Th 23, St 1, Gb 14, Liv 3, and Gb 34 for red, swollen, painful eyes.

For hepatitis, use with Liv 14, Liv 8, Liv 3, Liv 4, Gb 24, Gv 14, Gv 9, Bl 18, Bl 19, Bl 20, St 36, Sp 9, and Sp 6.

For hypertension, use with Gb 20, Co 11, St 36, Liv 3, Liv 2, Th 17, taiyang, Ht 7, Sp 6, Kd 3, Gb 34, Sp 9, St 40, Pc 6, Cv 4, and Cv 6.

For numb feet, use with Gb 38, Gb 35, Gb 39, Gb 40, Bl 60, and Kd 3.

Use with Ht 7, Gb 21, Pc 6, Gv 20, and Kd 1 for insomnia.

Use with Liv 1, Liv 14, Liv 13, Cv 12, St 36, Bl 18, Bl 11, and Bl 25 for colic.

Applications:

1) Take his right straight with your p'eng as you strike straight in to Gb 25 between the 11th and 12th rib tips. Allow your left palm to take over his right forearm as your right palm slams into Liv 13. This combination is a death strike (fig. 173). When these points have been struck, the stomp onto Liv 2 seems to concentrate the effect of the strike, and death is imminent.

2) From a grappling situation, stomp onto Liv 2. This will shock his system so much that you will be able to take him down for perhaps a "sleeper" hold (a choke hold used in grappling, wherein the neck is squeezed to stop the flow of blood to the brain, thus causing KO in as little as two seconds).

LIV 3 (LIVER POINT NO. 3)

Chinese name:

Taichong (supreme assault or great pouring)

Location:

On the dorsum of the foot, between the ossa metatarsal 1 and 2 in the depression posterior to the metatarso-phalangae. A very sore spot just up from Liv 2 between the big and second toes, slightly toward the big toe.

Connections:

Takes transverse luo from Gb 37.

Direction of strike:

Straight down onto the point from above.

Damage:

This is an "earth, shu, and yuan point." (Again, a yuan point is one that draws upon ancestral qi. Shu means transporting; it is a collective name for the five welling stream points.) A strike right on Liv 3 will immediately immobilize the attacker. The local pain is just too much, and great qi drainage occurs. A feeling of drainage right up to the forehead is felt. This strike causes the recipient to feel totally disoriented and "out of it."

Set-up point:

Liv 3 is a particularly potent point, both in healing and damaging. We could use any of the Gb points to set up Liv 3—Gb 15 in particular. When Liv 3 is struck, you will feel "something" (a feeling, or pain) right up at Gb 15.

Antidote:

Place the patient on the ground and rub the whole abdomen area downward as he breathes out. Repeat this until the drained or nauseated feeling has gone (fig. 174).

Healing:

Used for uterine bleeding, hernia, enuresis, retention of urine, pain in the anterior aspect of the medial malleolus, fullness of the hypochondriac region, deviation of the mouth, infantile convulsions, epilepsy, headache, migraine, vertigo, insomnia, hypertension, hepatitis, mastitis, irregular menstruation, thrombocytopenia (decreasing blood platelets), and soreness of the joints in the extremities.

Traditional indications include sore throat; pain of the eyes, chest, and ribs; lower back pain, abscess of the breast, irregular menstruation, continuous sweating after childbirth, retention of urine, failing eyesight, and jaundice.

Traditional functions are to soothe the liver and gallbladder, regulate the circulation of qi and blood, work as a sedative to stop pain, and open up the channels. It is an earth point of the liver meridian, a yuan source point, and a shu stream point. To massage, press and hold, or do clockwise or counterclockwise rotations for xu or shi conditions. You can also do fingertip percussion on the point.

For headache, use Liv 3 with Gb 20 Gb 21, Gv 20, Co 4, Co 11, St 36, Gb 34, Gb 14, taiyang, yintang, Gb 1, Th 23, and Gb 11; add Liv 14, Bl 18, Bl 19, and Bl 20 for migraine.

Use with Cv 4, Cv 5, Cv 6, Cv 7, Bl 18 Bl 17, Bl 20, Sp 6. Liv 2, Sp 9, and Liv 4, for menstrual irregularity or pain. For soreness of the joints of the extremities, use it with Co 11, Co 4, St 36 Gb 34, Sp 10, and Sp 6.

Use with Gb 20, Gb 20, Th 17, Si 19, Pc 6. Cv 12, St 36, and Kd 3 for vertigo.

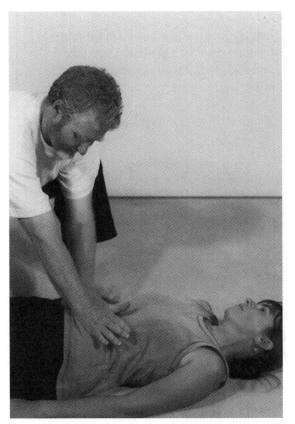

Figure 174

Applications:

1) This point can be accessed by a grab and sudden violent finger pressure, as in a grappling situation where you are able to grab the foot, when someone perhaps has pinned you face down and is trying to get a damaging leg lock on you. You must apply instant and great pressure using a thumb or other fingers. The great pain that this will inflict will at least give you time to get him off you.

2) Slam his right forearm at Lu 5, with your left palm as your right palm attacks to Gb 15. Now, stomp onto Liv 3 point with your right heel.

LIV 4 (LIVER POINT NO. 4)

Chinese name:

Zhongfeng (middle seal).

Location:

1 cun anterior to the medial malleolus, midway between Sp 5 and St 41, in the depression on the medial side of the anterior tibialis tendon. Above the tubercle of the navicular bone, medial to the anterior tibialis tendon (in a straight line from the web of the big and second toes, where the foot joins the ankle).

Connections:

None.

Direction of strike:

Into the ankle at 45 degrees, usually using a heel kick.

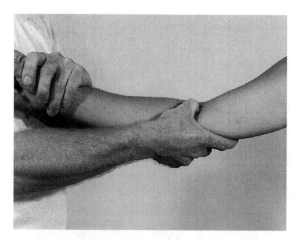

Figure 175

Damage:

This point is relatively difficult to get to; however, the effect is almost the same as that of a kick to the groin—local pain and ankle damage. This point will stop a fight if the strike is hard enough. It can also be used as a set-up strike to a groin shot or a Liv 14 shot.

Set-up point:

Lu 5 or neigwan, straight in. This will first drain energy sufficiently to enhance the attack to Liv 4.

Antidote:

For local damage, see a doctor. If qi damage is suspected—perhaps the recipient is sobbing uncontrollably or is extremely angry (well, you have just kicked him in the foot!)—apply thumb pressure down onto Lu 5 (fig. 175).

Healing:

Innervation is by a branch of the medial dorsal cutaneous nerve of the foot and the medial cutaneous nerve of the calf. Irrigation is by the dorsal venous network of the foot and the anterior malleolar artery. Used for pain in the external genitalia, seminal emission, retention of urine, hepatitis, pain of hernia, lower abdominal pain, and disease of the ankle and surrounding tissue.

Figure 176

Traditional indications are nocturnal emissions, dripping urine, colic, jaundice with slight fever, lower back pain, and pain of the knee or ankle.

As a metal point of the liver meridian, a jing river point (traversing), and a root point of the liver channel, Liv 4's traditional functions are to spread liver qi and clear the channels.

For hepatitis, you might use Liv 4 with Bl 18, Bl 20, Liv 14, and Liv 2. For enlargement of the liver and spleen, use with Liv 13, Liv 14, Bl 20, Bl 21, Bl 18, Cv 12, St 36, and SP 4,

Use with St 36, Co 10, Bl 3, Bl , Lu 1, Cv 17, and Cv 12 to improve immunity of the body.

For goiter or thyroid problems, use it with Cv 22, Lu 2, Lu 14, Co 11, Cv 17, Gb 20, Gv 14, Si 11, Th 13, Lu 3, St 42; use moxa on all points.

For painful urination, use Lu 7, Bl 17 Bl 18, Bl 20, Bl 23, Bl 27, Cv 3, Cv 6, and Cv 4 with the point. Use these same points for retention of urine.

To help with difficult labor, use this point with Sp 12, St 30, Co 4, Sp 6, Gb 21, Bl 31, and Bl 32.

To massage, press and hold, rotate clockwise or counterclockwise for xu or shi conditions, or do fingertip percussion over the point.

Applications:

This point could be used against a kick, but I wouldn't recommend it, as you would have to make a serious error by *not* coming straight in. However, if you are caught unaware, and you have to block the roundhouse kick, for instance, you could strike the inside of the ankle using a one-knuckle punch or a heel palm. You could then do the right thing and move in quickly to enhance the Liv 4 shot and strike to the groin (fig. 176).

LIV 5 (LIVER POINT NO. 5)

Chinese name:

Tigou (worm eater's groove).

Location:

5 cun above the tip of the medial malleolus, on the medial aspect near the medial border of the tibia. One-third of the length from the tip of the malleolus to the midpoint of the knee (5 cun above the ankle bone on the inside of the lower leg).

Connections:

This is a transverse luo point to Gb 44 and Gb 40.

Direction of strike:

This point must be struck using a slicing motion or an arc down the leg.

Damage:

First, the recipient of a strike to Liv 5 will feel nausea, and then cramping of the abdomen. If the strike is hard enough, other muscles will also cramp up. It's enough to stop the fight. Liver damage will also occur later in life, so do not play around with this point!

Set-up point:

Neigwan, preferably on both forearms. (See application below.)

Antidote:

Lie the patient down and apply palm pressure downward and into the ground onto Liv 13 on both sides.

Healing:

Innervation is by the anterior branch of the saphenous nerve and is located just posterior to the great saphenous vein.

Used for irregular menstruation, dysuria (difficult or painful urination), hernia, leg pain, endometritis, retention of urine, orchitis, and sexual dysfunction.

Traditional indications include irregular menstruation; abnormal uterine bleeding; vaginal discharge; swollen, painful testicles; prolapsed uterus; impotence; difficult urination; and lower back pain.

Traditional functions, as a luo point of the liver channel, are to spread liver qi, benefit the qi,

Figure 177

Figure 178

clear the channels, eliminate damp heat from the genitals, and, when combined with Cv 3, to reduce the fire of the liver. Because it is a luo point, Liv 5 can also treat colic, swelling of the testicles caused by xu conditions, and itching in the pubic region in shi conditions of the liver or gallbladder. Liv 5 is a connecting point to the divergent meridian of the gallbladder.

To massage, press and hold or do clockwise or counterclockwise rotations for xu or shi conditions. Use with Liv 8, Liv 3, Cv 4, Cv 3, and Cv 6 for orchitis.

For intercostal neuralgia, use with Th 6, Gb 34, Gb 24, Liv 14, Gb 40, Liv 2, Liv 3, Bl 18, Bl 17, Liv 13, St 40, Sp 9, Pc 6, and jiaji points corresponding to the level of pain (extra point).

For CVA resulting in slurred speech, use with Pc 4, Gv 15, Ht 6, Ht 5, Pc 6, Cv 23, Kd 6, Cv 14, Kd 1, and jaiji points from T3 to T5.

For impotence, use with Cv 4, Cv 6, Bl 3, Bl 18, Bl 43, Sp 6, Ht 7, Gv 4, Kd 3, Liv 3.

For lower back pain, use with Bl 25, Bl 26, Bl 23, Bl 54, Gb 30, Bl 40, and Gb 34.

Applications:
1) A bagwazhang entering method can be used as an excellent set-up and strike when he perhaps comes in with a two-handed attack or is simply standing in an on-guard stance. Rush in and strike his right neigwan with your right palm. Instantly, while you are still moving in, strike to his Liv 5 point with your right heel. Instantly, turn your waist and strike with your right palm to his right neigwan as your right heel attacks to the Liv 5 point on his right leg. (fig. 177).
2) You can use this point for a groin shot against a kick. He perhaps strikes with a straight front kick. You strike Liv 5, slicing it downward with your right palm. Then, using the power of your waist turning, strike with your right elbow to his groin (fig. 178).

116

LIV 6 (LIVER POINT NO. 6)

Chinese name:
Foot zhongdu (middle metropolis).

Location:
7 cun above the medial malleolus, or 2 cun above Liv 5, on the medial aspect near the border of the tibia.

Connections:
None.

Direction of strike:
Strike inward and downward at the inside of the lower leg. This point can be accessed either with the foot or with the hand, as in the case of blocking a kick.

Damage:
This is a xie cleft point, so it is an accumulation point for qi. Striking this point will cause local pain as well as muscle spasm in the leg. Struck directly, it will cause nausea with an energy drainage. If it is struck hard enough, the recipient will have to sit down to recover. This is a good point to strike to when you just want to stop the situation and not really do that much damage.

Set-up point:
A little poke in to Liv 13 will set up this point. Perhaps you are in a grappling situation, close enough to poke Liv 13 on either side. Immediately after the poke, slice down onto the inside of his leg with the side of your shoe.

Antidote:
Hold and press neigwan down the inside of the forearm toward the fingers. This will have an immediate effect on the nausea.

Healing:
Innervation is by the branch of the saphenous nerve, and irrigation is by the great saphenous vein.

Used for uterine bleeding, hernia, acute hepatitis, and paralysis of the lower limbs.

As a xie cleft point of the liver, its traditional function is to treat acute problems of the liver and its channel (e.g., trauma to the genitals from a kick or other type of blow).

To massage, press and hold, do rotation clockwise or counterclockwise for xu or shi conditions, do fingertip percussion, or, as part of a treatment for circulation in the lower leg, you can slide finger or thumb along the edge of the tibia, passing through Kd 8, Sp 6 Liv 5, Liv 6, Sp 8, and Sp 9. For hepatitis, use with Bl 18, Bl 17, Bl 19, Bl 20, Liv 14, Liv 2, and Liv 3. (Liv 6 is the strongest point to use in acute hepatitis.)

For intercostal neuralgia, use with Th 6, Liv 5, Gb 34, Bl 18, Liv 14, Bl 19, Gb 24, and the relevant jaiji points (extra points).

For trauma to genitals or the liver channel, prick Liv 1 and get a spot of blood while just "holding" Liv 6. Use Liv 6 with Liv 5 for gout or bunions.

Applications:
You are in a closed situation. Use your elbow to poke into Liv 13. Now, using the foot opposite the elbow you used, scrape down the inside of his lower leg, covering Liv 6.

LIV 7 (LIVER POINT NO. 7)

Chinese name:
Xiguan (knee's hinge).

Location:
Posterior and inferior to the medial condyle of the tibia, in the upper portion of the medial head of the gastrocnemius muscle, 1 cun posterior to Sp 9. (In the middle of the inside of the leg, where the knee hinges.)

Connections:

None.

Direction of strike:

In from the inside of his lower leg, just below the knee and in a slightly forward direction. This is a somewhat difficult point to strike correctly because of the direction of the strike.

Damage:

There is great local pain when this point is struck correctly. The pain will rise up into the ears and cause loss of balance. This is an excellent set-up point for any major attack. It can be accessed either with the foot or by finger pressure when in a grappling situation.

Set-up point:

Use either neigwan or the mind point (an extra point on the inside of the jaw), or even St 9, to set up this point.

Antidote:

Place your palms over either side of his head and stroke them down the front of his body to the waist using mild pressure. This will stop the rising pain to the ears (fig. 179).

Healing:

Irrigation is by the posterior tibial artery, and innervation is by the branch of the medial sural cutaneous nerve and, deeper, the tibial nerve.

Used for pain in the medial aspect of the knee, strong recurrent headache, and arthritis of the knee.

Massage techniques include pressing and holding, rotating clockwise or counterclockwise for xu or shi conditions, or you can do percussion on this point.

For knee problems, use with Sp 10, Sp 9, Sp 6, Liv 8, Liv 3, St 34, St 35, St 36, Gb 34, and *xiyan* (an extra point on the patella ligament, on the side opposite of St 35).

For recurrent headache, use with Gb 20, Gb 21, Gb 14, Gb 24, Gb 34, Gv 20, Liv 2, Liv 3, Liv 4, St 36, Gb 10, Gb 8, Gb 41, Bl 18, Bl 19, Bl 17, Bl 20, Bl 25 Gv 14, and Kd 1.

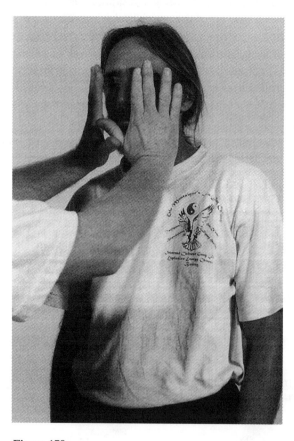

Figure 179

Figure 180

Applications:

1) In defense of his right straight reverse punch, slam his outer forearm with both hands, as in the beginning posture from the large san-sau (a training method from taiji). Use your right heel to low hook kick to Liv 7 (fig. 180).

2) If the fight has gone to the ground, you could use this point with violent finger pressure to cause him to release a grip.

LIV 8 (LIVER POINT NO. 8)

Chinese name:

Ququan (crooked spring).

Location:

On the medial side of the knee joint. When then knee is flexed, the point is above the medial end of the transverse popliteal crease, posterior to the medial condyle of the tibia, on the anterior border of the insertion of semimembranosus and semitendinosus.

Connections:

None.

Direction of strike:

Strike inward to the inside of the leg, just behind the knee.

Damage:

Liv 8 is a water point, which cools the system. Striking it will have the opposite effect of heating the system greatly. This will cause things like great nausea. It will also hinder the circulating qi in the liver channel. It will have an immediate affect upon the liver, causing it to "heat up," which will cause imbalance in the body.

Set-up point:

The liver fire point Liv 2 is used here. Stomp on the web between the big and second toe.

Antidote:

You can needle Liv 8, thus causing the fire to dissipate. Or you can stroke neigwan down the inside of the forearm.

Healing:

Innervation is by the saphenous nerve; irrigation anteriorly by the great saphenous vein. Also, the point is on the pathway of the genu suprema artery.

Used for prolapse of uterus, low abdominal pain, dysuria, pruritus vulvae (itching), mania, seminal emissions, pain in the external genitalia, pain in the knee and medial aspect of the thigh, vaginitis, prostatitis (inflammation of the prostate gland), nephritis, pain of hernia, and impotence.

Traditional indications include prolapsed uterus, itching and distension of the genitals, pain of the penis, painful and rough urination, dysentery, and knee pain.

Traditional functions: A he sea and water point (uniting point) of the liver channel. Benefits the bladder, clears and cools damp/heat, relaxes the muscle channels, clears the lower *jiao* (lower heating space), and relaxes the tendons and collaterals.

Used with Gb 27, Liv 3, Liv 4, Bl points in the sacrum, and Liv 6 for orchitis.

For pain from hernia, use with Liv 12, Sp 6, Liv 2, Liv 3, Liv 6, Gv 20, Sp 3, Bl 20, Bl 18, and St 30. (See Liv 7 for knee treatment.)

For mumps, you could use Liv 8 with Th 17, St 6, Co 4, Co 11, Lu 11, Co 1, Sp 10, Sp 6, Liv 2, and Lu 7.

For prostatitis, combine it with Sp 6, Cc 3, Cv 4, Cv 5, Cv 6, Bl 23, Bl 18, Bl 27, Liv 2, Liv 4, Bl 28, and jiaji points from T7 to L2.

For prolapse of the uterus, combine with Gv 20, St 30, Gb 28, Sp 6, Cv 6, Sp 9, Liv 3, abdomen zigong, Bl 20, Sp 3, St 36.

For impotence, use with Cv 4, Cv 6, Bl 23, Liv 3, Gb 25, Kd 3, Gv 20, Pc 6, Ht 7, St 36, Sp 6, and Sp 9.

To massage, press and hold or do rotation clockwise or counterclockwise for xu or shi conditions. Fingertip percussion is also applicable on this point.

Applications:

He attacks with a right straight. You might attack his right neigwan with your right palm, then load your waist to your right and attack to Liv 14 with your right elbow, and then use your right knee to attack to Liv 8 (fig. 181).

LIV 9 (LIVER POINT NO. 9)

Chinese name:

Yinbao (yin's wrapping).

Location:

4 cun above the medial epicondyle of the femur, between vastus medialis and sartorius.

Connections:

None.

Direction of strike:

Strike inward to the inside of the thigh.

Damage:

This is a common KO point that can be used effectively by most people with little knowledge. However, *I warn you here, do not use this point to show off; it can cause irreparable damage later in*

Figure 181

life (i.e., emotional problems). Struck hard enough, this point can kill through liver failure!

Set-up point:

The wrist is an excellent set-up point for this strike. You can either strike the back of the wrist at Th 4 or use a wrist lock to access the point.

Antidote:

If qi damage is suspected (diagnosed by uncontrollable weeping or laughing or extreme irritability), let's face it: he *would* be irritable because you have just kicked him in the leg! Treat Gb 41 with needles or thumb pressure straight in.

Healing:

Innervation is by the anterior femoral cutaneous nerve; the point is on the pathway of the anterior branch of the obturator nerve. Irrigation is on the lateral side the femoral artery and vein (deep) and the superficial branch of the medial circumflex femoral artery.

Used for irregular menstruation, dysuria, pain in the lumbosacral region referring to the lower abdomen, enuresis, and retention of urine.

Massage techniques are to press and hold the point, do rotation clockwise or counterclockwise for xu or shi conditions, or do fingertip percussion on the point.

For irregular menstruation, use Liv 9 with Liv 3, Liv 14, Sp 6, Cv 4, Cv 6, Gb 26, Bl 18, Bl 20, Sp 10, St 27, and St 28.

Use with Bl 25, Bl 26, Bl 54, Bl 52, Gb 29, Gb 30, Bl 40, Gb 34, Gb 27, Gb 28, and Sp 12 for low back pain referring to the lower abdominal region.

Use with Cv 2, Cv 3, Cv 4, Cv 5, Cv 6, Bl 23, Bl 28, Gv 4, Bl 53, and St 38 for retention of urine and enuresis.

Applications:

I have always said that locks and holds, no matter what type, are useless if you try to use them as your

Figure 182

Figure 183

main application. You must stun the attacker first, then get the lock or hold on. He attacks with perhaps a straight right. You should use your right p'eng block to his neigwan, and strike him with your left palm to Gb 25. This in itself is a good knockout strike, which will also cause great kidney damage and can even cause death. Slip your right palm over his right wrist, and, using your left palm to control his right elbow, lock his wrist in a small chi-na lock (fig. 182). Be sure to lock his elbow into your right axilla; this leaves your left hand free to do other damage. It is almost impossible to escape from this hold since you just have so much leverage on the wrist, which causes great qi drainage and local pain. As soon as he moves to try to do something to you, simply increase the pressure, causing him to fall down. To complete this method, kick to Liv 9 on his left leg with your right heel (fig. 183).

LIV 10 (LIVER POINT NO. 10)

Chinese name:
    Zuwuli (five measures of the foot).
Location:
    3 cun below St 30, on the lateral border of abductor longus, 1 cun below Liv 11.
Connections:
    None.
Direction of strike:
    Slightly upward into the inside of the upper thigh, just below the groin.
Damage:
    This is an excellent set-up point for one of the common KO shots. It will cause local pain and drain qi, thus putting the body into sleep mode. If struck hard enough, it could have an immediate effect upon the eyes, causing signals to be confused.

Set-up point:

Any of the liver points will also work as set-up for this point, as will any of the utility set-up points, such as neigwan.

Antidote:

Gb 35 is either needled or pressed quite hard inward, especially if eye confusion is suspected.

Healing:

Innervation is by the genito-femoral nerve and the anterior femoral cutaneous nerve; deeper, by the anterior branch of the obturator nerve. Irrigation is by the superficial branches of the medial circumflex femoral artery and vein.

Used for lower abdominal distension, retention of urine, lassitude, incontinence, eczema of the scrotum, and pain of the medial side of the thigh.

For massage, press, do clockwise or counterclockwise rotations for xu or shi conditions, do fingertip percussion over the point, or press and hold.

Use with Cv 2, Cv 3, Cv 4, Cv 5, Cv 6, Cv 9, Bl 28, Sp 6, Bl 23, Sp 9, Liv 4, Liv 3, St 36, and Gb 34, for lower abdominal distension, retention of urine, and incontinence.

Use with Liv 2, Liv 3, Liv 8, Sp 10, Ht 7, Gb 31, Bl 18, and Bl 17 for eczema of the scrotum.

Applications:

He might attack with a straight right front kick. Using a bagwazhang method, you slam the side of his calf on the outside at Gb 35. Step in with your left foot and slip your right forearm under his right leg as your left palm is lifted up ready to strike (fig. 184). Strike straight in to Liv 10 with your left palm (fig. 185). NOTE: The lifting of the leg will cause him to fall heavily onto his back.

Figure 184

Figure 185

LIV 11 (LIVER POINT NO. 11)

Chinese name:

Yinlian (yin's modest).

Location:

2 cun below St 30, on the lateral border of abductor longus, on the medial border of the thigh.

Connections:

Channel to Sp 12 and Sp 13 reunites at Liv 12.

Direction of strike:

Straight in to the point, outward from the groin.

Damage:

This point is interesting because it also has an effect upon the spleen. A strike to Liv 11 alone will cause the legs and even the arms to become weak, and it has even been known to cause the recipient to fall down because of leg weakness. The brain will also suffer, with the recipient having scattered thoughts, etc.

Set-up point:

Sp 17 is a good set-up here. It is one of the best qi drainage points if you can get at it. I have been struck here, and I couldn't carry on. I had to sit down until the qi had risen back up again.

Antidote:

Sp 1 is pressed, squeezed, or needled.

Healing:

Innervation is by the genito-femoral nerve, by a branch of the medial femoral cutaneous nerve, and, deeper, by the anterior branch of the obturator nerve.

Used for irregular menstruation, pain of the thigh, and pain of hernia.

For massage, press and hold the point or do rotation clockwise or counterclockwise rotations for

Figure 186

Figure 187

xu or shi conditions. You can also do fingertip percussion over this point, or press with both thumbs, releasing quickly and pulling the thumbs apart as you do.

For paraplegia associated with the femoral nerve, use jiaji points above the injury with Sp 12 with this point, as well as Bl 25, Bl 18, Gv 14, Gv 4, and Gv 20.

For irregular menstruation you can add this point to the formula shown in the Liv 9 treatments.

Applications:

You might be in the unfortunate position of a headlock. Your right (or left) fist, using the bent thumb, slams into Liv 11 through his legs (fig. 186). Now, as he loosens the grip, take your right palm around and, using the power of your waist, strike across his body to Sp 17 (fig. 187).

LIV 12 (LIVER POINT NO. 12)

Chinese name:

Jimai (urgent pulse).

Location:

Inferior and lateral to the pubic symphysis, 2.5 cun lateral to the Cv channel, at the inguinal groove lateral and inferior to St 30. (In a line lateral to the body from the top of the public bone out to the sides 2.5 cun).

Connections:

Connects to the genitals at Cv 2, Cv 3, and Cv 4, and reunites at Liv 13.

Direction of strike:

Straight in.

Damage:

This point has a strong effect upon the genitals, and when someone is struck here, it feels like a strike to the groin and is just as effective. It's easier to get to than the groin, as well. Struck hard enough,

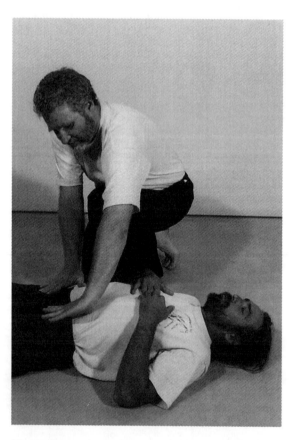

Figure 188

Figure 189

this point can kill. A light to medium shot will cause the genitals to bleed and do physical damage to the tendons and muscles at this area. It also has an effect upon the tantien and will cause the qi flow to the whole body to become erratic for a while. A good point to strike along with this point, although not a set-up point, is Gb 24. The effect is devastating when both are struck together.

Set-up point:

The navel (Cv 8), struck straight in, is an excellent set-up point.

Antidote:

Lie the recipient down and massage up and around the abdomen area on the opposite side of the groin from where the strike was. Repeat several times until the sick feeling has passed (fig. 188).

Healing:

Innervation is by the ileoinguinal nerve. Deeper, in the lower aspect, is the anterior branch of the obturator nerve.

Irrigation is by the branches of the external pudendal artery and vein, the pubic branches of the inferior epigastric artery and vein, and, laterally, the femoral vein.

Used for hernia, pain in the external genitalia, and prolapsed uterus.

Massage techniques are the same as for Liv 11.

Use with Liv 1, Liv 2, Liv 3, Liv 4, Liv 6, Liv 8, Cv 2, Cv 2, Cv 3, Cv 4, Cv 6, Ht 7, and Pc 6 for pain in the external genitalia.

Applications:

He attacks with a left straight. You block using a p'eng-type block onto neigwan, as your right heel kicks backward to Liv 12 (fig. 189).

LIV 13 (LIVER POINT NO. 13)

Chinese name:

Zhangmen (system's door).

Location:

On the lateral side of the abdomen, below the free end of the 11th rib. When the arm is bent at the elbow and held against the side, the point is roughly located at the tip of the elbow. This point is in the internal and external oblique muscles.

Connections:

There is an internal pathway to Liv 14, as well as to the gallbladder and dai mai meridians.

Direction of strike:

Straight in from the front. Usually, both points are struck—his left Liv 13 slightly before the right. It is not usually struck in from the sides, although I have heard of people doing this.

Damage:

Great physical damage is done here, as well as great electrical damage. This is one of the more dangerous points. I know of a case where an instructor struck a student at this point on a television show; they had to get a doctor from the audience to help the recipient, otherwise the student would have died. The spleen is easily ruptured with this strike immediately, as is the liver—thus this point's dangerous nature. It can also cause emotional disturbances later in life.

Set-up point:

No set-up point is needed here, although you could use both Lu 8 points in conjunction with this strike, causing even greater damage, since the qi would be drained greatly.

Antidote:

See a doctor because the physical damage is quite bad. For the emotional problems, treat Lu 5 with Lu 1, using light to medium pressure (although the physical damage will be more prominent immediately than the electrical).

Healing:

This point is innervated by its location slightly inferior to the 10th intercostal nerve and is irrigated by the 10th intercostal artery.

Used for vomiting, abdominal distension, diarrhea, indigestion, pain in the hypochondriac/costal and lumbar regions, enlargement of the liver and spleen, hepatitis, enteritis, and chest pain.

Traditional indications include diarrhea due to cold in the middle heater, turbid and cloudy urine, fullness in the chest and ribs, lumps and distension in the chest due to accumulation of qi, and prolonged jaundice that becomes black jaundice (yellow skin and dark facial complexion).

Liv 13 is a mu point of the spleen (alarm point), so its traditional functions include treating dysfunctions of the spleen/stomach complex (e.g., muscle wasting, anorexia, loose stool). Also, as a meeting point of the zhang (yin) organs (e.g., Liv, Ht, Kd, Sp, Lu, Pc) it can have a beneficial effect on their functions, and because it is a point where the liver and gallbladder channels intersect, it promotes the function of the liver, regulates the flow of qi and blood, relives retention of food, and helps the transformation and transportation function of the spleen.

Massage techniques include pressing straight down on the point, rotating clockwise and counterclockwise for xu or shi conditions, and pressing and releasing quickly with both thumbs,

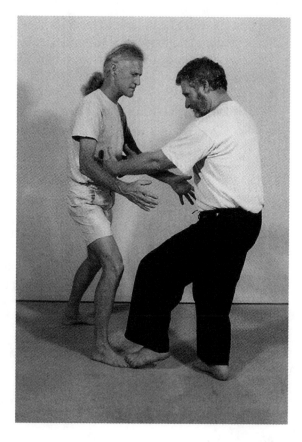

Figure 190

pulling the thumbs apart as you release the pressure. You can also hold this point with good effect or use it as part of massage that runs the dai mo.

For enlargement of liver and spleen, use this point with Liv 14, Gb 24, St 21, Cv 12, Bl 18, Bl 19, Bl 20, Bl 21, Liv 3, St 36, and Liv 4.

Use with Gv 14, Gv 9, Bl 18, Bl 19, Bl 20, Gb 34, Sp 6, Sp 9, Liv 2, Liv 3, Liv 4, Liv 14, Liv 6, St 36, Th 5, Sp 4, and Gb 40 for Hepatitis.

Use with Cv 14, Cv 12, Cv 9, Cv 5, St 21, Liv 14, Gb 26, St 25, St 28, St 36, Liv 3, Bl 18, Bl 20, Bl 23, and Bl 25 for distension of the abdomen; add Sp 4, Sp 6, Sp 9, and St 40 for diarrhea.

For intercostal neuralgia use with Th 6, Liv 5, Gb 34, Liv 14, Gb 24, Gb 40, Liv 2, Liv 3, Bl 18, Bl 19, Bl 17, St 40, Sp 9, Pc 6, and jiaji points at relevant levels.

Applications:
1) He attacks with perhaps both hands low. Using a bagwazhang method, slam both of his Lu 8 points downward with both palm heels. If you can also get a toe or heel onto Liv 3 at this point, it's even better. Now step in and thrust both of your knife-edge palms into both Liv 13 points (fig. 190). Alternatively, and only if the fingers and palms have been conditioned internally, thrust the fingers of both hands into the area of Liv 13 on both sides. This will do more damage, but most people never get to use the fingers, because they do not condition them.
2) He attacks with a straight right. Your left palm parries as your right elbow immediately strikes to his right Liv 13.

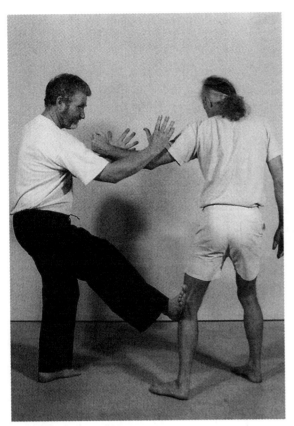

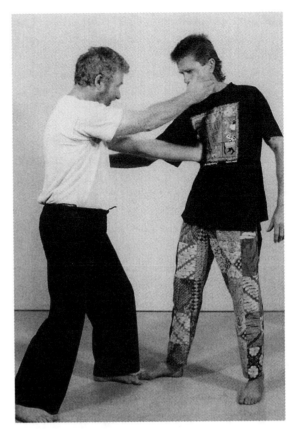

Figure 191   Figure 192

LIV 14 (LIVER POINT NO. 14)

Chinese name:

Qimen (expectation's door).

Location:

On the mamillary line, two ribs below the nipple, in the sixth intercostal space. This point is 6 cun above the navel and 3.5 cun lateral to Gv 14, near the medial end of the sixth intercostal space in the internal and external oblique muscles and the aponeurosis of the transverse abdominal muscle.

Connections:

Spleen channel and *yin wei mai* channel (an extra meridian). Liv 14 has an internal channel up through the head, around the mouth, and through the eyes to Gv 20.

Direction of strike:

Can be struck straight in or from outer to inner (i.e., laterally across the body).

Damage:

This point is used greatly in the martial arts because it is so deadly and relatively easy to get at. Needless to say, KO will occur when this point is struck—mainly because the recipient is dead! A strike to Liv 14 will cause mental problems, as well as heart problems (like stopping it!). It can cause the lungs to collapse. It can cause liver to stop functioning. Even a light strike here will do damage. When the strike to this point is a slice across the body from outside to inside, it will cause great emotional problems and energy drainage, as it stops the qi for a moment. Blindness can occur instantly or at some later time. Hence, this is one of the "delayed death touch points."

Set-up point:

Neigwan, or Lu 5, but both together is even better. See application below.

Antidote:

There is no antidote for this point, although you could see an acupuncturist if mental problems or emotional problems occur. If the strike is causing blurred vision and it was a lateral strike, you could massage the point in the opposite direction of the strike.

Healing:

Innervation is by the sixth intercostal nerve, and irrigation is by the sixth intercostal artery and vein.

Used for pain in the chest and hypochondriac regions, abdominal distension, fullness in the chest, hepatitis, enlarged liver, cholecystitis, pleurisy, nervous dysfunction of the stomach, and intercostal neuralgia.

Traditional indications include distension around the ribs, chest pain, vomiting, tidal fever, enlargement of the spleen as a result of prolonged tidal fever, and failure to discharge the placenta.

Traditional functions: it is a mu point of the liver, so it can treat syndromes of both the liver and gallbladder, relieve the retention of food, and regulate the circulation of qi and blood. Also, it is a point of intersection with the yin qiao mai (one of the eight extra channels).

Massage techniques include pressing and holding the point, rotating clockwise or counterclockwise for xu or shi conditions, and fingertip percussion over the point.

Use with Bl 17, Bl 18, B 19, Gb 34, Liv 2, Liv 3, Liv 4, Gb 43, Gb 44, St 36, and jiaji points from T 7 to T 10 for intercostal neuralgia.

For enlarged liver and spleen, use with Gb 24, Liv 13, Bl 18, Bl 19, Bl 20, Liv 2, Liv 3, Liv 4, Gb 34, St 45, St 44, Sp 10, Sp 9, and Sp 7.

For asthma or chest congestion with difficulty breathing, use Liv 14 with Bl 13, Bl 12, Bl 43, Bl 17, Bl 18, Bl 20, Bl 23, *dingchuan* (extra point), Lu 1, Lu 5, Lu 7, Lu 9, Co 4, Co 11, St 36, and Liv 3.

Use it with Pc 6, Pc 4, Pc 8, Ht 7, Cv 17, Cv 12, Cv 4, Liv 3, and St 36, for nervousness, anxiety, and depression.

Applications:

He attacks with a straight left. You use a taijiquan method of "lift hands" to trap and damage the elbow, slamming his neigwan point with your left palm while your right palm attacks to Si 8. Your right heel has also struck in to St 36 on his left leg (fig. 191). Your right palm pushes his left arm over to your left as the palm heel of your left hand strikes in to Liv 14 and your right fingers attack to St 9 (fig. 192).

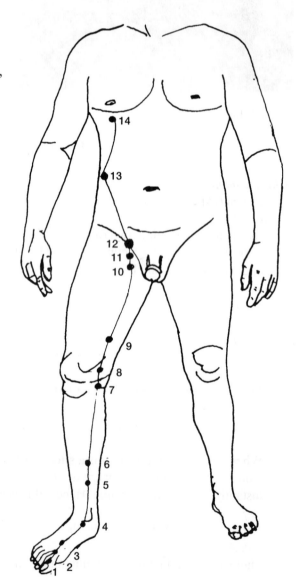

128

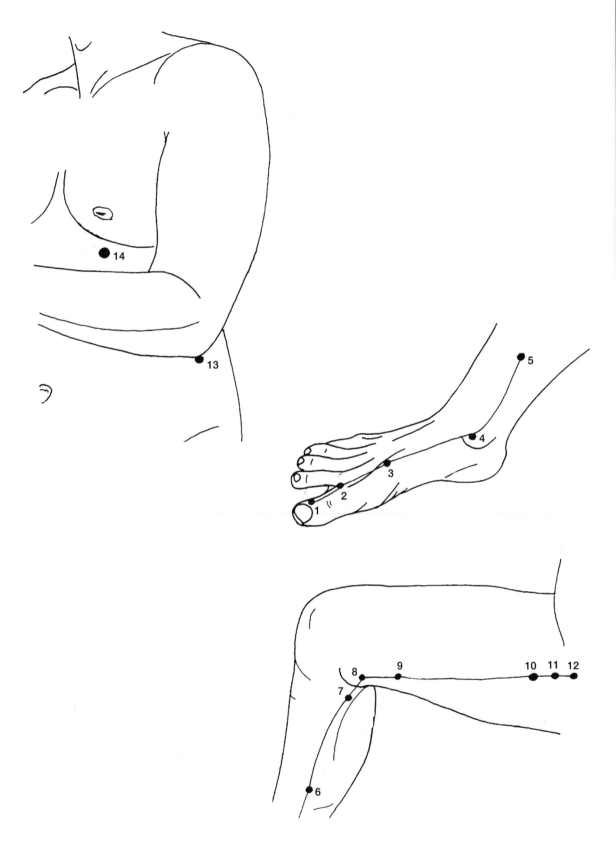

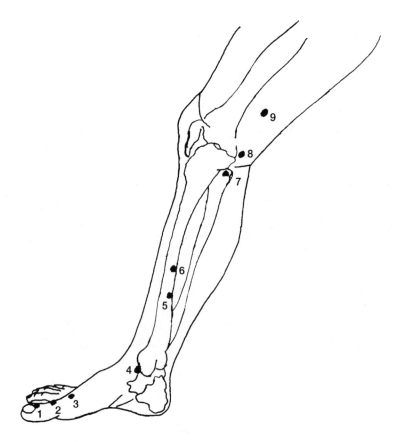

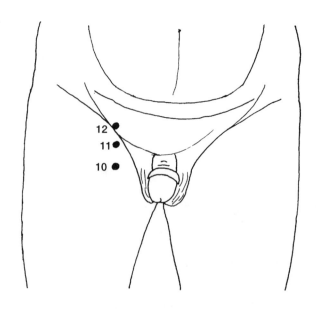

Chapter 3

The Bladder Meridian

The Chinese element for the bladder is water. Its yin counterparts are the kidneys, and its role in the social structure is the controller of fluid storage. The function of the bladder is to receive the waste fluids and expel them from the body. The bladder sphincter is controlled by kidney qi, so micturition (urination) is accomplished with the aid of the kidneys.

THE TCM VIEW

The TCM function of the bladder is to transform qi and remove water. Qi transformation takes place when the heat of the body acts upon the fluids, evaporating them into qi. This transformed qi then controls the amount of liquid leaving the body. If the transformation of qi is impaired in some way, urination problems occur. The function of qi transformation in the bladder is helped by the *san jiao,* or triple heater meridian, particularly the lower heating space. So the bladder is closely linked with the san jiao meridian, particularly the lower jiao.

The bladder meridian is the longest meridian, with many of the points, particularly on the back, very close together. Obviously there will be times when one point will do much the same as the one closest to it.

The bladder meridian seems to have more to do with spiritual matters than the other meridians—especially the points in the back. So many of the strikes to the back also have a secondary effect of "damaging the shen" (spirit). It is my belief, however, that nothing can harm the spirit (God part), and that what these strikes will likely do is cause difficulty or block communication between body, mind, and spirit.

The points in the back of the body are particularly dangerous. And the bladder meridian has more points in the back of the torso than any other meridian since it has two pathways side by side down the back. So, accessing the bladder points in the back is relatively easy once you have accessed the back.

BL 1 (BLADDER POINT NO. 1)

Chinese name:

Jingming (eyes bright).

Location:

0.1 cun superior to the inner canthus, in the medial palpebral ligament, and, in its deep position, in the rectus medialis bulbi. Outside corner of the eye.

Connections:

Gallbladder, small intestine, stomach, *yang qiao mai* (one of the eight extra meridians), *yin qiao mai*, (one of the eight extra meridians), and triple heater, spleen, and heart divergent meridians.

Direction of strike:

Into the corner of the eye on the nose side at a slight angle toward the nose.

Damage:

This point is particularly nasty. Its immediate effect for even a light strike is nausea, then a rapid energy loss and possible loss of sight. Because of its connections to many other meridians, internal qi damage is also done to those associated organs. Struck hard, it will stop the flow of qi, resulting in death.

Because this point stimulates the *wei qi* (which protects us externally from internal attack by disease, etc.), a strike here will cause the immune system to break down, thus causing damage later by disease. The whole energy system is put out of balance by a strike to Bl 1.

Set-up point:

A set-up point is not needed for this strike because it is so potent. However, neigwan will enhance its effects by draining energy, thus making it more lethal, if that is possible.

Antidote:

There is no antidote for a hard strike to this point. However, you could try the balancing method in Chapter 1 under "Antidote" for Gb 8 (placing both palms together over the head with three fingers touching, etc.) For nausea, use finger pressure to neigwan, down the inside of the forearm.

Healing:

Superficially, innervation is by the supratrochlear and infratrochlear nerves. Deeper, it is by the branches of the oculomotor and the ophthalmic nerves down the back. Above the point is the naso-ciliary nerve. Irrigation is by the medial angular artery and vein, the supratrochlear and infratrochlear arteries and veins, and, deeper and above, by the ophthalmic artery and vein.

Used for redness, swelling, and pain of the eye; lacrimation when attacked by wind; itching of the canthus; night blindness; color blindness; acute and chronic conjunctivitis, myopia, hypermetropia, astigmatism, atrophy of the optic nerve, optic neuritis, glaucoma, early stages of cataract, and keratoleukoma.

Traditional indications include red and sore eyes, polypus (polyps) extending into the eye, excessive tearing on exposure to wind, glaucoma, opacity of cornea, and obstructive membranes inside or outside the eye.

Traditional functions are to disperse wind, cool heat, clear the vision, and open the channels.

To massage, you can press and hold the point, rotate clockwise or counterclockwise for xu or shi conditions, or do a series of press and releases. Use with taiyang, qiuhou, and yiming (another extra point), Si 1, Co 4, Liv 2, Liv 3, Gb 43, and Gb 44 for cataracts and keratoleukoma.

Use with Bl 2, yuyao, Th 23, Gb 1, St 1, qiuhou, Gb 14, Gb 20, Gb 43, Gb 44, Liv 2, Liv 3, Gv 20, Co 4, Co 11, Gb 8, and taiyang for red, sore, and swollen eyes.

For hysteria, use with Pc 6, Ht 7, Gv 26, Si 3, Co 4, Liv 3, Lu 11, Liv 1, Sp 6, Co 11, Gb 30, Gb 34, Th 21, Th 17, Th 23, Gv 20, Kd 6, Kd 4, and Kd 1.

For psychosis, use with Gv 14, Gv 26, Gv 20, Gv 15, Gb 20, Gb 34, Cv 15, Cv 14, Cv 13, Cv 12, Pc 5, Pc 8, Pc 6, Th 6, St 40, Ht 5, Ht 7, Sp 6, Cv 5, Bl 39, Bl 18, Bl 20, Lu 11, Liv 3, Liv 2, *sishencong* (an extra point), and *anmien* (an extra point).

This is a point of intersection with the small intestine, stomach, yin qiao, and yang qiao channels. The colon channel also sends a branch from Co 20 to St 1 and Bl 1. This is also a branch point for the bladder meridian.

You can combine Bl 1 and the branch of the bladder meridian with Gb 37, the root of the gallbladder meridian, to treat eye disease.

Applications:

He attacks with a straight right. Slam his neigwan with your right palm. Your left now takes over the block as your right one-knuckle punch attacks to Bl 1.

BL 2 (BLADDER POINT NO. 2)

Chinese name:

Zanzhu (gathered bamboo/drilling bamboo).

Location:

In the supraorbital notch at the medial end of the eyebrow, in the frontalis and corrugator supercilii muscles.

Connections:

None.

Direction of strike:

Slightly upward into the upper part of the eye socket near the inner edge, just above Gb 1.

Damage:

Again, this point is extremely dangerous, as it is an extreme qi drainage point. Not only physical damage to the eye area but also great qi damage will result. A light strike here will cause headaches for months. When the point is struck in an upward way, the head feels as if it is exploding,, and KO, or even death, can occur when it is struck hard. The receipient will also experience nausea.

Set-up point:

No set-up point is needed here. However, neigwan could be used because it also drains qi.

Antidote:

Neigwan, rubbing down the forearm if there is nausea. If knocked out, use Gb 20 if breathing and pulse have not stopped. Use the "heart starter" method (below) or CPR if the heart has stopped. If none of the above work, try "bleeding" Kd 1. If you do not have a sharp object to bleed Kd, 1 use a very hard one-knuckle punch up into the point. This will release the stored qi from the kidneys to help the heart start.

Heart starter: press your thumbs quite hard down into St 11 (at the end of the collarbones near

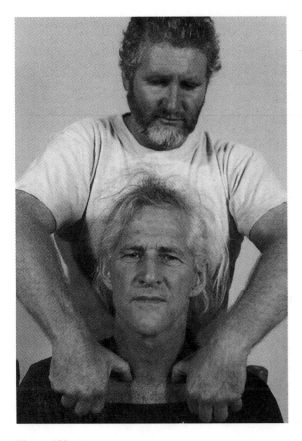

Figure 193

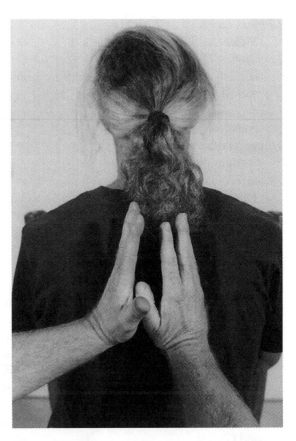

Figure 194

the neck) on both sides (fig. 193). Next, using both of your palms, strike in an arc to either side of each scapular, not touching the backbone (fig. 194).

Healing:

Used for headache; blurring and failing vision; pain in the supraorbital region; lacrimation in wind; redness, pain swelling of the eye; twitching of the eyelids; myopia; acute conjunctivitis; keratoleukoma; facial paralysis; and sinus.

Traditional indications include cold and hot headaches; headaches in the area around the eyebrows (sinus related); red, sore, swollen eyes; dizziness; excessive tearing; insanity; and infantile convulsions.

Traditional functions are to dispel wind, brighten the eyes, soothe the liver, stop pain, and invigorate the channels. Bl 2 is also a branch point for the small intestine meridian.

Massage techniques include pressing and holding the point, pressing and releasing a number of times, rotating clockwise or counterclockwise for xu or shi conditions, and pinching this point either alone or as a progression of pinches across the eyebrow.

Use with St 8, Gb 20, Gb 14, and Liv 3 for eye tic. For sinusitis, use with Co 20, Co 4, Co 11, Lu 7, Lu 5, yintang, St 36, Liv 2, Liv 3, and *bitong* (an extra point). For hyperthyroidism, use with Pc 5, Sp 6, Ht 6, Ht 7, Pc 6, Kd 7, St 2, Gb 20, and *shangtianzhu* (an extra point), *qiying* (an extra point), jiaji points from C 3 to C 5, Co 4, Liv 2, Liv 3, Liv 4, St 45, St 44, St 9, and Cv 23.

Applications:

1) You are perhaps in a grappling situation. Simply punch up into the corner of the eye socket on the top edge with a one-knuckle punch at Bl 2.

2) Take the outside of his left straight attack with your right palm, slamming it at Si 8. Use your elbow (or any other weapon) to strike up into Bl 2.

BL 3 (BLADDER POINT NO. 3)

Chinese name:

Meichong (eyebrow's pouring).

Location:

Directly above the medial end of the eyebrow, 0.5 cun within the anterior hairline, between Gv 24, and Bl 4.

Connections:

None.

Direction of strike:

Straight down into the head.

Damage:

This strike shocks the brain, causing a KO or a broken neck if the strike is hard enough. It is also an energy drainage point. Bl 3 is over the front part of the cerebrum, which pretty well controls all of the conscious physical functions of the body, so a strike here would cause loss of bodily control.

Set-up point:

Use neigwan.

Antidote:

For qi drainage, lightly press Gv 20 downward. For brain damage, see a doctor.

Healing:

Innervation and irrigation are the same as for Bl 1.

Used for headache, dizziness, epilepsy, and blocked nose.

To massage, press and hold the point, rotate clockwise or counterclockwise for xu or shi conditions, or you can do fingertip percussion on the point. You can do an on/off press on the point, with slow depression and fast release.

For headache, use with Gv 20, Gb 20, Gb 14, yintang, taiyang, Co 4, Co 11, Liv 3, Liv 4, St 36, and Gb 34.

Figure 195

Figure 196

For sinus, use with Co 4, Co 11, Lu 7, Lu 5, Co 20, bitong, taiyang, Liv 3, St 36, and St 40.

Use with Gv 20, Gb 20, Bl 18, Bl 23, Th 17, Co 4, Liv 3, Si 19, Pc 6, Cv 2, Kd 3, Liv 14, Liv 13, and Cv 4 for vertigo.

Applications:

If he is standing in a strong on-guard stance, rush in and slam his right neigwan with your left palm and immediately strike his left neigwan with your right palm. Now, the right palm is free to slam downward onto Bl 3 (fig. 195).

BL 4 (BLADDER POINT NO. 4)

Chinese name:

Quchai (discrepancy).

Location:

1.5 cun lateral to Gv 24, at the junction of the medial third and the lateral two-thirds of the distance between Gv 24 and St 8, within the natural hairline.

Connections:

None.

Direction of strike:

Straight in to the skull.

Damage:

This point will also shock the brain. Because it does not know what is happening, it then shuts the body down. You could easily strike to Bl 4 and Bl 3 with the same strike. The blow has to be substantial since this part of the skull is well protected. Physical damage to the neck will also occur.

Set-up point:

Neigwan.

Antidote:

Use the qi balancing method, or if physical damage has occurred, such as neck problems, see a doctor.

Healing:

Innervation is by the lateral branch of the frontal nerve; irrigation is by the frontal artery and vein.

Used for frontal vertical headache, blurring of vision, ophthalmoplegia, nasal obstruction, epistaxis, and eye disease.

Massage is the same as for Bl 3.

For blurred vision, use with Bl 5, Bl 1, Si 6, Co 4, Gb 20, Liv 3.

For sinus, use with Co 20, Co 11, Co 4, Lu 5, Lu 7, Gb 20, Bl 2, Bl 7, Bl 12, Bl 13, Gv 23, St 36, St 40, Liv 3, Sp 3, and yintang.

Use with Gb 14, yintang, Gv 20, Liv 2, Liv 3, Liv 4, St 36, Co 4, Co 11, and Pc 6 for frontal headache.

Applications:

He attacks with a straight right. Slam his right neigwan with your right palm, then rebound into a neurological strike to the side of his face. Now take his right elbow with your right palm. As your left palm takes his right wrist and bends the arm, you slip your right forearm into the "4" shape to form a reverse figure 4 lock and lift your right knee into Bl 4 (fig. 196).

BL 5 (BLADDER POINT NO. 5)

Chinese name:

Wuchu (five places).

Location:

1.5 cun lateral to Gv 23, directly above Bl 4, 1 cun within the natural hairline.

The distance from the midpoint of the anterior hairline to the midpoint of the posterior hairline is measured as 12 cun. If the anterior hairline is indistinguishable, it may be measured from the glabella (the extra point yintang, between the eyebrows) by adding another 3 cun.

Connections:

None.

Direction of strike:

Straight in to the head.

Damage:

Since Bl 5 is a little farther back than Bl 4, this strike needs less force. Local pain is felt, followed by a qi drainage that moves down the body, causing nausea when it reaches the stomach. KO will result if the point is struck hard enough.

Figure 197

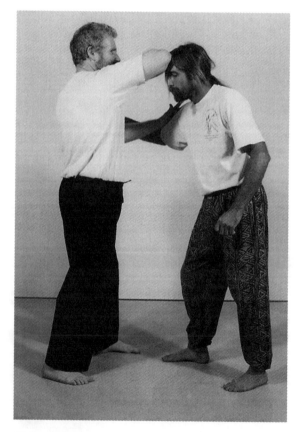

Figure 198

Set-up point:

Th 8 is a good set-up point since it will cause the brain to receive confused messages when Bl 5 is struck.

Antidote:

Treat Gb 40 either with needles or with finger pressure.

Healing:

Innervation and irrigation are the same as for Bl 4.

Used for headache, blurring of vision, epilepsy, vertigo, rhinitis, and sinusitis.

Massage as for Bl 3.

For visual problems, use with Gb 20, Bl 1, Bl 10 Gb 1, St 1, Co 4, Liv 3, Liv 2, and Bl 4.

For headache, use with Gb 20, Gv 20, yintang, Bl 6, Bl 10, Co 4, Co 11, Liv 2, Liv 3, Gb 41, Bl 66, Bl 67, and St 36.

Applications:

He attacks with a straight lunge with a knife. Using the knife defense principle of "evade, bump, and strike," you should move your center and strike (bump) to Th 8 on the outside of his forearm a little more than halfway up (fig. 197). Your left palm takes over the attack on the forearm as your right elbow strikes to Bl 5 (fig. 198). Then do something about the knife! The rule in knife defense is *never try to control or grab the arm that has the knife.* Bump it violently first, causing a shock wave to go into the brain, and in the ensuing split second when he is shocked, attack to a vital point, causing KO or death. Then take the knife.

BL 6 (BLADDER POINT NO. 6)

Chinese name:

Chengguang (support light).

Location:

1.5 cun posterior to Bl 5, 1.5 cun lateral to the Gv meridian, 2.5 cun above the natural hairline.

Connections:

None.

Direction of strike:

From front to rear of skull.

Damage:

This point is the one you bang when you are under the house fixing something and get up suddenly. The pain and qi drainage is great. You just have to sit down until the body's qi comes back to normal and the pain subsides. Bl 6 is right over the frontal fontanelle, so striking it will also cause damage to the skull structure, along with great pain and qi drainage.

Set-up point:

Co 14 is the best set-up for Bl 6. It is located down from the shoulder on the upper arm where the shoulder dips into the top of the biceps, and it is struck straight in. This point is a "receiver of qi," or an energy input point. So a strike here will prevent "ground or outer qi" from being transferred, causing great disorientation.

Antidote:

Rub Bl 6 back in the opposite direction lightly.

Healing:

Innervation is by the anastomotic branch of the lateral branch of the frontal nerve and the great occipital nerve. Irrigation is by the anastomotic network of the frontal artery and vein, the superficial temporal artery and vein, and the occipital artery and vein.

Used for headache, blurring vision, nasal obstruction, common cold, rhinitis, vertigo, and pannus (a disease of the eye).

Massage as for Bl 3.

Use with Bl 7, Bl 20, Gb 20, Co 4, Lu 7, Liv 3, and St 36 for watery nasal discharge and

Figure 199

Figure 200

mouth awry.

Use With Bl 2, Bl 3, Bl 4, Bl 5, Bl 7, Bl 9, Bl 10, Co 4, Co 20, Lu 7, Lu 5, Liv 2, Liv 3, and St 36 for nasal obstruction.

For blurred vision, use with Bl 1, Bl 4, Bl 5, Liv 3, Gb 1, St 1, St 36, Gv 20, and Gb 20.

Applications:

Stepping to your left, take his right straight with your left palm at Lu 8. Slam straight in with your right elbow to Co 14 (fig. 199). This will be enough to stop the fight. Your right palm grabs his neck and pulls him forward, exposing Bl 6 and loading your right elbow again. Strike to Bl 6 upward in a front-to-rear direction with the right elbow (fig. 200).

BL 7 (BLADDER POINT NO. 7)

Chinese name:

Tongtian (reaching heaven/penetrating heaven).

Location:

Draw a line approximately from the rear of the ear up to 1.5 cun from the middle line of the skull, or 1.5 cun posterior to Bl 6. The point is 1.5 cun posterior to Bl 6 and 1.5 cun lateral to the Gv meridian. 4 cun within the hairline. It is in the galea aponeurotica, 1 cun anterior to Gv 20.

Connections:

There are branches from Bl 7 to Gv 20, Gb 8, Gb 9, Gb 10, Gb 11, and Gb 12.

Direction of strike:

Straight in to the head from the side.

Damage:

This point literally knocks you senseless when struck. If it is only a medium strike, the brain is knocked into a state of confusion for a moment. Any harder and this confusion and senselessness lasts

Figure 201

longer. So it can be used as a point strike by itself or as set-up point for a more potent strike.

Set-up point:

Any of the utility set-up points, such as neigwan, can be used here. Points that work particularly well with this point are St 15 and St 16, struck straight in. This combination will increase the brain confusion by the action of St 15 and 16 on the heart.

Antidote:

Rest and a visit to a doctor are the only antidotes here.

Healing:

Innervation is by a branch of the great occipital nerve. Irrigation is by the plexus at the anastomosis of the superficial temporal and occipital arteries and veins.

Used for headache, dizziness, nasal obstruction, epistaxis, and rhinorrhea (persistent runny nose).

Traditional indications include congested, runny nose; loss of sense of smell; pain and heaviness at the vortex; dizziness; awry mouth; hemiplegia, and (commonly) migraine.

Traditional function is the elimination of wind from the upper part of the body.

Massage techniques are the same as for Bl 3.

Use with Gv 23, Co 20, Co 4, Lu 7, Lu 5, bitong, yintang, Liv 3, St 36, and Sp 4 for rhinitis.

(See Bl 6 for treatment of awry mouth and watery nasal discharge.) Use with taiyang, Gb 20, Gv 20, Co 11, Liv 2, Liv 3, St 36, and Gb 34, for headache.

For chronic sinusitis, use with Co 20, Bl 2, Gb 20, Co 4, Lu 7, Liv 2, Liv 3, Bl 12, Bl 13, Bl 20, Sp 4, Bl 4, and Gv 23.

Use with Gb 20, Gv 20, Gb 21, Co 4, Co 11, taiyang, Liv 4, Liv 2, Liv 3, and St 36 for migraine.

Applications:

He attacks with a straight right. Use a p'eng type of block. The left palm takes over at Si 8, upsetting the qi system of the whole body to begin with. Then the right palm strikes to Bl 7 (fig. 201).

BL 8 (BLADDER POINT NO. 8)

Chinese name:

Luoque (decline).

Location:

On the top of the head, 1.5 cun posterior to Bl 7, 1.5 cun lateral to the Gb meridian, 5.5 cun within the hairline.

Connections:

None.

Direction of strike:

This point is struck from the side into the skull. So you would be standing at the side of the opponent and striking from his right side, for instance, to his left side into the skull.

Damage:

Great local pain with a qi drainage down the side of the body where the strike was. A hard enough strike will cause KO. The recipient will experience nausea at least.

Set-up point:

Use neigwan with Lu 5. This will add to the drainage effect.

Antidote:

Rest. (You could also massage neigwan down the arm.)

Healing:

Innervation is by the branch of the great occipital nerve. irrigation is by the branches of the occipital artery and vein.

Used for dizziness, tinnitus, mental confusion, facial paralysis, rhinitis, goiter, and vomiting.

Massage techniques are the same as for Bl 3.

Use with Gv 20, Gb 20, Bl 2, Bl 3, Bl 5, Bl 6, Bl 7, Th 17, Si 19, St 36, Cv 12, Kd 3, Pc 6, Bl 18, Cv 6, Cv 4, Bl 23, and Kd 1 for vertigo.

For tinnitus, use with Th 17, Gb 20, Liv 2, Liv 3, Kd 3, St 40, Th 3, Si 17, Si 19, Gb 2, Si 2, Th 21, Liv 5, Gb 43, and Gb 44. For facial paralysis, use with Gb 20, Gb 4, Gb 5, Gb 6, St 5, St 6, St 8, Co 4, St 36, Liv 3, Liv 2, Liv 4, and Gb 34. Use with Pc 6, St 36, Liv 2, Liv 3, Liv 13, Liv 14, Cv 12, and Co 4 for vomiting.

Applications:

Figure 202

For a right hook, slam his arm at neigwan and at Lu 5 using your left and right palms. You have stepped to your left slightly as your right heel palm strikes to Bl 8 (fig. 202).

BL 9 (BLADDER POINT NO. 9)

Chinese name:

Yuzhen (jade pillow).

Location:

1.3 cun lateral to Gv 17, on the lateral side of the superior border of the external occipital protuberance.

Connections:

None.

Direction of strike:

Straight in to the skull from the back of the head, slightly downward.

Damage:

At a physical level, this point works much the same as Gb 19, in that it shocks the brain, causing KO. The electrical damage is slightly different, in that an accurate strike here using a smaller weapon will cause great qi drainage from the upper chest area, causing nausea at least and heart failure at most.

Set-up point:

This point has an unusual "set up." All of the normal set-up points will work, however, if you jerk the whole arm violently on the same side as the point, thus shocking the whole upper body. This will have a most distasteful effect, in that it will cause the recipient to have instant diarrhea!

Antidote:

Figure 203

Neigwan, rubbed down the arm or in conjunction with Gv 20, pressed lightly downward. Or Co 12 in conjunction with a squeeze on the tip of the index finger.

Healing:

Innervation is by the branch of the great occipital nerve. Irrigation is by the occipital artery and vein.

Used for headache, ophthalmoplegia, nasal obstruction, vertigo, and myopia.

Massage techniques are the same as for Bl 3, plus pressing and pulling the point laterally.

For headache use with Bl 10, Gb 20, Gb 21, Th 15, Si 13, St 3, Bl 12, Bl 11, Bl 13, Bl 43, Bl 17, Bl 18, Bl 19, Bl 20, Bl 21, Bl 60, Bl 58, Gb 34, Liv 3, Liv 2, and Liv 4.

Use with Gb 20, Co 4, Bl 1, St 1, St 2, St 36, Liv 3, and Gb 34 for myopia.

Applications:

Block his right attack with a p'eng-type block and instantly grab his wrist and elbow with your right and left hands, respectively. Using the power of your waist, jerk his arm violently to your right, trying to wrench his arm out of the shoulder joint. This also turns him so that Bl 9 is facing you, i.e., the back of his head is now in view. Strike straight in to Bl 9 using a downward one-knuckle punch or a downward heel palm (fig. 203).

BL 10 (BLADDER POINT NO. 10)

Chinese name:

Tianzhu (heavenly pillar).

Location:

1.3 cun lateral to Gv 15, within the posterior hairline on the lateral side of the trapezium in the origin of the trapezium and, in its deep position, in the semispinalis capitis muscle.

Connections:

There is a branch to Gv 17. This point is also an upper meeting point of the kidney and bladder divergent meridian.

Direction of strike:

Straight in to the back of the neck. This is the old rabbit chop.

Damage:

WARNING: *Do not play around with this point! It is a death point.* This is a most dangerous point. When we view the old James Bond movies, he always uses the chop to the back of the neck, because the director of those films knew that this point works. It will cause a KO at least. There will also be a "disconnected" feeling because of a resultant buildup of yang qi in the head, blocking emotional energy. The recipient will also feel as though there is no air getting from the lungs to the rest of the body. Use this point with St 9 and Cv 17, and you have a very dangerous cocktail. Death will occur instantly when these three points are struck. Bl 10 will cause death all by itself, however. The three points together stop the qi from flowing.

Bl 10 is just below the medulla oblongata, which is the lowest part of the brain stem and is about two centimeters long. (Besides being the major pathway for nerve impulses, it contains centers that regulate the heart and blood vessels, respiration, salivation, and swallowing.) The nerve fibers cross here, causing one side of the brain to receive information from the opposite side of the body. So the medulla oblongata is the control center for many vital bodily functions. The location of Bl 10 near the medulla oblongata could explain why this strike affects the breathing so much.

Set-up point:

Bl 10 doesn't need any setting up! It does fine all by itself. However, you could use St 9 and Cv 17 with this point to cause instant death. St 9 will affect the baroreceptor called "the carotid sinus," which signals to the heart to either stop or slow down because high blood pressure has been detected. Cv 17 drains energy from "the seat of power," or the diaphragm, so it will cause power to be lost all by itself.

Antidote:

If it was only a light tap to this point, perhaps use the revival method of pressing up into Gb 20 on both sides. This will bring yang qi back into the head, causing the recipient to come around. If it was a hard strike, there is not much hope of a revival. Even so, it is almost certain that the recipient will suffer brain damage, emotional damage, and physical damage for the rest of his life. He will experience continuous headaches at the very least!

Healing:

Innervation is by the great occipital nerve; irrigation is by the occipital artery and vein.

Used for headache, neck rigidity, nasal obstruction, pain in the shoulder and neck, hysteria, pharyngitis, and neurasthenia.

Traditional Indications include heavy, dizzy, and painful head; nasal congestion and swelling of the larynx; eye disease; seizures; and infantile convulsions.

Traditional functions are to dispel wind, invigorate the channels, and brighten the eyes, as well as to treat lower backache.

Massage techniques include pressing and holding the point or using clockwise or counterclockwise rotation for xu or shi conditions. You can also try pressing with the thumbs (one on each point) and then pulling the thumbs laterally for half an inch (or try the same thing except with the pull being downward for up to an inch). Finally, you can do fingertip percussion on this point.

You can combine with Si 17, Co 4, Co 11, *biantao* (an extra point), Lu 5, Lu 7, Lu 1, St 36, and Liv 2 for pharyngitis.

For chronic cough, combine with Co 11, Lu 9, Lu 5, Bl 12, Bl 13, St 36, and Liv 3.

For pain and stiffness in the neck, shoulders, and upper back, you might use it with Gb 20, Gb 21, Th 15, Si 13, Si 12, Si 3, Bl 11, Bl 12, Bl 13, Bl 17, Bl 18, Bl 58, Bl 60, and Gb 34. You can also use this type of treatment for cold wind penetration that might progress to common cold.

For occipital headache, use with Gb 20 , Gb 12, Gv 20, Gb 21, Th 15, Si 13, Si 3, Bl 17, Bl 18, Bl 19, Liv 2, and Liv 3.

Applications:

This point can be accessed with a direct strike from the rear, or, in a grappling situation, it is a wonderful point to access—one I have used on several occasions to great effect. One medium hit, and down he goes! You can use the thumb side of your palm to strike straight across Bl 10 (fig. 204).

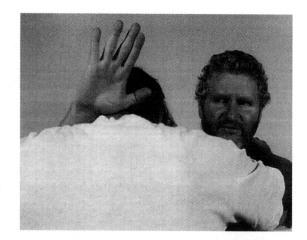

Figure 204

NOTE: When I get to this area of the bladder meridian, I am always of two minds: should I present these points or not? I am always slightly sickened at the ferocity of strikes to the back bladder points and what they cause. So I will present these points for the sake of interest, just so that people will know how dangerous they are and the awful damage they can do.

The back of the body holds the most dangerous points, although they are sometimes more difficult to get to than the frontal points. But when you know the methods to get at the back, you have to be really careful and be sure that you really want to inflict such damage.

BL 11 (BLADDER POINT NO. 11)

Chinese name:
Dashu (big shuttle).

Location:
1.5 cun lateral to the lower border of the spinous process of the first thoracic vertebra, about two finger breadths from the Gv meridian. Superficially, this point is located in the trapezius, rhomboid, posterior superior serratus muscles, and, in its deep position, in the longissimus muscle.

Connections:
Connection to the gallbladder .

Direction of strike:
Straight in from the back and slightly downward.

Damage:
Again, this is a deadly point, so do not play around with it! This point affects the bones and, therefore, also the kidneys. So it can be used as a set-up point for a bone strike (arm break, leg break, etc.). Immediate nausea results from the action on the kidneys, as does qi drainage. When Bl 11 is used in conjunction with St 37 and St 39, death occurs. And at some later stage, blood disorders can occur, like leukemia.

However, at this point, there is also a more bizarre effect. The recipient is cut off from the shen, or spirit. It is said in some older texts that the shen is damaged; but as I mentioned earlier, it is my belief that the shen cannot be damaged. When talking about this point, my main teacher, Chang Yiu-chun, simply said, "No God." So it is my view that we stop communication with the spirit by striking to this point, causing the recipient to go into immediate decline as a human being.

Set-up point:
Gb 25 is an excellent set-up point for Bl 11 because it's easy to get to and also sets up Bl 11 physically as it puts you in back of the opponent.

Antidote:
Either needle Kd 1 or strike it hard up into the foot.

Healing:
Innervation is by the medial cutaneous branches of the posterior rami of the first and second thoracic nerves and, deeper, their lateral cutaneous branches. Irrigation is by the medial cutaneous branches of the posterior branches of the first intercostal artery and vein.

Used for cough, fever, headache, aching of the scapula region, stiffness and rigidity of the neck, common cold, bronchitis, pneumonia, pleurisy, tuberculosis of the bones, arthritis, and numbness in the limbs.

Traditional indications include headache accompanied by chills, lower back pain, throat blockage, fullness in the chest, and shortness of breath, tidal fevers, infantile convulsions, pain and inability to bend the knee, stiffness along the spine, and general arthritis with deformity.

This point's traditional functions is as a point of intersection with the small intestine meridian, as an influential/meeting point for bones, and to treat wandering bladder.

To massage, press and hold the point; use rotation clockwise or counterclockwise for xu or shi conditions; do percussion with the fingertips or loose fists; press slowly and release quickly, rubbing laterally with the fingertips, knuckles, or the heel of the hand; rub back and forth across the point or lean on it with the elbow for a short time; and pinch this point to cause redness.

Use with Cv 17, Cv 22, Lu 1, Lu 5, Lu 7, Co 4, St 40, Liv 3, and Bl 43 for asthma.

Figure 205

Figure 206

For pneumonia, use with Bl 12, Bl 13, Lu 1, Lu 6, Liv 14, St 36, and Liv 3.

Use with Gb 20, Bl 12, Bl 13, Lu 7, Co 4, Co 11, and Liv 3 for common cold.

For the acute stage of infantile convulsions, use with Gv 20, Gv 16, Gv 14, Gb 20, Bl 12, Gv 4, Gv 3, Co 15, Pc 6, Gb 30, St 36, Gb 34, Liv 3, Liv 2, Co 4, Co 11, and Gb 21.

For broken bones, use this point with Gb 39, Gb 34, Liv 4, Sp 10, Sp 3, St 36, and corresponding points on the other side of the body.

Applications:

1) He might attack with a straight right, so you slam the outside of his elbow with your left palm at Si 8, stepping in a "V" shape to your left. Your right palm immediately attacks to Gb 25, causing kidney damage (fig. 205). You immediately step around behind the attacker and strike straight down into both Bl 11 points (fig. 206).

2) You could also have used your right foot to kick into St 37 and St 39 points on the lower leg before you attacked to Bl 11.

BL 12 (BLADDER POINT NO. 12)

Chinese name:

Fengmen (wind's door).

Location:

1.5 cun lateral to the lower border of the spinous process of the second thoracic vertebra. In the trapezius, rhomboid, and posterior superior serratus, and in the deep position the longissimus.

Connections:

This point is connected to the governing vessel.

Direction of strike:

Straight in from the rear and slightly downward.

Figure 207

Damage:

Again, this point causes great damage both physically and mentally. The qi circulation is immediately impaired and can take some time to readjust. A strike here opens up the spine to external attack. The Chinese say that the spine is attacked by "wind." Again, this point will have an effect upon one's communication with the shen. The recipient will, in the long run, get colds more easily and will not be able to shake them off. Socially, he or she will change emotionally over a number of years. (I know of people who have received strikes to this area from car accidents and have changed dramatically in personality over several years.)

Set-up point:

A slicing strike to Gb 24 will set up Bl 12 nicely. The strike must be from inside to outside across his body. So if you place your palm, for instance, onto the centerline of the body and wipe it outward to the side of the body, this is the direction of the set-up.

Antidote:

For any of the bladder strikes to the back, the utility qi balancing method (Chapter 1, under Gb 8) works to heal the internal qi and mind damage. (This method is covered in the previous chapters—placing the palms over the head and running them down the face to Cv 14, and so on.) You could also place both of your index and second fingers onto Bl 10 on both sides and hold (press in lightly) for seven seconds as you instruct the patient to breathe in. It is important to "think beautiful thoughts" at this time, so that healing qi will be dragged up from the ground and into the point. As the patient exhales, lessen the pressure. Then when he begins to inhale again, reapply the pressure.

Healing:

Superficially, innervation is by the medial cutaneous branches of the posterior rami of the second and third thoracic nerves; deeper, it is by their lateral cutaneous branches. Irrigation is by the medial cutaneous branches of the posterior branches of the second intercostal artery and vein.

Used for common cold, bronchitis, pneumonia, pleurisy, asthma, urticaria (a skin condition), shoulder and neck sprain, cough, fever, and upper back and neck stiffness and pain.

Traditional indications include headache, congested nose, cough due to cold, vomiting, belching, stiff neck, and pain in the chest and back.

Traditional functions include strengthening the dispersing action of the lungs, adjusting the circulation of qi, eliminating wind, relieving exterior symptoms, and opening the lungs.

Massage techniques are the same as for Bl 11.

Use with Gb 20, Gv 14, Bl 13, Co 4, Lu 7, Lu 5, Lu 1, and Cv 17 for influenza and the common cold.

Use with Bl 13, Bl 43, *dingchuan* (an extra point), Bl 17, Bl 18, Bl 23, Cv 17, Cv 22, Lu 1, Lu 5, Lu 9, St 36, and Liv 3 for asthma and bronchitis.

For pleurisy, use with Bl 13, Bl 43, Lu 6, Cv 17, Lu 1, Lu 7, St 36, and Liv 3.

For shoulder and neck stiffness and pain, use with Gb 20, Gb 12, Gb 21, Th 15, Si 13, Si 12, Si 10, Si 9, Si 3, Bl 11, Bl 13, Bl 43, Bl 17, Bl 18, Bl 60, Gb 34, and dingchuan.

For urticaria use with Co 11, Co 4, Lu 7, Sp 10, Liv 2, and Liv 3.

Applications:

Use the same method as for Bl 11, only use the right palm to strike across his Gb 24 point (fig. 207). Then attack to Bl 12 straight in and slightly downward.

BL 13 (BLADDER POINT NO. 13)

Chinese name:

Feishu (lungs hollow).

Location:

1.5 cun lateral to the lower border of the third thoracic vertebra. This point is in the trapezius and rhomboid muscles and, in its deep position, in the longissimus muscle.

Connections:

None.

Direction of strike:

Straight in to the back.

Damage:

This is a shu point, meaning it is an associated effect point on the bladder meridian. This point is directly related to the lungs and therefore will cause the lungs to be damaged. The lungs are part of the "power" system of the body, and so a strike to this point will greatly reduce power in the recipient, who feels as if he has had the proverbial kick in the guts—gasping for air and buckling over. The kidneys are also affected, as is the flow of qi, and especially the wei qi, which protects us from external pathogenic attack. So a strike here could cause the recipient to be more susceptible to diseases.

Set-up point:

Th 8 is used to set up Bl 13. This point will affect the production of blood and wei qi.

Antidote:

Needle Th 8 (see an acupuncturist and tell him that your wei qi and blood production have been damaged). You could use finger pressure; however, you have to be careful using finger pressure to Th 8 because this is one of the only points on the arm that cannot be built up to protect against physical attack.

Healing:

Innervation is by the medial cutaneous branches of the posterior rami of the third and fourth thoracic nerves and, deeper, by their lateral branches. Irrigation is by the medial cutaneous branches of the posterior branches of the third intercostal artery and vein.

Used for cough, asthma, hemoptysis, afternoon fever, night sweating, bronchitis, pneumonia, pulmonary tuberculosis, pleurisy, spontaneous sweating, upper back spasm from wind and cold invasion, and sore neck.

Traditional indications include hot sensation in the bones (yin xu-type condition) with night sweats, spitting of blood, wheezing cough, fullness in the chest and difficulty breathing, throat blockage, insanity, convulsions, and goiter.

As a shu point of the lungs, Bl 13's traditional functions include treating all lung conditions, readjusting the circulation of lung qi, eliminating wind, dispelling heat from the lungs, and activating the dispersing function of the lungs.

Massage techniques are the same as for Bl 11.

Used with Bl 12, Bl 43, Bl 17, Cv 17, Lu 1, Lu 7, Lu 5, Lu 9, St 40, and Liv 3 for cough.

See Bl 12 for treatment of asthma, influenza, common cold, pleurisy, and shoulder and neck stiffness and pain.

Use with *yishu* (an extra point), Bl 20, Bl 17, Bl 21, Bl 23, St 36, Kd 3, Lu 11, Lu 10, Cv 12, Kd 7, Kd 5, Sp 6, Cv 4, and jiaji points T 11/12 -T12/L1, and *pirexue* (an extra point) for diabetes.

For rhinitis and sinusitis, use with yintang, Co 4, Co 11, Lu 7, Lu 5, Co 20, bitong, Gb 20, Bl 2, Bl 12, Bl 20, Cv 12, St 36, Liv 3, and Liv 2.

Applications:

A backfist strike to Th 8 against his right straight attack. This places you to the rear of the attacker for an attack to Bl 13 straight in.

BL 14 (BLADDER POINT NO. 14)

Chinese name:

Jueyinshu (absolute yin hollow).

Location:

1.5 cun lateral to the lower border of the spinous process of the fourth thoracic vertebra. In the trapezius and rhomboid muscles and, deeper, in the longissimus muscle.

Connections:

None.

Direction of strike:

Straight in to the back.

Damage:

This point has a direct relationship with the pericardium meridian. A strike here will cause the heart to be affected in the short as well as in the long term because it affects the way that the pericardium protects the heart from perverse qi. This point also has an effect upon the relationship of the mind to the "shen" or spirit, and, depending upon how hard it is struck, will upset the "humanity" of the recipient. It will also affect the kidney *jing.* (Jing is the spare meridian energy that is stored in the kidneys. We make use of this condensed form of qi in both the martial and the healing arts, and whenever we need it, as in the case of an accident where the body has been traumatized. It is this jing that can bring the heart back to life.) Anyone who has diabetes or some other disease that affects the kidneys knows what a damaging effect weak kidneys have on the body. In many ways, we can still perform when other organs are not at peak condition, but with weak kidneys, your power is shot. And a strike to this point has an instant effect upon the overall power of the body by weakening kidney jing.

Set-up point:

Either use neigwan or Kd 25 or a slap downward to Gb 14.

Antidote:

Treat Kd 1, Ht 3, and Pc 6 (neigwan) individually with thumb or finger pressure.

Healing:

Innervation is by the medial cutaneous branches of the posterior rami of the fourth and fifth thoracic nerves and, deeper, their lateral branches. Irrigation is by the medial cutaneous branches of the posterior branches of the fourth intercostal artery and vein.

Used for rheumatic heart disease, neurasthenia, intercostal neuralgia, and upper back pain and spasm.

Traditional indications include pain in the chest caused by qi accumulation in the diaphragm, vomiting from qi counterflowing, coughing, and toothache.

Bl 14 is a shu point of the pericardium (the organ and the channel), so its traditional functions are to treat problems of emotional origin and of the Pc channel.

Massage techniques are the same as for Bl 11.

Use with Bl 15, Sp 6, St 36, Bl 43, Bl 17, Bl 18, Cv 17, Cv 14, Cv 15, Cv 12, Cv 4, Gb 25, Liv 14, and Liv 3, for rheumatic heart disease.

For chest pain, use with Ht 7, Cv 17, Liv 14, Gb 24, Cv 14, Bl 17, Bl 18, Liv 3, and St 36.

Use with Bl 15, Bl 18, Bl 17, Pc 6, Ht 7, St 36, and Liv 3 for migraine.

Use with Bl 18, Bl 17, Bl 19, Liv 6, Liv 14, Gb 24, Gb 34, Th 6, jiaji points T5 to T10, Sp 17, Liv 13, Liv 2, Liv 3, Liv 4, and Gb 36 for intercostal neuralgia.

Applications:

For the most part, the bladder points on the back can be accessed using the same applications, so I will give a couple of access methods here and then leave it up to you to decide how to get at the

Figure 208

Figure 209

points. Where there is a specific set-up and application, I will make note of it. Perhaps you should also take a look at your own katas to see which applications would be good to access the back. For the most part, the back points only require a strike straight inward.

Applications to access the back area:

1) He perhaps attacks with a straight right. Block using a p'eng-type block with your right forearm and strike to Gb 25 with your left palm (fig. 208). Now, grab his right wrist and pull violently to your right, turning the attacker so that his back is now in view for a bladder point strike to Bl 14 (fig. 209).

2) He might rush at you with both hands. You block onto the inside of both wrists at neigwan, and then, grabbing both of his wrists, pull him violently around so that his back is within view (fig. 210).

BL 15 (BLADDER POINT NO. 15)

Chinese name:

Xinshu (heart's hollow).

Figure 210

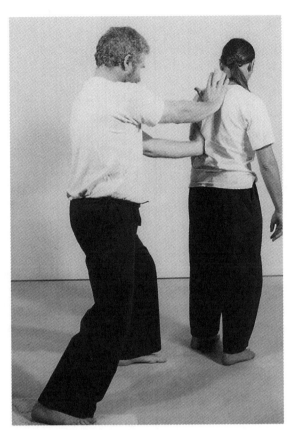

Figure 211

Location:

1.5 cun lateral to the lower end of the fifth thoracic vertebra. In the trapezius and rhomboid muscles and, deeper, in the longissimus muscle.

Connections:

This is a shu point of the heart.

Direction of strike:

Straight in to the back. It is much better to use a larger weapon for this point, such as a palm or palm heel.

Damage:

The heart is damaged with this strike. The immediate damage is heart failure. It will also have an effect upon the shen since the spirit is housed in the heart so it will affect social and emotional behavior and the humanity of the recipient where the shen is no longer in control. The seat of power (the lungs and the diaphragm) will also be damaged, thus immediately causing the effect of the old kick in the guts. Combine this point with any of the other back bladder points, and you have a really dangerous combination.

Set-up point:

You could use a strike to Ht 3, as this will set up the heart for the final attack. Or you could use Lu 5 because this will drain qi from the body.

Antidote:

Any method that will balance out the amount of yang and yin qi in the body will work as an antidote.

Healing:

Innervation is by the medial cutaneous branches of the posterior rami of the fifth and sixth thoracic nerves and, deeper, their lateral branches. Irrigation is by the medial cutaneous branches of the posterior branches of the fifth intercostal artery and vein.

Used for epilepsy, panic, palpitation, forgetfulness, irritability, cough, hemoptysis, neurasthenia, intercostal neuralgia, rheumatic heart disease, atrial fibrillation, tachycardia, psychosis, hysteria, and seizures.

Traditional indications include irritability and a depressed feeling in the chest and heart, chest pain, coughing, coughing blood, vomiting without eating, tidal fever, chills and fever, hot palms and soles of feet, spermatorrhea, night sweats, and absent-mindedness.

Its traditional function, as a shu point of the heart, is to tranquilize the mind and calm the heart and to invigorate the circulation of qi and blood.

Massage techniques are the same as for Bl 11.

Use with Cv 14, Pc 4, Pc 6, Ht 3, Ht 5, Ht 7, Liv 3, Liv 4, St 36, and Si 11 for angina.

Use with Bl 14, Sp 6, Pc 6, Co 4, St 36, Liv 2, and Liv 3 for rheumatic heart disease.

For pulmonary heart disease, use with Bl 17, Bl 18, Ht 7, St 40, Liv 3, Bl 20, and Sp 4.

For bronchial asthma, use with Bl 12, Bl 13, Bl 17, Bl 18, Bl 20, dingchuan, Lu 1, Lu 7, Cv 17, Kd 22, Kd 23, Kd 24, Kd 25, Kd 26, Kd 27, Liv 14, Liv 13, Gb 24, Liv 3, St 36, Co 4, and Kd 3.

Use with Pc 6, Ht 7, Bl 18, Bl 20, Bl 43, Liv 3, Co 4, Gv 20, and Kd 1 for hysteria.

Applications:

Get around the back of the opponent and strike to Bl 15 as well as to Bl 22 just up from the waistline. This combination has a particularly devastating effect since it also damages the triple heaters (fig. 211).

BL 16 (BLADDER POINT NO. 16)

Chinese name:

Dashu (governing hollow).

Location:

1.5 cun lateral to the lower border of the spinous process of the sixth thoracic vertebra. In the trapezium, latissimus dorsi, and longissimus muscles.

Connections:

Connects to Gv meridian.

Direction of strike:

Straight inward.

Damage:

Again, the communication with the shen is affected by the action upon the governing vessel. The "upper heavenly circulation" pathway, comprising the Gv and Cv meridians, plays an important role in the body's ability to communicate with the shen. So a strike here will not only cause qi drainage from the lungs, but will also affect the recipient's self-perception, emotional behavior, and social behavior. The Effects of this strike are not immediate unless the strike has been very hard. But the qi drainage will occur sometime later, causing the recipient to feel very weak. *Be warned: if this strike is done in the afternoon or early evening, it could cause death if the qi drainage occurs after midnight.*

Set-up point:

Neigwan or Th 8 will suffice here.

Antidote:

If you think that this point has been struck (e.g., accidentally during training), you must keep an eye on the recipient. If he begins to feel weak in the afternoon or early evening, you must administer the antidote immediately!

First, you must build up your own qi by doing perhaps a three-circle qigong (fig. 212). Stand for longer than 15 minutes in this position (my video *Basic Qigong* MTG 10 covers this in detail). Or you could do the power qigong as follows. (1) Stand with feet parallel and shoulder width apart, hands over your head (fig. 213). (2) Inhale as you

Figure 212

Figure 213

Figure 214

Figure 215

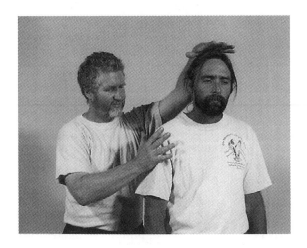

Figure 216

turn your waist, not your hips, to your left. Your eyes will follow the movement as your right palm touches your left (fig. 214). As your palms touch, exhale. (3) Now, turn your waist to your right and inhale, taking your right palm away from your left. (4) As you turn further, your left palm now reunites with your right palm, your eyes look in that direction, and you exhale (fig. 215). (5) Inhale as you turn your waist back to the front, open your palms to the position of when you began, and lower your head so that the eyes look straight ahead. (6) Breathe normally—slowly and deeply—for five minutes.

For the antidote, place your left palm onto his Gv 20 point and your right palm onto Co 14 on his "qi intake" point at the shoulder (fig. 216). Don't do anything; just stand there relaxed and the healing will happen naturally. You are only being a transmitter for ground qi. Your left palm will begin to vibrate, sometimes violently, depending upon how damaged his qi is. You will know when to stop because the vibration will begin to subside.

Healing:

Innervation is by the dorsal scapular nerve, the medial cutaneous branches of the posterior rami of the sixth and seventh thoracic nerves, and, deeper, their lateral branches.

Irrigation is by the medial posterior branches of the sixth intercostal artery and vein and the descending branch of the transverse cervical artery.

Used for cardiac pain, abdominal pain, intestinal noises, spasms of the diaphragm, mastitis alopecia (hair loss), pruritis, psoriasis, endocarditis, and pericarditis.

Traditional indications include hot and cold chest pain, abdominal pain, intestinal noises, and rebellious qi.

This is as a shu or transporting point of the Gv meridian, so its traditional function is to boost the qi in the channel or drain excess qi from the channel.

Massage techniques are the same as for Bl 11.

Use with Bl 13, Bl 17, Bl 18, Sp 10, Liv 2, Liv 3, St 36, St 25, Lu 7, Co 1, Co 2, Co 4, and Co 11 for psoriasis.

Use with Cv 17, Co 4, Co 11, Bl 17, Bl 18, Liv 14, Sp 18, St 15, Si 1, Liv 3, Liv 4, Sp 6, St 36, Pc 6, and Th 10 for mastitis.

Use with Pc 6, St 36, Sp 4, Sp 3, Liv 3, Liv 2, St 44, St 45, Cv 12, Cv 4, Cv 5, St 25, St 21, Liv 14, and Liv 13 for abdominal pain with borborygmus.

Applications:

Kd 27 works very well with this point, so in this case I will give an application. Slam his right straight with your left palm at Si 8. Stepping to your left diagonally, attack to Bl 16 with your right elbow as your right knee attacks to Gb 27 (fig. 217).

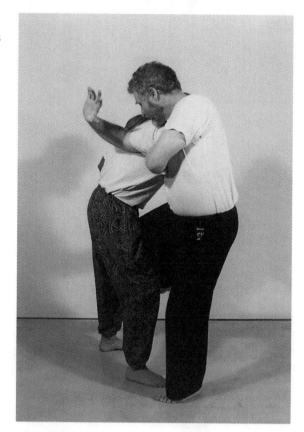

Figure 217

BL 17 (BLADDER POINT NO. 17)

Chinese name:

Geshu (diaphragm's hollow).

Location:

1.5 cun lateral to the lower border of the spinous process of the seventh thoracic vertebra. At the inferior margin of the trapezium and in the latissimus dorsi and longissimus muscles.

Connections:

None; a shu point of the diaphragm and esophagus.

Direction of strike:

Straight in and slightly downward into the back if you wish to affect the seat of power, or slightly upward if you wish to affect the upper heater and, therefore, the blood.

Damage:

The damage here is great in that it will affect the power of the body. In the case of a downward strike, immediate loss of power is felt in the legs especially, then rising up into the arms. Should the strike be upward, the person will have trouble eating and swallowing.

Set-up point:

The set-up for a downward strike should be Lu 5. The set-up point for an upward strike should be a downward strike right on top of the stomach. This works really well if the recipient has a huge belly.

Antidote:

Deep breathing is the only antidote for this strike.

Healing:

Innervation is by the medial branches of the posterior rami of the seventh and eighth thoracic nerves and, deeper, their lateral branches.

Irrigation is by the medial branches of the posterior branches of the seventh intercostal artery and vein.

Used for vomiting, hiccups, difficulty swallowing, asthma, cough, hemoptysis, afternoon fever, night sweating, anemia, chronic hemorrhagic disorders, spasm of the diaphragm, urticaria, tuberculosis of the lymph glands, and stomach cancer.

Traditional indications include chills and fever, hot sensation in the bones (a yin-deficient condition) with night sweats, coughing or spitting of blood, abdominal distension or lumps, lassitude, hyperosmia (high sensitivity to smells), and hemorrhage.

Traditional functions are to invigorate blood circulation, dispel fullness from the diaphragm, pacify the stomach, tonify weakness of whole body, and expand the chest. As a shu point for the diaphragm, it is an influential point for blood, thus its ability to transform congealed blood and generally regulate blood.

Massage techniques are the same as for Bl 11.

Use with Gv 22, Gv 17, Gv 14, St 36, Bl 18, Gb 34, and Liv 3 for spasm of the diaphragm.

For anemia, use with Gv 14, Bl 20, Bl 21, Bl 15, Sp 10, St 36, Liv 3, and Sp 3.

For cough or asthma, use with Lu 9, Lu 1, Cv 17, Lu 7, dingchuan, Gb 21, Liv 3, Bl 12, Bl 13, Bl 14, Bl 43, Bl 18, and St 36.

Use with St 11, Cv 22, Cv 12, Pc 6, Pc 8, St 36, St 44, St 25, Cv 4, and Cv 6 for hiccups.

Use with Bl 20, Bl 18, Bl 23, Bl 22, Sp 10, Sp 6, Sp 4, Sp 3, Liv 1, Cv 4, Cv 6, Liv 4, Liv 3, Liv 2, and St 36 for abnormal uterine bleeding.

Applications:

He might attack with a straight right, so you slam his Lu 5 point at the elbow with the back of your right palm. Now, pull the arm to your right violently with your right palm, thus turning his back to you as you strike straight in and down or up with your left palm.

BL 18 (BLADDER POINT NO. 18)

Chinese name:

Ganshu (liver's hollow).

Location:

1.5 cun lateral to the lower border of the spinous process of the ninth thoracic vertebra. In the latissimus dorsi muscle and between the longissimus and ilio-costalis muscles.

Connections:

None. Liver shu point.

Direction of strike:

Straight in.

Damage:

Striking to this point with a smaller weapon, such as a one-knuckle punch, will allow wood to invade earth (the exact opposite of what healing does at this point). This will cause great nausea in the stomach and intestine area. This strike can also cause momentary or permanent blindness due to the action upon the liver, as Bl 18 is a liver shu point. It also affects the gallbladder. Immediate KO occurs with this strike, as the brain thinks that the liver and gallbladder have been damaged greatly and so shuts the system down while it works out what is wrong.

Set-up point:

You could use Liv 13 or a stomp onto the web of the big and second toe at Liv 3.

Antidote:

Massage Liv 3 since this is an earth point. Or you could massage or needle Bl 18 directly (straight in with clockwise circular motions).

Figure 218

Figure 219

Healing:

Innervation is by the medial cutaneous branches of the posterior rami of the ninth and 10th thoracic nerves and, deeper, their lateral branches. Irrigation is by the medial branches of the posterior branches of the ninth intercostal artery and vein.

Used for jaundice, pain in the hypochondriac region, hematosis, epistaxis, redness of the eye, blurring vision, night blindness, pain in the back, mental confusion, epilepsy, chronic and acute hepatitis, cholecystitis, stomach disease, intercostal neuralgia, neurasthenia, and irregular menstruation.

Traditional indications include nosebleed, spitting blood, eye disease, jaundice, and pain and lumps in the chest and abdomen.

As a shu point of the liver, this point's traditional functions are to soothe the liver and gallbladder, eliminate damp heat, remove stagnation of qi, and brighten the eyes.

Massage techniques are the same as for Bl 11.

Used with Liv 2, Liv 3, Liv 4, Liv 13, Cv 12, St 36, Pc 6, and *yiming* (an extra point) for acute or chronic hepatitis.

For dulling eyes, use with Bl 1, Gv 20, St 1, Gb 1, Liv 3, Gv 4, and Gb 20.

Use with Bl 30, Bl 16, Bl 17, Bl 19, Bl 20, Liv 14, Liv 4, Liv 2, Liv 3, Sp 6, Sp 10, Gb 34, Gb 43, and Gb 44, for cirrhosis of the liver.

Use with Kd 3, Bl 23, Bl 11, Bl 17, Gb 39, Liv 2, and Liv 4 for acute leukemia.

Use with Gv 20, Gb 20, Th 17, Si 19, Liv 3, Pc 6, Cv 6, Cv 4. Kd 1, Cv 12, Kd 3, St 36, yintang, Gv 14, and Gv 16 for vertigo.

Applications:

He might again attack with a straight right. You should slam his elbow at Si 8 with your left palm as your right palm slams into Liv 13 (fig. 218). Now both of your palms are free to attack to Bl 18 and a little higher up at Bl 15 (fig. 219).

154

Chinese name:

Danshu (gallbladder's hollow).

Location:

1.5 cun lateral to the lower border of the spinous process of the 10th thoracic vertebra. In the latissimus dorsi muscle, between the ilio-costalis and longissimus muscles.

Connections:

None.

Direction of strike:

Straight in.

Damage:

This point works in much the same way that Bl 17 does, only it has a greater effect upon the digestive system and so greater nausea is felt. Should you wish to stop the fight instantly, then this point will work, and a light to medium strike will not cause too much real damage. However, the nausea that is caused is enough to stop the fight. Combine it with Gb 25 or Liv 14, and the recipient is in real trouble! This point has also been known to also result in spasm in the middle of the back, causing the attacker to have to discontinue the confrontation because he is doubled up in pain.

Set-up point:

Gb 24 or Liv 14, not so much as set-up points, but as points that work well with Bl 19.

Antidote:

Thumb pressure to neigwan down the inside of the forearm, deep and covering perhaps a 2-inch distance. If Gb 25 and Liv 14 have also been attacked, then apply CPR and find a hospital, if he is not already dead.

Healing:

Innervation is by the medial cutaneous branch of the posterior rami of the 10th and 11th thoracic nerves and, deeper, their lateral branches. Irrigation is by the medial posterior branches of the 10th intercostal artery and vein.

Used for jaundice, bitter taste in the mouth, pain in the chest and hypochondriac region, pulmonary tuberculosis, afternoon fever, hepatitis, cholecystitis, gastritis, roundworm in the bile duct, tuberculosis of the lymph glands, abdominal distension, and sciatica.

Traditional indications include headache with chills, bitter taste in the mouth, dry vomiting, sore throat, distension and fullness in the abdomen and chest, pain in the flanks, yellow eyes, jaundice, hot sensation in the toes with low-grade fever (yin-deficient consumptive disease), swelling of the axillary lymph glands, and sperm in the urine (yin-deficient condition).

As a shu point of the gallbladder, its traditional functions are to eliminate heat from the liver and/or gallbladder, pacify stomach qi, dispel fullness from the diaphragm, and regulate qi.

Massage techniques are the same as for Bl 11.

Use with Liv 14, Liv 13, Cv 12, Gb 43, Gb 44, Liv 2, Liv 3, dannamgxue, Pc 6, Gb 34, Gb 24, St 36, and jiaji points T 8 and T 9 on the right side for cholecystitis.

For sciatica or low back pain, use with Bl 25, Bl 26, Bl 52, Bl 40, Gb 34, Gb 29, and Gb 30.

Use with Gb 24, Liv 14, Liv 13, Liv 3, Gb 41, Bl 20, Bl 18, Bl 17, and St 36 for distension and fullness in the chest and abdomen.

Use with Gv 20, Gb 20, Gb 21, Gb 10, Gb 14, Gb 18, Gb 34, taiyang, Gb 41, Liv 3, Liv 2, Gb 43, Gb 44, Bl 12, Bl 13, and Si 13 for headache.

Applications:

Use both palms to strike to Gb 25 and Liv 14. Grab an arm and swing him around to get at Bl 19 straight in.

BL 20 (BLADDER POINT NO. 20)

Chinese name:

Pishu (spleen hollow).

Location:

1.5 cun lateral to the lower border of the spinous process of the 11th thoracic vertebra. In the latissimus dorsi muscle, between the longissimus and ilio-costalis muscles.

Connections:

None.

Direction of strike:

Straight in.

Damage:

This is quite an amazing point to strike. It is commonly called the "vomit point" in dim-mak circles. This point attacks just about every organ in the whole body and also attacks earth (the center of the body). It will cause great nausea and vomiting by attacking the stomach and digestive organs. In addition, it will attack the liver and gallbladder and, in particular, the spleen, which causes the liver to become "hot." One of the jobs for the spleen is the transportation of qi; hence this point's ability to attack all organs. The liver becomes hot and so affects earth, which in turn damages the spleen further, and so a vicious cycle is set up. *Do not play around with this point!*

Figure 220

Set-up point:

Strike to Spleen 17 from the outside to the inside of the torso. *This combination is deadly!*

Antidote:

Have an acupuncturist work on the spleen and healing earth. Also work on the liver to get the heat out. Eat watermelon. (Watermelon is a very yin type of food, which will counter the yang. It is a common treatment for many heat-related disease states.)

Healing:

Innervation is by the medial cutaneous branches of the posterior rami of the 11th and 12th thoracic nerves and, deeper, their lateral branches. Irrigation is by the medial posterior branches of the 11th intercostal artery and vein.

Used for gastritis, ulcers, prolapsed stomach, nervous vomiting, indigestion, hepatitis, enteritis, edema, anemia, enlargement of liver and spleen, chronic hemorrhagic disease, prolapsed uterus, urticaria, weakness of the limbs, abdominal distension, jaundice, diarrhea, dysentery, indigestion, and pain in the back.

Traditional indications include constriction of the esophagus (plumb stone throat), diarrhea, dysentery, edema, abdominal distension, lumps in the chest, and jaundice.

As a shu point of the spleen, its traditional functions include regulating spleen qi, promoting the transformation and transportation function of the spleen (T&T of food and fluids), eliminating damp, pacifying the stomach, reinforcing blood, expelling water (damp/edema from spleen yang deficiency), harmonizing the blood, and nourishing qi (ying qi).

Massage techniques are the same as for Bl 11.

Use with Bl 17, Bl 23, Bl 18, Bl 13, Sp 6, Cv 12, St 36, Kd 3, Lu 11, Lu 10, Cv 4, Bl 21, yishu, pirexue, Kd 7, and Kd 5 for diabetes.

Use with Bl 18, Gv 14, Sp 1, Cv 13, Sp 10, and St 36 for nosebleeds.

For stomachache, nausea, and vomiting, use with Pc 6, St 36, Cv 12, Cv 14, Cv 11, Cv 9, Cv 4, St 44, St 43, St 4, Bl 21, Bl 18, Bl 19, Bl 17, Sp 9, Sp 4, Liv 2, Liv 3, St 40, and jiaji points from T 8 to T 12.

Use with Gv 20, Cv 12, Cv 6, Cv 4, abdomen zigong, Gb 26, Sp 6, St 36, Liv 3, St 30, Sp 9, Liv 8, and Gb 28 for prolapsed uterus.

For anorexia, use with Sp 3, Liv 3, St 36, Cv 12, Cv 4, Cv 6, Liv 14, Bl 21, Bl 17, Bl 18, Pc 6, Ht 7, and Co 4.

Use with Bl 25, Bl 22, Bl 21, Bl 19, Bl 18, Bl 17, Cv 12, Cv 4, St 25, St 40, St 36, Sp 9, Sp 4, Liv 3, Sp 15, Gb 26, Co 4, and Th 4 for diarrhea, dysentery, and abdominal distension.

Applications:

Take his right strike with your right p'eng-type block. This will open up Sp 17 for a shot. The right palm now attacks to Sp 17 (fig. 220). Your left palm is now free to attack Bl 20 straight in.

BL 21 (BLADDER POINT NO. 21)

Chinese name:

Weishu (stomach's hollow).

Location:

1.5 cun lateral to the lower border of the spinous process of the 12th thoracic vertebra. In the lumbodorsal fascia, between the longissimus and ilio-costalis muscles.

Connections:

None.

Direction of strike:

Straight in.

Damage:

Great power loss is felt when this point is struck. Again, extreme nausea is felt as well as liver damage.

Set-up point:

Use any of the gallbladder points to set up this strike.

Antidote:

Neigwan, pressed down the inside of the forearm.

Healing:

Innervation is by the medial cutaneous branch of the posterior ramus of the 12th thoracic nerve and, deeper, its lateral branch. Irrigation is by the medial posterior branches of the subcostal artery and vein.

Used for pain in the chest/hypochondriac and epigastric regions, abdominal distension, nausea, vomiting, borborygmus, indigestion, stomachache, gastritis, prolapsed stomach, ulcer, pancreatitis, hepatitis, enteritis, loss of appetite, insomnia, and pain along the spine.

Traditional indications include difficulty in swallowing, regurgitation of food, infant vomiting of milk, abdominal pain from cold conditions in the stomach, diarrhea, edema (feels like a drum to touch), and vomiting.

As a shu point of stomach, its traditional functions include adjusting stomach qi, dispelling damp, and removing obstructions and stagnation.

Massage techniques are the same as for B 11.

Use with Bl 20, Bl 18, Bl 17, Bl 19, Cv 12, Cv 10, Cv 9, St 21, St 25, St 36, St 44, St 45, and Liv 3 for chronic gastritis.

Use with Bl 20, Bl 23, Bl 24, Gv 4, Cv 12, Cv 4, Cv 6, St 36, and Sp 3 for cold obstruction of the stomach causing pain and distension. (Moxa is the best thing to use on the points for this condition.)

For pain in the chest/hypochondriac and epigastric regions, use with Bl 17, Bl 18, Bl 19, Bl 20, Bl 22, Bl 40, Cv 12, Cv 10, Cv 9, St 21, Liv 14, Liv 13, Gb 24, Gb 26, St 36, Liv 3, Sp 9, Sp 4, and Liv 4.

Use with St 36, Sp 3, Cv 12 Liv 3, Bl 20, Bl 23, Bl 18, Bl 13, Pc 6, and Gv 20 for loss of appetite.

Applications:

You could use an old grappler's trick of coming in hard and high, then going low just as the opponent tries to strike you. Take his waist and take him down, landing him on his face with you on top. Strike straight into Bl 21.

BL 22 (BLADDER POINT NO. 22)

Chinese name:

Sanjiaoshu (triple heater's hollow).

Location:

1.5 cun lateral to the lower border of the spinous process of the first lumbar vertebra. In the lumbodorsal fascia, between the longissimus and ilio-costalis muscles.

Connections:

None.

Direction of strike:

Either upward into the back or downward. Upward there will be an effect on the middle heater, and downward there will be an effect upon the lower heater.

Damage:

This is a special point for the metabolism of water. It also affects the whole triple heater—literally the whole body's qi flow. So a strike here has not only instant effects such as extreme qi drainage, but also long-term effects on functions such as body lubrication, which in turn could cause joint diseases, for instance.

Set-up point:

Use either Gb 14 downward or slam Lu 5 to enhance the drainage effect, or grab and violently twist Lu 8 with Ht 5.

Antidote:

The whole body must be rebalanced using one of the qi balancing methods. Another qi balancing method not already mentioned is the "seven stars balancing." The seven stars are the seven qi (energy) input points in the body. There is a move from the taijiquan form called "step forward to form seven stars." Many people have translated this as "to protect the seven openings," or "to attack his seven points," etc. But the real meaning of this posture is to open the body to the seven qi input points to take in external qi. At birth we are given an amount of qi that cannot be built upon from within; it must be built up by adding "external qi." At a very basic level, external qi can simply come from what we eat or drink, and the quality of those things determines the quality and

Figure 221

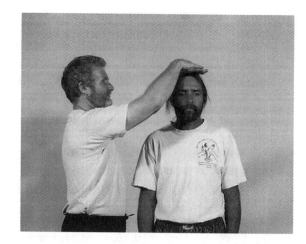

Figure 222

amount of qi taken in. However, opening up the seven qi input points through the seven stars qigong is another, more powerful way of taking in external qi (fig. 221). The seven star qi input points are Gv 20, (the crown), Si 16 on both sides of the neck, Co 14 on the shoulders, and Gb 30 at the buttocks. This makes seven points, counting the symmetrical points (Si 16, Co 14, and Gb 30). To cause a qi balance, we simply have to place our hands upon each of these points for 10 seconds and relax, doing nothing special. If you begin making funny sounds and trying to think about the energy being balanced, etc., nothing will happen. Stand in front of your patient and place both of your palms onto Gv 20. If you are male, place your right palm on top of the left, and if you are female, place your left palm on top of your right (fig. 222). For the rest of the points, simply place your left palm on the patient's right Si 16 and your right palm on the left Si 16, and so on, down the body.

Healing:

Innervation is by the lateral cutaneous branch of the posterior ramus of the 10th thoracic nerve and, deeper, by the lateral branch of the posterior ramus of the first lumbar nerve. Irrigation is by the medial posterior branches of the first lumbar artery and vein.

Used for abdominal distension, borborygmus, indigestion, vomiting, diarrhea, dysentery, edema, pain and stiffness of the lower back, gastritis, enteritis, nephritis, ascites, urinary retention, enuresis, neurasthenia, and stagnation of fluids in the abdomen.

Traditional indications include dizziness and headache, vomiting, indigestion, abdominal distension with intestinal noises, diarrhea, edema, and jaundice.

Traditional functions, as a three heater shu point, include regulating the passage of water, mostly for water movement in the lower heater; regulating the transforming function of qi; and resolving damp conditions.

Massage techniques are the same as for Bl 11. You can also vibrate this point with the fingertips, the heel of the palm, etc..

Use with Bl, 24, Bl 25, Bl 28, Cv 3, Cv 4, Cv 5, Cv 6, St 28, St 36, St 40, Sp 4, Sp 9, Sp 6, Liv 3, Bl 66, and Bl 67 for acute or chronic nephritis.

Use with Bl 40, Bl 54, Bl 53, Bl 26, Bl 25, Bl 24, Bl 23, Bl 21, Bl 20, Bl 19, Bl 18, Bl 17, and Gb 34 for lower back pain.

With Bl 25, Bl 20, Bl 23, Gv 4, Cv 4, St 25, St 28, Sp 15, St 37, Sp 4, Sp 9, Liv 2, and Liv 3, for diarrhea or dysentery.

For edema, use with Sp 6, Sp 4, Sp 9, St 40, St 36, St 28, Cv 9, Lu 7, Bl 20, Bl 28, Liv 3, Cv 12, Liv 13, and Gb 26.

Application:

Same as for Bl 21.

BL 23 (BLADDER POINT NO. 23)

Chinese name:

Shenshu (kidney's hollow).

Location:

105 cun lateral to the lower border of the spinous process of the second lumbar vertebra. In the lumbodorsal fascia, between the longissimus and ilio-costalis muscles.

Connections:

Kidney divergent.

Direction of strike:

Straight in. However, this strike works slightly better if you put a slight twist onto it (i.e., as your palm makes contact with the point, twist your right palm clockwise or your left palm counterclockwise).

Damage:

This is the shu point of the kidneys, so great kidney damage results—not as much as a strike to Gb 25, but enough to cause considerable kidney failure or blood in the urine. I have had personal experience with a technique that I will show under "Applications" for this point called "kidney damaging method." The recipient was hospitalized because of kidney damage and blood in the urine. The damage to this point is instant, and the recipient will be unable to carry on. If it is quite a hard strike, he will fall instantly. If he does not receive medical help, the kidneys will slowly fail, causing death. *Again, be warned: this strike should not be played around with, especially after noon!*

(This point in particular will be more effective in the part of the day when yang is going yin.) Another effect of this strike, little known to most instructors, is an excessive buildup of yang energy in the upper heater, resulting in fainting and eventual death!

Set-up point:

You can use neigwan as your blocking method.

Antidote:

See a doctor, and seek out TCM help for the kidneys. You will have to have acupuncture and take Chinese herbs. There are also many "off-the-shelf" herbal remedies specifically for the kidneys.

Healing:

Innervation is by the medial cutaneous branch of the posterior ramus of the first lumbar nerve and, deeper, the lateral branch of that nerve. Irrigation is by the medial posterior branches of the second lumbar artery and vein.

Used for seminal emission, impotence, enuresis, irregular menstruation, leukorrhea, low backache, weak knees, blurring vision, tinnitus, deafness, edema, nephritis (kidney disease), nephroptosis (dropping of the kidney into the pelvis), renal colic, spermatorrhea, bronchial asthma, alopecia injury to soft tissue of the lower back, and sequelae (aftereffects) of infantile paralysis.

Traditional indications include deafness, deficient kidneys, loss of sperm, impotence, blood in the urine, edema, emaciation and thirst, seizures, tidal fever, lower back pain, and cold knees.

Traditional functions, as a shu point of the kidneys, include readjusting kidney qi, eliminating damp, strengthening the lumbar vertebrae, and benefiting the ears and eyes.

Figure 223

Figure 224

Massage techniques are the same as for Bl 22. Also, use this point as part of massage for the girdle meridian, or dai mo. (The patient should be in the supine position. The practitioner is positioned at the patient's side with one hand either side of the patient's waist, middle finger touching *ming men*, or Gv 4. Using some pressure, the practitioner pulls his or her hands apart and around to front of the patient's body, passing the middle finger through the points Bl 23, Gb 25, Liv 13, Gb 26, Gb 27, Gb 28, the extra point *qimen*, St 28, Kd 13, and Cv 4. Alternatively, the technique might run from Gb 26 to Sp 15, St 25, Kd 14, and Cv 8.) This type of treatment will help with overall yin and yang balance in the body, abnormal vaginal discharge, abdominal distension, and mental imbalance.

Use with Cv 3, Cv 2, Cv 4, Sp 6, Kd 7, Bl 58, Bl 35, Bl 18, abdomen zigong, Kd 2, Bl 66, and Bl 67 for nephritis.

Use with Bl 28, Cv 2, Cv 3, Sp 6, Bl 66, Bl 67, St 28, and Cv 9 for urinary tract infections.

For lower back pain and stiffness, use with Bl 18, Bl 19, Bl 20, Bl 21, Bl 22, Bl 24, Bl 25, Bl 26, Bl 54, Bl 40, Gb 29, Gb 30, and Gb 34.

For diabetes, use with Bl 20, Bl 21, Bl 13, yishu, St 36, Kd 3, Kd 7, Kd 5, Lu 11, Lu 10, Cv 12, Cv 4, Bl 17, pirexue, jiaji points T 11/12 and T 12/L 1, Sp 4, Sp 6, and Liv 3.

For bronchial asthma, use with Bl 13, Bl 12, Bl 43, Bl 18, Bl 20, Lu 1, Lu 5, Lu 7, Lu 9, Liv 14, Gb 24, Cv 17, Cv 4, Gb 25, Cv 22, dingchuan, Kd 22, Kd 23, Kd 24, Kd 25, Kd 26, Kd 27, Kd 3, Liv 3, and St 36.

Applications:

The kidney-damaging method. He attacks with a straight right, and you use a p'eng type of block straight in to neigwan using your right arm. You now kick your right foot backward and hook into Bl 23, swiveling on the ball of your left foot. The striking surface is the back of the heel (fig. 223). Now, as your right foot recovers, use it to stomp down onto Kd 10 at the back of his right knee (fig. 224). You could also use your right elbow to any number of points around the back of the head, such as Gb 12.

BL 24 (BLADDER POINT NO. 24)

Chinese name:

Qihaishu (sea of qi hollow).

Location:

1.5 cun lateral to the lower border of the spinous process of the third lumbar vertebra. In the lumbodorsal fascia, between the longissimus and ilio-costalis muscles.

Connections:

None. This point is the shu point for the "sea of energy."

Direction of strike:

This point can be struck straight in, but it will be damaged doubly if the strike is downward into the buttocks.

Damage:

The immediate damage from this strike is that the power in the legs goes, as does the power in the back. So the recipient falls down. This point does have a more sinister effect, however. I have known a number of people who have been struck in this area as a result of sports injuries, etc. The long term-effect is always the same: the lower heating space—that which is below the waistline—begins to grow, until the person is extremely overweight and has problems with heart disease as a result! The healing aspects of this point are the exact opposite—we use Bl 24 to alleviate obesity.

Set-up point:

Sp 19 is the obvious choice here because it takes power from the legs. If the left Sp 19 is struck straight in, then the right leg becomes weak, and vice-versa. You can also use finger pressure, as in a violent grab in a grappling situation.

Antidote:

Treat Kd 1 and Kd 10 either with pressure or needles.

Healing:

Innervation is by the medial cutaneous branch of the posterior ramus of the second lumbar spinal nerve and, deeper, by its lateral branch. Irrigation is by the posterior branch of the third lumbar artery and vein.

Used for lower back pain, hemorrhoids, irregular menstruation, functional uterine blooding, and paralysis of lower limbs.

Traditional indications include lower back pain, bleeding hemorrhoids.

Traditional functions include strengthening qi, regulating qi and blood, and strengthening the lower back and knees.

Massage techniques are the same as for Bl 22.

Use with Bl 23, Bl 25, Bl 26, Bl 18, Bl 54, Bl 40, Gb 34, Gb 29, Gb 30, and Bl 52 for lower back pain and stiffness.

For hemorrhoids, use with Gv 20, Bl 20, Bl 25, Gv 1, Gv 2, Sp 3, Gb 34, St 36, Cv 4, St 25, and Sp 15.

Use with Sp 1, Sp 6, Sp 3, Liv 4, Liv 2, Liv 3, Cv 4, Cv 6, St 36, Kd 15, St 27, St 28, St 29, Gv 20, Bl 18, Bl 17, and Bl 35 for irregular menstruation.

Use with Bl 22, Bl 23, Bl 46, Bl 47, Bl 25, Bl 27, Bl 26, Sp 6, Sp 9, Kd 3, Gb 34, Cv 3, Cv 4, and Gb 25 for renal colic.

Figure 225

Applications:

He attacks with a straight right, so you block it with your right palm as your left palm takes over the block. Now your right fingers can poke into Sp 19 (fig. 225). You can now get around behind easily, since his legs have gone, and strike downward to Bl 24 over the buttocks.

BL 25 (BLADDER POINT NO. 25)

Chinese name:

Dachangshu (large intestine's hollow).

Location:

1.5 cun lateral to the lower border of the spinous process of the fourth lumbar vertebra. In the lumbodorsal fascia, between the longissimus and ilio-costalis muscles.

Connections:

Connected to the colon via yang ming.

Direction of strike:

Downward into the hip area.

Damage:

This is the shu point of the colon, and, as such, can cause great colon damage. Immediate nausea is felt, so much so that the recipient cannot carry on. Great local pain is also felt at this point, thus draining qi from the lower heater. At a later time, if this condition is not fixed, the person will go into stagnation and then into decay as a result of the colon's inability to get rid of bad qi. (It is the job of the colon not only to get rid of physical waste, but also internal qi waste.)

Set-up point:

A one-knuckle punch straight in and down to the lower abdomen at St 26 will set up this shot. This

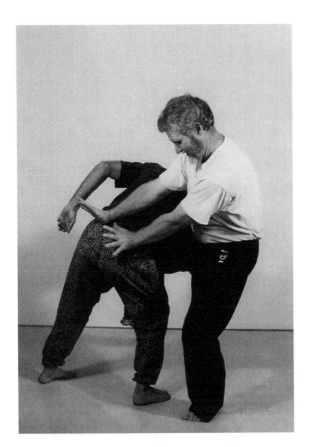

Figure 226

alone will be enough to stop the fight, but add Bl 25 and you have a most devastating method.

Antidote:

Pressure onto Co 10 with the left hand placed over Gv 20 will bring the colon back into balance.

Healing:

Innervation is by the posterior ramus of the third lumbar nerve. Irrigation is by the posterior branch of the fourth lumbar artery and vein.

Used for lower back pain and/or stiffness, pain of the sacroiliac joint, enteritis, dysentery, constipation, abdominal pain and distension, borborygmus, pain and or restriction of the shoulders when the pain is centered on Co 15.

Traditional indications include abdominal distension and intestinal noises, diarrhea, cutting pain around the navel, and difficult or painful defecation or urination.

Traditional functions, as a shu point of the large intestine, include promoting the function of that organ, invigorating the jing/luo, soothing the lower back and knees, and regulating the intestines and stomach.

Massage techniques are the same as for Bl 11. It is good to get into this point deeply with a knuckle or elbow and either do clockwise or counterclockwise rotations for xu or shi conditions or just rub back and forth across the point.

See Bl 23 for treatment of lower back pain.

Use with Co 4, Co 11, Co 14, Co 15, Gb 21, Th 15, Si 3, Si 13, Si 14, Si 9, Si 10, Si 11, Si 12, Bl 11, Bl 42, Bl 43, Bl 17, Bl 18, Gb 34, St 38, Gb 43, and Gb 44 for shoulder inflammation, pain, and loss of movement.

Use with Bl 20, Bl 23, Bl 54, Sp 4, Sp 9. St 40, St 36, St 25, St 28, Pc 6, Cv 12, Cv 4, Cv 6, Co 4, Co 11, St 37, Liv 3. Lu 5, Lu 7, and Sp 6, for loose stool or dysentery.

Use with Bl 24, Bl 23, Bl 22, Bl 21, Bl 20, Cv 12, Cv 4, Cv 6, Cv 9, St 36, St 25, St 21, St 37, Liv 13, Liv 3, Sp 3, and Sp 9 for borborgymus and abdominal distension.

Applications:

Perhaps he attacks with a right straight kick. You should move in immediately and slam the inside of his right knee with your right palm. Immediately, fold up the right arm and attack to St 26 with your right elbow. Take both hands under his right arm and, pulling him downward over your right knee, slam both palms into both Bl 25 points (fig. 226).

BL 26 (BLADDER POINT NO. 26)

Chinese name:

Guanyuanshu (hinge at the source).

Location:

1.5 cun lateral to the lower border of the spinous process of the fifth lumbar vertebra. In the sacro-spinalis muscle.

Connections:

None.

Direction of strike:

Straight in to the lower back.

Damage:

This point is the "shu of the door of vital essence." It is called the "life force" point because of its action upon the *chong mai*, one of the eight extra meridians. The immediate effect of a strike to Bl 26 is lower body damage, particularly to the leg on the side that was struck. An energy drainage will occur, causing nausea. In the long term, however, this strike is a bit more dangerous because it will affect the whole qi system and, in particular, the life force system. The qi flow in the chong mai will be damaged and slowly blocked so that the qi will have to find another route. Later in life, illness will start to creep in, meaning more hospital stays, operations, etc.

Set-up point:

Gb 31 straight in to the thigh will set up Bl 26 up nicely.

Antidote:

Any of the qi balancing methods will work as an antidote to this strike. Also, you could see a Chinese doctor to help with the damage to the chong mai.

Healing:

Innervation is by the posterior ramus of the fifth spinal nerve. Irrigation is by the posterior branches of the fifth lumbar artery and vein.

Used for abdominal distension, low back pain, diarrhea, chronic enteritis, diabetes, anemia, chronic peritonitis, cystitis, and sacroiliac pain or displacement.

Traditional indications include emaciation and thirst, lower back pain, frequent or painful urination, and enuresis.

Traditional functions are to regulate the lower jiao, (heater), strengthen the lower back and knees, and transform damp stagnation.

To massage, you can press straight into the point and hold, use rotation clockwise or counterclockwise for xu or shi conditions, press and vibrate, press into the point with an elbow and hold for three or four breaths or rock to and fro so that your elbow moves back and forth over the point, or do fingertip percussion on the point and around the whole sacroiliac joint.

Treat Bl 23 using needles or finger pressure for lower back pain and stiffness.

Use with Gv 4, Bl 32, Bl 23, Bl 33, Bl 18, Bl 20, Gv 3, Cv 4, Cv 6, Sp 6, Liv 3, St 36, Sp 8, Kd 15, Kd 11, Kd 27, Cv 3, Gb 26, Liv 14, and Pc 6, for loss of periods.

Use with Bl 23, Bl 28, Bl 18, Sp 6, Cv 2, Cv 3, Cv 4, Cv 5, Cv 6, Liv 8, Liv 3, St 29, St 28, jiaji points from T 8 to L 2, abdomen zigong, Kd 11, Kd 27, and Gv 20 for prostatitis.

Applications:

He might attack with a straight right. You should block that strike with either a left palm at Si 8 or a p'eng-type block to neigwan. Bring your left knee up into Gb 31 at the side of the thigh. Place it down and bring both hands into both Bl 26 points.

BL 27 (BLADDER POINT NO. 27)

Chinese name:

Xiaochangshu (small intestine's hollow).

Location:

At the level of the first posterior sacral foramen, 1.5 cun lateral to the Gv meridian. Between the origins of the sacro-spinalis and gluteus maximus muscle.

Connections:

This is a small intestine shu point, so it is connected to the small intestine.

Direction of strike:

Straight in to the lower back.

Damage:

The damage here is immediate. Nausea and even vomiting will occur with a medium to hard strike.

Figure 227

On a purely physical level, structural damage will also occur. In the immediate and long term, fire will rage in the heart, causing many ailments at both a physical and emotional level.

Set-up point:

Gb 14, struck upward, will enhance the fire in the heart part.

Antidote:

Eat watermelon; massage from the upper chest downward; massage neigwan.

Healing:

Innervation is by the lateral branch of the posterior ramus of the first sacral nerve. Irrigation is by the lateral posterior branch of the lateral sacral artery and vein.

Used for seminal emission, hematuria, enuresis, lower abdominal pain and distension, dysentery, constipation, enteritis, lower back pain, pain in the sacroiliac (small intestine joint), and disease of the sacroiliac joint.

Traditional indications include incontinence, blood in the urine, dark or red urine, dry mouth, emaciation and thirst, colic, and vaginal discharge.

Traditional functions, as a shu point of the small intestine, include opening and regulating the small intestine, eliminating damp, and cooling heat.

Massage techniques are the same as for Bl 26.

Use with Bl 11, Bl 17, Bl 18, Bl 20, Bl 25, Bl 26, Bl 53, Gb 34, Gb 39, Bl 40, Gb 29, and Gb 30 for small intestine joint problems.

See Bl 28 for hematuria, enuresis, incontinence, and so on.

Use with Co 4, Co 11, St 21, Sp 10, Sp 1, Liv 2, Gb 43, Gb 44, Cv 2, Cv 3, Cv 4, Si 1, Si 2, and Gv 14 for hematuria.

For colic, use with Bl 25, Bl 20, Bl 18, St 25, St 37, Cv 4, Cv 6, Cv 5, Cv 9, Co 4, Co 11, and Liv 3.

Applications:

Strike to Gb 14 upward in retaliation to his right- or left-handed attack. Spin him around and strike with your knee into Bl 27 while holding and pulling back his both shoulders (fig. 227).

BL 28 (BLADDER POINT NO. 28)

Chinese name:

Pangguangshu (bladder's hollow).

Location:

At the level of the second posterior sacral foramen, 1.5 cun lateral to the Gv meridian, in the depression between the medial border of the posterior superior iliac spine and the sacrum. The point is between the origins of the sacro-spinalis and gluteus maximus muscles.

Connections:

Shu point of the bladder.

Direction of strike:

Straight in to the lower back.

Damage:

A hard strike to this point will cause qi drainage and certain KO. At a deeper level, it will disrupt the body's mechanism for maintaining homeostasis because of the point's direct relationship to and direct effect upon the bladder. Striking this point will block the bladder's job of eliminating waste fluids, as well as its function of eliminating perverse energy such as excess heat, damp, or cold. This will prolong colds and flu, etc.

Set-up point:

The lower abdomen is the set-up point for this strike. A strike here, particularly to Cv 4 with a larger weapon such as the calf in a kick, will cause the major strike to be devastating in the immediate term as well as long term.

Antidote:

Seek medical help, especially if Cv 4 has been struck first, because death is imminent. If you have been struck in Bl 28 only, then have an acupuncturist penetrate the point 8 to 10 fen with a needle or burn moxa (7 to 15 cones) on the point. This will disperse stagnant qi in the lower heater and clear the bladder function.

Healing:

Innervation is by the medial branches of the dorsal rami of the first and second sacral nerves, and a communicating branch of the first sacral nerve. Irrigation is by the lateral posterior branches of the posterior sacral artery and vein.

Figure 228

Used for retention of urine, enuresis, diarrhea, constipation, pain and stiffness of the lower back, sciatica, diabetes, and disease of the urinogenital system.

Traditional indications include pain in the lumbar vertebra, loss of sperm, incontinence, dark and rough-flowing urine, and swelling and pain in the genitals.

As a shu point of the bladder meridian, its traditional functions are to promote the function of bladder, disperse qi of the lower jiao, soothe the back by benefiting the lumbar vertebra.

Massage techniques are the same as for Bl 26.

Use with Bl 23, Bl 27, Bl 26, Bl 25, Sp 9, Si 6, Cv 2, Cv 3, St 28, Cv 9, Cv 5, Bl 40, Bl 66, and Bl 67 for urinary tract infection.

Use with Bl 23, Bl 26, Bl 20, Bl 18, Bl 17, Cv 3, Cv 4, Cv 6, Cv 5, Cv 9, Cv 12, St 28, St 36, Kd 3, Liv 3, Gb 43, and Gb 44 for prostatitis.

Use with Bl 25, Bl 20, Bl 23, St 25, St 37, St 36, Bl 29, Cv 4, Bl 25, Bl 26, Bl 54, Bl 40, Gb 29, Gb 30, Gb 34, Bl 23, Bl 29, and Bl 35 for lower back pain and stiffness or sciatica.

Applications:

Take his left lower strike with a two-handed block and, swiveling on the ball of your left foot, slam your right calf across his lower abdomen at Cv 4 (fig. 228). Stomp down onto his left knee, placing your foot down to the rear so you are now facing the back of the attacker, and strike straight in to Bl 28 with both palms.

BL 29 (BLADDER POINT NO. 29)

Chinese name:

Zhonglushu (mid spine hollow).

Location:

At the level of the third posterior sacral foramen, 1.5 cun lateral to the governing meridian, between the origins of the sacro-spinalis and gluteus maximus muscles.

Connections:

None. A shu point of the sacrum.

Direction of strike:

Straight in to the sacrum.

Damage:

The sacrum is the large flat bone just above the coccyx (tailbone). It has great physical as well as spiritual importance. A strike straight in will adversely affect the structure of the whole body. The legs will not work correctly, and the recipient of a hard strike will have to sit down in great pain. However, in order to maintain a normally balanced system, we must have the qi "rising up the back." This is mentioned in all of the taijiquan classic sayings. When Bl 29 is struck, it damages this function and the qi will not rise up the back. As a result, the recipient will feel very tired and out of energy, especially after midday.

Set-up point:

St 11 and Lu 1 are the points to strike to set up this point, as they both work upon the overall power of the body. You can access both points with one strike downward, striking the collarbone with a claw-type weapon and the Lu 1 point with a heel palm at the same time.

Antidote:

For the physical damage, seek medical advice or an osteopath. For the spiritual damage, you will first have to have the physical damage fixed and then work with a qigong doctor to have the "gates" opened again (the three electrical gates that control the flow of qi up the backbone) since they will have been shut tight due to this attack. You can also do your own qigong to open the gates (included in my *Advanced Qigong* MTG 16 tape).

Healing:

Innervation is by the lateral branches of the posterior ramus of the third and fourth sacral nerves. Irrigation is by the posterior branches of the lateral sacral artery and vein and the branches of the inferior gluteal artery and vein.

Used for dysentery, hernia, pain and stiffness of the lower back, enteritis, and sciatica.

As a middle of back shu point, Bl 29's traditional functions involve treating mostly backache and the lower jiao.

Massage techniques are the same as for Bl 26.

Use with St 37, St 25, Sp 15, Bl 25, Bl 13, Bl 20, Cv 4, Cv 6, Co 4, Co 11, and St 36 for dysentery.

With Bl 25, Bl 26, Bl 54, Bl 52, Bl 40, Gb 34, Gb 29, and Gb 30 for pain and stiffness of the lower back or sciatica.

Applications:

Same application as for Bl 28, only strike to St 11 and Lu 1 as the set-up.

BL 30 (BLADDER POINT NO. 30)

Chinese name:

Baihuanshu (white circle's hollow).

Location:

At the level of the fourth sacral foramen, 1.5 cun lateral to the Gv meridian. In the gluteus maximus muscle and the inferior medial margin of the sacro-tuberous ligament.

Connections:

None.

Direction of strike:

Straight in to the lower back.

Damage:

The physical damage to the coccyx is obvious with this strike. However, again we have the spiritual damage caused to the whole body as we interrupt the flow of energy up the back. The dislocated or broken coccyx will end the fight.

Set-up point:

You could use the same set-up points as for Bl 29.

Antidote:

Obviously, see a doctor because of the broken coccyx. The spiritual damage can be helped in much the same way as for Bl 29.

Healing:

Innervation is by the inferior clunial nerve. Deeper, the point is located directly on the pudendal nerve. Irrigation is by the inferior gluteal artery and vein and, deeper, the internal pudendal artery and vein.

Used for seminal emission, irregular menstruation, leukorrhea, hernia, pain in the lower back and hip joint, endometritis, anal disease, sequelae of infantile paralysis, and sciatica.

Traditional indications include acute pain in the lumbar vertebra, debility of the legs and knees, loss of sperm, excessive uterine bleeding, vaginal discharge, colic, and painful defecation or urination.

Traditional function, as a shu point of leukorrhea, is to treat red or white vaginal discharge. Massage techniques are the same as for Bl 26.

Use with Bl 20, Gv 4, Cv 12, Cv 4, Cv 2, Cv 3, Cv 5, Cv 6, Cv 7, Gb 26, Gb 7, Sp 3, Sp 4, Sp 6, Sp 9, St 36, St 40, and Liv 3 for leukorrhea.

Use with Bl 57, Gv 1, Gv 20, Bl 20, Bl 17, St 36, Sp 3, and Liv 3 for prolapsed anus.

Use with Bl 25, Bl 26, Bl 53, Bl 54, Bl 52, Bl 40. Bl 58, and Gb 34, for arthritis of the lumbo-sacral region.

Use with Bl 25, Bl 26, Bl 23, Bl 50, Bl 51, Bl 52, Gb 29, Gb 30, Gb 34, Bl 54, Bl 40, Gb 44, Gb 43, and Gb 41 for sciatica.

Applications:

See Bl 29.

BL 31 (BLADDER POINT NO. 31)

Chinese name:

Shangliao (upper hole).

NOTE: The points Bl 31 to Bl 34 are collectively called *baliao,* meaning "eight seams."

Location:

In the first sacral foramen, roughly midway between the posterior superior iliac spine and the Gv meridian. In the sacro-spinalis and the origin of the gluteus maximus muscle.

Connections:

Connects to the gallbladder.

Direction of strike:

Straight in to the lower back.

Damage:

This point is closer to the spine than Bl 27, so it will cause considerable spine damage with a hard strike. Since it is above the sacrum, it will also cause spiritual damage.

Set-up point:

None. However, this point works well with Cv 4.

Antidote:

Qi balancing.

Healing:

Innervation occurs at the site where the posterior ramus of the first sacral nerve passes. Irrigation is by the posterior branches of the lateral sacral artery and vein.

Used for low back pain, irregular menstruation, prolapse of the uterus, leukorrhea, scanty urine, constipation, disease of the lumbo-sacral joint, sciatica, inducing labor, peritonitis, orchitis, paralysis of lower limbs, and sequelae of infantile paralysis.

Traditional functions, as a point of intersection with the Gb meridian, include regulating the lower heater and strengthening the lower back and legs.

Massage techniques are the same as for Bl 26.

Use with Bl 32, Co 4, Sp 6, Gb 21, Liv 3, and Bl 60 for induction of labor.

Use with Sp 6, St 36, Cv 4, Gv 12, Bl 23, Bl 24, Bl 25, Gb 1, Gb 6, Liv 3, and abdomen zigong for difficult menstruation. You could add this point to the formula for arthritis of lumbo-sacral region in Bl 30's treatment.

Applications:

Use the knee to strike to the point, or you could kick using the heel.

BL 32 (BLADDER POINT NO. 32)

Chinese name:

Ciliao (second bone). Part of baliao.

Location:

In the second posterior sacral foramen, about midway between the lower border of the posterior superior iliac spine and the Gv meridian. In the sacro-spinalis and the origin of the gluteus maximus muscle.

Connections:

Connection to the eight extra meridians and to Gb 30's internal pathway.

Direction of strike:

Straight in.

Damage:

This point is an interesting one. It will cause the legs to give way in the immediate term, and then the whole body will be weakened through a lack of qi. A hard strike will also cause paralysis of the muscles almost immediately. This point is also one of those that affect the communication with the shen.

Set-up point:

There is no set-up point, but you could use Sp 19 to enhance the effect on the legs.

Antidote:

Massage or needle the same point, Bl 32.

Healing:

Innervation occurs by its location on the course of the posterior ramus of the second sacral nerve. Irrigation is by the posterior branch of the lateral sacral artery and vein.

Used for lower back pain, irregular menstruation, leukorrhea, hernia, muscular atrophy, motor impairment and bi syndrome (the Chinese name for arthritic pain) of the lower extremities, induction of labor, orchitis, sciatica, sequelae of infantile paralysis, and peritonitis.

Traditional indications include nocturnal emissions, leukorrhea, and lower back pain and stiffness.

Traditional functions, as a point of intersection with the Gb meridian, include regulating the lower heater, tonifying the waist and knees, invigorating kidney qi, and removing blood stasis from uterus.

Massage techniques are the same as for Bl 26.

See Bl 31 for induction of labor.

Use with Sp 6, Bl 31, Bl 33, Bl 34, Cv 3, Cv 4, Liv 4, Liv 3, Bl 18, Bl 19, and Pc 6 for dysmenorrhea.

Use with Bl 31, Bl 33, Bl 34, Bl 35, Bl 25, Bl 26, Bl 40, Cv 12, Bl 18, Bl 19, Bl 20, Cv 9, Cv 5, St 28, Liv 2, Liv 3, Liv 4, Sp 9, and St 40 for peritonitis.

Use with Gv 1, Bl 31, Bl 33, Bl 34, Bl 25, Bl 35, Bl 20, Gv 20, St 37, Sp 3, and Liv 3 for hemorrhoids.

Applications:

You could kick using a round type of kick to his knee, which would not only turn him around but also take him down. Then you are free to attack to Bl 32 with any weapon you wish.

BL 33 (BLADDER POINT NO. 33)

Chinese name:

Zhongliao (middle hole). Part of baliao.

Location:

In the third posterior sacral foramen between Bl 29 and the Gv meridian. In the sacro-spinalis and the origin of the gluteus maximus muscle.

Connections:

None.

Direction of strike:

Straight in and slightly toward the backbone.

Damage:

The physical damage is much the same as for Bl 29; however, more spinal damage will occur with Bl 33 because it is closer to the spine, especially if the strike is aimed at a slight angle toward the backbone. The lower heater is damaged at a qi level, thus causing the elimination organs to malfunction.

Set-up point:

A quick shot to the lower abdomen around Cv 4 will suffice.

Antidote:

Perform the triple heater exercise, which will balance the energy in the whole body.

Triple heater qigong is performed as follows. (1) Stand with feet parallel and shoulder-width

Figure 229

Figure 230

apart. Place your tongue up on the hard palate and breathe in and out through the nose. (2) As in Figure 229, raise both of your palms slightly and breathe in. Squat down as your both palms make like they are scooping something up. Exhale. (3) Stand up and lift your palms up to chest height as you breathe in (fig. 230). You have stood up onto your toes. (4) Turn both palms downward and press down as you lower your heels and exhale. (5) Perform this routine again two more times.

This is for the lower heater.

When you have finished the third time and you have raised up again onto your toes with your hands facing upward at chest height, (1) turn both palms outward, away from you, and push out, extending your arms until both palms are out at your sides (fig. 231). (2) Turn the palms down and push down as you lower your heels and exhale. (3) Continue to squat and scoop, performing this routine, which works upon the middle heater, two more times. (4) When you have done it a total of three times, stand up again and scoop up to chest height.

Now, for the upper heater, instead of pushing your palms outward this time, (1) roll both palms over and push up over your head (fig. 232); (2) exhale as you push both palms down by your sides and lower your heels. Continue to squat until you have performed this routine three times. (My tape MTG 10, *Teach Yourself Basic Qigong,* covers this routine in more detail.)

Healing:

Innervation occurs by its location on the course of the posterior ramus of the third sacral nerve. Irrigation is by the posterior branches of the lateral sacral artery and vein.

Used for irregular menstruation, leukorrhea, lower back pain, dysuria, constipation, disease of the lumbo-sacral joint, sciatica, peritonitis, orchitis, paralysis of the lower limbs, and sequelae of infantile paralysis.

Traditional indications include nocturnal emissions, leukorrhea, and lower back pain and stiffness.

Again, this is a point of intersection with the Gb meridian, so its traditional functions are to regulate the lower heater and strengthen the lower back and knees.

Figure 231

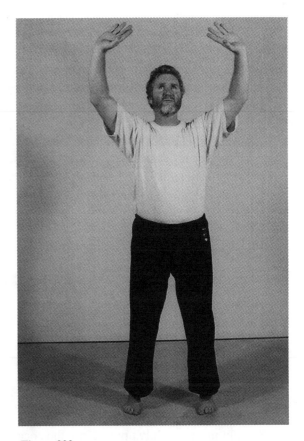

Figure 232

Massage is the same as for Bl 26.

(See Bl 32 for treatment of peritonitis, dysmenorrhea, and hemorrhoids.)

Use with Bl 31, Bl 32, Bl 34, Bl 35, Bl 25, Bl 26, Bl 54, Gb 29, Gb 30, Bl 40, and Gb 34 for lower back pain and stiffness, sciatica, and lumbo-sacral joint dysfunction.

Use with Bl 31, Bl 32, Bl 34, Bl 23, Bl 18, Cv 2, Cv 3, Cv 4, Cv 6, St 30, Liv 4, Liv 3, Liv 2, Liv 8, Liv 12, Gb 43, and Gb 44 for orchitis.

Applications:

Perhaps take his low right hook with your right palm, slamming it at Lu 5. Pull it over to your right and strike straight in to Cv 4. Then you are free to strike to Bl 33.

BL 34 (BLADDER POINT NO. 34)

Chinese name:

Xialiao (lower hole). Part of baliao.

Location:

In the fourth posterior sacral foramen between Bl 30 and the Gv meridian. In the sacro-spinalis and the origin of the gluteus maximus muscle.

Connections:

None.

Direction of strike:

Straight in.

Damage:

The damage here is the same as for Bl 33.

Set-up point:

Same as for Bl 33.

Antidote:

Same as for Bl 33.

Healing:

Innervation occurs by its location on the course of the posterior ramus of the fourth sacral nerve. Irrigation is by the branches of the inferior gluteal artery and vein.

Used for lower abdominal pain, constipation, dysuria, lower back pain, disease of the lumbo-sacral joint, sciatica, irregular menstruation, leukorrhea, peritonitis, orchitis, paralysis of lower limbs, and sequelae of infantile paralysis.

Traditional indications include leukorrhea, lower back pain and stiffness, and nocturnal emissions.

Traditional functions, as a point of intersection with the Gb meridian, are to regulate the lower heater and strengthen the lower back and knees.

Massage techniques are the same as for Bl 26.

(See other baliao points for suggestions of point combinations for different problems.)

Applications:

You could use the same technique as for Bl 33, but strike to Bl 34 instead.

BL 35 (BLADDER POINT NO. 35)

Chinese name:

Huiyang (meeting of yang).

Location:

0.5 cun lateral to the lip of the coccyx.

Connections:

None.

Direction of strike:

Straight in and slightly upward into the coccyx.

Damage:

A strike to this point causes obvious coccyx damage, which will result in elimination problems. Knockout is caused by the pain and qi drainage of having the coccyx broken. This point will also affect the "upper heavenly flow" of qi, so the "spiritual side" of the recipient will be damaged later in life.

Set-up point:

A kick to the groin in itself is not nice. This will suffice as the set-up point here.

Antidote:

For the spiritual disruption, balance the qi using one of the qi balancing methods.

Healing:

Innervation is by the coccygeal nerve, and irrigation is by the branches of the inferior gluteal artery and vein.

Used for leukorrhea, impotence, dysentery, hemafecia (blood in the stool), hemorrhoids, and pain in the lower back during menstruation.

Traditional indications include leukorrhea, impotence, loose stool, blood stagnation, and yang xu. Traditional functions are to move blood stagnation and tonify yang.

Massage techniques include straight press and hold, clockwise or counterclockwise rotations for xu or shi conditions, and fingertip percussion. You can also get in deeper with a knuckle or elbow.

Use with Bl 23, Gv 4, Gv 14, Gv 20, Bl 20, Gb 25, Cv 4, Cv 6, Kd 3, St 36, and Cv 12 for impotence and loose stool from yang xu.

Use with Liv 4, Sp 10, Kd 13, Kd 14, Kd 15, Bl 17, and Bl 18 for blood stagnation.

Use with Bl 31, Bl 32, Bl 33, Bl 34, Bl 30, Bl 20, Bl 18, Gb 26, Gb 27, Gv 4, Cv 2, Cv 3, Cv 4, Cv 5, Cv 6, Cv 7, Cv 9, Sp 6, Sp 9, Sp 4, St 40, St 36, and Liv 3 for leukorrhea.

Applications:

You can access this point from the front with a kick up and into the groin, the ball of the foot, or a toe reaching around to the coccyx.

BL 36 (BLADDER POINT NO. 36)

Chinese name:

Chengfu (receive support).

Location:

In the middle of the transverse gluteal fold below the buttock. At the inferior margin of the gluteus maximus muscle.

Connections:

None.

Direction of strike:

Upward into the buttock.

Damage:

This point has the capacity to send huge amounts of yang energy up and into the head when struck with a smaller weapon, thus causing nausea and even KO if struck hard enough. It is not a point that is often used, as it is difficult to get to and requires a great amount of pressure.

Set-up point:

None.

Antidote:

Strike downward onto Gb 21 and rub violently down the shoulders and out.

Healing:

Innervation is by the posterior femoral cutaneous nerve superficially, and, deeper, the sciatic nerve. Irrigation is by the comitans artery and vein of the sciatic nerve.

Used for hemorrhoids, pain in the lumbar/sacral/gluteal and femoral regions, sciatica, paralysis of lower extremities, retention of urine, and constipation.

Traditional indications include pain in lower back and legs, hemorrhoids, pain in the genitals, difficulty in urination, and swelling of the coccyx.

Massage techniques include pressing and holding the point or rotating clockwise or counterclockwise for xu or shi conditions. This is a very muscular area, so if the patient's knees are flexed to 90 degrees, you can stand on point and hold on to the feet of patient for support and balance. You can also get an elbow or knuckle in there. Or you can do press and release, with the press being a gradual increase of pressure and the release being very sudden. Use two thumbs for this and draw them apart as you release. You can do fingertip or loose fist percussion over this point.

Use with Bl 52, Bl 23, Bl 25, Bl 26, Bl 54, Bl 37, Bl 38, Bl 39, Bl 40, Gb 29, Gb 30, Gb 34, Gb 41 for sciatica and lower back pain.

Use with Bl 25, Bl 26, baliao points, St 25, St 37, Liv 3, and Co 4 for constipation.

Use with Bl 37, Bl 40, Bl 66, Bl 67, and Gb 34 for hamstring corck and trauma causing blood stasis.

Applications:

You will have to get around behind the opponent, which is not too difficult. Then strike in to Bl 35 with your toe or tip of shoe. You could also use a knee; however, this will require much power, because the knee is perhaps too large a weapon for this point.

BL 37 (BLADDER POINT NO. 37)

Chinese name:

Yinmen (door of abundance).

Location:

6 cun below Bl 36 on the line joining Bl 36 to Bl 40 in the semitendinosus muscle.

Connections:

None.

Direction of strike:

Straight in to the back of the thigh.

Damage:

There is not too much damage done here other than local damage to the leg. Some people say that this strike can cause paralysis of the leg; however, I have not experienced this.

Set-up point:

None.

Antidote:

None.

Healing:

Innervation is by the posterior femoral cutaneous nerve and, deeper, the sciatic nerve. Irrigation occurs by the point's location lateral to the third perforating branch of the deep femoral artery and vein.

Used for pain in the lower back and thigh, herniated disc, sciatica, occipital headache, paralysis of lower limbs, and paralysis.

Traditional indications include lower back pain that inhibits flexion and extension, and distension on the lateral side of the thigh.

Traditional functions include regulating the flow of qi and blood in the jing/luo and treating disorders of the waist and lower limbs.

Massage techniques are the same as for Bl 36.

Use with Bl 25, Bl 26, Bl 52, Bl 54, Bl 40, Gb 34, jiaji points lateral to L4/5 L5/Sl, Bl 20, Gv 14, and Si 3 for disk problems of the lumbar vertebra.

With Bl 40, Bl 25, Bl 26, Bl 23, Bl 39, Gb 34, Gb 29, Gb 30, for inability to bend or extend the lower back.

Applications:

Perhaps a hook kick to the back of the thigh.

BL 38 (BLADDER POINT NO. 38)

Chinese name:

Fuxi (floating xi).

Location:

1 cun above Bl 39 on the medial side of the tendon of biceps femoris. Locate the point with the knee slightly flexed.

Connections:

None.

Direction of strike:

Straight in to the back of the knee.

Damage:

This point presents the possibility for considerable local and internal damage. A strike here will cause great knee and leg damage, as well as damage to the elimination organs in the form of gastric problems. I heard of one chap who was kicked right on Bl 38 and immediately went to the toilet! Apart from the Bl 38 strike, you will probably also strike to Kd 10, which will cause even greater problems.

Set-up point:

Neigwan, as well as Kd 21 just lateral to Cv 14. In this instance, both are struck straight in.

Antidote:

Apply pressure to Co 10 and Co 12 at the same time.

Healing:

Innervation is by the posterior femoral cutaneous nerve and the common peroneal nerve. Irrigation is by the superior glenicular artery and vein.

Used for numbness of the gluteal and femoral regions, contracture of the tendons in the popliteal fossa, acute gastroenteritis, cystitis, constipation, and paralysis of the lateral aspect of the lower extremities.

To massage, press and hold, rotate clockwise or counterclockwise for xu or shi conditions, do fingertip percussion, press with lateral and medial movements, and press in with both thumbs slowly and release rapidly, pulling the thumbs apart as they leave the skin.

Use with Bl 25, Bl 26, Bl 53, Bl 54, Bl 36, Bl 37, Bl 39, Bl 40, Bl 57, Bl 66, Bl 67, Gb 34, Gb 33, Gb 32, Gb 31, Gb 30, and Gb 29 for numbness of the gluteal and femoral regions, contracture of tendons in popliteal fossa, and paralysis of the lateral aspect of lower extremities.

Applications:

He might attack with a right straight. You would strike his arm with your left and right palms at Lu 5 and neigwan, respectively. Now, swiveling on the ball of your left foot, hook kick with your heel to the back of his knee at Bl 38. (fig. 233).

Figure 233

BL 39 (BLADDER POINT NO. 39)

Chinese name:

Weiyang (commanding yang).

Location:

When the patient is prone, this point can be found 1 cun lateral to Bl 40 on the medial border of the tendon of biceps femoris in the popliteal fossa.

Connections:

None.

Direction of strike:

Straight in to the back of the knee.

Damage:

This point is closer to the back of the knee and acts on the bladder, causing the recipient to urinate on the spot! It will cause damage to the bladder, which will require medical attention or it will get worse as the person gets older. Knee damage is obvious. Kidney damage will also occur as a result of four points being struck with this strike: Bl 38, Bl 39, Bl 40, and Kd 10. WARNING: *This combination of points can cause death through kidney failure.*

Set-up point:

Use any kidney point as the set-up strike.

Antidote:

Have an acupuncturist look at the kidneys and treat as necessary. You might have also to take Chinese herbs.

Healing:

Innervation and irrigation are the same as for Bl 38.

Used for pain and stiffness of lower back, lower abdominal distension, dysuria, cramping of the leg and foot, nephritis, cystitis, chyluria (chyle in the urine), and spasm of gastrocnemius (a muscle in the back of the leg).

Traditional indications include fullness of the chest or abdomen, lower back pain extending to the abdomen, loss or retention of urine, hemorrhoids, and constipation.

As a lower he sea point of the triple heater meridian that benefits the bladder, its traditional functions include adjusting the lower heater, regulating the passage of water, transforming water, and benefiting the bladder.

To massage, flex the leg to 90 degrees and use the same techniques as for Bl 38.

Use with Bl 23, Bl 32, Bl 28, Cv 2, Cv 3, Cv 4, Cv 5, Cv 9, St 28, Bl 33, Sp 6, Bl 22, and Sp 9 for urinary retention or incontinence.

Use with Gv 4, Gv 3, Bl 31, Bl 32, Bl 37, Bl 40, Bl 54, jiaji points from Ll to L5, Gb 30, Gb 34, St 32, St 36, and Liv 3 for paralysis of leg.

See Bl 38 for lower back pain and stiffness, cramping, or contracture.

Applications:

Same as for Bl 38.

Bl 40 (BLADDER POINT NO. 40)

Chinese name:

Weizhong (commanding middle).

Location:

Midpoint of the transverse crease of the popliteal fossa, in the fascia of the popliteal fossa between the tendons of biceps femoris and semitendinosus. Locate the point in the prone position with the knee flexed.

Connections:

Connections to the lower meeting point of the bladder and kidney divergent meridians.

Direction of strike:

Straight in to the back of the knee.

Damage:

This point is the earth point and also a *he* (gathering together) point. A strike here will cause spasm in the tendons of the whole body if struck hard enough, or local spasm if light. At some later stage, nervous disorders will become apparent. Excessive yang energy will also cause heating problems within the body. This is not a point to play around with just to see what happens! Knockout has been known to occur when it is struck. There is an immediate rush of energy to the head, and blackout is possible.

Set-up point:

A strike to neigwan will cause the disorientation and confusion for a second or two, so in that time, strike to Bl 40 with devastating results.

Antidote:

Rub the shoulders down and away with pressure on Gb 21 points.

Healing:

Innervation is by the posterior femoral cutaneous nerve and the tibial nerve. Irrigation is by the femoral popliteal vein, in its deep position medial to the point the popliteal vein, in its deepest position the popliteal artery.

Used for lower back pain, motor impairment of the hip joint, contracture of the tendons in the popliteal fossa, muscular atrophy, motor impairment and pain in lower extremities, hemiplegia, abdominal pain, vomiting, diarrhea, heat exhaustion, acute gastroenteritis, sciatica, arthritis of knee, and spasm of gastrocnemius muscle.

Traditional indications include coma due to stroke, hemiplegia, stiffness and pain of lumbar region, seizures, leprosy, tidal fever, carbuncles, twisting pain in the chest and abdomen, vomiting, diarrhea, and acute lumbago.

As a he sea point and an earth point of the bladder meridian, Bl 40's traditional functions are to drain summer heat (when bled), relax the tendons, invigorate the collaterals, strengthen the lower back and knees, and clear heat from the blood.

Massage with the knee flexed, the same way as for Bl 38.

Used with Bl 25, Bl 26, Bl 54, Gb 29, Gb 30, and Gb 34 for lower back pain or stiffness.

Use with Bl 25, Bl 26, Bl 53, Bl 54, Bl 36, Bl 37, Bl 39, Bl 57, Bl 66, Bl 67, Gb 34, Gb 33, Gb 32, Gb 31, and Gb 30 for contracture of the tendons of the popliteal fossa.

For heat exhaustion, use with Gv 14, Gv 26, Co 4, Co 11, Sp 10, Liv 2, Gb 44, and Gb 43.

Use with Cv 6, Cv 4, Cv 3, Sp 6, Liv 1, Liv 3, Kd 10, Kd 2, Kd 3, Liv 4, St 36, Pc 6, Bl 18, Bl 19, Bl 20, and Bl 23 for irregular menstruation.

Applications:

A round type of kick using the instep. Or, if you are in a grappling situation, a one-knuckle punch here will cause the attacker to let go of any hold.

BL 41 (BLADDER POINT NO. 41)

Chinese name:

Fufen (appended part).

Location:

3 cun lateral to the lower border of the spinous process of the second thoracic vertebra. This is about four finger breadths (of the individual patient) lateral to the midline of the spine.

Connections:

None.

Direction of strike:

Straight in to the back.

Damage:

This point is opposite Bl 12, so you could easily strike both Bl 12 and Bl 41. This point, along with Bl 42 and 43, is right over what is known as the "power band." This is the area of the back that when struck damages the structure of the whole upper body. A strike here will seriously drain qi from the body, causing the recipient to fall down. Great local pain is also felt because this is an "electrical point."

Set-up point:

Sp 19 is a good point to strike along with Bl 41 since it weakens the legs.

Antidote:

Hold your palms on each shoulder and lift upward, then let it drop (fig. 234).

Healing:

Innervation is by the lateral cutaneous branches of the posterior rami of the first and second thoracic nerves and, deeper, the dorsal scapular nerve.

Irrigation is by the descending branch of the transverse cervical artery and the lateral branches of the posterior branches of the intercostal artery and vein.

Used for stiffness and pain of the shoulder/upper back and neck and numbness of the elbow and arm.

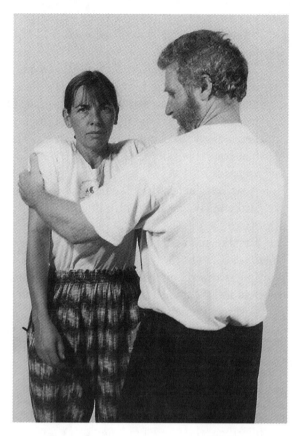

Figure 234

To massage, press straight in and hold; press and rotate clockwise or counterclockwise for xu or shi conditions; rub across the point (laterally and medially) with the fingertips, thumb, or the heel of hand; or do fingertip or loose fist percussion on the point. You can also get an elbow into this point (let your patient guide you as to how much pressure is tolerable). You'll get better access to the point if the arm is flexed behind the back. Press slowly with both thumbs and release quickly, pulling the thumbs apart.

Use with Gb 20, Gb 21, Gb 34, Th 15, Th 14, Si 3, Si 9, Si 10, Si 11, Si 12, Si 13, Si 14, Si 15, dingchuan, Bl 11, Bl 12, Bl 13, Bl 14, Bl 15, Bl 16, Bl 17, Bl 18, Bl 42, Bl 43, Bl 44, Bl 45, Bl 46, Bl 47, Bl 57, Bl 60, Bl 66, Bl 67, Si 1, Si 2, and Co 15 for pain and stiffness of the neck, shoulder, and upper back regions.

Use with Co 4, Co 7, Co 8. Co 9, Co 10, Co 11, Co 12, Co 13, Co 14, Co 15, Co 16, Si 3, Si 6, Si 7, Si 8, Si 9, St 10, Si 11, Si 12, and Si 13 for numbness, pain, and stiffness of the elbow and arm.

Applications:

You might strike straight in to Sp 19 with your right fingers as your left palm slams into his right neigwan. Flick your left palm over the top of his right forearm and swing it over to your right, thus turning him around so that his back is facing you. Strike straight in to Bl 41.

BL 42 (BLADDER POINT NO. 42)

Chinese name:

Pohu (soul's household).

Location:

3 cun lateral to the lower border of the spinous process of the third thoracic vertebra.

Used for pulmonary tuberculosis, cough, asthma, neck rigidity, pain in the shoulder and back, bronchitis, pleurisy, and atelectasis (collapsed lung).

Connections:

None.

Direction of strike:

Straight in to the back.

Damage:

This point does the same damage as Bl 41. However, more lung damage is done, thus draining more qi from the upper body. This point is also nearly parallel to the heart, so a sudden strike will also send a shock wave into the heart, thus causing it to stop either momentarily or forever!

Set-up point:

Same as for Bl 41.

Antidote:

Same as for Bl 41.

Healing:

Massage techniques are the same as for Bl 41.

See Bl 41 for treating upper back, neck, and shoulder pain and stiffness.

Use with dingchuan, Bl 12, Bl 13, Bl 43, Bl 44, Bl 45, Bl 17, Bl 18, Cv 22, Cv 17, Lu 1, Lu 2, Lu 3, Lu 4, Lu 5, Lu 6, Lu 7, Lu 8, Lu 9, St 36, Liv 3, Kd 22, Kd 23, Kd 24, Kd 25, Kd 26, and Kd 27 for cough, asthma, bronchitis, pleurisy, and so on.

Use with Gb 20, Bl 12, Bl 13, Bl 43, Bl 17, Lu 1, Lu 5, Lu 7, Co 4, Co 11, Cv 17, St 36, and Liv 3 for the common cold.

Applications:

Same as for Bl 41.

BL 43 (BLADDER POINT NO. 43)

Chinese name:

Gaohuangshu (vital's hollow).

Location:

3 cun lateral to the lower border of the spinous process of the fourth thoracic vertebra. At the end of the medial border of the spine of the scapula, in the trapezium and rhomboid muscles and, in its deep position, the ilio-costalis muscle.

Connections:

Connected to the upper heater.

Direction of strike:

Straight in to the back.

Damage:

This is the shu point of the "vital center" (that area just below the heart). A strike here will cause great weakness because it also affects the lung qi, draining it. The whole qi system is slowed down, i.e., the production of qi is slowed, thus causing the great weakness. The recipient will fall down from instant weakness.

Set-up point:

Attack to Lu 5 at the elbow.

Antidote:

You should have an acupuncturist place a slice of garlic over Bl 43 and then burn moxa over the point. You could also either massage St 36 or use moxa on it and Bl 43 together.

Healing:

Innervation is by the medial cutaneous branches of the posterior rami of the second and third thoracic nerves and, deeper, their lateral branches and the dorsoscapular nerve. In its deepest position it is innervated by the trunk of the fourth intercostal nerve. Irrigation is by the posterior branch of the fourth intercostal artery and the descending branch of the transverse cervical artery.

Used for pulmonary tuberculosis, cough, asthma, hemoptysis, night sweating, poor memory, seminal emissions, indigestion, bronchitis, pleurisy, neurasthenia, and general weakness caused by prolonged illness, upper back spasm, and pain.

Traditional indications include consumptive deficient disease, coughing of blood, hiccups, deficient spleen and stomach, nocturnal emissions, absent-mindedness, and pain along the spine.

Traditional functions are to regulate the lung qi, strengthen deficient conditions, and calm and strengthen the shen.

Massage techniques are the same as for Bl 41, but be careful if you use an elbow.

Use with dingchuan, Bl 12, Bl 13, Bl 17, Bl 18, Bl 23, Bl 42, Bl 44, Bl 45, Gv 22, Lu 1, Lu 5, Lu 7, Co 4, Pc 6, Cv 17, Kd 22, Kd 23, Kd 24, Kd 25, Kd 26, Kd 27, Kd 3, Cv 12, St 36, and Liv 3 for asthma, bronchitis, cough, and so on. Use with St 36, Sp 3, Gv 20, Lu 1, Cv 4, Cv 6, and Liv 3 for general weakness after prolonged illness.

See Bl 41 for treatment of pain and stiffness of the upper back, neck, and shoulders.

Applications:

He might attack with a right hook. Slam his Lu 5 point with your right back palm to cause him to become extremely weak and perhaps faint. If not, then pull him around so that you can now access his Bl 43 point and strike either one or both points straight in to the back to drop him.

BL 44 (BLADDER POINT NO. 44)

Chinese name:

Shentang (spirit's hall).

Location:

3 cun lateral to the lower border of the spinous process of the fifth thoracic vertebra.

Connections:

None.

Direction of strike:

Straight in to the back.

Damage:

This point is also a weakening point. A strong strike will cause the recipient to fall down because it shocks the lungs.

As with many of the bladder points, this one has a dire effect upon the spirit, disconnecting the human part with the "God" part. It is most difficult for someone who has been struck here to return to being a normal, loving human being again.

Set-up point:

Lu 5 is a good set-up point.

Antidote:

The same as for Bl 43.

Healing:

Innervation is by the medial cutaneous branch of posterior rami of the fourth and fifth thoracic nerves and, deeper, their lateral branches and the dorsal scapular nerve. Irrigation is by the posterior branches of the fifth intercostal artery and vein and the descending branch of the transverse cervical artery.

Used for asthma, cough, pain, and stiffness of upper back, bronchitis, intercostal neuralgia, and heart disease.

Massage techniques are the same as for Bl 41, but again, be careful if you use an elbow.

See Bl 43 for treating asthma, bronchitis, cough, etc.

Use with Pc 6, Ht 7, Pc 3, Cv 17, Liv 14, Bl 14, Bl 15, Bl 17, Bl 18, Bl 43, Liv 3, and St 36 for heart disease.

See Bl 41 for treating pain and stiffness of the upper back and shoulders, or use Bl 44 with Liv 14, Gb 24, Gb 34, Gb 41, Liv 2, Liv 3, and jiaji points of thoracic vertebra associated with the ribs involved.

Use with Gv 20, Gb 20, anmien, Ht 7, Pc 6, Bl 43, Liv 3, Bl 65, Bl 66, Sp 3, and Kd 16 for

Figure 235

mental illness, neurasthenia, depression, etc.

Applications:

The same as for Bl 43.

BL 45 (BLADDER POINT NO. 45)

Chinese name:

Yixi (surprise).

Location:

3 cun lateral to the spinous process of the sixth thoracic vertebra.

Connections:

None.

Direction of strike:

Straight in to the back.

Damage:

Again, this is a weakening point. If used in conjunction with Lu 5 or Lu 8 and Ht 5, it will cause great weakness from qi drainage.

Set-up point:

Lu 5 or Lu 8 and/or Ht 5.

Antidote:

Place your hand onto Gv 20 and apply light pressure downward into the head. You could also use the same antidote as for Bl 43.

Healing:

Innervation is by the medial cutaneous branches of the posterior rami of the fifth and sixth thoracic nerves and, deeper, their lateral branches. Irrigation is by the posterior branches of the sixth intercostal artery and vein.

Used for cough, asthma, pain in the shoulder and upper back, pericarditis, malaria, intercostal neuralgia, and hiccups.

Massage techniques include pressing and holding the point; rotating clockwise or counterclockwise for xu or shi conditions; pressing slowly with the thumbs and releasing quickly, pulling thumbs apart; doing fingertip percussion or loose fist percussion on the point; and rubbing the point medially and laterally with the tips of the fingers, the thumb, or the heel of the hand.

See Bl 43 for treatment of asthma, bronchitis, cough, etc. See Bl 41 for treatment of the upper back, neck, and shoulders.

Use with Gb 34, Sp 9, Si 3, Pc 5, Pc 6, Co 4, Co 11, Lu 7, Gv 10, Th 2, Gv 13, Gv 14, Bl 12, Bl 13, Gb 20, St 36, Liv 2, and Liv 3 for malaria.

Use with Bl 14, Bl 15, Bl 43, Bl 44, Cv 17, Pc 8, Pc 9, Th 1, and Th 2 for pericarditis.

Applications:

Perhaps you have used a p'eng type of block to his straight left. You should also strike in to Kd 25 to shock the kidneys. Then violently pull his wrist with your left palm, thus attacking Ht 5 and Lu 8, draining qi from the upper body. Pull him around and strike straight in to Bl 45 (fig. 235).

BL 46 (BLADDER POINT NO. 46)

Chinese name:

Geguan (diaphragm's hinge).

Location:

3 cun lateral to the lower border of the seventh thoracic vertebra, approximately at the level of the inferior angle of the scapula.

Connections:

None.

Direction of strike:

Upward into the scapula using a palm-heel strike.

Damage:

Great damage is done to the structure of the upper body, which will not allow him to continue the fight. This strike will also affect the heart and lungs, and the diaphragm or seat of power, bringing great qi drainage. Physically, you can also damage the muscular system around this area, causing chronic instant spasm, which will drop him quickly.

Set-up point:

Any of the qi drainage points will suffice here—Lu 5, Lu 8, neigwan, or Ht 5.

Antidote:

Bring qi back into the system by applying pressure downward onto Gv 20.

Healing:

Innervation is by the medial cutaneous branches of the posterior rami of the sixth and seventh thoracic nerves and, deeper, their lateral branches. Irrigation is by the posterior branches of the seventh intercostal artery and vein.

Used for difficulty swallowing, vomiting, belching, pain and stiffness of back, gastric hemorrhage, intercostal neuralgia, and esophageal spasm caused by blockage of liver qi.

Massage techniques are the same as for Bl 45.

Use with Pc 6, Ht 7, Liv 3. Liv 14, St 36, and Kd 1 for esophageal spasm causing vomiting, belching, or difficulty in swallowing.

Use with Bl 17, Bl 18, Bl 19, Bl 20, Bl 25, Bl 40, Bl 60, and Gb 34 for middle back pain and stiffness.

Use with Bl 21, Bl 20, Bl 19, Bl 18, Bl 17, Sp 10, Sp 1, Cv 12, Co 4, Pc 6, and Gb 26 for gastric hemorrhage.

Applications:

The same as for Bl 44.

BL 47 (BLADDER POINT NO. 47)

Chinese name:

Hunmen (soul's door).

Location:

3 cun lateral to lower border of the spinous process of the ninth thoracic vertebra.

Connections:

None.

Direction of strike:

Straight in to the back with a twist either clockwise for the right side or counterclockwise for the left side.

Damage:

A strike to this point causes great lung damage. The effect will be immediate: the recipient will fall down. However, there are prolonged effects with this strike, so be warned! The recipient could have lung deficiency lasting many years, causing not only emotional damage but physical conditions such as asthma, chronic bronchitis, and so on. Severe social or behavioral problems are also inherent to this strike because, again, it has a dire effect on the spirit or soul of the recipient. It is said of a strike to this point that the spirit is locked out and cannot return.

Set-up point:

Lu 5.

Antidote:

See an acupuncturist and have the lung deficiency looked at. For the physical damage, of course, see a doctor. For the emotional damage, you must have the lungs fixed immediately, as the longer it persists, the harder it is to fix. For the spiritual damage, you must have the door opened. An acupuncture needle is placed at Bl 46 and Bl 48, on either side of Bl 47, and at Bl 18. When the needles all begin to vibrate, this is the sign that the door has been reopened.

Healing:

Innervation is by the lateral branches of the posterior rami of the seventh and eighth thoracic nerves. Irrigation is by the posterior branches of the eighth intercostal artery and vein.

Used for pain in the chest/midback and hypochondriac regions, vomiting, diarrhea, neurasthenia, disease of the liver and gallbladder, pleurisy, and stomachache.

Massage is the same as for Bl 45.

Use with Bl 17, Bl 18, Bl 19, Bl 46, Bl 43. Bl 48, Bl 20, Bl 49, Liv 14, Liv 13, Liv 2, Liv 3, Liv 4, Liv 6, Gb 24, Gb 34, Gb 43, Bl 40, and Gb 44 for inflammation of the liver or gallbladder , pain in the chest/midback or hypochondriac regions, and stomachache.

Use with Pc 6, Bl 18, Bl 20, Cv 12, St 36, Liv 3, and Co 4 for vomiting, and add Bl 25, St 25, Sp 25, St 37, and Sp 4 for diarrhea.

Applications:

The same as for Bl 46.

BL 48 (BLADDER POINT NO. 48)

Figure 236

Chinese name:

Yanggang (yang's parameter).

Location:

3 cun lateral to the lower border of the spinous process of the 10th thoracic vertebra.

Connections:

None.

Direction of strike:

Straight in to the back. Usually struck in conjunction with Bl 49.

Damage:

A strike to this point obstructs the yang qi, causing long-lasting emotional problems, usually seen in the form of totally withdrawal. The immediate effect is that the lungs are damaged so that the recipient cannot breathe, causing him or her to fall down.

Set-up point:

Lu 5.

Antidote:

Place him in a sitting position and put his head between his knees if there is no obvious physical damage, such as broken ribs, etc.

Healing:

Innervation is by the lateral branches of the

posterior rami of the eighth and ninth thoracic nerves. Irrigation is by the posterior branches of the ninth intercostal artery and vein.

Used for borborygmus, abdominal pain, diarrhea, jaundice, hepatitis, cholecystitis, and gastritis. Massage techniques are the same as for Bl 45.

See Bl 47 for treatment of hepatitis, cholecystitis, etc.

Use with Bl 18, Bl 19, Bl 20, Bl 21, Bl 22, Gv 12, Liv 13, St 36, Sp 3, Sp 4, Liv 3, St 25, Cv 9, Cv 4, Cv 6, and St 21 for borborygmus and abdominal pain. Add St 25, Sp 15, Gb 26, St 37, and Sp 4 for diarrhea, and for gastritis add St 45, St 44, Liv 4, Liv 2, Gb 44, and Gb 43.

Applications:

Take his right straight with your right p'eng block as you are moving straight past the attacker. Then as his Bl 48 and 49 points are in view, strike backward with a right palm heel strike (fig. 236).

BL 49 (BLADDER POINT NO. 49)

Chinese name:

Yishe (lodge of ideas).

Location:

3 cun lateral to the lower border of the spinous process of the 11th thoracic vertebra.

Connections:

None.

Direction of strike:

Straight in to the back.

Damage:

This strike has the same effect as Bl 48 on the lungs. It also has an immediate effect upon the mind, causing the recipient to become confused and unable to carry through with ideas that pop up. So, in a martial sense, he might intend to strike you but will be unable to execute the necessary body movements.

Set-up point:

Lu 5.

Antidote:

The whole body must be rebalanced using one of the qi balancing methods.

Healing:

Innervation is by the lateral branches of the posterior rami of the 10th and 11th thoracic nerves. Irrigation is by the posterior branches of the 10th intercostal artery and vein.

Used for abdominal distension, borborygmus, diarrhea, vomiting, difficulty swallowing, hepatitis, cholecystitis, and gastritis.

Massage techniques are the same as for Bl 45.

Add this point to the formula for hepatitis given under Bl 47.

Use it with Pc 6, Ht 7, Co 4, Bl 18, Bl 17, Bl 46, Liv 14, Liv 13, Liv 3, St 36, and Kd 1 for difficulty swallowing.

Use with Bl 18, Bl 17, Bl 20, Bl 19, Bl 21, Cv 12, Liv 13, Liv 3, St 21, St 25, St 36, St 37, St 40, Gb 34, Gb 26, and Pc 6 for abdominal distension, borborygmus, diarrhea, vomiting, and lethargy.

Applications:

The same as for Bl 48.

BL 50 (BLADDER POINT NO. 50)

Chinese name:

Weicang (stomach's storehouse).

Location:

3 cun lateral to the lower border of the spinous process of the 12th thoracic vertebra.

Connections:

None.

Direction of strike:

Straight in to the lower back.

Damage:

This point attacks the stomach, both physically and qi-wise. Immediately, the recipient feels a "swelling" in the head caused by yang energy rushing upward. Immediate local pain will go away, only to return some minutes later as extreme pain across the lower back. This strike affects the "earth," and so the recipient loses his grounding and will easily be knocked over.

Set-up point:

Gb 14 upward.

Antidote:

Gb 21, pressed or struck downward.

Healing:

Innervation is by the lateral branch of the posterior ramus of the 11th thoracic nerve. Irrigation is by the posterior branch of the subcostal artery and vein.

Used for abdominal distension, pain in the epigastric region and the back, stomachache, and gastritis.

Massage is the same as for Bl 51.

Use with Pc 6, Cv 12, St 36, Bl 20, Bl 21, Bl 18, Cv 14, St 21, St 25, Bl 17, Liv 13, Liv 3, and jiaji from T 8 to T 12 for stomachache, abdominal distension, and epigastric pain.

Use with Bl 17, Bl 18, Bl 19, Bl 20, Bl 21, Bl 22, Bl 46, Bl 47, Bl 48, Bl 49, Bl 51, Bl 52, Bl 40, and Gb 34 for backache.

Applications:

Same as for Bl 48.

BL 51 (BLADDER POINT NO. 51)

Chinese name:

Huangmen (vitals' door).

Location:

3 cun lateral to the lower border of the spinous process of the first lumbar vertebra.

Connections:

None.

Direction of strike:

Straight in to the lower back.

Damage:

A little lower than Bl 50, this point attacks what is called the "vital centers." If it is used in conjunction with Bl 22 it will stop the heart.

Set-up point:

Lu 5.

Antidote:

Massage the point using counterclockwise circles on the right side and clockwise circles on the left side.

Healing:

Innervation is by the lateral branch of the posterior ramus of the 12th thoracic nerve. Irrigation is by the posterior branches of the first lumbar artery and vein.

Used for pain in the epigastric region, abdominal mass, constipation, mastitis, lower back pain, and paralysis of lower limbs.

To massage, press and hold the point; do rotation clockwise or counterclockwise for xu or shi conditions; press in slowly with the thumbs and release quickly, pulling the thumbs apart; do fingertip percussion on the point; and press with the heel of hand and rub medially and laterally.

Use with Bl 22, Bl 23, Bl 24, Bl 52, Bl 25, Bl 26, Bl 27, Sp 6, Sp 9, Kd 3, Cv 2, Cv 3, Cv 4, and Cv 5 for renal colic.

Use with Cv 14, Cv 12, Cv 9, Cv 7, Cv 6, Cv 5, Cv 4, Cv 3, St 21, St 25, St 29, Liv 3, Liv 13, Liv 14, Pc 6, Liv 4, St 36, Bl 20, Bl 21, Bl 18, and Bl 17 for epigastric pain, abdominal mass, and constipation.

Use with Bl 17, Bl 18, Bl 19, Liv 3, Liv 14, Cv 17, St 15, St 36, Sp 18, Si 1, and Sp 6 for mastitis.

Applications:

The same as for Bl 48.

BL 52 (BLADDER POINT NO. 52)

Chinese name:

Zhishi (lodge of the will).

Location:

3 cun lateral to the lower border of the spinous process of the second lumbar vertebra. In the latissimus dorsi and ilio-costalis muscles.

Connections:

None.

Direction of strike:

Straight in to the lower back.

Damage:

This strike is an interesting one because it causes physical as well as spiritual damage. When his right Bl 52 is struck, it will instantly weaken his left leg. Even a light to medium strike here will cause the leg to falter for a moment, enabling you to get in quickly for a more devastating shot. When his left Bl 52 is struck, it will damage his right leg. This is also a point for damaging the will. Whereas St 12 is the point for damaging his will to fight, this point damages the will to do anything.

Set-up point:

You could use St 12 because this will enhance the effect on the will and also drain qi from the lower body.

Antidote:

The legs will look after themselves, gaining qi in a few seconds, depending upon how hard the point is struck. The will must be worked upon, however, using acupuncture to St 12 and also to Bl 52.

Healing:

Innervation is by the lateral branch of the posterior ramus of the 12th thoracic nerve and the lateral branch of the first lumbar nerve. Irrigation is by the posterior branches of the second lumbar artery and vein.

Used for seminal emission, impotence, dysuria, edema, pain and stiffness of the lower back, nephritis, spermatorrhea, prostatis, eczema of the scrotum, painful urination, and paralysis of the lower limbs.

Traditional indications include vomiting, indigestion, incontinence, swelling and pain in the genitals, nocturnal emissions, and edema.

Massage techniques are the same as for Bl 51.

Use with Bl 53, Liv 4, Liv 8, Liv 12, Liv 1, Cv

Figure 237

2, Cv 3, and Cv 4 for pain and swelling of the external genitalia. Use with Bl 23, Bl 24, Cv 4, Cv 6, Gb 25, Kd 3, and Gv 4 for seminal emissions, impotence, and spermatorrhea; add Cv 2, Cv 3, Bl 27, Bl 28, Bl 25, Bl 20, Bl 18, and Liv 3 for dysuria, nephritis, and prostatis.

Use with Bl 23, Bl 24, Bl 25, Bl 26, Bl 53, Bl 54, Bl 40, Gb 34, Gb 30, and Gb 29 for stiffness and pain of the lower back.

Applications:
1) You could block any type of straight attack at neigwan and then attack using either a hammer fist or a claw-type weapon to St 12 (fig. 237).
2) Swing him around and strike to Bl 52 with one or both of your palms.

BL 53 (BLADDER POINT NO. 53)

Chinese name:
Baohuang (placenta and vitals).

Location:
3 cun lateral to the lower border of the spinous process of the second sacral vertebra, level with Bl 32.

Connections:
None.

Direction of strike:
Straight in to the buttocks.

Damage:
This point does much the same damage as Bl 28.

Set-up point:
The same as for Bl 28.

Antidote:
The same as for Bl 28.

Healing:
Innervation is by the superior cluneal nerves and, deeper, the superior gluteal nerve. Irrigation is by the superior gluteal artery and vein.

Used for borborygmus, abdominal distension, pain in the lower back, retention of urine, sciatica, and sacroiliac pain and misalignment.

To massage, press and hold; rotate clockwise or counterclockwise for xu or shi conditions; rub with the fingertips, knuckles, or elbow medially and laterally across the point; do fingertip or loose fist percussion on the point; or press slowly and release quickly, pulling the thumbs apart.

See Bl 52 for treatment of lower back pain and stiffness. You could also use that treatment plus Bl 20, Bl 27, Bl 28, Bl 29, Bl 30, and Bl 54 for misalignment of the sacroiliac joint.

For borborygmus and abdominal distension, use with Bl 20, Bl 21, Bl 22, Bl 23, Bl 24, Bl 25, Cv 12, Cv 6, Cv 4, St 21, St 25, St 26, St 27, St 28, St 29, St 30, St 36, Liv 3, Sp 9, and Liv 13.

Use with Bl 32, Bl 28, Bl 23, Bl 39, Bl 33, Cv 2, Cv 3, Cv 4, Cv 5, Cv 6, Sp 6, St 28, and Liv 3 for urinary retention.

Applications:
The same as for Bl 28.

BL 54 (BLADDER POINT NO. 54)

Chinese name:
Zhibian (order's edge).

Location:
Directly below Bl 53, 3 cun lateral to the spinous process of the fourth sacral vertebra. In the gluteus maximus muscle and the inferior margin of the piriformis muscle.

Connections:

None.

Direction of strike:

Straight in to the lower buttocks.

Damage:

If you are able to strike to Bl 54, 30, and 34, there will be a great qi drainage, causing the recipient to fall down. This is a three-point strike, so exercise caution do not play around with this method!

Set-up point:

Neigwan.

Antidote:

Apply light to medium pressure down onto Gv 20 while placing the other palm over the tantien point near Cv 4.

Healing:

Innervation is by the inferior gluteal nerve, the posterior femoral cutaneous nerve, and, lateral to this point, the sciatic nerve. Irrigation is by the inferior gluteal artery and vein.

Used for pain in the lumbosacral region, hemorrhoids, muscular atrophy, motor impairment and pain of the lower extremities, sciatica, disease of the reproductive organs and anus, and strained muscles of buttocks.

Traditional indications include pain in the lumbosacral region, painful urination, genital pain, hemorrhoids, and difficult defecation.

Massage techniques are the same as for Bl 53.

Use with Bl 25, Bl 26, Bl 53, Bl 36, Bl 37, Bl 38, Bl 40, Gb 29, Gb 30, Gb 31, Gb 32, Gb 33, Gb 34, Gb 39, Gb 41, Gb 43, and Gb 44 for sciatica.

Use with Cv 4, Cv 6, Bl 23, Bl 17, Bl 18, Bl 24, Bl 26, Bl 31, Bl 32, Bl 33, Bl 34, Bl 35, Kd 3, Liv 3, Liv 4, Sp 6, Gv 4, and St 36 for disease of the reproductive organs.

See Bl 52 for treatment of lower back pain and stiffness.

Use with Gb 29, Gb 30, Bl 53, Bl 36, Bl 40, Gb 34, Gb 41, Gb 43, and Gb 44 for strained muscles of the buttocks.

Applications:

You could use a palm strike or a knee strike here.

BL 55 (BLADDER POINT NO. 55)

Chinese name:

Heyang (confluence of yang).

Location:

2 cun directly below Bl 40, between the medial and lateral heads of the gastrocnemius, on the line that joins Bl 40 to Bl 57.

Connections:

None.

Direction of strike:

Inward and down slightly just under the back of the knee.

Damage:

This is one of those points that doesn't look like it would do much damage. However, the damage is great. It will cause leg damage from muscle spasm in the whole lower leg, and it will also cause a yang energy surge to the brain, resulting in blackout.

Set-up point:

Lu 5.

Antidote:

Massage the lower leg, including Bl 55, downward.

Figure 238

Healing:

Innervation is by the medial sural cutaneous nerve and, deeper, the tibial nerve. Irrigation is by the small saphenous vein and, deeper, the popliteal artery and vein.

Used for backache; aching, numbness, and paralysis of the lower extremities; abnormal uterine bleeding; and soreness from the lower back to the knee.

For massage, do a straight press and hold; rotate clockwise or counterclockwise for xu or shi conditions; press slowly with both thumbs and release quickly, pulling the thumbs apart; rub across the muscle fibers over the point; or flex the leg and do fingertip percussion on the point.

Use with Bl 25, Bl 26, Bl 53, Bl 54, Bl 36, Bl 37, Bl 38, Bl 39, Bl 40, Bl 56, Bl 57, Bl 58, Bl 60, Bl 63, Bl 65, Bl 66, Bl 67, Gb 34, Gb 35, Gb 36, Gb 37, Gb 38, Gb 39, Gb 41, and Liv 3 for backache; aching, numbness, and paralysis of the lower extremities; and soreness in lower back to knees.

Applications:

You could use a hook kick to Bl 55 with your right heel (or left) after you have blocked his right-hand attack (fig. 238).

BL 56 (BLADDER POINT NO. 56)

Chinese name:

Chengjin (support sinews).

Location:

In the center of the belly of the gastrocnemius, midway between Bl 55 and Bl 57. The gastrocnemius muscle consists of a lateral head, a medial head, and their single tendon of insertion. Each head is a thick muscular column, separated from the other by the back of the knee. As they descend, they come together. The medial head is larger and wraps around the leg more toward the front than does the lateral head. The muscular heads end at or slightly above the middle of the leg, where they attach to their tendon. The tendon descends and fuses with the tendon of the soleus, which lies just beneath it, forming the Achilles' tendon. The gastrocnemius muscle raises the heel, which lifts the body. It also assists, though minimally, in flexing the knee joint.

Connections:

None.

Direction of strike:

Straight in to the calf.

Damage:

As with all of the points on the calf, this point creates a shock to the whole system, thus making it good for getting out of holds, as in a grappling situation, etc. It can be struck with a toe kick straight in to cause great leg damage, especially to the muscles of the lower leg.

Set-up point:

Neigwan. St 9 also works very well with this point.

Antidote:

See a doctor because the damage with this point is purely physical—nerve damage and so on.

Healing:

Innervation: The medial sural cutaneous nerve and, deeper, the tibial nerve. Irrigation is by the small saphenous vein and, deeper, the posterior tibial artery and vein.

This point is used for pain in the leg, hemorrhoids, acute lower back pain, headache, and paralysis of lower limbs.

Massage techniques are the same as for Bl 55.

For headache, use with Gb 12, Gb 20, Gb 21, Th 15, Si 13, Si 3, Bl 10, Bl 11, Bl 12, Bl 13, Bl 41, Bl 42, Bl 43, Bl 17, Bl 18, Bl 19, Bl 40, Bl 55, Bl 57, Bl 58, Bl 59, Bl 60. Bl 62, Bl 63, Bl 64, Bl 65, Bl 66, Bl 67, Liv 3, Gb 34, Gb 41, Gb 43, Gb 44, Gv 20, Co 4, Co 11, Gb 14, yintang, taiyang, and Bl 1.

Use with Bl 23, Bl 25, Bl 26, Bl 52, Bl 53, Bl 54, Bl 40, Bl 55, Bl 57, Bl 58, Gb 29, Gb 30, and Gb 34 for lower backache. See Bl 57 for treatment of hemorrhoids.

Applications:

1) You could be in a grappling situation where he has pinned you. Take one arm across his neck and push into St 9 as your other hand grabs at Bl 56 and squeezes inward violently.

BL 57 (BLADDER POINT NO. 57)

Chinese name:

Chengshan (support mountain).

Location:

If patient lies prone, this point can be found by stretching the foot as if standing on tiptoe. This reveals a triangular shaped hollow in the middle of the calf, about midway between Bl 40 and the heel. The point is at the top of this triangle, at the lower border of the separation of the two bellies of the gastrocnemius muscle.

Connections:

None.

Direction of strike:

Straight in with a slight upward movement.

Damage:

This point, when struck, causes the whole leg to give way under the pressure of the body. It is a great point for when you are in a grappling situation, causing immediate pain with an "unknown factor" (i.e., the brain senses that something bad is happening but cannot quite work out what). So mixed signals go to the brain, causing the recipient to have to let go, etc. A good kick here will take out the leg and cause great lower leg damage. It can also cause anal problems later in life, causing the anus sphincter to become weakened.

Set-up point:

St 9 or neigwan work well with this point.

Antidote:

You should have the same point worked on by a good acupuncturist for the anal problems.

Healing:

Innervation and irrigation are the same as for Bl 56.

Used for lower back pain, spasm of the gastrocnemius, hemorrhoids, constipation, sciatica, paralysis of lower limbs, and prolapsed anus.

Traditional indications include sore throat, leg qi, hemorrhoids, vomiting and diarrhea, twisted muscles of the calf, and pain in lumbar spine.

Traditional functions include relaxing the tendons, invigorating the collaterals, regulating the qi in the yang organs, and treating hemorrhoids.

Massage techniques are the same as for Bl 55.

Use with Bl 20, Bl 30, Gv 1, Bl 56, Bl 35, Bl 34, Bl 33, Bl 32, Bl 30, Bl 53, Bl 54, Bl 25, Bl 26, *erbai* (an extra point), Gv 20, Sp 3, Liv 4, and St 36 for hemorrhoids, prolapsed anus.

Use with Gv 14, Co 11, Co 4, Liv 3, St 43, St 36, Pc 6, Cv 12, Sp 4, Gv 26, Bl 40, Gv 20, Pc 3, Pc 8, Kd 1, Si 3, Gb 34, Kd 7, Lu 9, Cv 6, and all the jing well points for heat exhaustion or sunstroke.

You can rub Pc 8 and up the Pc meridian to Pc 3 with alcohol or methylated spirits, then blow on the area to help cool body.

Use with Bl 25, Bl 26, Bl 52, Bl 53, Bl 54, Bl 40, Gb 29, Gb 30, and Gb 34 for lower back pain or sciatica.

Use with Bl 40, Bl 55, Bl 56, Bl 58, Bl 59, Bl 60, Bl 66, Bl 67, and Gb 34 for spasm of gastrocnemius muscle.

Applications:

Same as for Bl 56.

BL 58 (BLADDER POINT NO. 58)

Chinese name:

Feiyang (soaring flying high).

Location:

7 cun directly above Bl 60, on the posterior border of the fibula, approximately 1 cun inferior and lateral to Bl 57. In the gastrocnemius and soleus muscles.

Connections:

This point is a transverse *luo* (connecting point) point to Kd 3 and Kd 1 points.

Direction of strike:

Straight in to the leg from the side.

Damage:

This point is known as "the shock point" in dim-mak terms. A quick, violent grab or strike here and the recipient is shocked for a few moments while you have time to attack elsewhere. This point is great for grappling or for striking. You must, however, be fairly accurate. The leg will not work after a strike here. Also, the whole balance of yin and yang qi is upset with this strike; it can even cause temporary or permanent insanity when struck hard enough.

Set-up point:

St 9 or any of the other "shock points," such as Gb 25.

Antidote:

The same point is either needled or treated with moxa.

Healing:

Innervation is by the lateral sural cutaneous nerve of the calf. Irrigation is by the small saphenous vein and, deeper, the posterior tibial artery and vein.

Used for headache, blurring of the vision, nasal obstruction, epistaxis, lumbago, weakness of the leg, rheumatoid arthritis, nephritis, cystitis, beriberi, hemorrhoids, seizures, and lower back and leg pain.

Traditional indications include vertigo, nasal congestion, back and head pain, pain and weakness of the lower back and knees, pain in the calf, progressive painful joints, and insanity. It is much used for sciatica when the pain is on the side of the leg, as well as hemorrhoids.

Traditional functions are as a luo connecting point, so can treat back pain, headache, nasal congestion, nosebleed, and clear nasal discharge.

Massage techniques are the same as for Bl 55. These points in the calf muscle can also be treated with a straight push using the heel of the palm, while the other hand is placed on the shin and pulls up against the downward pressure of the pressing hand. The foot should be extended for this type of movement.

Use with Bl 52, Bl 23, Bl 24, Bl 25, Bl 26, Bl 53, Bl 54, Bl 40, Bl 62, Bl 63, Bl 64, Bl 64, and

Gb 34 for lower backache; add Bl 57, Bl 56, and Bl 55 for accompanying calf pain.

Use with Bl 1, Bl 65, Bl 60, Liv 3, Liv 14, St 1, Gb 1, T 23, and Kd 5 for blurring of vision.

Use with Cv 2, Cv 3, Cv 4, Cv 5, Cv 9, St 28, Bl 28, Sp 9, Kd 4, Kd 6, and Bl 23 for nephritis and cystitis.

Applications:

You could p'eng to his right straight using your right forearm, then get around behind for a toe kick straight in to the point. Or you could apply violent pressure as in a grappling situation.

BL 59 (BLADDER POINT NO. 59)

Chinese name:

Fuyang (tarsal yang).

Location:

3 cun directly above Bl 60 on the lateral aspect of the gastrocnemius muscle.

Connections:

Connection to the yang qiao mai meridian.

Direction of strike:

In from the side of the lower leg.

Damage:

This is an accumulation point (xie cleft). Apart from immediate physical damage to the lower leg, which will finish the fight, it has an effect upon the head and will cause headaches, eye damage, and a fullness of the head, resulting in blackout if struck hard.

Set-up point:

You could use Gb 31 straight in and then go straight down to Bl 59 with a double type of kick.

Antidote:

For the head type of damage, which will be longer lasting than the physical damage, see an acupuncturist.

Healing:

This point is innervated by the sural nerve and irrigated by the small saphenous vein and, deeper, the terminal branch of the peroneal artery.

Used for a heavy feeling in the head, headache, lower back pain, redness and swelling of the external malleolus, and paralysis of the lower extremities.

As a xie cleft point of the yang qiao mai and a point of intersection between the yang qiao and bladder meridians, its traditional functions include treating disease of the eye, tightness and spasm of muscles of the lateral aspect of the lower leg when those on the medial aspect are flaccid or atrophied (e.g., as in seizure or paralysis), and treating pain and stiffness of the lumbar region.

Massage techniques are the same as for Bl 58.

See Bl 57 for treatment of spasm in gastrocnemius.

Use with Gv 20, Gb 20, Gv 14, Bl 58, Bl 60, Liv 3, and Co 4 for heaviness of the head.

Use with Bl 60, Bl 61, Gb 34, Gb 40, Bl 67, Bl 66, Gb 43, Gb 44, and Gb 39 for redness, pain, and swelling of the exterior malleus.

Applications:

Same as for Bl 58.

BL 60 (BLADDER POINT NO. 60)

Chinese name:

Kunlun (Kunlun Mountains).

Location:

In the depression midway between the lateral malleolus and the Achilles' tendon, in the peroneus brevis muscle.

Connections:

None.

Direction of strike:

Usually a stomp straight down onto the ankle.

Damage:

This point is interesting because it has an effect upon the "power band" between the shoulder blades. A strike here will cause nervous disorders and an immediate weakening of the upper body. The arms just don't do what you want them to do. This is a "fire and jing" point so, traditionally, it will help balance out fire and water in the body. However, when struck using negative qi, this point will cause an imbalance in the whole body with extreme local pain, followed by an energy drainage causing the recipient to not be able to carry on with the fight.

Set-up point:

Sp 17 is an excellent point to use with this strike.

Antidote:

Massage up the length of the back of the leg with deep penetration.

Healing:

Innervation is by the sural nerve and irrigated by the lessor saphenous vein and the lateral posterior malleolar artery and vein.

Used for headache; neck rigidity; spasm and pain of upper back, neck, shoulders, and arm; blurred vision; epistaxis; pain in the heel; epilepsy in children; difficult labor; goiter; lower back pain; sciatica; paralysis of lower limbs; and disease of the ankle joint and surrounding tissue.

Traditional indications include headache and stiffness of the cervical vertebra, tidal fever, pain of lower back and buttocks, difficulty in childbirth, retained placenta, and infantile fright.

Traditional functions are to eliminate wind, remove obstructions from the collaterals, relax the tendons, and strengthen the waist As a fire point and a jing river point (transversing point) of the bladder meridian, it can cool heat and bring down fire.

To massage, use a straight press and hold, rotate the foot while pinching Bl 60 and Kd 3 together for ankle problems, press and rotate clockwise or counterclockwise for xu or shi conditions, or do percussion with one finger on this point.

Use with Gb 39, Gb 40, Gb 41, Gb 43, Gb 44, Bl 61, Bl 62, Bl 63, Bl 66, Bl 67, Gb 34, Bl 57, and Bl 58 for pain in the external malleus.

Use with Gb 20, Bl 10, Gb 21, Th 15, Si 13. Bl 11, Bl 12, Bl 13, Bl 17, Gb 34, and Si 3 for neck and shoulder spasm and stiffness, headache.

Use with Kd 3, Co 5, Pc 7, Bl 1, Si 3, Gb 1, Gb 16, Gb 43, Gb 44, Liv 2, Liv 3, Liv 14, St 1, and Th 23 for red eyes.

Applications:

A kick or stomp to the point is sufficient, or you could set it all up by attacking to Sp 17 first.

BL 61 (BLADDER POINT NO. 61)

Chinese name:

Pushen (serve and consult).

Location:

Posterior and inferior to the external malleus, directly below Bl 60 in the depression of the calcaneum at the junction of the red and white skin. Just above the heel on the outside of the foot.

Connections:

Yang qiao mai

Direction of strike:

Straight down just under the ankle on the side of the heel.

Damage:

The point is also an energy drainage point and will cause great local pain as well as qi drainage, forcing the recipient to sit down.

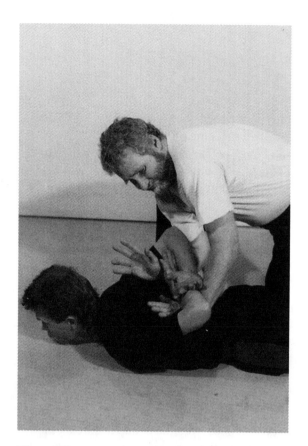

Figure 239

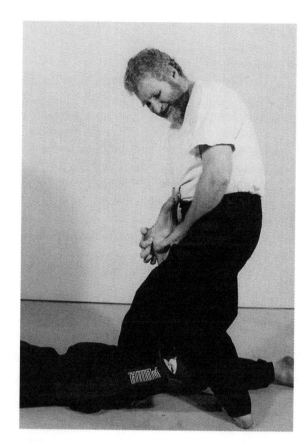

Figure 240

Set-up point:

Neigwan or Sp 17.

Antidote:

To bring the qi back, lie the patient on his belly and lock both arms around behind him in a double hammer lock. Now apply pressure upward, as if trying to apply the hammer locks (fig. 239).

Healing:

Innervation is by the external calcaneal branch of the sural nerve. Irrigation is by the external calcaneal branches of the peroneal artery and vein.

Used for lower back pain, pain in ankle and foot, paralysis of lower limbs, beriberi, and pain in the heel.

As a point of intersection with the yang qiao mai, its traditional function is to influence that channel.

To massage use a straight press with the thumb or knuckle and hold, rotate clockwise or counterclockwise for xu or shi conditions, or you can do fingertip percussion on the point. This point is also a good one to moxa for heel strike (inflammation of the bursa in this region). Use it with press and hold or rotation plus moxa in conjunction with Bl 60, Bl 59, Bl 58, Bl 57, Bl 56, Bl 55, Bl 40, Gb 34, Kd 3, Kd 4, Kd 5, Kd 6, Bl 66, and Bl 67 for heel strike or inflammation of the heel bursa, heel spur, etc.

Use with Gb 29, St 36, Sp 6, Gb 39, Sp 4, St 42, Liv 3, and Kd 6 for leg qi (edema of the leg), aka beriberi.

Applications:

If you should be the aggressor and are perhaps trying to apply some kind of leg lock, you could apply a strike to Bl 61 to lessen his resistance to the lock so that you are able to take the lock fully (fig. 240).

BL 62 (BLADDER POINT NO. 62)

Chinese name:

Shenmai (extending/expressing vessel).

Location:

In the depression at the inferior margin of the lateral malleus of the ankle.

Connections:

Yang qiao mai.

Direction of strike:

Pressure straight in just under the ankle bone and slightly forward.

Damage:

All of the foot points are very painful and, as such, drain qi, but none so much as this one. This is also one of those bladder points that acts upon the shen. So a strike by way of a stomp or kick will affect the way the recipient communicates with his spirit. It will also cause tendon and nerve damage, and it may even cause mental illness and "sleep/wakening" disorders. This is the "master point" for the yang qiao mai channel, which is the one that accelerates the yang energy. This channel will be affected adversely, causing great anger, red face, and so on, as a result of too much yang qi getting to the head. This is what will cause the mental disorders and such.

Set-up point:

A strike upward to Gb 14 will have a doubling effect for this strike.

Antidote:

Drain the yang qi from the head by pressing downward to the Gb 21 points (strike them) and then brushing off the shoulders violently.

Healing:

Innervation is by the sural nerve, and irrigation is by the external malleolar arterial network.

Used for mental confusion, epilepsy, headache, dizziness, insomnia, backache, aching of lower extremities, meningitis, Ménière's disease, psychosis, and arthritis of the ankle.

Traditional indications are lateral and midline headache, dizziness, tinnitus, palpitations, loss of speech due to stroke, hemiplegia, mouth and eyes awry, and insanity.

Traditional functions, as a confluent (master) point of the yin qiao mai, are to clear the mind, relax the tendons, invigorate the channels, and clear obstruction from the yin qiao mai. When used with Si 3 to activate yin qiao, it will treat disease of the inner canthus of eye, neck, ear, shoulder, small intestine, and bladder.

To massage, press and hold, do rotation clockwise or counterclockwise for xu or shi conditions, or do fingertip percussion.

Use with Th 17, Si 19, Th 21, Gb 2, Gb 12, Gb 20, Gb 7, Gb 8, Gb 9, Gb 10, Gb 11, Si 3, Th 3, Th 5, Th 6, anmien, Liv 3, and Kd 3 for tinnitus or Ménière's disease (you might add Gv 20 for the latter problem).

Use with Gb 20, Bl 2, Gb 1, Co 4, Liv 3, Kd 3, Sp 6, Bl 18, Bl 63, Liv 2, St 36, St 1, and the extra point *qiuhou* for early stages of glaucoma.

Use with Gv 14, Gb 20, Cv 17, Cv 15, Cv 13, Pc 5, Pc 6, Th 6, St 40, Gb 43, Gb 44, Liv 2, Liv 3, Kd 3, Pc 8, St 25, Liv 4, Co 4, Lu 7, Si 3, Ht 7, and Pc 3 for psychosis.

Applications:

Again, this point can be used in a grappling situation where you are pinned, etc. Or you could simply kick to the point to cause him to become so angry with yang head qi that a very light strike upward onto Gb 14 will cause him to fall down.

BL 63 (BLADDER POINT NO. 63)

Chinese name:

Jinmen (golden door).

Location:

Anterior and inferior to Bl 62, in the depression lateral to the cuboid bone.

Connections:

Yang wei mai.

Direction of strike:

Stomp to the side of the foot just under that big tendon running down the side of the foot to the toes.

Damage:

This is another xie cleft point. A strike here will cause mental illness, although not to the extent that Bl 62 will. It is not a good point for self-defense, since it has to be fairly accurate and doesn't cause that much local pain, relatively speaking. It also has an effect upon the wei qi, which protects the body from pathogenic attack, etc.

Set-up point:

Neigwan.

Antidote:

Needle Bl 62 or use finger pressure.

Healing:

Innervation is by the lateral dorsal cutaneous nerve of the foot and, deeper, the lateral planter nerve. Irrigation is by the lateral planter artery and vein.

Used for epilepsy, infantile convulsions, backache, pain in the external malleolus, paralysis of lower extremities, and pain at the bottom of the foot.

Traditional functions include influencing the yang wei mai channel since it begins at this point. Also, as a xie cleft point of the bladder meridian, it treats acute problems of both the channel and organ.

Massage is the same as for Bl 62.

Use with Bl 28, Bl 25, Bl 23, Cv 2, Cv 3, Cv 4, Cv 5, St 28, Sp 6, Liv 3, Bl 66, and Bl 67 for acute bladder infection.

Use with Gv 16, Gb 20, Gv 26, Gv 14, Bl 62, Kd 6, Pc 6, Pc 5, Ht 7, Ht 5, Co 4, Liv 3, Sp 6, Gb 34, Cv 14, Cv 12, St 40, Gv 24, and Sp 4 for epilepsy.

Use with Gb 34, Gb 39, Bl 60, Gb 40, Bl 62, Bl 66, Bl 67, Bl 65, Bl 57, and Bl 40 for paralysis of lower extremities.

Applications:

The same as for Bl 62.

BL 64 (BLADDER POINT NO. 64)

Chinese name:

Jinggu (capital bone).

Location:

On the lateral side of the dorsum of the foot, below the tuberosity of the fifth metatarsal bone, at the junction of the red and white skin, at the inferior margin of the lateral abductor digiti minimi pedis.

Connections:

Takes transverse luo from Kd 4.

Direction of strike:

Straight down onto the side of the foot.

Damage:

This is a *yuan* (or ancestral or source) point. It is normally used to calm the shen, but when attacked with negative qi, it will again affect the way the recipient communicates with the spirit. It will cause the recipient to feel quite weak from kidney damage.

Set-up point:

Neigwan or Lu 5.

Antidote:

Have an acupuncturist needle or use moxa or pressure on the same point on the other foot (the one that is not damaged from the stomp).

Healing:

Innervation and irrigation are the same as for Bl 63.

Used for epilepsy, headache, neck stiffness and pain, pain in the lower back and knees, myocarditis, and meningitis. Traditional indications include membrane over the eye, heaviness in the head and cold in the legs, stiff neck, palpitations, seizures, insanity, and tidal fever.

Traditional functions are to disperse wind, calm the spirit, and clear the brain. As a yuan source point of the bladder meridian, it can strongly tonify the qi of this organ.

To massage, press and hold the point, or you can use a thumb or knuckle or squeeze the point between the thumb and the fingers by clasping the whole foot, rotate clockwise or counterclockwise for xu or shi conditions, and do percussion with the fingertips or open hand using the ulnar side of the hand.

Use with Gb 29, Gb 30, Gb 31, Gb 32, Gb 33, Gb 34, Gb 35, Gb 36, Gb 7, Gb 38, Gb 39, Gb 41, Bl 25, Bl 26, Bl 53, Bl 54, Bl 37, Bl 38, Bl 39, Bl 40, Bl 57, St 40, St 41, Liv 3, St 36, Bl 60, and Ht 7 for CVA affecting the leg or for lower back pain that extends into the leg.

For neck stiffness, use with Gb 20, Bl 10, Gb 21, Th 15, Si 13, Si 3, Bl 11, Bl 12, Bl 13, Bl 17, Bl 43, Bl 18, dingchuan, Gb 39, Si 14, Gv 14, Bl 60, and Gb 34.

Applications:

None.

BL 65 (BLADDER POINT NO. 65)

Chinese name:

Shugu (restraining bone).

Location:

On the lateral side of the dorsum of the foot, posterior and inferior to the head of the fifth metatarsal bone, at the junction of the red and white skin.

Connections:

None.

Direction of strike:

Stomp straight down onto the side of the foot.

Damage:

This is a wood and shu point. A strike here will cause mental confusion, blurred vision, and, in the long run, continuous headaches. The eyes will slowly become worse. It will also have an adverse effect upon the wei qi.

Set-up point:

Gb 41, so you would stomp onto the foot twice.

Antidote:

Apply pressure to Gb 41 and Bl 65 simultaneously.

Healing:

Innervation is by the fourth common planter digital nerve and the lateral dorsal cutaneous nerve of the foot. Irrigation is by the fourth common planter digital artery and vein.

Used for headache, stiffness of the neck, malaria, seizures, mental illness, pannus that might present as blurring of vision, backache, and pain in the posterior aspect of the lower extremities.

As a shu stream point and a wood point of the bladder meridian, its traditional function is to treat damp problems, e.g., bi syndrome (arthritis).

Massage techniques are the same as for Bl 64.

Use with Gb 20, Bl 10, Gb 21, Th 15, Si 13, Si 14, Si 3, and Gb 34 for occipital headache.

Use with Pc 5, Pc 6, Co 11, Gv 13. Si 3, Gb 34, Sp 9, Co 4, Lu 7, Gb 20, and Liv 3 for malaria.

Use with Bl 25, Bl 26, Bl 53, Bl 54, Bl 40, Bl 57, Gb 29, Gb 30, and Gb 34 for lower back pain and stiffness.

Applications:

Obvious—just stomp on the foot.

BL 66 (BLADDER POINT NO. 66)

Chinese name:

Zutonggu (connecting valley of the foot).

Location:

In the depression anterior and inferior to the fifth metatarsal phalangeal joint.

Connections:

None.

Direction of strike:

Straight down onto the side of the little toe at the web.

Damage:

This is a water and yong point (spring or stream point), so it is a good set-up point. It will also cause blurred vision and headaches later.

Set-up point:

An attack to St 3 with two fingers will suffice here.

Antidote:

Same as for Bl 65.

Healing:

Innervation is by the planter digital proprial nerve and the lateral dorsal cutaneous nerve of the foot. Irrigation is by the plantar digital artery and vein.

Used for headache, neck rigidity, blurring of the vision (pannus), epistaxis, malaria, mental illness, and seizures.

As a water point and yong spring (gushing) point of the bladder meridian, its traditional function is to cool heat in either the channel or the organ. This point is often used with jing well point to shut pathogens out of the channel. It can also be used to accelerate qi in the channel, so it can be a good pep-up point.

To massage, squeeze between the thumb and the rest of the hand as you clasp the whole foot, press with the thumb or knuckle and hold, rotate clockwise or counterclockwise for xu or shi conditions, or strike the point with the fingertip or the ulnar side of the hand.

Use with Sp 5, Kd 21, Pc 6, Cv 12, St 36, and Liv 3 for predilection toward vomiting.

Use with Bl 2, Th 10, Ht 3, Ht 7, Bl 63, Sp 5, Liv 2, Bl 15, Si 3, Liv 3, Gb 34, Kd 3, and St 40 for seizures.

For back stiffness and pain, use with Bl 67, bladder points in the affected area, and Gb 34.

Applications:

Obvious.

BL 67 (BLADDER POINT NO. 67)

Chinese name:

Zhiyin (end of yin).

Location:

On the lateral side of the little toe, about 0.1 cun posterior to the lateral corner of the toenail.

Connections:

Takes transverse luo from Kd 4.

Direction of strike:

Stomp straight down onto the little toe in the nail area.

Damage:

This is a metal and cheng point and the root point of the extra meridian taiyang. It will have an adverse effect upon the muscles and tendons in the whole body and cause mental confusion as well as blurred vision. This point will have an adverse effect upon the fetus if the recipient is pregnant. It will also have an adverse effect upon the kidneys, causing weakness in the whole body.

Set-up point:

Any "wood or fire" element point is an excellent set-up point here.

Antidote:

Kd 1 pressed upward or Th 12.

Healing:

Innervation is by the planter digital proprial nerve and the lateral dorsal cutaneous nerve of the foot. Irrigation is by the network formed by the dorsal digital artery and planter digital artery.

Used for headache, nasal obstruction, epistaxis, ophthalmoplegia, feverish sensation in the sole of the foot, malposition of the fetus, difficult labor, and stroke.

Traditional indications include occipital headache, membrane and pain over the eye, nosebleed, clear nasal discharge, itching over the entire body, infantile convulsions, failure to discharge the placenta, and difficult labor.

As a jing well point and a metal point of the bladder meridian, one of its traditional functions is to control the superficial aspects of the body in order to quickly reduce shi conditions from the bladder channel and collaterals (e.g., swelling pain caused by trauma to the tendons or muscles). It would be best used in this situation as soon after the incident as is possible. It is also traditionally used to clear the mind, brighten the eyes, correct malposition of fetus, and regulate pregnancy and childbirth. Prick and bleed for trauma to the channel, but *not during pregnancy*. Probably best handled with extreme care during pregnancy.

Massage techniques are the same as for Bl 66, except that the striking method would not work on this point.

Use with Gb 10, Gb 20, Gb 21, Gv 14, *taiyang*, Bl 66, Co 4, Liv 3, Th 15, Si 13, and Si 14 for occipital headache. Use with Gb 20, Liv 3, Th 17, Si 19, Pc 6, Kd 3, Cv 12, Gb 16, Bl 8, Gv 20, Bl 62, and anmien, for head-spinning type of vertigo.

Use with Gb 21, Sp 6, Co 4, Gb 34, Bl 31, and Bl 32 for difficult labor.

Applications:

Obvious.

As you can see, the bladder points affect the shen greatly. Be careful with these points because they, more so than any of the other points, can cause long-lasting physical, mental, and spiritual damage.

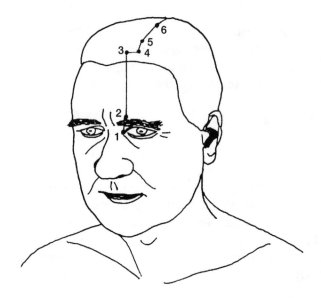

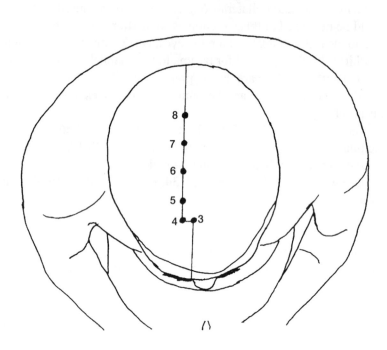

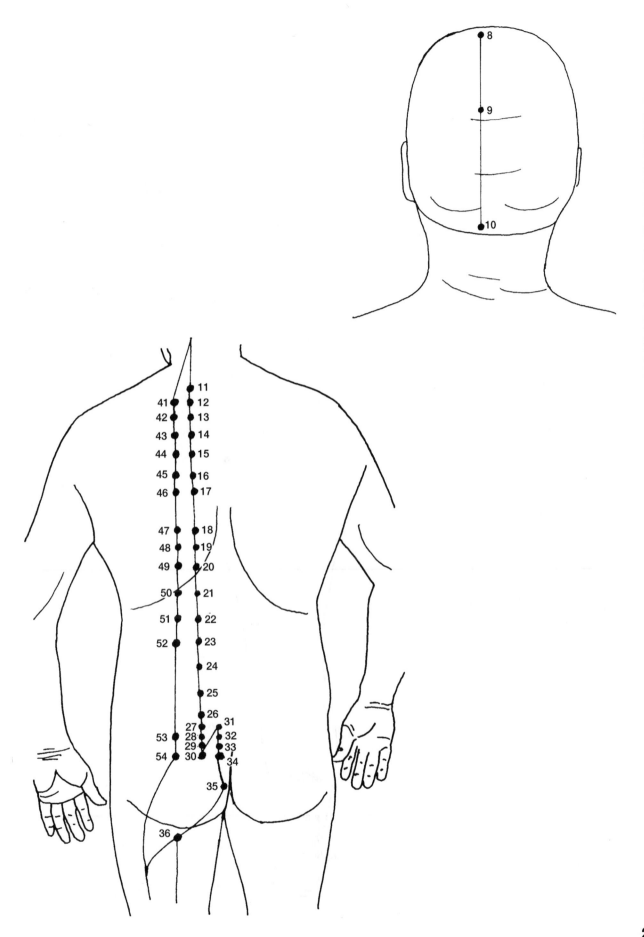

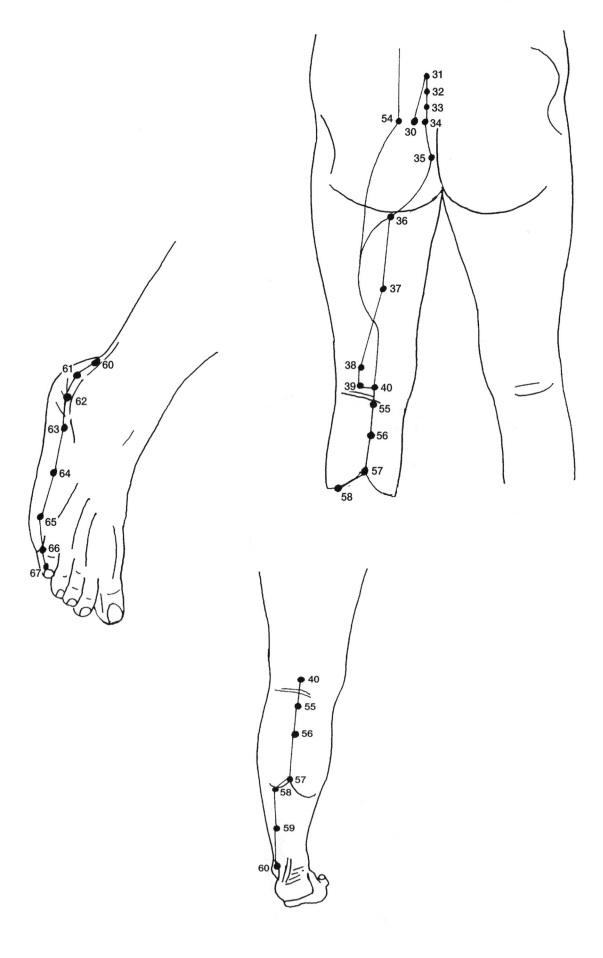

Chapter 4

The Kidney Meridian

The kidneys are responsible for filtering toxins, wastes, ingested water, and mineral salts out of the bloodstream. Kidneys are also responsible for regulating the acidity of the blood by excreting alkaline salts when necessary.

THE TCM VIEW

The kidneys are yin organs and are the "controllers of water distribution." Their opposite yang organ is the bladder, and their element is water. According to traditional Chinese medicine, their functions are as follows:

- To store jing and dominate reproduction, growth, and development
- To produce marrow, fill up the brain, dominate the bones, and manufacture blood
- To dominate water
- To control the reception of qi
- To opens the ear

Kidneys store jing in two forms—that which was given to us at birth (prenatal jing), and the "outside" jing that we gain from things like food, water, air, sun, earth, and so on. Jing is a purified or condensed form of qi. It's a little like having a bowl of water (qi) that you can do nothing with until you apply heat, which turns the water into steam (jing), which will enable you to run a steam engine, for instance. We are given a set amount of prenatal qi at birth, and that's our lot. We are given eight "lots" of qi, but as we grow older and perhaps do the wrong things, as humans do, our stored qi is depleted. By puberty, it is said that we have depleted about two to three lots, and by very old age, we finally use up the eighth lot and die.

There are certain things that we can do to hold off this natural depletion, however, such as practicing taijiquan and meditation, eating the right foods (those that were originally given to us to eat), drinking only pure water and breathing pure air, and, most important, thinking only good or pure thoughts. Impossible, you might say. Well, yes, but we can at least get some of it right and stave off the inevitable depletion of our last lot of jing. There are some masters who also believe, as I do, that we can give a little outside jing back to the "inside" or prenatal jing by doing all of these things.

Since the kidneys control the production and use of jing, it is very important that they are well kept. In fact, it is my belief that one can sort of "get by" with other organs that are not so healthy, but you just cannot get by with unhealthy kidneys, as in the case of diabetes.

In traditional Chinese medicine, the kidneys produce "marrow." But this marrow is unlike Western medicine's idea of marrow: it is the stuff that precedes either marrow or bone and is the common matrix of both. It is also the matrix of both brain and spinal cord.

The brain and spinal cord are called the "sea of marrow" in TCM. This means that kidney jing nourishes the brain and spinal cord. This brings good memory, clear vision, and clear thinking. If we are deficient in kidney jing, then we are dull and have dizziness, blurred vision, poor memory, tinnitus, and insomnia. Other organs also have these symptoms. For instance, "heart blood deficiency" will also cause insomnia, but it is a different type of insomnia. It keeps you awake all the time, whereas the kind caused by kidney deficiency will allow you only to take naps during the night. Many people with kidney disease have to urinate many times during the night, and, of course, this keeps them awake.

The kidneys also control the bones, so if you have good, strong kidneys, then your bones, particularly in the lower back and knees, are strong and healthy. The reciprocal occurs when the kidneys are not strong and producing strong kidney jing. This is also why people with kidney diseases are weak in the knees, legs, and lower back. Sexual function is also impaired or destroyed when the kidneys are not good. (The desire is there, but the penis will not become erect no matter how hard one tries!)

The kidneys also control the ears, which are the "opening" of the kidneys. This explains why many of us become short of hearing when we are old, because kidney jing has been depleted.

To help ailing kidneys and, therefore, ailing kidney jing, one must go back as close to scratch as possible. First, stop eating. Next, eat only fruit when you wish to begin eating again. Do not eat any form of salt, and drink pure water. You will be amazed at how quickly the kidneys can recuperate, given the help they need. From then on all of the other organs that were ailing because of the poor kidneys will begin to revitalize, and a new life will begin.

The kidneys are the home of *ming men*, or the door of life. All vital functions are under the control of ming men. Ming men can be called an external function of the kidneys. Ming men is called "primary yang" or "true fire," so although the kidneys are water in nature, they also house the strongest "fire" in the body, ming men. A decline in the fire of ming men can manifest in many ways. In males, it causes a withering of yang, cold jing, and impotence. In females it causes the uterus to become cold and weak, as well as bringing on leukorrhea and/or infertility. A lessening of the fire in ming men may also impair the digestive function of the stomach and spleen, causing an inability to absorb food and, as a result, diarrhea.

KD 1 (KIDNEY POINT NO. 1)

Chinese name:

Yongquan (gushing spring).

Location:

In the depression appearing on the sole of the foot when the foot is in plantar flexion. If you divide the sole into thirds from the base of the second toe to the heel, it is approximately at the junction of the anterior and middle third. The point is between the second and third metatarsal bones in the aponeurosis of the sole. Medial to it are the tendons of the flexor digitorum pedis, longus, and brevis, and the second lubricalis pedis muscle. In its deep position, the point lies in the interossei plantares muscle.

Connections:

Takes transverse luo from Bl 58 and internal meridian pathway from Bl 67.

Direction of strike:

Kd 1 would be a good place to strike if it weren't under the foot! So we do not regard it as a dim-mak point, but as a healing point only, especially in the area of antidote and revival. Even if one were able to get at Kd 1 to strike it, the amount of pressure needed is great. This point is sometimes bled to effect a revival from death.

Damage:

Since I have never been taught that Kd 1 is a dim-mak point, I will not cover any damage that a strike here might cause. However, as an emergency point, its powers are great. It releases stored qi to the body, thus bringing about a kind of kick-start. If, for instance, a person has been struck or has been in a car accident and CPR is not working to revive him, it is probably because the trauma to the system has been so great that it has drained the body's qi, leaving none available to start the heart and respiratory functions. Kd 1 is like having an extra battery in your car when the main one has failed. You can access stored qi by applying a very hard one-knuckle punch to Kd 1 or by sticking something sharp into the point, causing it to bleed. Then go back and try the CPR. There have been instances where this method has worked in starting the heart, only to have the patient die later because the trauma was just too great. One of my students, a surgeon, has even used this method in surgery. When all efforts had failed to revive a patient, he rushed around to the patient's foot and stuck his scalpel up into Kd 1, starting the heart! He was written up in medical journals for this.

Set-up point:

None.

Antidote:

This *is* an antidote point.

Healing:

Innervation is by the second common plantar digital nerve. Irrigation is by the anastomosis of the lateral planter and anterior tibial arteries in the plantar arch.

Used for headache at the vertex, dizziness, blurring of the vision, sore throat, dryness of the tongue, aphonia (loss of voice), dysuria, dyschezia, infantile convulsion, feverish sensation in the sole of the foot, loss of consciousness, shock, heat exhaustion, insomnia, stroke, hypertension, psychosis, mental illness, seizures, and paralysis of the lower limbs.

Traditional indications include vertigo, headache at the vertex, blurred vision, swollen throat, dry tongue, nosebleed, difficult urination and defecation, diarrhea, colic, edema, infantile convulsions, insanity, hot soles of the feet, and pain at the tip of the toes.

Kd1 is a jing well point and a wood and cheng point point of the kidney meridian. Its traditional functions are to bring down qi and drain shi conditions, tonify yin, pacify fire, tranquilize the mind, calm the heart, open the sensory orifices, and render the effects of resuscitation when bled as an emergency point.

To massage, press with the fingers, thumb, and elbow and hold; rotate clockwise or counterclockwise for xu or shi conditions, or do percussion with fingertips or a loose fist. You can also lie patient prone on a soft but firm surface and stand on this point with your heels or the ball of your foot.

Use with moxibustion (the procedure of burning moxa) for insomnia, and you could also press Ht 7 (*shenmen*) on the wrist and Pc 6.

Use with Liv 3, St 36, Gb 20, Co 11, Liv 2, Ht 7, Pc 6, Th 17, Sp 6, Gb 34, Cv 4, Cv 6, St 40, Gv 14, taiyang, Bl 14, Bl 17, Bl 18, Bl 20, and Bl 23 for hypertension.

Use with Liv 3, St 36, Gv 20, Gb 20, Th 17, Pc 6, Co 4, Kd 3, Liv 14, and Liv 2 for vertigo.

Prick and bleed as an emergency point when other emergency procedures don't seem to be working, and press on Liv 3 and Gv 26 as well.

This point can be very effective for any condition where qi seems to be trapped in the upper heater.

Applications:

None.

KD 2 (KIDNEY POINT NO. 2)

Chinese name

Rangu (burning valley). 然谷

Location:

Anterior and inferior to the medial malleolus, in the depression on the lower border of the tuberosity of the navicular bone, anterior and inferior to the joint of the navicular, in the abductor hallucis muscle.

Connections:

None.

Direction of strike:

Usually a kick in to the side of the foot. The strike is not generally done straight down on top of the point.

Damage:

This is a fire and yong point. All such stream or spring points cause great damage to the rest of the body. Apart from local pain, a strike here could cause instant diarrhea, so make sure you are in front of the recipient! Being the fire point of the water channel, it usually creates a balance of yin and yang in the system. However, a strike using adverse qi will cause the reciprocal effect, creating confusion and adverse energy states that will allow disease to enter the body. A strike here will weaken kidney yang, which will weaken the whole system.

Set-up point:

A strike to Kd 10, the water point just behind the knee, will enhance the effect of this strike. In fact, it will cause it to become very dangerous!

Antidote:

Have an acupuncturist needle Kd 3 in conjunction with Kd 2.

Healing:

Innervation is by the terminal branch of the medial crural cutaneous nerve, by the medial plantar nerve, and by a medial cutaneous branch of the saphenous nerve of the calf. Irrigation is by the branches of the medial plantar and medial tarsal arteries and veins.

Used for pruritis vulvae, prolapse of the uterus, irregular menstruation, seminal emission, hemoptysis, diarrhea, swelling and pain in the dorsum of the foot, diabetes, tetanus, pharyngitis, and cystitis.

Figure 241

Traditional indications include congested throat, thirst and emaciation, jaundice, diarrhea with intestinal pain and noises, tidal fever, sterility in women, itching of the genital region, prolapsed uterus, and irregular menstruation.

As a yong spring (gushing) point and a fire point of the kidney channel, its traditional functions include reducing or tonifying qi, pacifying fire, strengthening the yin qiao mai meridian, and eliminating heat to cool the blood.

To massage, clasp hand over the dorsum of the foot and squeeze the thumb into Kd 2. You can also press straight into the point and hold, rotate clockwise or counterclockwise for xu or shi conditions, or do percussion with the fingertips or the ulnar side of the hand on the point.

Use with Kd 4, Kd 5, Kd 6, Kd 1, Bl 57, Bl 58, Liv 3, Sp 3, Sp 4, Gb 34, Bl 60, Bl 61, Bl 62, and Bl 63 for pain in the heel.

Use with Si 17, St 12, Bl 11, Bl 17, Lu 2, Lu 5, Liv 2, St 45, Co 1, Co 4, Lu 7, Co 11, Co 10, Lu 6, St 36, St 40, Gb 20, and Bl 12 for congested throat that feels blocked as a result of tonsillitis.

Use with Kd 3 Bl 23, Gv 4, Liv 3, Sp 6, Liv 5, Ht 7, CV 4, Cv 6, Gb 25, Gv 20, Si 5, and St 36 for impotence.

Use with Liv 2, Liv 3, Gb 31, Ht 7, Cv 4, Cv 6, Sp 9, Sp 6, Gb 43, and Gb 44 for itching of the genital region.

Applications:

He might attack with a straight right. You should block this using perhaps a strike to neigwan with your left palm and a strike to the middle of his biceps with your right knife edge. Immediately, your right instep kicks around behind the knee toward the inside of his leg (fig. 241). Now, withdraw that right foot and kick in from the side to Kd 2 with the toe of the right foot.

KD 3 (KIDNEY POINT NO. 3)

Chinese name:

Taixi (great creek/bigger stream). 太溪

Location:

In the depression between the medial malleolus and the tendo calcaneus, level with the tip of the medial malleolus. Above the ankle and just in from the Achilles' tendon.

Connections:

Takes transverse luo from Bl 58.

Direction of strike:

Straight in from the rear of the Achilles tendon to the inside of the foot, in toward the ankle bone. So the strike must come from the rear to the front.

Damage:

Extreme local pain, with the immediate effect of qi drainage and blackout if it is a hard strike. A hard strike here along with one to Kd 10 will cause the legs in particular to become weak. It will also weaken kidney jing and thus weaken the whole body in the long term, causing disease later in life. This strike will also damage the kidneys' function of capturing qi and storing it for emergency use.

Set-up point:

Kd 10.

Antidote:

The same point, Kd 3, on the other leg should be pressured or needled by a qualified acupuncturist. This will strengthen the zhang, or yin, and restore kidney qi and kidney yin, which will, in turn, cause all of the fluids in the body to flow correctly.

Healing:

This is one of the most frequently used healing kidney points. Innervation is by the medial crural cutaneous nerve; the point is on the course of the tibial nerve. Irrigation occurs anteriorly by the posterior tibial artery and vein.

Used for sore throat, toothache, deafness, hemoptysis, asthma, irregular menstruation, insomnia, seminal emission, impotence, frequency of micturition, pain in the lower back, nephritis, cystitis. spermatorrhea, tinnitus, alopecia, emphysema, neurasthenia, paralysis of lower limb (upturned foot), pain in the sole of the foot, and chronic laryngitis.

Traditional indications include throat blockage, toothache, asthmatic wheezing, abscessed breast, thirst and emaciation, dark urine, irregular menstruation, impotence, nocturnal emissions, lumbar vertebral pain, and constipation.

As an earth point, a shu stream point and a yuan source point of the kidney meridian, its traditional functions are to tonify kidney qi; pacify empty fire; promote the function of the uterus; strengthen the waist, back, and knees; and, most often, to strengthen the kidney function.

Massage techniques include pinching the Bl 60 and Kd 3 point (put more emphasis on Kd 3) holding and rotating the foot, pressing straight in to the point and holding, rotating clockwise or counterclockwise for xu or shi conditions, or doing fingertip percussion on this point.

Use with Liv 3, Liv 2, Si 19, Gb 2, Th 21, Gb 20, anmien, Th 17, Th 3, St 40, Bl 23, Cv 12, Sp 3, Co 4, Co 10, St 7, Gv 20, St 16, and Liv 14 for tinnitus

Use with Cv 4, Cv 6, Cv 12, Bl 23, Bl 20, Bl 18, Sp 6, Liv 3, St 36, Ht 7, Liv 5, Gv 4, Gv 20, Bl 17, and Gb 25 for impotence.

Use with Cv 22, Bl 12, Bl 13, Bl 43, Bl 17, Bl 18, Bl 20, Bl 23, dingchuan, Co 18, Lu 1, Lu 5, Lu 7, Co 4, Co 10, St 36, Liv 14, Liv 13, Liv 3, Gb 24, and Gb 25 for asthma and wheezing.

For toothache, use with Co 4, St 5, St 6, St 7, St 2, St 44, and Bl 11.

Applications:

Again, begin with a kick to the back of his knee at Kd 10, then kick down using the toe into Kd 3 (fig. 242).

KD 4 (KIDNEY POINT NO. 4)

Chinese name:

Dazhong (big goblet). 大鐘

Location:

Posterior and inferior to the medial malleolus, in the depression medial to the attachment of the tendo-calcaneus. Below Kd 3 and a little closer to the Achilles' tendon.

Connections:

Transverse luo to Bl 64 and Bl 67.

Direction of strike:

Same as for Bl 3.

Damage:

This point, when struck, will impede the flow of yang qi throughout the system, causing great weakness instantly. It creates a feeling of fullness to the point of exploding in the head.

Set-up point:

Neigwan.

Antidote:

Pressure to St 36 along with Kd 4 on the opposite leg.

Healing:

Innervation is by the medial crural cutaneous nerve; the point is on the pathway of the medial calcaneal ramus, derived from the tibial nerve. Irrigation is by the medial calcaneal branch of the posterior tibial artery.

Used for hemoptysis, asthma, pain and stiffness of the lumbo-sacral region, dysuria, pain in the heel, malaria, neurasthenia, hysteria, retention of urine, and soreness of the pharynx.

Traditional functions, as a luo connecting point of the kidney meridian, are to treat diseases affecting the bladder and kidney meridians.

Massage techniques are all the same as those used with Kd 3, with the exception of the pinch. In this case you would pinch Kd 4 and Bl 61, with emphasis on Kd 4.

Use with Ht 5, Liv 3, Cv 17, Cv 14, Lu 1, and Pc 8 for lack of interest in talking and excess sleeping. See Kd 2 for treatment of pain in the heel, etc.

Use with Kd 1, Co 4, Co 11, Co 18, St 9, Lu 7, Liv 2, Liv 3, St 10, St 11, St 12, Si 16, Si 17, St 44, and St 45 for sore throat.

Use with Bl 23, Bl 25, Bl 54, Sp 10, St 36, Sp 6, Cv 2, Cv 3, Gv 4, Gv 6, St 28, Liv 2, and Liv 3 for pyelonephritis, dysuria, or retention of urine.

Applications:

Perhaps block his oncoming right attack at neigwan with your right palm as you kick to Kd 4.

Figure 242

KD 5 (KIDNEY POINT NO. 5)

Chinese name

Shuiquan (spring). 水泉

Location:

1 cun directly below Kd 3, in the depression anterior and superior to the medial side of the tuberosity of the calcaneum.

Connections:

None.

Direction of strike:

Same as for Kd 4

Damage:

This is a xie cleft point, so in the healing area it will clear blockages by inserting a great amount of qi into the system. However, when struck using adverse qi, this point will bring about instant qi drainage, causing the recipient to fall down. Local pain is also great with this strike.

Set-up point:

Neigwan as well as Sp 8.

Antidote:

Needle Sp 8 with Bl 5

Healing:

Innervation and irrigation are the same as for Kd 4.

Used for irregular menstruation, prolapse of uterus, pruritus vulvae, hernia, frequency of urination, epilepsy, sore throat, insomnia, amenorrhea, and myopia.

Traditional functions, as a xie cleft point, are to treat acute injury, such as acute pain of the kidneys (e.g., renal colic).

Massage techniques are the same as for Kd 4.

Use with Kd 1, Kd 2, Liv 4, and Liv 3 for acute trauma, such as a blow to the kidney region that results in blood stagnation (bruising).

Use with Liv 3, Sp 6, Bl 23, Bl 18, Bl 20, Bl 17, Sp 3, St 36, Liv 6, Sp 9, Cv 4, Cv 6, Liv 2, Gb 26, Ht 7, and Cv 12 for amenorrhea.

Use with Bl 1, St 1, Gb 1, yuyao, Gb 20, Co 4, St 2, St 36, and Liv 3 for myopia.

Use with Bl 13, Bl 20, Bl 23, St 36, Kd 3. Lu 11, Lu 10, Bl 17, Bl 21, Gv 12, Gv 4, Kd 7, yishu, pirexue, Sp 3, and Gb 26 to help supplement other types of treatment for diabetes mellitus.

Use with Gv 20, abdomen zigong, Gb 26, Cv 4, Cv 6, Cv 12, St 30, Gb 28, Sp 6, Sp 9, Liv 3, Liv 8, Bl 20, Bl 23, Bl 18, Kd 6, Sp 3, and St 29 for uterine prolapse.

Applications:

You could first attack his forward leg with a kick to Sp 8, just below the knee on the inside of his leg, then bounce that same kick down to Kd 5.

KD 6 (KIDNEY POINT NO. 6)

Chinese name:

Zhaohai (shining sea). 照海

Location:

1 cun below the medial malleolus of the ankle, at the insertion of the abductor hallucis muscle.

Connections:

Yin qiao mai.

Direction of strike:

Straight in from the side of the ankle.

Damage:

This is a particularly painful strike, causing immediate qi drainage. Kd 6 is the master point of the yin qiao mai and is the coupled point of the *ren mai*, or conceptor vessel, both extra meridians. It will cause mental confusion immediately. It will also cause mental illness later in life, especially if used with its set-up point! However, the strike must be right on the point.

Set-up point:

Strike yin qiao mai 7 (draw a line from Cv 22 out to where to neck joins the shoulders and then go halfway on this line, and that's the point). The strike should be an angle in to the neck. This extra point is a very dangerous strike all by itself.

Antidote:

If the set-up point was struck hard, there is no antidote. However, if only Kd 6 has been struck, then massage the inside of the leg right up to the groin with medium pressure.

Healing:

Innervation is by the medial crural cutaneous nerve and, deeper, the tibial nerve. Irrigation, posterior and inferior to the point, is by the tibial artery and vein.

Used for pharyngitis, tonsillitis, neurasthenia, seizures, psychosis, irregular menstruation, prolapsed uterus, pruritus vulvae, hernia, frequency of urination, and insomnia.

Figure 243

Traditional indications include throat blockage, dry throat, eye pain, edema, irregular menstruation, vaginal discharge, prolapsed uterus, itching in the genital region, difficult labor, hemiplegia, seizures, and insomnia.

Kd 6 is a confluent (meeting) point of yin qiao mai, so together with Lu 7, its traditional functions are to tonify yin, ease the throat, benefit the chest, tonify lung yin, eliminate heat, calm the mind, promote the function of the uterus, and remove obstructions from yin qiai mai.

Massage techniques include pressing the point straight in and holding, rotating clockwise or counterclockwise for xu or shi conditions, or doing fingertip percussion on the point.

Use with Gv 14, Pc 6, St 40, Gb 34, Liv 3, St 36, Gv 26, Gv 16, Gb 20, Gv 12, Sp 6, Gv 14, Bl 62, Pc 5, Ht 5, Co 4, and Kd 1 for seizures.

Use with Bl 10, Co 11, Si 17, Co 4, St 40, Lu 7, Lu 5, St 36, Liv 2, and biantao for pharyngitis or tonsillitis.

See Kd 5 for treatment of prolapse of the uterus.

Use with Gv 3, Gv 4, Cv 6, Liv 3, Sp 6, Bl 18, Sp 10, Bl 54, Bl 23, Bl 25, Bl 17, Bl 20, Gb 26, and Sp 9 for irregular periods.

Applications:

Take his right straight with your left palm striking his arm toward you. Your right fingers will poke straight into yin qiao mai 7 (fig. 243).

KD 7 (KIDNEY POINT NO. 7)

Chinese name:

Fuliu (returning column/current).

Location:

2 cun directly above Kd 3, on the anterior border of the tendo calcaneus, posterior to the tibia. At the inferior part of the soleus muscle and in the medial part of the calcaneus.

Connections:

None.

Direction of strike:

Straight in from the inside of the lower leg.

Damage:

This is a metal and jing point. When struck, it will damage the kidneys by damaging the kidney jing. The recipient will feel an immediate rising of heat into the head from damaged kidneys, which can cause KO or extreme nausea. It will also have an effect upon the lungs and will drain energy from the body. This is one of those points that can also cause damage later in life.

Set-up point:

Ht 6 is a good set-up point since it will bring too much heat into the head.

Antidote:

Apply pressure to Ht 6 as well as Kd 7.

Healing:

Innervation is by the medial sural and the medial crural cutaneous nerves and, deeper, the tibial nerve. Irrigation occurs in the deep position, by the tibial artery and vein.

Used for diarrhea, borborygmus, edema, abdominal distension, swelling of the leg, muscular atrophy, weakness and paralysis of the foot, night sweating, spontaneous nephritis, orchitis, functional uterine bleeding (menstruation), urinary tract infections, leukorrhea, and lower back pain.

Traditional indications include edema, abdominal distension, pus and blood in the stool, urinary dysfunction, night sweats, absence of sweating, tidal fever, insanity, and pain of the lumbar vertebra.

This is a metal point and, thus, the mother point of the kidney meridian, and a jing river point. Its traditional functions are to treat cough (often), regulate the kidney qi, clear and cool damp heat, and tonify the back.

To massage, do a straight press and hold, press the point by pinching below the tendon, do clockwise or counterclockwise rotation for xu or shi conditions, or do fingertip percussion on this point.

Use with Ht 6, Lu 1, Bl 12, Bl 13, Bl 20, and Lu 7 to treat sweating-related disorders.

Use with Cv 9, Kd 9, St 36, Liv 14, Liv 13, Liv 4, Liv 3, Liv 2, Gb 24, Bl 17, Bl 18, Bl 19, Bl 20, and Bl 25 for cirrhosis of the liver.

Applications:

You might strike to his inside wrist to attack to Ht 6. You will, of course, get a number of good set-up points in this location, such as Ht 5, Lu 8, and even neigwan. Then kick to the inside of his lower leg at Kd 7.

KD 8 (KIDNEY POINT NO. 8)

Chinese name:

Jiaoxin (crossing letters). 交信

Location:

2 cun above Kd 3, 0.5 cun anterior to Kd 7, posterior to the medial border of the tibia.

Connections:

Yin qiao mai.

Direction of strike:

Straight in to the inside of the lower leg. You will also hit Kd 7 with this strike.

Damage:

This is another kidney point that will cause mental problems as well as sleeping disorders. I know three people who have been struck at Kd 8 during kickboxing matches and have not been able to sleep for days afterward. Combine this with Kd 7 (hard not to), and you have a most devastating strike. The immediate effect will be mental confusion.

Set-up point:

Any of the wrist drainage points will suffice here.

Antidote:

Lu 1 and Lu 5 pressured together.

Healing:

Innervation is by the medial crural cutaneous nerve and, deeper, the tibial nerve. Irrigation occurs in the deep position, by the tibial artery and vein.

Used for irregular menstruation, uterine bleeding, prolapse of the uterus, diarrhea, constipation, pain and swelling of the testes, retention of urine, and pain of the medial aspect of the lower limb.

This is a point of intersection with the yin qiao mai and is the xie cleft point for the yin qiao mai, so its traditional function is to treat acute problems associated with this channel, e.g., lower abdominal pain, pain along the waist to the genitals, hernia, leukorrhea, and tightness and spasm of the muscles along the medial aspect of the lower leg with flaccidity or atrophied muscles on the lateral aspect of this region, as in cases of seizure or paralysis.

Massage as for Kd 7.

Use with St 41, Gb 40, Kd 3, Bl 60, Gb 39, Gb 35, Gb 34, Gb 41, Sp 6, and Liv 3 for arthritis of the ankle.

Use with Cv 3, Cv 4, Cv 6, St 25, St 29, St 28, Liv 3, Sp 6, and Sp 9 for lower abdominal pain.

Use with Liv 1, Liv 2, Liv 3, Liv 4, Liv 8, Cv 3, and Cv 4 for pain and swelling of the testes (you might prick and get a spot of blood out of Liv 1 if the pain and swelling are severe).

Applications:

Same as for Kd 7.

KD 9 (KIDNEY POINT NO. 9)

Chinese name:

Zhubin (house guest). 築賓

Location:

On a line drawn between Kd 3 and Kd 10, this point is located about 5 cun above Kd 3, at the lower end of the belly of the gastrocnemius, around 2 cun posterior to the medial margin of the tibia, where the gastrocnemius forms the calcaneus tendon under the soleus muscle.

Connections:

None.

Direction of strike:

Into the calf and slightly toward the front of the leg.

Damage:

This is a xie cleft point, so the qi damage is great. It will cause immense pain in the short term and mental problems in the long run. The kidneys will be damaged, and a hard enough strike will cause KO, especially if the associated set-up point is used.

Set-up point:

Bl 1, struck straight up into the head.

Antidote:

Apply pressure down onto Gv 20 to bring yang qi back into the system.

Healing:

Innervation is by the medial sural cutaneous and medial crural cutaneous nerves and, deeper, the tibial nerve. Irrigation is in the deep position by the posterior artery and vein.

Used for mental disorders, pain in the medial aspect of the leg, nephritis, cystitis, orchitis, pelvic inflammatory disease, and seizures.

Traditional indications include insanity, colic, and pain along the medial aspect of the lower leg.

The extra meridian yinwei mai starts at this point, which is also a xie cleft point for the yinwei mai, so its traditional functions include treating acute problems of the yinwei mai, tonifying the kidney qi, calming the mind, and tonifying yinwei mai to treat problems of the heart, chest, and stomach (use it with Pc 6 and Sp 4 for these latter problems).

To massage, use a straight press and hold, rotate clockwise or counterclockwise for xu or shi conditions, or do fingertip percussion on this point.

Use with Sp 2, Sp 3, Sp 4, Liv 3, and Liv 4 for pain and swelling of the big toe and associated distal metatarsal bone.

Use with Bl 23, Kd 7, Cv 3, Cv 4, Liv 3, and Bl 25 for nephritIS.

Use with Cv 3, St 29, St 28, Bl 58, Kd 7, Bl 28, and Liv 2 for urinary infections.

Use with Bl 23, Bl 28, St 29, St 28, Gv 4, Gv 3, Gv 6, Sp 6, abdomen zigong, Bl 18, Liv 3, Kd 3, and Bl 17, for prostatitis.

Applications:

1) He might attack with a straight kick. You should move in and strike to Kd 9 with either your palm heel or with a one-knuckle punch.

2) First strike to Bl 1 using a one-knuckle punch upward into the head, then use a hook kick to Kd 9.

KD 10 (KIDNEY POINT NO. 10)

Chinese name:

Yingu (yin's valley).

Location:

On the medial side of the popliteal fossa, level with Bl 40, between the tendons of semitendinosus and semimembranosus when the knee is flexed.

Connections:

A divergent meridian leaves from this point, with the main meridian going internally to Gv 1. Then a lower branch goes to Cv 4 and Cv 3, and an upper branch connects to Cv 17 and the mouth.

Direction of strike:

Straight in to the back of the knee.

Damage:

As a water and he point, this one is very dangerous. It can cause kidney failure immediately, as well as a slow decay of the kidneys. Via its connection to Cv 17, it will cause the seat of power to be attacked, resulting in an immediate KO or weakening of the body. This strike can also cause impotence immediately or later. It can be used with other kidney or bladder points to do great damage to the kidneys. It can also affect the heart as well as the dai mai, thus damaging communication between upper and lower. So this point is not one to play around with!

Set-up point:

You could use Bl 23 with a hook kick and then stomp downward onto Kd 10.

Antidote:

See a doctor if there is blood in the urine or great pain is felt around the kidney area. See an acupuncturist if you cannot sleep at all.

Healing:

Innervation is by the medial femoral cutaneous nerve. Irrigation is by the medial superior glenicular artery and vein.

Used for impotence, hernia, uterine bleeding, pain in the medial aspect of the thigh and knee, disease of the urinogenital system, and arthritis of the knee.

As a he sea and water point for the kidney meridian, its traditional functions include tonifying the kidneys, dispelling heat, regulating the lower heater, and preventing pathogens from penetrating deeper into body (you might use it with jing well and ying spring points for the latter).

To massage, press and hold, do rotation clockwise or counterclockwise for xu or shi conditions, or do fingertip percussion on this point.

Use with Bl 40, Bl 39, Bl 38, Bl 57, and Gb 34 for pain and spasm at the back of the knee.

Use with Cv 6, Cv 4, Liv 1, Liv 3, Kd 2, Sp 6, Sp 2, St 12, St 10, Ht 1, Pc 3, Bl 54, Cv 3, Bl 23, Bl 18, Sp 10, and Bl 17 for abnormal uterine bleeding or irregular menstruation.

Use with Sp 9, Cv 6, Cv 2, Cv 3, Cv 4, Pc 7, Bl 28, Bl 25, Bl 23, Bl 18, and Liv 3 for difficult urination.

Applications:

See the application for Bl 23.

KD 11 (KIDNEY POINT NO. 11)

Chinese name:

Henggu (horizontal bone). 撗骨

Location:

5 cun below the umbilicus, on the superior border of the symphysis pubis, 0.5 cun lateral to Cv 2.

Connections:

Takes an internal branch from Cv 3. Also, chong mei.

Direction of strike:

Straight in just above the groin over the pubic bone to the side of centerline.

Damage:

This is the first of the kidney points to connect to chong mei, or the life force meridian. It also connects to the Cv meridian and has an effect upon the lower heater. This strike affects the kidneys, causing immediate local pain and KO, as well as kidney damage later. A strike to this area is sometimes worse than a strike directly to the groin.

Set-up point:

Kd 10 used in conjunction with Kd 11 is a dynamic strike, causing immediate damage to the lower heater.

Antidote:

Pressure to Kd 10.

Healing:

Innervation is by the branch of the iliohypogastric nerve. Irrigation is by the inferior epigastric artery and external pudendal artery.

Used for pain in the external genitalia, seminal emission, impotence, retention of urine, hernia, and urethritis.

As a point of intersection with the chong mei, its traditional functions are to treat problems such as male sexual irregularities (e.g., impotence), or female gynecological disorders. Chong mei is referred to as the sea of the 12 primary channels, so it has an influence on all of the viscera and thus connects all primary channels.

To massage, push straight into the point and hold, rotate clockwise or counterclockwise for xu or shi conditions, use a thumb or a knuckle to rub across the point, or do light fingertip percussion on the point.

Use with Cv 3, Cv 4, Cv 6, Gb 25, Bl 23, Sp 9, Sp 6, and Gv 20 for impotence, premature ejaculation, and spermatorrhea. Use with Sp 4, Pc 6, Kd 12, Kd 13, Kd 14, Kd 15, Kd 16, Kd 17, Kd 18, Kd 19, Kd 20, Kd 21, and Kd 27 to treat chong mei symptoms (e.g., deficient blood or qi

Figure 244

producing abnormal uterine bleeding, amenorrhea, impotence). You can hold Kd 11 and Kd 27 to balance the flow of qi in the kidney meridian or chest and abdomen. This will help balance the three heaters or to restore qi flow when abdominal scars are retarding its flow.

See Kd 12 for treatment of pain and swelling of the external genitalia.

Applications:

You could use the kidney damaging method mentioned earlier (Chapter 3, under Bl 23), by attacking to Bl 23 and then down to Kd 10 with the heel. As he is going down, you could strike to Kd 11 with a palm strike or one-knuckle punch (fig. 244).

KD 12 (KIDNEY POINT NO. 12)

Chinese name:

Dahe (great clarity). 大赫

Location:

4 cun below the umbilicus, 0.5 cun lateral to Cv 3.

Connections:

Chong mei.

Direction of strike:

Straight in to above the pubic bone.

Damage:

This point has an effect on the emotions and mind. The immediate effect is mental confusion caused by emotional being confusion. (This is a good time to make a follow-up strike!) A high level of qi drainage also occurs with a strike to this point, and KO will occur if it is hard enough. The emotional disorders caused by this strike will also show up physically in the form of extreme tension in the lower body, sexual problems, etc.

Set-up point:

Again, we could use Kd 10.

Antidote:

Bl 10 squeezed inward, along with Si 11 pressed inward.

Healing:

Innervation is by the branches of the subcostal nerve and the iliohypogastric nerve. Irrigation is by the muscular branches of the inferior epigastric artery and vein. Used for pain in the external genitalia, seminal emission, leukorrhea, and neuralgia of the spermatic cord.

As a point of intersection with the chong mei, its traditional functions are to influence that meridian's actions.

Massage techniques are the same as for Kd 11.

See Kd 11 for treatment of deficient qi and blood producing abnormal uterine bleeding, amenorrhea, impotence, and so on.

Use with Cv 4, Cv 6, Bl 23, Sp 6, Pc 5, Bl 52, Bl 18, Bl 20, Kd 3, Cv 3, Cv 1, Gb 25, Liv 3, St 36, Bl 15, and Gv 20 for spermatorrhea.

Use with Bl 23, Bl 28, Bl 18, Cv 4, Cv 3, Cv 6, Sp 6, Cv 20, Sp 9, Liv 3, and St 36 for prostatitis.

Use with Liv 4, Liv 8, Liv 12, Liv 1, Cv 3, St 30, and Kd 11 for pain and swelling of the external genitalia.

Use with Cv 3, Cv 4, Cv 6, Cv 9, Gb 26, Sp 9, Sp 6, St 36, Kd 13, Liv 2, Liv 3, St 29, Kd 7, abdomen zigong, Bl 23, Gv 4, and Kd 14 for leukorrhea.

Applications:

Same as for Kd 11.

KD 13 (KIDNEY POINT NO. 13)

Chinese name:

Qixue (qi's orifice).

Location:

3 cun below the umbilicus, 0.5 cun lateral to Cv 4.

Connections:

None.

Direction of strike:

Straight in to the lower abdomen.

Damage:

This point, apart from being very dangerous physically because it is in an area that offers little physical protection, also has an effect upon the life force meridian and upon the total energy of the body. A strike to this point drains qi greatly, knocking the recipient down immediately and causing long-term lack of energy, etc. A strong strike will cause KO or even death.

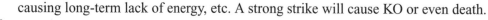

Figure 245

Set-up point:

Neigwan.

Antidote:

Tap on the back of the lower neck at that large vertebra Gv 14 (yang meeting point), using the fingers (fig. 245).

Healing:

Innervation is by the subcostal nerve. Irrigation is the same as for Kd 12.

Used for irregular menstruation, diarrhea, sterility, leukorrhea, and urinary tract infection.

As a point of intersection with the chong mei, its traditional functions are to influence that meridian's actions. Also, from the name and the location of this point, we can assume that, along with Cv 4 and perhaps ming men (Gv 4), it pertains to tantien.

Massage is the same as for Kd 11. You can also press slowly in on the point with both thumbs and quickly release as you pull the thumbs apart.

See Kd 12 for treatment of leukorrhea.

Use with Sp 6, Sp 8, Liv 3, Cv 4, Cv 6, Liv 14, Bl 18, Bl 17, Bl 23, Bl 25, and St 29 for irregular menstruation.

Use with Bl 23, Bl 28, Bl 25, Bl 32, Liv 2, Liv 8, Cv 3, St 28, Cv 2, and Sp 9 for urinary infection.

Use with Bl 23, Bl 20, Bl 18, Bl 17, Cv 4, Cv 6, Sp 6, and Liv 3 for sterility.

Applications:

You could use a back kick straight in to the lower abdomen after blocking his hand attack with your p'eng.

KD 14 (KIDNEY POINT NO. 14)

Chinese name:

Siman (four full). 四滿

Location:

2 cun below the umbilicus, 0.5 cun lateral to Cv 5.

Connections:

Chong mei.

Direction of strike:

Straight in with a slight angle toward the centerline of the lower abdomen.

Figure 246

Damage:

The instant you are struck here, you will feel a shot of pain go straight over to the centerline. This is the tantien being attacked via the chong mei meridian. If the strike is very hard, death will occur in about four minutes after an immediate KO.

Set-up point:

Neigwan, to drag qi to Pc 6, leaving Kd 14 open to attack.

Antidote:

None, unless you have a team of paramedics on hand within four minutes!

Healing:

Innervation is by the 11th intercostal nerve. Irrigation is the same as for Kd 12.

Used for uterine bleeding, irregular menstruation, postpartum abdominal pain, diarrhea, leukorrhea, sterility, and urinary tract infection.

Traditional functions are the same as for Kd 12 and Kd 13.

Massage techniques are the same as for Kd 13.

Use with Liv 4, Liv 3, St 25, Bl 18, Bl 25, and Bl 20 for hard, painful, drumlike abdomen.

Use with Sp 6, Bl 23, Bl 18, Bl 17, Bl 60, Cv 3, Cv 4, Cv 6, Cv 7, Bl 25, Sp 10, Sp 8, Liv 8, Liv 3, Liv 4, St 30, Co 4, Pc 6, Kd 12, St 29, St 36, Sp 3, Gb 21, and Gb 34 for amenorrhea where there once was untroubled menstruation.

Use with St 37, St 25, Sp 3, Sp 4, Bl 20, Bl 23, Bl 25, and Liv 2 for diarrhea.

Applications:

1) He might attack with a straight right, and you slam his right neigwan with your right palm, swivel on the ball of your left foot, and strike to Kd 14 with your right heel (fig. 246).

2) Alternatively, you could strike to his neigwan and then use your right knee to Kd 14.

KD 15 (KIDNEY POINT NO. 15)

Chinese name:

Zhongzhu (middle flow). 中注

Location:

1 cun below the umbilicus, 0.5 cun lateral to Cv 7.

Connections:

Chong mei

Direction of strike:

Straight in with a slight angle toward centerline.

Damage:

Again, we see this point affecting the life force meridian or chong mei. The strike will begin at Kd 15 but shoot straight across to chong mei. This strike has less of an effect upon tantien because the point is higher up and more protected by muscle. However, a good hard strike will cause a rising of qi to the whole neck area, so that the recipient feels like he has been choked!

Set-up point:

Neigwan and Lu 5. This combination will cause the brain to become confused, as qi is first drained, then added.

Antidote:

Qi balancing qigong performed by a qigong doctor.

Healing:

Innervation is by the 10th intercostal nerve. Irrigation is the same as for Kd 12.

Used for irregular menstruation, lower abdominal pain, constipation, and lower back pain.

Traditional functions are the same as for Kd 11. This point is also used during abdominal diagnosis. The point on the left, in particular, reflects the liver, and if very painful like a knife, it reflects liver blood stagnation.

Massage techniques are the same as for Kd 13, although if the point has come up as a sharp pain on the left, then use it in conjunction with Liv 4. (Use Liv 4 first, and then after the pain has diminished, use Kd 15.)

You can use this point with Pc 6, Cv 12, Sp 4, Liv 3, St 44, St 40, Gb 20, Bl 18, Bl 20, Bl 25, Bl 32, Bl 33, Bl 19, Bl 27, Bl 10, Cv 17, St 19, St 20, St 21, Gb 26, and St 36 for morning sickness, but care must be taken with the points over the abdomen during pregnancy (don't use deep pressure).

Use with Bl 25, Bl 18, Bl 53, Bl 26, St 25, Kd 16, Kd 17, Kd 18, Sp 15, St 37, Liv 3, Co 4, Liv 13, and Liv 14 for constipation.

For lower abdominal pain, use with Liv 4, Liv 3, Kd 16, Kd 14, St 25, St 26, St 28, St 29, St 30, Cv 4, Cv 3, Cv 2, Cv 5, Cv 6, Cv 7, St 36, and Sp 9.

Applications:

The same as for Kd 14.

KD 16 (KIDNEY POINT NO. 16)

Chinese name:

Huangshu (vital's hollow). 肓俞

Location:

0.5 cun lateral to the center of the umbilicus.

Connections:

Chong mei.

Direction of strike:

Straight in to the side of the navel.

Damage:

This point will normally balance the fire and water (yang and yin) of the system. When struck, apart from the damage to the chong mei, it will also have a psychological effect, producing alternate joy and fear. It will also cause extreme fatigue because the brain will think that a qi drainage has occurred.

Set-up point:

Neigwan.

Antidote:

Once the physical damage has abated, the patient must perform the posture from the taiji form called lotus kick. The weight is placed upon the left foot first, while the right foot is held past the body (fig. 247). Now, use the waist to throw your right foot over to your right while both of your hands slap the instep as they move to the opposite side (fig. 248). Place your right foot down and allow your hands to do an arc left and then right so that they end up over your right knee (fig. 249). Do this 10 times on both sides, morning and evening.

Healing:

Innervation is by the 10th intercostal nerve, and irrigation is the same as for Kd 12.

Used for abdominal pain, vomiting, abdominal distension, constipation, stomach spasm, pain of hernia, enteritis, and hiccups.

Figure 247

Figure 248

Figure 249

Traditional functions are the same as for Kd 11. This point is also part of a group of points used in demonic possession. In addition, it is used with Cv 9 during abdominal diagnosis to reflect the qi of the spleen.

Massage techniques are the same as for Kd 13. If the point is quite tender, use Sp 3, Sp 4, and St 36 first, then use Cv 12 with this point when the tenderness has subsided a little.

Use it with St 37, St 36, St 25, *lanweixue* (an extra point), Pc 6, Co 11, Sp 13, Bl 24, Bl 25, Bl 17, Liv 3, Bl 54, and Sp 10 for acute appendicitis.

Use with St 30, Liv 8, Liv 3, Liv 12, Sp 6, Kd 11, Gv 20, and Sp 3 for hernia.

Applications:

The same as for Kd 15.

KD 17 (KIDNEY POINT NO. 17)

Chinese name:

Shangqu (trade's bend). 商曲

Location:

2 cun above the umbilicus, 0.5 cun lateral to Cv 10.

Connections:

Chong mei.

Direction of strike:

Straight in to the stomach.

Damage:

Immediate KO from qi drainage and air blockage. (There are two types of choke KOs: an air cavity strike where the person is deprived of air and a blood cavity strike, and where the person is deprived of blood to the brain.) This strike shocks the whole of the stomach area, from the tantien right up the neck. If the strike is hard enough, it will cause death. It is possible, however, to build up this area to resist attacks by using "iron shirt" qigong. This is not just a muscular buildup as in "rippling abs," but a sinewy buildup, creating a sort of "barrel" of protection around the whole stomach area.

Set-up point:

St 3 straight up into the cheekbones.

Antidote:

Put the patient's head between his legs and press down onto his back for three seconds, release, then do it again.

Healing:

Innervated by the ninth intercostal nerve and irrigated by the branches of the superior and inferior epigastric arteries and veins.

Used for fullness of the abdomen, diarrhea, constipation, stomachache, colic, and peritonitis.

Massage techniques are the same as for Kd 13.

Traditional functions are the same as for Kd 11.

Use with Liv 5, St 36, St 25, Cv 12, Bl 25, Bl 20, Bl 18, Liv 3, Sp 3, Liv 13, Liv 14, St 21, Pc 6, and Co 4 for colic, stomachache, and fullness of the abdomen.

See Kd 15 to treat constipation.

Applications:

Take his right straight with your left palm, shooting it upward on the inside of his forearm as your right fingers poke upward into both St 3 points (fig. 250). Your left palm is now free to strike straight into Kd 17.

Figure 250

KD 18 (KIDNEY POINT NO. 18)

Chinese name:

Shiguan (stone hinge). 石關

Location:

3 cun above the umbilicus, 0.5 cun lateral to Gv 11.

Connections:

Chong mei.

Direction of strike:

Straight in to the midstomach.

Damage:

Again, this point is connected to the chong mei or life force meridian, so a strike here will cause KO through the qi drainage from the seat of power, the diaphragm. It also causes an increase of yang qi to the head, which will also cause a KO the opposite way.

Set-up point:

Neigwan, or Si 8.

Antidote:

Sit the recipient of this strike down and bend him forward. If the strike has been very hard, seek medical advice!

Healing:

Innervation is by the eighth intercostal nerve. Irrigation is by the branches of the superior epigastric artery and vein.

Used for vomiting, abdominal pain, constipation, postpartum abdominal pain, stomachache, hiccups, and spasm of the esophagus. Traditional functions are the same as for Kd 11.

Massage is the same as for Kd 13.

Use with Pc 6, St 36, St 21, Sp 3, Liv 3, Cv 12, Cv 14, Liv 14, Kd 20, Kd 24, Kd 25, Kd 26, Kd 27, Kd 16, Bl 20, Bl 18, Bl 19, and Bl 21 for vomiting, nausea, etc.

Use with Sp 6, St 25, Sp 9, Liv 3, Cv 4, Cv 6, Bl 23, Bl 25, Bl 20, Bl 18, Liv 4, and Sp 10 for postpartum abdominal pain.

Applications:

You could respond either to a straight attack on the outside at Si 8, or to a hook-type punch to neigwan. Then attack with a palm strike to Kd 18.

KD 19 (KIDNEY POINT NO. 19)

Chinese name:

Yindu (yin's metropolis).

Location:

4 cun above the umbilicus, 0.5 cun lateral to Cv 12.

Connections:

Chong mei.

Direction of strike:

Straight in.

Damage:

As we get closer to the area of the solar plexus or Cv 14, the damage gets greater. So this point's damage is on the verge of being very dangerous. A strike here shocks the whole upper body, causing a KO from qi drainage and air blockage. The diaphragm is attacked, so the loss of power is great, and the fight will be finished. A strong strike here will cause death!

Set-up point:

Neigwan struck toward you is a good addition to this point because it will drain qi. You could also strike to Kd 19 and then turn and strike to Bl 23, a combination that spells death. (See "Applications.")

Antidote:

Apply CPR if the recipient is dead. Using mild pressure, rub the whole upper torso upward from navel to upper chest on the centerline.

Healing:

Innervation and irrigation are the same as for Kd 18.

Used for borborygmus, abdominal distension and pain, emphysema, pleurisy, and malaria.

Traditional functions are the same as for Kd 11. From the name and the location of the point, we could possibly assume that this point and Cv 12 form a major plexus that, in the yogic tradition, would be thought of as the spleen chakra. Spleen and lungs form the most external of the yin divisions, *tai yin*. (Theoretically, there are six divisional pairings of the main meridians; in this case, the spleen and lungs are paired. This theory, which links up an arm yin and a leg yin channel or an arm yang and a leg yang channel, comes from the book *Shang Han Lun*, compiled btween 200 B.C. and 200 A.D. These pairings are seen as pathways from pathogenic penetration to different levels of

Figure 251

Figure 252

the body.) Spleen and lungs, together with the help of kidney yuan qi, supply the post-heaven nourishment (derived after birth) of the body as well as protective energy of the body that makes this a very important center.

Massage techniques are the same as for Kd 13.

Use with Cv 17, Cv 12, Lu 6, Lu 7, Lu 5, Lu 1, Bl 12, Bl 13, Co 4, Liv 3, and Kd 7 for emphysema or pleurisy.

Use with St 25, St 36, Sp 3, Liv 3, Liv 14, Liv 13, Cv 12, Bl 20, Bl 21, Bl 18, Bl 19, Bl 17, and Bl 25 for borborygmus and abdominal distension and pain.

Use with Gv 13, Gv 14, Gv 10, Pc 5. Pc 6, Co 11, Co 4, Si 3, Gb 34, Sp 9, Liv 3, Lu 7, and Kd 7 for malaria.

Applications:

He might attack with a right straight. You should block with your left palm and attack to Kd 19 with your right, as in Figure 251. Then, swiveling on your heels, turn and strike straight in to his kidney area at Bl 23 (fig. 252).

KD 20 (KIDNEY POINT NO. 20)

Chinese name:

Futonggu (connecting valley on the abdomen). 通谷

Location:

5 cun above the umbilicus, 0.5 cun lateral to Cv 13.

Connections:

Chong mei.

Direction of strike:

Straight in and a little toward the centerline.

Damage:

The same as for Kd 19, although there could be more damage since it is closer to Cv 14 and the solar plexus.

Set-up point:

Same as for Kd 19.

Antidote:

This point can be an irretrievable death point strike if struck hard. CPR is really the only antidote here.

Healing:

Innervation and irrigation are the same as for Kd 18.

Used for stiff neck, seizures, palpations, intercostal neuralgia, vomiting, diarrhea, abdominal pain and distension, and indigestion.

Traditional functions are the same as for Kd 11.

Massage techniques are the same as for Kd 13.

Use with Liv 14, Gb 24, Liv 2, Liv 3, Liv 5, Th 6, Gb 34, Gb 40, Bl 18, Bl 19, Bl 20, Bl 17, Bl 21, Pc 6, Sp 9, St 40, Liv 13, Kd 22, Kd 25, and jiaji points corresponding to the level of pain for intercostal neuralgia.

For palpitations, use with Pc 6, Cv 17, Liv 14, Liv 3, Bl 14, Bl 15, Bl 17, Bl 18, Ht 7, and St 36.

Use with Gv 12, Pc 6, St 36, Liv 3, Liv 13, St 21, Bl 20, Bl 18, Bl 19, and Bl 21 for vomiting, indigestion, etc.

Applications:

The same as for Kd 19.

KD 21 (KIDNEY POINT NO. 21)

Chinese name:

Youmen (secluded door/pylorus). 토티 門

Location:

6 cun above the umbilicus, 0.5 cun lateral to Cv 14.

Connections:

Chong mei.

Direction of strike:

Straight in and slightly toward the midline as for Kd 20.

Damage:

This is an extremely dangerous point because it combines the shock to the life force meridian (chong mei), as well as crossing over to Cv 14, which in itself is a very dangerous point strike. There will be instant heart stoppage and resultant death, especially if the point is struck between 11 A.M. and 1 P.M.

Set-up point:

A simple slap on the face will make this strike even more dangerous since the slap acts as a neurological shutdown, leaving the whole body vulnerable. When the strike to Kd 21 is felt, the nervous system gives up, as does the heart. So we have a double whammy here, with the heart and nervous system giving up at once!

Antidote:

There is no antidote! Many a cricket player has died as a result of being struck at Kd 21 and Cv 14 at midday. Not even immediate medical attention will suffice.

Healing:

Innervation is by the seventh intercostal nerve, and irrigation is the same as for Kd 18.

Used for abdominal pain, vomiting, diarrhea, intercostal neuralgia, distended stomach, stomach spasms, and chronic gastritis.

Traditional functions are the same as for Kd 11.

Massage techniques are the same as for Kd 13.

Use with Sp 5, Bl 66, Bl 18, Bl 20, Bl 19, Cv 12, Cv 13, Cv 14, St 21, St 36, Liv 3, and Pc 6 for predilection toward vomiting.

Use with Gv 20, Sp 3, St 36, Sp 9, Cv 4, Cv 6, Cv 12, Bl 21, Bl 20, Bl 18, Bl 19, Liv 14, Liv 13, Liv 3, Cv 9, and St 25 for stomachache, distended stomach, abdominal pain, etc. Use with Cv 12, Pc 6, Sp 4, Liv 3, St 44, St 36, St 40, Cv 11, Bl 20, Bl 18, Bl 21, and Bl 19 for morning sickness during the first five months.

Applications:

Any strike to this area will do. However, the strike is made even worse if a loose waist and attacking portion are used rather than the stiffer, karate-type attack.

KD 22 (KIDNEY POINT NO. 22)

Chinese name:

Bulang (stepping corridor). 步廊

Location:

In the fifth intercostal space, 2 cun lateral to the Cv meridian, approximately level to Cv 16.

Connections:

None.

Direction of strike:

Straight in.

Damage:

Again, this point is dangerous but not to the extent of Kd 21 because much more power has to be used to shock the heart, causing it to stop.

Set-up point:

Grab and jerk the wrist violently at H 5 and Lu 8. This will drain the heart and lungs of qi, thus causing great weakness and allowing the Kd 22 strike to have a much more lethal effect.

Antidote:

Place the palms on top of the head and use light to medium pressure downward. This will bring qi back up into the body. If the heart has stopped, use CPR.

Healing:

Innervation is by the anterior cutaneous branch of the fifth intercostal nerve and, deeper, the fifth intercostal nerve. Irrigation is by the fifth intercostal artery and vein.

Used for cough, asthma, pleurisy, intercostal neuralgia, rhinitis, gastritis, and bronchitis. Massage techniques are the same as for Kd 13.

Use with Th 6, Liv 5, Gb 34, Liv 14, Gb 24, Bl 18, Bl 19, Bl 17, St 40, Sp 9, Pc 6, and jiaji points at the level of the problem.

Use with Kd 23, Kd 24, and Kd 26 for intercostal neuralgia.

Use with Cv 17, Liv 14, Sp 18, St 15, Bl 18, St 18, St 16, Ht 1, Pc 2, Bl 44, Gb 21, SI 1, St 36, Bl 40, Liv 3, Liv 13, and Sp 6 for acute mastitis.

Applications:

1) A simple block with the left palm to his straight right, while the right palm attacks straight in to Kd 22.

2) Alternatively, you could take his hook left with your right palm and jerk it violently while your other palm attacks to Kd 20.

KD 23 (KIDNEY POINT NO. 23)

Chinese name:

Shenfeng (spirit's seal). 神封

Location:

In the fourth intercostal space, 2 cun lateral to Cv 17.

Figure 253

Connections:

None.

Direction of strike:

Straight in.

Damage:

This is one of those "spiritual points" that will damage the recipient's communication with his shen. It will also stop the heart and send a shock wave right into the upper chest area. As a result, he will be unable to carry on with the fight.

Set-up point:

Neigwan is good here, or you could use Lu 5 as an extreme qi drainage point just before the strike to Kd 23.

Antidote:

Use pressure all along both sides of the backbone, not touching the backbone, as a massage. This will reunite the patient with his spirit.

Healing:

Innervation is by the anterior cutaneous branch of the fourth intercostal nerve and, deeper, the fourth intercostal nerve.

Irrigation is by the fourth intercostal artery and vein.

Used for cough, asthma, a sensation of fullness in the chest and hypochondriac region, mastitis, pleurisy, intercostal neuralgia, and bronchitis.

From its name and its location proximal to Cv 17 (which is seen in the yogic tradition as being the region of the heart chakra), this point, in conjunction with *shendu*, or Gv 11, probably forms the energetic orb of the heart chakra traditionally.

Massage techniques are the same as for Kd 13. You can also use a loose fist to do percussion on this point.

Use this point with St 16, Gb 41, St 18, St 36, St 39, Liv 8, Sp 18, Gb 41, Sp 10, St 44, St 45, and Liv 1 for breast abscess.

Use with Lu 1, Lu 5, Lu 7, Co 4, Co 11, Cv 17, Bl 12, Bl 13, Bl 43, Bl 18, Liv 14, Liv 3, St 36, Kd 22, Kd 24, Kd 25, Kd 26, and Kd 27 for asthma, bronchitis, pleurisy, and so on.

Applications:

Use a one-knuckle right-handed attack to Kd 23 as your left hand grabs his right wrist and jerks it violently (fig. 253).

KD 24 (KIDNEY POINT NO. 24)

Chinese name:

Lingxu (spirit's ruins). 靈墟

Location:

In the third intercostal space, 2 cun lateral to Cv 18.

Connections:

None.

Direction of strike:

Straight in above the pectoral with a slightly downward direction.

Damage:

This is another one of those spiritual points that will affect the communication between God and man. It will also stop the heart.

Set-up point:

Ht 3.

Antidote:

A complete qi balancing is required when the communication between God and man is affected. If the heart has stopped, use CPR.

Healing:

Innervation is by the anterior cutaneous branch of the third intercostal nerve and, deeper, the third intercostal nerve. Irrigation is by the third intercostal artery and vein.

Used for cough, asthma, pain and fullness in the chest and hypochondriac region, mastitis, intercostal neuralgia, bronchitis, and vomiting.

Massage techniques are the same as for Kd 13.

Use with Liv 14, Liv 13, Gb 24, Liv 3, Gb 34, Gb 41, Bl 17, Pc 6, Bl 18, Bl 19, Bl 20, Bl 21, Cv 12, and Cv 14 for pain and fullness of chest and hypochondriac regions.

See Kd 23 for treatment of asthma, bronchitis, and so on. See Kd 22 for treatment of intercostal neuralgia.

Applications:

Take his right straight with your left palm on the outside while your thumb knuckle (with a closed taijiquan fist) attacks his Ht 3 point toward you. Your right palm will now rebound and strike slightly downward onto Kd 24.

KD 25 (KIDNEY POINT NO. 25)

Chinese name:

Shencang (spirit's storage).

Location:

In the second intercostal space, 2 cun lateral to Cv 19.

Connections:

None.

Direction of strike:

Straight in and slightly downward into the chest.

Damage:

This point will also affect the lungs, causing immense grief and fear instantly, as well as physical weakness. For this reason, it will work well as a set-up point. It also affects the spirit, so at some later time, the communication between God and man will be disrupted, making for emotional disorders. The qi will be scattered with no direction.

Set-up point:

Lu 5. This combination is one of the best for qi drainage.

Antidote:

Rub both arms upward on the inside of the forearms and apply pressure to Gv 20.

Healing:

Innervation is by the anterior cutaneous branch of the second intercostal nerve and, deeper, the second intercostal nerve. Irrigation is by the second intercostal artery and vein.

Used for cough, asthma, chest pain, bronchitis, vomiting, and intercostal neuralgia.

Traditional indications include cough and asthma from kidney deficiency.

Massage techniques are the same as for Kd 13.

Use with St 9, Lu 1, Lu 7, Co 4, Co 10, Bl 11, Bl 12, Bl 13, Kd 7, Bl 43, Bl 17, Bl 18, and Liv 3 for severe coughing and wheezing that won't stop.

See Kd 23 for asthma, bronchitis, etc.

See Kd 22 for treatment of intercostal neuralgia.

Applications:

Strike his Lu 5 point in retaliation to his right hook. Then use that same elbow to strike downward into Kd 25.

KD 26 (KIDNEY POINT NO. 26)

Chinese name:

Yuzhong (amid elegance). 彧中

Location:

In the first intercostal space, 2 cun lateral to Cv 20.

Connections:

None.

Direction of strike:

Straight in and down.

Damage:

This point will also affect the lung qi and cause immediate qi drainage. If enough pressure is used, it will bring about a KO. The recipient feels immediately tired, to the point that he must sit down.

Set-up point:

Lu 5.

Antidote:

Same as for Kd 25.

Healing:

Innervation is by the anterior cutaneous branch of the first intercostal nerve, the medial supraclavicular nerve and, deeper, the first intercostal nerve. Irrigation is by the first intercostal artery and vein.

Used for cough, asthma, sensation of fullness in the chest and hypochondriac regions, bronchitis, vomiting, and intercostal neuralgia.

Massage techniques are the same as for Kd 13.

See Kd 22 for treatment of intercostal neuralgia.

See Kd 23 for treatment of asthma, bronchitis, fullness of the chest, etc.

Use with Gv 12, Cv 14, St 21, St 36, Liv 3, Liv 13, Pc 6, Bl 20, Bl 21, Bl 18, Bl 19, Bl 25, and Gb 41 for vomiting.

Applications:

The same as for Kd 25.

KD 27 (KIDNEY POINT NO. 27)

Chinese name:

Shufu (hollow residence). 俞府

Location:

In the depression at the lower border of the clavicle, 2 cun lateral to Cv 21.

Connections:

None.

Direction of strike:

Upward into the collarbone, usually using a one-knuckle punch.

Damage:

Great damage is done with this strike, along with qi drainage and severe local pain. KO will occur with a hard strike. An imbalance between left and right sides of the body will develop gradually, and if left untreated it will cause mental instability in later life, along with physical imbalance.

Set-up point:

Lu 5.

Antidote:

A complete qi balancing is required to stop the imbalance from getting worse.

Healing:

Innervation is by the medial supraclavicular nerve. Irrigation is by the anterior perforating branches of the internal mammary artery and vein.

Used for cough, asthma, chest pain, bronchitis, vomiting, abdominal distension.

Massage techniques are the same as for Kd 13. In addition, you can hold Kd 11 and Kd 27 as part of a balancing technique for the trunk of the body.

Use with Gv 22, Cv 17, Lu 1, Kd 7, Bl 43, Bl 12, Bl 13, Bl 14, Bl 15, Bl 17, Bl 18, Liv 3, Lu 7, Co 4, and Ht 7 for coughing and wheezing induced by rheumatic heart disease.

Use with Gb 20, Gv 14, Bl 10, Bl 13, Bl 17, Bl 43, Cv 22, Cv 13, Lu 9, St 36, Gv 12, Cv 12, Lu 8, St 40, Liv 3, and Co 10 for whooping cough.

Use with Pc 6, Pc 5, Ht 8, Pc 4, Pc 3, Cv 12, Gv 6, St 25 St 36, Cv 4, St 29, Cv 9, St 28, Kd 7, Kd 5, Sp 9, Liv 13, Bl 18, Bl 13, Cv 11, Co 4, Cv 22, Bl 15, Bl 14, and Liv 14 for chronic heart failure.

Use with Cv 17, Liv 14, Liv 3, Sp 18, St 15, St 36, Sp 6, Pc 7, Si 1, Bl 40, Bl 18, Bl 17, and Gb 21 for acute mastitis.

Applications:

He might attack with a hook punch. You should strike his right Lu 5 with your left knife edge, while your right one-knuckle punch attacks up into Kd 27.

This brings us to the end of the kidney meridian. The kidneys are one of the most sensitive organs in one's body, and some of the most deadly points lie along this meridian. Most of the points, however, require a degree of accuracy in order to gain the effects mentioned in this chapter.

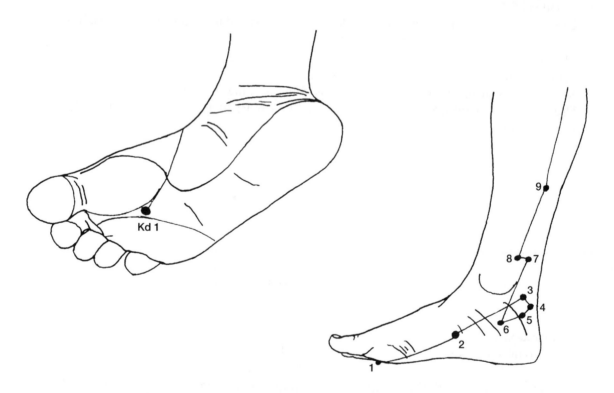

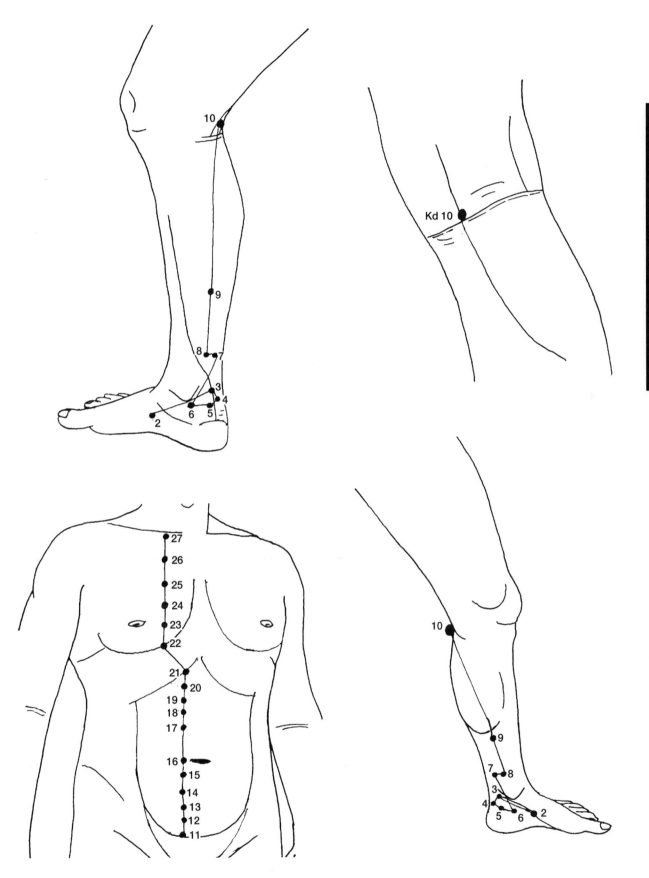

Kd 10

Chapter 5

The Stomach Meridian

The stomach is a flexible bag surrounded by muscle. It lies on the left side of the abdomen, under a dome-shaped, muscular sheet called the diaphragm. Full, the stomach can contain up to 1.5 liters of food, which enters the stomach from a muscular tube called the esophagus. The food can be stored in the stomach for up to four hours. The muscles in the stomach wall contract and relax, thus mixing the food with digestive substances called enzymes. This produces a liquid called chyme, which passes into the small intestine.

The action of the stomach can be affected by many things, including the emotional state. Tests have shown that the stomach will contract when a person is feeling angry, so that no normal stomach action will take place. So the mind has the ability to stop all digestion when the person is not in a fit state to be digesting.

THE TCM VIEW

Traditionally in Chinese medicine, the stomach is a yang organ and has the Chinese element of earth. In the "social order," the stomach is in control of "ripening and rotting." The stomach also aids the spleen in its function of transporting and transforming. The spleen moves in an upward direction, while the stomach moves downward, so both balance each other out in the earth element.

The collective functions of the stomach are called "stomach qi" in TCM. After it breaks down the food, the stomach sends it down to the small intestine for further digestion, so we are told that stomach qi descends. And if the descending function of the stomach is faulty, this may cause nausea, vomiting, and other stomach disorders.

The stomach meridian runs from head to foot, so it has many points that are easily accessible for the martial arts. Basically, when a stomach point is struck, it damages the "earth" of the recipient, cutting his connection to earth and effecting a great qi drainage, causing nausea so great that the recipient has to lie down. Several points on the St meridian are above important internal organs, and so strikes to these points will cause quite dangerous things to happen within the body. The most dangerous part of the stomach meridian is in the neck area, where a number of points can cause death easily when struck in the correct direction or KO with even a light blow. St 9, for instance, is situated right over the carotid sinus, which is a nerve ending of the vagus nerve. (I will cover this point and nerve in the section on St 9.) The vagus nerve is very important to dim-mak. It is the 10th cranial nerve, branching off of the medulla oblongata and extending upward and downward into the abdomen. An important nerve, the vagus divides into several branches that innervate vital structures in the body. These branches are the auricular, bronchial, cardiac (inferior and superior), celiac, esophageal, gastric, hepatic, laryngeal (recurrent and superior), meningeal, pharyngeal, and pyloric.

ST 1 (STOMACH POINT NO. 1)

Chinese name:
Chengqi (contain tears).

Location:
Between the eyeball and the midpoint of the infraorbital ridge. The point is above the inferior border of the orbit, in the orbicularis oculi muscle In its deep position within the orbit are the rectus inferior bulbi and the oblique inferior bulbi muscles.

Connections:
Co, Cv, Gb, upper meeting point of stomach/spleen divergent meridian. There is an internal path from Co 20 to Bl 1, then St 1.

Direction of strike:
St 1 is always struck straight in to the lower eye socket, using a small weapon such as a one-knuckle punch.

Damage:
St 1 is one of the more sensitive points and will be damaged easily by even a light blow to the area. Even a light blow is often enough to cause extreme nausea and drain qi from the upper body. A medium strike here will cause a KO, and a hard strike can cause death. This is a point that will slow the flow of *yang ming* qi (stomach and colon channels) through its connection to Co 20 and will drain the yang qi from the body in general. The liver is also affected by a strike to St 1 because not only does the liver control the eyes, but whatever happens to the eye area also has an effect upon the liver.

Set-up point:
Slam down onto Th 8, this will double the effect.

Antidote:
Neigwan rubbed upward on the inner forearm.

Healing:
Innervation is by a branch of the infraorbital nerve, the inferior branch of the oculomotor nerve, and the muscular branch of the facial nerve. Irrigation is by the branches of the infraorbital and ophthalmic arteries and veins.

Used for redness with swelling and pain of the eye, lacrimation when in wind, night blindness, facial paralysis, twitching of the eyelids, acute and chronic conjunctivitis, myopia, hypermetropia, astigmatism, convergent squint (esotropla), color blindness, glaucoma, cataracts, keratitis, retinitis pigmentosa, and inflammation or atrophy of the optic nerve.

Traditional indications include sore eyes, excessive tearing, opacity of the cornea, myopia, eyelid tic, mouth and eyes awry.

St 1 is a point of intersection with yang qiao mai, and the ren mai, colon channel, and liver

Figure 254

channel all have branches that pass through this point, so its traditional function is to influence these channels.

Massage techniques include a pushing straight and holding or clockwise or counterclockwise rotation for xu or shi conditions.

Use with Gb 20, Bl 1, *qiuhou* (an extra point), Co 4, Liv 3, Bl 18, Bl 23, St 36, Gb 37, Liv 2, Liv 14, and Gb 1 for optic neuritis or atrophy.

Use with Gb 20, Co 4, Bl 1, Gb 8, taiyang, Gb 37, St 3, Gb 1, Gb 43, Gb 44, Liv 2, Liv 3, Liv 5, and Gv 14 for conjunctivitis or red, swollen eyes.

For myopia, use with Gb 20, Co 4, Bl 1, St 36, St 2, Bl 2, Bl 4, Bl 5, Kd 5, Co 6, and Liv 3.

Applications:

Perhaps he attacks with a straight right. You will slam his forearm with your left palm as your right one-knuckle punch attacks straight in to St 1 (fig. 254).

ST 2 (STOMACH POINT NO. 2)

Chinese name:

Sibai (four whites).

Location:

Approximately 1 cun directly below St 1 in the infraorbital foramen between the orbicularis oculi and the quadratus labii superior muscles.

Connections:

None.

Direction of strike:

Downward into the cheekbone.

Damage:

Again, this point is quite sensitive and will cause considerable local pain and qi drainage, resulting in a KO and severe nerve damage. When struck, one feels a sinking sensation in the chest and then into the legs, which will become weak as a result of the downward draining qi.

Set-up point:

Same as for St 1.

Antidote:

Same as for St 1.

Healing:

Innervation is by a branch of the facial nerve, and the point is found directly on the infraorbitial nerve. Irrigation is by the branches of the facial and infraorbital artery and veins.

Used for redness and pain in the eye, facial paralysis and pain, twitching of the eyelids, allergic facial swelling, trigeminal neuralgia, keratitis, myopia, sinusitis, roundworm in the bile duct, and facial spasm.

Traditional indications are red, sore eyes, membrane over the eye, headache, dizziness, and mouth and eyes awry.

Traditional functions include eliminating wind, clearing vision and brightening the eyes, spreading liver qi, benefiting the gallbladder, relaxing the tendons, and relieving pain.

To massage, press and hold the point or do rotations clockwise or counterclockwise for xu or shi conditions. Light fingertip percussion is also good on this point.

Use with St 4, St 5, St 6, Gb 20, Liv 3, Gb 34, Co 4, St 36, Gb 14, St 44, and St 8 for facial paralysis or spasm.

For red, swollen eyes, use with Bl 1, St 1, Th 23, Gb 1, Liv 2, Liv 4, Gb 37, and Co 4.

Use with Co 4, Co 10, Co 11, Co 20, bitong, Lu 7, Liv 2, Liv 3, St 36, and Lu 5 for sinusitis.

Applications:

Same as for St 1, only use a downward one-knuckle punch. You can use the palm heel to gain access easily to both St 1 and St 2, and in this case, where both points are struck, it is best to use the downward blow and attack both points.

ST 3 (STOMACH POINT NO. 3)

Chinese name:
Juliao (great seam).

Location:
Directly below St 2 at the level of the lower border of the ala nasi, on the lateral side of the naso-labial groove. Either of the two lateral flared portions of the external nose.

Connections:
Colon meridian.

Direction of strike:
Up and into the cheekbones.

Damage:
When struck hard enough, this strike will send a shock wave up into the front of the brain, causing disorientation. It will also cause great nausea.

Set-up point:
Neigwan.

Antidote:
Rub neigwan up the inside of the forearm.

Healing:
Innervation is by the branches of the facial and infraorbital nerves. Irrigation is by the branches of the facial and infraorbital arteries and veins.

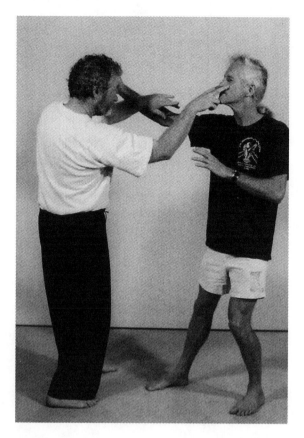

Figure 255

Used for facial paralysis, twitching of the eyelids, epistaxis, toothache, swelling of the lips and cheeks, rhinitis, and trigeminal neuralgia.

As a point of intersection with yang qiao mai, its traditional function is to influence that meridian. Massage techniques are the same as for St 2.

Use with St 1, yuyao, Liv 3, Gb 20, St 36, and Pc 6 for twitching of the eyelids. (Bl 1, Gb 1, and Th 23 would also help.)

For facial paralysis or spasm, use with Gb 20, Gb 14, St 4, Co 4, Gv 26, St 36, St 44, Co 19, taiyang, *jiachengjiang* (an extra point), Gb 34, Liv 3, and Si 3.

Use with Co 4, St 44, St 2, St 5, and St 6 for toothache.

Applications:
Use the posture from taijiquan called "sit back ready." Block his right hook or straight with your left palm as your right one-knuckle punch strikes up into St 3 (fig. 255).

ST 4 (STOMACH POINT NO. 4)

Chinese name:
Dicang (earth granary).

Location:
Lateral to the corner of the mouth, directly below St 3, in the orbicularis oris muscle and, in its deep position, in the buccinator muscle.

Connections:
Colon.

Direction of strike:
Straight in to the corner of the mouth using a small weapon.

Damage:

Again, this strike will shock the whole system when struck hard enough, causing a KO. However, this strike must be quite accurate.

Set-up point:

Si 8.

Antidote:

Do a complete qi rebalancing.

Healing:

Superficially, innervation is by the branches of the facial and infraorbital nerves; deeper it is by the terminal blanch of the buccal nerve. Irrigation is by the facial artery and vein.

Used for facial paralysis, trigeminal neuralgia, excessive salivation, spasm of the eyelid, and deviation of the mouth.

Traditional indications include mouth and eyes awry, muteness, drooling, eye tic.

As a point of intersection with the colon channel and the yang qiao mai, this point's traditional function is in facial acupuncture to treat the medial thigh region.

Massage techniques are the same as for St 2.

Use with St 6, Co 20, Co 4, St 5, St 36, St 44, Co 19, Liv 3, Th 17, Gb 34, taiyang, and St 8 for facial paralysis.

Use with Cv 24, Co 4, St 36, Sp 3, and Liv 3 for excessive salivation.

Use with St 5, St 6, Co 4, Liv 3, Gb 20, St 3, and Si 3 for awry mouth.

Applications:

Slam the outside of his right elbow with your left palm as your right one-knuckle punch attacks to the right corner of his mouth at St 4. (Of course, you have also stepped to your left to avoid his attack.)

ST 5 (STOMACH POINT NO. 5)

Chinese name:

Daiying (big welcome, or big meeting).

Location:

Anterior to the angle of the mandible, on the anterior border of the masseter muscle, in the groovelike depression appearing when the cheek is bulged, 0.5 cun anterior to St 6.

Connections:

Gallbladder.

Direction of strike:

Straight in to the lower part of the jaw and slightly back toward the back of the head.

Damage:

Any strike to this area of the jaw will cause a KO, especially if the point is associated with the Gb meridian. Obvious jaw damage is also apparent. But the primary damage is in the shock to the brain that jaw strikes cause. (This is why the jaw is always a common target in the movies.) St 9 is a great KO point. It sends a shock wave of qi into the brain, causing dizziness at least and KO at most, not to mention a broken jaw, etc. The direction must be straight in from the side to have the greatest effect. This point also has a connection to St 9 via St 1 and St 8, which is why it is called "great meeting." So we can get a KO from both the action upon the heart via the carotid sinus at St 9 and from too much yang qi to the brain. This point is called a "big point" since it has abundant qi and blood: hence the great amount of qi going into the brain when struck.

It must also be mentioned that the stomach has vagus nerve endings entering at its base. A strike to St 9 will also have an effect upon the vagus nerve, making this point one of the better KO points.

Set-up point:

Neigwan to drain qi. You could also use Si 8 or Lu 5 for this one. All will work equally well.

Antidote:

Depending on how bad the strike was, you might have to use CPR or one of the revival methods shown earlier in this book. Note that time will usually bring the recipient around as well.

Healing:

Innervated by the facial and buccal nerves and irrigated anteriorly by the facial artery and vein.

Used for trismus (lockjaw), deviation of the mouth, swelling of the cheek, parotitis (swelling or infection of one or both saliva glands), and toothache.

A branch of the Gb meridian runs from Gb 1 down to St 5, looping back up to the infraorbital region and down again to the neck where it rejoins the main channel, so St 5's traditional functions are to influence the Gb meridian.

Massage techniques are the same as for St 2.

Use with St 6, Cv 24, Co 4, Gb 34, Liv 3, Gb 21, Si 13, and Si 3 for lockjaw.

See St 4 for treatment of awry mouth and facial paralysis.

Use with St 2, St 3, St 4, St 6, St 7, Si 18, Si 3, Co 4, Liv 3, Gb 43, Gb 44, and Gb 34 for swollen cheeks.

See St 3 for toothache.

Applications:

Bob under his right attack and cut across with your right fist over the top of his right forearm to St 5.

ST 6 (STOMACH POINT NO. 6)

Chinese name:

Jiache (jaw vehicle).

Location:

One finger breadth anterior and superior to the lower angle of the mandible, where the masseter attaches at the prominence of the muscle when the teeth are clenched.

Connections:

Gallbladder.

Direction of strike:

In to the jaw at an angle of about 45 degrees toward the backbone.

Damage:

All strikes to the tip of the jaw are dangerous. First of all, a strike to St 6 will cause an instant KO. (It is the classic KO, with every movie star from John Wayne to Sean Connery having made this strike famous.) The reason it works so well is that this point is very close to the "mind point," which will stop signals from getting to the brain from the central nervous system. A strike here will also cause concussion by way of a shock to the brain, bringing about KO, nausea, and loss of memory. A concussion is a violent jar or shock to the brain that causes an immediate change in its function and can include loss of consciousness. For a mild concussion, the signs and symptoms include temporary loss of consciousness, memory loss, and emotional instability. For a severe concussion, the signs and symptoms include prolonged unconsciousness, dilated pupils, change in breathing, disturbed vision and equilibrium, and memory loss. The extent of injury can only be determined by a physician. If the concussion is mild, the injured person may be sent home after examination, but only if a responsible person is present to stay with the injured person and watch for serious symptoms. Follow the doctor's instructions carefully if you are the responsible person, as there are several symptoms to watch for and report to the doctor. The first 24 hours after the injury are critical, but serious aftereffects can appear later. The total extent of the injury may not be apparent for 48 to 72 hours. However, complete recovery is likely with early diagnosis and treatment.

Set-up point:

You want to drain the qi before a strike to the tip of the jaw around St 6, so you could use neigwan or Lu 5 as a set-up point.

Antidote:

Use one of the main "heart starters" (pressure downward to St 11 or a very hard strike to Kd 1 at the base of the foot with a small weapon) if the heart has stopped, or use Gb 20, squeezing upward into the head.

Healing:

Innervation is by the great auricular nerve and the facial and masseteric nerves. Irrigation is by the

Figure 256

Figure 257

masseteric artery and vein. Used for facial paralysis, swelling of the cheek, toothache, trismus, pain and stiffness of the neck, mumps, and temperomanibular arthritis.

Traditional indications include toothache, locked jaw, mouth and eyes awry, stiff neck.

Traditional functions are to disperse wind, remove obstructions from jing luo, adjust circulation of qi, and clear heat from yang ming.

Massage techniques include pressing and holding the point and rotating clockwise or counterclockwise for xu or shi conditions. Also, doing fingertip percussion on this point can be useful; press slowly with both thumbs and release quickly, pulling the thumbs apart.

Use with Co 4, Gb 34, St 5, Gb 21, Liv 3, Pc 6, Ht 7, and Cv 24 for locked jaw or spasm of the masseter muscle.

Use with Th 17, Co 4, St 5, Liv 3, and Co 11 for acute parotitis.

Use with Th 17, St 4, St 2, St 5. St 7, St 8, Co 4, Gv 26, St 18, Gb 14, Liv 3, St 40, St 36, Gb 34, and Pc 6 for facial paralysis from CVA.

Applications:
1) You could open the attacker up using the penetration punch (fig. 256) and then continuing to the jaw at St 6 (fig. 257).
2) Or you could simply attack straight across in defense of his right straight, cutting over his right forearm and up to strike St 6 at a 45-degree angle.

ST 7 (STOMACH POINT NO. 7)

Chinese name:
Xiaguan (lower hinge).
Location:
In the depression at the lower border of the zygomatic arch, anterior to the condyloid process of the

237

mandible, located with the mouth closed. Below this point is the parotid gland and the origin of the masseter muscle.

Connections:

Point of intersection with the Gb meridian.

Direction of strike:

In at an angle of about 45 degrees just in front of the earlobe.

Damage:

Again, this point is a qi drainage point and will cause KO when struck with a smaller weapon such as a one-knuckle punch. A feeling like a tickle in the throat down the front of the same side of the neck is felt, followed by a loss of power in the legs. Ear problems are also apparent with this strike, and they can last for years.

Set-up point:

Neigwan or Lu 5. A hard strike on top of the head will also act as a very good set-up for this point.

Antidote:

Treat Co 10 with mild to heavy thumb pressure.

Healing:

Innervation is by the zygomatic branch of the facial nerve and the auriculotemporal nerve and, at its deepest position, the mandibular nerve. Superficially, irrigation is by the transverse facial artery and vein and, deeper, the maxillary artery and vein.

Used for deafness, tinnitus, otorrhea (discharge from the ear), facial paralysis, toothache, motor impairment of the jaw, trigeminal neuralgia, temporomandibular arthritis, spasm of the masseter muscle, and otitis media.

Traditional indications include toothache, tinnitus, earache, pus in the ear, deafness, dislocated jaw, and mouth and eyes awry.

Traditional functions are to eliminate pathogenic wind, invigorate the jing luo, and soothe and remove obstructions from the joints.

Massage techniques are the same as for St 6.

Use with Th 17, Th 21, Th 3, Si 19, Gb 20, Gb 41, Si 3, Gv 20, and Kd 3 for deafness.

Use with St 6, St 5, St 3, St 44, Co 4, Kd 3, and Bl 11 for toothache.

Use with Co 4, Gb 34, St 5, St 6, Gb 21, Gv 26, Liv 2, Liv 3, St 3, Gb 20, Liv 14, and Bl 18 for lockjaw.

Applications:

Same as for St 6. Or you could block his right straight with your right palm, then bring that same palm back into St 7 using a backfist strike.

ST 8 (STOMACH POINT NO. 8)

Chinese name:

Touwei (head support, head safeguard).

Location:

0.5 cun within the anterior hairline at the corner of the forehead. 4.5 cun lateral to the Gv meridian. The point is found in the galea aponeurotica on the superior margin of the temporalis muscle.

Connections:

There is an internal path from St 8 to Gv 24.

Direction of strike:

Straight down onto the side of the head, usually using a palm strike.

Damage:

Because it is a stomach point, this point will cause concussion with more nausea than any of the other head strikes. Great local pain is felt along with a qi drainage, then KO. Death can occur if this strike is hard enough.

Set-up point:

Any type of damage to the elbow on the side of the head to which you are about to strike will work well as a set-up here.

Antidote:

Apply finger pressure straight inward to Gv 24. (Or use any of the Western medicine treatments for concussion.)

Healing:

Innervation is by the branch of the auriculotemporal nerve and the temporal branch of the facial nerve. Irrigation is by the frontal branches of the superficial temporal artery and vein.

Used for headache, blurring of vision, ophthalmoplegia, lacrimation when exposed to wind, migraine headache, psychosis, and facial paralysis.

Traditional indications include sore eyes with excessive tearing, blurred vision, spasm of the eyelid, headache, dizziness, and wheezing accompanied by irritability and fullness of the chest.

As a point of intersection with the gallbladder and colon meridians and yangwei mai, its traditional functions are to dispel wind, relieve pain, and brighten the eyes.

Massage techniques are the same as for St 6.

For psychosis, use with Co 4, Pc 6, Ht 7, Si 3, Liv 3, Liv 2, Liv 4, Kd 1, Gv 14, Gb 20, Cv 13, Cv 14, Cv 15, Cv 17, Pc 5, Th 6, St 40, Bl 18, Bl 19, Bl 14, Bl 15, Bl 25, Pc 8, Sp 6, Gv 20, yintang, Co 11, and Kd 4.

Use with Lu 7, Co 4, Co 11, Gb 20, Gv 20, Liv 2, Liv 3, St 36, Cv 12, Gb 14, and Gb 21 for migraine headaches.

Use with Bl 1, Bl 2, Liv 3, St 1, St 2, St 3, St 4, Gb 14, and Gb 20 for eyelid tic.

Applications:

You could block his right straight with your right p'eng-type block and then, using your left hand upon his elbow, pull with your right palm and push with your left palm to damage the elbow before striking straight down onto St 8 with your right palm.

ST 9 (STOMACH POINT NO. 9)

Chinese name:

Renying (man's welcome).

Location:

Level with the tip of the Adam's apple, just on the course of the common carotid artery, on the anterior border of the sternocleidomastoideus muscle. In the platysma muscle, 1.5 cun lateral to the laryngeal prominence at the meeting of the anterior margin of the sternocleidomastoid and the thyroid cartilage.

Connections:

Bladder and colon.

Direction of strike:

In to the neck at an angle toward the backbone.

Damage:

St 9 is one of the major dim-mak points. It is easy to get to, and its effect is devastating, ranging from KO for a light blow to death for a heavy blow. St 9 is situated right over the carotid sinus. The carotid sinus is a baroreceptor, responsible for detecting an increase in blood pressure. When it detects this increase, it sends a signal via the vagus nerve, of which it is a part, to the vasomotor center of the brain, which initiates a vasodilatation and slowing of the heart rate to lower the blood pressure to normal.

The martial artist is concerned with a phenomenon called the *carotid sinus reflex*, the decrease of the heart rate as a reflex reaction from pressure on or within the carotid artery at the level of its bifurcation. This reflex starts in the carotid sinus, a pocket in the wall of the carotid artery at its division in the neck. Carotid sinus syndrome is a temporary loss of consciousness or a KO that sometimes accompanies convulsive seizures because of the power of the carotid sinus reflex when pressure builds up in one or both carotid sinuses (or from a strike). This syndrome can be activated artificially by striking to the area of the carotid sinus, St 9.

I have done extensive research on the carotid sinus, seeking out the most knowledgable people in the world. I wanted to know exactly why it causes a person to black out (sometimes even when only stroked in this area). Other people have knocked themselves out when they have turned their heads suddenly because of a hypersensitive carotid sinus. In striking to St 9, we fool the brain into believing that deadly high blood pressure is present. (In many cases, high blood pressure *is* present when one is struck in this area because of the carotid artery being pinched.) My research told me that this was not a point to be played around with, as many people were doing at that particular time, usually to show what good martial artists they were, purely for ego. Some people discovered that they could effect an easy KO by striking to this part of the neck; however, none knew why the KO occurred. Nor did they know the dangers of such strikes. I wrote an article about nine years ago showing the dangers of such strikes and exactly why the KO occurred. It was the first such article, I believe, that showed the medical implications of such a strike. Since then, martial artists have been a little more careful when executing these KOs. But KOs should never be done just to show off. They should only be used in a self-defense situation because the dangers are great. For instance, a recipient can die several years later from stroke caused by the gradual disintegration of the internal wall of the carotid artery (hence the "delayed death touch" phenomenon). The martial artist is able to use a very common medical procedure to his or her advantage. Many doctors will perform the procedure of tweaking the carotid sinus with the fingertips in order to bring the blood pressure down. However, this procedure should only be done if the patient is about to die from high blood pressure! It is a very dangerous procedure!

One of my students in Argentina is a master surgeon. He and his team were performing an operation on the carotid sinus to remove a tumor! However, as an example of the sensitivity of the carotid sinus, when they so much as touched the sinus, the heart rate dropped dramatically. So they were in a dilemma about how to operate without killing the patient.

St 9 also has an effect upon emotional energy and, in the long run, will cause the recipient to have a "detached" feeling of floating, a disconnection between head and body.

It is a medical fact that striking St 9 on the right side will have a greater effect than on the left side. Western medical science cannot explain this, but TCM and dim-mak can. The right side of the body is considered to be yang, while the left side which is relatively yin. When striking to St 9 point on the right side, we attack the yang side after having set up the point with a yin strike to Pc 6. This yin strike has a far greater affect on the yang side of the body because it is opposite.

First Observations of a St 9 Knockout

Here we have the first observations by doctors of a St 9 strike back in 1940 (Jokl 1941):

In July 1940 there was an opportunity to observe for the first time a knock out caused by a strike to the right carotid sinus in a fencer. This case, which to our knowledge is the first observation of its kind, appears to be of great physiological interest. The padded tip of the blade first hit the victim beneath the right clavicle. [No particular points were struck here, but this is the area of "the power band," which, when struck, takes all power from the upper body and is in keeping with the effects of these two strikes on the fencer.]

The blade subsequently bent over and the tip slipped over the clavicle, and with a sharp impact, hit the right carotid sinus [St 9] from below. The victim immediately lost control over his movements. He stumbled backward, his arms dropped, his knees bent and he fell to the ground unconscious. More than one second had elapsed between being struck and losing consciousness. He was weak for four hours afterward after regaining consciousness some 3 minutes later!

What happened to the recipient is in keeping with the St 9 strike, and most people who receive such strikes, either from irresponsible martial artists in seminars or accidentally in sports, for instance, report similar effects. (Some people are affected more or less, depending on the sensitivity of their carotid sinus.)

Figure 258

Set-up point:

There are really only three set-up points for St 9. The first one is neigwan, or Pc 6. I have experimented under controlled situations and have found that the St 9 shot works anywhere, anytime. However, with the set-up of neigwan, the KO is effected using much less pressure. Pc 6 must be struck either straight in or in a direction that is slightly toward you. The other set up points are Lu 8 and Ht 5. These are usually activated by grabbing the wrist and jerking violently, thus draining qi from the body.

Antidote:

The antidote to a St 9 shot is to squeeze Gb 20 (in back of the skull) upward into the head, which will bring yang qi back into the head. If the recipient has been knocked out and the heart has not recovered, then you must use CPR, of course, and, failing that, you must use one of the heart-starting methods discussed elsewhere in this book.

Healing:

Innervation occurs superficially by the cutaneous cervical nerve and the cervical branch of the facial nerve, and, deeper, by the sympathetic trunk. Laterally, it is by the descending branch of the hypoglossal nerve and the vagus nerve. Irrigation is by the superior thyroid artery, the anterior jugular vein, and, laterally, the internal jugular vein, at the bifurcation of the internal and external carotid arteries.

Used for high or low blood pressure, asthma, goiter, distension and soreness in the throat, speech impediment, dizziness, and facial flushing.

Traditional indications include swollen throat, cough, wheezing, swelling of the neck, scrofula, and delirium.

Traditional functions are to regulates the qi and blood and benefit the throat.

To massage, press and hold only one side at a time or do rotations clockwise or counterclockwise for xu or shi conditions. NOTE: *Be very careful with this point!*

Use with Si 17, Co 4, Co 11, St 36, Kd 3, Pc 6, Sp 6, Co 18, and Liv 3 for goiter.

For hypertension, use with Co 11, St 36, Pc 6, Ht 7, Liv 2, Liv 3, Sp 10, Bl 17, Bl 18, Bl 15, and Liv 14.

Use with Gv 26, Liv 3, St 36, Pc 6, Gv 25, and Gv 20 for hypotension.

Applications:

There are many ways to access St 9, so here is one of the best. He attacks with a right hook. Swivel on your heels and strike his right neigwan point in a direction that is away from him. A split second later, your right knife edge will cut into St 9 point in the correct direction, toward the backbone (fig. 258). Done correctly, this will cause death! Done lightly, it will cause KO.

ST 10 (STOMACH POINT NO. 10)

Chinese name:

Shuitu (water prominence).

Location:

At the anterior border of the sternocleidomastoideus, midway between St 9 and St 11.

Connections:

None.

Direction of strike:

Straight in to the neck from the side at an angle of about 45 degrees.

Damage:

This point had always stood in the shadow of St 9. It is, however, just as dangerous as St 9 and, when struck exactly on the point, is considered by many doctors to be even more dangerous. A hard strike here causes an immediate rush of yang qi to the head, causing KO. In addition, the face goes red and the tongue turns blue. This strike adds qi to the head; there is also an immediate shock to the head area. The recipient will fall down a split second afterward. Combined with neigwan, you have a most dangerous strike.

Set-up point:

Neigwan.

Antidote:

Strike downward onto Gb 21 on each shoulder and swipe violently outward to the shoulders.

Healing:

Innervation occurs by the cutaneous cervical nerve superficially and, deeper, by the superior cardiac nerve issued from the sympathetic nerve and the sympathetic trunk. Irrigation is by the common carotid artery.

Used for sore throat, asthma, disease of the vocal cords, and goiter.

Massage techniques are the same as for St 9. (Again, *care should be taken with this point.*)

Use with Gb 20, Gv 14, Bl 11, Cv 22, Gv 4, Th 3, Bl 10, Gv 12, Bl 12, Cv 23, St 9, Gv 3, Gb 26, Liv 2, Liv 3, Sp 6, Co 4, Co 11, Kd 7, Ht 7, Ht 6, St 2, and Pc 6 for enlarged thyroid.

Use with Co 4, Co 11, Co 18, Liv 2, and St 40 for sore throat.

Applications:

Same as for St 9.

ST 11 (STOMACH POINT NO. 11)

Chinese name:

Qishe (qi's residence).

Location:

At the superior border of the sternal extremity of the clavicle, between the sternal head and the clavicular head of the sternocleidomastoideus muscle, directly below St 9.

Connections:

Travels internally to Gv 14 from this point.

Direction of strike:

Downward into the "clavicle notch." You can access this point from above the clavicle or from under the clavicle (from on top is better).

The clavicle, or collar bone, is a long, slightly curving bone that forms the frontal (anterior) part of each shoulder (pectoral) girdle. Located just above the first rib on each side of the ribcage, clavicles attach to the sternum in the middle of the chest and, laterally, to the acromion of the scapula (forming the acromioclavicular joint).

Damage:

St 11 is called the "heart starter" because it does just that in emergency situations. However, this point

Figure 259

will change whatever state the patient was in before being struck here. So if someone is awake (as in an attacker), then this point will stop his heart. If his heart has stopped, hard thumb pressure into the collarbone at this point will sometimes be enough to start the heart again. Because a strike downward into St 11 will stop the heart, it is not a point to play around with. Combine this strike with a clockwise strike to his left pectoral and a counterclockwise strike to his right pectoral at St 15 and 16 points, and you have a very dangerous heart stopper.

Set-up point:

Use Ht 3, struck toward you, as the set-up point.

Antidote:

CPR.

Healing:

Innervation is by the medial supraclavicular nerve and the muscular branch of the ansa hypoglossi. Irrigation occurs, superficially, by the anterior jugular vein and, deeper, by the common carotid artery.

Used for sore throat, asthma, pharyngitis, goiter, and scrofula.

To massage, press and hold the point or do rotation clockwise or counterclockwise for xu or shi conditions.

Use with Co 4, qiying, Cv 22, Co 11, Gb 20, Th 3, Cv 17, Gv 14, biliao, St 10, St 9, Co 18, Cv 23, Liv 2, Liv 3, St 40, Sp 10, Bl 18, and Bl 17 for simple goiter.

For pharyngitis, use with Co 4, Co 11, Lu 5, Lu 7, Co 18, Th 17, Si 16, Cv 23, Cv 22, and Cv 17.

Applications:

You can use a hammer punch or a one-knuckle punch down onto the clavicle or a claw-type weapon that digs into the top of the clavicle at the notch. To access the set-up point, you could take his right straight with your left palm while your right thumb knuckle attacks to Ht 3 (fig. 259).

ST 12 (STOMACH POINT NO. 12)

Chinese name:

Quepen (empty basin).

Location:

In the midpoint of the supraclavicular fossa, 4 cun lateral to the Cv meridian, or in the depression at the middle of the superior border of the clavicle and directly above the nipple.

Connections:

This is where Gv 14 reunites via the internal pathway. The meridian travels internally to St 30, Th, Gb, Co, Si, Cv and Lu (divergent meridians).

Direction of strike:

Downward into the clavicle, usually using a claw type of weapon, a one-knuckle punch, or a hammer fist.

Damage:

This is an interesting point since it is used to take the will to fight away. Anyone who has been struck here will agree on this—you just cannot carry on fighting after this point has been struck because

243

usually the clavicle, which is quite a weak bone, will break, causing great local pain and energy drainage. Also, since it is associated with Gv 14 (meeting place of yang), it affects the communication between yin and yang in the whole body and drains yang qi. It can be used with St 11 to cause great qi loss. It can be used in a grappling situation to stop the fight or in an attacking situation where you have to block and reattack, etc.

Set-up point:

Lu 5 is a good drainage point to use with this strike, as is neigwan. Or, if the situation lends itself to a downward strike to Cv 17, then all the better.

Antidote:

Use any of the qi balancing methods mentioned in earlier chapters. (See a doctor if the clavicle is broken, of course.)

Healing:

Innervation is by the intermediate supraclavicular nerve superficially; deeper, it is by the supraclavicular portion of the brachial plexus. Irrigation is by the transverse cervical artery.

Used for cough, asthma, sore throat, pain in the supraclavicular fossa, hiccups, intercostal neuralgia, and scrofula.

Massage techniques are the same as for St 11.

Use with Si 17, Lu 11, Co 4, Co 11, Bl 11, Bl 12, Bl 17, Lu 2, Lu 5, Liv 2, St 44, St 45, Kd 1, Kd 2, Liv 3, Sp 10, Cv 22, and Cv 23 for acute tonsillitis where the throat is blocked with hot and cold sensation.

Use with Kd 7, Lu 1, Liv 3, Lu 5, Lu 9, Liv 14, Gb 21, Kd 27, Kd 11, Bl 13, Bl 43, and dingchuan for sports-induced asthma.

Applications:

You could use a triple strike here (i.e., block and attack his right hook with your right palm at Lu 5, draining qi; then use a quick elbow shot to Cv 14 followed by a right claw to St 12.

ST 13 (STOMACH POINT NO. 13)

Chinese name:

qihu (qi's household).

Location:

At the middle of the inferior border of the clavicle, on the mamillary line (4 cun lateral to the Cv meridian).

Connections:

None.

Direction of strike:

Up under the clavicle directly below St 12.

Damage:

Whereas St 12 drains qi, St 13 adds yang qi to the head, causing loss of balance to the falling down point. With most of the St points, it will also cause great nausea. This is one of those points where the qi is said to enter the meridian, so a strike here also unbalances the yin and yang energy in the whole body.

Set-up point:

Neigwan struck upward on the inside of the forearm.

Antidote:

Rub neigwan in the opposite direction or use Gb 21 pushing downward.

Healing:

Innervation is by the branches of the supraclavicular nerve and the anterior thoracic nerve. Irrigation is by the branches of the thoracoacromial artery and vein and, superiorly, the subclavicular vein.

Used for asthma, cough, fullness of the chest, bronchitis, hiccups, and intercostal neuralgia.

To massage, press and hold the point, rotate clockwise or counterclockwise for xu or shi conditions, rub across the point, or press slowly with both thumbs and release quickly, pulling the thumbs apart. Fingertip percussion can be used on this point.

Use with Lu 1, Lu 5, Lu 7, Lu 9, Co 4, Co 10, Cv 17, Kd 7, Kd 27, Liv 14, Liv 3, St 36, Bl 12, Bl 13, Bl 17, and Bl 18 for asthma, bronchitis, cough, etc.

Applications:

Block the inside of his right forearm at Pc 6 upward with your left palm while your right one-knuckle punch attacks to St 13 upward under the clavicle.

St 14 (STOMACH POINT NO. 14)

Chinese name:

Kufang (storehouse).

Location:

In the first intercostal space, on the mamillary line, 4 cun lateral to Cv 20.

Connections:

None.

Direction of strike:

Strike slightly downward onto the top of the pectoral. Usually using a palm heel strike.

Damage:

Immediately, the recipient feels a sickly feeling in the whole chest area, quickly growing to full nausea. The strike must be fairly hard to have an effect, though.

Set-up point:

Neigwan.

Antidote:

Rub neigwan up the forearm.

Healing:

Innervation is by the branch of the anterior thoracic nerve. Irrigation is by the thoracoacrominal artery and vein and the branches of the lateral thoracic artery and vein.

Used for sensation of fullness and pain in the chest and hypochondriac region, cough, bronchitis, intercostal neuralgia.

Massage techniques are the same as for St 13.

Use with Bl 12, Bl 13, Bl 17, Bl 20, Lu 1, Lu 7, Lu 5, Cv 17, St 13, St 12, Cv 14, Lu 10, and Si 1 for bronchitis, cough, etc.

Use with Liv 2, Liv 3, jiaji points level with the region of pain, Bl 17, Bl 18, Bl 19, Bl 20, Liv 14, Gb 24, and Cv 17 for intercostal neuralgia.

Applications:

Take his right hook and strike neigwan toward you as your right palm slams downward onto the upper pectoral.

ST 15 (STOMACH POINT NO. 15)

Chinese name:

Wuyi (room screen).

Location:

In the second intercostal space, on the mamillary line, 4 cun lateral to Cv 19.

Connections:

None.

Direction of strike:

There are several directions for this strike, the most effective being a clockwise strike on his left side and a counterclockwise strike on his right side. The palm is used, and as it makes contact, twist your

Figure 260

Figure 261

elbows, squeezing inward to make the circles on either pectoral. You can also strike these points straight in or with a downward action. The result is the same in stopping the heart.

Damage:

Stops the heart when struck along with and at the same time as St 16, which is just below it, so both points can be struck with the palm.

Set-up point:

Use neigwan, pulling it toward you on both sides usually, in retaliation to a two-handed attack.

Antidote:

CPR.

Healing:

Innervation occurs on the course of the branch of pectoralis major derived from the anterior thoracic nerve. Irrigation is by the same vessels as St 14.

Used for cough, asthma, fullness and pain in the chest, mastitis, bronchitis, and intercostal neuralgia. Massage techniques are the same as for St 13.

Use with Liv 14, Liv 3, St 18, Cv 17, Sp 18, St 36, and Sp 6 for mastitis. St 15 can also be used with the St 13 or St 14 treatment of asthma, bronchitis, and cough.

Applications:

He might come at you with both hands. Both of your palms open up underneath both of his forearms at both neigwans, which you strike toward you. You immediately bring both palms back in and strike to both sides at St 15 and 16 with a twisting motion (figs. 260 and 261).

ST 16 (STOMACH POINT NO. 16)

Chinese name:

Yingghuan (breast's window).

Location:

In the third intercostal space, on the mamillary line, 4 cun lateral to Cv 18.

Connections:

None.

Direction of strike:

The same as St 15.

Damage:

Same as St 15.

Set-up point:

Same as St 15.

Antidote:

Same as St 15

Healing:

Innervation is by the branch of the anterior thoracic nerve. Irrigation is by the lateral thoracic artery and vein.

Use for cough, asthma, fullness and pain of the chest, mastitis, bronchitis, and intercostal neuralgia.

Massage techniques are the same as for St 13, if the breast tissue is full at this point then only gentle pressure should be used and percussion should be avoided.

Use with Cv 17, Liv 14, Liv 3, Liv 2, St 15, Sp 18, St 36, Bl 17, Bl 18, Bl 19, Si 1, Pc 6, and Gb 21 for mastitis.

You can add this point to the formulas for asthma, bronchitis, and cough shown under St 13 and St 14.

Applications:

Same as St 15.

ST 17 (STOMACH POINT NO. 17)

Chinese name:

Ruzhong (middle of breast).

Location:

In the middle of the nipple in the fourth intercostal space.

Connections:

There is a connection with the upper heater.

Direction of strike:

Straight in using a smaller weapon.

Damage:

This point when struck has a devastating effect and will cause death when a medium to hard strike is used. (In acupuncture, it is only ever given as a reference; it is not to be needled, nor is moxa to be used on it.) The strike must be accurate to within a millimeter, though. Immediately there is a sensation moving up the left side of the neck (if the left nipple is struck and vice versa) and over the top of the back of the head to the other side of the forehead, followed by an extreme qi drainage resulting in KO and loss of memory. If the strike has been hard enough, it could also result in mental illness that gets worse with age. *This is not a nice point, and should never be played around with!*

Set-up point:

It needs no set-up point; however, a tap to the side of the jaw will enhance the effect.

Antidote:

See a Chinese doctor (a Western doctor will not usually know what has happened). You must tell the doctor that you have been struck in St 17 (if you are able to, or have someone else do it for you). Mention the mental disintegration, etc.

Healing:

Innervation is by the anterior and lateral cutaneous branches of the fourth intercostal nerve. Irrigation is by a branch of the right and left subclavian arteries and veins or the branches of the intercostal arteries and veins.

This point is used only for a landmark, and while some sources claim moxibustion can be used in some circumstances, and it certainly has implications in erotic massage, I would not use it in any way in my clinic other than as a landmark (there are 8 cun between the nipples).

Applications:

Strike the point straight in at the nipple. You could also use two one-knuckle punches to both sides! Place your palms on top of his forearms and slam them downward (fig. 262), then bring both one-knuckle punches back up into both St 17 points, leading slightly with your right fist (i.e., it strikes a split second before the left one).

ST 18 (STOMACH POINT NO. 18)

Chinese name:

Rugen (breast root).

Location:

In the fifth intercostal space, directly below the nipple.

Connections:

None.

Direction of strike:

Straight in just under the nipple.

Damage:

I have read that this point is quite dangerous. However, it is my belief that those who say this are confusing this point with Liv 14. St 18 must be struck quite hard to have any effect. Those effects are headache, nausea, and, if struck on the left side, a shock directly to the heart. If you combine this strike with Liv 14, which is easy since Liv 14 lies just below St 18, then the effect is far greater in terms of qi drainage.

Set-up point:

Neigwan.

Antidote:

Rub neigwan back up the inner forearm.

Healing:

Innervation is by the branch of the fifth intercostal nerve. Irrigation is by the fifth intercostal artery and vein.

Used for cough, asthma, mastitis, deficient lactation, pain in the chest, bronchitis, and cholecystitis. Massage techniques are the same as for St 13.

Use with Cv 17, Si 1, Bl 18, Bl 20, St 36, Liv 3, Pc 6, and Co 4 for insufficient lactation.

Also, add this point to the formula for mastitis listed under St 16.

Applications:

Same as for St 17.

Figure 262

Chinese name:

Burong (uncontainable).

Location:

6 cun above the umbilicus, 2 cun lateral to Cv 14.

Connections:

None.

Direction of strike:

Straight in and slightly toward the outside of the body just under the ribcage.

Damage:

If St 18 was not too exciting, then St 19 is just the opposite. This strike attacks the seat of power, as does Cv 17, only this strike is even more damaging to the diaphragm because it strikes to the muscles that work the diaphragm, causing the recipient to feel as if he has no power at all and fall down. If this strike is hard enough it will cause death from suffocation.

Set-up point:

Neigwan combined with "the mind point."

Antidote:

Lie the patient down and apply pressure upward from the navel to the upper chest, using medium pressure. See a doctor!

Healing:

Innervation is by the branch of the seventh intercostal nerve. Irrigation is by the branches of the seventh intercostal artery and vein, the branches of the superior epigastric artery and vein.

Used for abdominal distension, vomiting, gastric pain, anorexia, gastrectasia, and intercostal neuralgia.

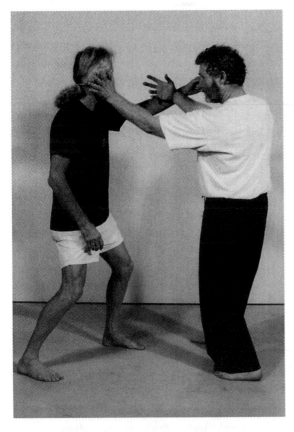

Figure 263

Figure 264

Massage techniques are the same as for St 13.

Use with Cv 12, Pc 6, Sp 4, Liv 3, St 44, Gb 20, Bl 18, Bl 20, Bl 25, Cv 17, Cv 16, St 20, St 21, Gb 26, and Liv 14 for morning sickness.

Use with St 36, Liv 3, Bl 20, Bl 19, Bl 18, Bl 25, Bl 23, Cv 12, Liv 13, Ht 7, Pc 6, Cv 4, Lu 1, Lu 9, St 21, and St 25 for anorexia.

Applications:

Strike his left neigwan with the back of your right palm as your left palm attacks to his right "mind point" (fig. 263). Now your right one-knuckle punch attacks to St 19 (fig. 264).

ST 20 (STOMACH POINT NO. 20)

Chinese name:

Chengman (support fullness).

Location:

5 cun above the umbilicus, 2 cun lateral to Cv 13 and 1 cun below St 19.

Connections:

None.

Direction of strike:

This strike does much the same damage as St 19, only the direction of the strike must be straight in this time.

Damage:

Attacks the seat of power, causing KO or death.

Set-up point:

Mind point.

Antidote:

Get to a hospital.

Healing:

Innervation and irrigation same as for St 19.

Used for gastric pain, abdominal distension, vomiting, anorexia, acute and chronic gastritis, intestinal noises, colic, and indigestion.

Massage techniques are the same as for St 13 with no percussion or very light percussion (better to use fingertip vibration).

For anorexia, use with St 21, St 22, plus the formula for anorexia listed under St 19.

Use with St 36, Pc 6, St 21, Liv 13, St 25, Liv 3, Cv 12, Cv 14, Cv 9, and St 37 for gastric pain, abdominal distension, and vomiting.

Applications:

Same as for St 19.

ST 21 (STOMACH POINT NO. 21)

Chinese name:

Liangmen (door of the beam).

Location:

4 cun above the umbilicus, 2 cun lateral to Cv 12.

Connections:

None.

Direction of strike:

Straight in.

Damage:

This point can be protected somewhat by the abdominal muscles; however, it is also an "electrical point," so it will have an effect regardless. It causes great local pain and qi drainage, as well as stomach and spleen problems due to its effect upon the yang qi of those organs.

Set-up point:

No set-up point, but it can be used with St 36 to enhance the effect of pain.

Antidote:

Rub the whole lower leg downward to the foot.

Healing:

Innervation is by the branch of the eighth intercostal nerve. Irrigation is by the branches of the eighth intercostal and the superior epigastric artery and veins.

Used for gastric pain, vomiting, anorexia, loose stool, stomach ulcers, stomachache, acute and chronic gastritis, and nervous dysfunction of the stomach.

Traditional indications include pain in the stomach cavity, abdominal pain caused by accumulation of qi, colic, and prolapsed anus. Traditional functions include promoting the function of the stomach and spleen. Used a lot for epigastric pain when the pain is more lateral.

Massage techniques are the same as for St 20.

Use with Pc 6, St 36, Cv 12, Cv 14, Cv 11, Bl 21, Bl 20, Bl 19, Bl 17, Sp 6, Sp 4, St 40, St 43, St 44, Sp 9, Liv 3, Cv 4, Liv 13, St 19, St 20, St 22, St 23, and St 24 for stomachache.

Use with St 37, St 40, Sp 4, Sp 3, Sp 9, St 25, Bl 25, Bl 23, Bl 20, Cv 12, Cv 9, and St 28 for loose stool.

Use with Pc 6, Liv 14, Liv 3, Cv 12, Bl 20, Bl 21, Ht 7, and Bl 14 for nervous dysfunction of the stomach.

Applications:

You could block his right straight on the outside with your right p'eng-type block as your right heel attacks downward at St 36. Then your one-knuckle punch attacks straight in to St 21.

ST 22 (STOMACH POINT NO. 22)

Chinese name:

Guanmen (gate).

Location:

3 cun above the umbilicus, 2 cun lateral to Cv 11.

Connections:

None.

Direction of strike:

Straight in.

Damage:

This strike attacks the communication between upper and lower. So there is confusion over what the lower body is doing. A feeling of something draining from lower body is also apparent until the power to the legs has gone.

Set-up point:

Use this point with Gb 25 for a devastating effect, like death!

Antidote:

Kd 1.

Healing:

Innervation and irrigation are the same as for St 21.

Used for abdominal distension and pain, borborygmus, diarrhea, anorexia, edema, and lack of appetite.

Massage techniques are the same as for St 20.

Use with St 21, St 20, St 19, St 23, St 24, St 25, Cv 10, Cv 12, Cv 4, St 36, St 40, Sp 9, Pc 6, and Liv 3 for pain and distension of the abdomen, borborygmus, etc.

Use with Gv 20, Cv 17, Cv 12, Cv 6, Cv 4, St 36, Sp 3, Liv 13, Liv 3, St 25, St 21, Bl 20, Bl 25, Bl 18, and Bl 17 for lack of appetite.

Applications:

You could use both palms against his right attack. Then your right palm attacks from side to Gb 25, followed by your right elbow to St 22.

ST 23 (STOMACH POINT NO. 23)

Chinese name:

Taiyi (great yi).

Location:

2 cun above the umbilicus, 2 cun lateral to Cv 10.

Connections:

None.

Direction of strike:

Straight in.

Damage:

Same as for St 22. Plus there is an adverse effect upon the bladder, causing problems both immediately and in later life. The recipient is likely to urinate when struck here with a smaller weapon such as a one-knuckle punch.

Set-up point:

Any bladder point or Gb 25 can be used to set up this point.

Antidote:

Co 10 used with Ht 7 squeezed back up the forearm at the same time.

Healing:

Innervation is by the branches of the eighth and ninth intercostal nerves. Irrigation is by the branches of the eighth and ninth intercostal and the inferior epigastric arteries and veins.

Used for mental disorders, irritability, restlessness, gastric pain, indigestion, intestinal pain, hernia, and enuresis.

Massage techniques are the same as for St 20.

Use with Cv 14, Gb 20, Gv 15, Cv 14, St 40, Pc 5, Pc 6, Ht 5, Th 6, Sp 6, Gv 20, Bl 58, St 24, Liv 3, Bl 18, Bl 20, Bl 14, Bl 15, Co 4, Co 11, Pc 8, Kd 4, Kd 1, Ht 7, Gb 34, Liv 4, Liv 5, Th 17, and Bl 1 for mental disorders.

Use with Liv 14, Liv 2, Liv 3, Bl 18, Bl 17, Bl 20, Cv 12, St 36, Pc 6, Ht 7, St 25, Bl 25, and Bl 14 for restlessness and irritability.

See St 22 for treatment of gastric pain and indigestion.

Applications:

Same as for St 22.

ST 24 (STOMACH POINT NO. 24)

Chinese name:

Huaroumen (door of slippery flesh).

Location:

1 cun above the umbilicus, 2 cun lateral to Cv 9.

Connections:

None.

Direction of strike:

Straight in using a smaller weapon.

Damage:

This point is protected by the abdominal muscles; however, it will have an electrical effect that affects the colon. In other words, it will cause the recipient to defecate not too soon after the strike, but with great pain.

Set-up point:

Co 10 will enhance the effect upon the colon.

Antidote:

Co 10 squeezed inward.

Healing:

Innervation is by the branch of the ninth intercostal nerve. Irrigation is by the branches of the ninth intercostal and the inferior epigastric arteries and veins.

Used for mental disorders, vomiting, gastric pain, acute and chronic gastritis, and insanity.

Massage techniques are the same as for St 20.

See St 23 for treatment of mental disorders.

Use with St 23, St 22, St 21, St 20, St 19, Cv 14, Cv 12, Cv 9, Pc 6, St 36, Sp 9, Sp 3, Liv 3, St 25, Bl 25, Bl 20, Bl 23, Bl 21, Bl 18, and Bl 17 for gastric pain, vomiting, gastritis, etc.

Applications:

Use a right backfist against his right straight attack. Your left palm now also slams into Si 8 at his elbow as your right one-knuckle punch attacks straight in to St 24.

ST 25 (STOMACH POINT NO. 25)

Chinese name:

Tianshu (heaven's axis).

Location:

2 cun lateral to the center of the umbilicus.

Connections:

None.

Direction of strike:

Straight in at an angle that goes toward the center of the body.

Damage:

A "mu colon point," St 25 will affect the colon. It is on the border of protection and no protection (i.e., the torso is well protected by muscle, but below the navel there is relatively little protection.) A hard strike to this point can cause KO. It will also cause diarrhea on the spot. This is a point that is capable of causing emotional disorders as well as the physical symptoms that go with emotional disorders, because it upsets the communication between shen and zhang fu (solid organs), in this case between the shen and the gallbladder and triple heater. First the recipient will feel pain that will grow in a circle outward from the strike, then he will feel a great power loss.

Set-up point:

Co 10.

Antidote:

Rub the outer forearm heavily downward, with attention to Co 10.

Healing:

Innervation is by the branch of the 10th intercostal nerve. Irrigation is by the branches of the 10th intercostal and the inferior epigastric arteries and veins.

Used for abdominal pain, diarrhea, dysentery, constipation, borborygmus, abdominal distension, edema, irregular menstruation, acute and chronic gastritis or enteritis, intestinal paralysis, peritonitis, roundworm in the intestinal tract, endometritis, and lower back pain.

Traditional indications include vomiting, diarrhea, abdominal pain, constipation, vaginal discharge with blood, irregular menstruation, dripping of turbid urine, infertility, and abdominal obstruction or lumps due to accumulation of qi and blood.

As a front mu point of the colon, its traditional functions are to regulate and facilitate the functioning of the colon, regulate qi and eliminate stagnation of qi and blood, and regulate menstruation. Reflects problems with the colon when palpated.

Massage techniques are the same as for St 20.

Use with Kd 5, Liv 3, Cv 4, Cv 6, Liv 4, Bl 18, Gb 26, and Sp 6 for irregular menstruation.

Use with St 37, St 40, Sp 4, Bl 25, Bl 23, Bl 20, Gv 20, and St 21 for diarrhea, borborygmus, etc.

Use with Th 6, Pc 6, Gv 12, Bl 20, Bl 18, Bl 21, St 36, Liv 3, St 21, and Co 4 for vomiting, nausea, and loose stool.

See St 26 for other things this point can treat.

Applications:

You could slam his Co 10 point with your right backfist and use your left palm to pull his right arm out of the way as your right palm slams into St 25. Or you could use a knee to St 25 by pulling him onto your knee.

ST 26 (STOMACH POINT NO. 26)

Chinese name:

Wailing (outer tomb).

Location:

1 cun below the umbilicus, 2 cun lateral to Cv 7.

Connections:

None.

Direction of strike:

Straight in.

Damage:

This strike will cause much the same damage as St 25, as it is still right over the colon, although there will be a little more physical damage as it is further down into the lower body. A hard strike will cause blackout, as it is an intestine strike. (There are three parts of the body that will cause a knock out when struck or in pain—the gallbladder, the intestines, and the ureter.

Set-up point:

Co 10.

Antidote:

Same as for St 25.

Healing:

Innervation and irrigation are the same as for St 25. Used for abdominal pain, hernia, and painful menstruation.

Massage techniques are the same as for St 20.

Use with St 25, St 27, St 36, St 37, St 40, Liv 3, Cv 4, Cv 6, Cv 9, and Cv 12 for abdominal pain.

Use with Liv 4, Liv 3, Cv 4, Cv 6, Sp 9, Sp 6, Bl 18, Bl 19, and Bl 17 for painful menstruation.

Use with Liv 8, Liv 5, Liv 4, Liv 12, Sp 6, St 23, St 27, St 28, St 29, St 30, Liv 3, Liv 8, St 36, Cv 12, Bl 20, and Gv 20 for hernia.

Traditional function is as a diagnostic tool. When pressed in conjunction with St 25 and Kd 15 (not Kd 16), if painful on the left side, it can reflect liver disharmony. If painful on the right side when pressed along with St 25, it can reflect a lung problem. Redness and darkness, or paleness with inverted tissue may also be a reflection of heat (if the former) or cold, weakness (if the latter).

Applications:

Same as for St 25. You could also use a back or a front kick to this point as well as to St 25.

ST 27 (STOMACH POINT NO. 27)

Chinese name:

Daju (the great or big, huge).

Location:

2 cun below the umbilicus, 2 cun lateral to Cv 5.

Connections:

None.

Direction of strike:

Straight in and slightly angled toward the midline.

Damage:

In this instance, the strike will disrupt the communication between the shen and the colon/stomach. It will cause emotional problems immediately, and if not treated by an acupuncturist, it will grow into emotional problems, such as not letting go of unwanted emotions (allowing them to grow and fester!) and obsessiveness to extremes. In the immediate, it will also cause great pain and qi loss—and KO if it is hard enough.

Set-up point:

St 36 or Co 10, or both.

Antidote:

For the emotional problems, have an acupuncturist treat St 27 along with Lu 1.

Healing:

Innervation is by the 11th intercostal nerve. Irrigation is by the branches of the 11th intercostal artery and vein and, laterally, the inferior epigastric artery and vein.

Used for lower abdominal distension and pain, dysuria, hernia, seminal emission, intestinal obstruction, retention of urine, and cystitis.

Traditional indications include abdominal distention and pain, hernia, and spermatorrhea.

Massage techniques are the same as for St 20.

Traditional functions are the same as for St 26.

See St 26 for treatment of hernia.

Use with Cv 12, Cv 6, Cv 4, Cv 10, St 21, St 30, St 25, St 29, Sp 14, Sp 15, Sp 16, Gv 4, St 36, jiaji points from the eighth thoracic to the second lumbar, Liv 3, Liv 2, Bl 20, Bl 18, Bl 17, and Ht 7 for polio where abdominal muscles are paralyzed.

Use with Cv 4, Cv 3, Cv 6, St 28, St 36, Sp 6, Sp 10, Liv 3, Liv 4, Bl 18, and Bl 17 for difficult or painful menstruation.

Applications:

Same as for St 26. This point is still high enough for a palm shot.

ST 28 (STOMACH POINT NO. 28)

Chinese name:

Shuidao (water way).

Location:

3 cun below the umbilicus, 2 cun lateral to Gv 4. In the rectus abdominis muscle and its sheath.

Connections:

None.

Direction of strike:

Straight in and slightly toward the midline.

Damage:

This strike is dangerous. It will immediately cause KO through the action on the colon, causing an "explosion" in the lower heater that will grow outward to the rest of the lower abdomen. Needless to say, repeated strikes to any of the lower abdomen points can cause bowel cancers later in life! This point really shocks the whole lower heater, causing damage to the elimination system.

Set-up point:

Co 10.

Antidote:

Have an acupuncturist work on "lifting" points that will lift the colon up, since this strike usually causes a prolapsed colon.

Healing:

Innervation is by the branch of the subcostal nerve. Irrigation is by the branches of the subcostal artery and vein, and, laterally, by the inferior epigastric artery and vein.

Used for lower abdominal distension, hernia, retention of urine, nephritis, cystitis, ascites, and orchitis.

Traditional indications include distension and fullness of the lower abdomen, heat and constriction in the triple heater, lack of urine, pain leading to the genitals, and edema.

Traditional functions are to eliminate damp from the lower heater, cool damp heat, benefit the bladder, and treat damp anywhere in the body. It can also be used in abdominal diagnosis to reflect fluid retention, etc.

Massage tehcniques are the same as for St 20.

Use with Kd 6, Bl 22, Bl 23, Bl 28, Gv 4, Bl 20, Gv 2, Cv 3, Gv 5, Gv 9, Sp 9, Sp 4, Kd 7, Kd 11, St 36, Sp 11, and Sp 12 for fluid retention.

See St 27 for treatment of difficult or painful menstruation. Use with Bl 32, Bl 39, Cv 3, Sp 6, Bl 23, Bl 22, Bl 28, Bl 33, Gv 2, Cv 4, Liv 4, and Liv 3 for urinary retention or incontinence.

Applications:

Same as for St 27. Or you could get around behind the attacker using any of the grappling-type movements (see my earlier book, *How to Fight a Grappler and Win*) and then use a quick pulling movement with both arms, where the fingers of both hands dig into both St 28 points. This is often enough to cause KO.

ST 29 (STOMACH POINT NO. 28)

Chinese name:

Guilai (return).

Location:

4 cun below the umbilicus, 2 cun lateral to Cv 3, in the lateral margin of the rectus abdominis muscle, the internal oblique muscle, and the aponeurosis of the transverse abdominis muscle.

Connections:

None.

Direction of strike:

Straight in and slightly in to the midline.

Damage:

This is a special point for the genitals. It is opposite Cv 3, which is a meeting point for the three "yins." It will affect the circulation of kidney qi, which in turn will affect the power of the whole body. It will cause stagnation of qi and thus a gradual loss of health. The immediate effect is a KO by the action upon the genitals; hard enough will cause death.

Set-up point:

None.

Antidote:

See a doctor and acupuncturist. Obviously a strike to this area will cause great physical problems, which should be attended to immediately.

Healing:

Innervation is by the iliohypogastric nerve. Irrigation is by the inferior epigastric artery and vein on the lateral side.

Used for abdominal pain, hernia, amenorrhea, prolapse of the uterus, irregular menstruation, inflammation of the adnexa, endometritis, and orchitis.

Traditional indications include colic, lack of menstruation, infertility, vaginal discharge, orchitis, and dysmenorrhea.

Traditional functions are to move stagnation of blood from the uterus and move stagnant qi and blood.

Massage techniques are the same as for St 20.

Use with Gb 27, Liv 3, Cv 2, Cv 3, Cv 4, Cv 6, Liv 4, Liv 5, Liv 6, Liv 8, Gb 21, and St 30 for retraction of the testicles. Use with Gb 26, Sp 6, Liv 2, Liv 3, Sp 9, Gv 4, Gv 6, St 36, and Kd 7 for leukorrhea.

Use with Gv 4, Bl 23, Co 4, Bl 25, Sp 6, Sp 8, Sp 10, Kd 14, Gv 4, Cv 3, Cv 6, St 36, Bl 18, Bl 20, and Bl 17 for amenorrhea.

Applications:

The same as for St 28.

ST 30 (STOMACH POINT NO. 30)

Chinese name:

Qichong (pouring qi).

Location:

5 cun below the umbilicus, 2 cun lateral to Cv 2, superior to the inguinal groove on the medial side of the femoral artery. In the aponeurosis of the external and internal oblique muscles, and the lower region of the transverse abdominis muscle.

Connections:

Gb, Bl, and Cv. This is where the internal branch from St 12 reunites with the St meridian and is the lower meeting point of St/Sp divergent meridian.

Direction of strike:

Straight in and slightly toward the midline.

Damage:

This is the "sea of nourishment" point along with St 36. It is also a point of the chong mai, or life force meridian. It circulates yuan qi to the stomach and hence to earth. A strike here will lower the body's ability to fight off disease and cause a gradual overall decline of qi to the internal organs. It will also hinder the free flow of qi. (The opposite occurs when St 30 and 36 are treated in a healing way.) This strike will cause KO immediately, and death can occur when a very heavy strike is taken. Even after medical treatment, the damage continues to mount if the person is not treated by an acupuncturist as well.

Set-up point:

Lu 5 or St 36.

Antidote:

Treat the same point on the opposite side of the attack, along with St 36.

Healing:

Innervation is by the ilioinguinal nerve. Irrigation is by the branches of the superficial epigastric artery and vein and, laterally, by the inferior epigastric artery and vein.

Used for pain and swelling of the external genitalia, hernia, irregular menstruation, and diseases of the reproductive organs.

Traditional indications include pain in the penis or testicles, colic, excessive bleeding, infertility, and disorders related to childbirth.

As a point of intersection with the chong mai, it can have a strong influence on the qi and blood flow in the body. (Chong mai connects all of the kidney points on the abdomen and is in some ways is seen as the origin of all the other extra meridians.) Massage tehcniques are the same as for St 20.

Use with Gv 20, Gb 28, SP 6, Cv 6, SP 9, Liv 3, Liv 4, Liv 8, Bl 20, Bl 18, Bl 17, Kd 6, and Cv 12 for prolapsed uterus. Use with Bl 31, Bl 32, Co 4, Sp 6, Liv 4, Sp 12, and Gb 21 for difficulty in labor.

Use with Gv 2, Bl 28, Gv 1, Bl 31, Bl 34, Bl 25, Bl 26, Bl 53, Bl 54, Bl 40, and Gb 34 for lower back pain.

Applications:

Strike the point with the knee or with a palm strike, although for the most damage to occur a smaller weapon should be used, such as a one-knuckle punch.

ST 31 (STOMACH POINT NO. 31)

Chinese name:

Biguan (hip hinge or thigh gate).

Location:

Directly below the anterior superior iliac spine, in the depression on the lateral side of the sartorius muscle when the thigh is flexed, level with the perineum. Inferior and medial to the great trochanter of the femur, between the satorius and the tensor fascia lata muscles.

Connections:

None.

Direction of strike:

Straight in to the top of the thigh.

Damage:

This point is called the "leg-draining point" because that's what it does. It will greatly decrease the qi to the legs, causing the recipient to have to sit down or else fall down! This point can be used as an excellent set-up for a physical leg strike because bones will break easily when this point has been struck first.

Set-up point:

If you were using St 31 as the main strike, then you could use any of the qi drainage points, such as Lu 5 or Pc 6.

Antidote:

Apply medium pressure to St 31 on the opposite leg with the thumb. Then massage down the outside of the leg and up the inside of the leg using medium pressure.

Healing:

Innervation is by the lateral femoral cutaneous nerve. Irrigation is by branches of the lateral circumflex femoral artery and vein in the deep position.

Used for pain in the thigh, muscular atrophy, motor impairment and numbness and pain of the lower extremities, lymphadenitis of the inguinal lymph glands, arthritis of the knee, and lower back pain.

Traditional indications include atrophy or blockage of the muscles of the thigh and buttock, inhibited movement of the leg muscle due to sinew tension, lower back pain and cold knees, numbness of the leg, infantile paralysis, and the after effects of wind stroke.

Its traditional function is as a very important point for qi circulation in the legs.

Massage techniques include pressing and holding the point; rotating clockwise or counterclockwise for xu or shi conditions; pressing in slowly with both thumbs and releasing quickly, pulling the thumbs apart; doing percussion with fingertips or a loose fist; and pulling across the point.

Use with Gb 29, Gb 30, Gb 31, Gb 32, Gb 34, St 32, and St 34 for pain or numbness in the thigh. Add St 36, Bl 20, Sp 3, and Liv 3 for leg atrophy.

Use with Bl 36, Bl 40, Gb 34, Bl 25, Bl 26, Bl 53, Bl 54, and Gb 30 for arthritis of the hip joint.

Applications:

He attacks with a straight right, and you slam his arm at Th 8 with your right backfist as your left palm strikes to Si 8 at the elbow (fig. 265). The right palm now rotates back to strike straight in to St 31 (fig. 266). It's OK to strike using the palm in this instance because of the nature of this method. Normally you would not use the palm this low.

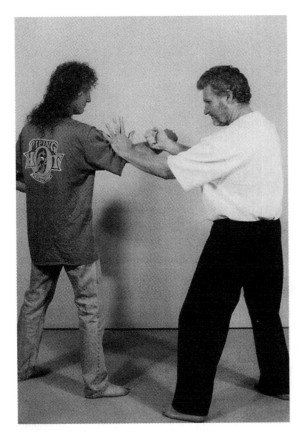

Figure 265

Figure 266

ST 32 (STOMACH POINT NO. 32)

Chinese name:

Futu (hidden rabbit).

Location:

6 cun above the laterosuperior border of the patella, on the line connecting the anterior superior iliac spine and the lateral border of the patella. At the lateral anterior aspect of the femur, in the middle of the belly of the rectus femoris muscle.

Connections:

None.

Direction of strike:

Straight in to the front of the thigh.

Damage:

This strike is called, in dim-mak terms, leg-paralyzing point. It can be struck with a palm straight across the thigh. Alternatively, with an implement such as a stick, the strike must be 180 degrees across the thigh (laterally, not at an angle). It paralyzes the leg and shocks the whole system, and it will cause KO when done hard enough because the brain is shocked for a moment, not knowing what has happened.

Set-up point:

Attack the lower forearm downward, away from his body (see "Applications").

Antidote:

Provided that this strike has not been too great, he will get over it given time. It is really a physiological strike that attacks the femoral nerve.

Healing:

Innervation is by the anterior and lateral femoral cutaneous nerves. Irrigation is by the lateral circumflex femoral artery and vein.

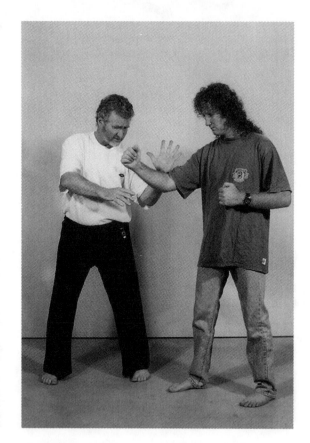

Figure 267

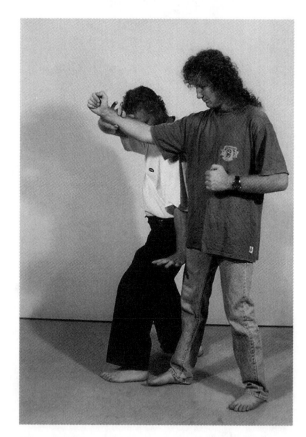

Figure 268

Used for pain in the lumbar and iliac regions, coldness of the knee, paralysis or motor impairment and pain of the lower extremities, arthritis of the knee, and urticaria.

Traditional indications include pain in the waist and groin, numbness of the lower limbs, leg qi (beriberi). Massage techniques are the same as for St 31.

See St 31 for treatment of pain or numbness of the thigh.

Use with St 34, St 35, St 36, Gb 34, Liv 3, Gb 41, and xiyan on the medial side of the knee.

With Sp 10, Sp 9, and Sp 6 for knee problems.

Applications:

1) He attacks with a straight right. You slam his forearm downward with your left palm as you step in with your left foot, turning your foot in the same direction that the attacker is facing (fig. 267). Now, your right foot steps around to his rear so that you are now facing the same direction that he is, and your right palm takes over this block as your left palm strikes across St 32 (fig. 268).

2) Or you could simply attack straight in to St 32 in retaliation to a kick.

ST 33 (STOMACH POINT NO. 33)

Chinese name:

Yinshi (yin's market).

Location:

3 cun above the laterosuperior border of the patella, on the line connecting the anterior superior iliac spine and the lateral border of the patella.

Connections:

None.

Direction of strike:

Straight in just above the knee.

Damage:

Great local pain and subsequent qi drainage from the leg. This is also an electrical point that will send a rush of qi to the head, causing confusion and possible blackout if the strike is hard enough.

Set-up point:

Jerk the wrist violently at Ht 5 and Lu 8 just before you kick to the point.

Antidote:

Needle St 36 or use medium finger pressure.

Healing:

Innervation is by the anterior and lateral femoral cutaneous nerves. Irrigation is by the descending branch of the lateral circumflex femoral artery.

Used for numbness or soreness and motor impairment of the lower extremities and arthritis of the knee. Massage techniques are the same as for St 31.

Use with formula for knee problems under St 32, also add to formula for pain and numbness of the thigh under St 31.

Applications:

You could use a palm strike here, but it is getting a bit low for hand techniques. So use a heel kick to St 33 after taking his hand attack and jerking his wrist violently.

ST 34 (STOMACH POINT NO. 34)

Chinese name:

Liangqiu (ridge mount or beam mount).

Location:

2 cun above the laterosuperior border of the patella, between the rectus femoris and the vastus lateralis muscles of the thigh.

Connections:

None.

Direction of strike:

Straight in just above the knee.

Damage:

This is a xie cleft point (stores *zhen* or meridian qi) that normally promotes the circulation of qi to the whole body. However, when struck using adverse qi, it has the reverse affect, so power is lost through a hindrance of qi and blood. Local pain and loss of leg power is apparent immediately.

Set-up point:

Any of the qi drainage points will suffice: Lu 5, neigwan, Ht 5, and Lu 8.

Antidote:

Any of the qi balancing methods, or you could needle or press St 34 in order to right the wrong.

Healing:

Innervation is by the anterior femoral cutaneous nerve and on the pathway of the lateral femoral cutaneous nerve. Irrigation is by the descending branch of the circumflex femoral artery.

Used for pain and swelling of the knee, motor impairment of the lower extremities, gastric pain, mastitis, gastritis, and diarrhea.

Traditional indications include pain in the lower back and leg, progressive swelling and pain of the knee, and swelling and pain of the breast.

Its traditional function is as a xie cleft (accumulating) point of the stomach meridian, so it can treat acute problems of both the organ and the channel, pacify the stomach, and clear the channels. It is the best point for pain of the stomach meridian or organ.

To massage the point, press and hold; rotate clockwise or counterclockwise for xu or shi conditions; press slowly with both thumbs and release quickly, pulling the thumbs apart; or do percussion with the fingertips or a loose fist.

Use with St 35, St 36, Sp 10, Sp 9, Sp 6, Liv 3, Gb 34, and medial xiyan for knee problems.

Use with Pc 6, Gv 12, St 21, Liv 13, Bl 20, Bl 21, Bl 18, St 36, St 44, St 45, Liv 3, or Liv 2 for gastritis, stomachache, etc.

Use with Gb 42, Cv 17, Liv 14, St 15, Sp 18, Sp 6, and Liv 3 for mastitis.

Applications:

The same as for St 33.

ST 35 (STOMACH POINT NO. 35)

Chinese name:

Dubi (calf nose) or xiyan (eyes of knee).

Location:

When the knee is flexed, the point is in the depression below the patella and lateral to the patella tendon.

Connections:

None.

Direction of strike:

Straight in just under the knee below the patella.

Damage:

This point is a special point for knee problems in acupuncture. It is a trauma point. A strike here will produce local pain and knee injury, immediately followed by severe kidney qi drainage and damage, causing immediate loss of power and tiredness.

Set-up point:

Kd 10.

Antidote:

Massage Kd 5 and Kd 10.

Healing:

Innervation is by the lateral sural cutaneous nerve and the articular branch of the common peroneal nerve. Irrigation is by the arterial and venous network of the knee.

Used for pain or numbness and motor impairment of the knee and for leg qi.

Traditional indications include pain of the knee, leg qi, and paralysis of the lower limb.

Traditional functions are to invigorate qi and remove obstructions from the jing lou (channels and collaterals).

Use the following massage technique. Facing the client, clasp the leg with the knee bent and press on this point and also the medial xiyan point with the thumbs. The fingers will be grabbing the back of the knee and pressing on Bl 40, Bl 39, and Kd 10. Move the hands in a circular fashion as if reeling in or out on a fishing line. You can also just press with thumb or fingers on the point, do clockwise or counterclockwise rotations for xu or shi conditions, or do fingertip percussion.

See St 34 for treatment of knee disorders, etc.

Applications:

It's difficult to get at both the set-up point and the major point. However, if the attacker is kicking you, then you can take his leg and strike behind his knee with your on knee, followed by a strike to just below the knee with your palm.

ST 36 (STOMACH POINT NO. 36)

Chinese name:

Zusanli (three measures of the leg).

Location:

3 cun below St 35, one finger breadth from the anterior crest of the tibia between the tibialis anterior and the tendon of the extensor digitorum longus pedis.

Connections:

A branch from here to the middle toe.

Direction of strike:

In from the side of the lower leg.

Damage:

This point is a major point in acupuncture and in dim-mak. It is an earth and he point and sea of nourishment point along with St 30. A strike here will cause great weakness, which, left untreated, will slowly get worse. It will also damage the spleen. There is obvious immediate physical leg damage and pain, but it is the internal organ problems this strike causes that are the main object of the attack.

Set-up point:

St 30.

Antidote:

Treat the same point on the other leg along with St 30.

Healing:

Innervation occurs superficially by the lateral sural cutaneous nerve and the cutaneous branch of the saphenous nerve. Deeper, it is by the deep peroneal nerve. Irrigation is by the anterior tibial artery and vein.

Used for gastric pain, vomiting, abdominal distension, indigestion, borborygmus, diarrhea, constipation, dysentery, mastitis, dizziness, mental disorders, hemiplegia, beriberi, aching of the knee joint, ulcers, acute and chronic enteritis, acute pancreatitis, indigestion and other disorders of the digestive system, hemiplegia, shock, general weakness, anemia, hypertension, allergies, jaundice, seizures, asthma, enuresis, diseases of the reproductive system, and neurasthenia.

Traditional indications include abdominal pain and distension, vomiting, constipation or diarrhea, paralysis, seizures, abscessed breast, swelling of the limbs, difficult urination, pain and distension of the lower abdomen, and loss of urine.

Traditional function is as a he sea point and an earth point of the stomach meridian. It tonifies the spleen and stomach, regulates the qi and blood, strengthens weak and deficient conditions, and eliminates wind and damp.

Massage techniques include pressing and holding the point, rotating clockwise and counterclockwise for xu or shi conditions, doing fingertip percussion, and pressing slowly with both thumbs and releasing quickly, pulling the thumbs apart.

Use with Cv 12, Pc 6, Liv 3, St 21, St 25, Bl 20, Bl 18, Gv 4, and Co 4 for nausea, vomiting, abdominal distension, etc. Use with Co 4, Pc 6, Cv 12, St 25, Bl 25, Bl 32, and Liv 3 for acute intestinal obstruction.

Use with Bl 20, Bl 25, Bl 17, Bl 18, Cv 12, Liv 3, Lu 7, Lu 1, Cv 17, Gb 20, Co 11, and Co 20 for allergies.

Applications:

A heel kick just below the knee will suffice. You could perform a double kick—first to St 30 and then down to St 36.

ST 37 (STOMACH POINT N0. 37)

Chinese name:

Shangjuxu (upper void).

Location:

On the lower leg, 3 cun below St 36, in the tibialis anterior muscle.

Connections:

None.

Direction of strike:

Slightly downward onto the side of the shin, usually using a heel kick.

Damage:

This point damages the colon function. It can cause defecation immediately if struck hard enough. It will also drag too much qi into the legs, causing an imbalance in the whole system. This strike will also have an adverse effect on the flow of wei qi, so the immune system will slowly become ineffective. There is also obvious immediate pain and qi drainage.

Set-up point:

Bl 11 struck straight in to the upper back.

Antidote:

Apply pressure to the opposite St 37, as well as to Bl 11 on both sides.

Healing:

Innervation is by the lateral cutaneous nerve of the calf and the cutaneous branch of the saphenous nerve and, deeper, on the pathway of the deep peroneal nerve. Irrigation is by the anterior tibial artery and vein.

Used for abdominal pain and distension, dysentery, borborygmus, diarrhea, appendicitis, hemiplegia, beriberi, enteritis, gastritis, and hemiplegia.

Traditional indications are deficient or weak conditions of the spleen and stomach, indigestion, leg qi, sharp pain in the intestines, diarrhea, and hemiplegia.

Its traditional function is as a lower he sea point of the colon, so this is the main point to treat the organ; plus it is also used to remove damp heat, relieve fullness of the chest, regulate the intestines and stomach, and eliminate accumulations and stagnation.

Massage techniques are the same as for St 36.

Use with St 25, Bl 25, Liv 3, Sp 9, Sp 10, Co 4, Co 11, Liv 2, Sp 15, and Gb 26 for dysentery.

Use with Liv 3, St 25, Liv 4, Bl 25, Bl 26, and Bl 20 for constipation.

Use with St 36, Liv 3, Cv 12, St 25, St 21, Bl 21, Bl 20, Bl 19, Bl 18, and Bl 17 for gastritis.

Applications:

You could be in a grappling-type situation and, as such, are able to strike using a one knuckle punch into Bl 11 on the upper back. Your heel now strikes down the front of the shin into St 37. The strike to Bl 11 is usually enough to cause any grappler to let go, enabling you to get at St 37.

ST 38 (STOMACH POINT NO. 38)

Chinese name:

Tiakou (line's opening).

Location:

8 cun below St 35 and 2 cun below St 37, midway between St 35 and St 41.

Connections:

Obviously the stomach points are all connected. However, there is a special connection to St 12 from this point.

Direction of strike:

Straight in and slightly downward along the side of the shin.

Damage:

This is an interesting point. I have tested this strike and have found that it has a dire effect upon the power of the upper body, especially the shoulders. In some cases the arms would not work after this strike and had to be treated using the antidote of St 12.

Set-up point:

Any good violent jerking of the arms works really well to set up the effect of damaging the shoulders.

Antidote:

St 12, using pressure downward into the clavicle—not too much pressure, however, for this will take away the patient's will to fight.

Healing:

Innervation and irrigation are the same as for St 37.

Used for muscular atrophy, motor impairment or pain and paralysis of the leg, shoulder pain, arthritis of the knee, stomachache, and enteritis.

Traditional indications include perifocal inflammation of the shoulder.

Massage techniques are the same as for St 36.

Use with Co 15, Co 14, Co 11, Co 4, Gb 21, Th 15, Si 13, Si 12, Si 11, Si 10, Si 9, Ht 1, Th 14, Th 13, Gb 34, St 36, and St 40 for shoulder pain with inability to lift the arm.

Use with St 36, St 37, St 40, Gb 34, and Liv 3 for shin splints (inflammation of the tibialis anterior).

Applications:

You could use a claw-type action on the clavicle and then a kick down to St 38, or a hammer fist onto the clavicle, which will drain so much qi that he will have to stop the fight anyway!

ST 39 (STOMACH POINT NO. 39)

Chinese name:

Xiajuxu (lower void).

Location:

9 cun below St 35, 3 cun below St 37, one finger breadth out from the anterior crest of the tibia.

Connections:

None.

Direction of strike:

Straight in from the side of the lower leg.

Damage:

This point affects the small intestine and will also cause paralysis of the legs when struck hard. It will also have an effect upon the wei qi, causing problems with the immune system later as well.

Immediate great pain when this point is struck directly.

Set-up point:

Si 8.

Antidote:

Apply pressure to the elbow area, in particular Si 8. Treat the leg if physical damage has occurred, of course.

Healing:

Innervation is by the branches of the superior peroneal nerve and the deep peroneal nerve. Irrigation is by the anterior tibial artery and vein.

Used for lower abdominal pain, backache referring to the testis, mastitis, muscular atrophy, motor impairment or pain and paralysis of the lower extremities, acute and chronic enteritis, and hepatitis.

As a lower he sea point of the small intestine, its traditional function is to treat disease of the Si organ and channel.

Massage techniques are the same as for St 36.

Use with Bl 25, Bl 26, Bl 53, Bl 54, Sp 12, Sp 13, Gb 27, Gb 28, Gb 29, Gb 30, Bl 52, Bl 38, Bl 39, Bl 40, and Gb 34 for lower back pain referring to the testis.

See St 38 for treatment of shin splints.

Use with Cv 4, St 25, Cv 12, Bl 27, Bl 25, Bl 26, Bl 20, Liv 3, and Pc 6 for blockage of the small intestine.

Applications:

Strike at Si 8 outside of his elbow in defense of his hand attack. Then chop downward onto his shin area with your heel at St 39.

ST 40 (STOMACH POINT NO. 40)

Chinese name:

Fenglong (abundance and prosperity).

Location:

8 cun superior and anterior to the external malleolus, about 1 finger breadth posterior or lateral to St 8, between the lateral side of the extensor digitorum longus pedis and the peroneus brevis muscles.

Connections:

Transverse luo to Sp 3 and Sp 1.

Direction of strike:

In from the side of the lower leg.

Damage:

Apart from local pain and qi drainage, this point also has an effect upon the spleen. It will cause a great imbalance between stomach and spleen and so weaken the body. This is a classic point for treating epilepsy. I have not heard of any instances where a strike here causes epilepsy; however, given the nature of this point, it could.

Set-up point:

Sp 10.

Antidote:

Have an acupuncturist treat the same point, St 40, on the opposite leg. You might also treat using finger pressure to Sp 10.

Healing:

Innervation is by the superficial peroneal nerve, and irrigation is by the branches of the anterior tibial artery and vein.

Used for chest pain; asthma; excessive sputum; sore throat; muscular atrophy; motor impairment, pain, paralysis, or swelling of the lower extremities; headache; dizziness; mental disorders; epilepsy; coughing; abundant mucous; beriberi; amenorrhea; and abnormal uterine bleeding.

Traditional indications are cough with excessive sputum, fluid retention anywhere in the body, epilepsy, and mental disorders.

St 40 is a low connecting point of the stomach meridian. Its traditional functions are to transform phlegm and dampness, calm the spirit, tranquilize the mind, and eliminate phlegm fire from the stomach.

Massage techniques are the same as for St 36.

Use with Bl 13, Bl 12, Bl 17, Cv 17, and Lu 7 for cough with abundant phlegm.

Use with Gv 20, Ht 7, Gb 20, Liv 3, anmien, Kd 1, Cv 12, Bl 14, Bl 20, and Gb 21 for insomnia and vertigo.

Use with Bl 13, Bl 12, Bl 43, dingchuan, Cv 22, Lu 1, Lu 5, Lu 7, Co 4, Liv 3, Liv 14, Sp 21, Kd 22, Kd 23, Kd 24, Kd 25, Kd 26, Kd 27, Bl 17, Bl 20, Bl 18, Bl 23, and Kd 7 for asthma, bronchitis, etc.

Applications:

You could use a double kick, first to Sp 10 just above the knee on the inside of the leg, then rebound that kick down to St 40.

ST 41 (STOMACH POINT NO. 41)

Chinese name:

Jiexi (release stream).

Location:

At the junction of the dorsum of the foot and the leg, between the tendons of the extensor digitorum longus and hallucis longus, approximately at the level of the tip of the external malleolus.

Connections:

None.

Direction of strike:

Usually a stomp down onto the top of the foot at the place where it joins with the leg.

Damage:

This is one of those points that seem harmless enough but have a great effect upon the whole body when struck. It is a fire and jing point. This strike will affect the stomach greatly, causing extreme nausea—enough to stop the fight. It will also drain qi from the lower extremities of the body, greatly weakening the legs.

Set-up point:

A violent slap onto the forearms (either side) will suffice.

Antidote:

Finger pressure to St 31.

Healing:

Innervation is by the superficial and deep peroneal nerves. Irrigation is by the anterior tibial artery and vein.

Used for headache, nephritis, enteritis, seizures, disease of the ankle and surrounding tissue, drop foot, edema of the head and face, dizziness and vertigo, mental disorders, and motor impairment or pain and paralysis of the lower extremities.

Traditional indications are headache, vertigo, eye disease, pain in the mouth, seizures, distended abdomen, severe palpitations, and pain of the foot and ankle.

This is a jing river point and a fire point of the stomach meridian. Its traditional functions are to tonify the stomach and eliminate cold damp.

Massage techniques are the same as for St 36.

Use with Bl 23, Kd 7, SP 9, Cv 2. Cv 3, Cv 4, Bl 66, and Bl 67 for nephritis.

Use with Gb 40, Bl 60, Kd 3, Liv 4, Sp 5, and Gb 34 for problems with the ankle.

Use with Gb 14, St 8, yintang, taiyang, St 44, St 45, Co 4, Co 11, Liv 3, Liv 2, and Gb 41 for headache.

Applications:

He might attack with both hands low, and you slam both of his forearms with both of your palms using great force, then stomp down onto the top of his foot (either one) at St 41.

ST 42 (STOMACH POINT NO. 42)

Chinese name:

Chongyang (pouring yang).

Location:

Distal to St 41 at the highest point of the dorsum of the foot, in the depression between the second and third metatarsal bones and the cuneiform bone.

Connections:

There is a branch from here to Sp 1. This point also receives transverse luo from Sp 4.

Direction of strike:

Stomp straight down onto the top of the instep.

Damage:

This is an electrical as well as a physiological point. The strike will cause nerve damage with an immediate electrical shock wave rushing up the whole leg. It is also a yuan, or source point. It will cause great qi loss and enough local pain to stop anyone from attacking further.

Set-up point:

Same as for St 41.

Antidote:

Pressure St 31 as with a St 41 strike, but because this is a source point, you also need to massage the whole stomach meridian up the leg from foot to pelvis.

Healing:

Innervation occurs superficially by the medial dorsal cutaneous nerve of the foot, derived from the superficial peroneal nerve and, deeper, the deep peroneal nerve. Irrigation is by the dorsal pedis artery and vein of the foot and the dorsal venous network of the foot.

Used for facial paralysis, muscular atrophy and motor impairment of the foot, redness and swelling of the dorsum of the foot, headache, toothache, malaria, insanity, fever, and lack of strength in the arms or legs.

As a yuan point of the stomach meridian, its traditional function is to build the yuan qi of that organ/meridian.

Use with Sp 4, St 36, Sp 9, Sp 6, St 40, Liv 3, Gb 39, Gb 29, and St 44 for leg qi.

Use with Co 4, Cv 22, Co 11, Gb 20, Th 3, Lu 2, Co 14, Liv 4, Cv 17, Gv 14, St 11, Lu 3, Th 13, St 9, and Cv 23 for goiter.

Applications:
Same as for St 41.

ST 43 (STOMACH POINT NO. 43)

Chinese name:
Xiangru (sinking valley).

Location:
In the depression distal to the junction of the second and third metatarsal bones, directly above the lateral side of the second toe.

Connections:
None.

Direction of strike:
Straight down onto the top of the foot, back from the second toe.

Damage:
This is a wood and shu point and normally promotes the free flow of qi all over the body. However, when struck using adverse qi, it will cause the reverse, resulting in such a loss of power that the recipient must sit down, as well as great local pain and qi drainage. It can even cause things like rheumatism later in life.

Set-up point:
Neigwan because of its qi drainage properties.

Antidote:
Press St 36.

Healing:
Innervation is by the medial dorsal cutaneous nerve of the foot. Irrigation is by the dorsal venous network of the foot.

Used for facial and general edema, borborygmus, abdominal pain, pain and swelling of the dorsum of the foot, conjunctivitis, and hysteria.

Traditional indications consist of general aching.

As a wood point and a shu stream point of the stomach meridian, its traditional function is to eliminate wind from the channels.

To massage, press and hold, do rotations clockwise or counterclockwise for xu or shi conditions, do fingertip percussion, or you can use your index or middle finger and vibrate this point.

Use with St 37, St 36, Co 4, Pc 6, Co 11, lanweixue, Sp 3, Bl 25, St 25, Bl 26, Bl 24, Sp 9, and Kd 16 for acute appendicitis.

Use with Pc 6, St 36, Cv 12, St 21, St 25, Liv 13, Bl 20, Bl 21, Bl 25, and Liv 3 for stomachache.

Applications:
The same as for St 41.

ST 44 (STOMACH POINT NO. 44)

Chinese name:

Netting (inner court).

Location:

Proximal to the web margin between the second and third toes, in the depression distal and lateral to the second metatarsodigital joint.

Connections:

None.

Direction of strike:

Strike down onto the web of the second toe.

Damage:

This is a water and yong point (spring or stream point). Striking this point will affect the way the qi is sent all over the body, so a strike here will cause power loss and great local pain. This strike has a strange effect in that it causes the recipient to feel as if he has been struck in the jaw. This could cause the brain to think that the jaw has been struck and cause KO. If left unchecked, this strike will cause all kinds of qi balance problems that will only get worse.

Set-up point:

Neigwan.

Antidote:

Have an acupuncturist use needles to balance the qi between water and earth.

Healing:

Innervation occurs where the lateral branch of the medial dorsal cutaneous nerve divides into two digital nerves. Irrigation is by the dorsal venous network of the foot.

Used for toothache, deviation of the mouth, epistaxis, abdominal pain or distension, diarrhea, dysentery, pain and swelling of the dorsum of the foot, febrile diseases, trigeminal neuralgia, tonsillitis, stomachache, acute and chronic enteritis, pain of intestinal hernia, and beriberi.

Traditional indications include toothache, nosebleed, eye pain, paralysis of the mouth, lockjaw, throat blockage, ringing in the ears, abdominal distension, diarrhea, red or white dysentery, blood in the urine, and wind rash.

This is a water point and a ying spring (gushing) point. Its traditional functions are to cool and drain heat from the stomach, regulate the qi, suppress pain, promote digestion, remove obstruction from the intestines, and clear and relieve fullness from the stomach.

To massage, pinch the web between the thumb and forefinger, press and hold, do rotations clockwise or counterclockwise for xu or shi conditions, or use fingertip percussion.

Use with Co 4, St 2, St 3, St 5, and St 6 for toothache.

Use with Gb 41, Cv 3, Cv 4, Cv 6, Sp 9, St 25, Liv 4, Liv 3, St 36, Bl 25, and Bl 26 for distension in the lower abdomen.

Use with St 45, Liv 2, Liv 3, Liv 4, St 25, Cv 12, St 21, Liv 13, Co 4, Co 11, St 36, Bl 20, and Bl 21 for gastritis.

Applications:

A stomp on the second toe.

ST 45 (STOMACH POINT NO. 45)

Chinese name:

Lidui (strict exchange).

Location:

On the lateral side of the second toe, about 0.1 cun posterior to the corner of the nail.

Connections:

Transverse luo from Sp 4.

Direction of strike:

Stomp on the second toe.

Damage:

This strike has some dire affects. It is a metal and cheng point and will have a great effect upon the muscles and tendons, so it can be used as a set-up point for a joint lock where the tendons and muscles are being attacked. It will cause mental confusion and has been known to cause the nose to bleed profusely.

Set-up point:

St 36.

Antidote:

Squeeze the tip of the other second toe.

Healing:

Innervation is by the dorsal digital nerve derived from the superficial peroneal nerve. Irrigation is by the arterial and venous network formed by the dorsal digital artery and vein of the foot.

Used for facial swelling, deviation of the mouth, toothache, epistaxis, distending sensation of the chest and abdomen, cold in the leg and foot, febrile disease, dream-disturbed sleep, mental confusion, ischemia of the brain, neurasthenia, tonsillitis, hepatitis, indigestion, and hysteria.

This is a jing well point and a metal point.; its traditional function is to disperse heat in yang ming.

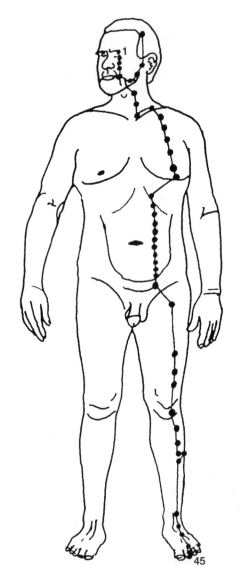

Traditional indications include gastritis, tonsillitis, and febrile disease.

To massage, pinch the point between the knuckle of the thumb and the forefinger. You can do rotations clockwise or counterclockwise for xu or shi conditions.

Use with St 44, Liv 3, and St 34 for acute trauma to the stomach meridian.

Add to formula for toothache listed under St 44.

See St 44 for treatment of gastritis.

Use with Si 17, Co 4, Co 11, Lu 11, Lu 2, Lu 5, Liv 2, Kd 1, Kd 2, Bl 7, St 12, Bl 11, and St 44 for acute tonsillitis.

Applications:

The same as St 41. Or if you were using it as a set-up point strike, simply stomp on the second toe, then come in and try to get the lock.

This is the end of the stomach meridian. Obviously there are points you will strike that are close to other points on adjacent meridians, etc. With most of the stomach points, you don't have to be that accurate to make them work; and if you are not accurate, you will probably get some other point.

270

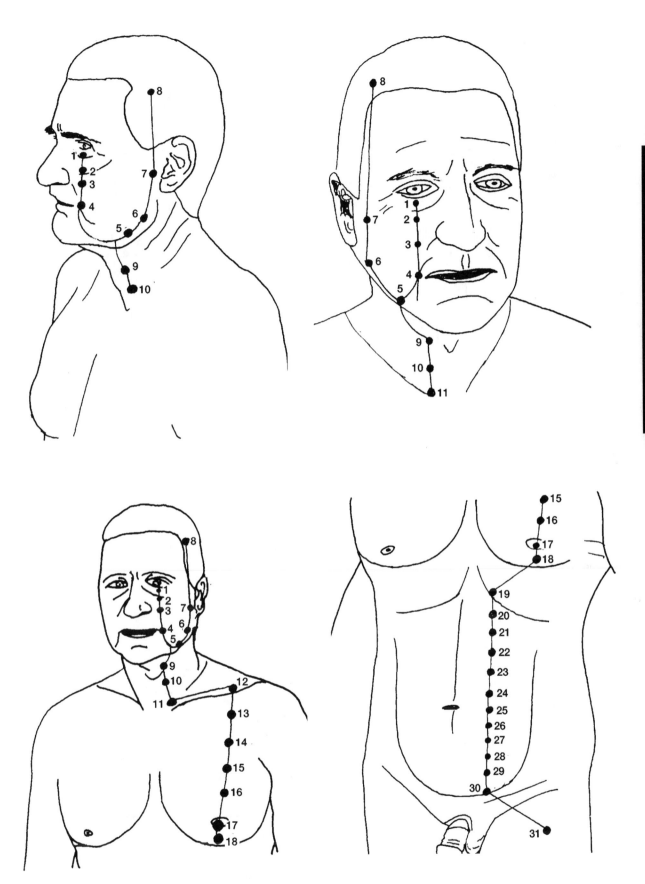

271

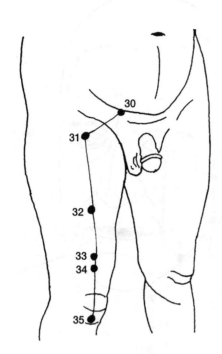

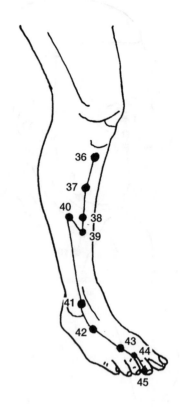

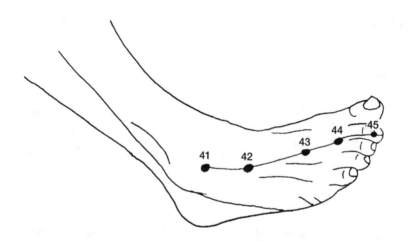

Chapter 6

The Spleen Meridian

The spleen is the only lymphatic organ whose job it is to filter blood. It takes away used-up blood cells from the blood, changes their hemoglobin to bilirubin, and then sends their iron back into the bloodstream to be used to make other blood cells.

THE TCM VIEW

Chinese element of the spleen is earth. Its *fu* (yang) organ is the stomach, and it is traditionally the controller of transport.

The traditional functions of the spleen are as follows:

- Dominates *yun hua* (transformation and transportation)
- Controls blood (holds it in the vessels)
- Dominates the muscles and the four limbs
- Opens into the mouth and manifests in the lips
- Controls the raising of qi.

The spleen is more important in TCM than in Western medicine. In fact, most of what is attributed to the stomach and intestines in Western medicine is actually considered to be caused by the spleen in Chinese medicine.

The spleen is crucial for digestion and transportation of the products of that transformation. If the function of the spleen is normal, there will be good appetite, good digestion, normal absorption, and normal bowel movement. If it is faulty, there will be no appetite, abdominal distension, poor digestion, lack of strength, and undigested food in the stool.

The spleen also controls transportation of qi extracted from food to all of the muscles in the body, particularly those in the limbs. If its function is impaired, there will be a lack of energy (strength) in the limbs in particular and a desire to lie down and rest most of the time.

The spleen controls the transportation and transformation of fluids. If the function of the spleen is impaired, fluids may accumulate, causing dampness, and there may be edema, particularly in the lower and middle parts of the body, with a feeling of heaviness.

The spleen controls the transportation of proper distribution of essences of qi extracted from food to various organs.

The spleen holds blood within the vessels and causes it not to extravasate. In addition to regulating the liver and the pumping action of the heart, the spleen must also hold the blood, and when this function is impaired, there can be hemorrhages of any kind, (e.g., nosebleeds, blood in the sputum and feces, broken blood vessels).

Muscles and limbs depend upon essences extracted from food, and it is the job of the spleen to cause this extraction. When this function is normal, the muscles will be thick and strong, and the four limbs will be warm and energetic (and vice versa when this function is impaired).

Chewing facilitates the spleen function of transformation and transportation. When the spleen function is strong and its qi is strong, the mouth tastes better and the lips are rosy and moist. If the spleen function is impaired, there may be an abnormal taste in the mouth (flat and sticky), a lack of appetite, and the lips will be pale and dry. If the spleen has heat, the lips could be dry with a sweet taste in the mouth. If the spleen qi is deficient, the lips will be pale.

The spleen has the job of holding things in place, particularly along the midline of the body, and producing a lifting effect. This function, called raising qi, is what makes sure that the organs are in their place. When this function is impaired, there may be prolapse of kidney, uterus, bladder, colon, and anus, as well as varicose veins.

SP 1 (SPLEEN POINT NO. 1)

Chinese name:
Yinbai (hidden white).
Location:
On the medial side of the big toe, about 0.1 cun posterior to the corner of the nail.
Connections:
Transverse luo from St 40.
Direction of strike:
A stomp straight down on the big toe.
Damage:
This is a wood and cheng point and a root point of tai yin (the greater yin division of spleen and lungs). This strike has a great effect upon the muscles and tendons because it is a control point for those. It is also a control point for the divergent meridians. Spleen damage will occur immediately, with a great energy drainage. There is a downward rushing feeling when struck, followed by nausea and loss of power caused by this point's connection with the lungs by being the root point of tai yin. So it drains qi from the lungs as well as the spleen. Often used to relax problems related to menstruation, this point also controls bleeding (in healing) in the gastrointestinal tract. As a result, a strike here using adverse qi will cause any bleeding to be worse and to be harder to stop, especially bleeding from, for instance, a knife strike to the stomach area. So this point can also be used as an excellent set-up for a knife attack!

This is also one of those points that will affect the communication between heaven and earth when struck, causing great confusion between mind and body. In healing it is also used as one of the major treatments for shock. When used as a dim-mak strike, however, the reverse happens, with the symptoms of shock becoming apparent more easily, even with a light to moderate strike to the head, for instance. So, again, this is an excellent set-up point for a major strike. Sp 1's effect upon the mind causes an inability to sleep soundly. (In healing, it is used to give a restful sleep.)

A word of warning: Sp 1 should never be used either in a dim-mak way or even for healing during pregnancy because it will have an adverse effect upon the uterus. In healing, it should never be used on a patient who suffers from diabetes because it will affect the balance of insulin/sugar.
Set-up point:
Mind point at the side of the jaw.

Antidote:

The opposite point Sp 1 (on the other foot) should be pressed or squeezed quite hard. Since this point has so much damage associated with it, it is advisable to see a Chinese doctor.

Healing:

Innervation is by the anastomosis of the dorsal digital nerve, derived from the superficial peroneal nerve and the plantar digital proprial nerve. Irrigation is by the dorsal digital artery.

Used for abdominal distension, uterine bleeding, mental disorders, dream-disturbed sleep, convulsions, and bleeding of the digestive tract.

Traditional indications include continuous nosebleed, spitting of blood, abnormal uterine bleeding, blood in urine or stool, and chronic infantile convulsions. Bleed for manic depression, and use moxa for excess dreaming or startled sleep and menorrhagia.

This is a jing well point and a wood point of Sp meridian. Its traditional functions are to tonify the spleen, regulate menstruation, calm the mind, regulate the blood, and strengthen the spleen's function of holding blood.

To massage, pinch the point between the knuckle of the thumb and the forefinger and hold. You can do rotations clockwise or counterclockwise for xu or shi conditions, and this is a good point to use moxa on, as with all jing well points, as you can prick it and get a spot of blood.

Use with Cv 6, Sp 10, Sp 6, Liv 3, Liv 4, Bl 18, Bl 20, Bl 17, Bl 23, Cv 4, and Gb 26 for abnormal uterine bleeding. Use moxa on this point for abnormal uterine bleeding (plus points like Gv 20, St 36, Sp 3, Cv 12, and Bl 20).

You can prick and bleed this point for manic depression, as well as using acupressure on points Liv 3, Liv 4, Kid 16, Sp 3, Cv 12, St 40, Sp 6, Bl 10, Bl 19, Bl 17, Bl 20, Bl 25, St 25, Gb 26, Gb 20, and yintang.

Applications:

Take his right straight, using both of your palms (the right one is palm toward you and yin shaped,

Figure 269

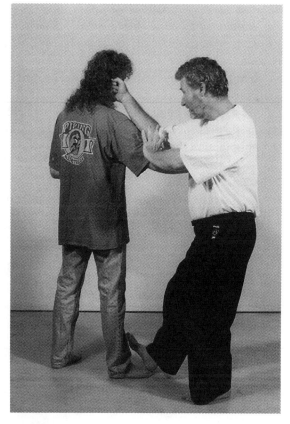

Figure 270

while left palm is facing away from you and yang shaped) (fig. 269). Now, your right palm strikes into the jaw at a 45-degree angle. Just after this, your heel will stomp down onto his right big toe, aimed slightly toward the right side or the side closest to the second toe (fig 270).

SP 2 (SPLEEN POINT NO. 2)

Chinese name:

Dadu (big metropolis).

Location:

On the medial side of the big toe, distal and inferior to the first metatarsodigital joint, at the junction of the red and white skin.

Connections:

None.

Direction of strike:

This point can be accessed either by stomping on the big toe just back from the largest part of the toe, or in a grappling type of situation where you might have access to the toes with your hands. In this case, a quick violent squeeze would be sufficient to cause the grappler to let go of any hold he might have applied.

Damage:

This is a fire and yong point and normally will strengthen the spleen. In this case where the point is used as a dim-mak strike, it will damage the spleen and weaken it, thus causing lack of power, nausea with vomiting, and a loss of memory in the long term if the condition is not treated. This strike will slow the flow of qi in the channel. It will also have an effect upon communication between heaven and earth. This point, like Sp 1, is also forbidden for healing during pregnancy.

Set-up point:

Neigwan will enhance the effects of nausea and loss of power.

Antidote:

Should someone be struck here by accident, you should treat neigwan by rubbing it up the inner arm. Then, you should treat the opposite Sp 2 by squeezing gently—but not if a woman is pregnant!

Healing:

Innervation is by the plantar digital proprial nerve derived from the medial plantar nerve. Irrigation is by the branches of the medial plantar artery and vein.

Used for abdominal distension, gastric pain, febrile disease with anhidrosis (lack of sweating in the presence of an appropriate stimulus), diarrhea, stomachache, edema of the limbs, apoplectic coma.

As a yong spring (gushing) point and a fire point of the spleen, its traditional functions are to sedate or to tonify.

To massage, press and hold the point, do rotations clockwise or counterclockwise for xu or shi conditions, or use fingertip percussion on this point.

Use with Gv 24, Gv 23, Gv 22, Gv 21, Gv 19, Gb 19, Gb 20, Si 5, Bl 67, Bl 63, Bl 62, St 36, Gv 20, Kd 1, yintang, Liv 3, Cv 12, and Sp 3 for dizziness.

Use with Cv 7, Cv 4, Cv 6, Sp 6, Bl 20, Bl 18, Sp 1, Bl 23, and Sp 10 for abnormal uterine bleeding.

Use with St 34, Cv 12, St 21, St 25, Liv 3, St 44, St 45, St 36, Bl 20, Bl 21, and Bl 25 for gastric pain.

Applications:

Should you have access to this point, as in a grappling situation, use the thumb to attack it by squeezing violently. Should you wish to attack it while standing up, strike using a heel kick to the inside side of the big toe, or you can stomp on it.

SP 3 (SPLEEN POINT NO. 3)

Chinese name:

Taibai (most white).

Location:

Proximal and inferior to the head of the first metatarsal bone, at the junction of the red and white skin.

Connections:

Transverse luo from St 40.

Direction of strike:

Straight in to the foot from inside (big toe side) of the foot. Usually attacked with a kick or with finger pressure, as in a grappling situation.

Damage:

This point will give immediate great pain resulting in qi drainage at the point, from the upper chest right down to the foot. The pain alone will be enough to cause a grappler to let go long enough for you to reattack. It is an earth, yuan, and shu point. The long-term effects are easy bruising, lack of memory, and muscle problems such as cramps, muscles becoming atrophied, etc. The immediate effect is a shock to the whole system, which in many cases can cause KO because of this shock. It can be used as a good set-up point strike for points that lie on the four sides of the torso.

Set-up point:

Th 8 is used as the set-up point strike. The shock from this strike is just being registered by the brain when the second strike to Sp 3 happens, completely confusing the brain.

Antidote:

Apply pressure to either side of the head. Just hold the palms on either side for some minutes until the pain and confusion have stopped (fig. 271). There was a chap at a gym where I was teaching once who

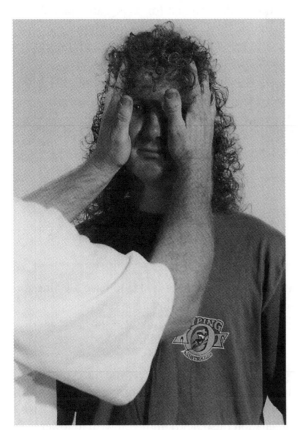

Figure 271

had dropped a heavy weight onto Sp 3 and was in a state of shock. So I applied this antidote for five minutes until he was okay. (The interesting thing is that this chap, prior to this treatment could not understand mathematics at all, having had this problem all of his life. After the treatment, he could perform instant mathematics in his mind and his comprehension had increased dramatically).

Healing:

Innervation is by the branches of the saphenous nerve and the superficial peroneal nerve. Irrigation is by the dorsal venous network of the foot, the medial plantar artery, and the branches of the medial tarsal artery.

Used for gastric pain, abdominal distension, sluggishness, dysentery, constipation, vomiting, diarrhea, beriberi, headache, edema, and acute gastroenteritis.

This is a shu stream (transporting) point of the spleen, an earth point, and a yuan source point of the spleen. It is the earth point of the earth organ/channel complex, so its traditional functions are to build digestion or ground someone who is off with the fairies. It eliminates both internal and external dampness and strongly tonifies the spleen.

Massage techniques are the same as for Sp 2.

You can also grab the whole foot between the thumb and forefinger with the thumb resting on Sp 3 and squeeze.

Use with St 36, Pc 6, Cv 12, Bl 20, Bl 23, Cv 4, Cv 6, and Cv 14 for vomiting, nausea, sluggishness, loose stool, and lack of energy.

Use with Bl 25, Bl 26, Bl 20, Bl 18, Bl 17, St 25, Sp 16, St 37, Liv 3, Liv 4, and Sp 6 for constipation.

Use with Pc 6, Ht 7, St 36, Liv 3, Gv 20, Kd 1, and Cv 12 to treat someone in shock (you could also add Gv 26).

Applications:

The same as for Sp 2.

SP 4 (SPLEEN POINT NO. 4)

Chinese name:

Gongsun (grandfather's grandson).

Location:

In the depression distal and inferior to the base of the first metatarsal bone, at the junction of the red and white skin or roughly 1 cun behind the joint of the big toe. At the anterior, inferior margin of the first metatarsal, in the abductor hallucis muscle.

Connections:

Transverse luo to St 42 and St 45.

Direction of strike:

In to the side of the foot, usually with finger pressure or a kick.

Damage:

This is a luo point and a master point for chong mai and a coupled point of yin wei mai. A strike here causes dizziness and immediate great local pain with associated qi drainage. This strike can cause KO and much later damage. The pain caused by this strike can last for days, cause sleepless nights, etc. I have noticed that with this strike, even analgesics will not stop the symptoms caused by the type of pain where the body scrunches up and becomes very tense. Because it is a master point of the extra meridian chong mai, it will greatly decrease one's life force. A gradual deterioration of the recipient's quality of life will become apparent, helped by the disruption of the yin and yang energies of the stomach/spleen. If the recipient is into things like yoga, qigong, taijiquan, etc., before the strike, the positive effects of this good practice will slowly diminish until he or she is finally receiving no benefit from it. One of the reasons for doing such meditations is to unite prenatal and postnatal qi, and this strike will stop this. The heart will also be damaged as a result of this strike. In fact, this point strike will have an adverse effect upon all of the organs, immediately and over a period. It is one of those points that you just shouldn't play around with.

Set-up point:

I don't know of any traditional set-up strikes particularly for this point. However, it has been my experience that a hard strike straight in to the inner forearm at neigwan will enhance the negative effects of this strike.

Antidote:

This is such a bad strike, with so many things being affected, that it is a good idea to have a Chinese doctor check you out should you be struck here. However, because of the damage done to stomach/spleen, there is a qigong that will suffice to help this area. The beginning is the same as for the previous qigong for the triple warmer meridian, which balanced out the qi in the body (see Chapter 3, under the antidote for Bl 33).

Squat down and scoop as before. When you are about to rise up onto your toes, you turn your right palm upward and your left palm downward. You have inhaled (fig. 272). Push your right palm upward until it is out of sight and your left palm downward until it is opposite your left hip (fig. 273). You have also risen up onto your toes. Hold this posture with an inhalation (also held) until you wish to lower your heels and your right palm back to the same position (on the other side of your body, of course) as your

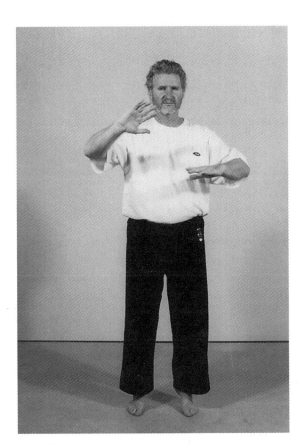

Figure 272

Figure 273

left palm. Exhale as you do this. Perform the whole thing on the other side (i.e., with your left palm going up and your right going down as you rise up). Altogether, do this three times on both sides.

Healing:

Innervation is by the saphenous nerve and the branch of the superficial peroneal nerve. Irrigation is by the medial tarsal artery and the dorsal venous network of the foot.

Used for gastric pain, vomiting, borborygmus, abdominal pain, diarrhea, dysentery, acute and chronic enteritis, endometritis, irregular menstruation, and foot and ankle pain.

Traditional indications include stomachache, hard intestines (like a drum) and abdominal pain, vomiting and diarrhea, tidal fever, and seizures.

Sp 4 is a luo point connecting the spleen and stomach channels. It is one of the eight confluent points (master and couple points that activate the extra meridians, e.g., Sp 4 is the master point of the chong mai, or penetrating vessel, and the couple point of the yinwei mai, while Pc 6 is the master point of the yinwei mai and the couple point of the chong mai). The chong mai and yinwei mai treat the heart, chest, and shoulder regions, so this point's traditional functions are to treat disease of the heart/chest and stomach, regulate the spleen and stomach, and invigorate the chong mai. It is better at stopping pain than Sp 3.

Massage techniques are the same as for Sp 3.

Use with St 36, Pc 6, St 34, Cv 12, Bl 20, Bl 25, Bl 21, Bl 18, Liv 13, Liv 3, St 44, and St 45, for gastric pain, diarrhea, vomiting, borborygmus, etc.

Use with Pc 6, Sp 6, Cv 7, Cv 4, Cv 3, St 25, Kd 15, Bl 25, Bl 26, Bl 18, Bl 20, Bl 23, Bl 17, Liv 4, Liv 3, Liv 13, and Liv 14 for endometritis or irregular menstruation.

Use with Sp 6, Sp 9, Sp 5, Kd 6, St 28, Cv 3, Cv 4, Cv 5, Cv 9, Bl 23, Bl 28, and St 40 for fluid retention.

Applications:

Same as for Sp 2. Or you could use a one-knuckle punch, then dig that knuckle into the point violently.

SP 5 (SPLEEN POINT NO. 5)

Chinese name:

Shangqiu (mound of commerce or merchant mound).

Location:

In the depression distal and inferior to the medial malleolus, midway between the tuberosity of the navicular bone and the tip of the medial malleolus.

Connections:

None.

Direction of strike:

Straight down on top of the ankle to the top of the foot at an angle of 45 degrees.

Damage:

This is a metal and jing point. It is a special point where the joints are concerned. So apart from the great damage that this point strike gives, it is also used as a set-up point for those other points, such as Sp 19, that will affect a joint (in the case of Sp 19, the opposite knee joint). It will cause great local pain resulting in qi drainage and power loss immediately. It will cause normally strong joints to give way immediately under mild pressure, such as in a joint lock, etc.

Set-up point:

Gb 27 works well with this point.

Antidote:

Apply pressure in the same direction on the other foot, or see an acupuncturist.

Healing:

Innervation is by the medial crural cutaneous nerve and the branch of the superficial peroneal nerve. Irrigation is by the medial tarsal artery and the great saphenous vein.

Used for borborygmus, abdominal distension, stiffness and pain of the tongue, constipation, diarrhea, pain of the foot and ankle joint, gastritis, enteritis, indigestion, beriberi, and edema.

Traditional indications include abdominal distension associated with deficient spleen, intestinal noises, diarrhea, constipation, stomachache, jaundice, breast pain, hemorrhoids, and colic. Traditional functions are to strengthen the spleen and stomach, transform damp stagnation, and as a jing river (traversing) point and metal point of the spleen, it can target joints.

Massage techniques are the same as for Sp 3.

Use with Sp 9, St 28, Bl 39, Bl 22, Bl 20, Bl 23, Cv 5, Cv 9, Kd 6, St 40, St 36, and Sp 4 for edema.

Use with Sp 9, St 25, St 44, St 45, Co 1, Co 2, Co 4, and Co 11 for chronic enteritis.

Use with St 41, Liv 4, Gb 34, Bl 60, Kd 3, and Gb 40 for foot pain.

Applications:

1) You would normally strike this point with your heel kick, which fits nicely into the area of the ankle joint on top of the foot a little to the inside of the leg.
2) You could take his right punch with your right palm and back kick straight down onto the point with your right heel.
3) Or you could avoid his attack, back kicking to Gb 27, and then, using the rebound from that kick, drop the same foot straight down onto his ankle joint.

SP 6 (SPLEEN POINT NO. 6)

Chinese name:

Sanyinjiao (three yin junction).

Location:

3 cun directly above the tip of the medial malleolus, on the posterior border of the tibia, on the line drawn from the medial malleolus to Sp 9. Between the posterior margin of the tibia and the soleus muscle and, in its deep position, in the flexor digitorum longus pedis muscle.

Connections:

Kidney and liver.

Direction of strike:

In to the lower inner side of the leg at an angle downward. Usually it would be a kick, although you could use this point in a grappling situation with violent finger pressure.

Damage:

This is the meeting point of the lower yin meridians. Immediately, great pain is felt with a dropping feeling from waist downward. (I know of an incident where a chap was kicked at this point and immediately defecated.) Great nausea is also felt immediately—so much so that the fight is over.

Set-up point:

The tip of the chin is struck as the set-up (no particular point, just punch him on the chin). It doesn't have to be hard, just enough to shock his system, as long as the Sp 6 strike comes directly after the chin strike. You can test this yourself by having a friend strike you gently on the tip of the chin, then rack his knuckles down the inside of your lower leg at Sp 6. When the set-up is done correctly, you will feel great pain even with a light blow to Sp 6, and you will be rubbing your leg for hours afterward.

Antidote:

Rub over Sp 6 on either leg upward for about 6 inches, using mild to light pressure until the effects have gone.

Healing:

Innervation occurs superficially by the medial crural cutaneous nerve and, deeper, in the posterior aspect, the tibial nerve. Irrigation is by the great saphenous vein and the posterior tibial artery and vein.

Used for borborygmus, abdominal distension, loose stool with undigested food, irregular menstruation, uterine bleeding, leukorrhea, prolapsed uterus, amenorrhea, sterility, difficult labor, seminal emission, pain of the external genitalia, hernia, dysuria, enuresis, muscular atrophy, insomnia, incontinence, hemiplegia, eczema, uticaria, neurodermatitis, neurasthenia, and motor impairment, paralysis, and pain of lower extremities,

This is a meeting point of the spleen, liver, and kidney meridians, so it can have an effect on all these channels.

Also, as a root area of the spleen meridian, its traditional functions are to reinforce the spleen to eliminate damp, promote the functions of the stomach and spleen, invigorate the circulation of qi and blood, remove obstructions from the jing-luo, strengthen the liver's free-going function, and benefit the kidneys. It is used a lot for insomnia.

Massage techniques include pressing and holding, doing rotations clockwise or counterclockwise for xu or shi conditions, pressing with both thumbs slowly and releasing quickly, pulling the thumbs apart, and doing fingertip percussion. This is a good point to use fingertip pressure and vibrate. Use with Liv 4, Liv 3, Gb 21, Bl 31, Bl 32, Co 4, and Bl 67 for difficult labor or induction of labor.

Use with Sp 10, Bl 17, Bl 35, Liv 4, Liv 3, Cv 12, Pc 6, St 36, Bl 25, St 25, Bl 15, Bl 18, Bl 20, and Liv 14 for Buerger's disease.

Use with Cv 4, Cv 6, abdomen zigong, Liv 3, Liv 4, Bl 18, Bl 23, Bl 25, Bl 26, Gb 26, Pc 6, and St 36 for menstrual irregularities.

Use with Cv 3, Cv 4, Cv 2, Cv 6, Cv 9, St 28, Bl 25, Bl 28, Bl 26, Sp 9, Liv 3, and Liv 4 for acute prostatitis.

Applications:

Take his left strike with your right palm and rebound off into his chin. Immediately "chop kick" with your right heel down, cutting into Sp 6.

SP 7 (SPLEEN POINT NO. 7)

Chinese name:

Lougu (sleeping valley).

Location:

6 cun above the tip of the medial malleolus, 3 cun above Sp 6, at the posterior margin of the tibia.

Connections:

None.

Direction of strike:

Straight in to the side of the lower leg.

Damage:

Great immediate pain and qi drainage.

Set-up point:

Neigwan.

Antidote:

Rub the leg upward at the lower leg.

Healing:

Innervation and irrigation are the same as for Sp 6.

Used for abdominal distension, borborygmus, urinary tract infection, and cold, numbness, and paralysis of the lower limbs. Massage techniques are the same as for Sp 6.

Used with Gb 30, Gb 29, Gb 34, Gb 39, Sp 6, Sp 3, St 36, St 41, Gb 38, Gb 35, Liv 2, Liv 4, Bl 60, Gv 14, Gv 12, Gv 9, Sp 9, Gb 41, and *bafing* (an extra point) for multiple neuritis where the lower limbs are involved.

Use with St 25, St 36, Cv 12, Cv 4, Cv 6, Bl 25, Bl 20, Bl 18, Liv 3, Sp 4, and St 21 for abdominal distension and borborygmus.

Applications:

The same as for Sp 6.

SP 8 (SPLEEN POINT NO. 8)

Chinese name:

Diji (earth's mechanism).

Location:

3 cun below the medial condyle of the tibia, on the line connecting Sp 9 and the medial malleolus, between the posterior margin of the tibia and the soleus muscle.

Connections:

None.

Direction of strike:

Straight in to the lower leg from the inside of the leg.

Damage:

This is a xie cleft point (accumulation point) for zhen qi (meridian qi or "real qi"). In healing, it is mainly used for uterine problems. When struck, however, it will cause an obstruction in the meridian and thus spleen problems such as stomach disorders, varicose veins, and bladder problems. A numbing of the lower leg is the immediate effect, with a full feeling around the point. Local pain is also felt. This point is often used as a set-up for a strike to the third eye point, just between the eyebrows. It is said that this combination will "explode the head" (direct translation). Needless to say, the fight is over when this combination has been used. However, one must have a certain higher level of fighting skills to use this combination.

Set-up point:

Although this point can be used as a major point strike, it is regarded as a set-up point itself and, as such, does not have a set-up point.

Antidote:

Place the left hand over the third eye point, using mild pressure downward into the forehead as the right hand applies mild pressure to Sp 8.

Healing:

Innervation is by the cutaneous branch of the saphenous nerve; deeper, the tibial is posterior to the point. Irrigation is by the great saphenous vein and the genu suprema artery. Posteriorly, it is by the tibial artery and vein.

Used for abdominal distension, edema, anorexia, dysentery, irregular menstruation, dysuria, seminal emission, dysmenorrhea, and abnormal uterine bleeding.

Traditional indications include distension of the abdomen and flanks, edema, difficult urination, irregular menstruation, colic, hemorrhoids, and nocturnal emissions.

As a xie cleft point of spleen meridian, its traditional functions are to treat acute problems of the stomach and spleen, harmonize the blood, and regulate the uterus.

Massage techniques are the same as for Sp 6.

Use with Co 4, Kd 13, Kd 15, Liv 4, Liv 3, Sp 6, Cv 4, Cv 6, Sp 10, Bl 18, Bl 17, Bl 25, Bl 23, and Sp 9 for irregular menstruation.

Use with St 25, Cv 4, Cv 6, Cv 12, Bl 20, Bl 25, Bl 18, Bl 21, St 36, Liv 3, Sp 4, and Sp 9 for abdominal distension, colic, etc.

Applications:

Here we could use one of the bagwazhang methods that makes use of both the feet and hands. As he attacks with perhaps a straight right, your right palm will slam his inner forearm at neigwan. He might attack again with his left hand, so your right palm again slams the inside of his left inner forearm at neigwan as your right heel scrapes down the inside of his right inner lower leg at Sp 8. Now you have set up this strike so your right palm attacks to the third eye point. This whole routine has only taken one second.

SP 9 (SPLEEN POINT NO. 9)

Chinese name:

Yinlingquan (fountain of yin spring).

Location:

On the lower border of the medial condyle of the tibia, in the depression between the posterior border of the tibia and the gastrocnemius in the upper part of the origin of the soleus muscle.

Connections:

None.

Direction of strike:

Straight in to the inside of the leg just below the knee.

Damage:

This is a water and he point (sea point, gathering together). There is great local pain when this point is struck right on target. It has the reverse effect of the healing, in that it will cause the body to fill up with water and, if not corrected using acupuncture or other Chinese medicine, will eventually lead to early death. This point is used also as a set-up point in the same way that Sp 8 is used. It is not such a good primary strike since it is relatively difficult to get to with much power unless you are a seasoned martial artist. A good, hard strike here will cause great nausea and is sometimes used in conjunction with Gb 34.

Set-up point:

Use Sp 19, as this will weaken the leg opposite the point, so a secondary strike to Sp 9 will cause the leg to give way easily.

Antidote:

Rub neigwan upward on the inside of the forearm.

Healing:

Innervation occurs superficially by the medial crural cutaneous nerve and, deeper, the tibial nerve.

Irrigation occurs anteriorly by the great saphenous vein and the genu suprema artery. Posteriorly, it is by the tibial artery and vein.

Used for abdominal distension, edema, jaundice, diarrhea, dysuria, incontinence, pain in the external genitalia, seminal emission, pain of the knee, ascites, retention of urine, urinary tract infection, irregular menstruation, impotence, beriberi, enteritis, and dysentery.

Traditional indications include distension of the abdomen, edema, diarrhea with undigested food, abdominal pain, retention or incontinence of urine, pain of the genitals, nocturnal emissions, and pain of the lower back and leg.

Traditional functions are to transform damp, relieve stagnation, benefit and adjust the lower jiao (burner), and eliminate damp heat from the lower jiao. It is a water point and a he sea point of the spleen meridian.

Massage techniques include pressing and holding, rotating clockwise or counterclockwise for xu or shi conditions, and doing fingertip percussion or vibration.

Use with Sp 10, Sp 6, Liv 8, St 34, St 35, St 36, Liv 3, Gb 34, and *xiyan* (an extra point) for knee problems.

Use with Cv 4, Cv 3, Cv 2, Cv 9, Sp 6, St 28, Cv 5, St 36, Bl 39, Bl 22, Bl 28, Bl 23, Kd 6, for retention of urine, ascites, incontinence of urine.

Use with Liv 4, Liv 3, Liv 14, Cv 4, Cv 6, St 25, St 36, Sp 6, Bl 25, Bl 23, Bl 20, Bl 18, Bl 17, and Sp 5 for irregular menstruation.

Applications:

Take his right straight with your right palm on the inside of his forearm as your left palm comes up underneath to take over this block, leaving your right fingers to poke straight into Sp 19. Your right heel can now attack to Sp 9, causing the leg to give way.

SP 10 (SPLEEN POINT NO. 10)

Chinese name:

Xuehai (sea of blood).

Location:

When the knee is flexed, the point is located 2 cun above the mediosuperior border of the patella, on the bulge of the medial portion of the quadriceps femoris, at the superior margin of the medial condyle of the femur, in the medial margin of the vastus medialis muscle. Another way of locating this point is to cup your right palm to the patient's left knee, with the thumb on the medial side and the other four fingers directed proximally. The point is located where the tip of your thumb rests.

Connections:

This is a point of chong mai.

Direction of strike:

Just above the knee straight in to the leg at an angle to the front of the thigh.

Damage:

This is called a shock point because it sends a shock throughout the system. The brain does not know what is happening for a second or two, which gives you time to get in with another attack. Just squeeze this point with your thumb and see what it does to you at that level. Now imagine the effect when this point is struck hard with, for instance, a heel. Sp 10 does not respond very well to a larger weapon such as an instep type of round kick. It must be a more accurate weapon, such as a heel or a fist, etc. Being a "special point" for the blood in the healing area, this strike has the reverse effect when struck, allowing the blood to become "reckless," which in turn allows pathogens to enter it.

Set-up point:

You should attack the outside of the forearm with a glancing blow back up the lower forearm.

Antidote:

Treat Sp 10 on the leg opposite the strike with squeezing pressure.

Healing:

Innervation is by the anterior femoral cutaneous nerve and the muscular branch of the femoral nerve. Irrigation is by the muscular branch of the femoral artery and vein.

Used for irregular menstruation, dysmenorrhea, amenorrhea, uterine bleeding, pain in the medial aspect of the thigh, eczema, uticaria, pruritis, neurodermatitis, and anemia.

Traditional indications are to dispel wind, dispel heat from the blood, and regulate circulation of ying (nourishing) qi and xue (blood).

Massage techniques are the same as for Sp 9.

Use with Liv 4, Liv 3, Co 4, Co 11, Sp 6, Sp 5, Sp 9, St 37, St 25, Bl 20, Bl 25, Bl 18, Bl 17, Pc 6, and Th 5 for ulcerative colitis, bloody dysentery, and irritable bowel syndrome.

Use with Co 4, Co 11, Lu 7, Lu 5, Liv 2, Liv 4, St 36, and Sp 6 for uticaria.

Applications:

You could use one of the taijiquan methods from the large san-sau. (I have covered this method in previous chapters. It is the first method from the two-person set known as large san-sau.) He attacks with a straight right, and you block using a blow that is moving upward on the outside of his forearm with your left palm. Your right palm immediately comes underneath and takes over the block and also slides up the outside of his forearm. Now your right heel attacks to his left Sp 10.

SP 11 (SPLEEN POINT NO. 11)

Chinese name:

Jimen (basket's door).

Location:

6 cun above Sp 10, at the medial aspect of the sartorius muscle on the line drawn between Sp 10 and Sp 12.

Connections:

None.

Direction of strike:

Straight in from the inside of the upper thigh.

Damage:

Struck with accuracy, this point can give much local pain and qi drainage. It will affect the way the spleen transports the qi, so power will also be affected. This point can be used as a set-up point strike for Cv 17.

Set-up point:

Neigwan struck straight in.

Antidote:

Place both palms on the top of the head at Gv 20 and apply mild pressure downward.

Healing:

Innervation is by the anterior femoral cutaneous nerve and, deeper, the saphenous nerve. Irrigation is by the great saphenous vein superficially and, deeper, on the lateral side, the femoral artery and vein.

Used for retention of urine, enuresis, pain and swelling in the inguinal region, and urethritis.

Massage techniques are the same as for Sp 9. You can also press in slowly with both thumbs and release quickly, pulling the thumbs apart. Use with Cv 2, Cv 3, Cv 4, Cv 5, Cv 9, St 28, Bl 28, Bl 25, Bl 23, Kd 6, Liv 3, and Sp 6 for urinary problems.

Use with Liv 1, Liv 2, Liv 4, Liv 6, Liv 8, Sp 12, Sp 13, Liv 11, and Liv 12 for pain and swelling in the inguinal groove.

Applications:

Use a knee or a toe strike to Sp 11 as you also block his hand attack, then rebound into a downward strike into Cv 17 with the palm heel. This will drain qi greatly from the seat of power, causing great loss of power.

SP 12 (SPLEEN POINT NO. 12)

Chinese name:

Chongmen (pouring door).

Location:

Superior to the lateral end of the inguinal groove, on the lateral side of the femoral artery, at the level of the upper border of the symphysis pubis, 3.5 cun lateral to Cv 2.

Connections:

Divergent meridian branches from this point. Receives branch of liver.

Direction of strike:

Straight in from the front of the body.

Damage:

This point is situated right over the femoral artery and can cause great internal damage to this artery. It is also near the femoral nerve and will cause the whole leg to be paralyzed. A strong kick to this region can also knock the head of the femur and ball joint right out of its socket, damaging the tendons and ligaments and causing great pain and immobilization. At some later stage in life, if not treated, this strike will prevent the body from being able to take as much qi from food, air, and water as it should and, as a result, disease and weakness are allowed to creep in.

Set-up point:

No set-up point is needed here, although any strike to the face will suffice to put the attacker off what is coming next in the kick to Sp 12.

Antidote:

Treat the same point, Sp 12, using needles .7 cun perpendicular. Or you could use finger pressure on the opposite point. This will treat the long-term effect of this strike. See a doctor if the physical damage is great.

Figure 274

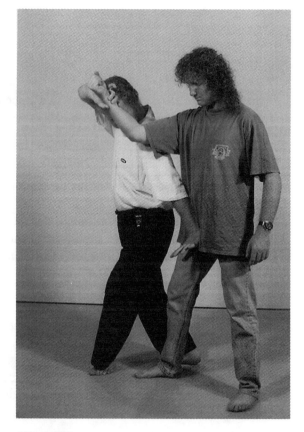

Figure 275

Healing:

Innervation occurs by the point's location just where the femoral nerve traverses. Irrigation occurs on the medial side of the femoral artery.

Used for abdominal pain, hernia, retention of urine, endometritis, and orchitis.

This is a point of intersection with the yinwei mai, so its traditional functions are to influence that meridian.

To massage, press and hold, do rotations clockwise or counterclockwise for xu or shi conditions, do fingertip vibration, or press in slowly with both thumbs and release quickly pulling the thumbs apart.

Use with jiaji points and Bl points one or two vertebra above and below the spinal injury, plus Liv 11 for paraplegia.

Use with St 37 St 25, Bl 25, Bl 24, Sp 9, Sp 6, St 3, Sp 10, lanweixue, Co 4, Co 11, Liv 3, and Liv 4, plus moxa painful regions of abdomen for chronic appendicitis.

Applications:

1) A straight back kick to the area just above the groin and to the side of the body.
2) Take his right straight with your left palm, with your left foot forward (fig. 274). Turn around in the opposite direction and allow your right foot to swing around to the rear as your right palm takes over the block and your left palm now attacks straight in to Sp 12 (fig. 275).

SP 13 (SPLEEN POINT NO. 13)

Chinese name:

Fushe (dwelling).

Location:

0.7 cun above Sp 12, 4 cun lateral to the Cv meridian.

Connections:

Liver and yin wei mai.

Direction of strike:

Straight in and slightly angled to the outer part of the body.

Damage:

This strike causes much the same damage as Sp 12. The only difference is that the point is closer to the femoral nerve, so the strike will cause considerable nerve problems, such as paralysis or nervous shutdown, if it's done hard enough.

Set-up point:

None.

Antidote:

Same as for Sp 12.

Healing:

Innervation is by the ilioinguinal nerve. Irrigation is the same as for Sp 12.

Used for abdominal pain, hernia, mass in the abdomen, inguinal lymphadenitis, adnexitis, pain in lower abdomen, and appendicitis.

This point is where the yinwei meridian, the spleen meridian, and the liver meridian converge and enter the abdomen, further connecting with the spleen, heart, and lungs; hence the name of "dwelling" or "converging house." Its traditional function is to influence these meridians.

Massage techniques are the same as for Sp 12.

Use with St 36, Kd 16, Pc 6, Co 4, Co 11, Bl 24, Bl 25, St 25, Liv 4, Liv 3, St 37, lanweixue, Bl 17, Bl 18, and Bl 53 for appendicitis.

Add to the treatment listed under Sp 11 for pain and swelling of inguinal groove.

Applications:

The same as for Sp 12.

SP 14 (SPLEEN POINT NO. 14)

Chinese name:

Fujie (abdomen's knot).

Location:

3 cun above Sp 13, 1.5 cun below Sp 15, on the lateral side of the rectus abdominis, 4 cun lateral to the Cv meridian.

Connections:

None.

Direction of strike:

Straight in.

Damage:

If you can get a strike in at this point when the recipient is not expecting it, it will have a great effect, shocking the whole body. It has been known to cause KO. The area is well protected by the external oblique muscles, however, which can be flexed to afford some kind of protection, especially if the attacker has been practicing iron shirt qigong.

Set-up point:

Sp 21 will put so much of a shock to the whole torso area that you may not even need to strike to Sp 14.

Antidote:

Internal damage can occur with this strike, especially to the colon and small intestine area, so watch out for signs of this damage (e.g., pain the lower abdomen, bleeding from the anus). Seek medical advice.

Healing:

Innervation is by the 11th intercostal nerve, and irrigation is by the 11th intercostal artery and vein.

Used for abdominal pain around the umbilical region, hernia, and diarrhea.

Massage techniques are the same as for Sp 12.

Use with St 25, St 37, Liv 4, Liv 3, Bl 25, Bl 26, Bl 20, Bl 18, Cv 5, Cv 7, Cv 9, and Kd 15 for pain around the umbilical region.

Use with Sp 4, Sp 3, St 36, St 37, Sp 6, Sp 9, St 25, St 28, Liv 13, Cv 12, Bl 20, Bl 25, Bl 23, Bl 22, and Bl 39 for diarrhea.

Applications:

He might attack with a straight right, so you would move quickly to your left, stepping with your left foot. You glance his attack with your right palm, which would then rebound into Sp 21. Your right palm now grabs around his upper back and pulls him forward onto your right knee at Sp 14.

SP 15 (SPLEEN POINT NO. 15)

Chinese name:

Daheng (big horizontal).

Location:

4 cun lateral to the center of the umbilicus, on the mammillary line, lateral to the rectus abdominis, in the external and internal oblique and the transverse abdominal muscles.

Connections:

Yin wei mai.

Direction of strike:

Straight in to the abdomen.

Damage:

Although this point strike will cause things like diarrhea and great nausea instantly, it is too well protected by the external oblique muscles, which can be built up to great proportions (especially true if the person has been practicing iron shirt). The strike has some shock value, but I would not be doing my job in teaching people how to defend themselves if I were to tell you to strike to this area. I would not advise you to attack to this region regardless of the attacker's abdominal strength. Many other martial arts systems advocate this strike, and you will see them in tournament, especially the noncontact variety, using the reverse punch with a loud yell and much bravado, striking to this area and gaining a point for doing so. I have invited many highly ranked martial artists to strike me in this region with little or no effect, to their great surprise. Plus, the way some martial artists attack, you can see the strike coming some seconds before, giving you plenty of time to prepare the area for the shock.

Set-up point:

None.

Antidote:

If you have been struck here while you are not expecting it and are experiencing some renal problems, squeeze the tip of your index finger quite hard and massage Co 10.

Healing:

Innervation is by the 10th intercostal nerve. Irrigation is by the 10th intercostal artery and vein.

Used for dysentery, constipation, pain in lower abdomen, and diarrhea.

This is a point of intersection with the yangwei mai, and its traditional function is to treat abdominal distension.

Massage techniques are the same as for Sp 12. You can also use it when running the dai mai as an alternative pathway from Gb 26. (Normally, when you run the dai mai, you start at Gv 4 and go to Bl 23, Bl 52, Gb 25, Liv 13, Gb 26, Gb 27, Gb 28, St 28, Kd 13, and Cv 4. Here you can go from Gb 26 to Sp 15 to St 25 to Kd 16 to Cv 8.)

Use with St 25, Liv 3, Liv 4, Bl 25, St 37, Bl 26, Bl 20, and Bl 18 for constipation or diarrhea.

Use with Cv 3, Cv 4, Cv 6, Cv 7, Cv 9, Sp 6, Sp 9, Liv 3, Liv 4, St 25, Kd 15, St 26, St 27, St 28, St 29, and St 30 for lower abdominal pain.

Applications:

Do not strike to this area.

SP 16 (SPLEEN POINT NO. 16)

Chinese name:

Fuai (abdomen's sorrow).

Location:

3 cun above Sp 15, 4 cun lateral to the Cv meridian.

Connections:

Yang wei mai.

Direction of strike:

Straight in and slightly angled in toward the centerline.

Damage:

This point too can be protected. However, if the recipient is caught unaware, a strike here can have devastating results, as it is in the area of the diaphragm. This strike can cause death by suffocation at the most. It will at least force the recipient to sit down to regain his breathing.

Set-up point:

You could use neigwan to take his mind off the Sp 16 strike.

Antidote:

Apply CPR if dead. Otherwise, sit him down and push his head between his knees.

Healing:

Innervation is by the eighth intercostal nerve, and irrigation is by the eighth intercostal artery and vein.

Used for abdominal pain, indigestion, constipation, dysentery, and pain in the region of the umbilicus. It is a point of intersection with the yangwei mai, so its traditional function is to influence that channel.

Massage techniques are the same as for Sp 12.

Use with St 25, St 37, Bl 25, Bl 20, Bl 23, Bl 26, Bl 18, Sp 15, St 36, Cv 12, Sp 6, Sp 9, Sp 4, and Liv 3 for constipation or dysentery.

Use with Liv 4, Liv 3, St 25, Liv 8, Sp 5, Sp 9, Gb 43, Gb 44, Bl 20, Bl 25, Bl 26, Bl 18, Bl 19, Bl 17, St 36, and St 34 for abdominal pain.

Applications:

1) Take his strike at neigwan and then rebound using an elbow to Sp 16.
2) You could slam his left leg (kick) at the side of his knee, causing great pain, then come straight in with a back elbow (i.e., a strike that uses the back part of the elbow rather than the front).

SP 17 (SPLEEN POINT NO. 17)

Chinese name:

Shidou (food's cavity).

Location:

6 cun lateral to the Cv meridian, or 2 cun lateral to the mammillary line, in the fifth intercostal space.

Connections:

None.

Direction of strike:

This point is one of the better qi drainage points. I have had personal experience with this one, and all you want to do is to lie down and rub the area. The direction must be from outside to midline. So if you are striking to his right Sp 17, you would strike it from his right to left over the point and into the pectoral.

Damage:

The damage is great, with local pain lasting for some hours. The qi drainage is so severe that you will just wish to lie down. This point can be struck with a number of weapons, including elbow and palm as the better ones. The elbow is well suited because of the direction of the strike. You can cause the heart to stop beating because of the percussive effect that travels straight into the heart. This is one of the most devastating strikes. However, it takes a little getting at because the arm must be raised first.

Set-up point:

Any strike to the lower forearm, especially at neigwan or Th 8 or at the wrist at H 5 or Lu 8, will cause the qi to be directed to these points while you strike to Sp 17. Sp 17 will work regardless of a set-up point, but it will be even better with one.

Antidote:

Massage the Sp 17 point in the opposite direction of the strike. Then rub the inside of the upper arm from armpit to elbow.

Healing:

Innervation is by the lateral cutaneous branch of the fifth intercostal nerve. Irrigation is by the thoracoepigastric vein.

Used for sensation of fullness and pain in the chest and hypochondriac regions, intercostal neuralgia, ascites, retention of urine, and gastritis.

Massage techniques include pressing and holding the point; doing rotations clockwise or counterclockwise for xu or shi conditions; pressing in slowly with both thumbs and releasing quickly, pulling the thumbs apart; and doing fingertip percussion and vibration.

Use with Liv 14, Gb 24, Liv 13, Cv 12, Liv 3, Liv 4, Liv 8, St 36, Pc 6, Co 4, Bl 17, Bl 18, Bl 19, Bl 20, Bl 21, Bl 22, Bl 25, and St 25 for fullness in the chest and hypochondriac regions and gastritis.

Use with St 28, Cv 5, Bl 22, Bl 39, St 40, Sp 3, Sp 4, Bl 20, Bl 28, Cv 2, Cv 3, Cv 4, Kd 6, Liv 3, Cv 12, St 25, and Bl 25 for ascites and retention of urine.

Applications:

Take his right straight with your right palm at neigwan as your left palm comes underneath to take over the block. Your left palm now controls his right arm as your right elbow is free to attack in the correct direction to Sp 17 (figs. 276, 277).

Figure 276

Figure 277

SP 18 (SPLEEN POINT NO. 18)

Chinese name:

Tianxi (heaven's stream).

Location:

2 cun lateral to the nipple or 6 cun lateral to the Cv meridian, in the fourth intercostal space.

Connections:

None.

Direction of strike:

Struck again in from the outside as for Sp 17; however, the angle of this strike is not as great, at about 45 degrees. (The Sp 17 shot was a little less than 180 degrees.)

Damage:

This is again a devastating strike, causing a shock wave to rise up into the head and around the whole upper torso with great qi loss. This strike can also stop the heart. You can test this point by using finger pressure only at the edge of the pectoral and note the pain caused even with finger pressure. If you are right on the point, you will also experience a feeling like a shiver going up in to the head and across the chest.

Set-up point:

Neigwan, as for Sp 17.

Antidote:

Place the palm onto the pectoral and rub, using mild pressure outward and down onto the biceps. The patient's arms should be at his side in order to do this.

Healing:

Innervation is by the lateral cutaneous branch of the fourth intercostal nerve. Irrigation is by the branches of the lateral thoracic artery and vein, the thoracoepigastric artery and vein, and the fourth intercostal artery and vein.

Used for sensations of fullness and pain in the chest, cough, mastitis, lactation deficiency, bronchitis, asthma, and hiccups.

Massage techniques are the same as for Sp 17.

Use with Cv 17, Liv 14, St 15, St 36, Sp 6, Liv 4, Liv 8, Liv 3, Bl 17, Bl 18, Bl 19, Si 1, Pc 6, Th 10, and St 18 for mastitis.

Use with Lu 7, Lu 5, Lu 1, Co 4, Co 11, Bl 12, Bl 13, Bl 43, dingchuan, Cv 22, Cv 17, Kd 22, Kd 23, Kd 24, Kd 25, Kd 26, Kd 27, Kd 11, Kd 7, Liv 3, Pc 6, Liv 14, Bl 17, and Sp 21 for fullness and pain in the chest, cough, bronchitis, and asthma.

Applications:

1) Do the same as for Sp 17, only bring your one-knuckle punch across to strike to the point instead of your elbow. This will decrease the angle, causing the greatest damage.

2) You could also block his right straight attack from the outside with your left palm, lifting his right arm slightly to allow access to Sp 18 with your right palm (fig. 278).

SP 19 (SPLEEN POINT NO. 19)

Figure 278

Chinese name:

Xiongxiang (chest home).

Location:

One rib above Sp 18, in the third intercostal space, 6 cun lateral to the Cv meridian.

Connections:

None.

Direction of strike:

Straight in to the shoulder and a little toward centerline, just above Sp 18.

Damage:

Usually struck with a finger jab, this point is interesting because it controls the power in the opposite leg. So if you strike to Sp 19 on his right side, his left leg will be weakened and vice versa. I was taught that the location for this point was a little more to the outside of the body in the shoulder crease, but I have not come across this location in any texts. The effect is the same, however, using both locations: great nerve damage to the shoulder area. This point can be used as a set-up for a leg kick, requiring little power to cause his leg to buckle. I have caused one chap's leg to quiver and bounce violently when this point was only squeezed.

Set-up point:

Use neigwan.

Antidote:

Push Liv 14 straight in. Liv 3 will also help with the leg damage.

Healing:

Innervation is by the lateral cutaneous branch of the third intercostal nerve, and irrigation is by the lateral thoracic artery and vein and the third intercostal artery and vein.

Used for a sensation of fullness and pain in the chest and hypochondriac regions, and intercostal neuralgia.

Massage techniques are the same as for Sp 17.

Use with Liv 14, Gb 24, Sp 21, Bl 17, Bl 18, Bl 19, Bl 20, Bl 21, Bl 43, jiaji points corresponding to the region affected (extra), Liv 3, Gb 43, Gb 44, Gb 34, Pc 6, Th 6, Liv 5, Gb 40, Liv 2, and St 40 for intercostal neuralgia and pain or fullness in the chest.

Applications:

It begins the same way as for the previous application for Sp 17, only now, the fingers of the right hand poke violently into Sp 19, followed by a right heel kick to the knee of his left leg. (If you had struck at his left Sp 19 point, you would have kicked with your left heel to the knee of his right leg.)

SP 20 (SPLEEN POINT NO. 20)

Chinese name:

Zhourong (encircling glory).

Location:

One rib above Sp 19, directly below Lu 1, in the second intercostal space, 6 cun lateral to the Cv meridian.

Connections:

None.

Direction of strike:

Straight in.

Damage:

This point will also affect the way the opposite leg functions, but to a lesser degree. It will cause great local tearing of the tendons in the shoulder, with little or no external damage. I once struck an opponent in a tournament at this point, and he could not carry on, although there were no visible signs of damage. The next day, he went to see a doctor who took X-rays, and to his astonishment, all of the tendons underneath the muscle were torn. The doctor had to ask how he acquired this damage. This point used with Liv 14 is a death combination. The whole body goes numb, and the lungs and heart stop.

Set-up point:

Neigwan.

Antidote:

Used with Liv 14, there is no antidote! If only Sp 20 is struck, rest and hold cold compresses onto the point for 20 minutes exactly, then release the compress for a further 20 minutes.

Healing:

Innervation is by the muscular branch of the anterior thoracic nerve and the lateral cutaneous branch of the second intercostal nerve. Irrigation is by the lateral thoracic artery and vein and the second intercostal artery and vein.

Used for a sensation of fullness in the chest and hypochondriac regions, cough, intercostal neuralgia, pleurisy, pulmonary empyema, bronchiectasis.

Massage techniques are the same as for Sp 17.

Use with the formula listed under Sp 19 for intercostal neuralgia and fullness of the chest.

Use with Si 15, Gv 12, Gv 9, Lu 6, Lu 7, Lu 5, Lu 1, Co 4, St 40, Lu 9, Cv 17, Bl 12, Bl 13, Bl 17, Bl 20, Bl 22, Bl 18, Bl 25, St 36, Sp 4, Sp 3, Kd 6, Kd 7, Liv 14, and Sp 21 for bronchiectasis, pleurisy, pulmonary empyema, (empyema by itself is more common), and cough.

Applications:

He attacks with either a hook right or straight. The fingers of your left hand will strike to Sp 20, thus blocking his attack also, as your right palm attacks to the opposite side of the body to Liv 14.

SP 21 (SPLEEN POINT NO. 21)

Chinese name:

Dabao (big wrapping).

Location:

On the midaxillary line, 6 cun below the axilla, midway between the axilla and the free end of the 11th rib, in the seventh intercostal space.

Connections:

All luo meridians. The main meridian flows internally to Lu 1.

Direction of strike:

In from the side of the upper torso.

Damage:

This point does amazing internal damage both electrically (qi wise) and physically. This point balances the whole body, left and right (especially torso) and inner and outer. A strike here spreads out over the chest, causing great imbalance to the qi system of the whole body. The recipient will fall into a coma if the strike is hard enough and will not recover until energy balancing is performed on him. Physically, the liver can be damaged, as well as the lungs, since this point is also connected to Lu 1. Rib breakage will also occur. This is not a point to be played around with! It is an excellent point to use with St 9 because the combination will cause KO and extreme spleen damage, plus the lungs will contract, causing suffocation.

Set-up point:

Neigwan.

Antidote:

Massage Sp 20 and 21 downward if the damage has not been great. Or squeeze Gb 20 points upward.

Healing:

Innervation is by the seventh intercostal nerve and the terminal branch of the long thoracic nerve. Irrigation is by the thoracodorsal artery and vein and the seventh intercostal artery and vein.

Used for pain in the chest and hypochondriac regions, asthma, general aching and weakness, and intercostal neuralgia.

The great luo of the spleen starts here and spreads across the chest and hypochondriac regions, supervising all the blood of the body. (The spleen is seen as the ruler of blood, although one source suggests that this meridian covers the whole body. A shi condition of this channel may cause general aches and pains throughout the body, whereas a xu condition may cause weakness in the muscles of the limbs and joints.)

Massage techniques are the same as for Sp 17.

Use with Cv 4, Sp 6, Cv 9, Cv 8, Cv 5, Cv 17, Cv 7, Gv 4, Cv 11, Cv 4, Cv 6, Kd 27, Kd 11, and St 13 for chyluria.

Add to any formula used to open up the chest.

Applications:

Use the same method as for Sp 17 or Sp 18. Or you could take his right straight, for instance, with your left palm as you move to your left, then strike straight in with your right elbow.

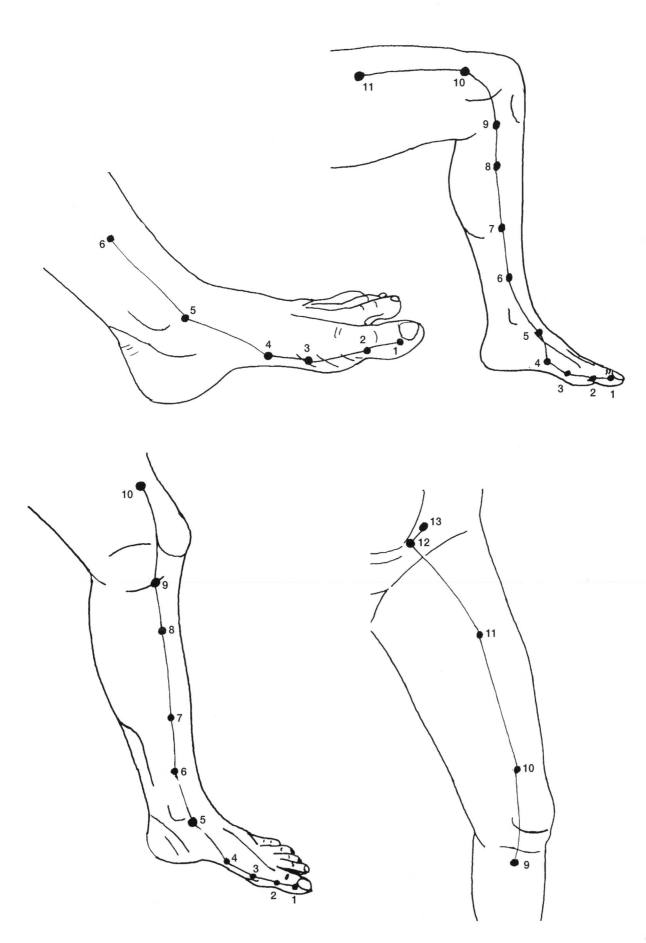

295

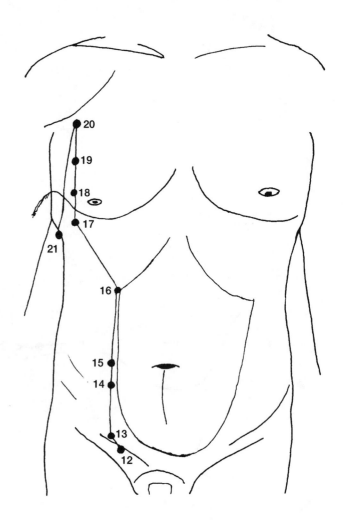

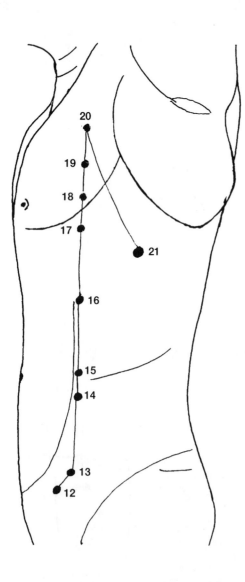

Chapter 7

The Heart Meridian

THE TCM VIEW

The heart is a yin (zhang) organ, its element is fire, and its fu organ is the small intestine. The heart's "official job" is the supreme controller of organs.

Most of what Chinese medicine says about the heart is in keeping with what Western medicine says. However, there is one big difference, and probably the most important one: that the heart houses the shen, or spirit. Chinese medicine states that the heart, not the brain, houses the "mind." The heart is the residence of the shen or spirit consciousness, awareness, mental clarity, memory, stored thoughts, and sleep. The shen is said to be reflected in the eyes.

The following five functions are affected by the heart:

- Mental activity
- Memory
- Consciousness
- Thinking
- Sleep

A strong heart leads to normal mental activity, clear consciousness, good memory, sharp thinking, and sound sleep. The reverse is true when the heart is not strong.

In Chinese medicine, each zhang organ dominates a certain tissue, with the heart dominating the blood vessels. The circulation of blood by pumping is accomplished by heart qi and zhong qi. Qi ensures an even, regular beat. So healthy or unhealthy blood vessels depend upon the state of the heart.

The heart's function of controlling the blood depends upon a healthy mind. The function of housing the shen depends upon a good supply of blood and nourishment to the heart. So there is a relationship of mutual dependence between the function of controlling blood and that of housing the shen. Deficient blood cause restlessness or an uneasy mind, insomnia, and poor memory. An uneasy, restless mind; emotional problems; sadness; or excess joy can cause a deficiency of blood supply to the heart, resulting in palpitation and poor complexion.

The state of the heart manifests in the face or complexion, which is said to be the expansion of the heart. So if the heart is healthy, there will be a good complexion. If the heart is deficient, the complexion will be pale or bluish purple.

The heart opens to the tongue, which is the associated organ and gives rise to the associated sense of taste and speech. The tongue is the mirror of the heart, with heart qi and shen giving rise to free mobility of tongue and clear speech. Hence, someone with too much "fire in the heart" will talk incessantly. Things like stuttering, difficult or weak speech, and aphasia could be the result of a weak heart. The state of the heart will also control the taste and color of the tongue. With a normal heart, the tongue is slightly pale red and in good shape; the taste will be good. If there is heat in the heart, the tongue will be dark red with a bitter taste. If the heart is blood deficient and weak, the tongue will be pale and swollen.

Acupuncture points along the meridian line of the heart can aid in the treatment of heart complaints, such as high or low blood pressure. They can also help eye and skin problems and alleviate symptoms of stress, anxiety, and tension.

DIM-MAK

The heart meridian is one of the most dangerous meridians because all of its points affect the heart directly. There are only nine points along the inner arm up to the axilla, and all will affect what the heart does, from a mild slowing to complete stoppage, depending upon which points have been struck and in what order, etc. We often use heart points as set-up points to other deadly points since the heart points can make the recipient feel really ill. Just ask any heart patient how he felt when he was having his first heart attack, and you will know what can be also achieved by striking to heart points.

If there are any points that are more deadly than others on this meridian, they would have to be Ht 3 and Ht 1.

HT 1 (HEART POINT NO. 1)

Chinese name:
Jiquan (summit's spring).
Location:
In the center of the axilla, on the medial side of the axillary artery, at the lateral, inferior margin of the pectoralis major muscle and, in its deep position, in the coraco-brachialis muscle
Connections:
This is a lower meeting point of the heart/small intestine divergent meridian. Takes an internal path of the meridian from the zhang (i.e., although the first point is the axilla, there is obviously a connection to the physical heart via an internal connection directly from the heart.
Direction of strike:
Straight up into the axilla, usually using a thumb knuckle or side of the forearm.
Damage:
This is one of the most dangerous heart points; a medium to heavy strike will stop the heart instantly. The point is right over the top of the axillary artery, and, as such, great artery damage is also done when this point is struck. The shen is affected, and the recipient feels as though he has been disconnected from God! Brain function is also affected, speech is impaired, and mental activity in general is severely affected. The emotional state of the recipient is also damaged greatly. This is all on top of immediate shoulder damage. (This point is traditionally used to cure "frozen shoulder" because of its ability to clear both external and internal qi of the meridian.)
Set-up point:
Si 8 is an excellent set-up point.
Antidote:
There is no known antidote other than CPR and immediate medical treatment.

Figure 279

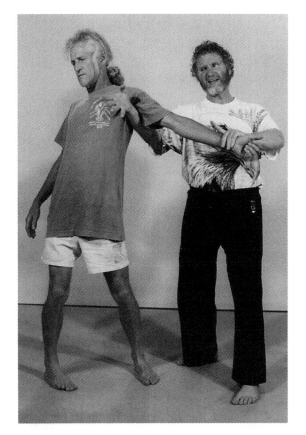

Figure 280

Healing:

Innervation is by the ulnar nerve, median nerve, and the medial brachial cutaneous nerve. Irrigation occurs by the axillary artery's location lateral to this point.

Used for pain in the costal and cardiac regions, scrofula, cold and pain in the elbow, arthritis of the shoulder, perifocal inflammation of the shoulder joint, angina pectoris, and intercostal neuralgia.

Traditional indications include chest pain and thirst, inability to raise the arm, full and painful ribs, jaundice, and depression.

Massage techniques include pressing and holding the point, doing rotations clockwise or counterclockwise for xu or shi conditions, rubbing back and forth in the direction of the scapula for frozen shoulder (look for the tense muscle), and doing fingertip percussion.

Use with St 38, Gb 34, Co 15, Co 14, Co 11, St 3, St 9, St 10, St 11, St 12, St 13, St 14, Th 13, Th 14, Th 15, Gb 21, Gb 20, *jianneling* (an extra point), and *naoshang* (an extra point) for frozen shoulder.

Use with Cv 7, Cv 14, Cv 17, Bl 14, Bl 15, Bl 17, Bl 18, Liv 14, Liv 4, Liv 3, St 36, and Pc 6 for angina pectoris. For this you can also look for a painful point medial and superior to Si 9, and another one around Si 11, both on the left only.

Applications:

He might attack with a low left hook to your lower right rib area. You should move to your right and slam his left arm at Si 8 with your right forearm as your left palm slams down on top of his forearm, causing considerable local pain and setting up the Ht 1 shot (fig. 279). Immediately grab his left wrist at Ht 5 and Lu 8, thus draining the qi from the organ, and with your right forearm or thumb knuckle, strike violently up into Ht 1 (fig. 280). NOTE: Your right palm, on the thumb side, could strike to St 9 at the same time if you used your forearm to strike to Ht 1.

HT 2 (HEART POINT NO. 2)

Chinese name:

Qingling (youthful spirit).

Location:

When the elbow is flexed, the point is 3 cun above the medial end of the transverse cubital crease (Ht 3), in the groove medial to the biceps brachii.

Connections:

None.

Direction of strike:

Straight in just beneath the biceps, slightly toward yourself, (i.e., down his upper arm toward his fingers).

Damage:

This point will slow the heart rate sufficiently to make him feel really ill. This point is also an excellent nerve point strike, affecting the whole arm and sending a shock wave into the upper body. KO has been effected using this point.

Set-up point:

Slap the outside of the forearm upward, covering Th 8.

Antidote:

Squeeze the little finger.

Healing:

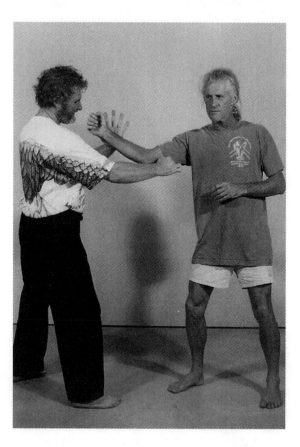

Figure 281

Innervation is by the medial antebrachial cutaneous nerve, the medial brachial cutaneous nerve, and the ulnar nerve. Irrigation is by the basilic vein, the superior ulnar collateral artery.

Used for yellowish sclera; pain in the hypochondriac region, shoulder, and arm; costalgia (pain localized in the ribs), and icteric sclera.

Massage techniques include pressing and holding the point, rotating clockwise or counterclockwise for xu or shi conditions, doing fingertip percussion or vibration, and pressing in slowly with both thumbs and releasing quickly, pulling the thumbs apart.

Use with the formula for frozen shoulder listed under Ht 1.

Use with Liv 14, Liv 4, Liv 3, Liv 8, Gb 24, Liv 13, Bl 17, Bl 18, Bl 19, Bl 20, and Bl 21 for hypochondriac pain.

Applications:

This application is also good for Ht 3. He might attack with a straight right. You should move slightly to your left and attack to his Th 8 point with your left palm. A split second later, your right thumb knuckle attacks to Ht 2 in a direction that is slightly toward you (fig. 281).

HT 3 (HEART POINT NO. 3)

Chinese name:

Shaohai (lesser sea).

Location:

When the elbow is flexed, the point is at the medial end of the transverse cubital crease, in the depression anterior to the medial epicondyle of the humerus, in the pronator teres and the brachialis muscles.

Connections:

None.

Direction of strike:

Into the inside of the elbow and slightly toward you, usually with a thumb-knuckle punch.

Damage:

This is a water and he sea point, and it is one of the more dangerous points. A strike here will have the immediate action of stopping the heart and damaging the tendon (nervous) system. The point is usually used to treat, among other things, stress, depression, and emotional disturbances, so this strike will have the reverse effect, causing long-term nervous and emotional disorders. It will unbalance the yin/yang relationship throughout the whole body. Someone who has been struck here and has not been treated will have a complexion like people who have smoked all their lives (like someone who is 35 years old but who looks like 65 years old!). This strike also works very well with the mind point on the side of the jaw—someone is knocked out very easily with a light slap on this point after Ht 3 has been struck. If struck in a proximal way, the mind point will cause high blood pressure. If struck straight in it will cause the heart to weaken over a period.

Set-up point:

The only set-up point that this strike needs is a sharp slap going up along the outer forearm.

Antidote:

Have an acupuncturist look at the whole energy system of the body and have it balanced out. You could try treating Ht 3 on the other arm, using finger pressure up the arm. Or you could try squeezing Ht 9.

Healing:

Innervation is by the medial antebrachial cutaneous nerve. Irrigation is by the basilic vein, the inferior ulnar collateral artery, and the ulnar recurrent artery and vein.

Used for cardiac pain, numbness of the arm, hand tremor, contracture of the elbow, pain in the axilla and hypochondriac regions, scrofula, neurasthenia, psychosis, intercostal neuralgia, ulnar nerve neuralgia, lymphadenitis, and disease of the elbow.

Traditional indications include headache and dizziness, stiff neck, toothache, vomiting, nodular growths in the neck, pain in the axilla, absentmindedness, madness, and debility of the limbs.

Traditional functions are to calm the spirit, regulate the heart qi, relax the tendons, invigorate and clears the channels and collaterals, and, as a water point and he sea point for the heart meridian, it can be used to cool the heart and its channel.

Massage techniques are the same as for Ht 2.

Use with Co 10, Co 11, Co 9, Co 8, Co 7, Co 6, Co 4, Ht 7, Si 3, Si 8, and Pc 3 for numbness or pain of the forearm and elbow.

Use with Sp 6, Pc 6, Pc 3, Ht 7, Ht 8, Cv 17, Liv 14, Liv 3, St 36, and Kd 3 for neurasthenia.

Use with Ht 7, Gv 20, and Sp 6 for absent-mindedness.

Applications:

The same as for Ht 2.

HT 4 (HEART POINT NO. 4)

Chinese name:

Lingdao (spirit's path).

Location:

On the radial side of the tendon of the muscle flexor carpi ulnaris, 1.5 cun above the transverse crease of the wrist when the palm faces upward.

Connections:

None.

Direction of strike:

Straight in.

Damage:

This is a metal and jing point, usually used for "local" problems in the healing area. A strike here adds fire to the heart and causes high blood pressure immediately.

Set-up point:

A sharp strike just under the heart, slightly to the left of the body.

Antidote:

This strike causes high blood pressure, which can cause a KO. In this case it is okay to lightly finger St 9, jiggling the fingers on the point, which will bring the high blood pressure down again.

Healing:

Innervation is by the medial antebrachial cutaneous nerve; the point is on the side of the ulnar nerve. Irrigation is by the ulnar artery.

Used for cardiac pain, sudden hoarseness, contracture of the elbow and arm, convulsions, chest pain, psychosis, hysteria, and neuralgia of the ulnar nerve.

Traditional functions: a metal point and jing river (traversing) point of the heart meridian.

Massage techniques are the same as for Ht 2.

Use with Ht 3, Liv 3, Liv 2, and Ht 6 for neuralgia of the ulna nerve.

Use with Ht 3, Ht 7, Pc 6, Liv 14, Liv 4, Liv 3, Bl 14, Bl 15, Bl 17, Bl 18, Bl 25, Sp 6, St 36, Cv 12, Sp 3, and St 40 for psychosis, hysteria, and so on.

Use with Ht 3, Ht 6, Ht 7, Pc 6, Cv 17, Liv 14, Liv 4, Liv 3, Bl 14, Bl 15, Bl 17, Bl 18, Sp 6, and St 36 for cardiac pain.

Applications:

Usually used with wrist grabs. If you can get a finger or two right on the point, then squeeze violently, this will work even better.

HT 5 (HEART POINT NO. 5)

Chinese name:

Tongli (reaching the measure).

Location:

When the palm faces upward, the point is on the radial side of the tendon of the flexor carpi ulnaris muscle, 1 cun above the transverse crease of the wrist, between the tendon of the flexor carpi ulnaris and the flexor digitorum superficialis manus muscle. In its deep position, it is in the flexor digitorum sublimis muscle.

Connections:

Transverse luo to Si 4 and Si 1.

Direction of strike:

Usually used with a violent wrist grab and shake. Or it could be struck straight in.

Damage:

This is a classic qi drainage point and works very well as a set-up point strike. In fact, it is used in acupuncture when qi drainage is called for, although acupuncturists will not work this point too hard since it could cause KO from qi drainage. It works very well with Th 12. This strike will weaken the elbow greatly.

Set-up point:

None, although Lu 8 works very well with this point and can be accessed along with Ht 5, as they are both on the wrist area.

Antidote:

Usually time will help. However you could needle Ht 6, the xie cleft point of the heart meridian, .3 cun perpendicular. Or you could pull Ht 5 distally, then rub Ht 3 proximally.

Healing:

Innervation and irrigation are the same as for Ht 4.

Used for palpitations, dizziness, blurring of vision, sore throat, sudden hoarseness, aphasia with

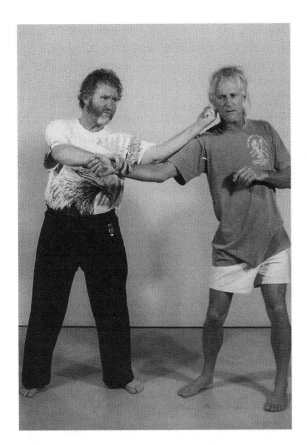

Figure 282

stiffness of the tongue, pain in the wrist and arm, chest pain, bradycardia, neurasthenia, psychosis, cough, and asthma.

Traditional indications include headache and dizziness, stiffness of the tongue, throat blockage, palpitations due to nervous fright, abnormal uterine bleeding, and incontinence.

As a luo connecting point of the heart meridian its traditional functions are to calm the spirit and regulate the heart qi. It is also is very good to bring down fire from the head caused by mental irritation. It is a special point for aphasia.

Massage techniques are the same as for Ht 2.

Use with Liv 2, Liv 4, Sp 6, Liv 14, Cv 4, Cv 6, St 36, St 29, St 28, St 27, St 26, St 25, Bl 26, Bl 25, Bl 23, Bl 20, Bl 19, Bl 18, Bl 17, and Bl 15 for excessive uterine bleeding.

Use with Ht 7, Pc 6, Bl 15, Bl 14, Bl 17, Bl 18, Cv 14, Cv 17, Liv 14, Liv 3, and St 36 for cardiac arrhythmia.

Use with Ht 3, Ht 7, Pc 6, Bl 14, Bl 15, Bl 43, Bl 17, Bl 18, Liv 14, Liv 4, Liv 3, Sp 6, Sp 9, Sp 4, St 40, and Kd 1 for psychosis.

Applications:

Block his low left attack with both arms. Your right palm slams down on top of his left wrist as your left outer forearm slams the inside of his left forearm. Now, your right palm grabs and shakes his left wrist area violently at Ht 5 as your left palm attacks to his mind point at the jaw (fig. 282). This is called p'eng in taijiquan.

HT 6 (HEART POINT NO. 6)

Chinese name:

Yinxi (yin accumulation).

Location:

On the radial side of the tendon of flexor carpi ulnaris muscle, 0.5 cun above the transverse crease of the wrist.

Connections:

None.

Direction of strike:

Also a grabbing-type motion on the wrist.

Damage:

Ht 4, 5, 6, and 7 are very close to each other and, as such, it is difficult to only get one. So it is common for all four points to be attacked at once with a grabbing and shaking motion. This will cause great qi loss and immobilization, just before a more dangerous attack to St 9, for instance. Ht 6 is the xie cleft point. If struck all by itself, it said to cause madness and weaken the heart.

Set-up point:

This is a classic set-up point.

Antidote:

Finger pressure to the opposite Ht 6 point up the inner arm.

303

Healing:

Innervation and irrigation are the same as for Ht 4.

Use for cardiac pain, hysteria, night sweating, neurasthenia, palpitations, and pulmonary tuberculosis.

Traditional indications are acute problems of the heart.

Traditional functions: a xie cleft point (accumulating point) of the heart, stops night sweating, treats acute phlegm disorders of the heart.

Massage techniques are the same as for Ht 2.

Use with Kd 7, Sp 6, Si 3, Bl 13, and Bl 15 for night sweating.

Use with Ht 3, Ht 7, Ht 8, Bl 14, Bl 15, Bl 17, Bl 18, Cv 17, Cv 14, Liv 14, Liv 4, Liv 3, St 36, Pc 6, and Co 4 for cardiac pain and palpitations.

Applications:

The same as for Ht 5.

HT 7 (HEART POINT NO. 7)

Chinese name:

Shenmen (spirit's door).

Location:

On the transverse crease of the wrist, in the articular region between the pisiform bone and the ulna, in the depression on the radial side of the tendon of the muscle flexor carpi ulnaris.

Connections:

Transverse luo from Si 7.

Direction of strike:

Straight in to the wrist or a wrist grab.

Damage:

This point has a great effect upon the shen. It is an earth, yuan, and shu point. This strike damages the shen's emotional control over the whole system. The fire element is totally unbalanced, causing too much heat to enter the system. The whole system becomes emotionally unstable and tense.

Set-up point:

Ht 3 works very well as the set-up for this point.

Antidote:

Take the opposite hand and squeeze shenmen (Ht 7) up along the inner forearm at the wrist about 1 inch. You can also squeeze Ht 3 lightly as you do this. This will restore the shen, and calmness will prevail. This point is particularly good for patients having seizures or epileptic fits, etc. I have used this point many times on patients having mild epileptic fits, in which they feel as though they are dying and turning green, etc. About five minutes of stroking shenmen and they are well again.

Healing:

Innervation and irrigation are the same as for Ht 4.

Used for cardiac pain, irritability, mental disorders, epilepsy, poor memory, palpitation, hysteria, insomnia, yellowish sclera, pain in the hypochondriac region, feverish sensation in the palms, excessive dreaming, heart disease, angina pectoris, paralysis of the hypoglossus muscle, and neurasthenia.

Traditional indications include idiocy and seizures, irritability and insomnia, vomiting blood, jaundice, pain in the ribs, loss of voice, and panting.

As an earth point, shu stream point, and yuan source point of the heart meridian, shenmen's traditional functions are to calm the spirit, pacify the heart, clear the channels, and act as a sedative.

Massage techniques are the same as for Ht 4. You can also pinch the pisiformbone between the thumb and forefinger and move clockwise or counterclockwise.

Use with Pc 6, Ht 3, Ht 5, Ht 6, Bl 15, Bl 17, Bl 14, Bl 18, Cv 14, Cv 17, Liv 4, Liv 3, Liv 8, St 36, St 40, and Sp 3 for cardiac pain, angina pectoris, palpitations, poor memory, excessive dreaming, mental disorders, etc.

Use with Sp 6, Liv 3, Sp 9, Cv 4, Cv 6, Bl 25, Bl 53, Bl 26, Bl 23, Bl 20, Bl 18, and Bl 17 for premenstrual tension.

Use with Liv 3, St 36, Sp 3, Gv 20, Gb 20, yintang, Gb 21, Pc 6, and Kd 3 to calm pre-exam nerves.

Applications:

The same as for Ht 5.

HT 8 (HEART POINT NO. 8)

Chinese name:

Shaofu (lesser residence).

Location:

On the palmar surface, between the fourth and fifth metacarpal bones. When the hand is supine and the fingers are cupped in a half-fist, this point is found on the palm just below the tip of the little finger. Between the fourth and fifth metacarpal bones, in the fourth lumbrical muscle and the tendon of the flexor digitorum sublimis muscle. In its deep position, it is in the interosseous muscle.

Connections:

None.

Direction of strike:

Straight in to the palm. It is usually used with a small ch'i-na strike.

Damage:

This point also upsets the shen and the emotional stability. It's not a point that I would use in a tight situation. (Use the small circle ch'i-na lock, as described in the application section.) It is a fire and yong point, and when struck it upsets the heart qi, so the heart is damaged. As a sideline, this point strike will upset the body's clock, showing symptoms of jet lag! (It can also be used to combat jet lag in the healing sense.)

Set-up point:

None.

Antidote:

Use the opposite Ht 8 with finger pressure.

Healing:

Innervation is by the fourth common palmar digital nerve, derived from the ulnar nerve. Irrigation is by the common palmar artery and vein.

Used for palpitations, pain in the chest, twitching and contracture of the little finger, feverish sensation in the palm, skin pruritis, dysuria, enuresis, rheumatic heart disease, cardiac arrhythmia, angina pectoris, and hysteria. Traditional indications include palpitations, chest pain, spasm of the little finger, itching of the groin, difficult urination, and incontinence.

Traditional functions, as a fire point and a ying spring (gushing) point of the heart meridian, are to clear heat from the heart, calm the spirit, and regulate the heart.

Massage techniques are the same as for Ht 4. You can also squeeze this point between the thumb and forefinger.

Use with Ht 4, Ht 3, Ht 6, Ht 7, Bl 14, Bl 15, Bl 17, Bl 18, Cv 14, Cv 17, Sp 6, Liv 3, Liv 4,

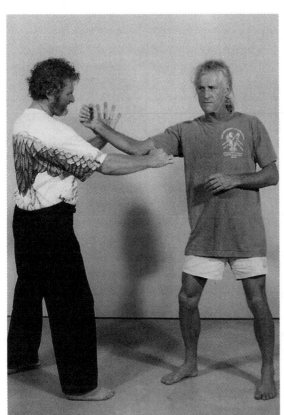

Figure 281

THE HEART MERIDIAN

305

Liv 8, St 36, Pc 6, and Pc 3 for hysteria, rheumatic heart disease, palpitations, and itching in the groin region.

Use with St 36, Cv 2, Cv 3, Cv 4, Cv 5, Cv 9, St 28, Bl 28, Bl 25, Bl 22, Bl 39, and Kd 11 for retention of urine.

Applications:

Slam his right neigwan with your left palm as your right palm attacks to St 9. Now your right hand takes a small ch'i-na lock on his small finger as your fingers dig into Ht 8 (fig. 283).

HT 9 (HEART POINT NO. 9)

Chinese name:

Shaochong (lesser pouring).

Location:

On the radial side of the little finger, about 0.1 cun posterior to the corner of the nail.

Connections:

Takes transverse luo from Si 7.

Direction of strike:

Squeeze the little finger.

Damage:

Although this point works very well, it is difficult to get to without opening yourself up to an attack. It is usually used in the healing area as an emergency point or revival point. It is a wood and cheng point. It has to be struck very hard to work as anything other than as a healing point, so even if you do attack this point, you could *help* the attacker, not hurt him! If struck really hard, this point will shock the heart for a moment to enable you to get in with another strike. It is not a point I would use martially in a tight situation. It is, however, an excellent heart healing point.

Set-up point:

None.

Antidote:

Use Ht 3.

Healing:

Innervation is by the palmar digital proprial nerve derived from the ulnar nerve. Irrigation is by the arterial and venous network formed by the palmar digital proprial artery and vein.

Used for palpitations, cardiac pain, pain in the chest and hypochondriac regions, mental disorders, febrile disease, loss of consciousness, apoplectic coma, hysteria, infantile convulsions, and high fever.

Traditional indications include vaginal discharge.

As a jing well point and a wood point of the heart meridian, it tonifies heart qi.

To massage, squeeze the patient's last small finger knuckle with your thumb and your forefinger and hold, do rotations clockwise or counterclockwise for xu or shi conditions, and burn a rice-grain-size piece of pure, refined moxa on the point to tonify heart qi.

Use with Lu 1, Cv 7, Liv 14, Liv 3, and Bl 17 for chest pain.

Applications:

None.

This brings us to the end of heart meridian. This meridian has a few excellent points; however, many of them are used primarily for healing.

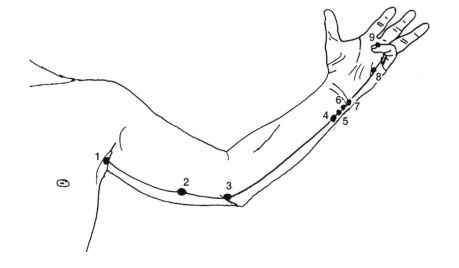

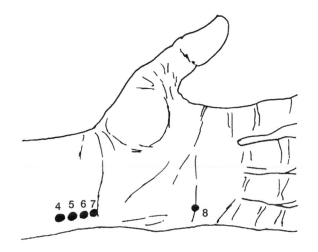

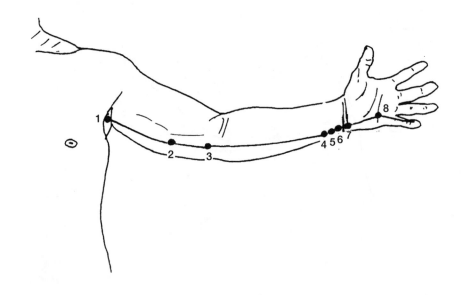

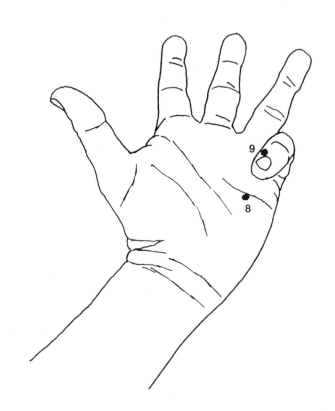

Chapter 8

The Small Intestine Meridian

THE TCM VIEW

The small intestine is a yang organ. The Chinese element of the small intestine is fire. Its yin counterpart is the heart. Its official job is to control the separation of pure and impure.

The small intestine receives food from the stomach and stores it for further digestion. In addition, it partially digests that food, taking nutrients from it and then passing it on to the colon. It also separates the clean from the dirty (i.e., it takes the clean or refined, usable part of the food that, after absorption, is taken by the spleen to all parts of the body, and it transfers the "dirty" part, or the wastes produced by digestion, to the colon or bladder). The small intestine also separates bodily fluids, some of which are sent to the bladder for excretion and some to the colon for reabsorption. This process is undertaken by the small intestine but it is controlled by kidney yang.

It is also important to note that the function of the small intestine is also to separate pure from impure mental functions. It has the ability to separate pure thoughts from useless thoughts, something that we as martial artists or healers must pay attention to. Useless thoughts and mental activity only waste qi. So the small intestine also clears up internal pollution.

In dim-mak, the small intestine meridian includes some very dangerous points, especially those around the head and neck. There are also some excellent set-up points, particularly those along the arm. Of these points, Si 16 and 17 would probably be the most dangerous. In general, strikes to the small intestine meridian will cause heat to build up in the heart.

SI 1 (SMALL INTESTINE POINT NO. 1)

Chinese name:
   Shaoze (lesser marsh).
Location:
   On the ulnar side of the little finger, about 0.1 cun posterior to the corner of the nail.
Connections:
   Transverse luo from Ht 5.
Direction of strike:
   This is a small fingertip squeeze. It is not a point that I would use in a serious situation, although it can have some startling effects if you are able to get at it.

Damage:

This is a metal and cheng point; it controls the muscle/tendino and divergent meridians. It is more of a healing point than a dim-mak point, and it can be used to produce and to improve the quality of breast milk. This strike can work as a delayed death touch because it can affect the body's defenses over time. It will cause the recipient to become very angry since it causes heat in the heart.

Set-up point:

None.

Antidote:

If you think you have been damaged here, see an acupuncturist and have your wei qi looked at.

Healing:

Innervation is by the palmar digital proprial nerve and the dorsal nerve derived from the ulnar nerve. Irrigation is by the arterial and venous network formed by the palmar digital proprial artery and vein and the dorsal digital artery and vein.

Used for febrile disease, loss of consciousness, lactation deficiency, sore throat, cloudiness of the cornea, headache, mastitis, and pterygium.

Traditional indications include fever and chills with no sweating, headache, chest pain, shortness of breath, pain in the ribs, jaundice, swollen breasts, membrane over the eye, and deafness.

Traditional functions are to disperse wind heat and facilitate the flow of milk. As a jing well point and a metal point of the small intestine, it can tonify or sedate.

To massage, squeeze this point between the knuckle of your thumb and your forefinger and hold. In addition, you can do rotations clockwise or counterclockwise for xu or shi conditions, and you can prick and bleed it to treat trauma or mastitis.

Use with Bl 1, Gb 1, St 1, qiuhou, Co 4, taiyang, Liv 2, Liv 3, Liv 4, and Liv 8 for pterygium.

Use with taiyang, Cv 17, Liv 14, Liv 3, Sp 6, St 36, St 15, Sp 18, Bl 17, Bl 18, and Bl 19 for sore, swollen breasts or deficiency of lactation.

Use with St 2, St 3, St 9, Si 10, St 11, St 12, St 13, St 14, Si 15, St 16, Gb 21, Th 14, Th 15, Gb 20, Gb 34, Bl 12, Bl 13, and Bl 43 for neck and shoulder pain that extends down the back of the arm.

Applications:

None.

SI 2 (SMALL INTESTINE POINT NO. 2)

Chinese name:

Qiangu (forward valley).

Location:

When a loose fist is made, the point is distal to the metacarpophalangeal joint, at the junction of the red and white skin.

Connections:

None.

Direction of strike:

Straight in from the side of the palm at the base of the small finger.

Damage:

This is a water and yong point. A strike here will cause heat to rise in the body, which will cause all kinds of problems, including heart disease, sores on the lips and tongue, and general ill health. Again, this is not a point that I would use in a tight situation unless I were to use the small finger as a ch'i-na locking hold. Its main function in dim-mak is as a controlling point, used when one does not really wish to do great damage immediately (as in the case of a bouncer, etc.). One can never be sure about what is working here—whether it is purely the little finger being bent that causes the pain or the point that you are also attacking while doing the finger lock.

Set-up point:

None.

Antidote:

You could needle the opposite point (on the other hand) 1 fen perpendicular. This will create a cooling effect on the liver, kidneys, and heart by taking fire away. This is the exact reverse of what this point does in the dim-mak area.

Healing:

Innervation is by the dorsal digital nerve and the palmar digital proprial nerve derived from the ulnar nerve. Irrigation is by the dorsal digital artery and vein arising from the ulnar artery and vein.

Used for numbness of the fingers, febrile disease, pannus, tinnitus, congested throat, and mastitis.

As a ying spring (gushing) point and a water point of the small intestine, its traditional functions are to cool heat and drain pathogens out of the channel.

Massage techniques include pressing and holding the point and doing rotations clockwise or counterclockwise for xu or shi conditions.

Use with Co 16, Co 15, Co 14, Co 11, Co 4, Ht 1, Si 3, Si 9, Si 10, Si 11, Si 12, Si 13, Gb 21, Si 16, St 38, and Gb 34 for inability to raise the arm.

Use with formula listed under Si 1 for mastitis.

Use with Gb 20, Bl 10, Gv 14, Gv 16, Bl 12, Th 17, Gv 20, Co 19, Co 20, Gb 2, Si 3, Gb 43, Gb 44, Kd 3, and St 40 for tinnitus.

Applications:

He attacks with his right hand. You should block with your right p'eng type of block and slam him in the face with your left palm. Your right palm now grabs his little finger and bends it greatly, thus causing great pain. Your right thumb will also dig into Si 2 as you are taking this lock.

SI 3 (SMALL INTESTINE POINT NO. 3)

Chinese name:

Houxi (black creek).

Location:

When a loose fist is made, the point is proximal to the head of the fifth metacarpal bone on the ulnar side, in the depression at the junction of the red and white skin. Lateral to the abductor digiti minimi manus.

Connections:

None.

Direction of strike:

Straight in to the side of the palm, just back from the little finger web.

Damage:

This point will cause considerable damage, but again it is not easy to get at. It is a wood and shu point and a master point for the dai mai. This strike will cause a breakdown in communication between heaven and earth, and thus between upper and lower body. The senses will become confused immediately, and the nerves and tendons will tense up, making this an excellent set-up point for a lock. This point will also have an adverse effect upon the liver. Immediately, there will be great pain and qi drainage. It is also a great controlling lock point.

Set-up point:

None.

Antidote:

Needle or finger pressure the opposite point on the other hand.

Healing:

Innervation is by the dorsal branch derived from the ulnar nerve. Irrigation is by the dorsal digital artery and vein, the dorsal venous network of the hand.

Used for headache, neck rigidity, congestion of the eye, deafness, contracture and twitching of the elbow/arm and fingers, febrile disease, epilepsy, malaria, night sweating, psychosis, hysteria, intercostal neuralgia, low back pain, and deaf mutism.

Traditional indications include red and painful eyes, membrane on the eye, tinnitus, deafness, jaundice, madness, tidal fevers, and finger spasm.

As a shu stream (transporting) point, a wood point of the small intestine, and a master point for the governing channel, it can treat disease of the inner canthus, neck, ear, shoulder, small intestine, bladder, and spine; relax the channels; open the Gv meridian; clear the mind; eliminate wind heat; relax the tendons and muscles; and treat malaria via the Gv meridian. Massage techniques include pressing and holding the point, doing rotations clockwise or counterclockwise for xu or shi conditions, and using fingertip percussion.

Use with Si 13, Si 14, Si 9, Si 10, Si 11, Gb 20, Gb 21, Th 15, Bl 11, Bl 12, Bl 13, Bl 43, Bl 17, Bl 18, Bl 60, and Gb 34 for neck and shoulder pain.

Use with Gv 14, Co 4, Co 11, Lu 7, Pc 5, Gv 13, Pc 6, Gv 10, Sp 9, Gb 34, Liv 2, Cv 17, St 36, and Sp 10 for malaria.

Use with Bl 25, Bl 26, Bl 53, Bl 54, Bl 40, Bl 58, Gb 29, Gb 30, Gb 34, Gb 41, Gb 39, and Bl 62 for painful legs.

Applications:

The same application as for Si 2. Or, since this point is further up the palm, you could even strike to the side of the palm with a knife-edge strike.

SI 4 (SMALL INTESTINE POINT NO. 4)

Chinese name:

Wangu (wrist bone).

Location:

On the ulnar side of the palm, in the depression between the base of the fifth metacarpal bone and the triquetral bone. Lateral to the origin of the abductor digiti minimi manus.

Connections:

Takes transverse luo from Ht 5.

Direction of strike:

Straight in to the side of the palm.

Damage:

Like Si 3, this point has some dangerous properties; however, it is not a point that I would use in a tight situation since it is difficult to get at. It is a yuan point and is used in healing for gallbladder-related problems. The long-term effect of this strike will be a loss of innovation or the ability to form ideas. It will also affect the heart by causing heat to accumulate because it also has an effect upon the bladder. Immediately, it will cause an energy loss, so it is a good controlling point. Another long-term effect is sore, itchy, burning eyes.

Set-up point:

None.

Antidote:

Treat the opposite hand at Si 4 with a needle, 3 fen perpendicular, or moxa (three to seven cones). In a pinch, you could use finger pressure.

Healing:

Innervation is by the dorsal branch of the ulnar nerve. Irrigation is by the posterior carpal artery (the branch of the ulnar artery) and the dorsal venous network of the hand.

Used for headache, neck rigidity, cloudiness of the cornea, pain in the hypochondriac region, jaundice, febrile disease, arthritis of the wrist/elbow and fingers, tinnitus, diabetes, gastritis, and cholecystitis.

Traditional indications include headache, hot conditions without sweating, throat blockage, emaciation and thirst, pain in the ribs, jaundice, and inhibited movement of the fingers.

As a yuan source point for the small intestine, its traditional functions are to invigorate taiyang (the greater yang division of the Bl and Si channels), disperse damp heat from the small intestine and so treat cholecystitis and jaundice, and treat hypochondriac pain.

Massage techniques are the same as for Si 3. You can also press with both thumbs slowly and release quickly, pulling the thumbs apart, or use vibration with the tips of the fingers or thumb.

Use with Bl 20, Bl 21, Bl 23, Bl 18, Bl 17, Cv 4, Cv 6, Cv 12, Liv 13, St 36, Sp 6, Sp 3, Sp 4, Liv 3, Lu 1, and Sp 9 for diabetes.

Use with Si 5, Si 3, Si 1, Si 2, Si 8, Gb 34, and Th 4 for pain in the wrist.

Applications:

The same as for Si 3.

SI 5 (SMALL INTESTINE POINT NO. 5)

Chinese name:

Yanggu (valley of yang).

Location:

On the ulnar side of the wrist, in the depression between the styloid process of the ulna and the triquetral bone.

Connections:

None.

Direction of strike:

Either a strike straight in to the extreme medial edge of the wrist crease or a violent grab and jerk at the wrist.

Damage:

This is a fire and jing point. It is an excellent set-up point for a more dangerous strike, such as to St 9, Si 16, St 15, or Cv 14. All points will cause death when Si 5 is activated first. A hard strike here, however, has the ability to cause what is known as yang madness, a buildup of stagnant yang qi in the head.

Set-up point:

None.

Antidote:

Needle the opposite Si 5 2 fen perpendicular or burn three to five cones of moxa on the point.

Healing:

Innervation is by the dorsal branch of the ulnar nerve. Irrigation is by the posterior carpal artery.

Used for swelling of the neck and submandibular region, pain in the wrist and the lateral aspect of the arm, febrile disease, parotitis, insanity, deafness, and tinnitus.

This is a jing river (traversing) point and a fire point of the small intestine. Its traditional functions include regulating the qi of the small intestine and treating damp heat in the knees (i.e., swollen/painful and hot knees).

To massage, press and hold the point, do rotations clockwise or counterclockwise for xu or shi conditions, use fingertip percussion or vibration, or press in slowly with both thumbs and release quickly, pulling the thumbs apart.

Use with Si 13, Si 14, Si 15, Si 16, Si 1, Si 2, Si 3, Si 4, Si 6, Si 7, Gb 21, Gb 20, Gb 34, Th 15, Th 16, and Gb 41 for pain and swelling of the neck and submandibular regions. Use with Sp 10, Sp 9, Sp 6, St 34, St 35, St 36, St 40, Gb 34, xiyan, and Liv 3 for damp-heat-type swelling and pain in the knees.

Use with Si 4, Th 4, Th 5, Pc 7, Co 4, Lu 7, Si 6, Si 7, and Gb 34 for pain in the wrist.

Applications:

Block his oncoming attack, then jerk his wrist violently as you strike him at Cv 14 with a palm heel strike.

SI 6 (SMALL INTESTINE POINT NO. 6)

Chinese name:
Yanglao (nourishing the old).

Location:
Dorsal to the head of the ulna. When the palm faces the chest, the point is in the bony cleft on the radial side of the styloid process of the ulna. On the dorsal aspect of the ulna, above the head of the ulna at the wrist, between the tendons of the extensor carpi ulnaris and the extensor digiti minimi manus muscles.

Connections:
None.

Direction of strike:
Straight in or strike across the wrist area from the inside of the wrist to the outside thumb side.

Damage:
This is a xie cleft point, and a strike here using adverse qi will cause the tendons in the whole body to become tense. I read of one documented case where a person who was chopped at this point had his knee ligaments torn, and there was no leg attack at all. This point can also cause failing vision or an instant temporary blindness, which makes it an excellent set-up point.

Set-up point:
None.

Antidote:
Needle the opposite point on the other hand 3 fen obliquely toward Pc 6. Or use thumb pressure in the same direction.

Healing:
Innervation is by the anastomotic branches of the posterior antebrachial cutaneous nerve and the dorsal branch of the ulna nerve. Irrigation is by the terminal branches of the posterior interosseous artery and vein (the dorsal venous network of the wrist).

Used for blurring of vision; aching of the shoulder, back, elbow, and arm; arthritis of the upper limbs; hemiplegia; stiff neck; lower back pain; hernia pain; and eye disease.

Traditional indications include pain in the shoulders and arm, blurred vision, and restriction of movement in the lumbar region.

As a xie cleft point of the small intestine, its traditional functions are to treats acute problems of the organ and channel, relax tendons and ligaments, remove obstructions from the collaterals, and clear the vision. It is a root of the small intestine meridian.

Massage techniques are the same as for Si 5.

Use with Pc 6, St 36, Sp 4, Cv 12, Liv 3, Bl 20, Bl 18, Bl 19, Bl 17, Liv 14, and St 21 for belching.

Use with Bl 1, Gb 1, Th 23, yuyao, St 1, Liv 3, and Co 4 for eye disease.

Use with Pc 6, Si 9, Si 10, Ht 1, Gb 34, Gb 21, Th 15, Th 14, Co 15, Co 16, jianneling, naoshang, and St 38 for shoulder problems.

Applications:
Use this as a set-up point for any of the more dangerous strikes. You can strike it with a one-knuckle punch as he attacks with that hand, or it can be used in a locking type of situation.

SI 7 (SMALL INTESTINE POINT NO. 7)

Chinese name:
Zhizheng (branch of uprightness).

Location:
5 cun proximal to the wrist, on the line joining Si 5 and Si 8.

Connections:
Transverse luo to Ht 9 and Ht 7.

Figure 284

Direction of strike:

Straight in to the ulna about halfway up the forearm.

Damage:

This is the first of the Si dangerous point strikes. It will add much yang qi to the heart and cause great immediate pain. A strike here can cause permanent blindness over a period. There is an immediate buildup of heat in the heart, causing great nausea and fainting. This is not a point to be played around with!

Set-up point:

You could use any of the lower-numbered Si points as the set-up. Points that work really well with Si 7 are Cv 14, Ht 3, Ht 1, St 15, and Gb 14.

Antidote:

Use any of the lower numbered points on the Si meridian to take the heat out of the heart. Or you could use finger pressure to Ht 5.

Healing:

Innervation occurs, superficially, by the branch of the medial antebrachial cutaneous nerve, and deeper, on the radial side, by the posterior interosseous nerve. Irrigation is by the terminal branches of the posterior interosseous artery and vein.

Used for neck rigidity, contracture and twitching of the elbow, pain in the fingers, febrile disease, mental disorders, and neurasthenia.

As a luo connecting point of the small intestine meridian, its traditional functions are to treat joint looseness, atrophy of muscles in the elbow and arm, long, finger-shaped warts, and scabies.

Massage techniques are the same as for Si 5.

Use with Si 3, Gb 20, Gb 21, Bl 10, Th 15, Si 13, Si 14, Si 15, Si 16, Bl 11, Bl 12, Bl 13, Bl 14, Bl 15, Bl 16, Bl 17, and Bl 18 for neck rigidity.

Use with Co 11, Co 10, Th 10, Th 11, Si 8, Co 15, Th 14, Co 4, Si 3, Th 3, and Gb 34 for contracture and twitching of the elbow.

Applications:

A straight right is aimed at you. Step to your left to avoid the attack and at the same time strike to his Si 7 point with your left palm. Your right palm strikes to Gb 14 a split second after this (fig. 284).

SI 8 (SMALL INTESTINE POINT NO. 8)

Chinese name:

Xiaohai (small sea).

Location:

Between the olecranon of the ulna and the medial epicondyle of the humerus. The point is located with the elbow flexed.

Connections:

None.

Direction of strike:

Straight in at the inner elbow.

Damage:

Again, this is a very dangerous point strike. It is an earth and he point. It will cause considerable pain and qi drainage, and when struck at the same time as Lu 5, it will cause KO or even death. It can also be used as an excellent controlling point using violent finger pressure, which has the ability to immobilize an opponent to the point that he will drop to the ground. There will also be continuing headaches until an acupuncturist has treated this situation. Other points that work really well with Si 8 are neigwan, Si 16, the mind point, and Cv 4. A No. 1 neurological strike also works wonders with this point. (A neurological strike causes the nervous system to shut down briefly. A No. 1 neurological strike is done with the palm to points around the eye and cheekbone.)

Set-up point:

Neigwan struck straight in.

Antidote:

Have an acupuncturist needle any of the lower Si points.

Healing:

Innervation is by the branches of the medial antebrachial cutaneous nerve and the ulna nerve. Irrigation is by the superior and inferior ulna collateral arteries and veins and the ulna recurrent artery and vein.

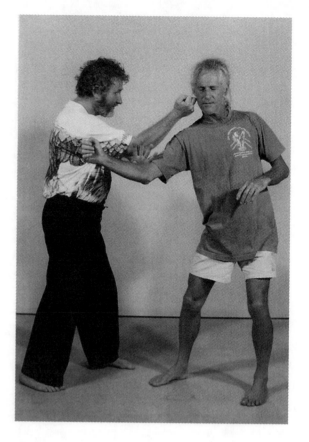

Figure 285

Used for swelling of the cheek, pain in the nape of the neck and the lateroposterior aspect of the shoulder and arm, epilepsy, neuralgia or paralysis of the ulna nerve, psychosis, and chorea (St. Vitus' Dance).

As a he sea (uniting) point and an earth point of the small intestine, its traditional functions include draining excess qi from the small intestine and having an earthing or stabilizing effect (just as the small intestine is responsible for separating pure from impure in both the physical and the mental/emotional aspects of our being).

Massage techniques are the same as for Si 5.

Used with Si 7, Si 1, Si 2, and Si 3 for ulna nerve paralysis. Use with Si 3, Si 9, Si 10, Si 11, Si 12, Si 13, Si 14, Si 15, Si 16, Gb 20, Gb 21, Th 15, Th 16, Bl 11, Bl 12, Bl 13, dingchuan, Bl 17, and Gb 34 for pain in the nape of the neck and the lateroposterior aspect of the shoulder and arm.

Applications:

He attacks with a straight right. You step to your left and strike his Si 8 point at the elbow with your right backfist. Your left palm again strikes to this point as your right palm attacks to the mind point or neurological shutdown point No. 1 (fig. 285).

SI 9 (SMALL INTESTINE POINT NO. 9)

Chinese name:

Jianzhen (shoulder chastity).

Location:

Posterior and inferior to the shoulder joint. When the arm is adducted, the point is 1 cun above the posterior end of the axillary fold, at the lateral margin of the scapula below the infraglenoid tubercle. In the posterior deltoid muscle and, in its deep position, in the teres major muscle.

Connections:
    None.
Direction of strike:
    Straight in to the lower back of the shoulder just up from the axilla crease.
Damage:
    An immediate rush of energy to the head, causing great nausea and fainting, a buildup of stagnant qi at the base of the skull at Gb 20 is also apparent, causing the head to feel as if it is exploding.
Set-up point:
    Neigwan struck toward yourself.
Antidote:
    Finger pressure at Ht 5 and Lu 8.
Healing:
    Innervation is by the branch of the axillary nerve and, deeper, in the superior aspects, the radial nerve. Irrigation is by the circumflex scapular artery and vein.
    Used for pain in the scapular region, pain and motor impairment of the hand and arm, disease of the shoulder and shoulder joint, and excessive perspiration in the armpits.
    Traditional indications include pain in shoulder blades, pain in the arm that inhibits movement, tinnitus, deafness, toothache, and swelling of the mandible.
    To massage, abduct the arm and press then adduct the arm while still holding the press; do rotations clockwise or counterclockwise for xu or shi conditions; do fingertip, loose fist or ulnar side of the hand percussion; use fingertip vibration, or press in slowly with both thumbs and release quickly, pulling the thumbs apart.
    Use with Si 10 Th 14, Si 11, Si 12, Si 13, Si 14, Gb 34, Gb 21, Th 15, and Si 3 for shoulder problems that are more on the posterior aspect.
    Use with Co 4, St 44, St 5, St 6, St 1, St 2, St 3, Kd 3, Bl 11, and Gb 39 for toothache.
Applications:
    He attacks with a right hook. Your left palm attacks neigwan down his inner forearm. A split second later, your right hand will pull his arm around so that his back is facing you. Your left palm now takes over the block as your right palm attacks straight in to Si 9.

SI 10 (SMALL INTESTINE POINT NO. 10)

Chinese name:
    Naoshu (scapula's hollow).
Location:
    When the arm is adducted, the point is directly above Si 9, in the depression inferior and lateral to the scapular spine. In the deltoid muscle posterior to the glenoid fossa of the scapula and, in its deep position, in the infraspinatus muscle.
Connections:
    Yang qiao mai and yang wei mai.
Direction of strike:
    Straight in and slightly downward, just below the top of the shoulder and in line with the axilla crease.
Damage:
    This strike will do great immediate physical damage due to the accumulation of tendons and muscles at this point. The damage is so great that it can cause KO from the qi drainage and pain. There is also extreme scapular damage.
Set-up point:
    Liv 14 struck straight in.
Antidote:
    Keep the patient still and see a doctor! It is important not to move the patient too much, especially if Liv 14 has been struck.

Healing:

Innervation is by the posterior cutaneous nerve of the arm, the axillary nerve, and, deeper, the suprascapular nerve. Irrigation is by the posterior circumflex humeral artery and vein and, deeper, the suprascapular artery and vein.

Used for aching and weakness of the shoulder and arm, pain and motor impairment of the hand and arm, disease of the shoulder and joint, and excessive perspiration in the armpits. Traditional indications include chills and fever, inability to raise the arm, and soreness and lack of strength in the arm. This is a shoulder shu point, so its traditional functions are to treat shoulder problems.

To massage, press and hold, do rotations clockwise or counterclockwise for xu or shi conditions, press in slowly with both thumbs and release quickly, pulling the thumbs apart, do percussion with fingertips or loose fist, do fingertip vibration. Also, with some individuals you can lean on this point with your elbow, while others are very sensitive and you need to move deeper slowly. See Si 9 for treatment of shoulder problems, etc.

Use with Ht 6, Ht 7, Lu 7, Bl 13, Bl 14, Bl 15, Bl 17, and Bl 18 for excessive sweating of armpits.

Applications:

He attacks with a straight right, and your left palm parries it back up his outer forearm as you step to your left. Your right one-knuckle punch attacks to Liv 13. Your right palm now moves back under his right arm to grab at the elbow, pulling him around so that your left palm can strike at Si 10.

SI 11 (SMALL INTESTINE POINT NO. 11)

Chinese name:

Tianzong (heaven's ancestor).

Location:

In the infrascapular fossa, at the junction of the upper and middle third of the distance between the lower border of the scapular spine and the inferior angle of the scapula. In the infraspinatus muscle.

Connections:

None.

Direction of strike:

Straight in to the scapular.

Damage:

This point is one of the major point strikes on the back because it is capable of taking out the whole arm and draining much qi. Even a medium strike here, with either a large weapon such as a palm or a small one such as a finger, will cause considerable damage to the back and arm. Immediately, you feel something like an electrical shock running down your arm, and then the paralysis sets in. I received this strike in my early training days, and my left arm was out of action for one week! I was given the antidote and was told that it would be okay in one week, and it was.

Set-up point:

Drain the qi by striking to Lu 5.

Antidote:

Grab the shoulder with both hands and squeeze using medium pressure, then slide both hands—still holding that grip down the outside of the whole arm—10 times. You must also repeat this three times per day for two days (fig. 286).

Healing:

Innervation is by the suprascapular nerve. Irrigation is by the muscular branches of the circumflex scapular artery and vein.

Figure 286

318

Used for pain in the scapular region and in the lateroposterior aspect of the elbow and arm.

Traditional indications include pain in the shoulder and shoulder blade, fullness in the chest and ribs, severe hiccups, and swelling in the cheek and jaw.

Traditional functions are to disperse fullness from the chest, eliminate stagnation of qi from the hypochondrium, and treat the shoulder. Also, the point on the left side is used as an alarm point for heart problems, and the point on the right side can reflect problems with Gb, Co, and Si.

Massage techniques are the same as for Si 5.

Use with Co 15, Th 14, Si 9, Si 10, Si 3, Gb 21, Si 6, Gb 34, Bl 13, Bl 12, Bl 42, Bl 43, Bl 17, and Bl 18 for shoulder inflammation.

Use with Cv 17, Liv 14, Liv 3, Si 18, Si 1, St 15, and Sp 18 for insufficient lactation or mastitis.

Applications:

He attacks with a right hook, and you slam the inside of his right elbow with your right back palm at Lu 5, thus draining qi. This strike could cause KO anyway. Turn your right palm down and hook his right arm over to your right, thus exposing his back. Slam him in Si 11 with your left palm.

SI 12 (SMALL INTESTINE POINT NO. 12)

Chinese name:

Bingfeng (holding wind). (*Bing* means to recieve, *feng* means wind. This point is also translated as "facing or controlling wind.")

Location:

In the center of the suprascapular fossa, directly above Si 11. When the arm is lifted, the point is at the site of the depression.

Connections:

Colon, gallbladder, and triple heater.

Figure 287

Direction of strike:

Straight down onto the rear of the shoulder.

Damage:

This point, when struck quite hard, will cause an energy rush to the head that can cause KO. There will be a sickly feeling in the upper body for some time afterward. The scapular can be knocked out of position with tendon damage as well.

Set-up point:

Strike Gb 14 upward to enhance the effect of this strike.

Antidote:

If bone or tendon damage is done, it will have to be healed medically. The energy rush can be treated by striking Gb 21 mildly downward and then rubbing out to the end of the shoulders.

Healing:

Innervation is by the lateral suprascapular nerve and the accessory nerve and, deeper, the suprascapular nerve.

Irrigation is by the suprascapular artery and vein.

Used for pain in the scapular region, numbness and aching of the upper extremities, inflammation of the supraspinatus tendon, and soreness and pain in the back of the shoulder.

Traditional functions are to eliminate wind and treat shoulder problems. This is a meeting point of the triple heater, colon, and gallbladder channels.

Massage techniques are the same as for Si 10.

See Si 9 and Si 8 for shoulder, neck, and upper back treatment.

Use with Gb 21, Gb 20, Co 16, Si 3, Th 15, Si 3, and Gb 34 for inflammation of the supraspinatus tendon.

Applications:

Take his straight right with your left palm sliding up the inside of his right arm as your right palm slams his Gb 14 point upward. Now bring your right elbow down onto the top of his shoulder toward the rear onto Si 12 (fig. 287).

SI 13 (SMALL INTESTINE POINT NO. 13)

Chinese name:

Quyuan (crooked wall).

Location:

On the medial extremity of the suprascapular fossa, around midway between Si 10 and the second thoracic vertebra spinous process. On the superior margin of the spine of the scapula, in the trapezium and supraspinatus muscles.

Connections:

None.

Direction of strike:

Straight down onto the top of the shoulder, closer to the neck than Si 12.

Damage:

This point is more dangerous than Si 12 in that it will drain qi rather than add it. The recipient will feel like something is draining from the whole upper body, which will cause the fight to be over. The lungs can be damaged with this strike, and scapular damage is also imminent with a medium to hard strike.

Set-up point:

The point to use with Si 13 is Cv 14 straight in. It is more of a helping point than a set-up point. The two points work really well together since death will occur when both are struck. It is important to strike Cv 14 before Si 13.

Antidote:

None. Try CPR. This is an extreme death point.

Healing:

Innervation is by the lateral branch of the posterior ramus of the second thoracic nerve and the accessory nerve superficially. Deeper, it is by the muscular branch of the suprascapular nerve.

Irrigation is by the descending branches of the transverse cervical artery and vein and, deeper, the muscular branch of the suprascapular artery and vein.

Used for pain and stiffness of the scapular region, inflammation of the tendon of the supraspinatus muscle, disease of the soft tissue of the shoulder joint, and neck stiffness with inability to turn the head to one or both sides.

Traditional indications include pain in the shoulder and shoulder blade, muscle spasms, and blockage conditions.

Traditional functions are to eliminate wind and relax the tendons and muscles.

To massage, press and hold the point; do rotations clockwise or counterclockwise for xu or shi conditions; press in slowly with both thumbs and release quickly, pulling the thumbs apart; lean on the point with the elbow; rub laterally across the point; use fingertip or loose-fist-type percussion; and do fingertip vibration.

Use with Gb 20, Bl 10, Gb 21, Th 15, Si 14, Si 15, Si 12, Si 11, Si 10, Si 9, Si 3, Co 4, Bl 60, and Gb 34 for shoulder problems and neck rigidity.

Use with the above formula plus Bl 12, Bl 13, Bl 14, Bl 43, Bl 17, Bl 18, Bl 19, Bl 20, Bl 25, Pc 6, Cv 17, Liv 3, and Ht 7 for stress-related neck and shoulder pain or stiffness.

Applications:

Avoid his attack and slam him into Cv 14, followed by an elbow down onto Si 13.

SI 14 (SMALL INTESTINE POINT NO. 14)

Chinese name:

Jianwaishu (shoulder's outer hollow).

Location:

3 cun lateral to the lower border of the spinus process of the first thoracic vertebra, on the vertical line drawn upward from the medial border of the scapula.

Connections:

None.

Direction of strike:

Straight down onto the shoulder.

Damage:

This point strike will put a shock into the upper body, causing the lungs and heart to falter. Extreme nausea with vomiting will result. Later it will even cause death if untreated, especially if used with Cv 14.

Set-up point:

Again, use Cv 14 as a helping point. These two also work very well together.

Antidote:

None.

Healing:

Innervation is by the medial cutaneous branches of the posterior rami of the first and second thoracic nerves and the accessory nerve, superficially. Deeper, it is by the dorsal scapular nerve. Irrigation is by transverse cervical artery and vein.

Used for stiffness and pain of the upper back and shoulder regions and neck rigidity.

Traditional indications include shoulder problems and neck stiffness.

Traditional functions include eliminating wind, clearing through the channels, and relaxing the tendons and muscles.

Massage techniques are the same as for Si 13.

See Si 13 for treatment of shoulder and neck problems.

Use with Gb 20, Gb 21, Th 15, Si 13, Bl 12, Bl 13, Bl 43, Bl 17, Bl 18, Bl 20, Bl 23, Kd 7, Cv 22, Cv 17, Lu 1, Lu 7, Liv 3, Gb 34, Liv 14, and dingchuan for asthma or bronchitis.

Applications:

The same as for Si 13.

SI 15 (SMALL INTESTINE POINT NO. 15)

Chinese name:

Jianzhongshu (mid-shoulder hollow).

Location:

2 cun lateral to the lower border of the spinous process of the seventh cervical vertebra (Gv 14). At the end of the transverse process of the first thoracic vertebra. Superficially in the trapezium and, in its deep position, in the levator scapulae muscle.

Connections:

None.

Direction of strike:

Straight down onto the top of the shoulder.

Damage:

A severe qi drainage from the upper body will result, causing KO if the strike is quite hard. Nervous damage can occur as well since it is quite close to the backbone at the neck. There will also be nausea.

Set-up point:

A very hard slam onto the inner wrist will set up this point. This targets no particular point; however, a whole bunch of points will be struck here, which will drain qi.

Antidote:

Place your palm onto the top of the head and press downward.

Healing:

Innervation and irrigation are the same as for Si 14.

Used for bronchitis, asthma, bronchiectasis, stiff neck, pain in the upper back and shoulder, and cough.

Traditional indications include coughing, spitting blood, blurred vision, fever and chills, and consumption in infants from drinking milk.

Traditional functions are eliminating wind and clearing the channels.

Massage techniques are the same as for Si 13.

Use with Gv 12, Gv 9, Lu 6, Bl 13, Bl 12, Cv 17, Lu 7, Co 4, Lu 1, Liv 3, Liv 13, Bl 17, Bl 18, and Bl 19 for bronchiectasis.

Add to the formula for asthma, cough, and bronchitis listed under Si 14.

See Si 13 for treatment of shoulder and neck stiffness and pain.

Applications:

Slam his right wrist (or left) with your right palm on the inside of his wrist. Hook your right palm over his wrist immediately and swing his arm to your right, thus exposing his back. Now strike straight down onto Si 15 with your right knife-edge strike.

SI 16 (SMALL INTESTINE POINT NO. 16)

Chinese name:

Tianchuang (heaven's window).

Location:

In the lateral aspect of the neck, on the posterior border of the sternocleidomastoid muscle, posterior to Co 18, 3.5 cun lateral to the laryngeal prominence.

Connections:

None.

Direction of strike:

Straight in to the neck from the side.

Damage:

This is a "window of the sky point." It is one of the more deadly Si points, causing instant death when struck hard. Medium strikes will cause emotional imbalance and heart problems. A strange side effect of this strike is that the recipient will laugh when struck! This is because of the imbalance of emotions when the shen is disconnected from the body. This is a point that is not to be played around with! If you are one of those people who go around knocking people out in demonstration, *do not use this point*—as death can occur really easily.

Set-up point:

Lu 8, Ht 5, and Lu 5.

Antidote:

None. However, if the strike has been medium and emotional imbalance is happening, see a Chinese doctor to have the heart reunited with the shen.

Healing:

Innervation is by the cutaneous cervical nerve and the emerging portion of the great auricular nerve. Irrigation is by the ascending cervical artery.

Used for deafness, tinnitus, sore throat, stiffness and pain in the neck, and goiter.

To massage, press and hold; do rotations clockwise or counterclockwise for xu or shi conditions; press in slowly with both thumbs and release quickly, pulling the thumbs apart; rub laterally across the point; or do fingertip percussion with care.

Use with Gb 3, St 7, St 2, Gv 20, Gb 20, Gv 22, Th 17, Th 21, Gb 4, Co 5, Th 1, Th 2, Th 3, Si 19, and Gb 3 for tinnitus and deafness.

Use with Gv 14, Gb 20, Gv 20, Cv 15, Cv 13, Pc 5, Pc 6, Th 6, St 40, Ht 5, Ht 7, Sp 6, sishencong, Liv 3, Sp 3, Cv 12, St 36, Kd 1, Kd 3, Gb 21, and yintang for psychosis with hallucinations.

Applications:

Slam his right hook with your both knife edges at the wrist (Lu 8 or Ht 5, or both) and at Lu 5 at the elbow. This will more than likely cause KO. Now, bring your left knife edge back to strike straight into Si 17 under the tip of the jaw while your left knife edge strikes to Si 16. You will want to be really serious about this application because instant death will occur!

SI 17 (SMALL INTESTINE POINT NO. 17)

Chinese name:

Tianrong (heaven's contents).

Location:

Posterior to the angle of the mandible, in the depression on the anterior border of the sternocleidomastoid muscle and the inferior margin in the posterior belly of the digastric muscle.

Connections:

None.

Direction of strike:

Up and into the angle of the jaw.

Damage:

Again, this is one of the more deadly points. It is very close to the vagus nerve and will cause **KO** quite easily. It is also right over the external carotid artery, which will cause a "blood KO." This is a "window of the sky point"; when it is struck, the head feels like it will explode, especially if the strike is a lock around the neck using the knife edge of the palm. This is a well known neck locking point in jujutsu and has been demonstrated a number of times in public. Just a quick blow up under the angle of the jaw, and it's a KO.

Set-up point:

Si 16 works really well with Si 17 and can be struck just prior to a neck lock.

Antidote:

Gb 20 squeezed up and into the skull.

Healing:

Innervation occurs through the anterior branch of the great auricular nerve and the cervical branch of the facial nerve. Deeper, it is by the superior cervical ganglion of the sympathetic trunk. Irrigation is by the external jugular vein anteriorly. Deeper, it is by the internal carotid artery and the internal jugular vein.

Used for deafness, tinnitus, tonsillitis, pharyngitis, distention and soreness of the neck, asthma, foreign body lodged in the throat, sensation in the throat as if there were something lodged in it, and swelling of the neck and cheek.

Traditional indications include deafness, tinnitus, plumb pit throat, swelling and soreness in the neck, and severe coughing.

As a point of intersection with the gallbladder channel, its traditional functions are to spread the qi of the wood and activate the jing luo.

Massage techniques include pressing and holding the point; rotating clockwise or counterclockwise for xu or shi conditions; pressing in slowly with both thumbs and releasing quickly, pulling the thumbs apart; doing light, single fingertip tapping on the point; or running a finger down the anterior edge of the sternocleidomastoid muscle to the medial end of the clavicle.

Use with Co 4, Co 11, Lu 5, Lu 7, Lu 11, Lu 8, St 44, Gb 20 Bl 10, Bl 12, St 9, Liv 2, Liv 3, and Sp 10 for tonsillitis or pharyngitis.

Use with Gb 20, Gb 14, St 4, St 2, Co 4, Gv 26, taiyang, St 36, St 44, St 4, Co 19, Th 17, Bl 2, Th 23, Gb 7, St 5, St 6, Gb 1, Gv 20, Gb 34, Gv 20, and Gb 21 for facial paralysis.

Use with Liv 3, Pc 6, Liv 14, Bl 18, Bl 17, Gb 21, Gb 20, Cv 12, Co 4, Ht 7, Liv 1, Sp 6, Co 11, Gb 34, Cv 22, Lu 11, and Kd 6 for sensation of obstruction in the throat with difficulty in swallowing.

Applications:

He attacks with a right hook. Slam his neigwan point on his right arm with your right knife edge as your left palm takes over this block. Your right palm now attacks to Si 16. Your right palm grabs him around his neck and pulls him into a head lock as the left palm strikes up into the jaw angle at Si 17.

SI 18 (SMALL INTESTINE POINT NO. 18)

Chinese name:

Quanliao (cheek seam). (*Quan* means zygoma, and *liao* means foramen.)

Location:

Directly below the outer canthus, in the depression on the lower border of the zygoma, level with Co 20.

Connections:

Triple heater and gallbladder.

Direction of strike:

Angled at about 45 degrees into the cheekbone from the front.

Damage:

Using a smaller weapon such as a one-knuckle punch, this strike will cause KO. It shocks the brain and causes a rush of qi up the back of the neck to the brain, causing confusion and, hence, the KO.

Set-up point:

Use Lu 5 for the set-up.

Antidote:

Place the index fingers of both hands over both Gb 14 points and apply medium pressure straight in to the forehead.

Healing:

Innervation is by the facial and the infraorbital nerves. Irrigation is by the branches of the transverse facial artery and vein.

Used for facial paralysis, twitching of the eyelids, toothache, yellowish sclera, trigeminal neuralgia, and spasm of the facial muscles.

Traditional indications are to relieve pain in the face.

Traditional functions are to dispel wind and act as a sedative to stop pain.

To massage, press and hold; do rotations clockwise or counterclockwise for xu or shi conditions; press in slowly with both thumbs and release quickly, pulling the thumbs apart; apply light fingertip percussion or vibration; or you can run from Bl 1 down the side of the nose to Co 20, then out along the inferior edge of the zygoma through Si 18 and out to Gb 2, down through Si 17, and down the anterior edge of the sternocleidomastoid muscle to the clavicular notch.

Use with formula listed under Si 17 for facial paralysis.

Use the run-down from Bl 1 to the clavicular notch plus Si 19, Co 4, Th 2, Th 3, Th 4, Th 5, Th 6, Th 7, Th 8, Th 9, Th 22, Th 20, Th 21, Kd 3, St 40, and Si 3 for deafness or tinnitus.

Use with St 5, St 6, St 44, Co 4, St 2, St 3, and Co 20 for toothache.

Use with Co 4, Liv 3, St 5, St 6, St 3, St 7, St 8, taiyang, St 36, Gb 34, Gb 20, Gv 20, and Gb 3 for spasm of facial muscles.

Applications:

Slam his right arm at Lu 5. Your left palm now takes over this block as your right fist does a penetration punch into his left Si 18.

SI 19 (SMALL INTESTINE POINT NO. 19)

Chinese name:

Tinggong (palace of hearing).

Location:

Between the tragus and the mandibular joint, where a depression is formed when the mouth is slightly open. At the anterior of the middle of the tragus and the posterior margin of the condyle of the mandible.

Connections:

Gallbladder and triple heater via internal pathways within the ear.

Direction of strike:

Straight in from the side of the face.

Damage:

This point should do great damage, and I have been told that it causes the brain to shut down the body. However, it has been my experience that this point does nothing at all. (Of course, if one were to hit it with a hammer, who knows?) But this point seems to do nothing more than give someone a headache and tinnitus! It is well protected by bone here. A little lower, it's a different story, though. Gb 2 is a very dangerous point.

Set-up point:

None.

Antidote:

None, take an aspirin!

Healing:

Irrigation is by the branch of the facial nerve and the auriculotemporal nerve. Irrigation is by the auricular branches of the superficial temporal artery and vein. Used for deafness, tinnitus, otorrhea, deaf-mutism, otitis media, and inflammation of the external ear canal.

Traditional indications include seizures and insanity, tinnitus, deafness, pus in the ear, toothache, and pain in the chest and abdomen.

Traditional functions are to remove obstructions from the jing luo and soothe the ears.

To massage, press and hold; do rotations clockwise or counterclockwise for xu or shi conditions; press in slowly with both thumbs and release quickly, pulling the thumbs apart; and run the forefinger from Th 21 down the edge of the jaw to Si 17, then move down the anterior edge of the sternocleidomastoid muscle to the sternal notch.

Use with Th 21, Gb 2, Th 4, Si 3, Th 17, Gv 15, Th 5, Th 3, Gb 20, Liv 2, Liv 3, St 40, Kd 3, Bl 23, St 7, Si 17, Gb 21, Gv 20, Bl 8, and Bl 10 for deafness or tinnitus.

Add to the formula listed under Si 18 for toothache.

Use with Liv 3, St 5, St 6, St 8, Gb 34, Co 4, and Gb 21 for lockjaw.

Applications:

The same as for Gb 2.

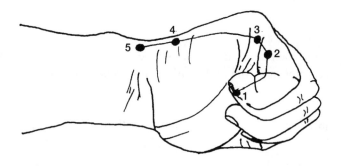

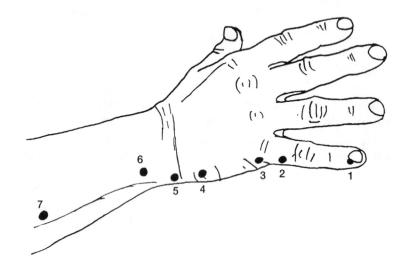

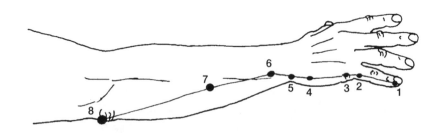

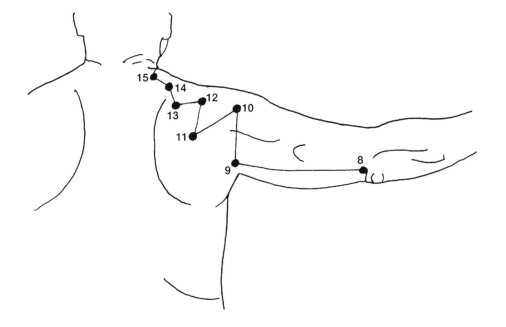

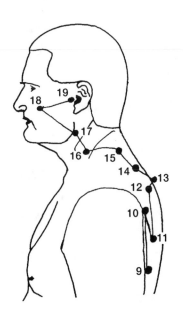

327

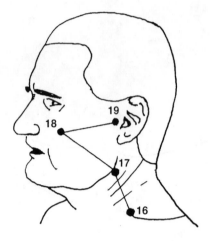

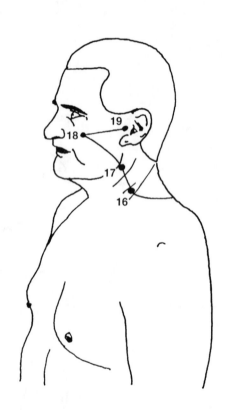

Chapter 9

The Lung Meridian

THE TCM VIEW

The lung is a yin organ, and its opposite yang organ is the colon (large intestine). Its role in the body society is the "controller of qi." Its Chinese element is metal. It has a descending and dispersing function and regulates the water passages. It dominates the skin and hair and opens into the nose.

Respiration and the domination of qi are the most important functions of the lungs. Constant inhalation of clean qi and exhalation of dirty qi are vital for normal oxygenation of tissue.

The lungs play an important part in the refinement of qi and the spreading of that refined qi all over the body. The essence of food and liquid from the spleen (*gu* qi) flows up into the chest and combines with clean inhaled qi, or respiration. In the lungs these combine to form zhong qi (qi of the chest), so the thorax is often called "the sea of qi." Zhong qi via the lungs provides nourishment for the whole body. So there is a saying in Chinese medicine: "All qi belongs to the lung." When the lungs are strong, the voice is strong and affirmative, but with weak lungs the voice is soft and unassertive.

The lungs also control "the 100 vessels" (blood vessels). The heart pushes the blood, but it must rely upon the qi from the lungs to perform this job. So the blood and the qi are inseparable; where the qi goes, the blood follows.

The lungs are the uppermost and outermost (the skin) organ in the body. Due to the latter, they are the first organ to be invaded by external pathogenic factors. Because the lungs are the highest organ in the body, their qi must flow downward. They also send fluids downward to the kidneys and bladder for excretion or to be recycled. When the lung qi does not flow down, it causes congestion in the chest with breathlessness, asthma, etc. If the lungs fail to send down fluids, this could contribute to edema, mainly in the face and arms.

The dispersing function of the lungs is the first to be affected by a pathological condition. This function has two aspects. The first is concerned with the wei qi (that qi that flows around the outside of the body, protecting it from external pathogenic attack. The lungs scatter the wei qi all over the body, especially to the skin, so the lungs are connected to the skin in this way. When the body is attacked by "wind/cold," most of the heavy cold symptoms (e.g., headaches, blocked sinuses, sneezing) are caused by the fact that the presence of wind/cold in the skin interferes with the lungs' dispersing function. Because the qi cannot be dispersed, the whole body feels blocked. The second aspect involves bodily fluids. After separation, the spleen sends the fluids to the lungs, which distribute them throughout the whole body. The lungs normally vaporize bodily fluids, which are then distributed all over the skin in the form of fine mist. This is the process of sweating. If this function is impaired and there is a shi (excess) condition, then the pores will be blocked with no sweating. And if there is a xu (deficient) condition, then there will be too much sweating.

The skin and hair depend upon the lung for their nourishment. So if the function of dispersing and regulating water passages is impaired, the skin will be flaccid, rough, and dry. The hair (body hair included) will be withered. The opposite will occur when this function is strong.

The sense of smell is controlled by the lungs and also the spleen. If the lungs are not good, the sense of smell will be weak and the nose will be blocked. If the lungs are affected by much heat, the nose will be red and the nostrils will flare.

LU 1 (LUNG POINT NO. 1)

Chinese name:

Zongfu (central residence).

Location:

Zhong means middle and *fu* means place; this refers to the middle jiao, where the lung channel starts. The qi of the spleen and stomach are gathered into the Lu meridian at this point. The point is below the acromial extremity of the clavicle, 1 cun directly below Lu 2, 6 cun lateral to the Cv meridian, in the first intercostal space. In the pectoralis major and minor muscles and, in its deep position, in the internal and external intercostal muscles.

Connections:

This is a point of intersection with the spleen channel. It receives internal meridian from Sp 21. The deep pathway of the lung meridian passes through Cv 9, Cv 12, and Cv 13, then to Lu 1.

Direction of strike:

Straight in and slightly upward toward the clavicle.

Damage:

The lung points all do great damage. Lu 1 must be struck with a smaller weapon, such as a one-knuckle punch. There will be great qi drainage and thus great local pain, which will slowly spread over the whole chest area due to this point's connection to Sp 21. A strike here will hinder the progress of gu qi, that which is made from food and liquid. So apart from the immediate effect of extreme pain in the whole chest area, there is the long-term effect on the gu qi. As a result, although the recipient is taking food, the qi from that food is going nowhere, and so health and life-style are slowly diminished.

Set-up point:

Lu 5.

Antidote:

Treat Lu 1 on the opposite side of the body with finger pressure or have an acupuncturist needle 3 fen laterally. Careful here, though: bones could also be broken.

Healing:

Innervation is by the intermediate supraclavicular nerve, the branches of the anterior thoracic nerve, and the lateral cutaneous branch of the first intercostal nerve. Irrigation, on its superiolateral side, is by the axillary artery and vein and the thoracoacromial artery and vein.

Used for cough; asthma; pain in the chest, shoulder, and back; fullness in the chest; bronchitis; pneumonia; and pulmonary tuberculosis.

Traditional indications include coughing and wheezing, coughing blood and pus, throat blockage, congested nose, excessive sweating, and tumors and nodular growths on the neck.

As a mu (alarm) point of the lungs, this point's traditional functions include diagnosis, as well as treatment, of lung pathologies and dispersal of fullness of the chest.

Massage techniques include pressing and holding the point; rotating clockwise or

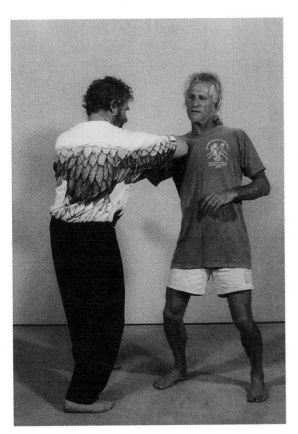

Figure 288

counterclockwise for xu or shi conditions; pressing in slowly with both thumbs and releasing quickly, pulling the thumbs apart; and doing fingertip percussion or vibration.

Use with Lu 7, Lu 5, Lu 6, Bl 13, Bl 17, Bl 43, Bl 12, Bl 18, dingchuan, Bl 23, Kd 7, Liv 14, Cv 17, and St 40 for bronchitis or asthma.

Use with Co 4, Co 11, Lu 5, Lu 6, Lu 9, Lu 10, Sp 10, Bl 17, St 36, and Liv 3 for coughing up blood.

Use with Co 15, jianneling, naoshang, Gb 21, Th 14, Co 4, Co 11, and Co 14 for shoulder pain.

Use with Pc 6, Cv 17, Liv 3, Liv 14, Bl 43, Bl 17, Bl 18, and Bl 12 for fullness in the chest.

Applications:

Attack his hook right with your right back palm at Lu 5. Immediately rebound, turning your waist to your right, and come back with the tip of your right elbow to Lu 1 slightly upward (fig. 288).

LU 2 (LUNG POINT NO. 2)

Chinese name:

Yunmen (cloud's door).

Location:

In the depression below the acromial extremity of the clavicle, between the pectoralis major and the deltoid muscles, 6 cun lateral to the Cv channel.

Connections:

Colon.

Direction of strike:

There are two directions for this point: either upward into the clavicle or down on top of the clavicle.

Damage:

When this point is struck upward into the clavicle, it produces a devastating effect upon the qi system of the whole body. It causes great internal damage with little external appearance. The pain is tremendous, and the strike will cause a KO or even death through qi drainage.

When the point is struck from the top above the clavicle, the collarbone will be broken, along with the qi drainage and even more pain! However, because the collarbone is able to take some of the pressure from this strike, even though it breaks, the likelihood of death is lessened. The downward strike will stop a confrontation really fast, though.

Set-up point:

Lu 5 along with *xishang*, a new point located 8 cun above the transverse crease of the wrist on the inner forearm about 2 cun down from the elbow crease. This point strike will affect the heart and cause power loss. Combine it with Lu 5 and you have one of the better set-up combinations. You must, however, slice down from Lu 5 down the forearm, covering xishang.

Antidote:

Apply only light finger pressure to the opposite xishang and Lu 5 while holding (placing a finger over) Lu 2 on the opposite side.

Healing:

Innervation is by the intermediate and lateral supraclavicular nerve, the branches of the anterior thoracic nerve, and the lateral cord of the brachial plexus. Irrigation is by the cephalic vein, the thoracoacromial artery and vein, and inferior to the axillary artery.

Used for cough; asthma; pain in the chest, shoulder, and arm and fullness or pain in the chest; and perifocal inflammation of the shoulder.

Traditional functions: *Yun* refers to the qi of the lungs. This point is on the upper part of the chest and serves as a door for qi of the lungs. This point is also used for paralysis of the arm as a result of CVA.

Massage techniques are the same as for Lu 1.

Use with the formulas for asthma, chest fullness and pain, and shoulder pain listed under Lu 1.

Use with Co 15, Co 14, Co 11, Pc 3, *bizhong* (an extra point), Pc 6, *baxie* (extra), Co 4, Pc 8, Gb 34, Th 10, St 40, Liv 3, Co 10, Th 4, Si 5, and Pc 7 for paralysis of the upper extremities and pain or restriction of the arms.

Applications:

Slam his right hook with your left knife edge at Lu 5 and slice down over xishang as your right one-knuckle punch attacks straight up and into Lu 2. Or you could use a hammer fist down onto Lu 2 via the clavicle.

LU 3 (LUNG POINT NO. 3)

Chinese name:

Tianfu (heaven's residence).

Location:

On the medial aspect of the upper arm, 3 cun below the end of the axillary fold, on the radial side of the biceps brachii, 6 cun above Lu 5.

Connections:

None.

Direction of strike:

Straight in just below the biceps on the outside of the upper arm where the skin just turns from white to a darker color.

Damage:

Immediately there is an effect like an electrical shock that goes up and down the arm causing momentary or long-lasting paralysis of the arm. Being a "window of the sky" point, it will also totally upset the balance between heaven and earth, or head and body, causing great emotional problems that will only get worse if left untreated. Emotionally caused problems such as confusion and loss of memory will occur at a later stage. This strike will also give an extreme case of instant vertigo!

At a healing level, this point is a really good one for nosebleed, using mild finger pressure over the point on both arms.

Set-up point:

Lu 5 and/or xishang. Same as for Lu 2.

Antidote:

Either use finger pressure gently on the opposite Lu 3 or have an acupuncturist take a look at the problem. Also press Lu 2 (the "happy point"). Or you could squeeze the tip of the thumb while pressing in on Lu 9.

Healing:

Innervation is by the lateral brachial cutaneous nerve at the place where the musculocutaneous nerve passes through. Irrigation is by the cephalic vein and the muscular branches of the brachial artery and vein.

Used for asthma, epistaxis, pain in the medial aspect of the arm, and bronchitis.

Massage techniques are the same as for Lu 1. Use with Gb 20, Bl 17, Sp 10, Sp 1, Gv 14, Gv 20, Sp 3, and Lu 4 for epistaxis. Use with asthma and bronchitis treatment listed under Lu 1.

Use with Co 15, Co 14, Co 12, Co 11, Lu 4, Lu 5, Lu 6, Co 4, and Gb 34 for pain in the medial aspect of the arm.

Applications:

You could simply slam his inner lower forearm to set up this strike, then bring your left hammer fist to strike straight in to Lu 3. Or you could take his right straight with your left palm glancing upward on the outer forearm while your right hammer fist attacks to Lu 3.

LU 4 (LUNG POINT NO. 4)

Chinese name:

Xiabai (gallantry).

Location:

Xia means to press from both sides, and *bai* means white. When both arms are hanging freely, this point is precisely on both sides of the lungs, on the medial aspect of the upper arm, 1 cun below Lu 3, on the radial side of the biceps brachii.

Connections:

None.

Direction of strike:

Straight in to the upper arm just below Lu 3.

Damage:

This point immediately does the same as Lu 3, only the local pain and electrical shock is a little worse. This is also a great nerve strike that can cause the brain to shut down the body, not knowing what has happened. Emotional problems will also occur later, but they won't be as severe as with Lu 3.

Set-up point:

Lu 5.

Antidote:

If the nerve damage has occurred, see a doctor. Or use Gb 20 if neurological shutdown has occurred.

Healing:

Innervation is by the lateral antebrachial cutaneous nerve and the radial nerve. Irrigation is by the branches of the radial recurrent artery and vein, the cephalic vein.

Used for asthma, epistaxis, pain in the medial aspect of the arm, bronchitis, cough, and fullness in the chest. Use with Cv 13, Cv 12, St 21, St 25, Pc 6, St 36, Liv 4, Liv 3, St 44, and St 45 for acute perforation of gastric and duodenal ulcer with chest pain, dry heaves, and irritability. Use with Co 4, Co 11, Co 20, yintang, Gb 20, Sp 10, Lu 11, and Lu 3 for nosebleed.

See Lu 3 for treatment of pain in the medial aspect of the arm.

Applications:

Same as for Lu 3.

LU 5 (LUNG POINT NO. 5)

Chinese name:

Chize (cubit marsh).

Location:

Chi means ruler or ulna, and *ze* means marsh. The *chi* part of the name refers to the ulnar aspect (from the wrist to the elbow). The point is in the depression of the elbow fossa at the ulna aspect. The qi of the channel is infused here, like water flowing into a marsh. On the cubital crease, on the radial side of the tendon of the biceps brachii. The point is located with the elbow slightly flexed, in the origin of the brachioradialis muscle.

Connections:

None.

Direction of strike:

Straight down into the inside of the elbow joint.

Damage:

This point can cause great damage to the whole system. It can cause KO when struck, for instance, with a back palm and using a "dead arm" (where the arm is totally loose with no tension at all and is thrown at the target making use of the heaviness of the arm itself). It can be used (as I have already mentioned several times) as a set-up point, or it can be used all by itself as a devastating strike. The whole upper body is put out of balance, both physically and qi-wise. A strong strike can also cause brain damage. Because this is a he point, it will take qi away from the lungs when struck rather than used for healing. And as the lungs are part of the power system of the body, you will lose power instantly.

Set-up point:

None. This is usually a first-strike point.

Antidote:

Needle the opposite Lu 5, as this will bring qi into the lungs. Even finger pressure will work to a degree. Go straight in and the patient will feel an immediate energy surge in the lungs and thus a regaining of power.

Healing:

Innervation is by the lateral antebrachial cutaneous nerve and the radial nerve. Irrigation is by the branches of the radial recurrent artery and vein, the cephalic vein.

Used for cough, hemoptysis, afternoon fever, asthma, fullness in the chest, sore throat, spasmodic pain in the elbow and arm, pneumonia, pleurisy, erysipelas, and swelling and pain in the throat.

Traditional indications include asthma, spitting blood, chest pain, throat blockage, and fullness in the chest.

Traditional functions are to drain heat from the lungs, suppress and regulate rebellious lung qi, cool heat, and stop bleeding. As a he sea and water point of the lungs, it also soothes asthma.

Massage techniques include pressing and holding, rotating clockwise or counterclockwise for xu or shi conditions, pressing in slowly with both thumbs and releasing quickly, pulling the thumbs apart, and doing fingertip percussion.

Use with Lu 9, Lu 1, Co 4, Bl 13, Lu 6, Pc 5, Lu 10, Ht 7, Pc 8, Gv 14, Liv 8, Kd 3, Kd 2, Liv 3, Bl 18, Bl 20, and Sp 10 for coughing blood.

Use with Lu 7, Co 4, Co 11, Cv 17, Cv 22, Bl 12, Bl 13, Bl 43, Bl 17, Bl 18, Bl 20, Bl 23, Kd 7, Liv 3, Liv 14, Cv 12, *dingchuan*, Lu 1, and St 40 for asthma, bronchitis, etc. Use with Co 11, Gb 34, Co 10, Co 9, and Co 4 for pain and spasm of the elbow.

Applications:

He attacks with a right low hook. You use your right back palm and slam the inside of his right elbow with it. However, you must be certain that your palm and right arm have no tension or this strike will only cause mild damage. This is not a point to play around with!

LU 6 (LUNG POINT NO. 6)

Chinese name:

Kongzui (opening maximum or supreme hole).

Location:

On the palmar aspect of the forearm, on the line joining Lu 9 to Lu 5, 7 cun above Lu 9. The point is in the brachioradialis muscle, in the lateral margin at the upper extremity of the pronator teres muscle and the medial margin of the extensor carpi radialis brevis and longus muscles.

Connections:

None.

Direction of strike:

Straight in to the upper inner forearm with a slight distal direction.

Damage:

Lower arm paralysis is immediate with a hard strike. The recipient will feel as though he has been struck in the lungs. This is a xie cleft point. A strike here causes the reverse effect of healing using this point. It is an emergency point and can release much needed qi to the lungs in an emergency, such as being struck in the lungs. So this point can be used as an aftershot, following a strike to the attacker's lung area. The body calls for its reserve of qi, but it is unavailable because of the second strike to Lu 6. The recipient of such a strike could die within minutes.

Set-up point:

Strike straight in to Cv 14. This is sure death!

Antidote:

If Cv 14 (or a strike to the lungs) has been used as the set-up, you have to work fast because death is imminent. You must mobilize the emergency lung qi by working on the opposite Lu 6 point, either fingering it or needling it 5 fen. Then use CPR if breathing and pulse have already stopped.

Healing:

Innervation is by the lateral antebrachial cutaneous nerve and the superficial ramus of the radial nerve. Irrigation is by the cephalic vein and the radial artery and vein.

Used for cough, asthma, hemoptysis, sore throat, pain and motor impairment of the elbow and arm, pneumonia, and tonsillitis.

Traditional indications include headache, absence of sweating, spitting blood, loss of voice, sore throat, belching, pain in the elbow and arm, and difficulty in bending the arm.

As a xie cleft (accumulating) point of the Lu meridian, it treats acute disorders of the lung and its channel, regulates lung qi, makes lung qi descend, eliminates heat, and stops bleeding and pain.

Massage techniques are the same as for Lu 5.

Use with Lu 7, Co 11, Co 4, St 36, Liv 3, Bl 12, Bl 13, Bl 17, Cv 17, Liv 3, and Lu 5 for colds and flu.

Use with Kd 7, Co 4, St 36, Bl 13, Cv 17, Liv 3, Lu 7, and Lu 1 for chills and fever with no sweating.

Use with Co 4, Co 11, Lu 5, Lu 7, Lu 10, Lu 11, Co 1, Co 2, Co 3, Co 5, Co 7, Co 18, St 44, and St 45 for sore throat and loss of voice.

Applications:

Take his straight right with your left palm as your right palm strikes straight in to Cv 14. Then it rebounds back onto Lu 6 using a hammer fist strike.

LU 7 (LUNG POINT NO. 7)

Chinese name:

Lieque (broken sequence or every deficiency).

Location:

Superior to the styloid process of the radius, 1.5 cun above the transverse crease of the wrist, in the depression. When the index fingers and the thumbs of both hands are crossed with the index finger of one hand placed on the styloid process of the radius of the other, the point is in the depression under the tip of the index finger, between the tendons of the brachioradialis and the abductor pollicis longus muscles.

Connections:

Transverse luo to Co 4 and Co 1

Direction of strike:

Straight down onto the wrist area about 1.5 cun back from the wrist crease.

Damage:

Although this strike is "only on the wrist," it is quite a nasty one, since it creates great pain and qi drainage. Even heavy finger pressure here, as in the case of a lock, will cause great pain. The qi drainage and pain are so bad that the recipient has to sit down. I know of one instance where a KO occurred with only a light strike. A strike here will upset the balance of yin and yang between the lung and colon, causing artificial grief with much sobbing. Also, the ability to learn physical things will be impaired and will get worse as time goes by.

Set-up point:

Kd 6 struck downward on the lower leg.

Antidote:

The lung/colon qi must be rebalanced. To do this you must know the lung/colon qi-balancing massage. You must also know which points are the balancing points for each meridian. For the lung, the balancing point is Co 11. For the colon, the balancing point is Lu 9. So first you place your left *laogung*, or Pc 8, onto his Lu 9 point and just hold it there. Now, your right laugung point will rub along the whole of the colon meridian from lowest numbered point to highest. The right palm must not actually touch the skin, but get as close to the skin as possible. You do this three times.

Now do the lung meridian. Place your left laugung point onto Co 11 and rub your right laugung over the lung meridian from lowest number to highest, same as you did for the colon. Do this three times. Then do the whole thing on the other arm.

This is a healing method for someone who has too much grief, is weeping all the time and has an inability to learn physical things. (In fact, in my video No. MTG 88 I teach all six qi balancing massages for each meridian pair.)

Healing:

Innervation is by the lateral antebrachial cutaneous nerve and the superficial ramus of the radial nerve. Irrigation is by the cephalic vein and branches of the radial artery and vein.

Used for headache, neck rigidity, cough, asthma, sore throat, facial paralysis, trismus, weakness of the wrist, and urticaria.

Traditional indications include headache, panting, swelling of the pharynx, hemiplegia, mouth awry, wind rash, blood in the urine, and acute edema of the limbs.

Traditional functions are to strengthen the dispersing function of the lungs, dispel wind/cold, remove obstruction and invigorate the jing luo, and clear and regulate the Cv meridian. It is a luo connecting point of the lung, master point of the Cv meridian, and couple point of the yin qiao mai.

When used with Kd 6 it will tonify yin, soothe a sore throat, and activate the descending function of the lungs in a more dynamic way than Lu 9.

Apply direct qi (pressure) upward for headache and to tonify the Lu qi, and downward to treat pain in the thumb.

Massage techniques include pressing and holding the point; rotating clockwise or counterclockwise for xu or shi conditions; pressing in slowly with both thumbs and releasing quickly, pulling the thumbs apart; clasping the wrist so your fingers are on the ulnar side and your thumb is on the styloid process and squeezing and/or rotating the fingertip or open hand ulnar-side-type percussion.

Use with Lu 8, Lu 9, Co 4, Co 11, Pc 6, and Th 5 for burning sensation in the palm.

Use with Kd 6, Kd 3, Sp 9, Cv 2, Cv 3, Cv 4, Cv 5, Cv 9, St 28, Bl 39, Bl 22, Bl 28, Bl 23, Bl 20, Sp 6, Liv 3, and St 40 for edema, retention of urine, and fluid imbalances in general. See Lu 6 and Lu 5 for treatments of cough, colds, asthma, bronchitis, etc.

Use with Lu 11, Lu 10, Co 4, Co 5, and Gb 34 for pain in the thumb.

Use with Pc 6, Ht 7, St 36, Co 4, Liv 3, Bl 13, Bl 14, Bl 15, Bl 17, Bl 18, Bl 19, Bl 20, and Bl 23 for excess sadness or melancholy.

Applications:

He comes in with a right-handed attack. You avoid the attack and stomp straight down onto the inside of his ankle with your right heel. Now your right knife edge strike comes across to strike straight in to Lu 7.

LU 8 (LUNG POINT NO. 8)

Chinese name:

Jingqu (across the ditch).

Location:

1 cun above the transverse crease of the wrist, in the depression on the radial side of the radial artery.

Innervation is by the lateral antebrachial cutaneous nerve and the superficial ramus of the radial nerve.

Connections:

None.

Direction of strike:

This point is usually used along with Ht 5 as a qi drainage, setup point. The two points are usually grabbed and jerked violently, thus taking qi away from other more vulnerable points. Usually, any face strike will suffice after these points have been attacked. They are classic qi drainage points by themselves or together.

Damage:

Great qi drainage, thus setting up other points for attack. Ht 5 by itself has been known to cause KO when needled too much, the same as Lu 8. Lu 8 is a metal and jing point. This is the horary point of the channel. As such, when it is struck it will cause the qi to be disrupted in the channel when it is supposed to be active during the 24-hour cycle. Thus the lungs will not be at their peak throughout the day. This qi imbalance will get worse as each day passes until a healing is effected. Sleep will be affected greatly, especially between 3 and 5 A.M. This will be coupled with the need to urinate, because the bladder meridian is at the opposite side of the horary cycle and, as such, will have the least amount of qi available to it at this time.

Set-up point:

None.

Figure 289

Antidote:

Work on the opposite Lu 8 and also on Liv 3 using finger pressure, or have an acupuncturist needle both points.

Healing:

Innervation is by the lateral entebrachial cutaneous nerve. Irrigation occurs laterally by the radial artery and vein.

Used for cough, asthma, sore throat, pain in the chest and wrist, and bronchitis.

As a jing river point and a metal point of the Lu meridian, its traditional function is to tonify or sedate.

To massage, press and hold (be careful not to depress the artery), do rotations clockwise or counterclockwise for xu or shi conditions, and flick the point with the forefinger.

Use with Bl 17, Co 4, Co 11, Co 18, Lu 6, Lu 5, and Liv 2 for sore, swollen throat.

Use with Lu 7, Lu 9, Lu 10, Lu 11, Co 4, and Co 11 for burning sensations in the hand.

Use with Gb 21, Co 11, Co 10, Co 8, Co 13, Gb 34, Co 4, Th 4, and Gb 20 for arm pain caused by cold wind.

Applications:

Block his low left attack with both palms (fig.

337

289). Your right palm is on top while your left is underneath. Your right palm attacks to Lu 8 while your right palm attacks Ht 5. Now, grab the wrist with your right palm and jerk it violently as you attack to the side of his face with your left backfist.

LU 9 (LUNG POINT NO. 9)

Chinese name:

Taiyuan (great abyss or bigger deep hole).

Location:

At the transverse crease of the wrist, in the depression on the radial side of the radial artery. At the lateral aspect of the tendon of the flexor carpi radialis muscle and the medial aspect of the tendon of the abductor pollicis longus muscle.

Connections:

Transverse luo from Co 6.

Direction of strike:

Down into the wrist just above the thumb mount distally into the palm.

Damage:

This is again a great qi drainage point. It is an earth, yuan, and shu point and a special meeting point of pulse (arteries and veins). It must be struck right on the point, so it is not one that I would use in a tight situation, although it works quite well as a set-up point, causing great local pain and qi drainage. It will cause respiration to become erratic, so that the recipient thinks he is going to be suffocated.

Set-up point:

None.

Antidote:

Finger pressure the opposite Lu 9 back along the inner forearm toward the elbow until breathing has become normal again.

Healing:

Innervation is by the lateral antebrachial cutaneous nerve and the superficial ramus of the radial nerve. Irrigation is by the radial artery and vein.

Used for asthma, cough, hemoptysis, sore throat, palpitations, pain in the chest and the medial aspect of the forearm, bronchitis, whooping cough, influenza, pulmonary tuberculosis, and disease affecting the radial side of the wrist joint.

Traditional indications include headache, toothache, pain in the eyes, membrane on the eyes, coughing blood, chest pain, and pain and debility of the wrist.

This is root area of the Lu meridian, a shu stream (transporting) point and earth point of the Lu meridian, a yuan source point of Lu meridian, and one of the eight influential points/meeting points of the blood vessels. It eliminates wind, resolves phlegm, strengthens the lung function, stops coughing, and tonifies lung yin. Use for long-standing problems.

Massage techniques are the same as for Lu 8.

Use with Lu 1, Bl 12, Bl 13, Bl 17, Bl 20, Cv 17, Cv 12, Cv 6, Cv 4, St 36, Sp 5, Liv 3, Sp 6, Co 4, Gb 20, Gb 21, and Th 4 to build lung qi in those who have frequent colds and lack of energy or stamina.

Use with Lu 7, Co 4, St 40, Cv 17, Cv 12, Bl 13, Bl 17, Bl 20, and Pc 6 for wind phlegm-type cough.

Use with Gv 20, Sp 3, St 36, Bl 20, Sp 10, Sp 1, Sp 6, and Bl 17 for tendency toward varicose veins.

Applications:

He attacks with a straight right. You move to your right and hammer the inside of his wrist with your right knife edge distally. Now you are free to attack any of the face points, such as a neurological shutdown point on the side of the cheek.

LU 10 (LUNG POINT NO. 10)

Chinese name:
Yuji (fish border).

Location:
On the radial aspect of the midpoint of the first metacarpal bone, at the junction of the red and white skin (the lighter colored and darker colored skin). In the lateral abductor pollicis brevis and opponens pollicis muscles.

Connections:
None.

Direction of strike:
Straight in to the thumb mount; however, this is not a point I would use in self-defense.

Damage:
This is not a point to use in a realistic fighting situation. If struck very hard, it will cause heat to rise in the lungs, causing coughing. It is more of a healing point and is used to eliminate heat from the lungs, thus easing sore throats, etc. It is a fire and yong point.

Set-up point:
None.

Antidote:
Should the lungs have heat, squeeze the tip of the thumb at the edge of the nail at Lu 11.

Healing:
Innervation is by the superior ramus of the radial nerve. Irrigation is by the venules of the thumb draining to the cephalic vein. Used for cough, hemoptysis, sore throat, fever, laryngopharitis, tonsillitis, hoarseness, asthma, and infantile malnutrition syndrome.

Traditional indications include coughing, throat blockage, spitting blood, loss of voice, emotional disturbance, tidal fever, abdominal pain, and pain in the chest and back.

This is a fire point and a ying spring (gushing) point of the lungs. Its traditional functions are to cool heat in the lungs, benefit the throat, and eliminate fire from the head caused by depression (e.g., lots of crying and general sadness).

Massage techniques are the same as for Lu 5. Use with Co 16, Lu 5, Co 4, Co 11, Sp 10, Bl 17, Bl 13, Liv 2, and Sp 3 for hemoptysis.

Use with Co 41 Co 11, Co 18, Co 1, Co 2, Lu 5, Lu 7, Lu 11, St 44, St 45, and Th 2 for sore throat.

Use with Lu 9, Sp 6, Bl 13, Bl 20, Lu 7, Cv 17, and Liv 3 for tidal fever.

Applications:
None.

LU 11 (LUNG POINT NO. 11)

Chinese name:
Shaoshang (lessor merchant).

Location:
On the radial side of the thumb, about 0.1 cun posterior to the radial corner of the nail.

Connections:
Transverse luo from Co 6.

Direction of strike:
This, again, is not a point I would use, it is right on the end of the thumb. It is really for healing only.

Damage:
This is a wood and cheng point and can be used for the healing of muscles and tendons. If struck with perhaps a hammer, it will drain qi from the upper body and can cause emotional problems later in life. It is more used for throat and tonsils in particular. It is also used to increase the wei qi to the surface of the skin when external pathogenic attack is imminent.

Set-up point:

None.

Antidote:

If this point has been struck, by a hammer for instance, you should either needle the point or bleed the opposite point. Never use moxa on this point.

Healing:

Innervation is by the terminal nerve network formed by the mixed branches of the lateral antebrachial cutaneous nerve and the superficial ramus of the radial nerve, as well as the palmar digital proprial nerve of the median nerve. Irrigation is by the arterial and venous network formed by the palmar digital proprial artery and veins.

Used for cough, asthma, sore throat, epistaxis, contracture and pain of the fingers, febrile disease, loss of consciousness, mental disorders, tonsillitis, parotitis, common cold, pneumonia, stroke, fainting, and infantile indigestion.

Traditional indications include apoplectic delirium, coughing, cervical swelling with throat blockage, mumps, swollen patchy tonsils, and fever and external symptoms.

Traditional functions: As a wood point and jing well point of the Lu meridian, it eliminates wind heat from the lung, benefits the pharynx, expels the exterior (symptoms that have existed for two to five days), and also revives a person who has fainted.

To massage, hold the thumb between the forefinger and the knuckle of your thumb and squeeze, do rotations clockwise or counterclockwise for xu or shi conditions, or, for mental illness or epistaxis, burn three to five rice-grain-size cones of refined pure moxa on this point.

Use with Co 4, Co 11, Lu 5, Lu 8, Liv 2, St 36, Lu 10, and Lu 6, and bleed Lu 11 (prick and drain two or three drops of blood) for acute tonsillitis.

Use with Co 4, Co 11, Lu 5, Lu 7, Cv 17, Bl 12, Bl 13, Bl 17, St 40, Liv 3, and Sp 4 for colds and flu with thick, yellow discharge.

Applications:

None.

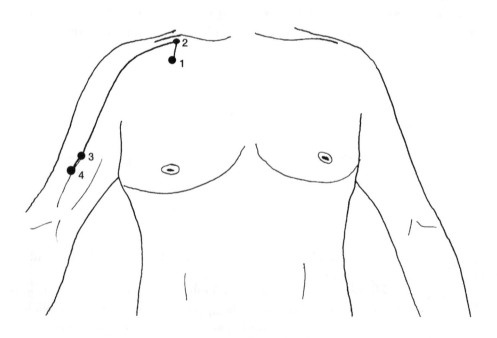

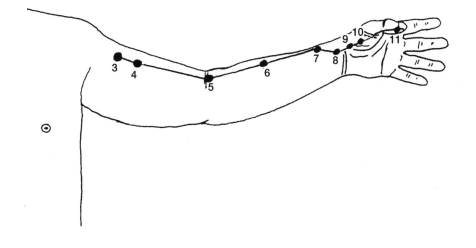

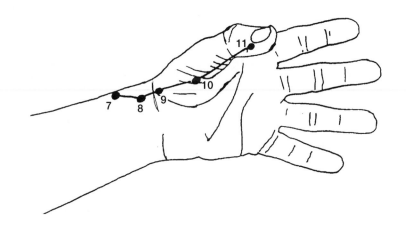

Chapter 10

The Colon Meridian

THE TCM VIEW

The colon has the Chinese element of metal. It is a yang organ, and its counterpart yin organ is the lung. The colon's official role is the controller of expelling waste.

The colon receives the waste from the small intestine. It absorbs some liquids and then transforms the remainder into feces to be expelled. The anus is controlled by kidney jing and is called the "door of strength."

The colon also has other duties in waste control. It is also responsible for getting rid of wasteful thoughts. In fact, constipation can sometimes be related to clinging to wasteful thoughts and habits, and thus impeding change. So the health of the colon is directly related not only to a healthy body but also to mental health in helping the individual to change.

In dim-mak, there are several important points on the colon meridian that can be used as set-up points or as dangerous points in their own right. Co 10 is one of the main set-up points and works quite well all by itself. Co 12 is an excellent point strike, as is Co 14 (a qi input point and one of the "seven star" points for qi input into the body). Co 17 and 18 are very dangerous points, while Co 19 and 20 are also excellent "electrical" point strikes.

CO 1 (COLON POINT NO. 1)

Chinese name:
    Shangyang (trade or merchant yang).
Location:
    On the radial side of the index finger, about 0.1 cun posterior to the corner of the nail.
Connections:
    Takes transverse luo from Lu 7, and there is a connecting pathway internally from Lu 11.
Direction of strike:
    I would not use this point in a tight situation. You would have to bite the tip of the finger, and nowadays, with things like AIDS and hepatitis C running rampant, this is not a good method of self-defense.
Damage:
This is a metal and cheng point and is only ever used in the healing art. It clears wind/heat. It is an

emergency point for coma and should be bled for this purpose. In fact all cheng points are bled. It will also drag qi to the extremities to strengthen the outer limbs.

Set-up point:

None.

Antidote:

None.

Healing:

Innervation is by the palmar digital proprial nerve derived from the median nerve. Irrigation is by the arterial and venous network formed by the dorsal digital arteries and veins. Used for toothache, sore throat, swelling of the submandibular region, numbness of the fingers, febrile disease, loss of consciousness, apoplectic coma and deafness.

This is a jing well point and a metal point of the lungs. Its traditional functions are to clear wind/heat, move stagnation in the channel, use as an emergency point, and treat stroke.

To massage, hold the forefinger between the thumb and your forefinger and squeeze, do rotations clockwise or counterclockwise for xu or shi conditions, or prick and bleed (one to three drops). You can also do rice-grain-size cones of refined pure moxa for qi and yang xu conditions.

Use with Co 2, Co 4, St 44, St 45, St 2, St 3, St 5, St 6, Kd 3, Bl 11, and Gb 39 for toothache.

Use with Pc 6, Th 5, Lu 11, Th 1, Si 1, Pc 9, *baxi* (an extra point), *shang baxi* (an extra point), Co 4, Lu 7, Pc 7, Th 4, Si 3, Si 4, Si 5, Si 6, St 36, Gb 41, and St 40 for numbness of the fingers.

You can prick and bleed (a couple of drops) from all the jing well points, except those in the heart channel, for loss of consciousness.

Applications:

None.

CO 2 (COLON POINT NO. 2)

Chinese name:

Erjian (between two).

Location:

Er means two and *jian* means clearance. *Jian* here indicates the point. This is the second point on the colon meridian. On the radial side of the index finger, distal to the metacarpophalangeal joint, at the junction of the red and white skin in the depression.

Connections:

None.

Direction of strike:

This point can be used in the case of a hand lock along with Co 3, although I would not advise this instead of a more normal palm lock. You have to have very strong hands to activate and to cause damage with these two points.

Damage:

It is a water and yong point and, as such, can be used as a set-up point for Co 5 (fire). It is an excellent point to relieve constipation. Should you be able to get one finger exactly onto Co 2 and also dig one finger into Co 5, this can cause KO. However, while you are doing this, he will probably knock you out!

Set-up point:

None.

Antidote:

None.

Healing:

Innervation is by the dorsal digital nerve derived from the radial nerve and the palmar digital proprial nerve derived from the median nerve. Irrigation is by the dorsal digital and palmar digital proprial arteries and veins, derived from the radial artery and vein.

Used for blurring of vision, epistaxis, toothache, sore throat, febril disease, facial paralysis, and trigeminal neuralgia.

As a water point and ying spring (gushing) point of the colon meridian, its traditional functions are to cool heat and increase or decrease qi flow.

To massage, press and hold the point, do rotations clockwise or counterclockwise for xu or shi conditions, or do fingertip percussion on the point.

Use with Co 1, Co 4, Co 11, St 36, St 40, Sp 9, St 37, Liv 2, Liv 3, St 25, Bl 25, Bl 20, Bl 18, Bl 17, Cv 12, Cv 6, Cv 4, Sp 10, Gb 43, Gb 44, Liv 4, Sp 4 and Sp 5 for irritable bowel syndrome where there is blood and mucous in the stool.

Use with St 6, St 5, Gv 26, Lu 7, Lu 9, Co 4, St 4, Th 23, taiyang, Gb 34, and Gb 41 for facial paralysis with mouth and eyes awry.

Use with Gv 20, Kd 3, Kd 4, Kd 6, Liv 10, Sp 6, St 36, and yintang for excessive sleepiness.

Applications:

None.

CO 3 (COLON POINT NO. 3)

Chinese name:

Sanjian (between three).

Location:

San means three, and *jian* means clearance. Here jian indicates the point; this is the third point on the colon meridian. When a loose fist is made, the point is on the radial side of the index finger in the depression proximal to the head of the second metacarpal bone.

Connections:

None.

Direction of strike:

Squeeze the index finger just back from the palm. But again, it's not a point I would use in fighting.

Damage:

Use with Co 2. It is a wood and shu point. A good strike here, if you can get it, can cause temporary blindness. However, I must warn you that this is very difficult to achieve.

Set-up point:

None.

Antidote:

Finger pressure to the opposite Co 3 point.

Healing:

Innervation is by the superficial ramus of the radial nerve. Irrigation is by the dorsal venous network of the hand and the branch of the first metacarpal artery.

Used for ophthalmia, toothache, sore throat, redness and swelling of the fingers and the dorsum of the hand, trigeminal neuralgia, painful eyes, and malaria.

Massage techniques are the same as for Co 2.

As a wood point and shu stream (transporting) point of the Co meridian, its traditional functions are to expel wind and damp conditions (e.g., treat aching joints).

Use with Si 17, Co 11, Co 4, Lu 11, Gb 20, Lu 5, St 9, Si 16, Liv 2, Lu 10, St 40, and Liv 3 for tonsillitis or sore throat.

Use with Co 2, Gb 34, Gb 20, Lu 7, St 40, Sp 9, Liv 3, Gb 43, Gb 44, Gb 39, Bl 11, Bl 13, Bl 12, Th 4, Th 5, Th 3, Bl 40, Bl 65, and Bl 66 for arthritis-type joint problems.

Use with Co 4, St 44, Gb 10, Gb 14, St 3, and St 6 for toothache.

Applications:

None.

CO 4 (COLON POINT NO. 4)

Chinese name:

Hegu (adjoining valleys).

Location:

Between the first and second metacarpal bones, approximately in the middle of the second metacarpal bone on the radial side. Roughly between the second metacarpal bone and the end of the crease created when the thumb is adducted, in the dorsal interroseus muscle and, in its deep position, in the transverse head of the abductor hallucis muscle.

Connections:

Transverse luo from Lu 7.

Direction of strike:

Straight in just above the web of the thumb and index finger.

Damage:

This point does some damage in qi drainage and local pain. It can be used as a set-up point to a Lu 1 shot or to a Liv 14 shot. Struck right on the point with a smaller weapon such as a one-knuckle punch, this point will cause confusion in the brain. However, this is not easy because that strike must be very accurate.

Set-up point:

None.

Antidote:

Using thumb pressure on the opposite Co 4, squeeze the point distally using mild pressure.

Healing:

Innervation is by the superficial ramus of the radial nerve and, deeper, the palmar digital proprial nerve derived from the median nerve. Irrigation is by the venous network of the dorsum of the hand, proximally, right on the radial artery piercing from the dorsum to the palm of the hand.

Used for headache, redness with swelling and pain of the eye, epistaxis, toothache, facial swelling, sore throat, contracture of the fingers, pain of the arm, trismus, facial paralysis, febrile disease with anhidrosis, hidrosis, amenorrhea, delayed labor, abdominal pain, constipation, dysentery, common cold, disease of the sensory organs, hemiplegia, neurasthenia, and pain in general.

Traditional indications include headache, pain in the eyes, membrane on the eyes, nosebleed, deafness, toothache, facial edema, throat blockage, mouth and face awry, locked jaw due to stroke, tidal fever, wind rash, scabies, miscarriage, and abortion.

As a yuan source point of the colon, this point's traditional functions are to strongly reinforce the qi of the channel, eliminate wind/heat or wind/cold (perhaps a little better for wind/heat), relieve exterior symptoms, activate the dispersing function of the lungs, activate the function of the intestines, treat all symptoms of the face, relieve pain, and clear the channels.

Massage techniques include pressing and holding the point, rotating clockwise or counterclockwise for xu or shi conditions, and doing fingertip percussion.

Use with Gv 20, Gb 20, Liv 3, Gb 14, taiyang, yintang, Gb 21, and Gb 34 for headache.

Use with Lu 7, Lu 5, Co 11, Co 20, Gb 20, Cv 17, Bl 13, Bl 17, and Liv 3 for cough, colds, etc.

See Co 2 for treatment of facial paralysis.

See Co 1 for treatment of toothache and numbness of the fingers.

See Bl 1 for treatment of eye problems.

Use with Co 11, Co 14, Co 15, Gb 21, jianneling, naoshang, Gb 34, and St 38 for treatment of anterior shoulder pain and restriction.

Use with Sp 6, Bl 31, Bl 32, and Gb 21 for induction of labor.

Use with Pc 6, St 36, Cv 12, Liv 3, St 21, St 25, Bl 20, Bl 18, Bl 25, Sp 3, and Sp 4 for nausea and vomiting.

Figure 290

Applications:

He might try to grab you around the neck. You take his right or left hand and, grabbing the whole hand, apply pressure onto Co 4 as you bend his wrist backward (fig. 290). Now you are able to strike straight in to Lu 1 (or slightly upward into the upper chest) using a one-knuckle punch.

CO 5 (COLON POINT NO. 5)

Chinese name:

Yangxi (adjoining valley).

Location:

Yang refers to the yang mountains created by the tendons in this area, and *xi* means brook. The depression of this point is like a brook in the mountains. On the radial side of the wrist, when the thumb is tilted upward, the point is in the depression between the tendons of the extensor pollicis longus and brevis.

Connections:

None.

Direction of strike:

Usually used as a wrist lock along with Si 2.

Damage:

This is one of the "natural" short-out points with Si 2 that will cause great pain and allow you to put someone down onto his knees easily. Applying pressure straight across the back of the wrist diagonally will short out Co 5 and Si 2 (fire and water respectively).

Set-up point:

None.

Antidote:

As soon as the both points are released, the action of the short-out across Si 2 and Co 5 will cease to have any effect, but the damage to the wrist and fingers has already been done.

Healing:

Innervation is by the superficial ramus of the radial nerve. Irrigation is by the cephalic vein and the radial artery and its dorsal carpal branch.

Used for headache, redness with swelling and pain of the eye, toothache, sore throat, pain of the wrist, ophthalmia, tinnitus, deafness, and infantile indigestion.

Traditional indications include headache, red and painful eyes, membrane over the eye, deafness, throat blockage, toothache, pain in the root of the tongue, pain in the wrist, and inability to flex the arm at the elbow.

As a fire point and jing river (traversing) point of the large intestine, it can cool heat and treat cough. Massage is the same as for Co 4.

Use with Si 5, Bl 1, St 1, Gb 1, Gb 14, Gb 43, Gb 44, Th 23, Liv 2, Liv 3, Co 4, Co 11, and Gb 20 for red, swollen, and painful eyes.

Use with Lu 7, Th 4, Si 5, Pc 7, and Gb 34 for tenosynovitis of the wrist.

Use with Si 17, Liv 14, Liv 3, Bl 17, Bl 18, Bl 43, Bl 13, Cv 17, dingchuan, Lu 7, and Lu 5 for fullness in the chest with breathing difficulty.

Applications:

Take his right straight with your right palm as your left palm comes under to take over the block (fig.

Figure 291

Figure 292

291). Your right palm now attacks to the side of the face to cause neurological shutdown (fig. 292). Your left palm now takes the fingers as your right palm slips in behind to create the short circuit. You have a very powerful wrist lock, and pulling both hands downward will break the fingers easily because of the short circuit (fig. 293).

CO 6 (COLON POINT NO. 6)

Chinese name:
Pianli (partial order).
Location:
3 cun above Co 5 on the line joining Co 5 and Co 11. On the radial side, the lateral antebrachial cutaneous nerve and the superficial ramus of the radial nerve, on the ulnar side, the posterior antebrachial cutaneous nerve and the posterior antebrachial interosseous nerve. *Pian* means divergence, and *li* means passageway. This is where a collateral separates and diverges to the Lu meridian.
Connections:
Transverse luo to Lu 9 and Lu 11.

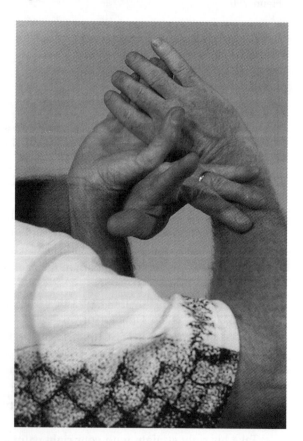

Figure 293

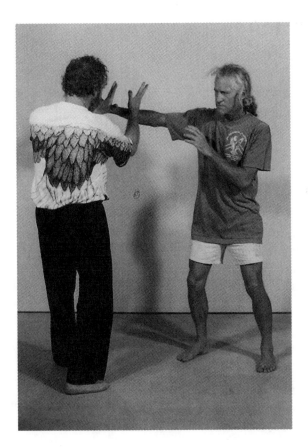

Figure 294

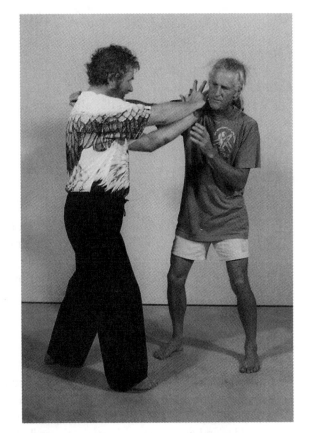

Figure 295

Direction of strike:

Straight down onto the thumb side of the outer forearm.

Damage:

This point causes great qi drainage and local pain. When struck hard enough it will cause KO. Communication between the upper and lower heaters is upset greatly, causing internal damage to the flow of qi. In the long term, emotional disturbances will build up because this strike prevents the elimination of both bad emotions and bad thoughts.

Set-up point:

Co 3 and Co 6 are struck at almost the same time, as in a double knife-edge strike.

Antidote:

Needle the opposite point 3 fen, or use finger pressure distally on the point.

Healing:

Irrigation is by the cephalic vein. Innervation is by the superficial ramus of the radial nerve.

Used for epistaxis, deafness, aching of the hand and arm, edema, facial paralysis, and tonsillitis.

Traditional functions derive from being a luo connecting point of the colon meridian.

Massage the same way as for Co 4. You can also press in slowly with both thumbs and release quickly, pulling the thumbs apart, and try flicking on the point with the forefinger.

Use with Co 11, Co 10, Co 9, Co 8, Co 7, and Co 4 for pain of the forearm.

Use with Co 4, Co 11, St 36, St 5, St 6, St 8, Gv 26, Cv 24, Gb 14, Liv 2, Liv 3, and Gb 34 for facial paralysis.

Use with Sp 10, Gb 20, Co 4, Co 11, Liv 2, Sp 1, Sp 3, Gv 20, and Co 20 for epistaxis.

Applications:

He attacks with a hook punch where the outer forearm is pointing toward you. His small finger is facing upward. Use your knife edges to strike within a split second of each other to Co 3 and Co 6 (fig. 294). Now, both knife edges rebound across the neck at Co 17 and 18 (fig. 295).

349

CO 7 (COLON POINT NO. 7)

Chinese name:

Wenliu (warm slide).

Location:

When a fist is made with the ulnar side downward and the elbow flexed, the point is 5 cun above Co 5.

Connections:

None.

Direction of strike:

Straight down onto the forearm.

Damage:

This is a xie cleft point, meaning that it is an accumulation point. A strike here will cause local pain and qi drainage. It will cause pain along the whole channel and, if struck hard enough, can cause a KO. Used with any of the neurological shutdown points, in particular No. 1 across the jaw, it will cause KO even with a mild blow. This is an excellent set-up point for a Co 11 shot.

Set-up point:

Neurological shutdown points.

Antidote:

Use Gb 20.

Healing:

Innervation is by the posterior antebrachial cutaneous nerve and the deep ramus of the radial nerve. Irrigation is by the muscular branch of the radial artery, the cephalic vein.

Used for headache, facial swelling, sore throat, borborygmus, abdominal pain, aching in the shoulder and arm, stomatitis, parotitis, and glossitis.

This is a xie cleft point of the Co meridian, so its traditional function is to treat acute disorders of the organ and channel. *Wen* means warm, and *liu* means circulation, so this point is able to warm the channel and promote circulation and is good for treating cold pain of the elbow.

Massage techniques are the same as for Co 6.

Use with Co 1, Co 2, St 37, St 25, Bl 25, Bl 20, Cv 12, Liv 3, Liv 2, and Lu 7 for inflammatory conditions of the large intestine.

Use with Co 15, Co 14, Co 11, Co 4, Co 1, Co 2, Gb 21, jianneling, naoshang, Gb 34, and St 38 for acute injury to the anterior of the shoulder.

Use with Co 4, Co 11, St 44, St 45, Liv 2, and Liv 3 for stomatitis.

Applications:

Take his right straight with your right palm, the left one taking over immediately. The right palm now strikes to the side of his jaw, then straight down onto Co 7 using the knife edge across the forearm.

CO 8 (COLON POINT NO. 8)

Chinese name:

Xialian (lower integrity).

Location:

4 cun below Co 11. *Xia* means inferior, and *lian* means edge; the point is inferior to Co 9, on the dorsal side of the forearm, close to the radial aspect.

Connections:

None.

Direction of strike:

Straight down onto the upper forearm.

Damage:

Same as for Co 7. This is not a xie cleft point, but it does cause a KO when struck really hard. Use this point with Lu 1, and it will enhance the shot tenfold! The power of the whole body is drained when these two points are struck slightly after each other, Lu 1 first.

Set-up point:

Lu 1.

Antidote:

Massage Lu 1 on the opposite side downward using the thumb.

Healing:

Used for pain in the elbow and arm, abdominal pain, headache, painful eyes, vertigo, and mastitis.

Massage techniques are the same as for Co 6.

Use with Co 11, Co 10, Co 9, Co 7, Co 4, Gb 34, Co 1, Co 2, Liv 3, Gb 43, and Gb 44 for tennis elbow, or repetitive strain injury of the forearm.

Use with Co 4, Cv 17, Liv 3, St 15, St 36, Sp 18, Sp 21, Si 1, Si 2, Bl 18, Bl 17, Liv 4, St 18, Pc 6, Th 10, Kd 22, and Bl 40 for mastitis.

Applications:

Block his hand attack and strike slightly upward into Lu 1 with a one-knuckle punch, then straight down onto Co 8 with a knife edge.

CO 9 (COLON POINT NO. 9)

Chinese name:

Shanglian (upper integrity).

Location:

3 cun below Co 11. *Shang* means superior, and *lian* means edge; the point is superior to Co 8 on the dorsal side of the forearm, close to the radial aspect.

Connections:

None.

Direction of strike:

Straight down onto the forearm using a knife-edge strike.

Damage:

This strike will cause paralysis of the hand and arm, and again, if used along with Lu 1, it will cause such power loss that the fight will be over.

Set-up point:

Lu 1.

Antidote:

Same as Co 8.

Healing:

Innervation and irrigation are the same as for Co 8.

Use for aching of the shoulder region, motor impairment of the upper extremities, numbness of the hand and arm, borborygmus, hemiplegia, sprain, intestinal noises, and abdominal pain.

Massage is the same as for Co 6.

Use with St 36, Gb 34, Gb 30, Gb 29, Bl 25, Bl 26, St 25, Cv 6, Cv 4, Cv12, and Gb 26 for fullness in the flanks and abdomen.

Use with Gb 21, Co 11, Co 10, Co 8, Co 13, Lu 8, Gb 34, Co 4, and St 36 for pain in the arm as a result of exposure to wind/cold.

Applications:

The same as for Co 8.

CO 10 (COLON POINT NO. 10)

Chinese name:

Shousanli (arm's three measure).

Location:

2 cun below Co 11 on the radial aspect of the radius, in the extensor carpi radialis brevis and longus muscles.

Connections:

None.

Direction of strike:

This is a major dim-mak strike, either by itself or as a set-up point. Strike straight in to the point on the upper forearm. Or strike slightly upward or slightly downward, causing different reactions.

Damage:

This strike will paralyze the arm, and in some cases it will stop the heart. It causes a shock wave to rise up the arm into the upper body, and it will cause KO if struck hard enough. Usually it is used with St 9 for a death blow! This point will affect the whole Co meridian, especially around the arm, neck, and face, which is why St 9 works really well with this point. When the point is struck slightly upward, the lower body will lose qi and there will be nausea. We have had several martial artists who have received a whack on Co 10 go down and turned slightly green. When it is struck slightly downward (down the forearm toward the fingers), the bowels may work on the spot! When it is struck straight in, the lower abdomen will go into spasm, the arm will become paralyzed, and there may be residual diarrhea for a number of days.

Set-up point:

None. Use it as a set-up point.

Figure 296

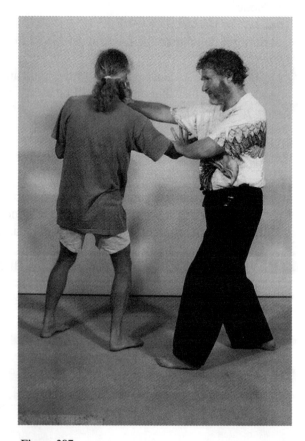

Figure 297

When you do not know the direction of the strike, take both arms at around Co 10 and squeeze all the fingers together (squeeze the whole upper arm). Or squeeze Co 1 and press Co 4 for an upward strike. For a downward strike, massage the opposite Co 10 in the same direction using medium pressure. Squeeze Co 1. If the strike was straight in, use the knuckles to scrape (massage) down the outside of the forearm on both arms.

Healing:

Innervation is the same as Co 7. Irrigation is by the branches of the radial recurrent artery and vein.

Used for abdominal pain, vomiting and diarrhea, pain in the shoulder region, motor impairment of the upper extremities, ulcer, stomachache, and indigestion.

Traditional indications include toothache, loss of voice, swelling of the mandible and cheek, scrofula, vomiting with diarrhea, hemiplegia, and it is much used for arm problems and edema of the arms.

Massage is the same as for Co 6, and you can also do loose fist percussion on this point.

Use with Cv 12, St 36, Liv 2, Liv 3, Co 4, Gb 29, Bl 17, Bl 18, and Bl 20 for gastric or duodenal ulcers.

Use with St 36, Cv 12, St 21, Liv 3, Liv 14, Liv 13, St 25, Gb 26, St 37, Sp 3, Bl 20, Bl 25, Bl 18, Bl 19, Bl 17, and Bl 21 for lumps in the abdomen due to stagnant food.

Use with Co 15, Co 14, Co 4, Co 16, Gb 21, jianneling, and naoshang for anterior shoulder pain and stiffness.

Applications:

He attacks with a straight right. You step to your left and attack Co 10 with your right backfist (fig. 296). Your left palm takes over this strike as your right knife edge strikes straight in to St 9. This is a death-point combination (fig. 297).

CO 11 (COLON POINT NO. 11)

Chinese name:

Quchi (crooked pool).

Location:

When the elbow is flexed, the point is in the depression at lateral the end of the transverse cubital crease, midway between Lu 5 and the lateral epicondyle of the humerus. On the radial aspect of the elbow at the origin of the extensor carpi radialis muscle and the radial side of the brachioradialis muscle.

Connections:

None.

Direction of strike:

Straight in to the back of the elbow.

Damage:

This is a major point because it is an earth and he point. It normally calms and regulates the whole system, but when struck using negative qi, it will have the reverse effect. Not only will the elbow joint be damaged as a result of purely physical damage, but the whole joint system of the body can be made weaker. The point also can cause diarrhea and vomiting. This point will also upset the balance between the shen and the body. However, you must be aware that you may also damage your own hand on the target elbow! So use a palm strike here.

Set-up point:

Co 7.

Antidote:

Massage the opposite Co 11 and squeeze Co 1.

Healing:

Innervation is by the posterior antebrachial cutaneous nerve and, deeper, on the medial side, the radial nerve. Irrigation is by the branches of the radial recurrent artery and vein. Used for pain in the elbow and arm, motor impairment of the upper extremities, scrofula, uticaria, abdominal pain, vomiting, diarrhea, dysentery, febrile disease, sore throat, arthritic pain of the upper limbs, hemiplegia, hypertension, high fever, measles, anemia, allergies, goiter, and skin disease. Traditional indications include red and painful eyes, toothache, throat blockage, nodular growths in the neck, goiter, hives, wind rash, dry parched skin, hemiplegia, light menstrual flow, windstroke, and heat in the Co meridian.

As an earth point and a he sea point of the stomach meridian, its traditional functions are to eliminate wind and exterior conditions, cool heat, resolves damp, regulate the blood and qi, remove obstructions from and soothe the joints, and serve as a cooling point for internal heat as well as wind/heat.

Massage techniques are the same as for Co 10.

Use with Gb 20, Gb 21, Bl 10, Gv 20, Gb 14, Co 4, yintang, taiyang, Liv 3, St 36, Gb 34, and Gb 41 for headache.

Use with Co 4, yintang, Lu 11, Lu 8, Lu 5, Bl 17, Sp 10, and St 36 for measles.

Use with Gv 20, Bl 14, Bl 15, Bl 17, Bl 18, Bl 20, St 36, St 40, St 9, Gv 14 Liv 2, Liv 3, Liv 4, and Liv 8 for hypertension.

Use with Co 4, Lu 7, Ht 7, Pc 6, Liv 3, Liv 2, Liv 4, St 36, Gb 34, and Cv 17 for smoking and other drug withdrawal.

Use with Co 4, Gb 20, Gb 21, Bl 12, Bl 13, Bl 43, Bl 17, Lu 7, Cv 17, Lu 5, Lu 8, and Lu 6 for colds and flu-type symptoms.

Use with Co 4, Lu 10, Lu 11, Lu 5, Lu 8, Cv 22, Liv 2, Bl 13, and Bl 17 for sore throat, loss of voice, etc.

Applications:

He attacks with a right, and you use the knuckles of your right backfist to strike straight into Co 7. Your right palm now grabs around his right wrist as your left palm strikes straight in to Co 11 and your right palm pulls backward violently, thus breaking the elbow joint.

CO 12 (COLON POINT NO. 12)

Chinese name:

Zhouliao (elbow seam).

Location:

When the elbow is flexed, the point is superior to the lateral epicondyle of the humerus, around 1 cun superolateral to Co 11, on the medial border of the humerus at the origin of the anconeus muscle and the lateral margin of the triceps muscle. *Zhou* means elbow, and *liao* means foramen; the point is at the elbow close to the foramen.

Connections:

None.

Direction of strike:

Straight in and slightly downward over the lump of the elbow.

Damage:

Great qi drainage when struck downward into the elbow. This point is struck with the knife edge of the palm, which strikes with the palm facing slightly downward and then rolls over to palm up as it strikes, thus causing more of a cutting action on the point. This point works so well that few people will be able to continue after being struck here.

Set-up point:

None.

Antidote:

Grab both points and squeeze gently downward.

Healing:

Innervation is by the posterior antebrachial cutaneous nerve, and, deeper, on the medial side, the radial nerve.

Irrigation is by the radial collateral artery and vein.

Used for pain/contracture and numbness of the elbow and arm and inflammation of the lateral epicondyle of the humerus.

Traditional indications include pain in the elbow and arm, spasm or numbness of the arm, and lassitude. Massage techniques are the same as for Co 11. Use with Gb 34, Gb 43, Gb 44, Co 4, Co 1, Co 2, Co 11, and Co 10 for inflammation of the lateral epicondyle of the humerus.

Use with Co 15, Co 11, Co 4, Th 6, Th 13, Si 4, Gb 34, St 40, Bl 39, St 28, Cv 5, Cv 2, Cv 3, Cv 9, Kd 6, Sp 9, and Bl 22 for multiple neuritis resulting in numb hands.

Applications:

He attacks with a low left hook. Your left palm strikes to Co 12 just above the elbow and continues to cut inward to just over the elbow lump. This would be followed by a strike to St 9 with the same hand, or into Liv 14 with both hands, the right palm pushing in behind the left palm to assist in the power.

CO 13 (COLON POINT NO. 13)

Chinese name:

Shouwuli (five measures on the arm).

Location:

Superior to the lateral epicondyle of the humerus, 3 cun above Co 11, on the line connecting Co 11 with Co 15.

Connections:

None.

Direction of strike:

Straight in to the outer side of the upper arm, usually with a knife edge.

Damage:

This point is more of a nerve point strike, which inflicts great pain and nervous shock. The pain will grow very quickly until the recipient has to give up because of this pain. This strike does not have to be that hard, either, although a hard strike will impose the greatest pain.

Set-up point:

None.

Antidote:

Rub the whole outer, upper part of the arm downward with medium pressure.

Healing:

Innervation is by the posterior antebrachial cutaneous nerve, and deeper, the radial nerve. Irrigation is by the radial collateral artery and vein.

Used for contracture and pain of the elbow and arm, scrofula, coughing blood, pneumonia, and peritonitis.

Some texts forbid needling here, claiming that if it is needled five or six times in a lifetime, then death will result. Others urge extreme caution to avoid the artery if needling this point. Massage and moxa are traditionally used on this point.

Massage techniques are the same as for Co 6.

Use with Co 4, Co 11, Lu 9, Sp 10, Bl 17, Lu 6, and Bl 13 for coughing up blood.

Use with Co 12, Co 14, Co 15, Co 11, Co 4, Co 2, Co 1, Gb 34, Th 4, Th 6, Th 13, and Th 14 for contracture and pain in the elbow and upper arm.

Applications:

Take his left strike with your right palm, moving it over to your left. This will load your right elbow, which now comes back to strike straight in to Co 13, causing the fight to be finished.

CO 14 (COLON POINT NO. 14)

Chinese name:

Binao (arm and scapula).

Location:

On the radial side of the humerus, superior to the lower end of the deltoid muscle, on the line connecting Co 11 to Co 15. *Bi* means arm, and *nao* means muscle prominence of the arm; thus, this point is on the muscle prominence of the arm.

Connections:

A internal branch to Th 13.

Direction of strike:

Straight in to just under the shoulder on the upper arm.

Damage:

This point strike causes great qi damage to the whole body being one of the "seven star" points. The seven star points (Gv 20, Co 14 points, Si 16 points, and Gb 30 points) are those that take energy in from the outside. They are used in qigong stances as qi input points. A strike to Co 14 will block energy from entering the body and cause weakness and extreme emotional problems due to the mind's knowing that something really bad has happened but not quite knowing what.

Set-up point:

Co 12.

Antidote:

Place the palms on top of the head at Gv 20 and press downward lightly. Then hold both palms over each of the pairs of seven star points for 30 seconds.

Healing:

Innervation is by the posterior brachial cutaneous nerve and, deeper, the radial nerve.

Irrigation is by the branches of the posterior circumflex humeral artery and vein and the deep branch of the brachial artery and vein.

Used for pain in the shoulder and arm, scrofula, paralysis of the upper limbs, and disease of the eye.

Traditional indications include chills and fever, pain in the shoulder and upper back inhibiting the lifting of the shoulder, and scrofula.

Traditional functions are to clear the channels and the vision.

Massage techniques are the same as for Co 10.

Use with Bl 1, St 1, Gb 1, Th 23, yuyao, Co 4, Liv 3, and Gv 20 for disease of the eyes.

Use with Co 15, Co 11, jianneling, naoshang, Gb 34, St 38, Gb 43, Gb 44, Liv 4, Liv 8, Bl 25, St 37, and St 25 for anterior shoulder problems.

Applications:

He attacks with a right attack to your midsection. Your right palm strikes his right Co 12 point downward and then hooks over his arm to throw it over to your right, thus exposing his right side. Your right elbow now attacks straight in to Co 14.

CO 15 (COLON POINT NO. 15)

Chinese name:

Jianyu (shoulder bone).

Location:

Anteroinferior to the acromion, in the middle of the upper portion of the deltoid muscle. When the arm is in full abduction, the point is in the anterior depression of the two depressions appearing at the anterior border of the acromioclavicular joint. *Jian* means shoulder, and *yu* means corner; the point is at the corner of the shoulder.

Connections:

This is the departure point of the divergent meridian.

Direction of strike:

Straight down onto the tip of the shoulder, just a little up on the shoulder.

Damage:

Not a great qi damage point; it is more used for healing. However, a good hard strike here will either break or dislocate the shoulder, so it is a good physical shot.

Set-up point:

None.

Antidote:

Medical treatment.

Healing:

Innervation is by the lateral supraclavicular nerve and the axillary nerve. Irrigation is by the posterior circumflex artery and vein.

Used for pain of the shoulder and arm, motor impairment of the upper extremities, rubella, scrofula, hemiplegia, hypertension, perifocal inflammation of the shoulder joint, and excessive sweating.

Traditional indications include wind dampness in the shoulder, hemiplegia, wind rash (urticaria), lack of arm strength, goiter, and it is used a lot for wind stroke.

Traditional functions are to eliminate wind and remove obstructions from the jing-luo, soothe the joints, and serve as a crossing point of yin qiao mai.

To massage, press and hold; do rotations clockwise or counterclockwise for xu or shi conditions; press in slowly with both thumbs and release quickly, pulling the thumbs apart; and do fingertip or loose fist percussion. Cupping this point can give immediate relief to shoulder problems where there is an inability to lift the arm.

Use with Co 4, Co 11, Co 5, Gb 20, Lu 7, Lu 5, St 36, and Liv 3 for wind rash.

Use with Co 14, Gb 20, Gb 21, Th 15, Si 3, Si 13, Si 14, Si 15, Si 9, naoshang, jianneling, St 38, St 37, Bl 25, Bl 17, Si 10, Bl 43, Gb 34, Co 1, Co 2, Co 3, Co 4, and Co 10 for shoulder problems.

Use with moxa on Cv 24, St 6, Lu 7, Lu 9, Lu 10, and Si 5, and massage Co 41, St 44, Kd 3, St 7, and Gb 21 for toothache. This is also a crossing point of the bladder muscle meridian.

Applications:

Same as for Co 14, only slam down onto the shoulder.

CO 16 (COLON POINT NO. 16)

Chinese name:

Jugu (great bone).

Location:

In the upper aspect of the shoulder, in the depression between the acromial extremity of the clavicle and the scapular spine. In the trapezium and supraspinatus muscles. *Ju* means huge, and *gu* means bone; the clavicle was called jugu in ancient times.

Connections:

Point of yang qiao mai. There is an internal pathway to Si 12, Gv 14, and St 12, and then a branch to St 25.

Direction of strike:

Straight down near the collarbone from the back.

Damage:

Great qi drainage and physical damage to the clavicle. This point must be struck very hard, though. It is difficult to strike the exact spot, so I usually suggest using a larger weapon, such as a palm strike, and hoping for the best (although a thumb-knuckle punch is the best weapon for this point).

Set-up point:

Co 12.

Antidote:

Seek medical treatment because the clavicle will probably be broken. Place the palms onto the top of the head at Cv 20 and use light pressure downward.

Healing:

Innervation occurs, superficially, by the lateral supraclavicular nerve, the branch of the accessory nerve, and, deeper, the suprascapular nerve. Irrigation is deep, by the suprascapular artery and vein.

Used for pain in the shoulder, pain and motor impairment of the upper extremities, spitting blood, scrofula, and diseases of the shoulder joint and surrounding soft tissue.

Traditional indications include pain in the arm and shoulder inhibiting movement, frightened convulsions, spitting blood, scrofula, and nodular growths on the neck.

Traditional functions are to disperse congealed blood and clear the channels. It is a crossing point of the yang qiao mai.

Massage techniques are the same as for Co 15, though cupping is also used here. Use with Ht 1, Th 14, Bl 43, Si 9, Si 10, Si 11, Si 12, Si 13, Si 14, Si 15, Co 15, Si 3, Gb 34, Co 11, Th 4, Th 6, and Bl 25 for perifocal inflammation of the shoulder joint.

Use with Lu 6, Lu 5, Lu 10, Co 4, Co 11, Sp 10, Bl 17, Bl 13, Liv 4, Liv 2, Liv 8, and Co 13 for coughing up blood.

Applications:

Same as for Co 15, only use a thumb-knuckle punch down onto the shoulder slightly toward the front of the body.

CO 17 (COLON POINT NO. 17)

Chinese name:

Tianding (heaven's vessel).

Location:

On the lateral side of the neck, superior to the midpoint of the supraclavicular fossa (St 12), around 1 cun below Co 18, on the posterior border of the sternocleidomastoideus muscle. *Tian* means heaven, and *ding* is the term used by the ancient Chinese for a cooking vessel with 2 loop handles. Here tian implies upper, and the head looks like a *ding* (wok).

Connections:

Reunion point of the internal pathway.

Direction of strike:

In to the base of the neck at a 45-degree angle. Same direction as for St 9.

Damage:

This is one of the most dangerous points, which, when struck, will cause death. The blood will be blocked, the qi will be blocked, and the brain will be shocked. Not even CPR will revive a person who has been struck here.

Set-up point:

Neigwan or Co 12.

Antidote:

None!

Healing:

Innervation occurs superficially by the supraclavicular nerve. The point is on the sternocleidomastoideus muscle just where the cutaneous cervical nerve emerges. Deeper innervation is by the phrenic nerve. Irrigation is by the external jugular vein.

Used for sore throat, laryngitis, scrofula, goiter, tonsillitis, and paralysis of the hypoglossus muscle.

To massage, press and hold, do rotations clockwise or counterclockwise for xu or shi conditions; press in slowly with both thumbs and release quickly, pulling the thumbs apart; and do fingertip percussion.

Use with Bl 10, Gb 20, Co 4, Co 11, Lu 5, Lu 10, Lu 11, Lu 6, Co 1, Co 2, Sp 10, Bl 12, Cv 22,

Liv 2, and Liv 3 for sore throat, tonsillitis, laryngitis, etc.

Use with Si 17, Co 11, Co 4, St 44, St 45, Gv 14, and Lu 5 for acute tonsillitis.

Use with Bl 12, Bl 60, Co 4, Th 1, Gb 20, Gv 20, Liv 3, Th 3, Bl 10, and Gb 21 for headache and dizziness.

Applications:

Use any of the strikes that I have already mentioned to this area of the neck, such as to St 9, cutting into the neck with the knife edge. Strike the inside of his right forearm with your left palm as your right knife edge cuts straight into Co 17.

CO 18 (COLON POINT NO. 18)

Chinese name:

Futu (support the prominence).

Location:

On the lateral side of the neck, level with the tip of the Adam's apple, between the sternal head and the clavicular head of the sternocleidomastoideus muscle. *Fu* means side, and *tu* means prominence; here, tu refers to the prominence of the larynx since the point is beside it.

Connections:

Upper meeting point of the lung and colon divergent meridians.

Direction of strike:

Again, this is at an angle of 45 degrees, same as for Co 17 and St 9.

Damage:

This is again one of the most deadly points to strike. It is close to St 9, so you could easily strike both points simultaneously, causing death immediately with no chance of revival! Do not play around with this point; even a light blow will cause great damage! It is a window of the sky point. The emotions will be affected long after this strike, with a blocked feeling in the throat, a detached feeling between the mind and body, and emotions such as grief running rampant.

Set-up point:

Co 12.

Antidote:

Have an acupuncturist needle this point 4 fen perpendicular for the emotional and detached problems. However, if this point is struck hard along with St 9, there is no antidote!

Healing:

Innervation is by the great auricular nerve, cutaneous cervical nerve, lessor occipital nerve, and the accessory nerve. Irrigation is deeper, on the medial side, by the ascending cervical artery and vein.

Used for cough, asthma, sore throat, hoarseness, scrofula, goiter, excessive mucous, difficulty swallowing, distended feeling in the throat; used for anesthesia during thyroid operations.

Traditional indications include coughing and wheezing, excessive mucous, difficulty swallowing, sounds in the throat (like a duck). It is used to ease the throat and treat goiter.

To massage, press and hold; do rotations clockwise or counterclockwise for xu or shi conditions; press in slowly with both thumbs and release quickly, pulling the thumbs apart; do fingertip percussion (with care); and use all the fingers to run down from the mastoid process to the sternoclavicular notch, depressing the sides and the center of the sternocleidomastoideus muscle (do only one side at a time).

Use with Cv 22, Kd 3, Kd 7, Lu 7, St 36, Liv 14, Liv 3, Sp 21, Bl 43, Bl 17, Bl 13, and St 40 for asthma.

Use with Cv 22, Co 4, Cv 17, Lu 1, Lu 7, Lu 8, Bl 13, Bl 17, Liv 3, Co 11, and Lu 5 for cough, sore throat, and hoarseness.

Use with Bl 10, Gb 20, Gb 21, Th 15, Si 3, Si 13, Si 15, Bl 11, Bl 13, Bl 17, Bl 18, Gb 34, and Bl 60 for stiff, painful neck.

Applications:

The same as for Co 17. Or you could block his low left attack with both arms (fig. 298). Now, hold

Figure 298

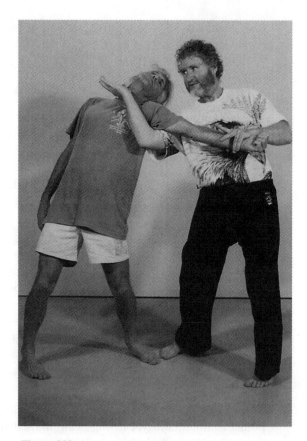

Figure 299

his left wrist with your left palm and strike up under his left arm so that the thumb side of your right palm strikes across Co 18 and St 9 (fig. 299).

CO 19 (COLON POINT NO. 19)

Chinese name:
    Heliao (grain seam).
Location:
    Directly below the lateral margin of the nostril, level with Gv 26, in the fossa canine of the superior maxilla, at the junction of the quadratus labii superioris muscle. The point is also called *kouheliao*. *Kou* means mouth, *he* means grain, and *liao* means foramen (the grain/food enters the stomach through the mouth); this point is in the foramen above the mouth.
Connections:
    None.
Direction of strike:
    Straight in above the top lip.
Damage:
    This is a shock point. It will cause the recipient to go into shock. A hard strike will cause KO. Usually a backward (palm upward) thumb-knuckle punch is used here.
Set-up point:
    Co 12.
Antidote:
    Press inward and slightly upward into Gv 26, about two-thirds of the way up in the space between the lip and the bottom of the nose.

Healing:

Innervation is by the anastomotic branch of the facial nerve and the infraorbital nerve. Irrigation is by the superior labial branches of the facial artery and vein.

Used for epistaxis, nasal obstruction, deviation of the mouth, rhinitis, and facial paralysis.

Traditional indications include ulceration of the nose, extra tissue in the nose, nosebleed, and locked jaw.

Massage techniques include pressing and holding the point; rotating clockwise or counterclockwise for xu or shi conditions; pressing in slowly with both forefingers and releasing quickly, pulling the thumbs apart; and using gentle fingertip percussion.

Use with St 4, St 5, St 2, St 6, Gb 14, St 7, St 8, Gb 34, Gb 43, Gb 44, Liv 3, Gv 20, Gb 20, taiyang, and *qianzheng* (an extra point) for facial paralysis.

Use with yintang, Lu 7, Sp 10, Co 4, Co 11, Co 6, Co 2, Liv 2, Liv 3, St 36, and Gb 20 for nosebleed.

Use with St 3, St 44, Co 4, Co 1, Co 2, Co 3, Co 5, Kd 3, and Bl 2 for toothache.

Applications:

He attacks with a left straight. Take it with your right palm, cutting downward onto Co 12. (This could cause KO by itself.) You have stepped forward with your right foot. Turn your right foot in and, stepping with your left foot around to his rear so that you are now facing in the same direction as the attacker, bring your right thumb-knuckle punch (palm facing upward) into Co 19.

CO 20 (COLON POINT NO. 20)

Chinese name:

Yingxiang (welcome fragrance).

Location:

In the nasolabial groove, at the level of the midpoint of the lateral border of the ala nasi in the quadratus labii superior muscle and, in its deep position, at the border of the apertura piriformis.

Connections:

Internal path to St 1 and Gb 14.

Direction of strike:

Inward just next to the nose and slightly away from it.

Damage:

This point is in such a position on the cheekbone that it will cause KO. It is not a death point, but will suffice to stop an argument.

Set-up point:

Co 12.

Antidote:

This point is more of a healing point for mucus and eye problems, etc. It is also used to heal any problems associated with a strike to the same point.

Healing:

Innervation is by the anastomotic branch of the facial and infraorbital nerves. Irrigation is by the facial artery and vein and the branches of the infraorbital artery and vein.

Used for nasal obstruction, epistaxis, rhinorrhea, deviation of the mouth, itching and swelling of the face, roundworm in the bile duct, and facial paralysis.

Traditional indications include nosebleed, tissue in the nose, runny nose, inability to distinguish odors, facial swelling and itching, and mouth and eyes awry.

Traditional functions are to open the nasal passages and disperse wind/heat. It is a crossing point of the stomach meridian.

Massage techniques include pressing and holding and doing rotations clockwise or counterclockwise for xu or shi conditions. To help drain the sinuses, use as part of a rub with the forefinger from Bl 1, down the lateral sides of the nose to Co 20, then laterally out through St 3, St 6, and down over the angle of the jaw through Si 17, St 9, to Cv 22.

Use with Co 4, Ht 7, Gb 20, Gv 20, St 44, and St 45 for itchy, swollen face.

Use with Co 4, Co 11, Lu 5, Lu 7, St 36, Bl 2, Bl 4, Bl 6, Bl 7, Bl 9, Bl 10, Bl 13, St 36, and bitong for sinus congestion, blocked nose, etc.

Applications:

Take his right hook with your left palm and strike to Co 20 with your one-knuckle punch in a counterclockwise circle, causing the blow to move away from the nose to the outside of the head.

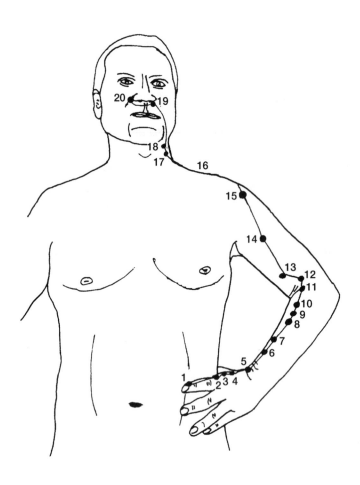

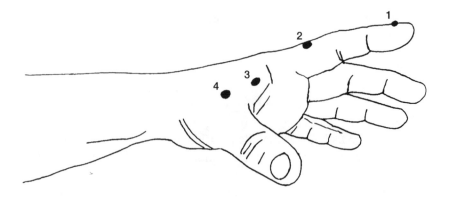

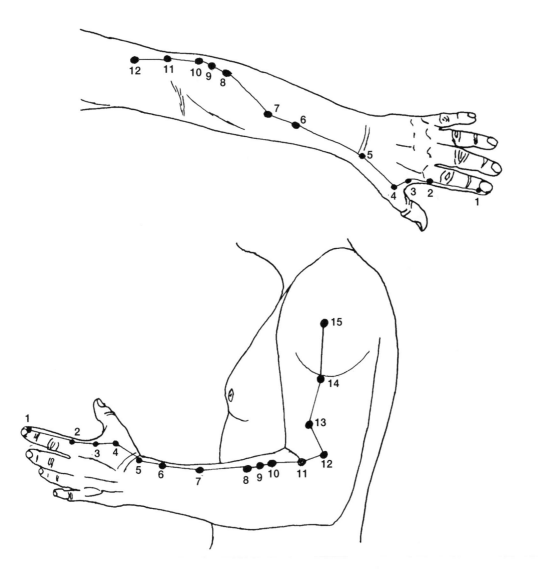

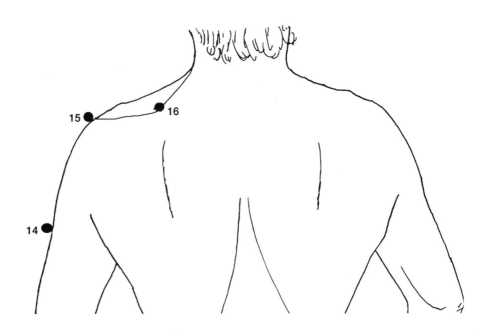

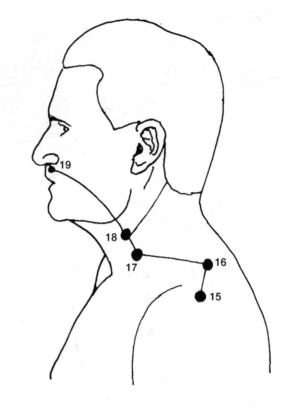

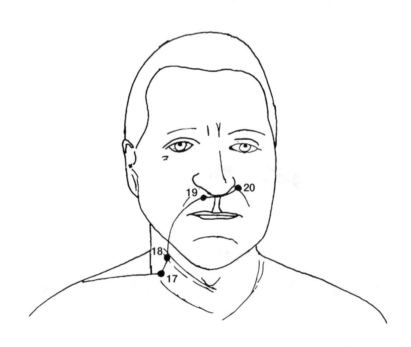

Chapter 11

The Triple Heater Meridian

THE TCM VIEW

The Chinese element for the triple heater is fire. The triple heater's yin associated meridian is the pericardium. The official role of the triple heater is the controller of heating.

The triple heater is not so much an organ as it is a function, and, as such, there is no Western medicine equivalent. There are three "heating" spaces in the body, as follows: upper (from diaphragm to head), middle (from diaphragm to navel), and lower (from navel down). The upper space is concerned with the heart and mind. Where qigong is concerned, the upper heater also has to do with respiration. The middle heater has to do with the stomach, spleen, liver, and gallbladder. Where qigong is concerned, it has to do with digestion. The lower heater has to do with the kidneys, bladder, small intestine, and colon. In qigong, it has to do with elimination. The upper heater is concerned with the distribution of blood, qi, and air. The middle heater is concerned with absorbing nutrients from food and digesting. The lower heater is concerned with expelling waste.

The three spaces are areas of work, which creates heat. When we work on the triple heater meridian in qigong, we must work on the three individual spaces with three different qigong methods. When the three spaces are said to be balanced or in harmony, then the whole body is in harmony. The ideal situation is to have an equal amount of yin and yang energy in each of the three spaces. One of the first qigongs we do each morning is the triple heater qigong to make for a balanced and relaxed day.

There is a relationship between the three heaters (jiao). The upper heater is like a mist that rises from the cooking pot (middle heater) and acts like a condensing plate, dispersing and descending the mist rising from the middle. It corresponds to heaven.

The middle heater is like the cooking pot where things are soaked and decomposed. It corresponds to earth.

The lower heater is like an aqueduct for the flowing of water, as in a swamp from which water is drained away. It also contains the kidneys, which are responsible for fluid movement as well as the sexual function. It corresponds to man.

The triple heater meridian is the epitome of the fact that all of the organs and meridians are interconnected and if one organ or meridian is not in balance then the whole organism is also out of balance. Because the Th is representative of the whole body, if one portion is unbalanced, then so is the whole body. Although these points in acupuncture are used mainly for meridian problems, they can also be added to a specific organ ailment to enhance the treatment.

In dim-mak, the Th meridian is a very important one. The points on this meridian are excellent set-up points as well as major points, some of which are extremely deadly. Because of the nature of the Th meridian, when one point is struck the whole body will be out of balance immediately.

TH 1 (TRIPLE HEATER POINT NO. 1)

Chinese name:
Guanchong (gate's pouring).

Location:
On the lateral side of the ring finger, around 0.1 cun posterior to the corner of the nail. *Guan* means bend; since the ring finger cannot be stretched out alone, guan here is referring to the ring finger. *Chong* means gushing, the point is near the tip of the ring finger and is the jing well point where qi of the meridian originates and gushes upward along the channel.

Connections:
Takes transverse luo from Pc 6 and branch from Pc 8.

Direction of strike:
This point is on the little finger side of the ring finger. It is not used as a dim-mak point, but more in the healing area. It is a metal and cheng point. It is a controlling point for muscles and tendons and divergent meridians.

Damage:
To receive a blow to the ring finger, perhaps you might hit it with a hammer. You will cause an imbalance in the meridian, which will cause your day to be "off." It will not kill you, but it will have to be dealt with if balance is to be regained.

Set-up point:
None.

Antidote:
Do the triple heater qigong (taught in Chapter 3, under the antidote for Bl 33).

Healing:
Innervation is by the palmar digital proprial nerve derived from the ulnar nerve. Irrigation is by the arterial anevenous network formed by the palmar digital proprial artery and vein.

Used for fever, laryngitis, conjunctivitis, headache, stiffness of the tongue, sore throat, irritability, and redness of the eyes.

As a jing well point and a metal point of the triple heater meridian, its traditional functions are to dispel wind/heat conditions, as well as move excess in the channel as a result of a trauma (e.g., punch or kick to the yang aspect of the arm).

To massage, use the knuckle and forefinger to squeeze the point.

Use with Cv 24, Bl 49, Kd 2, Kd 3, Sp 6, Bl 13, Bl 23, St 36, Lu 11, Lu 10, Bl 17, Bl 21, Cv 12, Cv 4, and jiaji points lateral to T10/11 and T11/12 for diabetes where thirst and emaciation are problems.

Use with Gb 20, Bl 10, St 9, Co 17, Si 16, St 6, Bl 11, Bl 12, Si 15, Gb 21, Co 4, Co 11, Th 17, Th 3, Co 3, Lu 11, Co 2, and Co 1 for acute tonsillitis.

Applications:
None.

TH 2 (TRIPLE HEATER POINT NO. 2)

Chinese name:
Yemen (fluid's door).

Location:
Proximal to the margin of the web between the ring and small fingers. The point is located with a clenched fist.

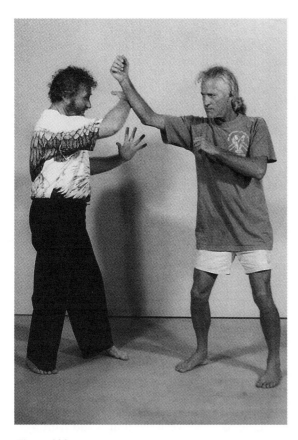

Figure 300

Connections:
> None.

Direction of strike:
> You could use this point in a small ch'i-na lock, digging the thumb into the point as you lock the small finger backward. Straight in at the web of the little finger and ring finger.

Damage:
> This point will do internal damage and help the lock to work even better. This lock can be used by small children on adults to literally take them to their knees. This is a water and yong point and will cause great qi disruption to the body when attacked, especially the movement of fluids throughout the body. It is not a point that I would count on in a tight situation, however, as it is very difficult to get at.

Set-up point:
> None.

Antidote:
> Should this point cause qi damage or too much fluid to build up, you should needle the opposite point (Th 2) on the other hand 1 fen obliquely.

Figure 301

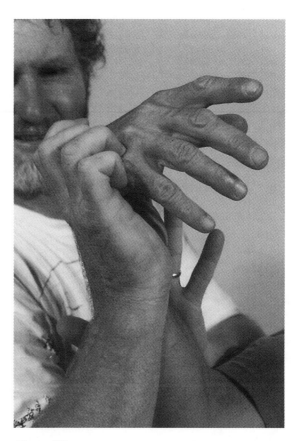

Figure 302

Healing:

Innervation is by the dorsal branch of the ulnar nerve. Irrigation is by the dorsal digital artery of the ulnar artery.

Used for headache, redness of the eyes, deafness, sore throat, pain in the hand and arm, malaria, laryngopharyngitis, and pain and swelling of the fingers.

Th 2 is a ying spring (gushing) point and a water point of the Th meridian. *Ye* means water, and *men* means door; this is the rong (ying) spring point of this channel, and it has the function of regulating water passage like a door.

To massage, press and hold, or do rotations clockwise or counterclockwise for xu or shi conditions.

Use with Th 16, Th 17, Si 19, Gb 20, Kd 3, Gb 41, Gv 20, and Th 21 for deafness.

Use with Lu 10, Lu 11, Co 4, Lu 7, Lu 5, Co 11, and Liv 2 for sore throat.

Use with Co 4, Co 11, Liv 2, Liv 3, Bl 1, St 1, Gb 1, Gb 14, and Gb 20 for red, sore eyes.

Applications:

Block his attack with your right p'eng block as your left palm guards his right hand (fig. 300). Now, quickly slide your right palm down his arm and take his little finger, pressing your thumb into Th 2 (fig. 301 and 302).

TH 3 (TRIPLE HEATER POINT NO. 3)

Chinese name:

Zhongzhu (middle island).

Location:

When the hand is palm down, the point is on the dorsum of the hand between the fourth and fifth metacarpal bones, in the depression proximal to the metacarpophalangeal joint in the fourth interosseous muscle.

Connections:

None.

Direction of strike:

This point is also not a point I would use; however, those who are adept at taking locks and holds (not recommended in the Montaigue system of fighting) could use this point as an adjunct to a small ch'i-na lock on the little finger.

Damage:

This is a wood and shu point and will have an effect upon the hearing when struck. It will also help in the execution of a finger lock, making it work much better and causing more damage. It also has an effect upon the sides of the body, so you could use this point to cause the attacker to buckle in at the sides and then strike the side of the body, especially at Gb 25, causing great internal damage and KO.

Set-up point:

Th 8 works very well with this point.

Antidote:

To help with the ears, massage the point straight in to the point of slight pain.

Healing:

Innervation is by the dorsal branch of the ulnar nerve. Irrigation is by the dorsal venous network of the hand and the fourth dorsal metacarpal artery.

Used for deaf-mutism, tinnitus, deafness, headache, pain in the shoulder and back, intercostal neuralgia, red eyes, sore throat, pain of the elbow and arm, motor impairment of the fingers, and febrile disease.

Traditional indications include pain in the shoulder, back, elbow, and arm; inability to bend the fingers; headache; tinnitus; blurred vision; and acute strain of the lower lumbar region.

Figure 303

This is a root of Th meridian, a shu stream (transporting) point, and a wood point of the Th meridian. Its traditional functions are to regulate qi circulation, dispel pathogenic heat, soothe the ear, and stimulate the thyroid. *Zhong* means middle, and *zhu* means a small plot of land in water; the point is in the middle of the five shu points, and the qi of the channel flows like water into a pool.

To massage, press and hold, do rotations clockwise or counterclockwise for xu or shi conditions, and do fingertip percussion.

Use with Th 21, Th 17, Gb 20, Gv 20, Liv 2, Liv 3, St 40, Kd 3, Bl 23, Si 4, Si 5, Si 9, Si 2, Co 5, Gb 43, Gb 11, Bl 8, and Co 10 for tinnitus and deafness.

Use with Th 2, Co 4, Bl 1, St 1, St 45, St 44, Liv 2, Liv 3, Gb 1, Gb 43, and Gb 44 for red, sore eyes.

Use with Gb 20, Gv 20, Gb 21, Liv 3, Liv 2, Co 4, Co 11, Gb 44, St 36, Bl 18, and Bl 17 for migraine headache.

Applications:

Slam his left straight with your right palm at Th 8. Slide your right palm down until you can lock his little finger, digging your own ring finger into Th 3. This will cause his body to bend as your left palm attacks to his face and your right knee attacks to his left side at about Gb 25 (fig. 303).

TH 4 (TRIPLE HEATER POINT NO. 4)

Chinese name:

Yangchi (pool of yang).

Location:

Yang is as in yin and yang, and *chi* means pool; the point is in a depression on the back of the wrist, and the qi (yang) flows like water into a pool here. Located at the junction of the ulna and carpal bones, in the depression lateral to the tendon of extensor digitorum communis muscle. With the hand supine, this point can be found directly above the transverse crease on the dorsal side of the wrist, in a hollow above the third and fourth metacarpal bones, between the tendons of extensor digitorum and extensor digiti minimi manus muscles.

Connections:

Transverse luo from Pc 6.

Direction of strike:

Straight in on the little finger side of the back of the palm near the wrist crease.

Damage:

This is a yuan point. It will cause damage to the tendons and to the "life force." It is not good to be struck here if you have had either a vasectomy or a hysterectomy. It will cause great pain and qi drainage. It is an excellent set-up point, if you can get at it. Th 4 must be struck right on the point, using a smaller weapon such as a one-knuckle punch. The qi drainage can be so bad that the recipient has to sit down.

Set-up point:

None. This point can be used as a set-up to Gb 25.

Antidote:

Massage or needle (3 fen) the opposite point on the other hand to fix the tendon problems and life force problems. Apply mild pressure downward onto the crown of the head for the qi drainage and consequent nausea.

Healing:

Innervation is by the dorsal branch of the ulnar nerve and the terminal branch of the posterior antebrachial cutaneous nerve. Irrigation occurs inferiorly by the dorsal venous network of the wrist and the posterior carpal artery.

Used for pain in the wrist, shoulder, and arm; malaria; deafness; tonsillitis; and common cold.

Traditional indications include thirst and dryness in the mouth, red and swollen eyes, throat blockage, deafness, tidal fever, and pain and weakness of the wrist.

As a yuan source point of the triple heater meridian, its traditional functions are to strongly reinforce the yang qi of the body, relax the tendons, invigorate and clear the channels and collaterals, reinforce the three jiao, promote the function of the chong and ren mai in strengthening qi and controlling xue (blood), and relieve heat. It is used a lot in Japan to tonify yang.

Massage techniques are the same as for Th 3. Use with Pc 7, shang baxi, baxi (extra), Co 4, Si 3, Si 5, Gb 34, Gb 41, and St 36 for arthritis of the wrist, fingers, and hands.

Use with St 36, Kd 3, Lu 9, Liv 3, Bl 23, Bl 20, Bl 18, Bl 17, Bl 13, Sp 3, Gv 4, Gv 14, Gv 20, Cv 4, and Cv 12 to pick up yang qi after a long-term disease or in old age when yang has declined but yin is still strong.

Use with Gb 2, Si 19, Th 21, Gb 20, anmien, Kd 3, and Bl 23 for deafness.

Applications:

He attacks with a right straight. Move to the outside (your left) and, using a backfist strike, hit the point with your right largest knuckle. Then bring that same palm back under to Gb 25. This would result in death or kidney failure causing death at most or extreme nausea at least.

TH 5 (TRIPLE HEATER POINT NO. 5)

Chinese name:

Waiguan (outer gate).

Location:

2 cun above Th 4, between the radius and ulna and the extensor digitorum and extensor hallucis longus muscles.

Connections:

Transverse luo to Pc 7 and Pc 9.

Direction of strike:

Straight in to the little-finger side of the outside of the forearm.

Damage:

When struck, this point makes you feel like collapsing or lying down. The qi drainage and pain are incredible when it is struck right on with a smaller weapon. This is a luo point and a master point of yang wei mai, so it has a connection with many other meridians. It will unbalance the yin and yang of the body.

Set-up point:

None.

Antidote:

Massage or needle the opposite point or perform the triple heater qigong.

Healing:

Innervation is by the posterior antebrachial cutaneous nerve and, deeper, the posterior interosseous nerve of the radial nerve and the anterior interosseous nerve of the median nerve. Irrigation is deep by the posterior and anterior interosseous arteries and veins.

Used for febrile disease, headache, pain in the cheek and hypochondriac regions, deafness, tinnitus, motor impairment of the elbow and arm, pain of the fingers, hand tremor, common cold, pneumonia, parotitis, enuresis, stiff neck, hemiplegia, and migraine.

Traditional indications include pain in the fingers inhibiting grasp, hand tremors, swollen throat, tinnitus, deafness, febrile disease, pain in the ribs, constipation, and headache.

As a luo connecting point of the Th meridian, a master point (meeting point) of the yang wei mai, and a couple point of the dai mai (girdle channel), its traditional functions are to treat disease of the outer canthus, back of the ear, cheek, neck, and shoulder; dispel wind; relieve exterior symptoms; relax the tendons; invigorate the channels and collaterals; remove obstruction from the yang wei mai; and cool hot conditions.

Massage techniques are the same as for Th 3.

Use with Gb 34 , Th 6, Liv 14, Bl 17, Bl 18, Bl 19, Bl 20, Cv 17, Liv 2, Liv 3, Liv 13, Gb 24, Sp 21, St 36, St 44, and St 45 for intercostal neuralgia.

Add to formula for deafness under Th 4.

Use with Gv 20, Gb 20, Co 4, Lu 7, Bl 12, Bl 13, Cv 17, Lu 1, and St 36 for common cold.

Applications:

The same as for Th 4; only after the point has been struck, grab the whole arm with your left and right hands and strike to his right hip with your left knee. Th 5 will cause the hips to become weak.

TH 6 (TRIPLE HEATER POINT NO. 6)

Chinese name:

Zhigou (branch supporting ditch).

Location:

3 cun above Th 4, 1 cun above Th 5, between the radius and ulna and the extensor digitorum and extensor hallucis longus muscles. With the palm down, the point is found on the radial side of the extensor digitorum muscle. *Zhi* means limbs, and *gou* means ditch; here zhi is referring to the upper limbs, and the ditch is between the radius and ulna.

Connections:

None.

Direction of strike:

Same as for Th 5.

Damage:

This is a fire and jing point. When struck using adverse qi, this point will weaken the sides of the body and cause intestinal problems at some later stage. In the long term, it will hinder the flow of qi throughout the body and cause heat to rise in the middle and upper heaters, resulting in mental and breathing problems. Immediately, though, the strike will cause intense pain and qi drainage, to the point where the recipient will have to sit down. It is usually used as a set-up point, however.

Set-up point:

None.

Antidote:

The opposite point on the other arm must be needled 5 fen perpendicular or massaged deeply.

Healing:

Innervation is by the posterior antebrachial cutaneous nerve and, deeper, the posterior interosseous nerve of the radial nerve and the anterior interosseous nerve of the median nerve. Irrigation is by the posterior and anterior interosseous arteries and veins.

Used for sudden hoarseness, tinnitus, deafness, aching and heavy sensation of shoulder and back, vomiting, constipation, angina intercostal neuralgia, pleurisy, and insufficient lactation.

Traditional indications include soreness and heaviness in the shoulder and arm, chest pain, belching, swollen throat, acute pain in the ribs and axilla, vomiting and diarrhea, constipation, cholecystitis, hypochondrium pain, and herpes zoster. As a jing river (traversing) point and a fire point of the Th meridian, its traditional functions are to regulate qi circulation, dispel stagnation and retardation, remove obstruction from the intestines, and harmonize and cool the three jiao (heaters).

Massage techniques are the same as for Th 3, plus pressing in slowly with both thumbs and releasing quickly, pulling the thumbs apart.

Use with St 36, St 37, St 25, Cv 12, Liv 13, Bl 25, Bl 26, Bl 20, Liv 3, Sp 15, and Bl 18 for chronic constipation.

Use with Cv 17, St 36, St 18, Sp 18, Liv 3, Si 1, Bl 18, Bl 20, and Liv 14 for insufficient lactation.

Use with Gb 34, Gb 43, Gb 44, thoracic jiaji points, Bl 17, Bl 18, Bl 19, Bl 20, Liv 2, Liv 3, St 44, Liv 14, Gb 24, and Liv 13 for intercostal neuralgia, cholecystitis, herpes zoster, and hypochondrium pain.

Applications:

The same as for Th 5.

TH 7 (TRIPLE HEATER NO. 7 POINT)

Chinese name:

Huizong (meeting of the clan).

Location:

3 cun proximal to the wrist, about 1 finger breadth lateral to Th 6 on the radial side of the ulna.

Connections:

None.

Direction of strike:

Straight in.

Damage:

This is a xie cleft point or an accumulation point. A strike to any xie cleft point causes the qi to explode everywhere, causing great qi disruption all over the body. So this is an excellent set-up point. Immediately, there is great pain, to the point that the recipient has to sit down.

Set-up point:

None.

Antidote:

Needle or massage the opposite point 3 fen perpendicular.

Healing:

Innervation is by the posterior and medial antebrachial cutaneous nerves and, deeper, the posterior and anterior interosseous nerves. Irrigation is by the posterior interosseous artery and vein.

Used for deafness, pain in the arms, and seizures.

H*ui* means meeting, and *zong* means gathering. This is the xie cleft point of the triple heater meridian, where the qi of the channel gathers, and its traditional function is to treat acute disorders of the three heaters.

Massage techniques are the same as for Th 6.

Use with Gb 2, Th 17, Th 21, Si 19, Kd 3, Gb 20, Gv 20, Co 4, Th 5, Th 6, and *yilong* (an extra point) for sudden deafness. Use with Co 4, Co 11, Th 5, Th 6, Th 8, Th 9, and Gb 34 for pain in the forearm.

Applications:

Same as for Th 6, then strike straight in to St 9.

TH 8 (TRIPLE HEATER POINT NO. 8)

Chinese name:

Sanyangluo (three yang connection).

Location:

4 cun above Th 4, between the radius and ulna and between the exterior digitorum and the origin of the abductor pollicis longus muscles.

Connections:

None.

Direction of strike:

Straight in to the point.

Damage:

This is one of the only points that cannot be built up to resist attack. (For instance, Co 10 can be built up by striking oneself as in many of the bagwazhang forms.) A strike here can cause death if it is hard enough. Th 8 with Cv 24 and Pc 6 is a deadly combination. There is immediate qi drainage with great pain and an itchy feeling that rises up into the chest and then into the head.

Set-up point:

Use neigwan.

Antidote:

If only Th 8 has been struck, then either massage the opposite point or needle it 5 fen perpendicular. If the combination has been used, there's not much you can do apart from years of acupuncture treatment and qigong (if the person survives!).

Healing:

Innervation and irrigation are the same as for Th 7.

Used for sudden hoarseness, deafness, pain in the hand and arm, aphasia, and postoperative pain associated with pneumonectomy.

Traditional indications include deafness, sudden muteness, pain in the forearm inhibiting movements, and lassitude.

Traditional functions are to clear the channels and sensory orifices.

Massage techniques are the same as for Th 6.

Use with Gb 20, Gv 20, Gb 21, Th 15, Si 13, Si 3, Gb 34, and Liv 3 for headache.

Use with Th 6, Bl 66, Gv 20, Cv 22, Cv 23, Gv 26, yintang, Liv 3, and Lu 1 for sudden muteness.

Applications:

Strike his right neigwan with your right palm. Hook that palm over his arm and pull it violently over to your right as your left palm strikes straight in to Th 8. Your right palm now attacks straight in to Cv 24 with a one-knuckle punch.

TH 9 (TRIPLE HEATER POINT NO. 9)

Chinese name:

Sidu (four ditch).

Location:

When the hand is palm down, the point is 5 cun below the olecranon (elbow), between the radius and ulna and the extensor carpi ulnaris muscle of the forearm.

Connections:

None.

Direction of strike:

Straight in to the upper forearm on the outside.

Damage:

This is more of a nerve and muscular strike when struck using a smaller weapon. It will take out the arm that us struck. There is also a feeling of sinking. In fact, the strike has been known to cause a person to fall down because of the qi drainage at this point.

Set-up point:

None.

Antidote:

None. Time usually fixes this strike. Or you could simply massage the whole region gently until the pain has stopped.

Healing:

Innervation and irrigation are the same as for Th 7.

Used for sudden hoarseness, deafness, toothache, pain in the forearm, headache, paralysis of the upper limbs, neurasthenia, and vertigo.

Traditional indications include sudden deafness, toothache in the lower jaw, loss of voice, obstructed pharynx, and pain in the forearm.

Massage is the same as for Th 6.

Use with Gb 20, Gv 20, Gb 8, taiyang, Co 4, Co 11, Liv 3, Gb 14, Gb 1, and Gb 21 for headache.

Use with yuyao, Bl 2, Pc 6, Gb 14, Bl 66, Bl 67, Th 1, Th 2, Liv 2, and Co 4 for supraorbital neuralgia.

Use with Co 10, Co 8, *yingxia* (an extra point), jiaji points in the upper back, Gb 34, Th 14, Co 15, and Gv 14 for paralysis of the wrist.

Traditional functions: *Si* means four, and *du* means river or ditch (the Yangtze, the Yellow, the Huaihe, and the Jishui rivers were called *sidu* in ancient times); the qi of the meridian is able to irrigate many more regions when it reaches this point.

Applications:

As he attacks, strike the point with your backfist or a knife edge strike.

TH 10 (TRIPLE HEATER POINT NO. 10)

Chinese name:

Tianjing (heaven's well).

Location:

When the elbow is flexed, the point is in the depression about 1 cun superior to the olecranon of the elbow. In the cavity above the olecranon at the posterior aspect of the lower end of the humerus and the superior margin of the olecranon prominence of the ulna, in the tendon of the triceps muscle.

Connections:

None.

Direction of strike:

Straight in to the back of the elbow.

Damage:

This is an earth and he point. A strike here will damage the communication of the whole system because this point attacks all three heaters. Weak areas of the body will begin to show up after a short time. I know of one athlete who received a blow at this point. He used to be a high jumper! He is no longer a high jumper because his legs became weakened. And although acupuncture helped to restore power, his legs were never back to full power. He is now an excellent javelin thrower. Continuous headaches are also a symptom of being struck at this point. Of course, the elbow is also damaged and could be broken.

Set-up point:

Use Th 8.

Antidote:

See a Chinese doctor and tell him or her that you have been struck at Th 10. The triple heater qigong will also help, and in most cases performing the qigong morning and night over a period of about one year is all you will need.

Healing:

Innervation is by the posterior brachial cutaneous nerve and the muscular branch of the radial nerve. Irrigation is by the arterial and venous network of the elbow.

This point is used for soft tissue disease of the elbow; migraine; tonsillitis; urticaria; scrofula; pain in the costal and hypochondriac regions; neck, shoulder, and arm pain; and epilepsy.

Traditional indications include pain in the neck, shoulder, and back; pain in the eyes; headache; deafness; throat blockage; tidal fever; and insanity.

Traditional functions: as an earth point and a he sea (uniting) point of the Th meridian, this point will strengthen the overall functions of the Th meridian. It also enhances the communication within the bodily system.

Massage techniques are the same as for Th 6.

Use with Cv 17, Liv 14, Liv 3, Bl 17, Bl 14, Bl 15, Bl 18, and Bl 46 for chest blockage with heart pain.

Use with Co 11, Ht 3, Co 10, Co 9, Si 8, Co 4, and Gb 34 for disease of the elbow.

Use with Gv 20 and *zaojian* (an extra point), use 5 to 7 cones of moxa on thin slices of ginger for scrofula.

Applications:

Strike his Th 8 point with your right backfist as he attacks with perhaps a right straight. Your left palm now attacks straight in to the elbow joint as your right palm pulls his wrist backward, thus also breaking the elbow.

TH 11 (TRIPLE HEATER POINT NO. 11)

Chinese name:

Qinglengyuan (cooling gulf).

Location:

1 cun above Th 10.

Connections:

None.

Direction of strike:

Straight in to the rear of the elbow, slightly (about 1 cun) above Th 10.

Damage:

This point can be used to weaken the elbow joint. In fact, most elbow breaks can be made using this location rather than the more common one of right on the elbow. The reason is that this point weakens the elbow joint in particular.

Set-up point:

Same as for Th 10.

Antidote:

See a doctor if the elbow is broken.

Healing:

Innervation is by the posterior brachial cutaneous nerve and the muscular branch of the radial nerve. Irrigation is by the terminal branches of the median collateral artery and vein.

Used for pain in the shoulder and arm, headache, and pain in the eyes.

Qing means cool, *leng* means cold, and *yuan* here means deep water. The function of this point is to eliminate heat from the sanjiao (three heaters), as if the patient were in cool deep water.

Massage techniques are the same as for Th 6.

Use with Th 23, Gb 1, Bl 1, St 1, Liv 2, Liv 3, Co 4, Gb 43, Gb 44, St 45, St 44, Gv 20, and Co 11 for pain and redness of the eyes.

Use with Th 13, Th 14, Gb 34, Th 15, Gb 21, Si 3, Si 10, and Si 11 for shoulder pain extending down the posterior aspect of the arm.

Applications:

The same as for Th 10, only strike 1 cun above Th 10 with the left palm.

TH 12 (TRIPLE HEATER POINT NO. 12)

Chinese name:

Xiaoluo (melting luo river).

Location:

On the line joining the olecranon and Th 14, midway between Th 11 and Th 13.

Connections:

None.

Direction of strike:

Straight in and using a backward/forward motion (like sawing) across the point. This has the effect of causing a nerve point strike as well as a qi strike.

Damage:

The damage here is to the whole arm. This point is used as a set-up point to drain qi from the whole body as well as a major point for arm locks and breaks. It is very easy to take the largest man down using this point in conjunction with an arm lock. When struck in a slightly upward direction, it will cause a huge amount of qi to be pumped into the head; thus it has the potential to cause a KO.

Set-up point:

Th 8.

Antidote:

Grab the whole triceps on each side and squeeze gently until the arm has returned to normal. An alternative treatment is to take hold of the wrist of the arm that was struck and shake it gently. Next rub down the outside of the forearm, then slap it at Co 10 and then at Th 8 gently with the flat of your palm.

Healing:

Innervation is by the posterior brachial cutaneous nerve and the muscular branch of the radial nerve. Irrigation is by the median collateral artery and vein.

Used for headache, stiffness and pain of the neck, pain in the arm, toothache, and seizures.

Traditional functions: *xiao* here means to eliminate, and *luo* means marsh. This point pertains to the triple heater (san jiao) meridian and its functions of regulating water passages and metabolism of fluids).

Massage techniques are the same as for Th 6.

Use with Gv 17, Bl 7, Cv 22, Cv 23, Sp 6, Liv 2, Liv 3, Liv 4, Co 41, Co 18, St 9, Gb 20, and Th 3 for goiter-type growth on the front of the neck.

Use with Th 13, Th 14, Th 11, Th 2, Th 1, and Gb 34 for pain in the triceps.

Applications:

To his right straight, use your right p'eng. Step to your left and grab his right wrist as the back of your left forearm saws across Th 12, using great pressure downward as well, to take him down to the ground.

TH 13 (TRIPLE HEATER POINT NO. 13)

Chinese name:

Naohui (shoulders meeting).

Location:

On the line joining the olecranon process (Th 10) to Th 14, 3 cun below Th 14, in the depression on the posterior inferior aspect of the deltoid muscle. *Nao* means muscle prominence of the upper arm.

Connections:

This is a point of wang wei mai and also receives a channel from Co 14.

Direction of strike:

Straight in.

Damage:

This is a point of the extra meridian yang wei mai, and, as such, can be used with other points to form devastating multiple strikes. It is also connected to Co 14, making for a most dangerous combination when these two points are struck. We have an energy (qi) input point (Co 14) and a Th point (Th 13) being struck one after the other (Co 14 first), blocking the "mother" qi, as well as unbalancing the whole qi system. After this strike, the fight is usually over.

Set-up point:

Th 8.

Antidote:

If the recipient is able to stand, have him stand in the seven stars qigong (described in Chapter 3, under the antidote for Bl 22). Otherwise have an acupuncturist treat him.

Healing:

Innervation is by the posterior brachial cutaneous nerve, the muscular branch of the radial nerve, and, deeper, the radial nerve. Irrigation is by the median collateral artery and vein.

Used for pain in the shoulder and arm and goiter.

Massage techniques are the same as for Th 6, and you can also do loose fist or open hand percussion on this point.

Use with Th 10, Th 11, Th 12, Th 14, and Gb 34 for weakness in flexing the elbow.

Use with Liv 3, Lu 3, St 11, Pc 5, Sp 6, Ht 6, Kd 7, Co 4, Pc 6, Bl 2, St 2, St 9, St 18, Gb 20, and Gv 14 for hyperthyroidism with swollen throat.

See Th 14 or Co 15 for treatment of shoulder problems.

Applications:

He attacks with a left straight. You strike his Th 8 point with your right palm to damage and block. Your waist has turned to your left, loaded and ready for your left elbow to come back across his Co 14 point. The waist has now loaded to your right, allowing your right palm to strike straight into Th 13.

TH 14 (TRIPLE HEATER POINT NO. 14)

Chinese name:

Jianliao (shoulder seam).

Location:

Posterior and inferior to the acromion, in the depression about 1 cun posterior to Co 15 in the deltoid muscle. *Jian* means shoulder, and *liao* means foramen; this point is in a foramen on the shoulder.

Connections:

Point of yang wei mai, and a path to Si 12.

Direction of strike:

Straight in to the back of the shoulder.

Damage:

This is also a yang wei mai point, so a strike here also has an effect upon many other points, including Si 12. There will be great scapular damage, along with a feeling of nausea caused by the connection to Si 12. This point is well protected, but a percussive strike that will send a shock wave inside the body will get in where a normal physical strike will not.

Set-up point:

Si 12.

Antidote:

You could massage the whole scapular region, including Si 11 and Si 12, then work on neigwan down the inside of the inner forearm.

Healing:

Innervation is by the muscular branch of the axillary nerve. Irrigation is by the muscular branch of the posterior circumflex humeral artery.

Used for heavy sensation in the shoulder, pain in the arm, hemiplegia, hypertension, excessive sweating, and perifocal inflammation of the shoulder joint.

To massage, press and hold; do rotations clockwise or counterclockwise for xu or shi conditions;

press in slowly with both thumbs and release quickly, pulling the thumbs apart; or do percussion with the fingertips, a loose fist, or the ulna side of an open hand.

Use with Th 13, Si 10, Si 9, Si 11, Si 13, Bl 43, Bl 17, Bl 13, Bl 11, Gb 34, St 38, Ht 1, and Bl 57 for perifocal shoulder joint.

Use with Si 11, Si 5, Th 10, Th 11, Th 12, Th 13, Co 4, and Gb 34 for arm pain.

Use with Co 15, Co 11, Co 4, Th 5, Th 14, Co 10, Th 4, Th 3, Gb 34, *bizhong* (an extra point), *zhitan* (an extra point), Gv 26, Kd 1, Pc 8, Gb 20, Pc 6, Gv 4, Bl 23, Liv 3, Bl 18, Bl 20, and Bl 17 for sequelae of CVA. .

Applications:

Strike his right neigwan with your right palm as he attacks with a right straight. Immediately, pull his arm across to your right, thus exposing his back. With your left palm, strike down onto Si 11, and, a split second later, Th 14.

TH 15 (TRIPLE HEATER POINT NO. 15)

Chinese name:

Tianliao (heaven's seam).

Location:

Midway between Gb 21 and Si 13, on the superior angle of the scapula. *Tian* means heaven, and *liao* means foramen; upper is referred to as heaven, and the point is in a foramen above the shoulder blade.

Connections:

A point of yang wei mai. Receives meridian from St 12. There is also an internal path to St 12, Cv 17, Cv 12, and Cv 7, returning to Cv 14.

Direction of strike:

Straight down on top of and slightly back from the shoulder.

Damage:

Because of the connection with St 12, this point will lessen the will to fight. However, because it is a Th point, it will do much more than that: it will also damage the whole qi system. It will also bring local pain all over the upper back area, causing a sick feeling in the stomach.

Set-up point:

Th 8 or St 12.

Antidote:

Triple heater qigong, or you could massage the opposite point on the shoulder.

Healing:

Innervation is by the accessory nerve and the branch of the suprascapular nerve. Irrigation is by the descending branch of the transverse cervical artery and, deeper, the muscular branch of the suprascapular artery.

This point is used for pain in the shoulder and arm, pain and stiffness of the neck, inflammation of the supraspinatus tendon, pain and soreness in the region of the scapula, and fever.

This is a point of intersection with the *yang wei mai*. It relaxes the tendons, invigorates the channels and collaterals, and soothes the joints.

Massage techniques are the same as for Th 14.

Use with Gb 20, Gb 21, Si 13, Si 14, Si 15, Si 3, Bl 11, Bl 12, Bl 13, Bl 43, Bl 17, Bl 18, Gb 34, Bl 60, dingchuan, Gv 14, bailao, and Bl 10 for occipital headache, neck and shoulder pain and stiffness, asthma, and inability to turn the head.

Use with Si 3, Si 9, Si 10, Si 11, Si 12, Si 13, Si 14, Si 16, Gb 34, and Gb 21 for inflammation of the suprascapular tendon.

Applications:

Strike St 12 using a claw palm downward This will take his will to fight away. Using that same claw on the clavicle, pull him around so that his back is now facing you. Strike straight down onto both Th 15 points.

TH 16 (TRIPLE HEATER POINT NO. 16)

Chinese name:

Tianyao (heaven's window).

Location:

Posterior and inferior to the mastoid process, on the posterior border of the sternocleidomastoid, level with Si 17 and Bl 10. Near the hairline, in the posterior margin at the insertion of the sternocleidomastoid muscle.

Connections:

Upper meeting point of the triple heater and pericardium divergent meridians. Takes an internal meridian from Gv 14.

Direction of strike:

Straight in from the side of the neck, just back from the angle of the jaw.

Damage:

Here we have one of the more dangerous point strikes. This will cause a KO all by itself by shocking the brain. It will also cause death if it is struck hard. It is a window of the sky point, and, as such, will place too much yang qi into the brain, causing confusion or KO. Emotional problems will also instantly seem far greater than they are. Many people who have been struck here say that they forgot the reason for beginning the confrontation in the first place. This is the major point of all the window of the sky points and, as such, it is very dangerous and should be avoided at all costs unless your life is threatened!

Set-up point:

Th 8.

Antidote:

None. Although, to treat the emotional disturbance caused by a strike to this point, you should have a Chinese doctor treat the same point.

Healing:

Innervation is by the lesser occipital nerve, and the point is irrigated by the posterior auricular artery.

Used for dizziness, facial swelling, sudden deafness, blurring of vision, neck rigidity, tinnitus, and sore throat.

Traditional indications include sudden deafness, sore eyes, constricted throat, excessive dreaming, and scrofula.

To massage, press and hold the point; do rotations clockwise or counterclockwise for xu or shi conditions; do fingertip percussion; and press in slowly with both thumbs and release quickly, pulling the thumbs apart.

Use with Si 19, Th 2, Th 21, Th 17, Th 7, Th 6, Th 5, Th 3, Th 2, Kd 3, Co 4, St 40, and Gv 20 for deafness and tinnitus.

Use with Th 17, Co 4, Co 11, Lu 5, Lu 7, Cv 22, St 9, and Si 17 for sore throat.

Use with St 5, St 6, Si 17, St 44, Si 18, Co 4, Co 11, St 4, St 45, Co 1, and Co 2 for facial swelling.

Traditional functions: *tian* means heaven, and *yao* means window. This point is on the upper lateral aspect of the neck and is used to open the upper aperture; thus it is likened to a heavenly window.

Figure 304

Applications:

He could attack with a right. You step to your left and strike Th 8 with your right backfist. Your left palm comes across to also slam his right forearm to take over the block as your right knife edge strikes straight across Th 16 (fig. 304).

TH 17 (TRIPLE HEATER POINT NO. 17)

Chinese name:

Yifeng (shielding wind or wind screen).

Location:

Posterior to the lobe of the ear, in the depression between the mandible and mastoid process.

Connections:

Gb and Si meridian branches enter the ear and Si 19 then travels to Th 21, 22, and 23.

Direction of strike:

This strike must travel from the rear of the head to the front, into just below the back of the earlobe.

Damage:

Here we have one of the most deadly strikes. It is difficult to get at if you don't know how, but when it is struck, there is no return! However, this point can also be used as a controlling point for doormen or bouncers, police, etc. In fact, it was used in Australia by police against protesters who were trying to avoid having their school closed down. When I saw this on the TV news, I was horrified that policemen were using this point against innocent people who were just sitting on the ground. The police would come up behind them one by one and stick their fingers in behind the ears and lift upward. They had the wrong direction, but it still worked to get them up on their feet! They had doctors on the TV saying that this was perfectly harmless! Little did they know that if the direction was changed slightly, they could have killed people!

If you are attacked by someone who is perhaps under the influence of drugs of alcohol, slap his face at a neurological shutdown point, then, holding his head still with one hand, take your other hand and, using the fingers, stick them into the point and pull forward. He will go with you! If he should resist or try to strike you, dig a little deeper and he will fall to the ground.

Set-up point:

Slam Th 8 upward on the outside of the forearm.

Antidote:

None. Even CPR will not work when this point is struck in the correct direction.

Healing:

Innervation is by the great auricular nerve and, deeper, the site where the facial nerve perforates out of the styomastoid foramen. Irrigation is by the posterior auricular artery and vein and the external jugular vein.

Use for tinnitus, deafness, deaf-mutism, parotitis, temporomandibular arthritis, toothache, sore eyes, facial paralysis, swelling of the cheek, and trismus.

Traditional indications include tinnitus, deafness, swelling of the cheek, convulsions, mouth and eyes awry, locked jaw, blurred vision, and membrane over the eye. This point is also much used for facial paralysis.

This is a point of intersection with the Gb meridian. Its traditional functions are to dispel wind, invigorate the channels and collaterals, soothe the ears, and benefit hearing and vision. *Yi* means shielding, and *feng* means pathogenic wind; because this point is behind the earlobe, it is the place for shielding off pathogenic wind.

Massage techniques are the same as for Th 16.

See Th 16 for treatment of deafness, tinnitus, and sore throat. Use with St 6, Co 4, Liv 2, Liv 3, Lu 7, and Gb 20 for parotitis.

Use with St 7, St 6, St 5, St 36, Gb 34, Liv 3, Gb 21, Gb 20, and Co 4 for temporomandibular arthritis.

Use with Ht 5, Liv 3, St 36, Gv 20, Co 4, and Lu 7 for sudden loss of voice.

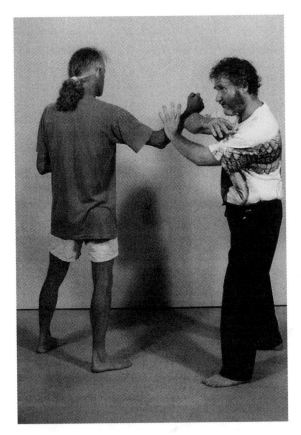

Figure 305

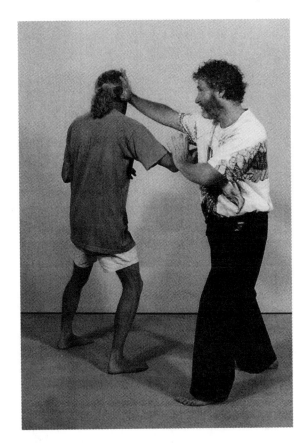

Figure 306

Applications:

Unless you can get around behind the attacker and strike him from the rear to get the correct direction, you will have to know the taijiquan method of striking to this point. It comes from the posture known as *arn* (push) right. This is the very first attacking movement from the Yang-style taijiquan form.

He attacks with a straight right. You step quickly to your left with your left foot parrying his right forearm and slamming Th 8 point back up his arm. Notice that your right palm is already getting ready, coming up underneath your left arm (fig. 305). You have turned your waist to your right. As you turn your waist back to the left, your right palm strikes to behind his ear at Th 17 in the correct direction (fig. 306).

TH 18 (TRIPLE HEATER POINT NO. 18)

Chinese name:

Qimai (feeding the vessels).

Location:

In the center of the mastoid process, at the junction of the middle and lower thirds of the curve by Th 17 and Th 20, posterior to the helix at the root of the auricle.

Connections:

None.

Direction of strike:

Straight in to the side of the head back from the ear.

Damage:

This is also a very dangerous strike because the brain is shocked. A hard strike here can cause death. KO will occur with a medium strike here.

Set-up point:

Also Th 8 upward on the outer forearm.

Antidote:

If death has occurred, try CPR or the heart starter (mentioned earlier and also in my other books on dim-mak).

Healing:

Innervation is by the posterior auricular branch of the great auricular nerve. Irrigation is by the posterior auricular artery and vein.

Used for headache, tinnitus, deafness, and infantile convulsions.

Traditional functions: *qi* means convulsions here, and *mai* means channel or collateral. This point is behind the ear where the collaterals are distributed, and it is useful for treating convulsions.

Massage techniques are the same as for Th 16.

Use with Th 17, Si 19, Th 21, Gb 2, Gv 15, Cv 23, Co 4, Th 3, yiming, Kd 3, Liv 3, Pc 9, Th 9, Bl 23, Bl 18, and Bl 20 for deaf-mutism.

Use with Gv 20, Gb 20, Th 16, Th 17, Th 19, Th 20, Gb 8, Liv 3, Gb 41, Gb 43, Gb 44, Liv 4, Liv 8, and Co 4 for headache.

Applications:

The same as for Th 17, only bring the strike straight in to the head rather than in a back to front direction.

TH 19 (TRIPLE HEATER POINT NO. 19)

Chinese name:

Luxi (skull's rest).

Location:

Posterior to the ear, at the junction of the upper and middle thirds of the curve formed by Th 17 and Th 20, behind the helix or 1 cun above Th 18 behind the ear.

Connections:

None.

Direction of strike:

Straight in to the side of the head just above Th 18.

Damage:

Combine this strike with Th 18, and you have a recipe for death when a hard blow is felt. (Your palm can strike both points at the same time.) With a medium shot, the recipient is knocked out or totally disoriented. This is because of the location of the point with reference to the physical parts of the brain. The brain is shocked and shuts down.

Set-up point:

Th 8 struck upward.

Antidote:

CPR.

Healing:

Innervation is by the anastomotic branch of the great auricular nerve and the lessor occipital nerve. Irrigation is by the posterior auricular artery and vein.

Used for headache, tinnitus, earache, otitis media, and vomiting. This point is part of the branch region for the Th meridian. *Lu* means skull, and *xi* means tranquillity. The point is on the skull, and its traditional function is to calm the mind.

Massage techniques are the same as for Th 16.

Use with Pc 6, Cv 12, St 36, Bl 20, Bl 21, Bl 18, and Liv 3 to treat vomiting.

See Th 18 for treatment of deaf-mutism.

Use with Th 16, Th 17, Th 18, Th 21, Si 19, Th 3, Th 9, Kd 3, St 40, Gb 20, Gv 20, Gb 21, Gb 2, and Th 5 for tinnitus.

Applications:

The same as for Th 17, only straight in to the side of the head.

TH 20 (TRIPLE HEATER POINT NO. 20)

Chinese name:

Jiaosun (angle of regeneration).

Location:

Directly above the apex of the ear, within the hairline of the temple. *Jiao* here means corner, and *sun* means reticular collateral. This point is on the temporal region corresponding to the ear apex, where the reticular meridians are distributed.

Connections:

Connected to the gallbladder meridian. A point of intersection with the Gb and Co meridians. There is also an internal path of the meridian to Gb 5, Gb 4, Gb 14, Bl 1; then it encircles the cheek to Si 18.

Direction of strike:

Straight in to the side of the head just above the top point of the ear.

Damage:

This point must be struck fairly hard to have any effect. But when it does have an effect, it is substantial. The recipient will experience extreme dizziness and fall down, with great nausea. A KO will occur with a medium to hard strike.

Set-up point:

Th 8.

Antidote:

See a doctor.

Healing:

Innervation is by the branches of the auriculotemporal nerve, and irrigation is by the branches of the superficial temporal artery and vein.

Used for redness and swelling of the ear; redness, swelling, and pain of the eye; toothache; pannus; and parotitis.

As a point of intersection with the Gb and Co meridians, its traditional function is to influence those meridians.

Massage techniques are the same as for Th 16.

See Th 18 and Th 19 for treatment of tinnitus and headache.

Use with Co 4, Co 11, Gb 43, Gb 44, Gb 2, Th 21, Si 19, Si 1, Si 2, and Si 3 for redness and swelling of the ear.

Applications:

Slam his right neigwan with your right palm as he attacks with a straight right. Immediately pull his right arm around so that the side of his body is facing you. Now, your right palm will strike straight in to Th 20.

TH 21 (TRIPLE HEATER POINT NO. 21)

Chinese name:

Ermen (ear's door).

Location:

In the depression anterior to the supratragic notch and slightly superior to the condyloid process of the mandible. The point is located with the mouth open. *Er* means ear, and *men* means door; this point is in front of the ear, like a door to the ear.

Connections:

None.

Direction of strike:

In to just before the ear notch, a little above it and slightly angled toward the ear.

Damage:

This strike causes a sickly feeling to slowly move down the whole chest area, much like the feeling one gets when attacked in a controlling manner at Th 17. Struck hard, it will cause KO. This sickly feeling will turn into a nagging pain after some time, causing the recipient to feel like he is having a heart attack. You must use the antidote to right this condition.

Set-up point:

Th 8.

Antidote:

Apply finger pressure to St 15 and St 16, beginning with St 15 on both sides. The pressure should be almost to the point of pain.

Healing:

Innervation is by the branches of the auriculotemporal nerve and facial nerve. Irrigation is by the superficial temporal artery and vein.

Used for deafness, tinnitus, otorrhea, toothache, deaf-mutism, and temperomandibular arthritis.

Traditional indications include tinnitus, deafness, pus in the ear, toothache in the upper jaw, pain in the jaw, and headache. Traditional functions are to open the ear and disperse heat. You can use the root of the Gb meridian (Gb 42) in conjunction with the branch of the Th meridian (Th 21) for conditions such as tinnitus.

To massage press and hold the point; do rotations clockwise or counterclockwise for xu or shi conditions; or press in slowly with both thumbs and release quickly, pulling the thumbs apart.

Use with Si 19, Gb 2, Gb 42, Gb 20, Th 2, Th 3, Th 4, Th 5, Th 6, Th 7, Th 8, Th 9, Th 16, Th 17, Th 18, Th 19, Th 22, Kd 3, Gb 3, Gb 4, Gb 10, Gb 11, Gb 43, Gb 44, and St 40 for tinnitus, deafness, deaf-mutism, otorrhea, etc.

Use with Gb 20, Gb 14, Gb 12, Gb 41, Gb 43, Gb 44, Gb 34, Gb 21, taiyang, Co 4, Co 11, Th 1, Th 2, Th 3, and Th 5 for one-sided headache.

Applications:

Slam his right straight with your left palm at Th 8 upward on the forearm as your right one-knuckle punch attacks over the top to Th 21.

TH 22 (TRIPLE HEATER POINT NO. 22)

Chinese name:

Heliao (harmony's seam).

Location:

Anterior and superior to Th 21, level with the of the auricle, on the natural hairline of the temple where the superficial temporal artery passes.

Connections:

None.

Direction of strike:

Straight in to the side of the head, again angled slightly toward the back of the head.

Damage:

This point is much the same as Th 21, only there is also great local pain and qi drainage. Because of its location, it can cause KO, but the strike must be quite hard. Using a palm strike to this point, you will also get a number of other points like Gb 3, which when struck together will cause death.

Set-up point:

Th 8.

Antidote:

Place both palms onto the sides of the forehead and push backward toward the back of the skull, stretching the skin lightly. If death has occurred, of course, perform CPR.

Healing:

Innervation is by the branch of the auriculotemporal nerve, on the course of the temporal branch of the facial nerve. Irrigation is by the superficial temporal artery and vein.

Used for tinnitus, headache, heavy sensation of the head, lockjaw, and facial paralysis.

This is a point of intersection with the Gb and Si channels. *He* means harmony, and *liao* means foramen; the point is in the depression in front of the supratragic notch, and its traditional function is to improve hearing.

Massage techniques are the same as for Th 21.

Use with St 5, St 6, St 7, St 8, Gb 20, Gb 21, Gb 34, Co 4, Si 19, Liv 3, and Gb 41 for locked jaw.

See Th 21 for treatment of tinnitus, deafness, pus in ear, etc.

Applications:

The same as for Th 21, only use a palm instead of the one-knuckle punch.

TH 23 (TRIPLE HEATER POINT NO. 23)

Chinese name:

Sizhukong (silken bamboo hollow).

Location:

In the depression at the lateral end of the eyebrow, on the lateral border of the zygomatic process of the frontal bone, in the orbicularis oculi muscle. *Sizhu* means slender bamboo, and *kong* means space; the point is at the lateral end of the eyebrow, which looks like a slender bamboo, and it is in a shallow depression.

Connections:

There is a link from here to Gb 1.

Direction of strike:

This point must be struck downward, usually using a heel palm strike. It can also be struck with an alternative direction of downward and slightly toward the eye.

Damage:

When I first discovered this point (i.e., had it worked on me), I became very excited. This point is one of the very dangerous variety and will cause a KO very easily when struck in the correct direction. The heel of the palm must strike just above the corner of the eye in the hollow above the eye bone, then it glances downward over the side of the eye. You must catch the heel palm in that hollow striking to the upper edge of the eye bone. When struck right on, it doesn't need too much power to cause a KO. A hard strike will cause death, however. This point will drain qi dramatically from the lower heating space and also from the middle heating space. My 7-year-old son (at that time) was able to knock me out with a light blow to this area.

Immediately the recipient feels great local pain. A split second later, there is a sinking feeling in the chest and abdomen as the qi is drained, then the knees go and the KO occurs. Even after the recipient has been revived, the legs are shaky. When this point is struck slightly inward toward the eye, still with a downward motion, it can cause blindness.

Set-up point:

Either use neigwan or Th 8, depending on the technique used.

Antidote:

Squeeze Gb 20 points upward. If the alternative direction has been used, treat the opposite point, needling 3 fen horizontally toward Gb 3.

Healing:

Innervation is by the zygomatic branch of the facial nerve and the branch of the auriculotemporal nerve. Irrigation is by the frontal branches of the superficial temporal artery and vein.

Used for headache, blurring of vision, redness and pain of the eye, twitching of the eyelid, and facial paralysis.

Traditional indications include lateral and midline headaches, red eyes, vertigo, ingrown eyelash, blurred vision, seizures, and insanity.

Traditional functions are to dispel wind, stop pain, clear fire, and brighten the eyes.

Massage techniques are the same as for Th 21.

Use with Th 3, Gb 20, Gv 20, Co 4, Liv 3, Gb 41, Gb 34, Gb 21, Gb 14, and taiyang for migraine headache.

Use with Bl 1, St 1, Bl 2, Gb 1, Liv 2, Liv 3, Co 4, Gb 20, and yuyao for red, sore, swollen eyes.

Use with Th 22, St 2, St 4, St 8, St 6, St 44, St 36, Liv 3, Gb 34, Gv 20, Gb 21, and Bl 2 for facial paralysis.

Applications:

He attacks with a right hook. Slam his right neigwan with your left knife-edge palm as you right palm heel slams down onto Th 23.

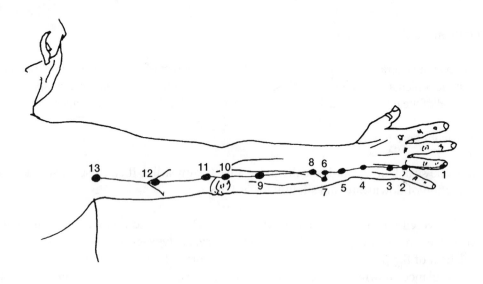

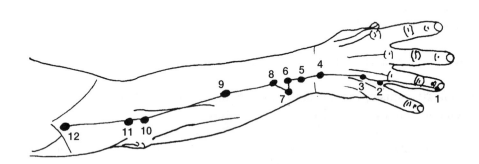

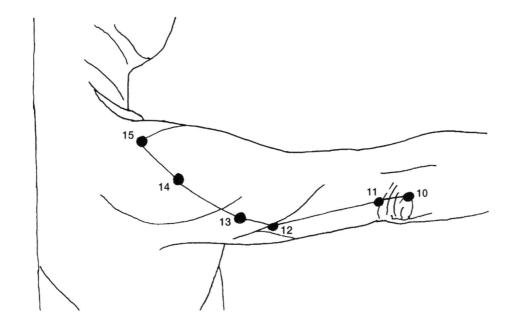

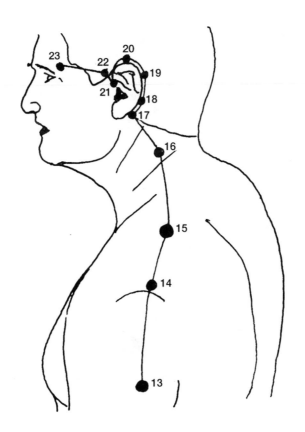

Chapter 12

The Pericardium Meridian

The pericardium is the sac that hangs around the heart to protect it. It consists of two layers of fibrous tissue with a small space between them. The inside layer covers the heart like skin, but the outer layer is much looser, allowing for the heart to move. The space between the two layers is filled with a thin layer of pericardium film, which is a lubricant between the heart and the sac. It also supports the heart and cushions it as it beats.

THE TCM VIEW

The Chinese element for the pericardium is fire. Its yang counterpart is the triple heater. Pericardium is yin, and its role in the social structure of the body is the protector or bodyguard of the supreme controller (heart).

When we are attacked by external pathogenic factors, it is usually from the external layers to the deep layers. When external pathogenic factors attack the heart, they have to invade the pericardium first, which causes sweating, fevers, delirium, restlessness, dry mouth, and dizziness. Ancient Chinese thought enlikened the relationship of the heart and pericardium to the emperor and his official who takes all the flak, thus protecting the emperor. It is widely thought nowadays that although external pathogenic factors may attack only the pericardium, internal emotional factors will attack the pericardium as well as the heart.

In dim-mak, the pericardium meridian is usually considered to be used for setting up other points because of Pc 6 or neigwan, which is the best known set-up point (as you have probably noticed, I have used it many, many times in this book). It is easy to get to, one must strike it to simply block an oncoming attack, and it is one of the best qi drainage points known. It is also a utility point in the healing area, used to calm the whole body, help with motion sickness and nausea, and help when someone is having a fit.

There are a few points on the Pc meridian, however, that are just as dangerous as some of the other points on other meridians. These are easy to get to and can be struck in a number of directions, causing different reactions. Because of its close relationship to the heart, the pericardium points will also affect the heart. One instance I remember well is that when I was teaching movement therapies at the New South Wales College of Natural Medicine in Sydney, Australia, one girl who was studying taijiquan with me as part of her TCM course had great difficulty performing the postures known as "brush knee twist step." This was more than your normal uncoordination; she actually vomited whenever she came to this particular posture. So I asked her if she had anything wrong with her heart. She said no, but that she did have a pericardium disease! The posture was trying to fix the problem and, in doing so, causing her great discomfort. That experience confirmed the close relationship between heart and pericardium.

There is another area of this relationship—that of internal striking (which I will cover in the second volume). It is actually possible to strike the pericardium, for instance, using the correct mental attitude and physical way of attacking. In this way, we can cause the attack to act like an external pathogenic factor that will search out and destroy the heart! In this chapter, however, I will only cover the basic strikes to the pericardium points.

PC 1 (PERICARDIUM POINT NO. 1)

Chinese name:

Tianchi (heaven's pool).

Location:

1 cun lateral to the nipple, in the 4th intercostal space. *Tian* means heaven, and *chi* means pool; the point is lateral to the breast, and the milk secreted from the breast is like nectar from a heavenly pool.

Connections:

Receives an internal path from the main meridian after it leaves Cv 7, Cv 12, Cv 13.

Direction of strike:

Angled slightly toward the middle of the body.

Damage:

Pc 1 is one of those points that will affect the heart whether struck on left or right side. It will also have an effect upon the lungs, causing coughing and an itchy feeling in the neck. It will drain qi from the heart and lungs, thus causing great damage to the whole system. It is a mu point of the pericardium, meaning that it is an alarm point. Tenderness here usually means that something is wrong with the organ. When it is struck, there *will* be tenderness. It is also a window of the sky point; thus it will have an effect upon the emotions. Used with Sp 17, this is a devastating double point strike, causing great internal damage with little or no external damage, and it can be used in cases where one does not wish to show physical damage! Death can occur when this combination is struck, and a cause of death is often hard to ascertain other than from a heart attack. This is not a point to play around with in demonstration! This point has also been known to affect the kidneys.

Set-up point:

All of the pericardium points are set up by neigwan (other than neigwan, of course).

Antidote:

You can massage using thumb pressure right over the opposite point; only medium pressure is used here. If the heart has stopped, use Kd 1 as the heart starter.

Healing:

Innervation is by the muscular branch of the anterior thoracic nerve and the fourth intercostal nerve. Irrigation is by the

Figure 307

thoracoepigastric vein and the branches of the lateral thoracic artery and vein.

Used for suffocating sensation in the chest, pain in the hypochondriac region, swelling and pain of the axillary region, angina pectoris, and intercostal neuralgia.

To massage, press and hold; do rotation clockwise or counterclockwise for xu or shi conditions; press in slowly with both thumbs and release quickly, pulling the thumbs apart; and do fingertip percussion on males.

Use with Cv 17, Cv 14, Liv 14, Liv 3, Pc 6, Bl 17, and Bl 18 for a stuffy sensation in the chest.

Use with Sp 21, Gb 22, Gb 23, Bl 17, Bl 18, Bl 19, Bl 16, Bl 15, Gb 41, Gb 43, Gb 44, and Ht 7 for swelling and pain in the axillary region.

Applications:

In defense against his right straight or hook, you would slam his right neigwan with your right palm, straight in this time, as your left palm comes underneath to take over the block. Now, your right hammer fist will slam into Pc 1 in the correct direction (fig. 307). Using this method, you do not have to know the correct direction since the technique itself dictates it.

PC 2 (PERICARDIUM POINT NO. 2)

Chinese name:

Tianquan (heaven's spring).

Location:

2 cun below the end of the anterior axillary fold, between the two heads of the biceps brachii muscle.

Connections:

None.

Direction of strike:

In from the inside of the upper arm.

Damage:

Again, this point will also affect the heart and can be used in conjunction with Lu 3 in a claw type of grab to cause great qi disruption and drainage. I have experienced this claw, and it will put someone on his knees if used correctly. Local pain and nerve damage are also apparent. The strike to Pc 2 can sometimes take the breath away, with the recipient exhaling and sinking at the same time.

Set-up point:

Neigwan.

Antidote:

Apply medium pressure, sliding from Cv 17 down to Cv 14 with the thumb or the heel palm.

Healing:

Used for pain in the cardiac region, distension of the hypochondriac region, cough, pain in the chest, back, and medial side of the upper arm, angina, and palpitations.

Traditional functions: *tian* means heaven and *quan* means spring. The qi of the meridian, originating from Pc 1 (tianchi), flows downward like spring water from heaven. This is a water and he point, which frees heart qi. It is also the main point used to remove heat from the blood. It adjusts the intestines and calms rebellious qi.

Figure 308

To massage, press and hold, do rotations clockwise or counterclockwise for xu or shi conditions, and do fingertip percussion.

Use with St 16, Sp 18, St 18, Kd 22, Bl 18, Ht 1, Bl 43, Bl 44, Gb 21, Cv 17, Pc 7, Si 1, Bl 40, St 36, Liv 3, Liv 14, and Th 10 for acute mastitis.

Use with jianneling, Pc 3, Gb 34, Co 15, Co 14, Co 4, Bl 17, Bl 14, and Bl 43 for pain in the medial upper region of the arm.

Applications:

You would probably use the "dragon prawn" method to defend against his straight attack. The right palm blocks at neiguan as the left comes underneath to take over the block. You slam him on the side of the jaw with your right back palm to effect a neurological shutdown, and then your right palm digs into the upper biceps of his right arm, the thumb going in to Pc 2 while the fingers go into Lu 3 (fig. 308).

PC 3 (PERICARDIUM POINT NO. 3)

Chinese name:

Quze (crooked marsh).

Location:

On the transverse cubital crease, at the ulnar side of the tendon of the biceps brachii muscle. *Qu* means curve, and *ze* means marsh; the qi of the meridian infuses into the shallow depression of the elbow like water flowing into a marsh.

Connections:

None.

Direction of strike:

Straight in to the point and slightly toward you down the arm, or slightly up the arm, depending upon what organs you wish to affect.

Damage:

This is a water and he point. It will affect the heart and intestines. It will add heat to the heart, causing long-term effects such as cold sores on the mouth and lips, too much talking about nothing, etc. It will also affect the emotions, especially later in life.

Here we have a triple strike if you also strike to Ht 3 and Lu 5, resulting in extreme qi drainage that would stop the heart and the lungs from working. So these three points are not to be played around with! All by itself, Pc 3 will drain energy and affect the heart when struck downward toward the wrist. It will affect the lungs when struck slightly upward in the opposite direction. All three points can be accessed with a knife-edge strike straight across the inside of the lower upper arm just above the elbow joint, angled slightly downward to get at Lu 5 as well. The triple strike is far more effective than using one or two of these points together.

Set-up point:

Pc 6.

Antidote:

Use Kd 1 to bring back the yang qi, then use the heart starter or CPR. If extreme nausea is the result, then pressure Pc 6 up the inside of the forearm.

Healing:

Innervation is by the median nerve, and irrigation is by the brachial artery and vein.

Used for gastric pain, vomiting, febrile disease, irritability, pain in the cardiac region, palpitations, pain in the elbow and arm, tremor of the hand, acute gastroenteritis, enteritis, rheumatic heart disease, myocarditis, bronchitis, and heat exhaustion.

Traditional indications include chest pain, being easily frightened, heat exhaustion, diarrhea with vomiting (acute gastroenteritis), fever, irritability, and fullness.

Traditional functions are to open up the heart, drain heat from the blood, and regulate the intestines. It is a water point and a he sea (uniting) point of the Pc meridian.

Massage with the arm slightly flexed. Press and hold, or do rotations clockwise or counterclockwise for xu or shi conditions.

Use with Pc 6, Pc 5, Cv 17, Bl 15, Bl 14, Bl 43, Bl 17, Bl 18, Liv 3, St 36, and Ht 8 for rheumatic heart disease.

Use with Pc 6, Pc 7, Cv 17, Bl 17, Bl 15, Bl 14, Bl 18, Co 4, Liv 3, Liv 14, Bl 23, and St 36 for chest pain.

Use with Pc 6, Co 4, Co 11, St 36, Cv 12, Cv 14, St 21, St 25, Bl 20, Bl 25, Bl 40 (best to prick with a sterile needle and extract a drop of blood from this point for this condition), and Liv 3 for acute gastroenteritis.

Applications:
To his right hook, using both knife edges, strike to neigwan with your left palm and to Pc 3, Ht 3, and Lu 5 with your right palm.

PC 4 (PERICARDIUM POINT NO. 4)

Chinese name:
Ximen (gate of the crevice).

Location:
5 cun above the transverse crease of the wrist, on the line connecting Pc 3 to Pc 7, between the tendons of the palmaris longus and flexor carpi radialis muscles, in the flexor digitorum superficialis manus muscle. In its deep position, it is in the flexor digitorum sublimus muscle.

Connections:
None.

Direction of strike:
Straight in to the inner forearm. You could also include Pc 5 and 6 in this strike.

Damage:
This point will affect the heart, especially if the recipient has an angina problem. In this case, the heart will stop immediately. In the case of a normal, healthy person, it will weaken the heart, opening it up to external pathogenic attack that will break through the pericardium easily.

The strike is made more effective if Pc 5 and 6 are included. Pc 4 is a xie cleft point, which will cause the heart to become tense and beat faster for no reason, causing high blood pressure. It also has an effect upon the shen or spirit.

Set-up point:
Pc 6.

Antidote:
Use the opposite xie cleft point on the opposite arm to calm the heart and to send stored qi into the whole chest area to remove the blockages caused by the strike.

Healing:
Innervation is by the medial antebrachial cutaneous nerve and, deeper, the median nerve—and, deepest, the anterior interosseous nerve. Irrigation is by the median artery and vein and, deeper, the anterior interosseous artery and vein.

Used for cardiac pain, palpitations, hematemesis (vomiting blood), epistaxis, furuncles (boils), rheumatic heart disease, myocarditis, angina pectoris, mastitis, pleurisy, spasm of the diaphragm, and hysteria.

Traditional indications include irritability and pain in the chest, depression, chest pain with vomiting, and fear of strangers.

As a xie cleft (accumulating) point of the Pc meridian, its traditional functions are to treat acute problems of the organ and channel (it is a special point for angina), pacify the heart and calm the spirit, regulate the qi, expand the diaphragm, and open the chest. *Xi* means cleft, *men* means door; this is a point where the qi of this meridian enters and exits.

Massage techniques include pressing and holding the point; doing rotations clockwise or counterclockwise for xu or shi conditions; pressing in slowly with both thumbs and releasing quickly, pulling the thumbs apart; and doing fingertip percussion on the point.

Use with Pc 6, Cv 17, Liv 14, Liv 3, St 36, Co 4, Bl 17, Bl 14, Pc 3, Pc 8, and Si 11 for angina.
Use with Co 4, Co 11, Th 8, Sp 10, and Bl 17 for hemoptysis.
Use with Pc 6, Pc 3, Pc 5, and Ht 8 for rheumatic heart disease.

Applications:
The same as for Pc 3.

PC 5 (PERICARDIUM POINT NO. 5)

Chinese name:
Jianshi (intermediary).
Location:
3 cun above the transverse crease of the wrist, between the tendons of the muscles palmaris longus and flexor carpii radialis, in the flexor digitorum superficialis manus muscle. In its deep position, it is in the flexor digitorum sublimis muscle.
Connections:
None.
Direction of strike:
Straight in to the lower forearm on the inside of the arm.
Damage:
This is a metal and jing point. It will have an effect upon the mind, causing it to become scattered and tense, verging upon mental illness. The heart will also be affected adversely. The heart-lung balance will be disturbed, thus draining qi and causing great weakness. Used with Pc 6 and Pc 4, this point has the potential to stop the heart! Digestion will also be affected greatly.
Set-up point:
Pc 6.
Antidote:
Massage the opposite Pc 5 point upward.
Healing:
Innervation is by the medial and lateral antebrachial cutaneous nerves, the palmar cutaneous branch of the median nerve, and, deepest, the anterior interosseous nerve. Irrigation is by the median artery and vein and, deeper, the anterior interosseous artery and vein.

Used for cardiac pain, palpitations, gastric pain, vomiting, febrile disease, irritability, malaria, mental disorders, epilepsy, swelling of the axilla, twitching or contracture of the elbow, pain of the arm, rheumatic heart disease, seizures, hysteria, and psychosis.

Traditional indications include chest pain, palpitations, stomachache and vomiting, tidal fever, yellow eyes, insanity, generalized scabies, and irregular menstruation.

This is a metal point and a jing river (traversing) point of the Pc meridian. Its traditional functions are to calm the spirit, harmonize the stomach, eliminate phlegm, dispel fullness in the chest, stop pain, and clear internal heat. It is also a special point for malaria. *Jian* means space, and *shi* means minister of the monarchy; the space is between the two tendons, and the pericardium is the minister of the heart.

Massage techniques are the same as for Pc 4.
Use with Bl 11, Sp 6, Co 4, Lu 9, Bl 20, and Gv 14 for tidal fever.
Use with Kd 1, Si 3, Co 4, Co 11, St 40, Bl 20, Bl 25, Cv 12, Gv 20, yintang, Sp 9, Kd 2, Pc 3, Pc 8, Ht 7, and Cv 17 for insanity.
Use with Sp 6, St 9, Co 4, Co 11, Cv 23, Ht 6, Kd 7, Bl 2, St 2, Gb 20, anmien, qiying, Liv 3, Liv 2, and St 36 for hyperthyroidism.
Applications:
The same as for Pc 4.

PC 6 (PERICARDIUM POINT NO. 6)

Chinese name:

Neigwan (inner gate).

Location:

2 cun above the transverse crease of the wrist, between the tendons of the palmaris longus and flexor carpi radialis muscles, in the flexor digitorum superficialis manus muscle. In its deep position, it is in the flexor digitorum sublimis muscle. *Nei* means inner, and *gwan* means pass; this point is an important site on the medial aspect of the forearm, like a passage where the qi on the meridian comes in and out.

Connections:

Transverse luo to Th 4 and Th 1.

Direction of strike:

Straight in, or downward.

Damage:

This is one of the best set-up points and is used a great deal in dim-mak and healing. It is a luo point and a master point for yinwei mai and a coupled point of chong mai. When struck, it will upset the yin-yang balance in the body, causing confusion internally. It can cause mental illness at most or mental instability and confusion at least. It is one of the best qi drainage points. This point is usually struck using a violent grab or a strike. It can be incorporated into wrist locks using the fingers to dig into the point, making the lock much easier to get on and to hold. This strike will cause great internal activity for no reason, so the heart will race for no reason, the lungs will try to take in more air for no reason, etc. A strike straight in will cause great nausea, and I have seen a recipient turn green and throw up when he was struck accidentally on this point.

Set-up point:

None.

Antidote:

Use the opposite neigwan, fingering it upward on the arm. Also, massage the opposite point on the outside of the forearm downward, using the second knuckle when the fist is closed, which is Th 6.

Healing:

Innervation and irrigation are the same as for Pc 5.

Used for cardiac pain, palpitations, gastric pain, vomiting, mental disorders, epilepsy, contracture and pain of the elbow and forearm, febrile disease, malaria, rheumatic heart disease, shock, angina pectoris, abdominal pain, spasm of the diaphragm, migraine, hyperthyroidism, hysteria, asthma, swollen and painful throat, and pain associated with surgery. Traditional indications include chest pain, disease of the chest, vomiting, nausea, disharmony between the stomach and spleen, tidal fever, jaundice, apoplexy, prolapsed rectum, and an attack by the liver on the stomach/spleen.

Traditional functions are to calm the heart and shen (spirit), regulate the qi, suppress pain, promote the function of the stomach, regulate the middle heater, open the chest, and open the yin wei mai. It is a master point of yin wei mai, and so has a profound effect on the three systems (cardiovascular, digestive, and mental/nervous). It is also a luo point of the Pc meridian and the root area of the Pc meridian.

Massage techniques are the same as for Pc 4.

Use with Co 4, Co 11, Cv 17, Cv 14, Cv 12, Bl 14, Bl 15, Bl 17, St 36, Liv 3, Liv 4, Liv 14, Ht 7, Sp 6, Bl 18, and Bl 20 for angina and chest pain.

Use with Co 4, Co 11, Lu 7, St 36, St 25, Cv 12, St 21, Liv 3, Liv 13, Sp 3, Sp 5, and Sp 9 for nausea, vomiting, and stomach flu.

Use with Pc 5, Ht 8, and Pc 3 for rheumatic heart disease.

Use with dingchuan, Bl 12, Bl 13, Bl 43, Bl 17, Bl 18, Cv 22, Cv 17, Cv 12, Cv 14, St 36, Liv 3, Liv 14, Lu 1, Lu 9, Lu 6, Lu 7, Co 4, Kd 7, Kd 3, and Bl 23 for asthma.

Use with Gv 25, Gv 20, Gv 14, Gv 4, St 36, Liv 3, Bl 14, Bl 17, Bl 15, and Kd 3 for low blood pressure.

Use with St 36, Ht 7, Co 4, Liv 3, Cv 12, Bl 20, Bl 18, Bl 17, Bl 43, Gv 20, Cv 17, and Liv 13 for shock.

Applications:

All of the techniques using neigwan that I have covered to great extent in this book.

PC 7 (PERICARDIUM POINT NO. 7)

Chinese name:

Daling (big tomb).

Location:

In the depression in the middle of the transverse crease of the wrist, between the tendons of the palmaris longus and flexor carpi radialis muscles, and in the flexor hallucis longus muscle and the tendon of the flexor digitorum sublimis muscle. *Da* means big or large, and *ling* means tomb or mound; the protrusion of the palmar root is quite large, like a mound, and the point is in the depression of the wrist proximal to it.

Connections:

None.

Direction of strike:

Straight in to the wrist.

Damage:

This is an earth, yuan, and shu point. A strike here will have an immediate effect upon the heart, shocking it sufficiently to enable a more deadly strike. So this point is used as a set-up point for strikes to other meridians, such as the heart. It will cause too much heat in the heart.

Set-up point:

None.

Antidote:

Finger pressure the opposite Pc 7 point on the opposite arm. This will cool the heart.

Healing:

Innervation is deep, by the median nerve. Irrigation is by the palmar arterial and venous network of the wrist.

Used for cardiac pain, palpitations, gastric pain, vomiting, panic, mental disorders, epilepsy, pain in the chest and hypochondriac regions, myocarditis, tonsillitis, insomnia, intercostal neuralgia, and disease and pain of the wrist joint.

Traditional indications include seizures, throat blockage, swelling of the axilla, spitting of blood, scabies, pain at the root of the tongue, and damp disease of the upper extremities.

This is a shu stream and earth point of the Pc meridian and a yuan source point of the Pc meridian, so its traditional functions are to strongly tonify the organ and the channel, clear the heart and calm the shen, harmonize the stomach, open the chest, and reduce fire in the heart.

Massage techniques are the same as for Pc 4.

Use with Ht 7, Gv 20, Kd 3, yintang (extra), St 36, Cv 12, Cv 17, Liv 3, Liv 1, and Kd 1 for insomnia.

Use with Cv 4, Sp 10, Co 4, Bl 17, Cv 2, Cv 3, Liv 2, Liv 3, Kd 2, and Bl 28 for blood in the urine.

Use with Cv 17, Pc 6, Pc 3, Liv 14, Liv 3, Bl 17, Bl 18, Gb 21, Sp 21, Gb 22, Liv 13, Bl 14, and Bl 15 for fullness and pain in the chest.

Applications:

As he attacks with a right straight or hook, slam his Pc 7 point at the wrist with your right knife edge, then use that same hand to attack to the neck.

PC 8 (PERICARDIUM POINT NO. 8)

Chinese name:

Laogong (labor's palace).

Location:

When the hand is placed palm upward, the point is between the second and third metacarpal bones, proximal to the metacarpophalangeal joint, on the radial side of the third metacarpal bone. With the fingers cupped in the palm in a half-fist, this point can be found in front of the tip of the middle finger between the second and third metacarpal bones. Below the point are the aponeurosis, the second lumbrical, and the superficial and deep tendons of the flexor digitorum muscles. In its deep position are the origin of the transverse head of the adductor hallucis muscle and the interossei muscle. *Lao* means labor, and *gong* means center; the hand is for labor, so here lao refers to the hand. The point is in the center of the palm.

Connections:

There is an internal path from this point to Th 1.

Direction of strike:

Straight in to the palm. However, this is not a point I would use in self-defense. It is more known for its healing qualities of cooling the heart.

Damage:

A fire and yong point. When this point is struck, it heats the heart. When used in healing, it cools the heart. This point is however, more known as the point where the qi emanates from, either for healing or for the martial arts. This is where the qi comes from when we put in either healing qi or disruptive qi. It doesn't matter whether he hand is open or closed, the qi still comes from this point. It can also be used as a balancing point for when we do meridian balancing on someone to balance the yin/yang energy in the body. This point on only the left hand is held over the earth point on each meridian, and then the other Pc 8 is rubbed down the length of the meridian.

Set-up point:

None.

Antidote:

If Pc 8 has been struck perhaps accidentally, apply finger pressure to the opposite Pc 8 straight in with a digging type of movement.

Healing:

Innervation is by the second common palmar digital nerve of the median nerve. Irrigation is by the common palmar digital artery.

Used for cardiac pain, mental disorders, epilepsy, vomiting, stomatitis, foul breath, fungal infection of the hand and foot, coma from stroke, heat exhaustion, angina, frightened fainting in infants, hysteria, excessive sweating of the palms, and numb fingers.

Traditional indications include chest pain, inability to swallow food, jaundice, hand tremors, "swan hands" (uncontrollable waving of the hands), madness, and ulcerated oral cavity.

This is a fire point and ying spring (gushing) point of the Pc meridian. Its traditional functions are to cool the heart and drain heat.

Massage techniques are the same as for Pc 4.

Use with Kd 26, Co 4, Gv 20, Liv 3, Liv 2, Gb 34, Gb 20, St 36, Cv 12, yintang, Si 3, Pc 6, Ht 7, Co 11, Liv 1, Kd 1, Sp 6, Kd 4, Kd 6, Lu 11, Th 21, and Ht 3 for hysteria.

Use with Pc 7, Pc 6, Cv 17, St 36, Liv 3, Liv 14, Bl 17, Bl 18, Ht 7, Bl 43, Bl 13, Bl 15, Gb 21, and Liv 4 for angina or depression.

This is an energy input and exit point and so can be used as an energy transference to transfer shi (excess) qi or stuck qi from an area of stagnation to an area of xu (deficiency). An example is somebody with frontal headache or someone who is spending too much time in his or her head (thinking, worrying, scamming, or just tripping out) and not enough time in the body digesting the content of thoughts or, for that matter, the stomach. In these cases, the left hand could be placed on the forehead (left hand is yin and the receiver of energy, while the right hand is yang and the giver of energy) and the right hand on the tantien (Cv 4 or guanyuan) or zhongwan (Cv 12). The breathing of both patient and practitioner should be in tantien and, if possible, in sync. After a while you may become aware of a pulsing in your laogong points, first the left and then the right (it doesn't really matter which one is felt first, that's just the way I feel it). Don't fix your mind on this sensation, or it will probably disappear. Keep your mind on the breathing. What you are doing is creating a pathway from the forebrain to the center of the body, taking shi from one place and putting it where there is xu. I would often visualize the flow of qi coming into my left hand and out my right, then up the Cv meridian of the person I was doing the balancing on. If you put too much concentration into this visualization, then you will lose the breath; better to stay with the breath in tantien and let the qi flow take care of itself. This is a good balancing treatment that is easy to do on yourself or another, and the results can at times be astounding. *Don't be demanding in your expectations, or you may miss any effect that is forthcoming.*

Applications:

None.

PC 9 (PERICARDIUM POINT NO. 9)

Chinese name:

Zhongchong (middle pouring).

Location:

In the center of the tip of the middle finger. Another location is 0.1 cun from the base of the middle fingernail on the radial side.

Connections:

Takes transverse luo from Th 5.

Direction of strike:

None.

Damage:

If you were to bang yourself on the longest finger, you might experience some heat in the heart (e.g., anger), which will cause you to jump around a bit and sprout profanities. This is a healing point, and I would not use it in a self-defense application. It is a wood and cheng point, and therefore is used in such emergency treatments as coma, and is usually bled.

Set-up point:

None.

Antidote:

None.

Healing:

Innervation is by the palmar digital proprial nerve of the median nerve. Irrigation is by the arterial and venous network formed by the palmar digital proprial artery and vein.

Used for cardiac pain, irritability, loss of consciousness, aphasia with stiffness of the tongue, febrile disease, heat stroke, infantile convulsions, feverish sensations in the palm of the hand, shock, coma, and angina.

Pc 9 is a jing well point and wood point of the Pc meridian. Its traditional function is to reduce fire from the heart, which results in a resuscitation affect (prick and bleed one or two spots of blood for this effect).

Zhong means middle, and *chong* means gushing; this point is at the tip of the middle finger and is the jing well point of this meridian where qi of the channel originates and gushes upward along the channel.

To massage, use the knuckle and the forefinger to squeeze the point at either location or prick and bleed to cool the heart and effect resuscitation.

Use with Cv 1 and Gv 26 as an adjunct to CPR in cases of drowning.

Use with St 36 and Gv 26 for fainting.

Use with Gv 26, Co 4, Liv 3, Gv 14, Pc 6, St 40, Kd 1, Gv 20, and sishencong for coma.

Use with Gv 25, Gv 26, Pc 6, Kd 1, St 36, Gv 20, Cv 4, Cv 6, and Liv 3 for shock.

Applications:

None.

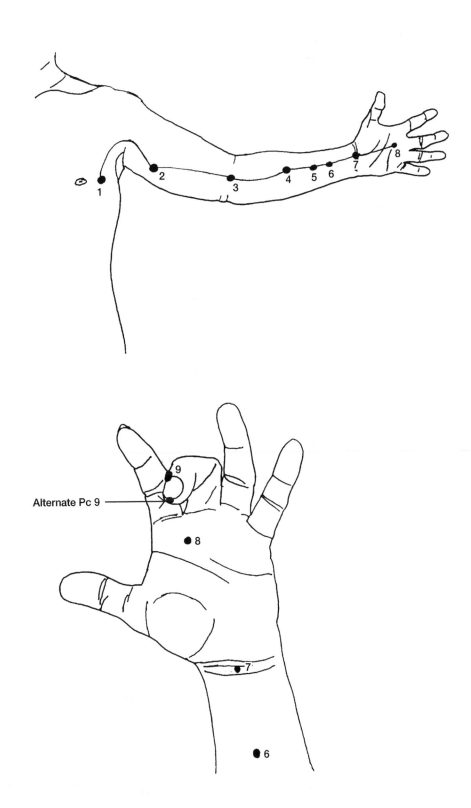

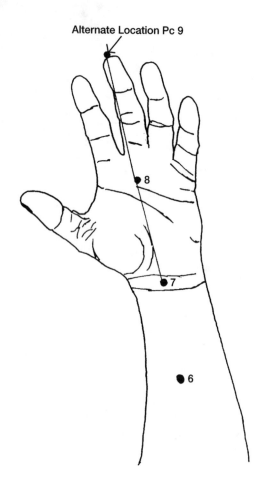

Alternate Location Pc 9

● 8

● 7

● 6

Medical

Glossary

The following medical reference is by no means complete. I have only included the anatomical terms and the disease states that are included in this encyclopedia and that most people would not be familiar with.

A

Addison's disease: This disease is caused by failure of the adrenal gland to secrete corticosteroid hormones and can be life threatening. Addison's disease (or syndrome) can be caused by a number of factors, such as tumor, autoimmune diseases, and infection.

Indications of this disease include weakness, a change in color of skin (mainly to a darker shade), cold sensitivity, loss of appetite, weight loss, and intestinal problems, to name a few. There is a Western treatment program that cures this disease.

adnexitis: A swelling of the adnexal organs of the uterus, i.e., the fallopian tubes and ovaries.

amenorrhea: The normal flow of blood and discharge called menstruation does not happen. Normally, for instance, during pregnancy and milk flow or before puberty and after menopause, this flow does not occur. However, with amenorrhea, the flow does not appear at all or stops for unnatural reasons. The former is normally caused by malfunction with the hypothalamus gland, the ovary or uterus, or the pituitary gland. The latter often occurs in athletes who achieve an extremely low percentage of body fat as a result of intense training and in women who have eating disorders.

ametropia: We get a wrong image at the back of the eyeball because the light is not bent the correct way upon entering the eye.

angina pectoris: A pain in the chest like a cramp that travels down the left side of the body, usually caused by a lack of oxygen to the heart. It is also linked with hardening of the arteries. The patient feels like he or she is dying from suffocation.

anhidrosis: An absence of sweating when one should be sweating under normal stimulus.

aphasia: Speech is lost due to a nerve problem, usually caused by injury or disease in the left side of the brain. It is not a problem of articulation, etc. It can be reversed, and in most cases speech returns.

aphonia: Loss of voice caused by disease of the larynx or mouth. It can be caused simply by overuse of the vocal chords.

apoplexy: Nowadays, we simply us the word "stroke." Apoplexy is a stroke with paralysis.

ascites: This disease can be caused by a number of factors. Mainly, though, it is caused by cirrhosis (liver disease). It is an abnormal amount of fluid in the abdominal cavity with large amounts of protein, and swelling of the abdomen.

atelectasis: The failure of a part of the lung to expand, as seen in many premature babies. It can happen in adults from inhaling foreign bodies or from bronchial cancer or tuberculosis, an internal blockage, etc. Physiotherapy can help this situation.

atrophy: Part of the body wasting away. This can be caused by disease or accident. Muscles can atrophy simply form lack of exercise. Restricted blood flow is also a factor.

B

borborygmus: Noises from within. Bowel or stomach noises, rumbling, or gurgling noises. Usually caused by a blockage of the small intestine.

beriberi: Is a dietary deficiency disease cased by a lack of vitamin B. The disease is characterized by neuritis, often with muscle atrophy, poor coordination, and eventual paralysis. Death may occur from heart failure. The disease is prevalent in those parts of the East where polished rice is the main food. Health is restored quickly when adequate amounts of vitamin B are given. (Also called "leg qi.")

Buerger's disease: An inflammatory condition of the arteries, especially in the legs, that predominantly affects young male cigarette smokers.

C

canthus: The corner of each eye where the upper and lower eyelids meet.

cholecystitis: Inflammation of the gallbladder, usually caused by a bacterial infection that results in great pain over the Gb and fever. Acute cholecystitis is usually associated with gall stones. An X-ray is usually taken to rule out other diseases, such as appendicitis.

choroiditis: An inflammation of the choroid layer of the eye (the layer of the eyeball between retina and sclera).

chorioretinitis: The outer membrane and retina of the eye are swollen, usually due to inflammation. Blurred vision and light sensitivity are some symptoms.

chyluria: Chyle in the urine. This gives a milky appearance. Chyle consists of certain digestive juices, which make their way into the urine from the small intestine.

conjunctivitis: Inflammation of the front of the eye, called the conjunctiva. Caused by infection, bacteria, or virus and spreads quickly to the other eye and to others who have close contact. Swelling, redness, and pus will also be present. This disease causes more discomfort than pain, and it can affect vision, but this is rare. (Also called pink eye.)

costal: Relating to a rib, near a rib.

Costalgia: Pain in the ribs. This term is very rarely used nowadays. (I guess they simply say, "Pain in the ribs"?)

Cushing's disease or syndrome: Overstimulation of the adrenal glands by excessive amounts of ACTH/corticosteroid hormones secreted by a tumor of the pituitary gland. Symptoms are excessive body hair growth, weight gain, reddened face and neck, osteoporosis, (loss of minerals from the bones), high blood glucose levels, and often mental disorders. This can also be caused by the use of steroid drugs over several weeks or longer.

D

dyschezia: Constipation caused by a voluntary urge not to defecate over a long period. The bowel is distended, and defecation is difficult and painful.

dysuria: Difficult and painful urination due to a bacterial infection of the urinary tract. Frequent urge and urination. It is usually helped by a large intake of fluid. This is a symptom of urethritis, cystitis, or proctitis.

E

edema: An excessive level of fluids in the body tissues. This used to be called dropsy, and years ago people would die of this disease. It is not that prevalent nowadays and is easily treated.

empyema: Pus in a body cavity, such as in the area between the lung and the membrane surrounding it. Caused by an infection like TB or pleurisy.

endometritis: Inflammation of the endometrium (the mucus membrane lining the uterus) caused by chronic or acute infection. It may also be caused by foreign bodies, such as parasites or bacteria. Sometimes happens after childbirth or abortion where the woman is fitted with an IUD.

enuresis: Lack of control over urination, usually in the evenings in bed.

epilepsy: Can be any one of a number of disorders of brain function. Characterized by sudden attacks of convulsions, or blackouts, or seizures, or all three. There is an uncontrolled discharge of electricity from the nerve cells on the surface of the brain. The cause is generally unknown.

F

febrile: Means the high temperature of the body as a febrile reaction to infection.

furuncle: This is a localized staphylococcal skin infection, usually occurring in a follicle of the hair. Pain and red swelling that exudes dead tissue. (Also called boils.)

frontal cortex: This is the most complicated part of your brain. It is responsible for intellect, personality, and learning. Judgment and reasoning and consciousness are also produced here. This area is directly affected by environment and upbringing.

G

glaucoma: High blood pressure within the eye. The normal flow of fluid between the cornea and aqueous humor (lens) is blocked. Acute glaucoma can result in blindness within two to five days; chronic glaucoma may take years to develop. Usually controlled by eye drops.

goiter: A swelling in the neck caused by an overgrown thyroid gland.

H

hemafecia: The presence of blood in the stool.

hematuria: A presence of blood in the urine at an abnormal level, caused by kidney diseases.

hematemesis: The act of vomiting blood.

hemiplegia: One side of the body is paralyzed.

homeostasis: The constant state within the body that is is naturally maintained, comprising body temperature, heartbeat, blood pressure and production, salt balance, breathing, and glandular secretions.

hypermetropia: Farsightedness. Near vision is more blurred than far vision.

hyperosmia: High sensitivity to smells.

hypochondriac region: Both sides of the upper abdomen and beneath the ribs.

hypoglossal nerve: A pair of nerves in the head that cause tongue movement and swallowing.

hyperopia: Same as hypermetropia, farsightedness. (U.S. terminology).

hyperosmia: A high sensitivity to smells.

I

ischaemia: The organ or part of the organ that receives inadequate blood supply caused by some restriction in the blood supply.

inguinal: Pertaining to the groin area.

K

keratitis: Inflammation of the cornea of the eye.

keratoleukoma: A firm nodule that appears mainly on the face and grows to 1 to 2 centimeters across in about six weeks.

L

lacrimation: Crying, or simply tearing. An excessive amount of tears as in crying.

lassitude: Wanting to sleep all day, no energy, etc.

leucorrhea: A white or yellowish discharge from the vagina. This can be normal during periods or during pregnancy.

lumbosacral plexus: The nerves that supply the legs and pelvic area.

lymphadenitis: Usually caused by a bacterial infection or circulating cancer cells causing inflammation of the lymph nodes.

M

micturition reflex: The urge to urinate. This is normal when the pressure of fluid rises in the urinary tract. Controlled naturally but uncontrolled as with infants.

menorrhagia: Longer and heavier than normal menstruation periods. Happens naturally at some time in a woman's reproductive life. If it continues, she should be checked out for cancer, etc. It may cause anemia if left too long without help.

myopia: Shortsightedness. Distant things are blurred.

myocarditis: Inflammation, either acute or chronic, of the heart muscle.

N

nebula: A scar or "spot" on the cornea, usually not causing light to be blocked. It is picked up only by an optometrist using specialized lighting.

Nelson's syndrome: A hormone disease that could follow the removal of the adrenal gland. Many call this disease Cushing's Disease.

nephritis: Kidney disease of any kind that has swelling or organ malfunction as its symptoms.

nephroptosis: Dropping of the kidney into the pelvis. This can occur in very thin women, for example.

neuralgia: Pain caused by diseases that affect the nervous system. (It is usual to place the affected portion of the body placed before "neuralgia," as in "facial neuralgia.")

neurasthenia: Psychological and physical conditions causing fatigue, irritability, headache, anxiety, dizziness, and intolerance to noises. Can be caused by a head injury or neurosis.

neurosis: Any long-term behavioral or mental disorder in which the patient is aware of it. (In other words, the patient maintains a connection with reality.)

neurodermatitis: A skin disorder usually found in anxious or nervous patients. The skin—especially around the forehead, forearms, nape of the neck, and legs—is hard and thickened as a result of scratching or rubbing.

O

ophthalmoplegia: Paralysis of the muscles of the eye. Can be either internal or external.

orchitis: Inflammation of the testis, either one or both. Can cause sterility if caused by mumps.

otorrhea: Any kind of discharge from the ear. Usually seen in chronic middle ear infections.

P

palpitation: A very fast beating of the heart in some people who are under stress and in heart patients.

pannus: The outer layers of the cornea become filled with blood vessels, usually as a result of inflammation of the cornea.

pancreatitis: A swelling of the pancreas, which can be caused by damage to the gallbladder or too much alcohol. The acute variety is often deadly. The chronic variety is also usually caused through alcohol abuse and is associated with diabetes.

parotid glands: A pair of the largest saliva glands, situated on the inside of the cheek below the outer ear.

parotitis: Swelling or infection of one or both saliva (parotid) glands. Mumps.

peptic ulcer: A breakdown of the lining of the digestive tract. Usually occurs when pepsin and acid are at unusually high levels.

pericarditis: The pericardium, or the membrane that surrounds the heart, is inflamed. Caused by injury, cancer, heart disease, etc. There are breathing difficulties and pain in the first stages. The second stages are more serious, with fluid gathering around the pericardium and a swelling on the outside of the body around the heart.

pleurisy: Inflammation of the linings of the lungs (*pleura*, an oily membrane that surrounds the lungs). Symptoms include pain in the lungs and shortage of breath. Can be caused by pneumonia, cancer, or tuberculosis.

polupus: Same as polyp. A growth, usually benign, proturuding from the mucus membrane. Commonly found in the nose.

pronator teres: The muscle in the forearm that turns the hand down or back (as in the yin- or yang-shaped hand).

prostatitis: Infection of the prostate gland, causing swelling with the urgent need to urinate. A burning sensation accompanies urination.

pruritus: Itching, or rather that which makes someone need to scratch, sometimes causing infection.

psychosis: A mental disorder that has a physical or emotional source. The patient may have illusions (mistaken beliefs) and/or delusions (false beliefs).

pterygium: A triangular overgrowth of the cornea, on the inner side, by thickened and degenerative conjunctiva. People from dry, hot, dusty climates are more prone to this disease. It very rarely interferes with vision.

ptosis: Eyelids that droop, either one or two of them, caused by a weakness of the muscle that raises them or malfunction of the nerve that triggers this muscle.

pyelonephritis: A bacterial infection of the kidney. Characterized by fever, chills, and a need to urinate frequently, this disease moves quickly. Can lead to kidney failure.

R

rhinitis: Nasal discharge caused by inflammation of the mucus membrane in the nose. A runny nose.

rhinorrhea: Mucus freely flowing from the nose. Or the release of spinal fluid after a head injury.

S

sclera: The hard stuff behind the eyeball (membrane) that keeps the eyeball in its shape. The white of the eye.

scrofula: An old name for tuberculosis of the lymph glands in the neck.

stye: An infection of a gland of the eyelid that forms pus.

T

tachycardia: When the heart contracts at a rate greater than 100 beats per minute at a regular rate.

temporalis: The muscle that closes the jaw; one of four muscles used for chewing.

thrombocytopenia: Too few platelets in the blood, causing bleeding into the skin, bruising easily and bleeding after injury.

tidal fever: A fever that comes and goes (like the tide).

tinnitus: Ringing in the ear, which could be a sign of acoustic injury.

trigeminal neuralgia: Stabbing pain in the face along the trigeminal facial nerve. Caused by pressure on the nerve.

trismus: A long-term spasm of the jaw muscles keeping the jaw tightly shut. As in tetanus. Also called lockjaw (informal).

U

urethraliga: Pain of the urethra.

urticaria: A skin condition where the skin erupts into wheals (or welts) of differing shapes and sizes with clear margins.

uveitis: Inflammation of any part of the uveal part of the eye. Could be caused by diabetes, trauma, infection, and could turn into glaucoma.

Glossary

Accumulation point: Where the qi accumulates so that it can be sent to different parts of the body.

Acupressure: A way of using the acupuncture points for healing without using needles; only the fingers are used to press the points.

Acupuncture points: Along each meridian or channel, there are points that offer less electrical resistance. These are the points that an acupuncturist will pierce with a metal needle in order to put into the body, qi or electricity from his or her own body. The points in this book are numbered with a system well accepted in the West. (Usually Chinese texts are numbered differently than are Western texts.)

Chen: A family in China whose style of taijiquan is becoming more popular in modern times. Many believe that it was the Chens who invented taijiquan, while others believe that they simply changed their form of Chinese boxing to be more in keeping with the taijiquan principles. Nowadays, Chen style is regarded as one of the four major systems of taijiquan.

Cheng point: An extremity point. (Many extremity points are used as emergency points.)

Chang Yiu-chun: One of only three disciples of Yang Shou-hou and teacher of the Erle Montaigue.

Chee Sau: Sticking hands. This is a training exercise in taijiquan that teaches students about hand techniques and reflex actions. Both partners join hands at both wrists and, using circling motions, try to attack each other from this short distance with punches and palm attacks. The very instant an attack is felt, the attackee reattacks, thus defending himself using an offensive method.

Chi: Ultimate, the pinnacle, as in t'ai chi ch'uan. (Do not confuse this with *ch'i,* or qi.)

Ch'i-na: The art of locking the joints. Jujutsu is a form of this. Taijiquan has its own version of it based solely upon the postures of the forms.

Chong mai: One of the eight extra meridians.

Chu King-hung: One of only three disciples of Yang Sau-chung and teacher of Erle Montaigue in the Yang Cheng-fu system.

Ch'uan: Fist, or boxing, as in t'ai chi ch'uan.

Cun: (Pronounced "tsoone.") A measurement of about 1 inch, used in acupuncture and dim-mak to locate points. The distance between the second and last knuckles on the middle finger when the finger is bent tightly.

Dai mai: The girdle meridian, which runs around the waist. An extra meridian.

Dim-mak points: The same points that are used in acupuncture, but they are used on a martial level, to kill or to heal.

Dim-hseuh: Another name for dim-mak.

Du mai: Governing (vessel) meridian. One of the eight extra meridians. Unlike the other six extra meridians, however, this one, along with the *ren mai*, or conceptor (vessel) meridian, has its own meridian and points.

Emergency points: Those points that are used in diagnostic procedures to determine whether a patient is in dire straits, or those that can be used in emergency situations, such as death.

External martial arts: Those such as karate, tae kwondo, and the kung-fu systems, such as Choy Lae-fut, Jow gar, and Hung gar, that had their beginnings at the Shao-lin temple in China.

Extra meridians: There are 12 main meridians in the body and eight "extra" ones. Whole medical practice has evolved in China using purely the eight extra meridians. These meridians also hold the key to some of the most deadly point strike combinations.

Extra point: These are acupuncture points that have either been discovered after the main meridian points were discovered or are not situated upon any particular meridian.

Extremity points: Those acupuncture points that are "at the extremities" of the body, such as Ht 9 at the tip of the little finger.

Fa-jing: Explosive energy, fa-jing is the "motor" of dim-mak. Without it, you just cannot use dim-mak. It is a way of attack using the whole body rather than just the portion of the body that is issuing the attack. It is very much like a sneeze. Your whole body sneezes, however, not just your nose.

Fen: About one-tenth of an inch, also used to measure acupuncture points.

Fu: Hollow organs, the yang organs.

He point: A sea point, or "gathering together."

Hun: The spiritual soul that lives in the liver.

Ho Ho-choy: Disciple of the great bagwazhang master Chiang Jung-chiao, and one of several teachers of the author in bagwazhang.

Ho ho ha ha kee kee ku ku: The call of the Australian kookooburra.

Internal martial arts: Those martial arts systems, such as taijiquan, bagwazhang, and h'sin-i ch'uan, that rely more upon an internal strength, making use of the flow of qi rather than relying upon brute strength.

Jeh: The will, which lives in the kidneys.

Jing point: Used for the river point.

Jing qi: The extra kidney qi that is stored in the kidneys and is used for resuscitation.

Ke, or ko: The controlling cycle of the five elements.

Large san-sau: A training exercise in taijiquan wherein both partners perform attacks and defenses in a set dance-like routine of attack and defense. Every posture from the taijiquan form is employed in this set. At an advanced stage, more free-style attacks and defenses are used.

Luo: A connecting point or meridian.

Mai: Meridian or channel.

Martial taijiquan: This is the second level of a taijiquan student's martial training. It is necessary to understand martial taijiquan in order to use it for healing others. This is where we learn how to use taijiquan for self-defense. It goes much deeper than simply knowing what each posture is used for.

Medical taijiquan: The highest level of one's internal martial arts training. This is where the practitioner is able to use taijiquan postures to actually heal someone of disease. It is not just the patient doing the postures himself, but the "doctor" using the martial arts application of each posture to heal disease.

Meridian: A channel along which "qi" (energy, electricity) flows. There are 12 main meridians and eight "extra" ones in the body. In this book, we deal with the 12 main meridians and only glance at the eight extras where necessary.

Ming: Translated as brightness or sunlight. *Yang ming*, for instance, is the sunlight yang division of stomach and colon.

MO: Abbreviation for meridian or channel.

Mu: To mobilize. Mu points are the alarm points on the meridian. Should one of these be very tender, it could indicate disorder in that meridian or organ.

Pauchi form: Cannon fist form. this is the solo version of the large san-sau. There are two sides, "A" and "B." At a solo level, the student performs the A and B sides without stopping. This is one of the best ways of learning about martial arts movement.

Po: The animal spirit, or the soul of the animal, which lives in the lung.

Push feet: The taijiquan practice of a set of movements of attack and defense practiced by two people using the feet. Both partners stand on one leg, joining the other leg at the Achilles tendon. Circling begins as one person tries to kick at the other's leg with his heel. The attackee defends by turning his body and thus pulling that attacking foot in an arc, thus forming a circle when the whole operation is repeated. At an advanced stage, hand attacks are also employed, all on one leg.

Push hands: The taijiquan practice of a set of movements of attack and defense practiced by two people using the hands. This is not a competition, but rather a training method that teaches the use of taijiquan as a self-defense art. It begins with simple pushing and defensive movements and becomes quite advanced in attack and defense. Beginners start with big, low, open stances. As they learn, the stances become more like those that would be used in a real street fighting situation. Punches, finger jabs, leg attacks are all part of this training method.

Qi: An internal energy that flows through the acupuncture meridians, bringing a life-giving force to every organ in the body. Qi is used for every movement and action of the body; without it we die.

Qigong: Literally, internal work; a means of gaining good health through certain stances used in conjunction with breathing methods. An integral part of one's taijiquan or any internal martial arts training. There are 2,000 different types of qigong, broken down into three categories: self-healing, martial arts, and medical.

Ren mai: Conceptor (vessel) meridian. One of the eight extra meridians. Unlike the other six extra meridians, this one, along with du mai, has its own meridian and points.

Self-healing taijiquan: This is where we all begin our taijiquan training. Each posture of the taijiquan form causes one of the main meridians in the body to be activated, thus beginning the self-healing process necessary for healing the internal organs.

Shao lin: Literally, "Little Forest"—a place in China where the monks of the Shao Lin monastery would study the martial arts as part of their training. It is believed that all of the hard-style martial arts, including karate, came from this temple.

Shen: The spirit that lives in the heart.

Shiatsu: The Japanese version of acupressure.

Shou: Literally, "hand" or "arm." Can be used as follows: *Shou shao yin* means "hand lesser yin," or the heart meridian.

Shu: This is a collective term for the five welling, stream, or antique points.

Shu Point: A transporting or "stream point."

Small San-Sau: The taijiquan way of learning about the main applications of the postures of the taijiquan kata or form up to the posture known as "single whip." One person is the attacker, throwing different types of punches in a set routine, while the attackee defends against these attacks using the postures from the form. At an advanced stage, the attacks and defenses will become free-style.

Stasis: A condition in acupuncture wherein the blood is stagnant.

Sun family: Sun Luc-tang learned several taijiquan systems and also bagwazhang and h'sin-i ch'uan. He then formed his own style of taijiquan, the "Sun system." He was better known for his bagwazhang, however.

T'ai: Meaning greater or supreme (as in t'ai chi ch'uan, or supreme ultimate boxing.) T'ai yang is the greater yang division of bladder and small intestine.

Tuite: The Japanese name for dim-mak.

Tui-na: The Chinese art of massage, which includes manipulating the acupuncture points and twisting the meridians to cause a healing.

Wudang Shan: A range of mountains in China's Hupei province that holds great religious significance to the "internal" styles of martial arts. One of the peaks of this range, also called Wudang Shan, is said to be where Chang San-feng founded the martial system of dim-mak, which later became known as h'ao ch'uan and, nowadays, taijiquan.

Wu family: Wu Quan-yu learned the Yang family system from Yang Lu-ch'an and passed it on to his son Wu Chien-chuan, who changed the system to become the Wu family system.

Wei qi: Protective energy.

Xie cleft point: An accumulation point.

Yang: In this book, we use the classical Chinese meaning for yang and yin, rather than the newer Japanese concepts of this term. So for our purposes, yang means expanding, light, male, open, warm, active.

Yang family: Yang Lu-ch'an founded the most famous system of taijiquan in the 1700s. His sons Yang Ban-hou and Yang Kin-hou also learned his system. Kin-hou's sons, Yang Cheng-fu and Yang Shou-hou, also learned their father's and grandfather's system. Cheng-fu changed it to what has become the most popular system of modern taijiquan. Shou-hou, on the other hand, refused to change the system. The author, Erle Montaigue, has trained extensively in both of these systems.

Yang Sau-chung: Sau-chung was the head of the Yang family until his death in May 1985. He was the eldest son of Yang Cheng-fu and was one of Erle's teachers.

Yang qiao mai: One of the eight extra meridians.

Yang wei mai: One of the eight extra meridians.

Yin: Dark, passive, female, closed, contracting, cool. It must be remembered that "yin and yang" can only ever be relative to each other. So Papua, New Guinea, would be considered yang to Sydney, Australia, which would be yin in this instance. However, Sydney is yang compared to Melbourne, which would be yin in this instance, and so on.

Yin qiao mai: One of the eight extra meridians.

Yin wei mai: One of the eight extra meridians.

Ying qi: Nourishing qi.

Yong point: Spring or stream point.

Yuan: Ancestral; origin or source.

Yuan point: A source point that draws upon yuan qi.

Zhang: Solid yin organ.

Bibliography

Chen, Jing. 1982. *Anatomical Atlas of Chinese Acupuncture Points*. Jinan, China: Shandong Science and Technology Press.

Ding, Li. 1991. *Acupuncture Meridian Theory and Acupncture Points*. Bejing, China: Foreign Language Press.

Jokl, Ernst. 1941. *The Medical Aspects of Boxing*. Pretoria, South Africa: L. van Schaik P/L.

Martin, Elizabeth, ed. 1994. *Concise Medical Dictionary, 4th edition*. Oxford, England: Oxford University Press.

Matsumoto, Kiiko, and Stephen Birch. 1986. *Extraordinary Vessels*. Brookline, MA: Paradigm Publications.

Rogers, Cameron and Carol. 1989. *Point location and Point Dynamics Manual*. Sydney, Australia: Acupuncture Colleges of Australia.

About

The Authors

Wally Simpson became interested in alternate health care in 1973. He earned a degree in reflexology and Swedish massage in 1977; went on to study Oriental massage, including shiatsu and Chinese massage, with various teachers in Australia, New Zealand, and Indonesia; and in 1980 set up a practice on the Gold Coast, Australia.

Meanwhile, he studied Traditional Chinese Medicine at the Australian Colleges of Acupuncture, Brisbane, graduating with a diploma of acupuncture in 1986 and a Bachelor of Acupuncture in 1987. In 1994 he received his diploma in Chinese herbal medicine.

Wally has studied and practiced yoga and meditation since the early 1970s and taijiquan for the past eight years—five of these in the Erle Montaigue system and the last two under the personal tutelage of Erle Montaigue.

Wally has always been a keen surfer and still enters into surfing competitions (at his age!). In fact sometimes on his way down the beautiful Queensland and Northern New South Wales coastline, he looks out there, pulls his car over, and has a quick surf before class. Wally used to be a "bricky," or a person who lays bricks for house building. This in itself says a lot about the man; he has experienced life—an important prerequisite for any internal healing/martial art!

Wally Simpson presently lives with his wife and child on the Gold Coast, Australia, and runs his private practice, where he has developed his own style of massage, incorporating aspects of Chinese massage, Japanese shiatsu, deep tissue massage, and manipulative techniques.

Erle Montaigue began his martial arts training when he was 11 years of age, training in karate and judo for a short while at the local police Boys' Clubs. His forte in these early years, however, was wrestling, which later led him to professional wrestling for a time. He was also an avid bodybuilder, later realizing the error of his ways.

In 1966, Erle was expelled from school for little more than being a rebel and painting the school yellow, among other "small" things. In1967 he took up a telephone maintenance course, where he met his first teacher of taijiquan, Mr. Wong Eog.

By the late sixties, Erle was married with two children. He was performing in stage plays and with his band, and he already had a No. 1 hit record, "Can't Wait for September," to his name. He was "expelled" from the telephone job for dying his hair green and singing on the job, so he took up music as a profession and became a rock and roll star, having several hit records and albums to his name by the early seventies.

In 1974, while performing as a nightclub entertainer, Erle left Australia for England, where he met his second taijiquan instructor, Mr. Chu King-hung, who took Erle on as one of his first students (if not the first). Chu King-hung is one of only three disciples of the late Yang Sau-chung (1909–1985), the eldest son of Yang Cheng-fu. Erle continued his acting career while in London, performing in several plays, musicals, and films before returning to Australia at the end of 1977.

In 1981 he traveled to Hong Kong, where his form was looked at by Yang Sau-chung, and where he studied with Ho Ho-choy, a direct disciple of bagwazhang Master Chiang Jung-jiao.

In 1982, after having taken up several occupations, including professional chauffeur and cab driver, he began teaching taijiquan in Sydney and became the chief of therapeutic movement at the NSW College of Natural Therapies. He opened his own school in Sydney in 1983.

The next year, Erle found his main internal martial arts master, Chang Yiu-chun, from whom he learned the secrets of dim-mak and h'ao ch'uan (taijiquan).

In 1985, Erle and eight of his students traveled to China to become the first Westerners ever allowed to view the All China National Wushu tournament, held in Yinchuan, Ningxia. There, he was tested by three of the world's leading internal martial arts experts and was granted the degree of "Master." He was the first Westerner to receive this honor.

Erle Montaigue has his own column in *Fighting Arts International*, the prestigious British martial arts magazine, and *Australasian Fighting Arts Magazine*, one of the longest-running quality martial arts magazines. His photo has appeared on the front cover of both of these publications, as well as that of *Karate/Kung-Fu Illustrated*, published in the United States. In addition, Erle has produced several books and a video with Paladin Press. Erle's magazine articles and books have helped change the way people view the internal fighting arts, and his 120 self-produced video titles have helped students learn from quality tapes when a teacher was not available. He currently serves as the editor of *Combat & Healing* magazine and heads the World Taiji Chinese Boxing Association, which has schools in more than 30 countries.

In 1995, Erle was invited to study with Liang Shih-kan, the leader and "keeper" of the now almost extinct forerunner to taijiquan, the Wutan Shan System of Boxing, thus becoming the only Westerner and one of only a handful of people to be taught the nine qi-disruptive methods.

Today, Erle and his second wife, Sandra, live with their three children, Ben, Eli, and Kataleenas, on their farm in Northern NSW on the caldera of one of the world's largest extinct volcanoes.

Readers wishing to contact either author may do so by writing to the following address:

MTG Video and Books
P.O. Box 792
Murwillumbah NSW 2484
Australia